T0353376

Enterprise Information Systems and the Digitalization of Business Functions

Madjid Tavana
La Salle University, USA

A volume in the Advances in Business Information Systems and Analytics (ABISA) Book Series

www.igi-global.com

Published in the United States of America by
    IGI Global
    Business Science Reference (an imprint of IGI Global)
    701 E. Chocolate Avenue
    Hershey PA, USA 17033
    Tel: 717-533-8845
    Fax: 717-533-8661
    E-mail: cust@igi-global.com
    Web site: http://www.igi-global.com

Library of Congress Cataloging-in-Publication Data

Names: Tavana, Madjid, 1957- editor.
Title: Enterprise information systems and the digitalization of business
  functions / Madjid Tavana, editor.
Description: Hershey, PA : Business Science Reference, [2017]
Identifiers: LCCN 2017001018| ISBN 9781522523826 (hardcover) | ISBN
  9781522523833 (ebook)
Subjects: LCSH: Management information systems.
Classification: LCC HD30.213 .E58145 2017 | DDC 658.4/038011--dc23 LC record available at https://lccn.loc.gov/2017001018

This book is published in the IGI Global book series Advances in Business Information Systems and Analytics (ABISA) (ISSN: 2327-3275; eISSN: 2327-3283)

British Cataloguing in Publication Data
A Cataloguing in Publication record for this book is available from the British Library.

All work contributed to this book is new, previously-unpublished material. The views expressed in this book are those of the authors, but not necessarily of the publisher.

For electronic access to this publication, please contact: eresources@igi-global.com.

Advances in Business Information Systems and Analytics (ABISA) Book Series

Madjid Tavana
La Salle University, USA

ISSN:2327-3275
EISSN:2327-3283

MISSION

The successful development and management of information systems and business analytics is crucial to the success of an organization. New technological developments and methods for data analysis have allowed organizations to not only improve their processes and allow for greater productivity, but have also provided businesses with a venue through which to cut costs, plan for the future, and maintain competitive advantage in the information age.

The **Advances in Business Information Systems and Analytics (ABISA) Book Series** aims to present diverse and timely research in the development, deployment, and management of business information systems and business analytics for continued organizational development and improved business value.

COVERAGE

- Information Logistics
- Business Decision Making
- Forecasting
- Legal information systems
- Data Analytics
- Big Data
- Business Process Management
- Geo-BIS
- Management information systems
- Decision Support Systems

IGI Global is currently accepting manuscripts for publication within this series. To submit a proposal for a volume in this series, please contact our Acquisition Editors at Acquisitions@igi-global.com or visit: http://www.igi-global.com/publish/.

Titles in this Series

For a list of additional titles in this series, please visit: www.igi-global.com

Business Analytics and Cyber Security Management in Organizations
Rajagopal (EGADE Business School, Tecnologico de Monterrey, Mexico City, Mexico & Boston University, USA)
and Ramesh Behl (International Management Institute, Bhubaneswar, India)
Business Science Reference • copyright 2017 • 346pp • H/C (ISBN: 9781522509028) • US $215.00 (our price)

Handbook of Research on Intelligent Techniques and Modeling Applications in Marketing Analytics
Anil Kumar (BML Munjal University, India) Manoj Kumar Dash (ABV-Indian Institute of Information Technology and Management, India) Shrawan Kumar Trivedi (BML Munjal University, India) and Tapan Kumar Panda (BML Munjal University, India)
Business Science Reference • copyright 2017 • 428pp • H/C (ISBN: 9781522509974) • US $275.00 (our price)

Applied Big Data Analytics in Operations Management
Manish Kumar (Indian Institute of Information Technology, Allahabad, India)
Business Science Reference • copyright 2017 • 251pp • H/C (ISBN: 9781522508861) • US $160.00 (our price)

Eye-Tracking Technology Applications in Educational Research
Christopher Was (Kent State University, USA) Frank Sansosti (Kent State University, USA) and Bradley Morris (Kent State University, USA)
Information Science Reference • copyright 2017 • 370pp • H/C (ISBN: 9781522510055) • US $205.00 (our price)

Strategic IT Governance and Alignment in Business Settings
Steven De Haes (Antwerp Management School, University of Antwerp, Belgium) and Wim Van Grembergen (Antwerp Management School, University of Antwerp, Belgium)
Business Science Reference • copyright 2017 • 298pp • H/C (ISBN: 9781522508618) • US $195.00 (our price)

Organizational Productivity and Performance Measurements Using Predictive Modeling and Analytics
Madjid Tavana (La Salle University, USA) Kathryn Szabat (La Salle University, USA) and Kartikeya Puranam (La Salle University, USA)
Business Science Reference • copyright 2017 • 400pp • H/C (ISBN: 9781522506546) • US $205.00 (our price)

Data Envelopment Analysis and Effective Performance Assessment
Farhad Hossein Zadeh Lotfi (Islamic Azad University, Iran) Seyed Esmaeil Najafi (Islamic Azad University, Iran) and Hamed Nozari (Islamic Azad University, Iran)
Business Science Reference • copyright 2017 • 365pp • H/C (ISBN: 9781522505969) • US $160.00 (our price)

www.igi-global.com

701 E. Chocolate Ave., Hershey, PA 17033
Order online at www.igi-global.com or call 717-533-8845 x100
To place a standing order for titles released in this series, contact: cust@igi-global.com
Mon-Fri 8:00 am - 5:00 pm (est) or fax 24 hours a day 717-533-8661

Table of Contents

Detailed Table of Contents

Chapter 1
Margee Hume, CQ University Australia, Australia
Paul Johnston, Care Systems, Australia

Aged care is projected to be the fastest-growing sector within health and community care industries with digital aged care growing in interest. Strengthening understanding of delivery and technology will assist in better delivery and reach more elderly in need through improved service delivery. In this we examine advance recent discourse on the role of knowledge management (KM) in digital aged care with the view to assist delivery of aged care. We advance knowledge by offering a unique view of KM from the perspective of 28 aged care stakeholders through in-depth interviewing and mental model pictorials. We offer advances in understanding for digital aged care and suggest practices for knowledge capture and management for aged care providers. We culminate the discussion by offering a digital agenda for aged care facilities and advance the discourse in this sector. Specifically reflections are offered for leadership and the consideration of the key players and links that should be developed in comprehensively capturing and disseminating knowledge digitally in the sector.

Chapter 2
Jessy Nair, PES University, India
D. Bhanu Sree Reddy, VIT University, India

The successful implementation of Enterprise Resource Planning (ERP) system is a challenge to many organizations. Though an intervention, ERP brings in large scale tangible and intangible benefits to an organization. It poses significant intervention on firm level endogenous dimensions; internal stakeholders, internal organization, business processes and technology. Though literature recognizes that ERP intervention brings about technological change during ERP implementation, hardly any article has conceptualized these interventions in evaluating its performance. Drawing on the Socio Technical system perspective the objective of this article is to conceptualize the ERP intervention on the endogenous dimensions of the organization and develop a comprehensive conceptual model to assess the success or failure of ERP system implementation. The conceptual model, Process-Variance and Adapted Socio-Technical (PVAST), proposed in this article will enable decision makers and practitioners to measure ERP project performance at every stage of its life cycle in a coherent method and adopt corrective measures.

This paper examines the alignment success factors necessary to improve logistics cost when implementing an ERP system taking a work system theoretical perspective. Organizations attempting to decrease logistics costs via an ERP implementation must consider the processes and activities involved in aligning participants, information, technology, and business process in these ERP implementations. We used a two-step approach, conducting a confirmatory factor analysis (CFA) to assess the psychometric properties of our measures and then conducting an independent sample t-test between two groups, one which experienced decreased logistic costs and the second which experienced the same or increasing logistic costs. This research has provided more insight into the practice of ERP implementations and has reemphasized the need to judge ERP success relative to impact on firm performance.

Chapter 4

Disruptive business models, such as software as a service and open source software, have made Enterprise Resource Planning (ERP) packages and related software more accessible for Small and Medium Enterprises (SMEs). However, the consulting required to configure an ERP to meet the specific needs of an organization remains a major financial burden for SMEs. One configuration task which is common to many ERPs is category configuration. With the help of automated category configuration support, managers of small businesses can perform category configuration on their own and reduce part of the consulting cost. This chapter presents the design of generic automation approaches for ERP category configuration, their implementation and their application to the open source ERP package ERP5. The approaches are based on similarity of example data, automatic vocabulary consolidation through Wikipedia redirects and (meta-) templates. The empirical evaluation through a laboratory experiment with one hundred test persons and a survey supports the validity, effectiveness and utility of the designed artefact.

Chapter 5

The increase of reliability and compliance of business processes is currently a major concern of organizations which simultaneously intend to achieve their organizational objectives and be compliant with external regulations. Thus, organizations are frequently looking for methods, tools and solutions which enable them to improve business compliance, and reduce the likelihood of situations that may jeopardize their operational performance and corporate image. This chapter aims to bring together a set of results and conclusions from a research project whose purpose was to conceptualize and validate an innovative solution which simultaneously monitors and audits organizational transactions executed in Enterprise Information Systems. A prototype was developed and deployed in a near-real environment. From the results, we conclude that the prototype offers Continuous Assurance services and is applicable to any organizational transaction, regardless of its type, dimension, business area or even its information system support technology. This independence is guaranteed by the abstraction level of an ontological model which is used to represent the organizational transaction we intend to monitor and audit. A case study enabled us to confirm the feasibility and effectiveness of the proposal in business compliance.

Chapter 6

Ebru E. Saygili, Yasar University, Turkey
Arikan Tarik Saygili, Izmir University of Economics, Turkey

The widespread usage of enterprise information systems (EIS) by various companies operating in different countries has led to digitalization of inter and intra-organizational business functions like customer relationship management (CRM) and supply chain management (SCM). This study considers current issues in EIS implementations in the context of enterprise resource planning (ERP) systems in different countries, industries and companies. Due to the increasing demands and varying needs of different parties, ERP implementations are getting more complex, which means considering a greater number and variety of critical success factors (CSFs). This study therefore reviews the current literature related to CSFs and their classifications before introducing a new conceptual model of 40 CSFs for successful EIS implementations.

Chapter 7

Aparna Raman, Management Development Institute, India
D. P. Goyal, Management Development Institute, India

Enterprise Information systems implementation is one of the most challenging parts of IT strategy for an organization, since implementation brings in efficiency in the system and justifies the investments made. Therefore, it becomes increasingly important to study the perspectives of implementation to understand the current dynamics. The purpose of this paper is twofold, first is to explore the type of literature that exists in information system implementation and secondly to determine the research methodologies incorporated therein for the information system field's implementation in specific. The basic content analysis is done to review the articles on information system implementation. A total of 47 articles were selected from peer reviewed journals and conferences. The study was conducted to assess the methodology used, the strategies followed along with the issues and challenges faced in the implementation. It presents an arena of the studies done in information system implementation in past 20 years (typically 1993 to 2013). The IMPLEMENT framework has been proposed to synthesize the literature finding for smooth functioning of IS implementation process. The factors influencing the adoption of information system innovation are described. The comprehensive framework for information innovation process is developed. This framework is then mapped to IMPLEMENT framework. This study would encourage the practitioners in the information systems domain to improve upon their organizational capability and incorporate other best practices.

Afzaal H. Seyal, Universiti Tecknologi Brunei, Brunei
Mohd Noah A. Rahman, Universiti Tecknologi Brunei, Brunei

The cardinal aim of this study is to assess the success of an Enterprise Resource Planning (ERP) system in investigating the role played by the top management and government support, external expertise, perceived benefits and the impact of business vision. This is a quantitative field study conducted on 150 business firms randomly selected from the Brunei Yellow Pages. In this study, 30% of the companies had practiced the ERP for more than one year. A statistical software package PSW-18 was used to analyse the data. The majority of the previous findings which include all contextual variables used were significant with an exception to the top management support which proved insignificant. Those results were compared with existing studies. The practical implications are discussed and a conclusion is drawn.

Mark Dale, Swinburne University of Technology, Australia

Enterprise architecture (EA) has provided organizations with powerful frameworks with which to plan, manage, model and coordinate the alignment of organizational IS/ IT portfolios with organizational strategy. However, for the benefits of EA to be realized, it needs to also contribute to the process of implementing the specified systems and platforms. Whilst implementation was seen by early authors as an integral aspect of the EA process, it has since generally been ignored by authors, or investigated through an ontological lens of discreet technical architecture activities that does not account for the social context of an EA implementation (EAI). Drawing on an actual case study of an EAI in a large Australian financial services organization, I examine the importance of the EAI process to the delivery of the systems and platforms specified in the EA plans and highlight an alternative perspective that has the potential to sensitize scholars and practitioners appreciate to the social context of an EAI.

Paul Hawking, Victoria University, Australia
Carmine Sellitto, Victoria University, Australia

Business Intelligence has been adopted across numerous industry sectors where the commensurate benefits have been reported as being significant to those that fall short of expectations. Indeed, an effective strategy that aligns company objectives and Business Intelligence has been shown to be an important factor in firm realizing organizational benefits. Using a case study approach, the paper documents the salient aspects of an energy company's Business Intelligence strategy that directly enhanced informational requirements. The firm's strategy embodied the adherence to certain guiding principles ensuring that the introduction of Business Intelligence directly addressed the company's needs. The paper presents a novel description of a company's Business Intelligence strategy that will provide valuable lessons for not only researchers, but also industry practitioners.

Businesses that purchase packaged application software – for example, an Enterprise Resource Planning system – must make choices about customization. Software vendors, anecdotal evidence, and practitioner-oriented research all recommend that organizations should customize software as little as possible, and instead adapt their processes to meet the "best practices" of the software. However, businesses continue to exceed their budgets on implementing and maintaining customized software, often to a significant extent. This suggests that either these organizations are making poor decisions, or that the conventional wisdom about customization is incorrect. In this paper we model the primary factors in the customization decision: "fit" between the desired business process and the packaged software; costs related to development, maintenance, integration, and performance; and benefits related to increased fit, integration, performance, and user acceptance. We use simulation techniques to illustrate the conditions under which customization is likely to provide value to the organization, as well as conditions under which customization should be avoided.

Chapter 12

This chapter presents the results and findings of a research project on innovation culture in Australian information technology sector organisations. The primary objective of this study was to establish the determinants of a successful enterprise innovation culture in organisations with a strong industry reputation for radical innovation initiatives. We obtained 244 responses from 102 member organisations of the Australian Information Industry Association (AIIA). The survey explored the internal and external characteristics of a successful innovative organisation. Both employees' and competitors' perspectives on "what makes a particular organisation a successful innovator" were the main focus. Our findings indicated that the absence of a successful innovation culture is a serious impediment to growth and success. However, preferences for the key innovation culture attributes varied significantly by executive functions, size of the organization and type of ownership structure. Thus, a mix of key innovation attributes should be deployed and tailored to each organisation, based on their industry and strategic objectives.

Chapter 13

Nastaran Mohammadhossein, Universiti Teknologi Malaysia, Malaysia
Mohammad Nazir Ahmad, Universiti Teknologi Malaysia, Malaysia
Nor Hidayati Zakaria, Universiti Teknologi Malaysia, Malaysia

The purpose of this study is to investigate the efficacy of customer relationship management (CRM) benefits for customers in relation to customer satisfaction. A model has been developed and empirically tested through data collected from a survey of 150 customers of three Malaysian companies. The results indicate that the benefits of CRM for customers have had a significant positive effect on their satisfaction towards marketing companies. Personalized services, responsiveness to customers' needs, customer segmentation, customization of marketing, multichannel integration, time-saving and improving customer knowledge are the benefits that we proposed would affect customer satisfaction and significantly improve marketing performance. Additionally, the results reveal that all the benefits found, with the exception of time-saving, enhanced customer satisfaction. This paper contributes to the existing literature by incorporating the benefits of CRM for customers, and the relationships of these benefits with their satisfaction in the proposed model.

Chapter 14

Chandra Sekhar Patro, GVP College of Engineering (Autonomous), India
K. Madhu Kishore Raghunath, National Institute of Technology, Warangal, India

Technology and world around have always been advancing time to time. One can speak of diverse areas to show how important IT is in daily business life, and of much Supply chain is one such area with more scope for Information Technology (IT) and has become a determinant of competitive advantage across the organizations. In order to survive in today's competitive environment the firms need to manage the future supply chain. In order to deliver quality information to the decision-maker at the right time and in order to automate the process of data collection, collation and refinement, the companies have to make IT an ally, harness its full potential and use it in the best possible means. IT is beneficial for cooperation and integration within the stakeholders of the supply chain. The chapter throw a light upon the stature of various technology based Tools in Supply Chain Management (SCM). The study also highlights the contribution of technology in helping to restructure the entire supply chain process to achieve higher service levels, lower inventory and the supply chain costs.

Chapter 15
Data Envelopment Analysis for Measuring and Evaluating Efficiency on IT Outsourcing

João Correia dos Santos, Instituto Superior Técnico, Portugal
Miguel Mira da Silva, Instituto Superior Técnico, Portugal

During the last decades, the IT service sector has been one of the fastest growing segment in the global economy, consequently, Information Technology (IT) outsourcing providers face several challenges: contracts are based on a multi-service configuration; high degree of variance between clients; market dynamism through rivalry, accelerated innovation, client requisites and relationship management. As a result, service providers employ several tools and methods to find the best fit between standardization (mainly for productivity increase) and customization (primarily for client satisfaction), because IT outsourcing operational context display a multi-input and multi-output set of variables that need to be known and managed, thus efficiency measurement is essential to delivery optimised IT operations. The purpose of this work is to identify, describe, evaluate and present a model based on Data Envelopment Analysis (DEA), which is a linear programming technique able to manipulate multiple inputs and outputs. DEA allows the identification of the most efficient operation that enables providers to set the best operational strategy to follow. To develop our research, design science research was applied, and eighteen contracts were used to evaluate our model's utility the results show the importance of quantitative measures in a dynamic business environment like IT outsourcing. This work is a major contribution for measuring efficiency in IT outsourcing operations.

Chapter 16

Sabrina Šuman, Polytechnic of Rijeka, Croatia
Alen Jakupović, Polytechnic of Rijeka, Croatia
Mile Pavlić, University of Rijeka, Croatia

Data modelling is a complex process that depends on the knowledge and experience of the designers who carry it out. The lack of designers' expertise in that process negatively affects the quality of created models which has a significant impact on the quality of successive phases of information systems development. This chapter provides an overview of data modelling, especially the entity relationship method, main actors in the modelling process, and highlights the main problems and challenges in this field. Knowledge based system for data modelling support has a potential to minimize and prevent most of the problems that occur in modelling process. Therefore, a systematic review of the existing KB systems, methods, and tools for the data modelling process is made. By summarizing their main characteristics, some important desirable features of the new KB system for data modelling support are identified. With this in mind, a new KB system for data modelling support is proposed, which applies formal language theory (particularly translation) during the process of conceptual modelling.

An understanding of how teams make decisions in the team environment is of utmost importance to organizational leaders. This research aims to determine the relationship that a shared leadership environment has on a team's approach to decision-making. A systematic review of past research efforts has shown that a strong relationship exists between the internal and external conditions of shared leadership and that a strong relationship exists between shared leadership and six sigma team decision-making principles and approaches. Furthermore, a review of the relationship between shared leadership and team decision making techniques has shown that the consensual approach is the most effective method to achieve the functional conditions of shared leadership. Based on the presented research, a model of decision-making in shared leadership environments is proposed for use by teams to determine the type of decision-making method that should be employed as a team's level of shared leadership increases. This model has been shown to have many practical applications for business as well as for academic research.

This paper presents the results of an exploratory study developed to identify the current CIO's main activities, to verify whether CIO's demographics and CIO's business context influence the perception of the importance of CIO activities and to identify CIO's main skills. The results show that managing projects, interacting with top management teams, optimizing business processes and making strategic decisions are main CIO's activities; and that the importance recognized to these activities is influenced by characteristics such as the CIO's age or the hierarchical structure of the organization. Regarding CIO's skills, understanding business processes and operations, and strategic thinking and planning, are the ones CIOs identified as being the most important.

Preface

In Chapter 1 titled "Mental Modelling Digital Aged Care and Service Management," Hume and Johnston show that aged care is projected to be the fastest-growing sector within health and community care industries and strengthening care-giving compliance, delivery and digital aged health care is not only vital to our social infrastructure and improving the quality of care, but also has the potential to drive long-term economic growth and contribute to the GDP through improved performance and service delivery. They argue that the key to responding to this pressure is increased empowerment and capability of leadership and management within the aged care workforce and offsetting practices through advance technological developments and knowledge creation. Digital health care and digital health care strategies are the focus of current health care discussion and investigation. How can we use digital disruption to improve delivery and enhance patient wellbeing? Aged care is becoming more diverse and complex advancing from residential care to incorporate community directed care. Thus, "aged care knowledge" and the information that feeds it is becoming increasingly heterogeneous placing more emphasis on the need for better Knowledge Management (KM) including its creation, storage access and diffusion to ensure high levels of care. They focus on aged care services as a national priority with this also a priority for many countries worldwide. With limited research related to KM in aged care, this chapter advances knowledge and offers a unique view of KM from the perspective of 28 aged care stakeholders. Using in-depth interviewing coupled with mental model pictorials, they explore where digital aged care may support knowledge capture and management for aged care providers. The chapter culminates in an offering some reflections for a digital agenda for aged care and advances the discourse in this sector. The Australian aged care system is seen as innovative globally and provides the benchmark for many countries developing reforms and strategies for aged care.

In Chapter 2 titled "Leveraging Enterprise Resource Planning Systems to Digitize Business Functions," Nair and Reddy conceptualize Enterprise Resource Planning (ERP) systems as an interaction between social and technical factors of a large organization. The chapter begins with a review of evolution of ERP to recognize the theme of the research. ERP implementation is based on organizational change that ERP brings about due to its intervention on the organization. From this standpoint, ERP implementation research can be classified into two major groups where ERP deployment corresponds to a technical system and ERP organizational intervention corresponds to a social system. Though ERP implementation is highly researched, a framework illustrating all its dimensions to enable the organizational decision makers to configure the most suitable combination of variables for a research theme is lacking. The chapter is significant in terms of theoretical rigor. The unique proposed framework named by the authors as Process Variance Adapted SocioTechnical (PVAST) model identifies variables known here as Critical Success Factors (CSF), a Variance perspective through grounded research methodology for ERP implementation.

The authors have presented the two premises where they compare and contrast the process and variance theoretical perspectives respectively to explain why any one of the perspectives used in isolation may not serve the purpose of evaluating the performance of ERP implementation from an organizational change viewpoint. They then cluster the identified CSF under SocioTechnical dimensions and analyze them based on process perspective. The focal point of this model is that the decision makers of the organization can cluster the CSF based on phase of lifecycle of ERP implementation. The authors have specifically leveraged the Leavitt's organizational change model to evaluate ERP performance through CSF since ERP is a technological intervention on the social structure of the organization. Integrating process-variance perspective with SocioTechnical perspective based on Leavitt's diamond model is an attempt to measure and monitor ERP performance and pinpoint areas where corrective actions need to be taken up during the ERP life cycle by the decision makers or practitioners in a coherent method.

In Chapter 3 titled "Improving Logistics Costs Through ERP Alignment," Muscatello, Parente, and Swinarski study ERP implementations and their impact on business on several dimensions. They argue that little work has been done linking logistics costs and ERP implementation factors. Taking a Work System Theoretical perspective, they examine the alignment success factors necessary to improve logistics cost. They use a two-step approach, conducting a confirmatory factor analysis (CFA) to assess the psychometric properties of our measures and then conducting an independent sample t-test between two groups, one which experienced decreased logistic costs and the second which experienced the same or increasing logistic costs. Organizations attempting to decrease logistics costs via an ERP implementation must consider the processes and activities involved in aligning participants, information, technology, and business process in these ERP implementations. Their research provides more insight into the practice of ERP implementations and has reemphasized the need to judge ERP success relative to impact on firm performance. This chapter is the first study exploring ERP success using Work System Theory to both hypothesize and empirically determine the causal link between critical success factors associated with alignment and logistics costs.

In Chapter 4 titled "Approaches for Automating ERP Category Configuration for SMEs," Wölfel presents automation of ERP implementation as a solution for making ERP packages more accessible for small businesses. His motivation comes from the fact that the ERP market is turning more and more towards Small and Medium Enterprises (SMEs) and that the cost of ERP implementation is still a major burden for them. When part of the implementation process can be automated, ERP packages become more affordable for SMEs. The author introduces the concept of category configuration as a general ERP implementation problem and describes the design and implementation of automation approaches to support managers of small businesses to perform an ERP category configuration on their own. The presented solution, the Category Configuration Support (CCS) system, was implemented with and applied to the open source ERP package "ERP5". It is based on innovative approaches from data science such as similarity of example data, automatic vocabulary consolidation through Wikipedia redirects and (meta-) templates. The solution was evaluated empirically for its validity, effectiveness and utility through a laboratory experiment. After introducing the general topic, the author compares the concept of ERP category configuration to other types of ERP package "tailoring". The reader should have a quick look at the exemplary category configuration for a small software company shown in appendix II which makes the concept much clearer. It is interesting to see how this concept exists in completely different ERP packages, such as SAP, OpenERP and ERP5. The author compares the challenge of automating category configuration to prior ERP configuration automation approaches. The mayor difference is that prior approaches focus on parametrization and therefore operate on a relatively small and well-defined value range and are therefore mostly implemented as rule-based systems. The range of possible values in category configuration on the other hand can be much larger. To tackle this specific challenge of automating category configuration, the author presents a new approach based on a questionnaire filled by the manager of a small company. The answers are used as input to a model built from an example data set consisting of 235 questionnaires already filled by managers of other small companies and ERP category configurations for these companies. Through a similarity measure, the model than outputs the most useful categories which the company manager uses to create his own category configuration. After describing the technical implementation of the designed automation approach – the CCS System – and its application to the open source ERP package ERP5, the author describes the empirical evaluation of the designed artefact. The laboratory experiment with 98 test persons indicates the validity, effectiveness and utility of the CCS System. Finally, the author summarizes the contributions of his research to theory and practice. He shows that the concept of category configuration is universal to ERP systems and the designed solution approach can be used for automating the configuration of categories of other ERP packages, not only ERP5. The main implication for practice is that the CCS System can reduce the financial burden of ERP implementation for SMEs. It streamlines part of the ERP package configuration process by enabling the management of a small business to create an effective ERP category configuration on its own.

In Chapter 5 titled "Continuous Assurance and Business Compliance in Enterprise Information Systems," Marques addresses business compliance and continuous assurance, which are very important and current organizational issues and concerns. The adoption of tools which enable organizations to improve business compliance and to reduce the likelihood of situations that may jeopardize their operational performance and corporate image, also allow them to simultaneously achieve their organizational objectives and be compliant with external regulations. The work described in this chapter is innovative and contributes to a new vision of organizational auditing focused on assurance services in transactions executed in digital format and supported by a business ontological model. It presents a conceptual architecture of an information system with continuous assurance services and describes some details about the prototype development. An innovative aspect of this solution is related to the fact that the author considered that there are different risk profiles (execution patterns used as reference) for each organizational transaction and developed a repository that manages the risk profiles of the transactions to monitor and audit, following an ontology. These risk profiles are important because they allow the prototype to compare these references with the data from the executions of monitored transactions and to produce auditing results in run-time. This view of monitoring, controlling and auditing of organizational transactions is innovative since there was no reference in the literature to any implementation of risk profiles repository in the aforementioned way. Another innovative aspect of this view is the attempt to provide assurance services to organizational transactions following the structure of an ontology, which presents the transaction at a very low level, contrary to what happens in most monitoring of transactions, which occur at a high level (for example, compare whether a completed transaction followed a set of established procedures). This chapter is interesting and relevant because the main results from a case study are presented. The case study includes the implementation of the prototype in a near-real organizational environment and the analysis of few hundreds of transactions made up of more than a thousand operations monitored and audited. From the results, the author concluded that the prototype offers continuous assurance services and is applicable to any organizational transaction, regardless of its type, dimension, business area or even its information system support technology. This independence is guaranteed by the abstraction level of an ontological model which is used to represent the organizational transactions we intend to monitor and audit. Finally, this work is contrary to the tendency of products to be advertised as continuous service providers, when in fact they only provide part of these services. This chapter ensures the feasibility of the development and the effective use of an information system with full continuous assurance services, having as support an ontological model, and which is considerably flexible and adaptable in order to be applicable to any digitally executed organizational transaction.

In Chapter 6 titled "Contemporary Issues in Enterprise Information Systems: A Critical Review of CSFs in ERP Implementations," Saygili and Saygili argue that the widespread usage of enterprise information systems (EISs) brings with it the digitalization of organizations' business functions while these systems' extended functionality integrates organizations and stakeholders. For example, new enterprise resource planning (ERP) software extensions include customer relationship management (CRM) and supply chain management (SCM). Given recent developments, the authors discuss contemporary issues in EIS concerning ERP systems various different countries, industries and companies. Due to the increasing demands and varying needs of different parties, ERP implementations are getting more complex, which has increased the number and variety of critical success factors (CSFs) needing consideration. In this paper, 40 CSFs are identified and re-categorized to develop a new conceptual model for explaining ERP implementation success. The model is derived from a comprehensive search through the most cited 17 articles concerning CSFs published between 1999 and 2013 which groups the 40 CSFs under four inter-related categories: Administration (8 CSFs), Project and Team Management (14), ERP Software (11) and Organization (7). The relationship between the categories is created through bridging CSFs. Some CSFs relate to external parties like consultants, vendors, country-specific regulations, customers and suppliers. Most previous studies have relied on literature reviews and case studies to identify CSFs, with only a very few empirical studies. The main limitation in this study was the difficulty of conducting empirical research to access primary data due to justified confidentiality issues raised by private enterprises. Nevertheless, the authors believe that exploring CSFs from stakeholders' perspectives will provide valuable insights that lead to more successful ERP system implementations.

In Chapter 7 titled "Extending IMPLEMENT Framework for Enterprise Information Systems Implementation to Information System Innovation," Raman and Goyal argue that organizations today strive to differentiate themselves to outperform themselves from their competitors. Information Systems innovation has helped the organizations to utilize their capability to the fullest. Further, Enterprise Information systems implementation is one of the most challenging parts of IT strategy for an organization, since implementation brings in efficiency in the system and justifies the investments made. Therefore, it becomes increasingly important to study the perspectives of implementation to understand the current dynamics. They study the literature of information system implementation, exploring the research methodologies and other factors influencing information system implementation. Further, the literature on information system innovation, the factors influencing overall information system implementation and based on the information, information system innovation process is deduced. The basic content analysis is done to review the articles on information system implementation. A total of 47 articles were selected from peer reviewed journals and conferences. The study was conducted to assess the methodology used, the strategies followed along with the issues and challenges faced in the implementation. It presents an arena of the studies done in information system implementation in past 20 years (typically 1993 to 2013). They propose the IMPLEMENT framework to synthesize the literature finding for smooth functioning of IS implementation process. The comprehensive framework for information innovation process is developed. This framework is then mapped to IMPLEMENT framework. Further, the ingenuity that innovation possesses has attracted a lot of researchers to think and study about what the information systems (IS) innovation is and how it relates to any organization. It applies to varied organizations, from private organizations to cater to the client requests to the public organizations overhauling their services to cater to the citizen and stakeholder needs. An information system is an important component, to improve product, processes and services. In today's dynamic and competitive business environment, success can only be achieved by providing new products, services, and solutions for consumers to provide radically better experience. The Information system innovation process framework is deduced in the study, through content analysis of 49 papers selected from peer reviewed journals. They then map the IMPLEMENT framework to the information system innovation process. This framework can serve as an aid both to the researchers and the managers. The researchers can further prove this model empirically, whereas the managers can understand the IS innovation process in an organization. The usage of IMPLEMENT framework in context of strategy based concepts such as information system innovation helps in establishing the extent to which this concept can be extended to contemporary and relevant contexts.

In Chapter 8 titled "Investigating Impact of Inter-Organizational Factors in Measuring ERP Systems Success: Bruneian Perspectives," Seyal and Rahman present a research to assess the success of an Enterprise Resource Planning (ERP) system in Brunei Darussalam. They first provide an understanding of ERP success factor among Bruneian businesses by assessing the validity of ERP success model of Ifinedo and Nehar within the context of Brunei Darussalam. They then study the various internal and external factors (business vision, top management support, external expertise, government support and perceived benefits) that contribute towards the success of ERP system. The majority of the previous findings which include all contextual variables used were significant with an exception to the top management support which proved insignificant. The significance of four (4) contextual variables in this study provide valuable insights on how businesses find them relevant in measuring ERP success. The business owners and regulatory authorities should focus on these and highlight them in planning seminars and road shows so that the organizations that are in the process of considering the ERP systems should consider it during the implementation phase as well.

In Chapter 9 titled "Re-Thinking the Challenges of Enterprise Architecture Implementation," Dale articulates the concept of enterprise architecture implementation (EAI) and differentiates EAI from enterprise architecture (EA) plan development. It puts forward a historical analysis of EA to demonstrate that early authors of EA frameworks, methods and tools did differentiate between EA plan development and EAI. EAI was seen as a product of EA plan development and was assumed to follow on immediately from EA plan development. A review of the EAI research indicates that EA plan development and EAI are distinct phases of work and that many organizations have difficulty transitioning from the development of their plans to the implementation of those plans. Whilst there is considerable literature attesting to the benefits of EA, the motivations for EAI are primarily to support a new organizational strategy and improve operational performance. However, organizations have little confidence in implementing their EA plans, the costs associated with EAI are too high and stakeholders lose interest in the EAI due to the protracted time required to deliver the systems and platforms specified in the technology selection plans. To date, much of the EAI literature has adopted a technical and rationalist approach to the challenges of EAI and ignored the relational aspects of an EAI. This chapter makes an important contribution to the area of EAI research and practice, by arguing that greater attention needs to be paid to the practices of architects that promote and inhibit connections with their stakeholders. In an EAI, architects will engage with a number of stakeholders from the business and technology who have a legitimate interest in the EAI. Based on the gaps in our knowledge of the social aspects of EAI and the emphasis on the technical aspects of EAI found in existing research, we need to improve our understanding of the practices of architects, including the relationships they build with their stakeholders and how this may affect the transition from the development of the EA plans to the implementation of those plans. While organizations continue to develop EA plans in order to benefit from the advantages of EA-enabled systems and platforms, many EAI initiatives continue to fail and more are likely to fail than succeed. Despite the active interest of organizations and governments in EA, academic interest in this area remains comparatively modest and tends to focus on EA frameworks, EA modelling approaches and methods, and the management of the EA function. The role of the interactions between architects and their stakeholders plays in the ability of architects to build support for and commitment to the systems and platforms specified in the EAI is under-investigated.

In Chapter 10 titled "Developing an Effective Strategy for Organizational Business Intelligence," Hawking and Sellitto contribute to understanding the growing importance of Business Intelligence in the modern-day enterprise. As an extension of firm's ERP system, Business Intelligence can provide significant benefits associated with allowing firms to access accurate, relevant and timely information that enhances corporate decision-making practices. The article uses a case study approach to clearly document and present the strategy an Australian energy company developed and used as part of their adoption of Business Intelligence. The paper is timely due to recent advent of big data and digital transformation practices—where Business Intelligence adoption has been touted as a powerful tool that can be used with in-memory data processing to enable competitive advantage. The case study is presented as a story, allowing the reader to understand some of the strategies the company adopted in confronting the various challenges and short-comings encountered. Indeed, one important component of the strategy was to adopt an enterprise approach to the use of Business Intelligence. This was initially achieved through the consolidation of existing Business Intelligence technologies and subsequent introduction of enterprise-wide data warehouse (EDW). Illustrative examples of the types of software considered and replaced are part of the case study— for instance, the discontinuance of the Business Objects environment was facilitated by SAP acquiring Business Objects. The case study presents insight into the developed an Information Management Strategy (IMS) to provide some overarching guiding principles for the implementation and use of Business Intelligence to ensure a closer alignment with company's needs. The IMS reflects a set of multi-faceted application points that can be used by researchers or practitioners per se to be better informed about not only the implementation process, but to also promote the alignment of business objectives. The authors make a relevant and timely contribution to the Business Intelligence domain by documenting the importance of business strategy aligning with the proposed solution. Although centered on the energy sector, the strategic approach reported could be usefully adopted by companies in other industry groups.

In Chapter 11 titled "To Code or Not to Code: Obtaining Value From the Customization of Packaged Application Software," Balint argue that packaged application software such as ERP promises many benefits in theory. Industry best business practices, professional support, and the elimination of the need to hire software developers are some examples. However, what these claims miss is that no two organizations are the same, and no two organizations implement the same package the same way. In his experience as an SAP consultant, the author witnessed many organizations whose implementation timelines and budgets were greatly exceeded due to the customization of ERP packages. In some cases, the organizations underestimated the amount of resources the custom development would take, a problem endemic to most software development. In other cases, the organization made poor choices when selecting the packaged software initially and tried to "close the gap" with customization. Most of the author's research is empirical, but data describing packaged software customization in different organizations are difficult to collect and quantify. Instead, the author decided to create a mathematical model of customization and to run simulations while changing the variables of interest. These variables include development and maintenance costs, the purpose of the development and the starting fit of the system. The results provide an interesting description of the effects that different types of custom development have on implementation outcomes. Custom development with the direct purpose of increasing fit, or with the intention of increasing user acceptance, can provide value to organizations. However, even under favorable circumstances the benefits of custom development do not outweigh the benefit of choosing the software package with the highest level of fit "out of the box". This research contributes to the literature on software development in two ways. First, while there is much research on ERP generally there is very little on customization. Project managers who are responsible for packaged software implementations often have to make difficult decisions on how much customization to do and how to prioritize it. ERP projects often use the FRICE framework (Forms, Reports, Interfaces, Conversions, Enhancements) to categorize this work. Instead, this paper approaches custom development by examining the impact of custom development on implementation and organizational outcomes. Second, while the era of huge ERP implementations is largely in the past, this research is more relevant than ever. As more organizations of all sizes are embracing information systems, the question of how much to customize continues to be important. Additionally, the Software as a Service model of application delivery continues to grow. This study should inform SAAS choices in terms of the amount of customizability available to organizations.

In Chapter 12 titled "Decoding Success Factors of Innovation Culture," Burdon, Kang, and Mooney review how successful organizations face the challenge of transforming a creative concept into a new service, product or process – in other words, the development of innovation. The authors chose to survey the Australian IT Industry Association members and assessed responses from 102 organizations. The technology sector was deemed especially relevant as it is often the vanguard of change - a fast moving, inventive and competitive industry whose advances often presage and underpin the innovative progress of many other markets. Because of the fast-changing nature of the IT industry, their approach to risk and reward is particularly pertinent, which encourages them to focus more of their innovation strategy on radical opportunities. Taking a creative idea and turning it into an innovative product requires the involvement of many people, not just the originators, and helps explain why fostering an innovation culture is particularly important. This involves action, collaboration and learning that can handle successive innovation processes – an intrinsic embedding of ways to differentiate acceptable and unacceptable behaviors plus prevailing systems governing decision-making, performance, success, failure, and rewards for a given context. The research confirmed that organizations where employees and competitors believed the organization had a strong innovation culture produced higher profit margins, superior financial metrics, high morale and recognition from peers and competitors. Thus, promoting the right social settings and values ensures an innovation culture that delivers new and improved products and services for customers, sustained improvements in service, better business models, effective branding, and more positive engagement at all levels. Conversely, less open contexts where processes, knowledge, resources, and personnel are more rigidly structured and closely regulated also tend to see a slowing in the pace and number of innovations realized. More specifically, the survey asked the respondents to assess their own organization's ability to meet ten key attributes. The research found that those organizations where their executives believed they had implemented the ten key issues to a high level strongly correlated with organizational growth rate, which was used as a surrogate for success. The most commonly esteemed attributes for successful organizations were the 'ability of the organization to communicate and align employee activities to the strategic plan', 'ability to create an inclusive interlinked culture' and 'ability to encourage learning and self-improvement in its people'. The chapter also explores differences in fostering an innovation culture, dependent on organizational size, ownership and the ability to build an innovation culture at all levels of the organization. In summary, this research shows a significant difference between the scores for Australian private and partnership organizations compared with those of the multinationals and ASX-listed organizations. Organizations that promoted 'self-improvement' and had an 'inclusive culture' were much more likely to have well-developed innovation cultures - and be recognized for this not only internally but also externally by other companies.

In Chapter 13 titled "Benefits of Customer Relationship Management on Customer Satisfaction: An Empirical Study," Mohammadhossein, Ahmad, and Zakaria assess the effectiveness of customer relationship management (CRM) benefits from customer point of view in relation to customer satisfaction. Main objective is defined as finding out the important benefits of CRM for customers based on the previous literatures. Personalized service, responsiveness to customer's needs, customer segmentation, customization of marketing, multichannel integration, time-saving and improving customer knowledge were proposed as important benefits which would affect customer satisfaction. The authors propose a model which has seven constructs that will influence customer satisfaction. The participants were 150 customers of three Malaysian companies (AEON, Tesco, PETRONAS). The authors find that customer satisfaction was positively related to all the CRM benefits found, except for time-saving. The correlations between using CRM and improve marketing performance were significant. The findings confirm that the companies that using CRM can improve their customer satisfaction. In addition, this paper contributes to the existing literature by incorporating the benefits of CRM for customers and the relationships of these benefits with their satisfaction in a proposed research model and empirically tested.

In Chapter 14 titled "Information Technology Paraphernalia for Supply Chain Management Decisions," Patro and Raghunath provide the readers with an insight into the world of Supply chain management after technology was encapsulated into it making organizations facilitate production and distribution with much easy, cost effective and moreover with better customer service. The companies are trying to improve their agility level with the objective of being flexible and responsive to meet the changing market requirements. The authors deal with the current scenario of supply chain management process and how it is managed keeping in mind the growing need of various stakeholders in this business. They also analyze how both supply chain management and Information Technology has gelled together for the benefit of stakeholders, by articulating the functional role of IT in supply chain processes in and around organization. Supply chain management emphasizes the overall and long-term benefit of all parties on the chain through co-operation and information sharing. Going ahead in this chapter, readers can gain some significant insights into the existing and emerging trends of Information Technology in Supply Chain Management process highlighting the advancements Information Technology has in SCM. Along with that we also observe the influence of these Information Technological trends on supply chain areas or to say as Supply Chain decisions like Location Decision, Inventory decision, Production decision, Transport/Distribution decisions. For the purpose the opinion of the employees of different companies has been analyzed to give a better understanding of the implementation of these emerging IT trends. The strategic and technological innovations in supply chain will impact on how organizations transact in future. Information and communication technologies are beneficial for co-operation and integration within the stakeholders of the supply chain. However clear vision, strong planning and technical insight into the transformational capabilities would be necessary to ensure that organizations maximize the technological potential for better supply chain management and ultimately improved competitiveness.

As we all know change is not easy and welcome and of course even in Supply Chain Management and after reading this chapter readers will be able interprets the various challenges that organizations come across while implementing Information Technology in Supply Chain Management. Finally, the chapter also discusses the impact and benefits of e-business technologies that helps to re-structure the entire supply chain process for achieving higher productivity and sustain the competitive market.

In Chapter 15 titled "Data Envelopment Analysis for Measuring and Evaluating Efficiency on IT Outsourcing Operations," dos Santos and da Silva deliver a model for efficiency measuring in IT outsourcing operations. A deep research on service operations was made, to identify the service dimensions and service items applicable to IT outsourcing operations, which displays a multi-input and multi-output set of variables that need to be known and managed, thus knowing what service dimensions and service items are available for IT outsourcing services configuration is essential to delivery optimised IT operations. Then, Data Envelopment Analysis (DEA), which is a linear programming technique able to manipulate multiple inputs and outputs, was used for efficiency measurement in IT outsourcing contracts (DMUs) to identify potential sources of inefficiency, recognizing best-practice DMUs for subsequent standardization of operations. During the research, authors, found several challenges, the first one was to gain access to real data to test the proposed model, and even with real data, not all the simulations were possible to execute, namely the multiple time periods also named as windows analysis (time series data). Secondly, the nomination of the seven service dimensions and the 23 service items can be considered excessive or minimalist depending on the research problem and service configuration to attain. However, according to the results obtained, they are found adequately complete, broad and capable of fitting in most scenarios of IT outsourcing operations. The developed research was based on design science research, and eighteen contracts were used to evaluate model utility, the results show the importance of quantitative measures in a dynamic business environment like IT outsourcing, which will allow IT outsourcing providers to identifying the "pain points" and act for efficiency improve in a multi-client environment.

In Chapter 16 titled "Knowledge-Based Systems for Data Modelling: Review and Challenges," Šuman, Jakupović, and Pavlić argue that data modelling is a complex and knowledge intensive process and show data modelling is appropriate for Knowledge-Based (KB) system approach because it is a non-algorithmic, non-trivial, and not fully deterministic nature. The primary benefits of introducing KB system into the process of a data modelling are: gathering rare and costly human expertise and performing and validating design activities. KB system also provides an explanatory system, which explains the rationale behind its actions and therefore educates the user. Finally, a KB system updates its knowledge base and so constantly improves itself. It is expected that KB system will help designers to create semantically high-quality data models. This will be achieved through the main KB system functionality: proposition of a data model based on the previous cases, user question-answering guidance, identification of the semantic errors in the data model, and advising users. This chapter argues about the main problems in the process of the data modelling and reviews some KB systems, methods, and tools for the data modelling. Reviewed KB systems are used for identification of their existing problems (for example too complex formalisation of the business description in natural language, too many questions to a user, no past data model repository etc.). Based on that, in the paper is proposed a conceptual model of the new KB system that tends to simplify input format in the form of the controlled natural language, uses case-based reasoning, creates a minimal number of specific questions to a user, and has an explanatory system. The main mechanism for developing a data model is a translation from one language into another. Business description is observed as the text-expressed knowledge in natural language that needs to be translated into the text-expressed knowledge in the data model formal language. A conceptual model of the new KB system is represented through a Logic model framework where its Purpose Context, Inputs, Activities, Outputs and Effects are identified.

In Chapter 17 titled "Six Sigma Project Teams and Rational Decision Making: A Shared Leadership Perspective," Galli, Szabat, and Kaviani argue that the concept of how teams make decisions in the team environment is a very important topic for all organizations and leaders to consider. More and more organizations rely on teams to complete a variety of projects, from new product development projects to process improvement projects, all of which impact the performance of the organization as a whole. Therefore, it is of the utmost importance that organizations and leaders understand how teams work and what styles they use to make effective and rational decisions. Only by understanding how teams make decisions and what makes them tick (in terms of performance and decision-making), will organizational leaders have the ability to help the teams to maximize their performance and therefore maximize the return on investment (ROI) to the organization. This research helped to build on the body of knowledge by studying and understanding the most common and effective forms of decision making methods that teams utilize to not only make timely decisions but also rational and quality decisions. A decision-making framework was developed that outlines the appropriate method of decision-making a team should use as a team's level of shared leadership increases. A team can utilize the findings from this research to more effectively plan how decisions should be made based on their level of team cohesion and style of team leadership present in the team environment. Team coaches or mentors can actively plan how they mentor and guide the teams they are responsible for. They can utilize the framework as an assessment tool to diagnose their team's performance and quality of decisions in order to adjust their style and level of coaching and mentoring, which in turn should help to maximize the quality and rationality of the team level decision-making.

In Chapter 18 titled "An Exploratory Study on the Influencers of the Perceived Relevance of CIO's Activities and Skills: An Update," Trigo and Soto-Acosta present a study which is the continuation of their research activity on the management of information systems and its main actor as the information systems manager commonly known as the Chief Information Officer (CIO). This study presents the activities and skills that 102 CIOs consider to be the most important for the performance of their profession. It is important to emphasize that this study is a rich study from the point of view of the respondents because they are experts in this domain, that of the management of information systems, knowing as nobody what the most important activities and competences. In addition to presenting a list of the most important activities and competencies, the authors also investigated whether the personal or company characteristics that CIOs belong to influence the perception of the importance of the activities performed by CIOs. This is an important aspect not previously investigated by the authors who tries to see if there is conditioning in the CIOs' responses in function of the characteristics described above. Regarding the contributions to the body of knowledge of the CIOs theme, the results show that managing projects, interacting with top management teams, optimizing business processes, and making strategic decisions are main CIO's activities; and that the importance recognized to these activities is influenced by characteristics such as the CIO's age or the hierarchical structure of the organization. Regarding CIO's skills, understanding business processes and operations, and strategic thinking and planning, are the ones CIOs identified as being the most important. Being this an explorative study, it would be also interesting to expand it with further studies considering other variables as, for instance, business sectors or business geographies.

Madjid Tavana
La Salle University, USA

Chapter 1
Mental Modelling Digital Aged Care and Service Management

Margee Hume
CQ University Australia, Australia

Paul Johnston
Care Systems, Australia

ABSTRACT

Aged care is projected to be the fastest-growing sector within health and community care industries with digital aged care growing in interest. Strengthening understanding of delivery and technology will assist in better delivery and reach more elderly in need through improved service delivery. In this we examine advance recent discourse on the role of knowledge management (KM) in digital aged care with the view to assist delivery of aged care. We advance knowledge by offering a unique view of KM from the perspective of 28 aged care stakeholders through in-depth interviewing and mental model pictorials. We offer advances in understanding for digital aged care and suggest practices for knowledge capture and management for aged care providers. We culminate the discussion by offering a digital agenda for aged care facilities and advance the discourse in this sector. Specifically reflections are offered for leadership and the consideration of the key players and links that should be developed in comprehensively capturing and disseminating knowledge digitally in the sector.

INTRODUCTION

Health informatics is a field of growing interest, popularity, and research. It deals with the resources, ICT (information and communications technology), and methods required to facilitate the acquisition, storage, retrieval, and use of information in the health sector. Currently, the tools include computers, formal medical terminologies such as tele-health monitors and information and communication systems, with knowledge management systems at the forefront of thought in health (Murray & Carter, 2005). This chapter embraces the important area of knowledge generation and informatics in aged care healthcare and introduces digital applications and channels for consideration. This chapter focuses on informing the advance of an analytics - driven operational systems and innovative KM hub practices for aged care

DOI: 10.4018/978-1-5225-2382-6.ch001

management and patient care services and advances on previous early work (Hume et al, 2014). Analytics is focused on communication and decision-making based on meaningful patterns in data gained from a methodological analysis. The chapter introduces the providers view of the digital pathways that will support knowledge management, decision support systems and data management in aged care and focuses on the importance of the diffusion pathways of knowledge to those in need.

Many countries including Australia are burdened with an ageing population (Venturato & Drew, 2010). This burden has created the need for policy reform and the introduction of new programs to improve the quality of life of senior citizens (Department of Health and Ageing, 2013). The changing industry needs are driven by a combination of changing demographics, changing care needs, increased funding for community care and restructuring by service providers to meet government reforms and initiatives. The recent reforms of aged care finding and delivery has created the need to exploit new information and knowledge to ensure innovative delivery and offer more innovative access to the aged. This need and the increased complexity of the information required to positon care at the forefront of consumer choice, encourages the need to be innovative in the management of knowledge ((Bailey & Clarke, 2001; Binney, 2000; Blair, 2002; Wiig, 1997) and the digital delivery of care. There is no doubt t some types of knowledge are efficiently managed such as patient medical records, funding reporting and basic accreditation records. However there is much data available that can enable better work practice and cost efficiencies that is not being accessed (Venturato & Drew, 2010; Sankaran, Cartwright, Kelly, Shaw, Soar, 2010) and digital practices that can enable this data to be used for more effective care.

The Australian Aged Care Sector

The aged sector needs are driven by a combination of demographics, changing care needs, increased funding for community care and restructuring by service providers to meet government reforms and initiatives. With 84% of community care packages and approximately 60% of residential aged care services, provided by not-for-profit (NFP) organizations (Productivity Commission, 2011) it is vital to assist and inform leadership, decision making and productivity improvements through advanced leadership techniques and decision making support such as KM (Bailey &Clarke, 2001; Binney, 2000; Blair, 2002). The notion of effective leadership and decision making warrants continued investigation. Previous work (Jeon, Merlyn, & Chenoweth, 2010; Cartwright, Sankaran & Kelly, 2008) identified that NFP aged care leaders require improved and supported decision making and knowledge support for leadership and performance was identified as an essential part of this (Riege, 2005). Knowledge supporting the accreditation process and ability to meet compliance expectations and standards was the primary focus of this knowledge support. While some KM systems and knowledge hubs have been developed in health they have failed to meet the requirements of the broader sector in a consistent manner with further research and advanced application required specifically in aged care (Pinnington, 2011; Hume and Hume 2008; Hume, Pope & Hume 2012; Hume Clarke & Hume, 2012).

Specifically, the research is:

- Not context specific to aged care;
- the KM business cases have been conducted in for profit firms and insufficiently flexible for use in NFP organizations and in particular health and faith based firms;
- Fail to embrace the aged care sector diversity, complexities and requirements of accreditation and quality of care; and

- Do not encompass the emergence of increased reporting requirements, client demand and flexibility required to deliver end-to-end aged care and community directed care.

The ABS has projected growth of the number of Australians aged 65 years or over to increase from the current 15 per cent to 21 per cent by 2026 and 28 per cent by 2056 (ABS 2012). This trend towards an ageing population poses social and economic challenges which are being responded to by the Australian Government through its *Living Longer Living Better* reform package (Department of Health and Ageing, 2013). The 2011 Productivity Commission report, *Caring for Older Australians* and the Commonwealth Department of Health and Ageing 2012 *Living Longer, Living Better,* aged care reform package, will be implemented between 2013 and 2022. The NFP providers in aged care sector employ nearly 900,000 staff, with support from 4.6 million volunteers (Productivity Commission 2010 and face continued funding and regulatory constraints, workforce shortages (Palmer, 2012), increasing frailty of clients and a rapidly increasing demand for complex professional and health services. These have been heralded major changes in the aged care sector (Comondor, Devereaux, Zhou, Stone, Busse, Ravindran, Burns, Haines, Stringer, Cook, Walter, Sullivan, Berwanger, Bhandari, Banglawala, Lavis, Petrisor, Schünemann, Walsh, Bhatnagar, Guyatt, 2009). These changes include an expansion of home care services and the introduction of a dementia supplement to support people with dementia receiving care at home and in residential care. In addition, recent changes to the Aged Care Funding Instrument (ACFI) for residential care aims to embed consumer-directed care principles into mainstream aged care program delivery and ensure the sustainability of facilities in regional, rural and remote areas. The reforms combine income and assets tests into a means-testing arrangement and introduced a lifetime cap on care fees (AIHW 2012). This reform package aims to deliver systems that provide older Australians with more choice, control and easier access to a full range of services, when and where they require it.

With these reforms come advanced management, leadership and business applications requirements for providers to meet the challenges and requirements of the future and comply with government legislation. The management of knowledge in aged care sectors is currently erratic and inconsistent and firms are suggested to be low on the capability maturity index KM considers the requirements and current practice of knowledge capture, storage, retrieval and diffusion (Davenport & Prusak, 2000) and the system assists current aged care providers in meeting the compliance and reporting needs of reforms and government legislation. A KM system also assists in creating flexibility catering for these and other imminent reforms and changes. Better management of knowledge and business intelligence will enable aged care providers in improved and streamlined patient management and service delivery (Lettieri, Borga, Savoldelli, 2004). The aged care sector is growing in most OECD countries; cost pressures and challenges of access and affordability are commonly reported. With the early baby-boomer generation now entering their late-60s, it is critical to incorporate technology-enabled solutions to facilitate the delivery of cost-effective aged care and address many of the challenges of managing this sector.

From any perspective, the Knowledge Management (KM) landscape is a complex one, not least in the diverse definitions of knowledge itself (Grant, 1996; Quintane et al., 2011; Tsoukas and Vladimirou, 2001; Spender, 2002; Crane, 2012). Despres and Chauvel (2002) counted 72 different KM theories, reporting scant agreement over the nature of knowledge, but a broad consensus that people are the cornerstone of KM with most treating knowledge work as social action. This status undoubtedly impacts on many of the other debates in KM: the definition of KM (Bouthillier and Shearer, 2002), ethical issues associated with the management of knowledge (Gourlay, 2006), the commodification and reification of knowledge (Smith, 2005), reportedly high failure rates (Virtanen, 2011), the question of how to measure knowledge value (Spender, 2002), whether knowledge is personal or organizational, or both, and cultural specificity (Despres and Chauvel, 2002). All of these issues have significant implications for research and practice in the aged care sector. The definition of knowledge is a prime catalyst for the ongoing debate (Quintane et al. 2011; Bhatt, 2001; Grant and Qureshi, 2006) and has sporned a widespread and sometimes esoteric body of research. Despite this research fragmentation, Nonaka and Takeuchi (1995) are still widely credited as the primary architects of modern organisational KM theory and practice through their profoundly influential book, "The Knowledge Creating Company," published in 1995 (Umemoto, 2002; Grant, 2007; Virtanen, 2011), yet this work still receives periodic criticism (Gourlay, 2006).

Part of the ongoing debate arguably stems from the assumptions on many theories: that knowledge can be identified as a singular thing or activity; that KM outcomes can be measured in some way; that the tacit knowledge can be made explicit and vice versa; that this phenomenon called knowledge resides predominately in people's heads, but that they must be motivated to share it. Others assume that what will work in one culture or organization will work in another; that with the right organizational structure, knowledge can be commanded and controlled; and perhaps, most significantly, that language, communication and social interaction are important.

A review of KM theory over the past 30 years since Senge (1990) shows the research landscape to be broad, complex, sometimes ambiguous and often confusing. Whilst it is recognised that industry and cultural differences will affect the design and management of the KM system, it is not clear how they can and should be tailored and managed holistically to drive the knowledge lifecycle in specific industries.

Examination of not for profit organisations (NFPs) and knowledge management (KM) in NFPs is undeveloped (Hume and Hume, 2008). In order to move forward in KM and aged care research, we must examine and understand the translation and integration of KM into this context and identify how KM can best be developed and adopted. Aged care is a growing and large sector in Australia and as such, research in this area warrants more attention. Previous research into large NFP firms identifies that KM is recognised in the firms as a practice that can support operations but it is often not viewed as a priority investment (Hume, Clarke and Hume, 2012).

McAdam (2001) and others compared small and large firms and the perception of KM over a decade ago, finding the large firm accepting of KM and its value whereas, the small and nonprofit sector firms were less advanced with an accidental approach to knowledge and low investment in KM approaches and systems (Desouza and Awazu, 2006). These researchers emphasised that small nonprofit firms like aged care facilities and small nonprofit operations servicing the community do not manage knowledge the same way as larger organisations and they do not merely scale-down practice to fit. Desouza and Awazu (2006) suggest limitations in managing knowledge and need to develop creative practices that fit their business constraints.

Hutchinson and Quintas (2008) reviewed the literature around SME firms introducing SMEs into the wider KM discussion. It was proposed that advanced research was warranted to understand knowledge benefits for SMEs with SMEs as it was a poorly understood area. They examined KM in the SME context and they supported the findings of others. They suggested most KM research has been conducted in large firms with SMEs relying heavily on informal knowledge. They did note a few anomalies with a few SMEs adopting more formalised KM strategies yet this was rare. Interestingly, Durst and Runar (2012) recently conducted a literature review of KM in SMEs. They found knowledge identification, knowledge storage/retention and knowledge utilisation were poorly understood in SMEs. The few studies found by Durst and Runar (2012) highlighted the benefits of KM yet offered minimal learnings on implementation and practice apart from the role of informal knowledge.

NFP researchers have suggested knowledge in a non-profit context is too unwieldy to manage without strategy and dedicated resourcing and therefore the management and operational focus for SME NFP's should be on core service delivery and fulfilling their firm mission (Riege, 2005). Ideally, developing a generic KM strategy and framework for these smaller non-profit firms could reduce the perceived costly and resource intensive approach to this practice for this sector. For the many different NFP enterprises that exist with differing purposes and practices, the relative ease of developing a "generic KM strategy" still remains complex.

Unlike previous research conducted, this research contributes to the discourse in this area by specifically examining SME NFPs. This research considers the previous research in SMEs and proposes that NFPs are not just scaled down large firms and may not be similar to a for-profit SME.

It is proposed that, like commercial for-proft SMEs, informal knowledge may be the basis of KM in the NFP setting. However, this research proposes that specific management of the transient and volunteer worker in NFPs contributes substantially to this (Borgonovi, 2008). It is proposed that the transient volunteer NFP worker is motivated by support of the social mission and the delivery of the mission rather than business profits and business operations thus undervaluing the role and processes involved with KM (Borgonovi, 2008). It is proposed that like the commercial SMEs, SME NFPs need to be creative in the management of knowledge. This research will contribute to knowledge by examining SME NFPs with this research building on the notion of informal/tacit knowledge in SMEs and advancing perception of the socialisation and its importance to knowledge capture and distribution in the NFP, SME.

This research aims to develop and inform a digital aged care from multiple perspectives through interviewing and mental modeling of stakeholders in the sector, this research will understand that digital aged care is more holistic than an IT system that supports knowledge capture and distribution and involves a number of enabling elements of knowledge strategy, people, process, leadership and culture that must be considered.

Aged Care, Health, and KM

KM is a foundation practice in the organization and informs what is valued as knowledge, capture and diffusion of it. Embracing knowledge management and decision support mechanism ensure improved productivity and efficiency (Vestal, 2005). Knowledge management (KM) is increasingly being discussed as a cornerstone of an organisation's ability to compete (Treleaven & Sykes, 2005). Despite the increasing recognition of the benefits of KM, a number of significant implementation challenges exist for consideration by both practitioners and academics especially in not for profits (NFPs) and sectors with low capability maturity for technological innovations and practices such as KM. The aged care sector is one such sector. Identifying the current KM needs and practices to inform the development of KM for future implementation and compliance is vital. This case presents and collates current knowledge capture, storage, retrieval and diffusion and builds the business case for the data needed to advance decision-making in aged care firms.

Many aged care organisations are being driven to adopt more commercial practices in order to improve their ability to effectively provide End to end care and delivery quality patient outcomes. Knowledge Management (KM) is one such "corporate" practice being explored to address the increasingly competitive environment, competitor intelligence and strategic intelligence (Haggie & Kingston, 2003). Although the concept of knowledge management may be basically understood researchers and managers are yet to explore and fully understand the complex inter-relationships of big data management, informatics, organizational culture, ICT, internal marketing, employee engagement and performance management as collective enablers on the capture, co-ordination, diffusion and renewal of knowledge in the aged care environment. This work advances the relationship of KM with those enabling elements offering a conceptual framework and implementation model to assist in planning and sustaining KM activity from integrated organizational and knowledge worker perspectives in aged care. The paper will emphasize an enduring integrated approach to aged care industry KM to drive and sustain the knowledge capture and renewal continuum. The paper will provide an important contribution on "*How to*" do KM in aged care and propose the need for interactive and Web 2.0 enabled knowledge hubs.

Aged care providers require leadership and innovation in Informatics and KM for Ageing and Aged-care to ensure productivity, innovation and growth and the ability to manage the imminent growth in the sector. Moreover, industry and consumer peak bodies have become more structured and planned in raising their concerns about aged care services (Reynolds 2009) and supporting and advising aged care providers. Aged care services are currently provided to more than 1 million people in Australia every year, through residential, community and flexible care services (Kane, 2003; Jeong & Keatinge, 2004). By 2050, it is expected that the number of Australians needing aged care services will increase to 3.5 million (Productivity Commission, 2011). As Australia's population ages at 20% per year with a predicted number of retirees by 2020 and the number of people reaching retirement doubling by 2030 and tripling by 2050, the aged care sector is under increasing pressure to ensure that quality aged care. Supporting providers, industry and consumer peak bodies with knowledge and data management frameworks will assist in moving them successfully into a new era of aged care. Many reports on ageing and the age (AIHW, 2012) identify the significant shortage in the current workforce trained to care for the needs of our nation's older adults, community care services and residential places. These places are predicted to grow explosively as more of the Baby Boomers retire and residential aged services will need to grow, evolve and innovate their service provision. Capital investment and allocation of capital is becoming increasingly hard for aged care providers and any measure which will assist in cost savings, improved service provision and efficiency such as KM is welcomed.

Managing the new advent of big data for known and sought knowledge and also having the ability to search for relevant but unknown sources will assist with industry transformation to improve productivity and enhance consumer directed care in the aged care services sector (AIHW 2012). Management of big data, knowledge, analytics and informatics are suggested to build services efficiency, improve quality of service and business profitability in many sectors especially knowledge intensive sectors like aged care and health (Hillmer, Wodchis, Gill Anderson Rochon, 2005; Tsai, Chien-Tzu, & Pao-Long, Chang, 2005; Vestal, 2005). It is widely believed that the use of information technology can reduce the cost of healthcare while improving quality and delivery (Manyika, Chui, Brown, Bughin, Dobbs, Roxburgh, and Hung Byers, 2011). The main issue with informatics and data management in this sector is the embryonic understanding of the data needed the ability to access the data, the storing of data, technology efficacy and how to use and integrate data and knowledge into the service delivery to improve service provision and patient outcomes. These are reinforced by the case of the Australian aged care sector.

Data and Method

The purpose of this research is to examine how KM and knowledge in operating in the aged care sector in Australia, what practices are required and preferred and provide a validation of the need for KM in an aged care NFP setting. This research reports qualitative findings from interviews of aged care stakeholders. These studies complete 28 interview subjects to ensure a consistent and complete set of responses.

The interviews selected subjects ranging from NFPs senior managers to operational staff. This reflected the leadership structure in the facilities accessed. Interestingly, in many facilities it was operational staff operation leading the facility on a regular basis. The questions, based on previous KM research, focused on the following areas:

- Do aged care NFP employees think KM assists in improving the understanding and management of information and knowledge in an aged care setting?
- Do aged care NFP organizations currently try manage the capture collection and diffusion of knowledge effectively using a KM system?
- How do you define knowledge; what is data in your sector what is known and what is recognized but not known?
- Do you have a KM Collection, Implementation and Diffusion Strategy?
- What is your perception of leadership style?
- Is knowledge performance management practiced?
- What is the culture in your facility?
- What is the culture of change?
- How do you leverage ICT and are you "technology enabled"?

The subjects were also asked to build a mental model and identify the key members of the digital aged care scope. Mental models can depict the motivation to thinking. They can offer the assumptions, generalizations and images that influence how we think about a subject and offer a view of the dominant logic, which determines the structure of the system. The subjects were asked to:

- Draw the pathways for the technology links you think are most beneficial for digital aged care.
- Circle the pathways that are not currently effective or existent.
- Highlight pathways and relationships between stakeholders where there are and will be adoption issues.
- Name any services or systems YOU are aware of in any pathways.

Figure 1 offers a summarized schematic of the key players identified. You will note the family and the patient feature prominently in the digital aged care landscape. This is a novel approach in information system and one which has not been used often to date. Identification of the key players suggests there are many links that need consideration in a digital aged care strategy.

EMERGING THEMES AND DISCUSSION

The interviews responses and early stage mental models were coded and analyzed through logical deduction by experts in the field. Each of the question areas lead to specific themes emerging with some leading to advanced discussions in the topic areas. These identified the following emergent theme areas

Figure 1. Key players in digital aged care

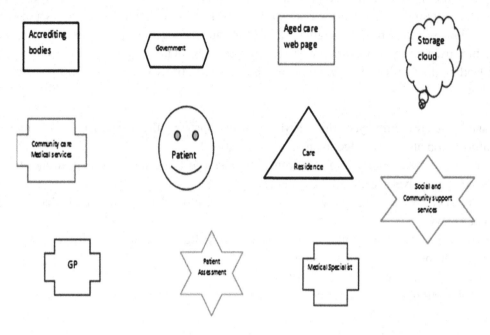

Lack of Leadership and Expertise in the Management of Knowledge

Current leadership in the sector is suggested to have little expertise in how to implement efficient KM strategies. This is compounded by a high turnover of staff, low technical efficacy and low capability maturity with these specifically hindering the adoption and implementation of KM strategies. The majority of subjects suggested that the understanding of the current capabilities and developing training strategies would assist in better knowledge definition, capture, storage and use. With this offering a real benefit to the sector. Discussions also suggested that the key players were little known with mental models offering many and varied players.

Nursing Manger Subject 6: My primary focus is on care and care delivery...I know I need to report care related issues however operational stuff get more confusing and timely...we need to have a better process and someone in charge to support it

Lack of Capability of Current KM Systems

The subjects suggested a lack of capability of current KM systems to meet the needs for efficient knowledge systems: Current KM/information support systems rely heavily on informal socialization and paper based systems with limited consistent document capture and storage, and limited formal engagement of staff. Many ICT systems lack the ability to manage knowledge and intelligence with very little understanding to date of Cloud technology and other virtual storage mediums. Improving the capability of accessing, storing massive amounts of data in its various forms would aid in providing efficiency and cost reductions for delivery. It was also identified that staff had relatively low technological efficacy, especially with more complex administration technology. Coupled with the informal nature of interactions and paper based recording KM was at a very embryonic stage with much tacit knowledge lost and much repetition with collection. Discussions also suggested that managers knew of few practices that could support digital aged care with mental models offering limited coverage of current practices.

Facility Manager Subject 9: We don't have much...some desktops in the facility...head office has more... we still use notes and store items in a large locked cupboard...there must be an easier way..but...

Limited Comprehensive Understanding of KM Process

Limited comprehensive understanding of what is knowledge, what needs to be stored and who are the key players in the knowledge process. Many subjects knew that they needed knowledge and that it was required for accreditation purposes however the specifics of who, what, where, when and why was overlooked. Mental models offered little coverage of current processes and practice that support KM in digital aged care.

Facility Manager Subject 9: I don't really understand the accreditation process apart from that we need to do it at local level...all things we do to improve the place, the care ....there is probably a whole lot of things we could collect but at this point we don't really have a system...or know what they are...I am sure it would help if we did...

Diverse Data Types

The subjects identified some specific types of data that they collected and they knew was relevant. The mental models offered a better understanding and clarity in this area with patient data and medical practice elements most prominent. The understanding of knowledge related to organizational systems, continuous improvement, (an essential component of accreditation) and specific needs for funding we found to be rudimentary.

Nurse Manager Subject 11: We must keep medical records and that is easy but what CI (continuous improvement) is very subjective there are all these headings and sections...we are not sure what we should collect and what we can ignore

CEO Small Facility Subject 15: We are learning as we go...I have sent most of the interested staff off to information sessions and they seem to be getting a better understanding of the ACSAA standards.... we are only a small facility...but they are still subject to interpretation...it would be good to all be on the same page

Interestingly, the most unknown data was management and service data especially ICT tools and data management factors that may assist in accreditation and continuous improvement capability. There was little patient data that the subjects were not aware of or did not recognize. This supports the need for stronger managerial training and leadership in the sector with clinical training for registered staff, satisfactory.

Managerial Implications

The discussion topic areas and mental model analysis lead to the following managerial implications. They include developing strategies to recognize knowledge and develop knowledge leaders and champions, developing interactive hubs, strategies to become a learning organization, ways to identify and understand key player and specific managerial areas of focus. Developing a better understanding of key stakeholders and the pathways of knowledge, capture, and diffusion in digital aged care is essential for moving forward.

It is Essential to Recognize Knowledge and Discover Knowledge Leaders

A key element of this project is that there is currently a wide gap between the potential of managing known information, acquiring information using big data and accessible data, analyzing the knowledge and its realization into business service provision and profits in aged care services. One of the hardest decisions is to know what data and information is of value to decision-making and should be acquired and stored and what information should be discarded. Data and information can come from many sources and can be tacit and or explicit and as such, the volume of data in the knowledge era is extensive. Figure Two identifies many of the areas where data can be gathered and proposed that as KM is better understood that each of these areas has a specific strategy for the capture and creation of knowledge in aged care.

Exploiting data captured from all paths of the internet and information can radically improve performance, if managers can locate it easily and use it to measure and inform problem solving. Firms that capture and store data well know radically more about their businesses and directly translate that knowledge into improved decision making and performance. Digital Aged care needs to consider KM and have a decision-making culture constructed on evidence based data. Clever KM systems have the ability to embrace the velocity and speed at which new data and information is entering the market with no question that technology enablement assists in the collection and storage of data and knowledge. Less consideration has been given to technology enablement for diffusion and the push of knowledge. Using a push knowledge strategy is the solution for unfamiliarity with knowledge especially known unknown data and unknown unknown data. This strategy needs knowledge champions (Jones, Herschel, & Moesel, 2003) and needs knowledge leaders (Wenger &Snyder, 2000) which appear few in the aged care sector. Knowledge leaders in the sector need to create and disseminate knowledge through hubs and identify the key areas of core business, external legislation and accreditation, industry metrics and practices, consumer metrics like satisfaction and quality and organizational successes and failures. Currently in the aged care sector this is limited.

The Data Flower proposed in Hume, Hume, Johnston, Soar and Whitty (2014) is not conclusive for all areas of data required in the sector however it introduces conceptually the areas identified by the subjects and shows how the capture, creation and diffusion is a feedback link for improved organizational performance and is the data flower and grows in relevance in this sector. Figure 2 shows the need for Knowledge champions work to support technology enablement and the practice of KM in the firm whilst also championing the role of knowledge in lessons learnt (Zuber-Skerritt, 2001) learning from practice, feedback and improving performance. When applied in this setting the data flowers will inform the building of links between the stakeholders as identified by the mental models.

Figure 2. Applied data flower

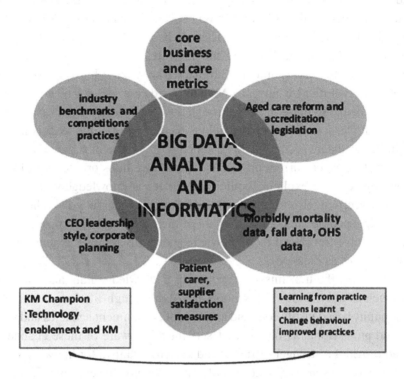

THE FUTURE OF KNOWLEDGE AND DIGITAL AGED CARE

A feature of globally competitive knowledge-based economies is that governments, universities, consumers and industry work together in these economies to create regional 'knowledge hubs'. Recent advances in the role of big data are topical and it proved very effective. Interactive big data capture and diffusion is now moving to real time and constant sourcing. Developing Knowledge hubs with real time collaboration via "subscribed" knowledge groups with constant pull and push. Creating knowledge networks is a solution to the support the leadership and decision making issues in the age care sector (Venturato, & Drew, 2010). Many facilities are managed by clinically trained staff that lack managerial and administrative training and knowledge supports systems would support the deficit (Salipante & Aram, 2003, O'Sullivan & McKimm, 2011). To create world best practice and position the Australian aged care system as the benchmark for global aged care knowledge sharing and diffusion of knowledge through a collaborative, inclusive aged care knowledge hub is vital. Improving diffusion through using social media and interactive web 2.0 platforms will improve access to known and unknown data.

Currently knowledge hubs are static and focused. They have been suggested to have three major functions: to generate knowledge; to transfer and apply knowledge; and to transmit knowledge to others in the community through education and training. Knowledge hubs have generated new and basic knowledge of relevance for many industries, both old and new and the knowledge-users provide a focus for knowledge-generation, transmission and diffusion. The early generations of knowledge hubs have captured and stored knowledge systematically with this knowledge accessed by a pull strategy i.e. the knowledge must be found and accessed by the user. Ideally a well-designed hub will link and portal all available knowledge foci. Unfortunately in many sectors and particular to the aged care sector, competing knowledge hubs have been created from different stakeholder perspectives simulating knowledge and creating competing knowledge hub "silos". These hubs are often disconnected with those in need ie "the knowledge user" and are difficult to find and navigate.

Exploring the notion of interactivity and web 2.0 enabled knowledge hubs supporting a diffusion push strategy would radically revolutionize current KM in the aged care sector. The notion of a push strategy would channel the knowledge to those in need through push web strategies of email, social media, webinars, forums, blogs discussion, alerts, pokes and rss feeds. Specifically, leadership, compliance and decision-making in the aged care sector would be supported by these next generation knowledge hubs. Irrespective of the existent of the current portals and knowledge hubs problems still exist based on the nature of the knowledge tacit or explicit. Explicit knowledge is knowledge that has been articulated, codified, and stored in a certain retrieval media. It can be readily transmitted to others. Conversely, tacit knowledge is knowledge, people are not often aware of the knowledge they possess nor how it can be valuable to others. Effective transfer of tacit knowledge generally requires extensive personal contact, regular interaction and trust as creation.

In the traditional setting, the transmission function of a knowledge hub takes place through educational institutions such as universities and schools but also through life-long learning processes that involve firms, community based institutions and a variety of government agencies and services including hospitals, clinics and professional associations. Users must be aware of these channels. Social media is underutilised and provides a stronger diffusive and viral mechanism for knowledge distribution. The aims are to maximse cooperation coordination, collaboration and conservation. Identifying the factors that influence the knowledge needs of aged care providers, advocates and associations, when considering and providing care, and the extent to which these preferences are met by current knowledge based services, is essential to capturing tacit and explicit knowledge.

Become a Learning Organization in Aged Care

The mental models begin to propose a system and a set of key players for KM for aged care services and a digital aged care KM implementation framework promoting a learning organization for the aged care sector. This chapter suggests that adopting lessons learnt philosophy will develop change behaviour and organisational rewiring. The importance of this is the involvement of people and the role that people play in generating and creating knowledge. Figure one offers the key players for learning organisations and improved performance, Knowledge leaders, knowledge champions and application of aged care health informatics (Senge, 1990; Senge, Roberts, Ross, Smith, and Kleinter, 1994) including capture and links to the patient, the family, all community and medical stakeholders are all essential for KM and digital aged care. The use of technology enabled analytics (KM) and infrastructure in aged care services improving leadership, social interactions and innovation in processes and availability and delivery through knowledge and lessons learnt are all essential for digital aged care. As suggested by many of the subjects the KM process needs to be simple process that is time effective and does not detract from care delivery.

Finally, the recommendations for management include the needs to address the four Management Challenges of KM implementation. Companies won't reap the full benefits of digital aged care and transition to using data, KM and Knowledge hubs unless they're able to manage change effectively and embrace lessons learnt philosophy and link pathways between the key players identified by the subjects mental models. Four areas are particularly important in that process. These are as follows:

Leadership

Companies succeed in the KM and big data era due to leadership teams that set clear goals, define what success looks like, and identify the correct needs. These leaders have vision and recognize opportunity and understand how the sector as a whole is developing. The customer orientation and internal marketing (Martinsons, & Hosley, 1993; Ballantyne, 2000) . This includes employees and other stakeholders. The successful participants in the aged care sector will be those with the ability to be flexible in changing the way their organizations make many decisions and develop a decision-making culture.

Key Players Considers, Knowledge Leaders, Data Experts, Patients, Family, Medical and Community Champions

As data becomes easily accessible and of low cost, the data experts and knowledge workers are of greater demand (Chong, 2005). Experts skilled in working with data are needed if the role of data and analytics is going to be incorporated in the business. The most valuable data experts will be those that can link the needs of the sector, the firm, the key players, data and design ways in which data can be used. These will be our knowledge leaders and champions.

Information and Communications Technology (ICT)

The tools available to handle the volume, velocity, and variety of big data have advanced substantially in recent times (Chong, 2005). There are many inexpensive, open source libraries that can aid the technologically minded in setting up a system. However, these technologies do require a skill set that is new to most IT departments, which will need to work hard to integrate all the relevant internal and external sources of data. In the aged care sector this skill set is at a lower capability so sourcing expert staff will be a priority

Evidence Based Decision Making Culture

Effective and performance oriented firms use evidence to make decisions. People who understand the problems need to be brought together with the right data, but also with the people who have problem solving techniques that can effectively exploit them.

FUTURE RESEARCH AND CONCLUSION

This paper has introduced the concepts of KM and the key players in digital aged care. The chapter has reported the findings of qualitative work that highlighted the current problems, current pathways, current players and the need for KM, KM champions and an easy and effective way to access knowledge. The chapter has offered the following considerations and recommendations and these are vital for a digital aged care system to be globally innovative and be the benchmark for many countries developing reforms and strategies for aged care.

Finally, testing and refining the elements of a dynamic, interactive digital aged care strategy and KM framework are essential for productivity. Developing a specific business cases for organisations and testing these in organizational settings using action research interventions and reflection will confirm the need and specifications of each system. For the sector to advance into the future further empirical work for digital aged care is essential for the sector.

ACKNOWLEDGMENT

This work is acknowledged as part of the Centre for Tourism and Regional opportunities as the result of sponsored pilot work discussed in the chapter.

REFERENCES

Australian Institute of Health and Welfare (AIHW). (2012). *Residential aged care in Australia 2010-11: a statistical overview, Aged care statistics series no. 36, Cat. No. AGE 68*. Canberra: AIHW.

Bailey, C., & Clarke, M. (2001). Managing knowledge for personal and organizational benefit. *Journal of Knowledge Management, 5*(1), 58–68. doi:10.1108/13673270110384400

Ballantyne, D. (2000). Internal relationship marketing: A strategy for knowledge renewal. *International Journal of Bank Marketing, 18*(6), 274–286. doi:10.1108/02652320010358698

Bhatt, G. D. (2001). Knowledge management in organizations: Examining the interaction between technologies, techniques, and people. *Journal of Knowledge Management, 5*(1), 68–75. doi:10.1108/13673270110384419

Binney, D. (2000). The knowledge management spectrum-understanding the KM landscape. *Journal of Knowledge Management, 5*(1), 21–32.

Blair, D. C. (2002). Knowledge Management: Hype, Hope or Help? *Journal of the American Society for Information Science and Technology, 53*(12), 1019–1028. doi:10.1002/asi.10113

Borgonovi, F. (2008). Doing well by doing good. The relationship between formal volunteering and self-reported health and happiness. *Social Science & Medicine, 66*(11), 2321–2334. doi:10.1016/j.socscimed.2008.01.011 PMID:18321629

Bouthillier, F., & Shearer, K. (2002). Understanding knowledge management and information management: the need for an empirical perspective. *Information Research, 8*(1), 8-1.

Cartwright, C., Sankaran, S., & Kelly, J. (2008). *Developing a New Leadership Framework for Not-For-Profit Health and Community Care Organisations in Australia*. Lismore, Australia: Southern Cross University.

Chauvel, D., & Despres, C. (2002). A review of survey research in knowledge management: 19972001. *Journal of Knowledge Management, 6*(3), 207–223. doi:10.1108/13673270210434322

Chong, C. S. (2005). Critical factors in the successful implementation of Knowledge Management. *Journal of Knowledge Management*, (June): 21–42.

Commision, P. (2010). Contribution of the Not-for-Profit Sector. Research Report, Canberra.

Comondore, V. R., Devereaux, P. J., Zhou, Q., Stone, S. B., Busse, J. W., Ravindran, N. C., & Guyatt, G. H. et al. (2009). Quality of care in for-profit and not-for-profit nursing homes: Systematic review and meta-analysis. *BMJ (Clinical Research Ed.)*, *339*(aug04 2), b2732. doi:10.1136/bmj.b2732 PMID:19654184

Crane, L. (2012). Trust me, Im an expert: Identity construction and knowledge sharing. *Journal of Knowledge Management*, *16*(3), 448–460. doi:10.1108/13673271211238760

Davenport, T. H., & Prusak, L. (2000). Working Knowledge: How Organisations Manage What They Know. Harvard Business School Press.

Department of Health and Ageing (Australian Government) (DoHA). (2012). Living Longer. Living Better. Aged care reform package. DoHA.

Desouza, K. C., & Awazu, Y. (2006). Knowledge management at SMEs: Five peculiarities. *Journal of Knowledge Management*, *10*(1), 32–43. doi:10.1108/13673270610650085

Durst, S., & Runar Edvardsson, I. (2012). Knowledge management in SMEs: A literature review. *Journal of Knowledge Management*, *16*(6), 879–903. doi:10.1108/13673271211276173

Eisenhardt, K. (1989). Building theories from case study research. *Academy of Management Review*, *14*(4), 532-550.

Eisenhardt, K., & Graebner, M. E. (2007). Theory building from cases: Opportunities and Challenges. *Academy of Management Journal*, *50*(1), 25–32. doi:10.5465/AMJ.2007.24160888

Glaser, B., & Strauss, A. (1967). *The Discovery of Grounded Theory: Strategies for Qualitative Research*. Chicago, IL: Aldine Publishing Company.

Gourlay, S. (2006). Conceptualizing knowledge creation: A critique of nonakas theory*. *Journal of Management Studies*, *43*(7), 1415–1436. doi:10.1111/j.1467-6486.2006.00637.x

Grant, K. A. (2007). Tacit knowledge revisited–we can still learn from Polanyi. *Electronic Journal of Knowledge Management*, *5*(2), 173–180.

Grant, K. A., & Qureshi, U. (2006, November). Knowledge Management Systems--Why So Many Failures? In Innovations in Information Technology, 2006 (pp. 1-5). IEEE.

Grant, R. M. (1996). Toward a knowledge-based theory of the firm. *Strategic Management Journal*, *17*(S2), 109–122. doi:10.1002/smj.4250171110

Haggie, J. K., & Kingston, J. (2003). Choosing a knowledge management strategy. *Journal of Knowledge Management*, (June): 33–56.

Haggie, K., and Kingston, J. (2003). Choosing your knowledge management strategy. *Journal of Knowledge Management Practice*, 1 – 20.

Hall, R. (2003). *Knowledge Management in the New Business Environment (A report prepared for the Australian Business Foundation)*. Sydney: ACIRRT, University of Sydney.

Hall, R. (2003). *Knowledge Management in the New Business Environment*. A report prepared for the Australian Business Foundation, ACCIRT, University of Sydney.

Hillmer, M. P., Wodchis, W. P., Gill, S. S., Anderson, G. M., & Rochon, P. A. (2005). Nursing home profit status and quality of care: Is there any evidence of an association? *Medical Care Research and Review, 62*(2), 139–166. doi:10.1177/1077558704273769 PMID:15750174

Hume, C., Clarke, P., & Hume, M. (2012). The role of knowledge management in the large non profit firm: Building a framework for KM success. *International Journal of Organisational Behaviour, 17*(3), 82–104.

Hume, C., & Hume, M. (2008). The strategic role of knowledge management in nonprofit organisations, International Journal of Nonprofit and Voluntary Sector Marketing. *Special Issue: Special Issue on Nonprofit Competitive Strategy, 13*(2), 129–140.

Hume, C., Pope, N., & Hume, M. (2012). KM 100: Introductory knowledge management for not-for-profit organizations. *International Journal of Organisational Behaviour, 17*(2), 56.

Hutchinson, V., & Quintas, P. (2008). Do SMEs do knowledge management? Or simply manage what they know? *International Small Business Journal, 26*(2), 131–146. doi:10.1177/0266242607086571

James, M., Chui, M., Brown, B., Bughin, J., Dobbs, R., Roxburgh, C., & Byers, A. H. (2011, May). Big data: The next frontier for innovation, competition, and productivity. McKinsey Global Institute. October 2012. *Harvard Business Review*, 59–69.

Jeon, Y. H., Merlyn, T., & Chenoweth, L. (2010). Leadership and management in the aged care sector: A narrative synthesis. *Australasian Journal on Ageing, 29*(2), 54–60. doi:10.1111/j.1741-6612.2010.00426.x PMID:20553534

Jeong, S., & Keatinge, D. (2004). Innovative leadership and management in a nursing home. *Journal of Nursing Management, 12*(6), 445–451. doi:10.1111/j.1365-2834.2004.00451.x PMID:15509274

Jones, N. B., Herschel, R. T., & Moesel, D. D. (2003). Using knowledge champions to facilitate knowledge management. *Journal of Knowledge Management, 7*(1), 49–63. doi:10.1108/13673270310463617

Kane, R. (2003). Definition, Measurement, and Correlates of Quality of Life in Nursing Homes: Toward a Reasonable Practice, Research, and Policy Agenda. *The Gerontologist, 43*(Supplement 2), 28–36. doi:10.1093/geront/43.suppl_2.28 PMID:12711722

Lettieri, E., Borga, F., & Savoldelli, A. (2004). Knowledge Management in Nonprofit Organizations. *Journal of Knowledge Management, 8*(6), 16–30. doi:10.1108/13673270410567602

Lettieri, E., Borga, F., & Savoldelli, A. (2004). Knowledge Management in non-profit organizations. *Journal of Knowledge Management, 8*(6), 16–30. doi:10.1108/13673270410567602

Martinsons, M., & Hosley, S. (1993). Planning a strategic information system for a market-oriented non-profit organization. *Journal of Systems Management, 44*(2), 14.

McAdam, R., & Reid, R. (2001). SME and large organisation perceptions of knowledge management: Comparisons and contrasts. *Journal of Knowledge Management, 5*(3), 231–241. doi:10.1108/13673270110400870

Miles, M. B., & Huberman, A. M. (1994). *An Expanded Sourcebook:Qualitative Data Analysis* (2nd ed.). Sage Publications International.

Murray, P., & Carter, L. (2005). Improving marketing intelligence through learning systems and knowledge communities in not-for-profit workplaces. *Journal of Workplace Learning, 17*(7), 421–435. doi:10.1108/13665620510620016

Murray, P., & Carter, L. (2005). Improving marketing intelligence through learning systems and knowledge communities in not-for-profit workplaces. *Journal of Workplace Learning, 17*(7/8), 421–435. doi:10.1108/13665620510620016

Nonaka, I., & Takeuchi, H. (1995). The Knowledge Creating Company. Oxford University Press.

Nonaka, I., & Takeuchi, H. (1995). The Knowledge Creating Company. Oxford University Press.

Oliver, S., & Kandadi, K. R. (2006). How to develop knowledge culture in organizations? A multiple case study of large distributed organizations. *Journal of Knowledge Management, 10*(4), 6–24. doi:10.1108/13673270610679336

OSullivan, H., & McKimm, J. (2011). Doctor as professional and doctor as leader: Same attributes, attitudes and values? *British Journal of Hospital Medicine, 72*(8), 463–466. doi:10.12968/hmed.2011.72.8.463 PMID:21841592

Palmer, E., & Eveline, J. (2012).Sustaining low pay in aged care work. *Gender, Work and Organization, 19*, 254–275.

Patton, Q. M. (1990). *Qualitative Evaluation and Research Methods* (2nd ed.). Sage Publications.

Pinnington, A. (2011). Leadership Development: Applying the same leadership theories and development practices to different contexts? *Leadership, 7*(3), 335–365. doi:10.1177/1742715011407388

Productivity Commission. (2011). *Caring for Older Australians*. Report No. 53. Final Inquiry Report, Canberra.

Quintane, E., Casselman, R. M., Reiche, B. S., & Nylund, P. A. (2011). Innovation as a knowledge-based outcome. *Journal of Knowledge Management, 15*(6), 928–947. doi:10.1108/13673271111179299

Raymond, L. (1985).Organizational characteristics and MIS success in the context of small business. *Management Information Systems Quarterly, 9*(1), 37–52.

Reynolds, A. (2009). *The Myer Foundation 2020: A Vision for Aged Care in Australia*. Fitzroy, Victoria, Australia: Outcomes Review, Brotherhood of St Laurence.

Riege, A. (2005). Three dozen knowledge sharing barriers managers must consider. *Journal of Knowledge Management, 9*(3), 18–35. doi:10.1108/13673270510602746

Salipante, P., & Aram, J. D. (2003). Managers as knowledgeable generators: The nature of practitioner-scholar research in the non-profit sector. *Nonprofit Management & Leadership, 14*(2), 129–150. doi:10.1002/nml.26

Sankaran, S., Cartwright, C., Kelly, J., Shaw, K., & Soar, J. (2010). Leadership of non-profit organisations in the aged care sector in Australia. *Proceedings of the 54th meeting of the International Society for the Systems Sciences.*

Senge, P. M. (1990). *The Fifth Dimension - The Art and Patience of The Learning Organisation.* New York: Doubleday.

Senge, P. M., Roberts, C., Ross, R. B., Smith, B. J., & Kleinter, A. (1994). *The Fifth Discipline Field Book: Strategies and Tools for Building a Learning Organisation.* New York: Doubleday.

Spender, J. C. (2002). Knowledge management, uncertainty, and an emergent theory of the firm. *The strategic management of intellectual capital and organizational knowledge,* 149-162.

Treleaven, L., & Sykes, C. (2005). Loss of organizational knowledge: From supporting clients to serving head office. *Journal of Organizational Change Management, 18*(4), 353–368. doi:10.1108/09534810510607056

Tsai, C-T., & Chang (2005). An integration framework of innovation assessment for the knowledge-intensive service industry. *International Journal of Technology Management, 30*(1-2), 85-104.

Tsoukas, H., & Vladimirou, E. (2001). What is organizational knowledge? *Journal of Management Studies, 38*(7), 973–993. doi:10.1111/1467-6486.00268

Umemoto, K. (2002). Managing existing knowledge is not enough. *The strategic management of intellectual capital and organizational knowledge,* 463-476.

Vasconcelos, J., Seixas, P., Kimble, C., & Lemos, P. (2005). Knowledge management in non-government organisations: A partnership for the future. *Proceedings of the 7th International Conference on Enterprise Information Systems.*

Venturato, L., & Drew, L. (2010). Beyonddoing: Supporting clinical leadership and nursing practice in aged care through innovative models of care. *Contemporary Nurse, 35*(2), 157–170. doi:10.5172/conu.2010.35.2.157 PMID:20950197

Vestal, W. (2005). Making sense of KM costs. *KM World, 14*(7), 8–11.

Virtanen, I. (2011). Externalization of tacit knowledge implies a simplified theory of cognition. *Journal of Knowledge Management Practice, 12*(3).

Wenger, E. C., & Snyder, W. M. (2000). Communities of practice: The organizational frontier. *Harvard Business Review, 78*(1), 139–145. PMID:11184968

Wiig, K. M. (1997). Integrating intellectual capital and knowledge management. *Long Range Planning, 30*(3), 399–405. doi:10.1016/S0024-6301(97)90256-9

Zuber-Skerritt, O. (2001). *Action Learning and action research: paradigm, praxis and programs. Effective change management using action research and action learning: Concepts, frameworks, process and applications.* Lismore, Australia: Southern Cross University Press.

KEY TERMS AND DEFINITIONS

Aged Care: Aged care in general practice is the management and care of the health of the elderly. The term 'frail aged' is used to describe aged people in need of substantial level of care and support.

Digital Health Care: Digital healthcare (also known as digital health) is an upcoming discipline that involves the use of information and communication technologies to help address the health problems and challenges faced by patients. These technologies include both hardware and software solutions and services.

Knowledge Capture: Knowledge capture is the process by which knowledge is converted from tacit to explicit form (residing within people, artifacts or organizational entities) and vice versa through the sub-processes of externalization and internalization.

Knowledge Dissemination: Knowledge dissemination is a crucial part of knowledge management because it ensures knowledge is available to those who need it.

Knowledge Management: Knowledge management is the efficient handling of information and resources within a commercial organization.

Mental Models: *Mental model* is an explanation of someone's thought process about how something works in the real world. It is a representation of the surrounding world, the relationships between its various parts and a person's intuitive perception about his or her own acts and their consequences.

Pull Factors: A pull strategy involves motivating customers to seek out your brand in an active process. "Getting the customer to come to you."

Stakeholders: *Stakeholders* can affect or be affected by the organization's actions, objectives and policies. Some examples of key *stakeholders* are creditors, directors, employees, government (and its agencies), owners (shareholders), patients and the community from which the business draws its resources and to whom it services.

Chapter 2
Leveraging Enterprise Resource Planning Systems to Digitize Business Functions

Jessy Nair
PES University, India

D. Bhanu Sree Reddy
VIT University, India

ABSTRACT

The successful implementation of Enterprise Resource Planning (ERP) system is a challenge to many organizations. Though an intervention, ERP brings in large scale tangible and intangible benefits to an organization. It poses significant intervention on firm level endogenous dimensions; internal stakeholders, internal organization, business processes and technology. Though literature recognizes that ERP intervention brings about technological change during ERP implementation, hardly any article has conceptualized these interventions in evaluating its performance. Drawing on the Socio Technical system perspective the objective of this article is to conceptualize the ERP intervention on the endogenous dimensions of the organization and develop a comprehensive conceptual model to assess the success or failure of ERP system implementation. The conceptual model, Process-Variance and Adapted Socio-Technical (PVAST), proposed in this article will enable decision makers and practitioners to measure ERP project performance at every stage of its life cycle in a coherent method and adopt corrective measures.

INTRODUCTION

Information Systems (IS) of organizations have evolved from disjointed business processes to a boundaryless and cross functional structure by transforming functional enterprises and organizing their independent functions into process value chains. ERP system software, an Information Technology (IT) driven initiative enables a value chain (Shehab, Sharp, Supramaniam & Spedding, 2004) based organization structure by allowing seamless flow of real time information across functional processes of the organization and empowering organizational stakeholders with precise decision making (Arnold, 2006). External

DOI: 10.4018/978-1-5225-2382-6.ch002

indicators like globalization of markets and operations (Gunasekaran, 2005) and competitive pressure; internal indicators such as increasing costs in inventory, administration and so forth, resulted in Hammer & Stanton (1999) claiming that organizations have to inevitably restructure into process enterprises by strategically orienting themselves in this manner to stay competitive. Henderson and Mitchell (2007) emphasize that while organizations develop their strategy and align resources for implementing strategy it is very pertinent that decision makers identify key dimensions internal to the organization. They further state that this will enable the organizations to develop organizational capabilities and the capabilities can be leveraged to shape the environment and match the organizational performance necessitated by the competitive business environment. A technological resource such as ERP is a strategic tool that results in organizational change while bringing about tangible and in-tangible benefits to the organization. Hence successful ERP intervention is therefore an outcome of high investments and organizations have achieved operational efficiencies, yet a large group of organizations have been unable to translate ERP implementations into a success (Nwankpa, 2015).

ERP as an application software is distinguished from other general software due to the tangible and intangible benefits it can bring about by its organizational impact. Review of literature of over a decade clearly points that even though ERP is an application software its implementation should not only consider technical perspective but interactions with social factors in an organizational context (see Figure 1).Therefore, organization stakeholders can consider internal factors like organizational context, stakeholders, culture, processes and external factors like globalization, competitiveness and customer requirements for successful implementation of ERP. Organizational change that occurs with ERP project necessitates organization stakeholders to implement ERP successfully and evaluate its performance. ERP intervention requires managing change brought about by implementing IS and the mutual interaction it has with the organization's socio-technical context, which is intertwined of technology, people (Davis & Olson, 1985), organizational context and processes (Uzoka, Abiola & Nyangeresi, 2008).

Figure 1. Evolution of ERP definition from technical to socio technical perspective

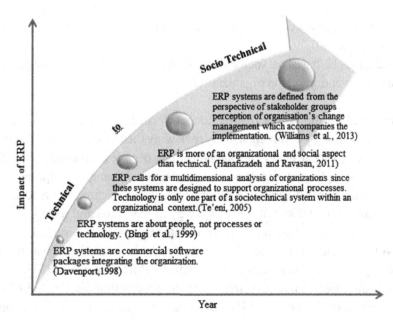

ERP systems are vendor developed software applications necessitating enormous monetary investment by the organizations for its implementation. Costs of ERP project constitute a larger amount (Janssens, Kusters, & Heemstra, 2008) which many organizations find difficult to estimate compared to the ERP software itself. Symons (2006) claims organizations are under increasing pressure from top management to demonstrate and improve the business value of their investments made for IT. The risk associated (Grant & Tu, 2005) with the intervention of ERP system monetarily as well as the organizational changes it brings about, implies that practice of only *post facto* performance evaluation in itself is inadequate. Emphasizing importance of evaluating IS, Beynon-Davies, Owens, & Williams (2004) claim organizations need to evaluate the IS during the life cycle of the IS development process and develop a framework to accommodate the evaluation process during every stage of development. Though the author's research question is contextual to IS development, this question is valid for ERP systems as well. Contemporary literature categorizes ERP implementation as either a process approach; performance of the system is evaluated through a series of phases or variance approach; identifies *a priori* Critical Success Factors (CSF) essential for success of ERP project. ERP implementation frameworks based on either approach defeats the purpose of mitigating risk because the former approach necessitates rigor in evaluation as ERP project transitions from antecedent to consequent phase. In the latter perspective, a CSF based framework is insufficient in addressing the performance of ERP implementation in each phase and taking appropriate corrective measures. The objective of the research is to address this conceptual gap in twofold: first, by developing an integrated framework of process and variance perspectives to identify CSF for each phase of ERP implementation and second, to categorize CSF into four dimensions; internal stakeholders, internal organization, business processes and technology. This will give a better perspective for stakeholders to take up corrective actions at each phase of ERP implementation. This research contributes to development of theory to measure the performance of ERP system implementation and develop associated concepts to evaluate the success or failure of ERP project. Theory development in this article sets a foundation for an empirical study with statement of propositions which are relationships between units observed or approximated in the empirical world, contains concepts, definitions and propositions (Bacharach; 1989; Kerlinger; 1988Pawar; 2009). Hence the following research questions arise:

1. What theoretical perspectives can be deliberated upon to conceptualize the dimensions to evaluate ERP success or failure?
2. Can these dimensions be based on sociotechnical organizational change perspective since ERP is a technological intervention on the organization?

The article is organized as follows. The first section sets forth the foundation and elucidates the gaps in analysing ERP implementation by comprehensively reviewing theoretical facets of ERP implementation methods based on process, variance and sociotechnical perspectives. Process perspective as pertinent to ERP projects describes implementation from an organizational change standpoint, factor perspective lists causal factors to be deliberated upon for ERP project and sociotechnical perspective describes ERP as an intervention on an organization that causes synergy in the social and technical endogenous environment. The subsequent section explains the merit of integrating process, variance and sociotechnical perspectives to develop an integrated conceptual framework that assists in measuring the performance of ERP system thereby reducing the risk associated with ERP implementation. Then we delineate the theoretical constructs and operationalize them to state the propositions associated with the study. The section that follows develops the proposed PVAST model explaining its elements and discussing the model's applications for practitioners and organization's decision makers. Finally we draw up conclusions, state the implications and explain the further scope of this research.

BACKGROUND: A COMPREHENSIVE STUDY OF ERP IMPLEMENTATION METHODS FROM A CHANGE PERSPECTIVE

Premise One: Process Approach to ERP Implementation- An Organizational Change Perspective

ERP restructures organization as value chain enabling information integration and the decision to implement such a technological artifact brings in both tangible and intangible benefits. This indicates the need to go beyond traditional project management principles (Holland & Light, 1999) as there is an inherent need to reengineer the organizations business processes which is accompanied by organizational change on core elements of organization. Stewart, Milford, Jewels, Hunter & Hunter (2000) refer to ERP as an intervention and change agent and recommend that organizations have a planned change management program that accommodates not only change of technology but also business processes, personnel and organization context to realize the benefits of ERP. Therefore it will be practical to consider Kurt Lewin's (1952) three step change management process model as it is profoundly used to theorize and institutionalize change in organizations. "It is a truly elegant and infinitely practical guide to the host of complex and sometimes baffling issues inherent in the change process" (Levasseur, 2001, pp. 71) where the change process in this model consists of three stages; first-unfreeze enables organizations to unlearn legacy processes and systems being practiced in the organization, second-transition is when the enterprise adopts new work practices and readies standards, systems and employees for the change and finally-refreeze the organization adapts to the new changes brought about in the organization by freezing the new ways of work and skills. Strong parallels can be drawn between Kwon & Zmud's (1987) stage model for IS and Markus & Tanis' (2000) emergent process model for ERP implementation with Lewin's generic model for change to manage technological intervention. Lewin's model can be used as a baseline and a practical guide to evaluate the success of ERP, since as a system it has to diffuse and evolve during the phases of the project.

Mapping Change Models

Figure 2 summarizes Kwon & Zmud's (1987) stage model and Markus & Tanis' (2000) ERP emergent process model with Kurt Lewin's (1952) change model for ERP implementation. The two models are mapped to Lewin's (1952) three step change management model to appreciate that IS implementation stage models are based upon organizational change. To assist organizations in the change process (Hawking, Stein & Foster, 2004) it befits to deliberate on a framework based on organizational change to successfully implement ERP. Kwon & Zmud's (1987) stage model for IT implementation follows six stages: initiation, adoption, adaptation, acceptance, routinization and infusion. This IT implementation research model is founded on Lewin's (1952) change model (Cooper & Zmud, 1990). The initiation stage is related to unfreeze stage, adoption and adaptation are linked to change stage and the acceptance, routinization and infusion stages are correlated to the refreeze stage in Lewin's change management model. This model was applied to study implementation of Materials Requirement Planning (MRP)

Figure 2. Mapping ERP implementation process with other implementation process

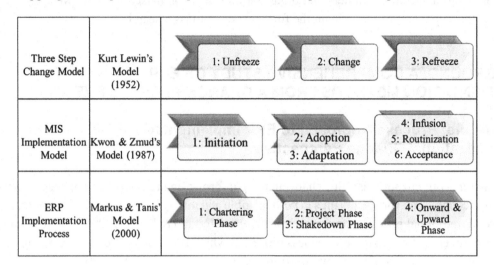

system by Cooper and Zmud (1990). MRP systems are specifically oriented towards the functional view of organizations where organizational changes were restricted to functional departments thereby being technically specific rather than organizational specific and therefore did not necessitate large scale process reengineering and change management. Markus & Tanis' (2000) model of ERP implementation consists of four phases namely; chartering: decisions regarding the business case and solution constraints; project: getting the system and end users started; shakedown: stabilizing, eliminating bugs, getting to normal operations; onward and upward: systems, supporting users, get results, upgrading system extensions. This model posits the necessary actions to be deliberated by decision makers in each phase of the ERP project where actions in each phase are mentioned *a priori*.

The above paragraphs illustrate IS implementation as an organizational change process while associating it to Kurt Lewin's change management model. This is referred to as process perspective and it helps us understand how ERP implementation efforts have happened and it therefore gives a moving picture about how we got from time 1 to time 2 (Aladwani, 2001). Several researchers fragment the implementation process into *a priori* stages or phases (Sabherwal & Robey, 1993). A synthesis of IS literature illustrated in Table 1 indicates that the number of stages or phases varies from at least three to six. Hence process approach seeks to understand outcomes by observing how events occur over time and in ERP transitions, processes may be conceived as sequence of events that occur over time (Boudreau & Robey, 1999) and though these events begin in a particular phase they may continue to overlap one another while another stage begins (Janssens, Kusters, & Heemstra, 2008). Boudreau & Robey (1999) affirm that an organization implementing ERP at any moment in time is influenced by conditions beyond its control and can achieve motivated behavior by way of plans and actions. As a result phase models are limited because they portray only one possible sequence of events through which all organizations are expected to progress. In the case of ERP implementation, the organization cannot risk the project by monitoring the success or failure *post facto*.

Table 1. Process perspective of ERP implementation

Reference: Author	Description of Phases	Number of Phases
Bhatti (2006)	Analysis, Installation, Final Preparation and Go Alive	4
Ehie & Madsen (2005)	Project Preparation, Business Blueprint, Realization, Final Preparation, Go Live and Support	5
Bajwa, Garcia, & Mooney (2004)	Awareness, Preparation, Selection, Implementation, Operation	5
Yusuf, Gunasekaran, & Abthorpe (2004)	Strategy and Direction, Planning Analysis and Early Deployment, Implementation	3
Aladwani (2001)	Knowledge Formulation Phase, Strategy Implementation Phase, Status Evaluation Phase	3
Esteves & Pastor (1999)	Adoption Decision Phase, Acquisition Phase, Implementation Phase, Use and Maintenance Phase, Evolution Phase, Retirement Phase	6
Ross (1998)	Design, Implementation, Stabilization, Continuous Improvement, Transformation	5
Kwon & Zmud (1987)	Initiation, Adoption /Adaption, Acceptance, Routinization, Infusion	6
Nolan (1973)	Initiation, Contagion, Control, Integration	4

Premise Two: Variance Perspective to ERP Implementation-Assessing Change Perspective Through *a priori* Factors

Literature points to majority of articles which identify requisite conditions or factors *a priori* to analyze the performance for successful ERP implementation. CSF are widely used in the information systems arena (Rockart, 1979) and within the context of ERP implementation context CSF are defined as factors needed to ensure a successful ERP project (Gibson, Holland, & Light, 1999; Parr & Shanks, 2000). An implicit goal of variance research is to establish the conditions necessary to bring about an outcome (Van de Ven & Poole, 2005) and is the focus of much of the research published in IS literature (March & Storey, 2008). Consequently, this article will interchangeably use the terms variance or factor perspective in the context of CSF. A review of literature confirms that the conditions necessary to evaluate the performance of ERP project are listed by way of "a laundry list of causal factors" (Richmond, 1993, pp.117). A majority of literature related ERP research is dedicated to listing CSF (Farzaneh, Vanani, & Sohrabi, 2013; Finney & Corbett 2007; Jarrar, Al-Mudimigh & Zairi, 2000; Markus & Tanis, 2000; Motwani, Subramanian, & Gopalakrishna, 2005; Nah, Lau, & Kuang, 2001; Soja 2006; Somers & Nelson, 2001; Toni & Klara, 2001; Zhang, Lee, Zhang, & Banerjee, 2002). Kini & Basaviah (2013) found CSF for large organizations and Small and Medium Businesses (SMB) similar.

Somers and Nelson (2001) argue that organizations must learn to identify the critical issues that affect the implementation process and know when in the process to address them effectively to ensure that the promised benefits can be realized and potential failures avoided. Rockart (1979) states that CSF are limited number of areas in which satisfactory results will ensure successful competitive performance for the individual, department or organization. While CSF identified *a priori* facilitates planning resources for successful ERP implementation, it adopts a rather static view, which limits its adequacy in explaining the dynamics of the implementation process (Aladwani, 2001) and it is unclear how these CSF inter-relate (Akkermans & van Helden, 2002), affirming this Esteves & Pastor (2001) report there is practical evidence that CSF do not have the same importance along the various phases of a SAP [Systems, Applications, and Products in Data Processing] implementation project. This is emphasized by Nah, Lau, & Kuang (2001) while developing a conceptual model for successful ERP project by listing eleven CSF across the phases of Markus & Tanis' model where they identified through an exploratory study, CSF that influences ERP implementation in various phases of ERP life cycle. A cumulative list of CSF clustered for each phase may not remain static over the life cycle of all ERP projects and also claim that organizations are influenced by exogenous factors that are beyond its control (Markus & Tanis, 2000). Tavana (2011) affirms this while describing the significance of considering an organization adapting to the ERP project through change and system in-built flexibility, organizations are influenced by dynamic environment and becomes essential to consider progressive changes that occur during the life cycle of ERP due to intervention of technology on people and organization. Hence it may be appropriate if CSF can be clustered into an integrated process variance framework where we can cluster CSF based on a model of organization that will enable the organization stakeholders identify and consider a plan of action to implement ERP.

Premise Three: SocioTechnical System Perspective to ERP Implementation – A Technological Intervention for Organizational Change

Conceptualizing ERP project as an organizational intervention creating change we draw Socio Technical (ST) system perspective to identify and define key constructs to analyse the performance of ERP system. ST system perspective began with the purpose of improving the Quality of Work Life (QWL) of workers on the production line (Mumford, 2006), the theory gradually found its application in design and implementation of new technologies (Dillon, 2000), clinical workplace (Wears & Berg, 2005), healthcare systems (Coiera, 2006) and computer information systems (Palvia, Sharma & Conrath, 2001). Recognizing significance of technological change in organization Appelbaum (1997) points to technology as an intervention and appraises the ST system theory to practitioners since this approach accommodates both social and technical elements of organization whereas Mumford (2006) considers ST system theory as a means for optimizing the intelligence and skills of human beings. ERP implementation is considered to rely on behavioural processes and actions (Al-Mudimigh, Zairi, & Al-Mashari, 2001) hence ST system can be a change perspective to examine interaction between social relationships of people with their environment explicitly organization and technical system using methods and materials.

ST system perspective is a synergy of social and technical subsystems and offers a standpoint to analyse performance of ERP implementation. We draw upon Leavitt's (1965) diamond model of organizational change and uncertainty due to its appeal and simplistic nature (Lyytinen, Mathiassen & Ropponen, 1996) to describe an organization as a social structure. Leavitt (1965) categorizes an organization as four distinct elements- task, actor, structure and technology interdependent to each other. Task refers to expected outcomes in terms of goals and deliverables (Lyytinen, Mathiassen & Ropponen, 1998), structure implies a means of communication, systems of authority and systems of work flow, actors refer to those participants involved that carry out tasks and technology is defined as any technical means, know-how and tools to carry out tasks (Lyytinen, Mathiassen & Ropponen, 1996). Grant & Mergen (1996) applied modified Leavitt's model to study the relation between task, technology, organization structure, people and an additional element of communication within a large corporation to reduce the cycle time of its products to keep up with the competition. Their evaluation of other organization frameworks reveals that Leavitt's ST system model was most appropriate since it is simple and explicit to stakeholders from diverse background in the organization. Leavitt's model is as illustrated in Figure 3. Here each element is interdependent on the other and any change in one element causes effects on other elements; in this case implementation of ERP involves changing the organization's technology component which automatically triggers changes in other components of the organization (Sarker, 2000).

To summarize, in premise one and two we compare and contrast the process and variance theoretical perspectives to explain why any one of the perspectives used in isolation may not serve the purpose of evaluating the performance of ERP implementation from an organizational change viewpoint. Since ERP is a technological intervention on the social structure of the organization it may be appropriate to leverage Leavitt's model to evaluate ERP performance through CSF. Integrating process-variance perspective with ST system based on Leavitt's diamond model is an attempt to monitor ERP performance and pinpoint areas where corrective actions need to be taken up during the ERP life cycle. DiMaggio (1995) argued that "many of the best theories are hybrids, combining the best qualities" (p. 392) of these approaches. This research article attempts to fulfil this gap in the literature. The following section discusses the research approach to evaluate performance of ERP implementation by integrating process and variance perspectives with ST system perspective.

RESEARCH APPROACH

The article is an exploratory study to conceptualize the performance of ERP implementation from process, variance and ST system perspectives. To review literature based on these perspectives we adopted

Figure 3. Leavitt's diamond model for sociotechnical change

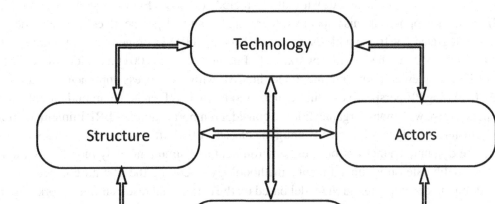

grounded theory approach. According to Wolfswinkel, Furtmueller, & Wilderom (2011) grounded theory approach enables to identify the key concepts to surface, instead of being deductively derived beforehand; the concepts emerge during the analytical process of substantive inquiry. With vast ERP implementation literature available Allan (2003) recommends a form of content analysis in grounded theory called coding to conceptualise the underlying issues amongst the 'noise' of the data. Key steps of this approach are: *open coding-* adopted to break down the data into distinct units of meaning called categories or concepts, *axial coding-* used to appreciate concepts in terms of their dynamic interrelationships which should form the basis for the construction of the theory and *selective coding-* adopted to identify and develop relations between the main categories (Goulding, 1999; Wolfswinkel, Furtmueller & Wilderom, 2011).

Integrated Conceptual Framework to Evaluate ERP Performance

In this section, we detail and develop an initial conceptual framework by integrating process and variance (PV) perspectives with sociotechnical (ST) perspective as described in the above premises. Literature review indicates that there have been significant efforts to group factors into dimensions and integrate under different frameworks to get a better understanding to analyse ERP implementation. Belassi and Tukel's (1996) empirical study to identify the factors for success or failure of projects highlights the significance of grouping factors based on criteria such as project elements, factors concerning project manager and team members, organization elements and external environmental elements to enable project managers understand the relationship between the grouped factors. Therefore, if CSF can be organized into dimensions, it will enable stakeholders to gain a better perspective of ERP project. ERP literature attempts to list such dimensions, another empirical study by Hanafizadeh and Ravasan (2011) chose to assess the first stage of ERP project-called ERP readiness assessment by leveraging McKinsey 7S framework by classifying the dimensions as hard and soft elements where the framework can be considered comprehensive and provides a specific list of factors for each of the elements: strategy, structure, systems, style, staff, skills and shared values for the readiness phase of ERP life cycle.

According to Sabherwal and Robey (1993) either phases or CSF approach during ERP project may not be conclusive to measure the performance of ERP implementation and they state that such a context as "cooking with a list of ingredients but without the recipe" (p. 449). Figure 3 shows the integrated conceptual framework proposed in this paper by integrating PV and ST perspectives. The left side of the schematic is an integrated PV framework (Nah, Lau & Kuang, 2001) leveraged from literature and the right side of this schematic is the ST framework. Nah, Lau and Kuang (2001) have identified CSF for each phases of ERP implementation and integrated the CSF with the process approach of Markus and Tanis' (2000). Collating PV perspectives with a generic model such as Leavitt's diamond model which is based on ST perspective will enable organizations to consider temporal nature of ERP implementation. It will enable in clustering and classifying CSF along the phases of ERP life cycle model. This will enable in adapting to the dynamic changes of business environment and simultaneously monitoring the ERP project. Next we deliberate on grounded theory methodology of coding the literature to identify constructs in an attempt to develop a research model based on the conceptual research framework, Figure 4.

Figure 4. Conceptual research framework: Integration of Process and Variance (PV) perspective with ST perspective

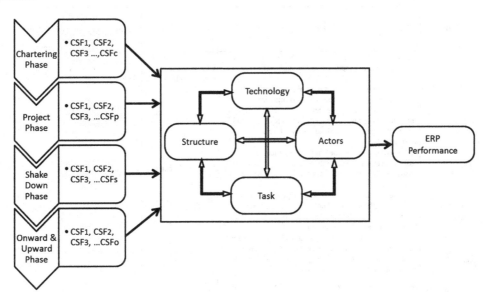

Adapted SocioTechnical (AST) System Model to Evaluate ERP Implementation

Literature search with appropriate keywords was conducted to identify articles in peer reviewed journals that analyse ERP implementation. This review is focused on two areas:

1. Articles associated to ERP implementation.
2. Articles that listed CSF for each phase of lifecycle model of ERP.

Initially, the articles that related to ERP implementation were analysed and summarised. Adopting the grounded theory approach, articles were reviewed for themes that emerged from the researchers' interpretation. A representative sample of reviewed articles and its summary is illustrated in Table 2. The emerging themes observed while reviewing the literature are stakeholders, organization, processes and technology. These themes are categorized and called concepts or constructs and this content analysis process of grounded theory is called open coding and the outcome of this open coding process resulted in four constructs.

For the next step, articles that list CSF for different phases (Dawson & Owens, 2008; Kronbichler, Ostermann & Staudinger, 2009; Motwani, Subramanian & Gopalakrishna, 2005; Nah, Lau & Kuang, 2001; Somers & Nelson, 2001) of ERP life cycle are considered for consolidating CSF. Table 3 summarises a list of 36 CSF obtained from the literature. To provide clarity and meaning to the four constructs, stakeholders, organization, processes and technology the CSF obtained through literature were clustered on the basis of their interrelationships and attributes using the process of axial coding. In the final step applying selective coding to data illustrated in Table 4, we observe an interrelationship between the constructs stakeholders and organization which is collated as social factors likewise we group processes and technology as technical factors and this defines a new SocioTechnical (ST) framework for ERP

Table 2. Consolidated concepts of sociotechnical Perspective for ERP implementation

Author	Summary	Context	Stakeholders	Organization	Processes	Technology / Technical
				Concepts		
Pan (2005)	Organization derives ES [Enterprise Systems] benefits through technical integration and re-engineering the processes.	Implementation of CRM systems, a module of ERP			√	√
Kamhawi (2007)	Empirical study of CSF in a developing country - Bahrain. Article stresses on dimensions such as organizational fit, process fit and BPR having significant influence on ERP implementation. Specifically employees resistance to ERP system during project needs to assessed for user acceptance.	ERP implementation	√	√	√	√
Janssens, Kusters, & Heemstra (2008)	ERP activities are classified into three dimensions: project, system and organization each of which have sub-clusters which depicts activities required to be taken up for successful ERP project	ERP implementation		√	√	√
Pries-Heje (2008)	The case study at a company adopted process model to implement ERP systems. The involvement of users the design and project activities caused a conflict of interest between the multiple stakeholders.	ERP implementation specifically assimilation stage	√	√		√
Uzoka, Abiola & Nyangeresi (2008)	Empirical study discusses organizational ERP software buying behaviour and emphasizes the involvement of organizational stakeholders for purchase process due to their awareness of business processes.	ERP software purchase decision making	√		√	
Yeoh, Koronios & Gao (2008)	Delphi study to develop or explore CSF for BI systems which is a module of ERP systems points to organizational factors more important than technological factors.	Implementation of Business Intelligence(BI) systems	√	√		
Hanafizadeh & Ravasan (2011)	McKinsey 7S framework to analyse readiness of an organization to avoid ERP project failure.	ERP readiness in the organization	√	√	√	√

Table 3. Representative list of CSF for ERP implementation

Key Authors	Nah,Lau & Kuang (2001),	Somers & Nelson (2001)	Motwani, Subramanian & Gopalakrishna (2005)	Dawson & Owens (2008)	Kronbichler, Ostermann & Staudinger (2009)
Critical Success Factors	• Top Management Support, • ERP Teamwork & Composition, • Effective Communication, • Project Management, • Business Plan & Vision, • Project Champion, • Change Management Program & Culture, • Appropriate Business & IT Legacy Systems, • BPR & Minimum Customization, • S/W Dev. Testing & Troubleshooting, • Monitoring & Evaluation of Performance	• Architecture Choices, • Clear Goals and Objectives, • Top Management Support, • Project Team Competence, • Use of Steering Committee, • Interdepartmental Communication, • Interdepartmental Cooperation, • User Training on Software, • Dedicated Resources, • Change Management, • Partnership with Vendor, • Use of Vendors' Tools, • Use of Consultants, • Education on new Business Processes, • Vendor Support, • Project Management, • Management of Expectations, • Project Champion, • Careful Selection of Package, • Data analysis & Conversion, • Business Process, Reengineering • Minimal Customization,	• Clear Understanding of strategic goals for ERP, • Commitment by Top Management, • Cultural & structural changes / Readiness, • Excellent Project Management, • ERP Package Selection that best with current business procedures, • Open information & communication Policy, • Exhaustive analysis of current business processes, • Importance of Data Accuracy, • IT leveragability & knowledge capability, • A great implementation team, • Focuses performance measures, • Appropriate celebration when project completed, • Post Implementation Audit, • Documentation and advertising ERP success, • Benchmarking	• Top Management Support, • Project Management, • ERP Team and Composition, • Effective Communication, • Business Plan & Vision, • Project Champion, • Appropriate Business & IT Legacy Systems, • Commitment to the Change, • A Vanilla ERP Approach	• Architecture Choices, technical implementation, technological infrastructure, • Vendor Support, • Top Management Support, • Project Management, • Project Champion / Empowered Decision Makers, • Team Composition & Teamwork, • Business Plan & Vision, • Partnership, • Interdepartmental Cooperation and Communication, • Change Management, • User Involvement / training, • Business Process Reengineering, • S/W Dev. Testing & Troubleshooting, • Legacy Systems Knowledge, • Deliverable dates / Smaller scope

Table 4. Final categorization of CSF under Adapted SocioTechnical (AST) framework

Social Factors		Technical Factors	
Stakeholder	**Organization**	**Processes**	**Technology**
Partnership with Vendor	Clear Goals and Objectives	Excellent Project Management	Architecture Choices
Top Management Support	Interdepartmental / Effective Communication	Exhaustive Analysis of Current Business Processes	Technical Implementation
Project Team Competence		Focuses Performance Measures	Technological Infrastructure
A Great Implementation Team and Competence & Teamwork	Interdepartmental Cooperation		Careful Selection of Package
	Dedicated Resources	Post Implementation Audit & Monitoring	Data Accuracy
Use of Steering Committee	Education on New Business Processes	Documentation and Advertising ERP Success	IT Leveragability & Knowledge Capability
User Training on Software	Cultural & Structural Change Readiness	Benchmarking	Appropriate Business & IT Legacy Systems
Vendor Support		BPR & Minimum Customization	
User Involvement & Training	Appropriate Celebration when Project Completed		Use of Vendors' Tools
	Business Plan & Vision	Deliverable Dates / Smaller Scope	S/W Development, Testing & Troubleshooting
Project Champion Empowered Decision Makers	A Vanilla Approach	Business Process Reorganization	
No of Factors: 9	No of Factors: 9	No of Factors: 9	No of Factors: 9

implementation. These four constructs can be mapped to equivalent dimensions of Leavitt's ST change model. The modified Leavitt's model with the new SocioTechnical (ST) framework is referred as Adapted SocioTechnical (AST) model (Figure 5) for assessment of ERP implementation. In the following section we discuss the conceptualization of constructs which are enablers of ERP performance and set forth the propositions for the proposed model. Setting limits to research in a conceptual paper by emphasizing theory (Schultz, Ginzberg & Lucas, 1994) answers what (constructs) and how (conceptual framework) (Whetten, 1989; Pawar, 2009) by setting directions to develop the propositions for the research article.

DELINEATING THE THEORETICAL CONSTRUCTS AND STATEMENT OF PROPOSITIONS

This section discusses and defines the five constructs of conceptual framework. The dependent variable is ERP performance which is a surrogate measure used to evaluate ERP success and independent variables are stakeholders, organization, processes and technology influencing the ERP performance. The constructs for the study is operationalized as shown in Table 5 and propositions are stated as a guide to enable in developing the research model.

Figure 5. Leavitt's diamond model and Adapted SocioTechnical (AST) constructs for ERP implementation

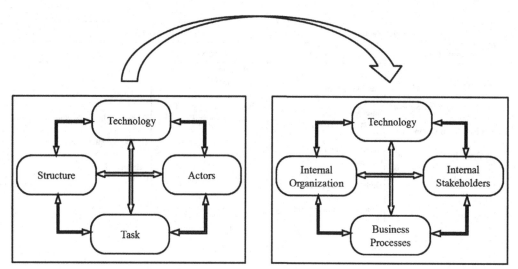

Social Factors (Stakeholder and Organization) and Technical Factors (Process and Technology)

AST framework developed in Table 4 displays CSF classified as social and technical dimensions. This emergent reaction between the social setting and technology is a phenomenon (Lee, 2000) that cannot be considered in isolation. As they interact with each other, it reinforces the need to look beyond technological perspective and study IT/IS implementation impact on humans and organizations and contribution of these interdependent elements by way of change on various contextual factors impacting the organization (Sarmento, 2005). Literature is opinionated with technology imperative which proposes that ERP technology being standardized software imposes organizations to adapt even though it is developed and implemented by humans to develop better explanations of human and machine interactions in organizations (Rose, Jones & Truex, 2005). However social imperative points out that new technology referred to as technical system has an effect on "users, the organisation, and work processes" and cannot be independent from the humans (Karsh, 2004). Hence by adopting a humane perspective to ERP project and relating it to "child rearing", managers who affiliate to technical side and the others who orient to human side of technology should communicate and co-ordinate as one unit to bring about successful organizational change (Tavana, 2011) and a symbiosis of social system and technical system will achieve the goals set if the combined systems is regularly monitored and controlled (Lee, 2004). In this research article we define the social dimension as consisting of two sub-systems- stakeholders and organization and the technical sub-system comprises of business processes and technology and evaluates ERP implementation through its performance grounded on the following statement:

The technical system is concerned with the processes, tasks, and technology needed to transform inputs to outputs. The social system is concerned with the attributes of people (e.g., attitudes, skills, values), the relationships among people, reward systems, and authority structures. It is assumed that the outputs of the work system are the result of joint interactions between these two systems. (Bostrom & Heinen, 1977, p.17)

Stakeholders to Internal Stakeholders

Stakeholders also referred to as actors (Keen, 1981; Leavitt, 1965) are group of people in an organization who share a pool of values that define what the desirable features of an IS are, and how they should be obtained (Beynon-Davies, Owens & Williams, 2004). Stakeholders are critical resource and necessitate a dedicated support (Orlikowski & Hofman, 1997; Zhang, Lee, Zhang & Banerjee, 2003). Employee's perception of the usefulness of the new system and acceptance of the new way of doing business (Beheshti & Beheshti, 2010) is modified by the attitudes of others to these behaviours (Coiera, 2006) and presence of the surrounding stakeholders, i.e. top management, project management, project champion, software vendor and consultants were identified as the root causes driving performance (Akkermans & van Helden, 2002). Boonstra (2011), for example has illustrated the impact of various stakeholders in each phase of ERP project life cycle so that their initiatives for the project can be planned by decision makers and defines stakeholders as "... any person or group who can affect or is affected by the EIS [Enterprise Information System] is a stakeholder (p.160)".

ERP project consultant and vendors are external players and their involvement begins well before pre-implementation stage by partnering with client in enabling them plan the type of implementation, modules of ERP system, business processes to be modified, training needs to adapt to new system and resources required for the project. They play a significant role by being part of ERP project which is referred by Markus, Axline, Petrie & Tanis (2000) as socially complex activities and they continue to assist organizations to assimilate the new systems. Therefore this study assumes consultant team and ERP vendors as internal stakeholders of a particular organization implementing ERP. It encompasses their perception towards project, usage of ERP system and attitude towards project stakeholders. Hence we rename our construct in AST model from stakeholders to internal stakeholders.

Proposition 1: Success of ERP implementation is related to performance of ERP and is positively related to the social perspective of internal stakeholders of an organization to ERP project.

Organization to Internal Organization

Lyttinen & Newmann (2008) argue that identifying business environment as a dimension can bring forward key elements that influence change in IS systems. Though the article calls upon consideration of internal and external organizational environment, this article deliberates on the internal organization context since it forms the controllable component and the decision makers are able to plan the resources to leverage the performance of ERP project. This is supported by Table 3 an exhibit of CSF represents endogenous organizational context. Organization strategies, mechanisms to communicate about ERP project and change management methods are made conducive to enable internal stakeholders adapt to ERP project. Duncan (1972) defines internal environment as consisting of those relevant physical and social factors within the boundaries of the organization.

An often overlooked aspect of ERP implementations is the effect that the new system will have on employees (Okrent & Vokurka, 2004) as a result, appropriate change methods and techniques that help individuals and groups make the best use of available technology are needed (Appelbaum, 1997). This is consistent with (Geels, 2004) that sociotechnical systems do not function autonomously, but are the outcome of activities of human actors and organizations. Another important aspect that effectively brings about change in organizations is culture (Grabski, Leech & Schmidt, 2011; Orlikowski & Hofman, 1997).

Culture is used as a means to understand organizations (Robey & Boudreau, 1999) and in the context of ERP implementation, culture signifies a mechanism of sharing values, believes and ideas among organizational stakeholders. Hence internal organization is defined as the endogenous organizational context planned for ERP implementation.

Proposition 2: ERP implementation success is related to ERP performance and is positively related to the internal organization from a social perspective.

Process to Business Processes

Implementing ERP application software (Rashid, Hossain, & Patrick, 2001) force companies to reengineer their business processes to accommodate the logic of the software modules for streamlining data flow throughout the organization. ERP system causes mutual interactions between IT and organization by pointing to the requirement that organizations must reengineer its business processes to fit the processes that the ERP software was programmed to manage (Lee, 2004). The Business Process Reengineering (BPR) paradigm is an enabler to bring about changes in business process. ERP deployment requires extensive effort (Al-Mudimigh, Zairi & Al-Mashari, 2001) to transform the business processes, bring about radical organizational change (Kwahk, 2006) and a thorough strategic thinking that allows companies to gain better understanding of their business processes (Ehie & Madsen, 2005). A business process in the context of ERP deployment can be defined as a method of identifying as-is business processes and configuring the ERP software for the new to-be business processes. Therefore, in this study we redefine processes in AST model as business processes.

Proposition 3: ERP implementation success is related to its performance and is positively related to processes from a technical perspective.

Technology

ERP implementations are usually large, complex projects, involving large groups of people and other resources, working together under considerable time pressure and facing many unforeseen developments (Akkermans & van Helden, 2002). The enterprise has its own thoughts, but the software of ERP has also certain thoughts, therefore, how to synthesize them is a critical work (Jing & Qiu, 2007). In this regard to bring about change effectively another key organizational context dimension is technology (Orlikowski & Hofman, 1997). The technical infrastructure is unlike other software systems where organization has to pay special attention to the existing technology, generically known as legacy systems and will be a good indicator of the nature and scale of potential problems (Finney & Corbett, 2007; Karsh, 2004).

Another issue faced by organizations relates to ERP customizations. Since ERP is vendor developed application software developed based on best practices of organizations worldwide while implementing ERP, nearly most organizations reengineer their processes and standardize them to meet the needs of ERP software rather than customizing the software to the requirements of the organization processes. Though ERP has the rich potential for customizing that distinguishes it from other packages (Klaus, Rosemann & Gable, 2000), while implementing ERP the objective of customization is to achieve a fit between the ERP system and the process that the system supports. This calls for decision makers to collaborate as a team with the top management and consultants to draw consensus while establishing a fit between the processes and technology (Parthasarathy & Anbazhagan, 2007). Hence we observe that technical systems cannot be stand-alone systems but must align with environment and involve sub-systems such as humans (Lee, 2000). This article defines organization's technology as the combination of hardware-software infrastructure (Whitworth, 2009) and software architecture framework.

Proposition 4: ERP implementation success is related to its performance and positively related to the technology from a technical perspective.

ERP Implementation Performance

ERP success or failure is a concern for organizations due to the risk associated with the project by way of investments made by the organization, acceptance of software by stakeholders, reengineering business processes, unlearning old practices and adapting to new systems. IS implementation can be defined in terms of management change and improvement (Schultz, Ginzberg & Lucas, 1998). This is consistent to the three theoretical premises based on change in this study. Therefore it is significant for IS professionals to understand how the implementation of such IS can bring about firm value through their performance (March & Storey, 2008).The full benefits of productivity improvement measures are realised when productivity is examined from two perspectives: operational efficiency of an *individual worker* or a *business unit* and effectiveness through *system performance* (Beheshti & Beheshti, 2010). Hence ERP implementation is viewed from the perspective of *internal stakeholder's* at all hierarchical

Table 5. Operational definition of conceptualized constructs to evaluate ERP performance

Constructs	Working / Operational Definition of Proposed PVAST Model
Independent Variables	
Internal Stakeholders	Defined as the attitude and perception of the members (top management, project team members, end users, vendors and consultants) who are part of the ERP project towards ERP deployment in the organization.
Internal Organization	The endogenous environment of organization is defined as a context where appropriate strategic planning process, effective communication tools, tools for decision making and change management methods and techniques is undertaken for ERP implementation.
Business Processes	Defined as the process of analysing as-is state of the organization and plan for the to-be processes on account of ERP implementation.
Technology	Tools (ERP system) required, its associated hardware, network, communication and software architecture framework for the organization to fulfil its objectives and end user to carry out their tasks.
Dependent Variable	
ERP Performance	The dependent variable. ERP success is measured with a surrogate measure, ERP performance. This surrogate measure is represented with three items to incorporate tangible (the cost of ERP did not outweigh the benefits), intangible benefits (ERP implementation has significant positive effectiveness for the business) and the organization gains with ERP implementation (improved overall business efficiency).

level of the organization and *business unit* which is *represented by constructs* of AST Leavitt's model in this study. ERP success during implementation is measured through *ERP performance* by evaluating the social and technical factors.

Proposition 5: ERP implementations success is related to ERP performance assessed through social and technical dimensions of organization.

THEORETICAL MODEL DEVELOPMENT AND DISCUSSIONS

In this section we propose a theoretical model that shows the relationship among the constructs. The proposed Process Variance and Adapted SocioTechnical (PVAST) model is illustrated in Figure 6. This PVAST model is an assimilation of three theoretical perspectives: process, variance and adapted sociotechnical. PVAST model is based on five constructs; one dependent variable: ERP implementation performance which enables in evaluating the success or failure of ERP implementation; four independent variables: internal stakeholders, internal organization, business processes and technology. The key for our research model is based on:

…the lessons that emerge in the interactive system effects between the technological [technical] and the organizational [social], where these lessons pertain to the management of information technology and the uses of information technology for managerial and organizational purposes. (Lee, 2000, p.vii)

The PVAST model is developed in two stages; firstly, integration of variance perspective under AST as illustrated in Table 4; and secondly, four instances of the above integrated model are generated for each phase namely chartering, project, shakedown and onward-upward. *CSF_X_Sx, CSF_X_Ox, CSF_X_Px* and *CSF_X_Tx* represent the CSF associated with internal stakeholders, internal organization, business processes and technology respectively, where *X* represents phases of implementation and *x* is number of CSF in the phase X. To illustrate this (see Figure 5), *CSF_C_S1* and *CSF_O_P6* represent the first CSF under internal stakeholder construct in chartering phase and sixth CSF under the business processes construct in the onward and upward phase respectively. This proposed model will facilitate to evaluate the performance of ERP project. This process of monitoring will also enable stakeholders of the project plan their resources based on temporal conditions of time and account for changes in CSF due to the dynamic competitive environment before the next stage of ERP project.

Uniqueness of PVAST model for ERP implementation is that it enables organization decision makers leverage simplicity of AST Leavitt's change model which can be understood easily by members with diverse backgrounds and frames of reference (Grant & Mergen, 1996). This is consistent with Alter's (2010, p. 3) view "a model that fosters better communication between business and IT professionals should consist of terms that are understandable to typical business professionals". Though the integrative model of Somers, Nelson, & Ragowsky (2000) is based on ST perspective view of organizations consisting of domains- actors, structure, technology, tasks and data, accounts for the external and internal environment of the organization, and is based on software life cycle model but it does not explain how the organization can apply the model to evaluate ERP implementation.

Figure 6. Proposed conceptual PVAST model for ERP implementation assessment based on Adapted SocioTechnical framework

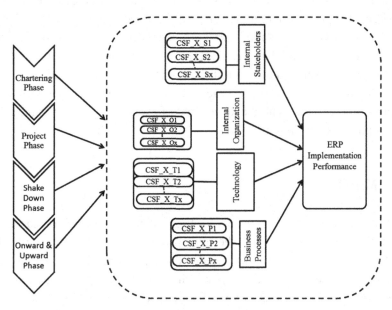

The proposed PVAST conceptual model allows an organization to gain perspective on the performance of ERP implementation can be powerful means of providing focus and improving the effectiveness of the systems efforts and will enable organization to diminish the risk associated with the technological interventions; nevertheless organizing CSF along the phases from a sociotechnical perspective enables stakeholders in conceptualizing ERP performance based on organization elements. This is consistent with Beheshti & Beheshti's (2010) call upon organizations if it wants to meet the challenges of the dynamic environment to consider ERP system as contained with people, management, strategic goals, business processes, the hardware and the ERP software. These components are the constructs of PVAST model and hence measuring ERP success with this model will enable organizations evaluate its performance.

CONCLUSION AND IMPLICATIONS

The objective of this research has been to develop a rich theoretical background to evaluate the success of ERP systems. An integrated PVAST conceptual model that associates process and variance perspectives with sociotechnical perspective in conjunction with an adapted Leavitt's change model has been theorized. The conceptual model draws on the synergy of social and technical dimensions of the organization to represent it as a social structure in Leavitt's adapted change model. The key constructs identified from this model are internal stakeholders, internal organization, business processes and technology. The article operationalizes the constructs by adopting the grounded theory approach and develops propositions for the study. The four instances of the PVAST model across the implementation phases (chartering, project, shakedown and onward-upward) enable decision makers to evaluate the success of ERP during its life cycle.

From an academic perspective this research has developed a novel integrated framework grounded on process, variance and sociotechnical perspectives to evaluate the success of ERP through its life cycle. The PVAST model enables practitioners to identify CSF for each phase in ERP life cycle model and cluster them under the adapted Leavitt's model and provides them a better standpoint to underpin areas where corrective measures are essential during planning, implementation and up-gradation of ERP system. The proposed model is developed by rigorously reviewing literature based on the grounded theory approach and further empirical study can be carried out to validate the proposed model. Future studies can extend the organization environment to take account of exogenous context to include concepts such as customers and suppliers as stakeholders.

ACKNOWLEDGMENT

The authors wish to thank anonymous reviewers for their valuable feedback on earlier versions of this research article. The feedback received from the reviewers has enabled us to improve this article substantially. The authors would also like to acknowledge the support received from the editor during this process. This chapter is a revised version of the research article "Conceptualizing Dimensions of Enterprise Resource Planning Systems Success: A SocioTechnical Perspective" published in the International Journal of Enterprise Information Systems, 10(1), 53-75.

REFERENCES

Akkermans, H., & van Helden, K. (2002). Vicious and Virtuous Cycles in ERP Implementation: A Case Study of Interrelations between Critical Success Factors. *European Journal of Information Systems*, *11*(1), 35–46. doi:10.1057/palgrave.ejis.3000418

Al-Mudimigh, A., Zairi, M., & Al-Mashari, M. (2001). ERP software implementation: An integrative framework. *European Journal of Information Systems*, *10*(4), 216–226. doi:10.1057/palgrave.ejis.3000406

Aladwani, A. M. (2001). Change management strategies for successful ERP implementation. *Business Process Management Journal*, *7*(3), 266–275. doi:10.1108/14637150110392764

Allan, G. (2003). A critique of using grounded theory as a research method. *Electronic Journal of Business Research Methods*, *2*(1), 1–10.

Alter, S. (2010). *Bridging the Chasm between Sociotechnical and Technical Views of Systems in Organizations*. Paper presented at the Thirty First International Conference on Information Systems, St. Louis, MO.

Appelbaum, S. H. (1997). Socio-Technical Systems Theory: An Intervention Strategy for Organizational Development. *Management Decision*, *35*(6), 452–463. doi:10.1108/00251749710173823

Arnold, V. (2006). Behavioral research opportunities: Understanding the impact of enterprise systems. *International Journal of Accounting Information Systems*, *7*(1), 7–17. doi:10.1016/j.accinf.2006.02.001

Bacharach, S. B. (1989). Organizational Theories: Some Criteria for Evaluation. *Academy of Management Review*, *14*(4), 496–515.

Bajwa, D. S., Garcia, J. E., & Mooney, T. (2004). An Integrative Framework for the Assimilation of Enterprise Resource Planning Systems: Phases, Antecedents, and Outcomes. *Journal of Computer Information Systems*, *44*(3), 81–90.

Beheshti, H. M., & Beheshti, C. M. (2010). Improving productivity and firm performance with enterprise resource planning. *Enterprise Information Systems*, *4*(4), 445–472. doi:10.1080/17517575.2010.511276

Belassi, W., & Tukel, O. I. (1996). A new framework for determining critical success/failure factors in projects. *International Journal of Project Management*, *14*(3), 141–151. doi:10.1016/0263-7863(95)00064-X

Beynon-Davies, P., Owens, I., & Williams, M. D. (2004). Information systems evaluation and the information systems development. *The Journal of Enterprise Information Management*, *17*(4), 276–282. doi:10.1108/17410390410548689

Bhatti, T. R. (2005, September). Critical success factors for the implementation of enterprise resource planning (ERP): empirical validation.*The Second International Conference on Innovation in Information Technology*, 110.

Bingi, P., Sharma, M. K., & Godla, J. K. (1999). Critical Issues Affecting an ERP Implementation. *Information Systems Management*, *16*(5), 7–15. doi:10.1201/1078/43197.16.3.19990601/31310.2

Boonstra, A. (2011). Aligning Systems, Structures and People: Managing Stakeholders. Managing Adaptability, Intervention, and People in Enterprise Information Systems, 157.

Bostrom, R. P., & Heinen, J. S. (1977). MIS Problems and Failures: A Socio- Technical Perspective Part I: The Causes. *Management Information Systems Quarterly*, *1*(3), 17–32. doi:10.2307/248710

Boudreau, M. C., & Robey, D. (1999, January). Organizational transition to enterprise resource planning systems: theoretical choices for process research. In *Proceedings of the 20th international conference on Information Systems* (pp. 291-299). Association for Information Systems.

Coiera, E. (2007). Putting the technical back into socio-technical systems research. *International Journal of Medical Informatics*, *76*, S98–S103. doi:10.1016/j.ijmedinf.2006.05.026 PMID:16807084

Cooper, R. B., & Zmud, R. W. (1990). Information Technology Implementation Research: A Technological Diffusion Approach. *Management Science*, *36*(2), 123–139. doi:10.1287/mnsc.36.2.123

Davenport, T. (1998). Putting Enterprise into the Enterprise system. *Harvard Business Review*, *76*(4), 1–11. PMID:10181586

Davis, G. B., & Olson, M. (1985). *Management information systems: Conceptual foundations, methods and development*. New York: McGraw Hill.

Dawson, J., & Owens, J. (2008). Critical success factors in the chartering phase: A case study of an ERP implementation. *International Journal of Enterprise Information Systems*, *4*(3), 9–24. doi:10.4018/jeis.2008070102

Di Maggio, P. (1995). What Theory is not. *Administrative Science Quarterly*, *40*(3), 391–397. doi:10.2307/2393790

Dillon, A. (2000). Group Dynamics Meet Cognition: applying socio-technical concepts in the design of information systems. In The New SocioTech: Graffiti on the Long Wall, (pp. 119-125). Springer Verlag.

Duncan, R. B. (1972). Characteristics of Organizational Environments and Perceived Environmental Uncertainty. *Administrative Science Quarterly, 17*(3), 313–327. doi:10.2307/2392145

Ehie, I., & Madsen, M. (2005). Identifying critical issues in enterprise resource planning (ERP) implementation. *Computers in Industry, 56*(6), 545–557. doi:10.1016/j.compind.2005.02.006

Esteves, J., & Pastor, J. (1999). An ERP lifecycle-based research agenda. *International Workshop in Enterprise Management and Resource. Planning: Methods, Tools and Architectures–EMRPS*, 1-12.

Esteves, J., & Pastor, J. (2001). Enterprise Resource Planning: An Annotated Bibliography. *Communications of the AIS, 7*(8), 1–51.

Farzaneh, M., Vanani, I. R., & Sohrabi, B. (2013). A Survey Study of Influential Factors in the Implementation of Enterprise Resource Planning Systems. *International Journal of Enterprise Information Systems, 9*(1), 76–96. doi:10.4018/jeis.2013010105

Finney, S., & Corbett, M. (2007). ERP implementation: A compilation and analysis of critical success factors. *Business Process Management Journal, 13*(3), 329–347. doi:10.1108/14637150710752272

Geels, F. W. (2004). From sectoral systems of innovation to socio-technical systems: Insights about dynamics and change from sociology and institutional theory. *Research Policy, 33*(6-7), 897–920. doi:10.1016/j.respol.2004.01.015

Gibson, N., Holland, C. P., & Light, B. (1999). Enterprise Resource Planning: A Business Approach to Systems Development.*Proceedings of the 32nd Hawaii International Conference on System Sciences.* doi:10.1109/HICSS.1999.772816

Goulding, C. (1999). *Grounded Theory: some reflections on paradigm, procedures and misconceptions.* Working Paper Series, Number WP006/99, ISSN Number ISSN 1363-6839, pp.1-26.

Grabski, S. V., Leech, S. A., & Schmidt, P. J. (2011). A Review of ERP Research: A Future Agenda for Accounting Information Systems. *Journal of Information Systems, 25*(1), 37–78. doi:10.2308/jis.2011.25.1.37

Grant, D., & Mergen, E. (1996). Applying quality to Leavitts framework to solve information technology problems: A case study. *Information Technology & People, 9*(2), 43–60. doi:10.1108/09593849610121598

Grant, D., & Tu, Q. (2005). Levels of enterprise Integration: Study Using Case Analysis. *International Journal of Enterprise Information Systems, 1*(1), 1–22. doi:10.4018/jeis.2005010101

Gunasekaran, A. (2005). Enterprise Information Systems & Organizational Competitiveness. *International Journal of Enterprise Information Systems, 1*(1), i–vi.

Hammer, M., & Stanton, S. (1999). How Process Enterprises Really Work. *Harvard Business Review*, 108–118. PMID:10662000

Hanafizadeh, P., & Ravasan, A. Z. (2011). A McKinsey 7S model-based framework for ERP readiness assessment. *International Journal of Enterprise Information Systems*, *7*(4), 23–63. doi:10.4018/jeis.2011100103

Hawking, P., Stein, A., & Foster, S. (2004, January). Revisiting ERP systems: benefit realization. In *System Sciences, 2004.Proceedings of the 37th Annual Hawaii International Conference on* (pp. 1-8). IEEE.

Henderson, R., & Mitchell, W. (1997). The interactions of organizational and competitive influences on strategy and performance. *Strategic Management Journal*, *18*(S1), 5–14. doi:10.1002/(SICI)1097-0266(199707)18:1+<5::AID-SMJ930>3.3.CO;2-9

Holland, C. P., & Light, B. (1999). A critical success factors model for ERP implementation. *IEEE Software*, *16*(3), 30–36. doi:10.1109/52.765784

Janssens, G., Kusters, R., & Heemstra, F. (2008). Sizing ERP implementation projects: An activity-based approach. *International Journal of Enterprise Information Systems*, *4*(3), 25–47. doi:10.4018/jeis.2008070103

Jarrar, Y. F., Al-Mudimigh, & Zairi, M. (2000). ERP Implementation Critical Success Factors–The Role and Impact of Business Process Management. ICMIT (pp. 122–127). IEEE.

Jing, R., & Qiu, X. (2007). A Study on Critical Success Factors in ERP Systems Implementation.*International Conference on Service Systems and Service Management*, 1-6. doi:10.1109/ICSSSM.2007.4280192

Kamhawi, E. M. (2007). Critical Factors for Implementation Success of ERP Systems: An Empirical Investigation from Bahrain. *International Journal of Enterprise Information Systems*, *3*(2), 34–49. doi:10.4018/jeis.2007040103

Karsh, B.-T. (2004). Beyond usability: Designing effective technology implementation systems to promote patient safety. *Quality & Safety in Health Care*, *13*(5), 388–394. doi:10.1136/qshc.2004.010322 PMID:15465944

Keen, P. G. (1981). Information systems and organizational change. *Communications of the ACM*, *24*(1), 24–33. doi:10.1145/358527.358543

Kerlinger, F. N. (1986). *Foundations of Behavioral Research* (3rd ed.). New York: Holt, Rinehart, & Winston.

King, J. L., & Kraemer, K. L. (1984). Evolution and Organizational Information Systems: An Assessment of Nolans Stage Model. *Communications of the ACM*, *27*(5), 466–475. doi:10.1145/358189.358074

Kini, R. B., & Basaviah, S. (2013). Critical Success Factors in the Implementation of Enterprise Resource Planning Systems in Small and Midsize Businesses: Microsoft Navision Implementation. *International Journal of Enterprise Information Systems*, *9*(1), 97–117. doi:10.4018/jeis.2013010106

Klaus, H., Rosemann, M., & Gable, G. (2000). What is ERP? *Information Systems Frontiers*, *2*(2), 141–162. doi:10.1023/A:1026543906354

Kronbichler, S. A., Ostermann, H., & Staudinger, R. (2009). A Review of Critical Success Factors for ERP Projects. *The Open Information Systems Journal*, *3*(1), 14–25. doi:10.2174/1874133900903010014

Kwahk, K. (2006, January). ERP acceptance: organizational change perspective. In *System Sciences, 2006. HICSS'06.Proceedings of the 39th Annual Hawaii International Conference on System Sciences* (*Vol. 8*, pp. 172b-172b). IEEE. doi:10.1109/HICSS.2006.159

Kwon, T. H., & Zmud, R. W. (1987). Unifying the Fragmented Models of Information Systems Implementation. In Critical Issues in Information Systems Research (pp. 227-51). John Wiley.

Leavitt, H. J. (1965). *Applying organizational change in industry: Structural, technological and humanistic approaches. In Handbook of Organizations*. Chicago: Academic Press.

Lee, A. (2000). Researchable Directions for ERP and Other New Information Technologies, Editors Comments. MIS Quarterly, 24(1), iii-viii.

Lee, A. S. (2004). *Thinking about Social Theory and Philosophy for Information Systems*. In L. Willcocks & J. Mingers (Eds.), *Social Theory and Philosophy for Information Systems* (pp. 1–26). Chichester, UK: John Wiley & Sons.

Levasseur, R. E. (2001). People Skills: Change Management Tools - Lewin's Change Model. *Interfaces*, *31*(4), 71–73.

Lewin, K. (1952). *Field theory in social science: Selected theoretical papers* (D. Cartwright, Ed.). London: Tavistock.

Lyytinen, K., Mathiassen, L., & Ropponen, J. (1996). A framework for software risk management. *Journal of Information Technology*, *11*(4), 275–285. doi:10.1057/jit.1996.2

Lyytinen, K., Mathiassen, L., & Ropponen, J. (1998). Attention Shaping and Software Risk – A Categorical analysis of Four Classical Risk Management Approaches. *Information Systems Research*, *9*(3), 233–255. doi:10.1287/isre.9.3.233

Lyytinen, K., & Newman, M. (2008). Explaining information systems change: A punctuated socio-technical change model. *European Journal of Information Systems*, *17*(6), 589–613. doi:10.1057/ejis.2008.50

March, S. T., & Storey, V. C. (2008). Design Science in the Information Systems Discipline: An Introduction to the Special Issue on Design Science Research. *Management Information Systems Quarterly*, *32*(4), 725–730.

Markus, M. L., Axline, S., Petrie, D., & Tanis, C. (2000). Learning from adopters experiences with ERP: Problems encountered and success achieved. *Journal of Information Technology*, *15*(4), 245–265. doi:10.1080/02683960010008944

Markus, M. L., & Tanis, C. (2000). The Enterprise System Experience– from adoption to success. In Framing the Domains of IT Management: Projecting the Future through the Past (pp. 173-207). Pinnaflex Educational Resources, Inc.

Motwani, J., Subramanian, R., & Gopalakrishna, P. (2005). Critical factors for successful ERP implementation: Exploratory findings from four case studies. *Computers in Industry*, *56*(6), 529–544. doi:10.1016/j.compind.2005.02.005

Mumford, E. (2006). The story of socio-technical design: Reflections on its successes, failures and potential. *Information Systems Journal, 16*(4), 317–342. doi:10.1111/j.1365-2575.2006.00221.x

Nah, F., Lau, J., & Kuang, J. (2001). Critical Factors for Successful Implementation of Enterprise Systems. *Business Process Management Journal, 7*(3), 285–296. doi:10.1108/14637150110392782

Nwankpa, J. K. (2015). ERP system usage and benefit: A model of antecedents and outcomes. *Computers in Human Behavior, 45*, 335–344. doi:10.1016/j.chb.2014.12.019

Okrent, M. D., & Vokurka, R. J. (2004). Process mapping in successful ERP implementations. *Industrial Management & Data Systems, 104*(8), 637–643. doi:10.1108/02635570410561618

Orlikowski, W., & Hoffman, D. (1997). *An Improvisational Model for Change Management: The Case of Groupware Technologies. In Inventing the Organizations of the 21st Century* (pp. 265–282). Boston, MA: MIT.

Palvia, S. C., Sharma, R. S., & Conrath, D. W. (2001). A Socio-Technical Framework for Quality Assessment of Computer Information Systems. *Industrial Management & Data Systems, 101*(5), 237–251. doi:10.1108/02635570110394635

Pan, S. L. (2005). Customer perspective of CRM Systems: A Focus Group Study. *International Journal of Enterprise Information Systems, 1*(1), 65–68. doi:10.4018/jeis.2005010105

Parr, A. N., & Shanks, G. (2000). A Taxonomy of ERP Implementation Approaches.*Proceedings of the 33rd Hawaii International Conference on System Sciences*, 1-10.

Parthasarathy, S., & Anbazhagan, N. (2007). Evaluating ERP implementation choices using AHP. *International Journal of Enterprise Information Systems, 3*(3), 52–65. doi:10.4018/jeis.2007070104

Pawar, B. S. (2009). *Theory building for hypothesis specification in organizational studies.* Sage Publications.

Pries-Heje, L. (2008). Time, attitude, and user participation: How prior events determine user attitudes in ERP implementation. *International Journal of Enterprise Information Systems, 4*(3), 48–65. doi:10.4018/jeis.2008070104

Rashid, M., Hossain, L., & Patrick, J. (2001). The Evolution of ERP Systems: A Historical Perspective. In L. Hossain, J. Patrick, & M. Rashid (Eds.), *Enterprise Resource Planning: Global Opportunities & Challenges* (pp. 1–16). Idea Group Publishing.

Richmond, B. (1993). Systems thinking: Critical thinking skills for the 1990s and beyond. *System Dynamics Review, 9*(2), 113–133. doi:10.1002/sdr.4260090203

Robey, D., & Boudreau, M. C. (1999). Accounting for the Contradictory Organizational Consequences of Information Technology: Theoretical Directions and Methodological Implications. *Information Systems Research, 10*(2), 167–185. doi:10.1287/isre.10.2.167

Rockart, F. (1979). Chief executives define their own data needs. *Harvard Business Review, 57*, 81–93. PMID:10297607

Rose, J., Jones, M., & Truex, D. (2005). Socio-Theoretic Accounts of IS: The Problem of Agency. *Scandinavian Journal of Information Systems*, *17*(1), 133–152.

Ross, J. W. (1998), *The ERP Revolution: Surviving Versus Thriving*. Centre for Information Systems Research, Research Report, CISR Working Paper No. 307, Sloan School of Management.

Sabherwal, R., & Robey, D. (1993). An Empirical Taxonomy of Implementation Processes Based on Sequences of Events in Information Systems Development. *Organization Science*, *4*(4), 548–576. doi:10.1287/orsc.4.4.548

Sarker, S. (2000). Toward a Methodology for Managing Information Systems Implementation: A Social Constructivist Perspective. *Informing Science*, *3*(4), 195–205.

Sarmento, A. (Ed.). (2004). Preface. In Issues of human computer interaction. IGI Global.

Schultz, R. L., Ginzberg, M. J., & Lucas, H. C. (1984). A structural model of implementation. In R. L. Schultz & M. J. Ginzberg (Eds.), *Management Science Implementation*. Greenwich, CT: JAI Press.

Shehab, E. M., Sharp, M. W., Supramaniam, L., & Spedding, T. A. (2004). Enterprise resource planning: An integrative review. *Business Process Management Journal*, *10*(4), 359–386. doi:10.1108/14637150410548056

Soja, P. (2006). Success factors in ERP systems implementations Lessons from practice. *Journal of Enterprise Information Management*, *19*(4), 418–433. doi:10.1108/17410390610678331

Somers, T. M., & Nelson, K. (2001, January). The impact of critical success factors across the stages of enterprise resource planning implementations. In *System Sciences, 2001.Proceeding of the 34th Hawaii International Conference on System Sciences*, 1-10. doi:10.1109/HICSS.2001.927129

Somers, T. M., Nelson, K., & Ragowsky, A. (2000). Enterprise Resource Planning (ERP) for the Next Millennium: Development of an Integrative Framework and Implications for Research. *AMCIS 2000Proceedings of the 2000 Americas Conference of Information Systems*, 998-1004.

Stewart, G., Milford, M., Jewels, T., Hunter, T., & Hunter, B. (2000). Organisational Readiness for ERP Implementation. *Americas Conference on Information Systems, AMCIS 2000 Proceedings*, 966 - 971. Retrieved from http://aisel.aisnet.org/amcis2000/291K

Symons, C. (2006). *Measuring the Business Value of IT, A Survey of IT Value Methodologies*. Forrester Research, Inc. Retrieved August 28, 2012, from http://www.cornerstone1.com/SAP/SAP_Forrester_Measuring_the_Business_Value_of_IT.pdf

Tavana, M. (2011). *Managing Adaptability*. Intervention, and People in Enterprise Information Systems; doi:10.4018/978-1-60960-529-2

Te'eni, D. (2005). In S. Nielsen & J. Beekhuyzen (Eds.), *Socio-technical aspects of ERP selection and implementation: The central role of communication. In Enterprise Systems in Academia* (pp. 1–21). Hershey, PA: IGP.

Toni, S. M., & Klara, N. (2001). The Impact of Critical Success Factors across the Stages of ERP Implementations.*Proceedings of the 34th Hawaii International Conference on Systems Science*.

Uzoka, F. M. E., Abiola, R. O., & Nyangeresi, R. (2008). Influence of product and organizational constructs on ERP acquisition using an extended technology acceptance model. *International Journal of Enterprise Information Systems*, *4*(2), 67–83. doi:10.4018/jeis.2008040105

Van de Ven, A. H., & Poole, M. S. (2005). Alternative approaches for studying Organizational Change. *Organization Studies*, *26*(9), 1377–1404. doi:10.1177/0170840605056907

Wears, R. L., & Berg, M. (2005). Computer technology and clinical work. *Journal of the American Medical Association*, *293*(10), 1261–1263. doi:10.1001/jama.293.10.1261 PMID:15755949

Whetten, D. A. (1989). What Constitutes a Theoretical Contribution? *Academy of Management Review*, *14*(4), 490–495. doi:10.2307/258554

Whitworth, B. (2009). *The Social Requirements of Technical Systems. In Handbook of Research on Socio-Technical Design and Social Networking Systems* (pp. 1–22). IGI Global; doi:10.4018/978-1-60566-264-0

Williams, J., Williams, M. D., & Morgan, A. (2013). A teleological process theory for managing ERP implementations. *Journal of Enterprise Information Management*, *26*(3), 235–249. doi:10.1108/17410391311325216

Wolfswinkel, J. F., Furtmueller, E., & Wilderom, C. P. (2011). Using grounded theory as a method for rigorously reviewing literature. *European Journal of Information Systems*, *22*(1), 45–55. doi:10.1057/ejis.2011.51

Yeoh, W., Koronios, A., & Gao, J. (2008). Managing the Implementation of Business Intelligence Systems: A Critical Success Factors Framework. *International Journal of Enterprise Information Systems*, *4*(3), 79–94. doi:10.4018/jeis.2008070106

Yusuf, Y., Gunasekaran, A., & Abthorpe, M. S. (2004). Enterprise information systems project implementation: A case study of ERP in Rolls-Royce. *International Journal of Production Economics*, *87*(3), 251–266. doi:10.1016/j.ijpe.2003.10.004

Zhang, L., Lee, M. K., Zhang, Z., & Banerjee, P. (2003, January). Critical success factors of enterprise resource planning systems implementation success in China. In *System Sciences.Proceedings of the 36th Annual Hawaii International Conference on System Sciences* (pp. 1-10). IEEE. doi:10.1109/HICSS.2003.1174613

KEY TERMS AND DEFINITIONS

Critical Success Factors: Critical Success Factors (CSF) are defined as factors needed to ensure a successful ERP project.

ERP Implementation: The intervention of ERP application system on the social and technical factors of an organization.

Process Perspective: The process perspective posits the necessary actions to be deliberated by decision makers in each phase of the ERP project where actions in each phase are mentioned *a priori*.

SocioTechnical Perspective: SocioTechnical perspective is a synergy of social and technical subsystems of an organization.

Variance Perspective: The process of establishing conditions necessary for the success of a project.

Chapter 3
Improving Logistics Costs Through ERP Alignment

Joseph R. Muscatello
Kent State University, USA

Diane H. Parente
Penn State, Erie, USA

Matthew Swinarski
Penn State, Erie, USA

ABSTRACT

This paper examines the alignment success factors necessary to improve logistics cost when implementing an ERP system taking a work system theoretical perspective. Organizations attempting to decrease logistics costs via an ERP implementation must consider the processes and activities involved in aligning participants, information, technology, and business process in these ERP implementations. We used a two-step approach, conducting a confirmatory factor analysis (CFA) to assess the psychometric properties of our measures and then conducting an independent sample t-test between two groups, one which experienced decreased logistic costs and the second which experienced the same or increasing logistic costs. This research has provided more insight into the practice of ERP implementations and has reemphasized the need to judge ERP success relative to impact on firm performance.

INTRODUCTION

Enterprise wide software solutions address the problem of disparate information in business organizations (Muscatello & Chen, 2008; Themistocleous, Zahir, & Love, 2004). They serve as the starting point for information capture and dissemination via a variety of mathematical models that continue to grow as technology innovation grows. Enterprise Resource Planning Systems have moved into the maturity phase of their lifecycle serving as the platform of choice for most manufacturing firms. In fact, ERP has shown a level of maturity where simple issues related to implementations are known by vendors and businesses (Han, Swanner and Yan., 2010; Capaldo and Rippa, 2009; Jacobs & Weston Jr., 2007).

DOI: 10.4018/978-1-5225-2382-6.ch003

ERP implementations frequently come with new software and hardware systems and business processes that substantially alter workflow and jobs (Monk and Wagner, 2013; Boudreau & Robey, 2005; Soh & Sia, 2005). These alterations change processes, job responsibilities and often lead to major training and other organizational initiatives. These organizational changes are usually positive, however, significantly higher value is achieved if the most appropriate types of information sharing are used, while other types of information sharing rather contribute to decreased value (Jonsson and Mattsson, 2013). Enterprise resource planning (ERP) systems have been used in integrating information and accelerating its distribution across functions and departments with the aim to increase organizations' operational performance. Thus, it is worth measuring ERP system performance based on its impact to critical performance of an organization (Shen, et al, 2015).

ERP initiatives lead to organizational improvement by more consistently providing information to organizations in a standardized, centralized, and cost efficient manner (Olson, Chae, & Sheu, 2005). Successful implementation of ERP systems, including new software and business processes, report positive benefits including greater efficiency and effectiveness at the individual employee and organizational levels (Muscatello & Chen, 2008; Olson et al., 2005; Venkatesh, 2008). Evidence also suggests that a firm's profitability increases after full implementation of an ERP system Hendricks, Singhal, & Stratman, 2007). Other benefits that have been documented include: drastic declines in inventory, increasing cash flow and working capital, improved customer service information, and an increased ability to manage the extended supply chain of suppliers, alliances, and customers as an integrated system Davenport & Brooks, 2004; Goodpasture, 1995; Muscatello, Small, & Chen, 2003).

ERP implementations require significant managerial and technical challenges, huge financial investments and impactful organizational change (Amid and Kohansal, 2014; Muscatello & Chen, 2008). ERP is a challenging project that causes major change and disruption for an extended period of time in the implementing firm (Boudreau & Robey, 2005;Soh & Sia, 2005). Despite annual investments of several billion dollars in ERP systems, estimates indicate that more than half of all ERP systems fail (Han, swanner and Yang, 2010) and such failures have been observed even in highly successful organizations, such as Hershey and Nike (Koch, 2002, 2004). ERP also has the reputation of being notoriously over-sold and under-delivered (Millman, 2004). Major Operational disruptions at Hewlett Packard, Whirlpool, Fox-Meyer Drugs and Hershey Foods have been caused by poor ERP implementations (Becerra-Fernandez et al., 2004). Therefore, a firm must be diligent and prudent in their implementation of an ERP system.

Supply chain is of significant importance when implementing ERP (Amid and Kohansal, 2014; Shaul and Tauber, 2013). Successful implementations will clearly affect the supply chain of a firm. Logistics, as defined by the Council of Supply Chain Management Professionals ("CSCMP Supply Chain Management," 2013), is the process of planning, implementing, and controlling procedures for the efficient and effective transportation and storage of goods including services, and related information from the point of origin to the point of consumption for the purpose of conforming to customer requirements. Several authors have pointed out that the importance of finding a better way to move product was identified as early as 1776 when Adam Smith detailed the connections between manufacturers and markets and transportation inefficiencies in The Wealth of Nations (Grawe, 2009).

The US Department of Transportation estimates final users purchase or consume 9% or close to $1 Trillion of the goods and services in the GDP basket to serve their transportation needs (2014). An effective logistics operation can provide a competitive advantage for a firm and increase market share (Monk and Wagner, 2013; Daugherty, Autry, & Ellinger, 2001; Mentzer, Keebler, Min, Nix and Smith, 2001). There is no wonder that businesses are diligently working to reduce their logistics costs as a huge area of opportunity.

Research on logistics and technology has focused on the ability to reduce costs and provide delivery solutions according to customer need (Randall, Nowicki, Whitman and Pollen, 2014; Grawe, 2009). The literature also addresses logistics technologies (e.g. EDI, RFID) (Barratt & Oke 2007), logistics programs (e.g. vendor managed inventory, cross-docking) (Chapman, Soosay, & Kandampully, 2003), supply chain management (SCM) (Monk and Wagner, 2013; Barratt & Oke 2007; Håkansson & Persson, 2004) and other types of innovations and their roles in logistics operations and relationships (Monk and Wagner, 2013; Grawe, 2009; Wagner & Bode, 2008). Research does show that ERP implementations support some SCM activities such as sourcing and the physical distribution system (Soh & Sia, 2005), however, they also show that ERP may not meet the SCM needs including supply and demand planning functionality which are critical to effective and efficient logistics practices (Amid and Kohansal, 2014; Bovet & Martha, 2003). Other research has shown that that the biggest challenge concerning the usage of an ERP is not technological, but relates more to issues of trust, collaboration, integration, lack of agility, poor user adoption, implementation timelines, and lack of customer focus. Consequently, understanding how an ERP influences each one of them, will highlight the importance and strategic value of ERP in terms of the logistics system efficiency (Folinas and Daniel, 2012). There is little research on the effect of ERP implementations on logistics costs and many firms, especially light manufacturers and value added warehouses, whose logistics costs may be very high compared to the total product cost, view ERP as unnecessary unless they can show logistic cost reduction.

Given the proportion of logistics costs in the GDP, it is critical to understand the effect of ERP implementation on logistics costs. In this research, we use work system theory to analyze the Critical Success Factors (CRF) of an ERP implementation, against logistics costs, to determine if there is a link between successful ERP implementation and reduced logistics costs. Therefore, our research question: Is there a difference in the importance of CRF's between successful and unsuccessful ERP implementation where success is defined by logistics costs?

THEORY OF WORK SYSTEMS

A work system is defined as a "system in which human participants and/or machines perform work using information, technology, and other resources to produce products and/or services for internal or external customers." (Alter, 2003, p. 368). Though Bostrom and Heinen (2003; Bostrom & Heinen, 1977a, 1977b) are credited with introducing the concept of work systems, the theory was first formally defined by Alter (1999). It was intended as a framework to help managers identify, implement, and evaluate IT-reliant systems in organizations (Alter, 2008). The theory presents both a static view of work systems, representing the current or proposed operations of a system, and a dynamic view of work systems, representing how a system evolves over time (Alter, 2003).

The context of this research, the static view, is depicted in Figure 1, comprised of nine elements: technology, information, participants, processes and activities, products and services, customers, infrastructure, environment, and strategy. The first four elements (technology, information, participants, processes and activities) are viewed as being internal to the work system while the last three elements (infrastructure, environment, and strategy) are viewed as being external to the work system. The remaining two elements (products and services and customers) may be solely external to the work system or they may be partially internal to the work system if they interact with the processes and activities of the work system. In addition, each of nine elements can be conceptualized as a meta-element with each

Figure 1. The work system framework
Adapted from Alter, 2003

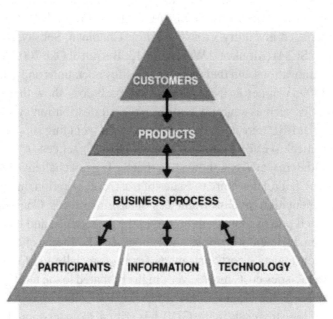

encapsulates a domain of conceptual sub-elements (Alter, 2006). For example, sub-elements under information may include income statements, purchase orders, invoices, and production schedules; while sub-elements under technology may include software, processors, and storage devices.

By its basic system nature, components of a work system must interact and must be properly aligned to achieve its business goals. The arrows within the work system framework depict the interaction and the needed alignment of paired elements and the possible causality. It is also possible to have multiple work systems, producing their own work products, all working together as component of a larger system to achieve various business goals (Alter, 2003). With respect to the Work System Framework as depicted in Figure 1, it is important to point out that connection from each internal work system elements of participants, information, and technology to the work system elements of products and service and customers is mediated by the processes and activities element. The processes and activities element also serves as the conduit for interaction between the three internal work system elements of participants, information, and technology (Alter, 2013). Therefore is it not surprising that at least one processes and activities element must be presents in the system and that these elements are central to a work system.

A key observation regarding Work System Theory, as compared to other system theories, is the emphasis on work performed and its evaluation in the context of the of business or organizational related outcomes such as revenue, efficiency, quality, and cost rather than information technology-related outcomes such as information quality, data accuracy, and system response time. In addition, the work produced is for consumption by the customer and as a result evaluation may also involve performance outcomes from the customer perspective (Alter, 2007, 2012). Viewing an information system as a work system, rather than simply as a technology, creates a theoretical perspective for establishing a direct link from the information system to business performance and customer satisfaction.

WORK SYSTEMS AND ERP

Business organizations conduct a variety of work activities such as selling products, procuring materials, manufacturing products, delivering finished products, providing services and creating financial reports. These activates often involve people, information, and technology. Therefore, these activities may be viewed as a work system with the entire business organization represented as multiple work systems networked together (Alter, 2003). In this same context of work systems, enterprise resource planning (ERP) systems have several interconnected modules with each module performing its own business activities. The modules are used by individuals to conduct work and share information and can also be considered as a set of interconnected work systems (Alter, 2013). Taking this perspective, one can make the theoretical argument that these systems have a direct relationship to business outcomes and related aggregate performance measures. However, if implementing ERP was as "simple" as configuring and installing the modules, major operational disruptions by poor ERP implementations would have never occurred at Hewlett Packard, Whirlpool, FoxMeyer Drugs and Hershey Foods (Becerra-Fernandez, Gonzalez, & Sabherwal, 2004). It has been noted in that the benefits of ERP cannot be realized without the proper alignment of the technical, personnel, informational and process aspects using principles of process orientation (Al-Mashari, Al-Mudimigh, & Zairi, 2003; Dezdar & Ainin, 2011).

CRITICAL SUCCESS FACTORS OF ERP SYSTEMS AND THEIR IMPACT ON ORGANIZATIONAL OUTCOMES

The literature has expanded with studies investigating the relationship between critical success factors (CSF) to various benefits associated with ERP systems. This expansion has led some researchers to try to delineate the numerous CSFs into more manageable sets of taxonomies, stages, factors and classifications as a means to better understand how select grouping of the factors impact ERP success (Dezdar & Sulaiman, 2009; Ehie & Madsen, 2005; Finney & Corbett, 2007; Ngai, Law, & Wat, 2008; Ram & Corkindale, 2014). More recently, there has been a focus on separating the benefits associated with ERP systems into two categories such as 'implementation outcomes' and 'organizational outcomes' (Law & Ngai, 2007; Ram & Corkindale, 2014; Ram, Corkindale, & Wu, 2013).

Given the large number of different critical success factors, it was decided to focus this research on the following: process re-engineering, personnel communication, technical support and training and education (Dezdar & Ainin, 2011; Dezdar & Sulaiman, 2009; Ngai et al., 2008; Ram & Corkindale, 2014). These CSFs were selected since they all relate to the use of alignment processes and activities among the four key internal work elements (technology, information, participants, processes and activities) associated with work systems. The organizational outcome measure of logistic cost was selected for four reasons (1) internal business measures are directly impacted by various processes and activities (including alignment), (2) internal business measures tend to be more reliable than perceived external customer measures, (3) internal cost measures tend to be more reliable than internal quality and satisfaction measures, and (4) to date there has been very little research investigating the impact of ERP systems on logistic costs. The arguments for the impact of the selected CSFs and logistic cost are provided next.

Alignment Through Technical Support

According to Rivard et al. (2004) technology increases response and helps coordinate actions, both major components to driving down logistic costs in ERP-enabled supply chains; however, such benefits are not possible in the presence of poor system design, implementation and maintenance. Firms with the right internal IT support capabilities can more effectively fit technology to processes and people (Davenport, 2000). An upgrade of current software may include new file structures, report writers, functional modules and other changes. Hardware upgrades may involve operating system changes, new functionality and new modules. But regardless of the type or level, managers must be proactive to insure that their technical employees can run the ERP system effectively (Muscatello & Chen, 2008). Not having sufficient technical capabilities can be catastrophic and lead to ERP system failure (Muscatello & Chen 2008). In our study, alignment through technical support was measured in three ways: (1) internal IT members understand custom ERP software programs, (2) the IT staff are able to efficiently implement ERP system upgrades, and (3) the IT staff are able to analyze the technical impact of proposed system changes. Based on this discussion we propose the following hypothesis:

H1: *Firms achieving lower logistics costs use technical support to properly align various elements of the ERP system.*

Alignment Through Processes Re-Engineering

Research has shown a strong correlation between process re-engineering and ERP success (Carton & Adam, 2003; Law & Ngai, 2007; Millman, 2004; Motwani, Mirchandani, Madan, & Gunasekaran, 2002; Muscatello et al., 2003; Olson et al., 2005). Reengineering of processes (as known as Business Process Redesign/reengineering or BPR) focuses the firm on identifying and improving the efficiency of critical operations, on restructuring important non-value-adding operations, and on eliminating inefficient processes (Hammer & Champy, 1993). Given that process re-engineering simplifies and improves work processes and activities {Harkness, 1996 #81}, it is likely that such improvements and simplifications in the ERP-enabled supply chain will likely decrease the costs associated with logistics. However, for process re-engineering to be most effective it involves a holistic approach to change which includes people, practice, responsibly, documents and technology. In our study, alignment through process re-engineering was measured in four ways: (1) business process redesign is performed before ERP implementation, (2) the operational processes of the ERP entity are formally documented, (3) business process redesign teams are cross functional, and (4) redesigned business processes are used to drive out inefficiency. Based on this discussion we propose the following hypothesis:

H2: *Firms achieving lower logistics costs use process re-engineering to properly align various elements of the ERP system.*

Alignment Through Personnel Communication

Managers have found ERP implementation projects to be one of the most difficult systems development projects (Kumar, Maheshwari, & Kumar, 2003). In part, this is due to the significant change that must occur in the organization. Olsen et al (2005) found that all jobs are going to change and employees need to adapt. Many people are resistant to change, so good organizational change management techniques have to be used. Additionally, it is difficult to implement any organizational change without cooperation. We might speculate the resistance is exacerbated given the magnitude of organizational change in an ERP system. The necessity of informing employees as to how the system can help them do their jobs better cannot be overstated (Olson et al., 2005). Effective communication and continuous support throughout the implementation has been noted to be beneficial by several researchers (e.g. Motwani et al., 2002; Muscatello et al., 2003; Sarkis & Sundarraj, 2003). Recent research has noted that organizational factors have a significant influence on supply chain management tool usage, of specific importance is the education level of the organization manager (Dabic, et al, 2013).

This is also supported by the Theory of Self-efficacy which, stated simply, is the employee's belief that they have the tools and capabilities to successfully accomplish their tasks. Failure to accomplish tasks correctly leads to inefficiencies, delays, and rework; all associated with increased logistic costs in ERP-enabled supply chains. In our study, alignment through personnel communication was measured in four ways: (1) employees understand how they fit into the new ERP entity, (2) management actively works to alleviate employee concerns about ERP, (3) the roles of all employees under the ERP system have been clearly communicated, and (4) an ERP support group is available to answer concerns about ERP job changes. Based on this discussion we propose the following hypothesis:

H3: *Firms achieving lower logistics costs use personnel communication to properly align various elements of the ERP system.*

Alignment Through Training and Education

ERP implementations bring radical process changes and have made providing sufficient and timely training to project personnel and users a critical requirement in ERP implementation (Davenport, 2000). Organizations must understand that when employees go through the skills assessment phase of the project, it usually uncovers employee deficiencies. Rectifying these deficiencies can be accomplished by: reassignment, outsourcing, termination and replacement, or in depth training of key employees and managers. Firms implementing ERP must provide fundamental ERP systems education if users are expected to complete tasks correctly (Plant & Willcocks, 2007; Sarkis & Sundarraj, 2003; Yusuf, Gunasekaran, & Abthorpe, 2004). Without proper training, employees take longer, produce errors, and have to redo work resulting in high logistic costs in the ERP-enabled supply chain. In our study, alignment through training and education was measured in three ways: (1) training materials have been customized for each specific job, (2) training materials target the entire business task, not just the ERP screens/reports, and (3) employees are tracked to insure they have received the appropriate ERP training. Based on this discussion we propose the following hypothesis:

H4: *Firms achieving lower logistics costs use training and education to properly align various elements of the ERP system.*

RESEARCH DESIGN

Based on a thorough review of the literature, the constructs identified by this study are well grounded in existing theory (Muscatello et al., 2003). The theoretical constructs were measured using items, anchored with a seven-point Likert scale, indicating the relative performance of each activity with respect to the ERP system (see Appendix for items).

In order to achieve a large enough sample size, a survey was conducted by mail in the United States, sampling members from the Institute for Supply Management (ISM), The National Association of Accountants (NAA), The American Productivity and Quality Center (APQC) and The Association for Operations Management (APICS).

In order to increase the response rate, a modified version of Dillman's total design method was followed (Dillman, 1978). Mailings were first class and included a cover letter, survey, and postage paid return envelope. All potential respondents were sent follow up reminder cards approximately three weeks after the initial mailing. The original mailing consisted of 973 surveys with 28 being returned unopened, making the sample 945. A total of 203 surveys were received for a response rate of 21.5%. This response rate is statistically valid and correlates well with other operations management (OM) empirical research. For example, Paulraj and Chen (2005) reported 23.2% and Krause et al (2001) reported 19.6%. The final response total was 197 after the researchers discarded six responses as unusable making the effective response rate 20.8% (197/945). The survey found that 156/197 respondents were involved in first time ERP implementations (see Table 1).

The respondent profile found that almost half the firms were end product manufacturers (49.4%) and had been in business for over 30 years (47.4%). Most of the respondents described themselves as middle managers (61.5%) followed by top executives (28.2%), and other others (10.3%). Small and large firms were well represented and fairly evenly distributed amongst respondents. The distribution is: Sales of over $20B (2.6%), $1B~$20B (25.0%), $500M~$1B (34.6%), $100M~$500M (23.1%), $10M~$100M (7.1%) and under $10M (7.7%). There were 500 or more employees at most firms (78.2%). Table 2 and Table 3 show the respondent and firm profiles.

The possibility of common methods bias is present in almost any type of survey research. Therefore, we used two statistical techniques to test for the possibility of common method bias including Harman's single-factor technique (Podsakoff & Organ, 1986) and Lindell and Whitney's (Lambert & Harrington,

Table 1. Survey distribution and results

Responses	Number
Distributed	978
Returned for incorrect address	28
Remaining	945
Received	203
Discarded	6
Total viable responses	197
Multiple ERP implementations	41
Final Sample	156

Table 2. Respondent profile

Title	Frequency	Percent
Manufacturing/Business Executives CEO,CFO,COO,CIO President, Vice-President, Director	44	28.2
Manufacturing/Business Middle Manager Purchasing Manager Operations/production Manager	96	61.5
Other Buyers, Planners Supervisors	16	10.3
Total	156	100.0

Table 3. Firm profile

Years in Operation	Frequency	Percent
Less than 5	7	4.5
6-15	29	18.6
16-30	46	29.5
30 or more	74	47.4
Total	156	100.0
Types of Products Produced	**Frequency**	**Percent**
Components	27	17.3
Sub-Assemblies	48	30.8
End Products	77	49.4
Other	4	2.6
Total	156	100.0
Annual Sales Volume	**Frequency**	**Percent**
Less than $10m	12	7.7
$10m-$100m	11	7.1
$100m-$500m	36	23.1
$500m-$1b	54	34.6
$1b-$20b	39	25.0
Greater than $20b	4	2.6
Total	156	100.0
Number of Employees	**Frequency**	**Percent**
Less Than 100	10	6.4
101-250	14	9.0
251-500	10	6.4
501- Up	122	78.2
Total	156	100.0

1990) marker variable technique. Harman's single-factor technique proposes that there is the potential for common methods bias if a factor analysis reveals that the total amount of extracted variance is substantially dominated by a single factor. A factor analysis using principal components analysis was conducted using all items in the model included in the analysis. This analysis generated seven factors having an eigenvalue higher than one with a total extracted variance of 69.4%. The first factor accounted for only 24.4% of the total extracted variance clearly indicating that there is no significant common methods variance in this data set. The Lindell and Whitney's (2001) marker variable technique requires the measurement of a "marker" variable that is theoretically unrelated to one or more variables in the research model. This technique proposes that statistically significant correlations between the marker variable and one or more variables in the model signal possible common methods variance (Malhotra & Kim, 2006). We used two markers; see Appendix for items. The test revealed only two significant correlations at the p=0.05 level. Marker item 1 had a significant (r=-0.149) correlation with the training item TR2 (training materials target the entire business task, not just the ERP screens/reports) and marker item 2 had a significant (r=-0.145) correlation with training item IT3 (The IT staff are able to analyze the technical impact of proposed system changes). Given only two significant correlations, out of 48, further confirms that there is not a substantial amount of common methods variance present in the current study.

METHODOLOGY

We used a two-step approach which involved first conducting a confirmatory factor analysis (CFA) to assess the psychometric properties of our measures and, second, conducting a sample t-test between two groups, one which experienced decreased logistic costs and the second which experienced the same or increasing logistic costs. The details regarding this two-step approach is provided next.

The CFA was conducted following Jayaram (1997) two-step approach of (1) testing each latent construct model in isolation, and (2) testing the models as a collection of correlated constructs. However, before proceeding to the CFA tests we first verified three important CFA assumptions: (1) ample sample size, (2) normality of each measure, and (3) identification of each model (J. Hair, W. Black, B. Babin, R. Anderson, & R. Tatham, 2006; Kline, 1998). Adequacy of sample size can be determined either in terms of (1) total sample size, or (2) number of cases per variable; Anderson and Gerbing (1988) suggested a minimum sample size of 150; while Bentler and Chou (1987) suggest a minimum of five cases per variable. Our sample size of 156 is above the minimum level of both established criteria. Examining the moments around and the means, and running tests on the kurtosis and skewness of the measures to check the normality of each measure revealed that some measures were negatively skewed. As a corrective approach and to keep all measure on the same relative scale we performed a log transfer of each measure (1- Log10 (7-Xr +1)). After the transformation all measures passed the normality condition. Finally, checking each model to ensure each was identified, in other words having a positive number of degrees of freedom, only two models were identified models: Process Re-engineering (PR) and Personnel Communication (PC). To create the identified models, paired construct models were constructed which involved combining Technical Support (TS) and Training and Education (TE) into one model; this resulted in three identified models for latent construct testing. The full correlated construct model was also identified.

The results for the three latent construct models are presented in Table 3. Analysis of the individual structural mechanisms measurement model indicated that all parameter estimates have the correct sign and are above the recommend 0.50 factor loadings value limit (Byrne, 1998). Assessment of the unidimensionality of each constructs was done using various fit indices; these fit indices include the Goodness of Fit Index (GFI.), Adjusted Goodness of Fit Index (AGFI.), Normed Fit Index (NFI), Relative Fit Index (RFI), Incremental Fit Index (IFI), Tucker Lewis Index (TLI), and Comparative Index (CFI) in addition to the Root Mean Square Error of Approximation (RMSEA). The analysis revealed all three latent construct models had model fit indices at or above the recommended values (J. Hair et al., 2006; Kline, 1998). The RMSEA values for all the four models was also at or below the recommended cutoff of 0.05 with p-values higher than 0.05, providing further evidence of good model fit.

To assess the discriminant validity of the constructs a full model was create containing the correlated collection of all constructs. The results of the full model are presented in Table 4 and reveal all parameter estimates, fit indices and the RMSEA with acceptable levels (Anderson & Gerbing, 1988; J. F. Hair, W. C. Black, B. J. Babin, R. E. Anderson, & R. L. Tatham, 2006). Overall, these results provide strong evidence of psychometric properties of our scales.

RESULTS

Having established the validity of the measurement models, we conducted a t-test comparing the ERP group that experienced a decrease in logistic costs and the ERP group which experienced no change or an increase in logistic costs across all six dimensions. Table 5 shows the results of the four comparisons revealing three significant differences and one weak significant difference.

Hypothesis 1 refers to the anticipated cause of technical support on logistic costs; with the results revealing that aligning various elements of the ERP system by technical support is associated with lower logistics costs. The results with respect to Hypothesis 2 reveal that properly aligning various elements of the ERP system through the use of re-engineered processes results lower logistics costs for the organization. Hypothesis 3 which examines the importance of personnel communication to employees with respect to role and job changes due to the ERP system was only weakly supported in helping the organization achieve improvements in logistic costs. Finally Hypothesis 4, which argues that the need to align ERP elements through training and education programs for employees will result in an increased likelihood of ERP success in terms of lower logistic costs, was also supported.

Table 4. Latent construct model test results

Measurement Model	Range of Std. Factor Loadings	GFI ≥0.90	AGFI ≥0.80	NFI ≥0.90	RFI ≈1.00	IFI ≈1.00	TLI ≥0.90	CFI ≥0.90	RMSEA	χ2, d.f., p-value
PR	0.78 - 0.64	0.99	0.96	0.97	0.96	1.00	0.99	1.00	0.044	2.60, 2, 0.272
PC	0.77 - 0.59	0.99	0.97	0.99	0.96	1.00	100	1.00	0.023	2.17, 2, 0.339
TS & TE	0.92 - 0.59	0.97	0.94	0.94	0.91	0.99	0.98	0.98	0.050	18.47, 14, 0.186
Full Model	0.86 - 0.57	0.90	0.86	0.94	0.91	0.97	0.97	1.00	0.033	181.37, 155, 0.072

Goodness of Fit Index (GFI.); Adjusted Goodness of Fit Index (AGFI.); Normed Fit Index (NFI); Relative Fit Index (RFI); Incremental Fit Index (IFI); Tucker Lewis Index (TLI); Comparative Index (CFI); Root Mean Square Error of Approximation (RMSEA).

Table 5. t-test results for ERP processes

Hypothesis	Constructs	Logistic Cost Improvement	Logistic Cost Same or Worse	
		N=100	N=56	t-values
H1	Technical Support	0.6756	0.5680	3.812***
H2	Process Re-engineering	0.6991	0.6057	3.437***
H3	Personnel Communication	0.6873	0.6388	1.966^
H4	Training & Education	0.6742	0.5936	2.826**

^ p > 0.100, * p > 0.050, ** p > 0.010, *** p > 0.001

DISCUSSION AND CONCLUSION

It is important to recognize that the success of the ERP implementation should ultimately be measured by its impact on firm performance. This article seeks to both theoretically and empirically provide such a linkage by examining four critical success factors (CSF) alignment associated with reduced logistics costs. Our result revealed three factors, process re-engineering, technical support and training and education are significant; while personnel communication was only weakly significant and project management was non-significant.

The significant results tell a clear story about the organizations that are successful in achieving lower logistic costs; these organizations consider technical complexity, business process change, and education as critical to ERP-enabled supply chain success as the results clearly show the importance of high technical support, training and education, and the need to incorporate process redesign and reengineering.

There was also a relatively weak support for the impact of personnel communication; however, this construct centers around providing support for changes in employee's role solely with respect to the ERP technology; we might see a stronger effect by examining additional the support this might have been given to employees about their overall role and responsibilities in the organization.

In summary, the results show that the ERP system is not simply a technology but rather a strategic and organizational system that engages in work to achieve benefits for the organization. This is in stark contrast to early ERP studies that believed the software would automatically drive organizational benefits such as lower logistic costs. The reality is that ERP systems require key alignment processes and activities to realize the gains promised.

Interestingly, organizations strongly believe that supplementing their internal staff with outside consultants is a must. This is likely a result of analyzing the catastrophic failures documented by firms who fail to understand the limitations of the current employees and management processes. Organizations should realize that ERP systems are more than basic software implementations and more about aligning key organization elements. This research has provided more insight into the impact of ERP systems on firm performance.

LIMITATIONS AND FUTURE RESEARCH

While there were a priori expectations for significance in Personnel Communication, the items used were of a technology-specific nature and did not capture a broader view. In future research, the survey items for Personnel Communication should be expanded to reflect alignment of information, processes and other participants. The research could also break down individual characteristics of Logistics and how they are impacted by ERP.

ACKNOWLEDGMENT

The authors would like to thank the reviewers and editors for their efforts.

REFERENCES

Al-Mashari, M., Al-Mudimigh, A., & Zairi, M. (2003). Enterprise resource planning: A taxonomy of critical factors. *European Journal of Operational Research*, *146*(2), 352–364. doi:10.1016/S0377-2217(02)00554-4

Alter, S. (1999). A general, yet useful theory of information systems. *Communications of the Association for Information Systems*, *1*(13), 1–70.

Alter, S. (2003). 18 reasons why IT-reliant work systems should replace the IT artifact as the core subject matter of the IS field. *Communications of the Association for Information Systems*, *12*(23), 365–394.

Alter, S. (2006). Work systems and IT artifacts - does the definition matter? *Communications of the Association for Information Systems*, *17*(1), 14.

Alter, S. (2007). Could the work system method embrace systems concepts more fully? *Information Resources Management Journal*, *20*(2), 33–43. doi:10.4018/irmj.2007040103

Alter, S. (2008). Defining information systems as work systems: Implications for the IS field. *European Journal of Information Systems*, *17*(5), 448–469. doi:10.1057/ejis.2008.37

Alter, S. (2012). *The work system method: Systems thinking for business professionals*. Paper presented at the IIE Annual Conference.

Alter, S. (2013). Work system theory: Overview of core concepts, extensions, and challenges for the future. *Journal of the Association for Information Systems*, *14*(2), 72–121.

Amid, A., & Kohansal, A. (2014). Organizational Levels Model for Measuring the Effectiveness of Enterprise Resource Planning System (Case Study TUGA Company, Iran). *Universal Journal of Industrial and Business Management*, *2*, 25–30.

Anderson, J. C., & Gerbing, D. W. (1988). Structural equation modeling in practice: A review and recommended two-step approach. *Psychological Bulletin, 103*(3), 411–423. doi:10.1037/0033-2909.103.3.411

Barratt, M., & Oke, A. (2007). Antecedents of supply chain visibility in retail supply chains: A resource-based theory perspective. *Journal of Operations Management, 25*(6), 1217–1233. doi:10.1016/j.jom.2007.01.003

Becerra-Fernandez, I., Gonzalez, A., & Sabherwal, R. (2004). *Knowledge management: Challenges, solutions, and technologies* (1st ed.). Upper Saddle River, NJ: Prentice Hall.

Bentler, P. M., & Chou, C.-P. (1987). Practical issues in structural modeling. *Sociological Methods & Research, 16*(1), 78–117. doi:10.1177/0049124187016001004

Bostrom, R. P., & Heinen, J. S. (1977a). MIS problems and failures: A socio-technical perspective. Part I: The causes. *Management Information Systems Quarterly, 1*(3), 17–32. doi:10.2307/248710

Bostrom, R. P., & Heinen, J. S. (1977b). MIS Problems and failures: A socio-technical perspective. Part II: The application of socio-technical theory. *MIS Quarterly, 1*(4), 11-28.

Boudreau, M.-C., & Robey, D. (2005). Enacting integrated information technology: A human agency perspective. *Organization Science, 16*(1), 3–18. doi:10.1287/orsc.1040.0103

Bovet, D., & Martha, J. (2003). *Supply chain hidden profits.* Mercer Management Consulting.

Byrne, B. M. (1998). *Structural equation modeling with LISREL, PRELIS, and SIMPLIS: Basic concepts, applications, and programming.* Mahwah, NJ: Lawrence Erlbaum Associates, Inc.

Capaldo, G., Rippa, P., 2009. A planned-oriented approach for EPR implementation strategy selection. *Journal of Enterprise information Management, 22,* 642 – 659.

Carton, F., & Adam, F. (2003). Analysing the impact of ERP systems roll-outs in multi-national companies. *Electronic Journal of Information Systems Evaluation, 6*(2), 21–32.

Chapman, R. L., Soosay, C., & Kandampully, J. (2003). Innovation in logistic services and the new business model: A conceptual framework. *International Journal of Physical Distribution & Logistics Management, 33*(7), 630–650. doi:10.1108/09600030310499295

Cliffe, S. (1999). ERP Implementation. *Harvard Business Review,* 16–17.

Dabic, M., Potocan, V., Nedelko, Z., & Morgan, T. R. (2013). Exploring the use of 25 leading business practices in transitioning market supply chains. *International Journal of Physical Distribution & Logistics Management, 43*(10), 833–851. doi:10.1108/IJPDLM-10-2012-0325

Daugherty, P. J., Autry, C. W., & Ellinger, A. E. (2001). The impact of resource commitment on reverse logistics. *Journal of Business Logistics, 22*(1), 107–124. doi:10.1002/j.2158-1592.2001.tb00162.x

Davenport, T. H. (2000). *Mission critical: Realizing the promise of enterprise systems.* Harvard Business School Publishing.

Davenport, T. H., & Brooks, J. D. (2004). Enterprise systems and the supply chain *Journal of Enterprise information Management, 17*(1), 8-19.

Dezdar, S., & Ainin, S. (2011). The influence of organizational factors on successful ERP implementation. *Management Decision, 49*(6), 911–926. doi:10.1108/00251741111143603

Dezdar, S., & Sulaiman, A. (2009). Successful enterprise resource planning implementation: Taxonomy of critical factors. *Industrial Management + Data Systems, 109*(8), 1037-1052.

Dillman, D. (1978). *Mail and telephone surveys: The total design method.* New York: John Wiley & Sons, Inc.

Ehie, I. C., & Madsen, M. (2005). Identifying critical issues in enterprise resource planning (ERP) implementation. *Computers in Industry, 56*(6), 545–557. doi:10.1016/j.compind.2005.02.006

Finney, S., & Corbett, M. (2007). ERP implementation: A compilation and analysis of critical success factors. *Business Process Management Journal, 13*(3), 329–347. doi:10.1108/14637150710752272

Flint, D. J., Larsson, E., Gammelgaard, B., & Mentzer, J. T. (2005). Logistics innovation: A customer value-oriented social process. *Journal of Business Logistics, 26*(1), 113–147. doi:10.1002/j.2158-1592.2005. tb00196.x

Folinas, D., & Daniel, E. (2012). Estimating the Impact of ERP Systems on Logistics System. *Enterprise Information Systems, 8*(3), 1–14. doi:10.4018/jeis.2012070101

Goodpasture, V. (1995). Easton steps up to the plate. *Manufacturing Systems, 13*(9), 58–64.

Grawe, S. J. (2009). Logistics Innovation: A literature-based conceptual framework. *The International Journal of Logistics Management, 20*(3), 360–377. doi:10.1108/09574090911002823

Hair, J., Black, W., Babin, B., Anderson, R., & Tatham, R. (2006). *Multivariate Data Analysis* (6th ed.). Upper Saddle River, NJ: Pearson Prentice Hall.

Hair, J. F., Black, W. C., Babin, B. J., Anderson, R. E., & Tatham, R. L. (2006). *Multivariate Data Anaalysis.* Upper Saddle River, NJ: Prentice Hall.

Håkansson, H., & Persson, G. (2004). Supply chain management and the logic of supply chains and nctworks. *The International Journal of Logistics Managmcnt, 15*(1), 15 26.

Hammer, M., & Champy, J. (1993). *Reengineering the corporation.* New York: Harper Business.

Han, J., Liu, R., Swanner, B., & Yang, S. (2010). *Enterprise resource planning.* Japansk produksjons-filosofi, Toyota Production.

Hendricks, K. B., Singhal, V. R., & Stratman, J. K. (2007). The impact of enterprise systems on corporate performance: A study of ERP, SCM, and CRM system implementations. *Journal of Operations Management, 25*(1), 65–82. doi:10.1016/j.jom.2006.02.002

Hill, S. (1997). The wait is over. *Manufacturing Systems, 15*(6), 11–X.

Jacobs, R. F., & Weston, F. C. Jr. (2007). Enterprise resource planning (ERP)—A brief history. *Journal of Operations Management, 25*(2), 357–363. doi:10.1016/j.jom.2006.11.005

Jonsson, P., & Mattsson, S. (2013). The value of sharing planning information in supply chains. *International Journal of Physical Distribution & Logistics Management, 43*(4), 282–299. doi:10.1108/IJPDLM-07-2012-0204

Kline, R. B. (1998). *Principles and Practice of Structural Equation Modeling*. New York: The Guilford Press.

Koch, C. (2002, November 15). Hershey's Bittersweet Lesson. *CIO Magazine*.

Koch, C. (2004, July 15). Nike rebounds: How (and Why) Nike recovered from its supply chain disaster. *CIO Magazine*.

Krause, D. R., Pagell, M., & Curkovic, S. (2001). Toward a measure of competitive priorities for purchasing. *Journal of Operations Management, 19*(4), 497–512. doi:10.1016/S0272-6963(01)00047-X

Kumar, V., Maheshwari, B., & Kumar, U. (2003). An investigation of critical management issues in ERP implementation: Empirical evidence from Canadian organizations. *Technovation, 23*(10), 793–807. doi:10.1016/S0166-4972(02)00015-9

Lambert, D. M., & Harrington, T. C. (1990). Measuring nonresponse bias in customer service mail surveys. *Journal of Business Logistics, 11*(2), 5–25.

Law, C. C. H., & Ngai, E. W. T. (2007). ERP systems adoption: An exploratory study of the organizational factors and impacts of ERP success. *Information & Management, 44*(4), 418–432. doi:10.1016/j.im.2007.03.004

Lindell, M. K., & Whitney, D. J. (2001). Accounting for common method variance in cross sectional research designs. *The Journal of Applied Psychology, 86*(1), 114–121. doi:10.1037/0021-9010.86.1.114 PMID:11302223

Malhotra, N. K., Kim, S. S., & Patil, A. (2006). Common method variance in IS research: A comparison of alternative approaches and a reanalysis of past research. *Management Science, 52*(12), 1865–1883. doi:10.1287/mnsc.1060.0597

Mentzer, J. T., Keebler, J. S., Min, S., Nix, N. W., Smith, C. D., & Zacharia, Z. G. (2001). Defining supply chain management. *Journal of Business Logistics, 22*(2), 1–25. doi:10.1002/j.2158-1592.2001.tb00001.x

Millman, G. J. (2004, May). What did you get from ERP and what can you get? *Financial Executive*, 38-42.

Monk, E. F., & Wagner, B. J. (2013). *Concepts in Enterprise Resource Planning*. Cengage Learning.

Motwani, J., Mirchandani, D., Madan, M., & Gunasekaran, A. (2002). Successful implementation of ERP projects: Evidence from two case studies. *International Journal of Production Economics, 75*(1-2), 83–96. doi:10.1016/S0925-5273(01)00183-9

Muscatello, J. R., & Chen, I. (2008). Enterprise resource planning (ERP) implementations: Theory and practice. *International Journal of Enterprise Information Systems, 4*(1), 63–78. doi:10.4018/jeis.2008010105

Muscatello, J. R., Small, M. H., & Chen, I. J. (2003). Implementing enterprise resource planning (ERP) systems in small and midsize manufacturing firms. *International Journal of Operations & Production Management, 23*(8), 850–871. doi:10.1108/01443570310486329

Ngai, E. W. T., Law, C. C. H., & Wat, F. (2008). Examining the critical success factors in the adoption of enterprise resource planning. *Computers in Industry, 59*(6), 548–564. doi:10.1016/j.compind.2007.12.001

Olson, D. L., Chae, B., & Sheu, C. (2005). Issues in multinational ERP Implementations. *International Journal of Services and Operations Management, 1*(1), 7–21. doi:10.1504/IJSOM.2005.006314

Paulraj, A., & Chen, I. J. (2005). Strategic supply management: Theory and practice. *International Journal of Integrated Supply Management, 1*(4), 457–477. doi:10.1504/IJISM.2005.006306

Plant, R., & Willcocks, L. (2007). Critical success factors in international ERP implementations: A case research approach. *Journal of Computer Information Systems, 47*, 60–71.

Podsakoff, P. M., & Organ, D. W. (1986). Self-reports in organizational research: Problems and prospects. *Journal of Management, 12*(4), 531–544. doi:10.1177/014920638601200408

Ram, J., & Corkindale, D. (2014). How critical are the critical success factors (CSFs)? *Business Process Management Journal, 20*(1), 151–174. doi:10.1108/BPMJ-11-2012-0127

Ram, J., Corkindale, D., & Wu, M.-L. (2013). Implementation critical success factors (CSFs) for ERP: Do they contribute to implementation success and post-implementation performance? *International Journal of Production Economics, 144*(1), 157–174. doi:10.1016/j.ijpe.2013.01.032

Randall, W. S., Wittmann, C. M., Nowicki, D. R., & Pohlen, T. L. (2014). Service-dominant logic and supply chain management: Are we there yet? *International Journal of Physical Distribution & Logistics Management, 44*(1/2), 113–131. doi:10.1108/IJPDLM-11-2012-0331

Rivard, S. (Ed.). (2004). *Information Technology and Organizational Transformation: Solving the Management Puzzle.* Oxford, UK: Elsevier Butterworth-Heinemann.

Sarkis, J., & Sundarraj, R. P. (2003). Managing largescale global enterprise resource planning systems: A case study at Texas Instruments. *International Journal of Information Management, 23*(6), 431–442. doi:10.1016/S0268-4012(03)00070-7

Segars, A. H. (1997). Assessing the unidimensionality of measurement: A paradigm and illustration within the context of information systems research. *Omega, 25*(1), 107–121. doi:10.1016/S0305-0483(96)00051-5

Shaul, L., & Tauber, D. (2013). Critical success factors in enterprise resource planning systems: Review of the last decade. *ACM Computing Surveys, 45*(4), 4. doi:10.1145/2501654.2501669

Shen, Y., Chen, P., & Wang, P. (2015). A study of enterprise resource planning (ERP) system performance measurement using the quantitative balanced scorecard approach. *Computers in Industry, 75*, 127–139. doi:10.1016/j.compind.2015.05.006

Soh, C., & Sia, S. K. (2005). The challenges of implementing "vanilla" versions of enterprise systems. *MIS Quarterly Executive, 4*(3), 373–384.

Supply Chain Management, C. S. C. M. P. (2013). Retrieved Jan 10, 2013, from http://cscmp.org/about-us/supply-chain-management-definitions

Themistocleous, M., Zahir, I., & Love, P. (2004). Evaluating the integration of supply chain information systems: A case study. *European Journal of Operational Research*, *159*(2), 393–405. doi:10.1016/j.ejor.2003.08.023

Transportation Statistics Annual Report. (2014). Bureau of Transportation Statistics.

Venkatesh, V. (2008). One-Size-Does-Not-Fit-All: Teaching MBA students different ERP implementation strategies. *Journal of Information Systems Education*, *19*(2), 141–146.

Wagner, S. M., & Bode, C. (2008). An empirical examination of supply chain performance along several dimensions of risk. *Journal of Business Logistics*, *29*(1), 307–325. doi:10.1002/j.2158-1592.2008.tb00081.x

Yusuf, Y., Gunasekaran, A., & Abthorpe, M. S. (2004). Enterprise information systems project implementation: A case study of ERP in Rolls-Royce. *International Journal of Production Economics*, *87*(3), 251–266. doi:10.1016/j.ijpe.2003.10.004

KEY TERMS AND DEFINITIONS

Alignment: The proper position or adjustment in relation to others.

Critical Success Factors: Outcomes from a project or process change that are paramount to the success of the project or process change.

Enterprise Resource Planning (ERP): A business software system that integrates core business processes.

Logistics: The coordination of moving and storage processes in a supply chain.

Manufacturing: The production of tangible goods using labor and machines.

Reengineering: Identifying and improving the efficiency of critical operations, on restructuring important non-value-adding operations, and on eliminating inefficient processes.

Technology: The creation and application of knowledge to create helpful tools.

Work Systems: System in which human participants and/or machines perform work using information, technology, and other resources to produce products and/or services for internal or external customers.

APPENDIX: MEASUREMENT ITEMS AND ASSOCIATED CONSTRUCT

Table 6.

Alignment Through Process Re-engineering (PR)	Mean	Std. Dev.
BP1. Business process redesign is performed before ERP implementation	5.48	1.302
BP2. The operational processes of the ERP entity are formally documented	5.42	1.349
BP3. Business process redesign teams are cross functional	5.57	1.197
BP4. Redesigned business processes are used to drive out inefficiency	5.70	1.104

Table 7.

Alignment Through Personnel Communication (EC)	Mean	Std. Dev.
PS1. Employees understand how they fit into the new ERP entity	5.70	1.115
PS2. Management actively works to alleviate employee concerns about ERP	5.63	1.159
PS3. The roles of all employees under the ERP system have been clearly communicated	5.56	1.182
PS4. An ERP support group is available to answer concerns about ERP job changes	5.51	1.087

Table 8.

Alignment Through Technical Support (TS)	Mean	Std. Dev.
IT1. Internal IT members understand custom ERP software programs	5.47	1.074
IT2. The IT staff are able to efficiently implement ERP system upgrades	5.33	1.209
IT3. The IT staff are able to analyze the technical impact of proposed system changes	5.44	1.235

Table 9.

Alignment Through Training and Education (TE)	Mean	Std. Dev.
TR1. Training materials have been customized for each specific job	5.44	1.148
TR2. Training materials target the entire business task, not just the ERP screens/reports	5.43	1.296
TR3. Employees are tracked to insure they have received the appropriate ERP training	5.47	1.172

Table 10.

Marker Items (MI)	Mean	Std. Dev.
MI1. Ineffective employees are moved or replaced if they are not able to adapt	4.53	1.402
MI2. Ineffective managers are moved or replaced if they are not able to adapt	4.77	1.445

Chapter 4
Approaches for Automating ERP Category Configuration for SMEs

Klaus Wölfel
Nexedi GmbH, Germany

ABSTRACT

Disruptive business models, such as software as a service and open source software, have made Enterprise Resource Planning (ERP) packages and related software more accessible for Small and Medium Enterprises (SMEs). However, the consulting required to configure an ERP to meet the specific needs of an organization remains a major financial burden for SMEs. One configuration task which is common to many ERPs is category configuration. With the help of automated category configuration support, managers of small businesses can perform category configuration on their own and reduce part of the consulting cost. This chapter presents the design of generic automation approaches for ERP category configuration, their implementation and their application to the open source ERP package ERP5. The approaches are based on similarity of example data, automatic vocabulary consolidation through Wikipedia redirects and (meta-) templates. The empirical evaluation through a laboratory experiment with one hundred test persons and a survey supports the validity, effectiveness and utility of the designed artefact.

INTRODUCTION

ERP packages and related systems are said to enable organisations to manage their resources efficiently and effectively by providing a total and integrated solution for their information processing needs (Nah, Lau, & Kuang, 2001). Due to technical and economical restrictions, ERP systems traditionally have been focused on larger organisations. In recent years, however, a turn of the market towards SMEs can be observed (Deep, Guttridge, Dani, & Burns, 2008). Adam and O'Doherty (2000) show that SMEs are as likely to be interested in ERP as multinational organisations. ERP packages are being viewed as a key factor for gaining competitive advantage in the SME sector, and empirical findings confirm these expectations (Koh & Simpson, 2007).

DOI: 10.4018/978-1-5225-2382-6.ch004

However, Morabito, Pace, and Previtali (2005) identify a lack of human and financial resources, as well as lock-in risks, as major problems that SMEs face when adopting ERP technology. They often do not have dedicated teams for implementation and software maintenance and cannot spend as much money on Information Technology (IT) as large enterprises, which in turn makes them more vulnerable to the risk of lock-ins in ERP packages and vendors when requirements change after implementation.

Business models in which SMEs access ERP functionalities through the Internet could alleviate the SME-specific problems and broaden the ERP market (Adam & O'Doherty, 2000). Since a some years, Software as a Service (SaaS) has been associated with this kind of business model (Hofmann, 2008). By providing applications directly through the Internet, SaaS eliminates installation and update tasks, thus saving clients from maintenance work and reducing IT expenses by on-demand pricing (Wang et al. 2008). Another "disruptive business model" mentioned by Hofmann (2008) is that of open source companies. Open source systems are considered a viable alternative for SMEs as they tackle their specific problems. They not only help to save license costs, but they also prevent lock-in. As their source code is free to everyone, they lower the barrier for third parties to perform modifications (Campos, Carvalho, & Rodrigues, 2007).

Despite these promising perspectives, consulting efforts remain a financial burden for an ERP implementation project (Janssens, Kusters, & Heemstra, 2007). Although ERP systems are cheaper and easier to implement for SMEs than for large enterprises (Morabito et al., 2005), SMEs may face challenges in affording major consulting support (Kinni, 1995; Snider, Da Silveira, & Balakrishnan, 2009). Open source ERP packages help to save license costs, but implementation costs often far exceed the costs for ERP package licenses. Thus, the greatest savings can be achieved during implementation (Timbrell & Gable, 2002).

To make implementation less complex and less costly, ERP vendors try to reduce the amount of knowledge required for implementation by various degrees: cutting down functionality, designing package templates or giving customers and system integrators a common implementation methodology (Timbrell & Gable, 2002). Functionality cut-down and package templates are static approaches and therefore only suit a defined group of companies sharing common business needs. A common implementation methodology does not permit the CEO of a small business to configure his ERP all on his own. This paper therefore proposes automated implementation support as an alternative or complementary approach to ERP package tailoring for small businesses. Off-the-shelf ERP packages are implemented mainly by configuration (Brehm, Heinzl, & Markus, 2001). An automated configuration support system can enable SMEs to perform parts of this configuration process on their own. Consulting costs can be saved or rather applied in a more tightly focussed fashion. Reducing the cost of ERP configuration would lessen the burden of the implementation process and make ERP more accessible for SMEs. Koch & Mitteregger (2014) find in an empirical study with data from an ERP provider that with increasing customization, the support effort also increases. If part of this customization is done by an SME on its own, later support costs could be saved because the SME better understands the customizations. ERP configuration demands extensive knowledge about the organisation, its structure and its requirements (Negi & Bansal, 2013). This knowledge is rather possessed by the own management of the organisation then by external consultants. Zach, Munkvold, & Olsen (2014) show that the owner-manager significantly influences ERP implementation in SMEs. Therefore this investigation follows the vision that a packaged ERP system could be configured by the management of an SME on its own thanks to an automated configuration support system based on a questionnaire.

One example of such a system is "ERP5 Configurator" which uses various wizards to automate the configuration of the open source ERP system ERP5. However, current technology does not support the configuration of categories, an important concept in ERP5 which is also common in other ERP packages. A review of existing approaches to automating ERP package configuration showed that none of them supports category configuration. To close this gap, this investigation follows a design-science research approach to generate and evaluate a new automated solution to suggest categories based on similarity of example data, templates and meta templates. Initially, a standardised questionnaire gathers the information which is typically asked by a consultant to the company management during an ERP implementation. Based on this information, the Category Configuration Support (CCS) system suggests possibly suitable configuration values for each kind of category which the user selects and extends.

The CCS system, together with the existing ERP5 Configurator technology, enables the management of an SME to create a basic ERP5 configuration on its own. In a SaaS-based setup, this basic configuration can later be refined by human consultants on demand over the Internet. The knowledge necessary to perform further tailoring with higher impact on the ERP system can be taught in a standardised consulting process based on mass customization (Wölfel, 2012).

The following sections begin with a classification of the different types of ERP package tailoring and the first definition of category configuration, a tailoring option which is particularly suited for automation. The requirements for an automated solution to the general problem of ERP category configuration are defined based on a review of prior approaches for automating ERP configuration. Next, the design-science methodology used is described. The following section presents the CCS system and its application to ERP5. The findings of the empirical evaluation of validity, effectiveness and utility of the created artefact are described before the paper concludes with discussing implications for theory and practice, limitations and future research.

BACKGROUND

The following section presents relevant knowledge to the problem at hand and a review of prior artefacts that have been created to solve similar problems (Gregor & Hevner, 2013). We introduce a classification of ERP package tailoring to identify the tailoring type most suitable for automation. Prior approaches for automating ERP configuration are reviewed to identify the gap in research which this investigation aims to fill.

ERP Package Tailoring

Adopting an ERP package requires its adaptation to the specific business needs of an organisation. ERP systems are often viewed as *off-the-shelf* software, which means that they are usually implemented by setting parameters in the package to adapt their functionality to business requirements. This form of implementation, called *configuration*, is usually distinguished from *modification,* which refers to changing the source code of a package. Modification is considered typical for *custom-built* software (Brehm et al., 2001).

Brehm, Heinzl, and Markus (2001) argue that ERP systems do not fit into this traditional distinction. They use the term *tailoring* to refer to both configuration and modification, as well as many options in between. They suggest a typology of nine different ERP tailoring types (Table 1). The order in which

Table 1. Typology of ERP tailoring types adapted from Brehm et al. (2001)

Tailoring Type	Description
Configuration	Setting of parameters to choose between different executions of processes and functions
Bolt-ons	Implementation of third-party package designed to work with ERP system and provide industry-specific functionality
Screen masks	Creating new screen masks for data in- and output
Extended reporting	Programming of extended data output and reporting options
Workflow programming	Creating of non-standard workflows
User exits	Programming of additional software code in an open interface
ERP programming	Programming of additional applications, without changing the source code (in a vendor's computer language)
Interface development	Programming of interfaces to legacy systems or third- party products
Package code modification	Changing the source-codes ranging from small changes to change whole modules

the tailoring types are presented in the table is roughly derived from the "impact" they have on the ERP system as well as on the ERP adopter, beginning with "lighter" tailoring types at the top of the table to "heavier" tailoring types at the bottom. For the ERP system, impact means how severely it is being changed if a tailoring option is applied. For the ERP adopter, impact means how much effect is required to employ a tailoring type. The lightest tailoring type is configuration, the heaviest type is package code modification. The value of benefits generated through custom development for packaged ERP systems continues to be debated (Balint, 2015). It can increase the fit between the business processes of the organisation and the ERP (Van Velsen, Huijs, & Van der Geest, 2008) as well as user acceptance (Pries-Heje, 2008;), but it can also increase the cost of maintenance and can decrease system performance if done poorly (Ng, 2013).

In previous work, we have discussed the nine tailoring types regarding their suitability for automation. We deduce the hypothesis that "the lower the impact of tailoring on the ERP system, the more likely it is that the tailoring is suitable for automation." Thus, *configuration*, the tailoring type with the lightest impact, is most suitable for automation (Wölfel & Smets, 2012).

Category Configuration

To make a contribution to generalized knowledge (Gregor & Hevner, 2013), an artefact for automated ERP configuration should focus on a configuration option which is common to many ERP packages. Category configuration fulfils this requirement particularly well. Categories are taxonomies used to classify business objects and to build hierarchies. Examples of similar category usage across different ERP packages can be found by comparing category definitions in ERP5 (Wölfel & Smets, 2012), OpenERP (OpenERP SA, 2014) and SAP CRM (SAP AG, 2014). Categories can be considered part of the reference data of an ERP package. Reference data defines collections of agreed-upon values which are used throughout the IT systems of an organisation. It defines common values which are referenced in business objects, represented by master data and business transactions, represented by transaction data (Dreibelbis et al., 2008).

Category configuration consists in the definition of taxonomies to model the structure of a company and the company's view of the world in an ERP system. In OpenERP, categories are configured directly using the user interface of the ERP (OpenERP SA 2014). In ERP5, categories can be alternatively defined using a spreadsheet which is later imported into the ERP (Wölfel & Smets, 2012). Category configuration is usually first done early in the ERP implementation and then refined later. The automation approach discussed in this paper is designed to support the initial category configuration in an early stage of the implementation process.

We will illustrate category configuration with the example of the category "function." This category is used in ERP5 to describe the functional structure of the adopting company and of the organisations with which it is doing business. Organisational functions are defined as nodes in the function tree, for example "factory," "warehouse," or "factory / warehouse." Functions of persons are represented by leaves, for example "factory / manager" or "shop / agent". Appendix II shows an excerpt of the category configuration for a small software company.

The degree of semantic strictness in which categories are defined varies from one ERP package to another. For classifying business partners, OpenERP uses one single category (OpenERP SA, 2014). It mixes different semantics, which in ERP5 are strictly separated into two different categories, "role" and "activity" (Nexedi SA, 2014). Similarly, SAP CRM's category "territory" (SAP AG, 2014) can mix semantics, which in ERP5 are separated into "group," "product line" and "region" (Nexedi SA, 2014). A category configuration using strict semantics can be automatically translated into a configuration using "relaxed" semantics, but not vice versa. To be generally useful, an approach for automating category configuration must thus be based on a category definition which is semantically as strict as possible. Therefore, the artefact created in this study is based on ERP5's categories which have been found to have stricter semantics than other ERP packages.

Prior Approaches for Automating ERP Configuration

To identify the need for a new solution to a problem, the applicability of prior approaches must be evaluated first. Few publications describe approaches for automating ERP configuration. This is because publishing an automation procedure requires explication of proprietary knowledge of ERP configuration, a role traditionally possessed by consultants. The relative rarity of ERP knowledge is the basis of the economic rent they gain from this knowledge. Consultants prefer to transfer this knowledge directly to clients instead of publishing it in a general form which could cannibalise future services to ERP adopters (Timbrell & Gable, 2002). Three prior approaches for automating ERP configuration have been identified:

- Hufgard (1994, pp. 215–221) describes an automated approach to supporting SAP R/3 configuration by step-by-step requirement specification: For a selected business area, a reduction checklist narrows the functional scope of the R/3 implementation and therefore reduces the amount of configuration requirements. Based on an assignment checklist, the rule-based system then proposes a combination of predefined business profiles. Finally, the system reports the requirement coverage of the selected profile combination to indicate which further configurations must be done manually to finish the configuration. The approach is commercially implemented in the "LIVE Kit" structure by IBIS Prof. Thome AG including more than a thousand questions and parameters (Thome & Hufgard, 2006, p. 84).

- Tsoi, Cheung, and Lee (2003) describe an expert system used to select and configure hard- and software components for enterprise applications. The rule-based system is less complex than Hufgard's because it avoids interdependencies between parameters by focussing on single-process enterprise applications instead of a complete ERP package. Besides rule-based inference, it uses case based reasoning to propose the user configurations from cases with similar requirements. Currently, it is only implemented as a prototype for a simple inventory management process.

Bucher and Meissner (2010) describe decision trees to support the configuration of different parameters of SAP ERP/APO inventory management. This approach is not implemented to date.

The comparison of prior approaches for automating ERP configuration with this study shows mayor differences (Table 2). The configuration objective in previous approaches focussed on *parameterisation,* or selecting *functionalities* or *components*. Parameters which are used to choose between different executions of processes and functions usually have a *small* value range. The possible parameter values and the conditions on which they depend are known in advance. Approaches focussing on parameterisation therefore use *rules* for knowledge explication. Value vectors which apply to the same set of rules are grouped in *templates*. The selection and combination of components for the inventory process supported by Tsoi, Cheung, and Lee's (2003) approach involves a larger range of possible values which are not known in advance. Therefore, their approach uses reasoning from *examples* in addition to rules and templates.

The range of possible values in category configuration can be much larger than for parameterisation or component selection. A rapid growth in the number of distinct values with the number of configured examples can be observed; for example, for the category "activity" (Figure 1). In 235 configurations, 7451 distinct categories can be found. Knowledge engineering approaches like rule-based systems are inefficient in this case because they hit a knowledge acquisition bottleneck (Sebastiani 2002). For every possible value, rules must be manually defined by an expert. An approach for automating category con-

Table 2. Comparison of ERP configuration approaches

Authors	Target System	Configuration Objective	Configuration Scope	ERP Implementation Approach	Target User	Type of Answers	Value Range	Knowledge Explication	State
Hufgard (1994); Thome and Hufgard (2006)	ERP Package	Function selection, parametrisation	Module-spanning	Requirements driven	Consultant	Nominal	Small	Rules, templates	Production (SAP, Siebel)
Tsoi, Cheung, and Lee (2003)	Inventory Management (Enterprise Application)	Component selection	Process-specific	Requirements driven	Inventory Manager	Nominal, numerical	Medium	Examples, rules, templates	Prototype (custom)
Bucher and Meissner (2010)	Inventory Management (ERP Module)	Parametrisation	Module-specific	Requirements driven	Consultant	Nominal	Small	Rules	Concept (SAP)
This study	ERP Package	Category configuration	Module-spanning	Business process improvement driven	Company executive	Nominal, numerical, textual	Large	Examples, rules, templates, meta templates	Beta (ERP5)

Figure 1. Growth of the activity structure

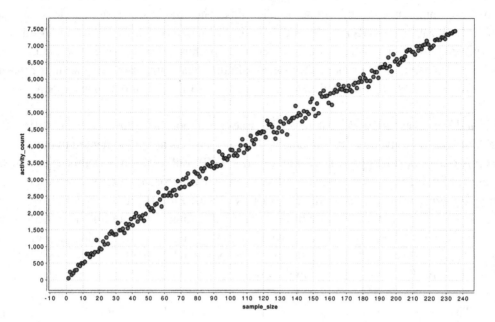

figuration therefore cannot be based on rules. Instead, it must be based on some form of learning from *example data* to suggest possibly suitable category values.

The explanatory variables for the automatic reasoning in prior approaches are fully known. Therefore, they use mainly questions with *nominal* and sometimes *numerical* types of answers. For category configuration, however, the explanatory variables which influence the suitability of certain category values for a particular configuration case are not entirely known in advance. An approach for automating category configuration must therefore be extensible to take explanatory variables into account which are identified later. It should also allow the use of questions with *textual* types of answers to allow the explication of explanatory variables whose possible values cannot be defined entirely in advance.

The target users of prior approaches for automating parameterisation are mainly consultants. They use the automation solution to perform a quick first ERP configuration together with the company staff. But, sufficient cost effects of automated category configuration can only be achieved if the approach enables the management of an SME to perform the configuration on its own. The questions of such an approach therefore must only ask organisation- and process-related information. No application system specific knowledge should be required to complete the questionnaire.

Previous studies follow a *requirement-driven* ERP implementation approach. Their questionnaires ask the user to define explicit requirements during the configuration process. This assumes that requirements and improvements of business processes in the course of the ERP implementation have already been defined for the ERP. To reach the aim of supporting the management of an SME to perform the category configuration on its own, a solution should be based on a *business process improvement driven* approach. Instead of asking for requirements, it should gather information on which business processes are currently not successful in the organisation and should be improved through the implementation of an ERP package.

To summarise, an automation approach for supporting the management of a company to perform a category configuration on its own must:

1. Support a large number of possible values for the target variables,
2. Support continuous extension of explanatory variables,
3. Support text answers,
4. Not require application system specific knowledge, and
5. Follow a business process improvement approach.

None of the prior studies found met all these requirements, as they were designed for other types of configuration options and focused mainly on consultants as target users for configuring ERP packages. The remainder of the paper examines the realisation of the requirements in an automated approach to effectively support category configuration.

RESEARCH APPROACH AND METHODOLOGY

The objective of this study is to better understand and solve the challenge of supporting the management of an SME to create a category configuration on its own. The study follows a design-science research approach. The idea of design-science is to better understand and solve human and organisational problems by creating innovative artefacts and applying them (Hevner, March, Park, & Ram, 2004). The artefact created in this investigation is referred to as a category configuration support (CCS) system. It is an automated approach to support the management of an SME to create a category configuration for an ERP package on its own. To validate the artefact, it is applied to the open source ERP package ERP5. The approaches implemented in the CCS System are generally applicable to other ERP packages. The application of the CCS System to ERP5 is exemplary.

The paper follows the publication schema recommended by Gregor and Hevner (2013). The study covers all phases of the design science research process (Offermann, Levina, Schönherr, & Bub, 2009). The research approach used follows the seven activities of the soft design science methodology (Baskerville, Pries-Heje, & Venable, 2009). The results of the first four activities have already been outlined: a specific problem is identified and expressed as a specific set of requirements (support ERP5 category configuration; aimed at the management of an SME). The requirements are abstracted and translated into a general problem (automating ERP category configuration). A general solution is designed and expressed in (five) general requirements. The next section describes the results of the remaining three activities: comparing the general requirements with the specific problem for fit, searching for components for a workable instance of a solution, and construction and application of a specific solution (the CCS system applied to ERP5).

This paper presents the latest iteration of the research process. A first iteration led to two approaches for automating category configuration, one based on knowledge engineering and one based on machine learning, which were prototypically implemented and validated through an example configuration case (Wölfel & Smets, 2012). A subsequent study allowed gathering 235 example configuration cases for further evaluation (Wölfel, 2014). The analysis of the example data showed that the approach from the first iteration did not solve the specific problem of ERP5 category configuration well enough for some kind of categories with a large number of possible values. Following Baskerville et al. (2009), this finding resulted in a re-expression of the specific problem and the final definition of requirements for a general solution in this latest iteration of the research process. The implications of these premises are outlined in the following section.

The artefact is designed based on expert knowledge, case studies, literature review and empirical evidence. Knowledge about the specific problem was gathered through expert interviews with ERP5 consultants followed by an analysis of the different category configurations of five companies which use ERP5 in production. A review of literature on prior configuration approaches and a comparison with category configuration in other ERP packages led to the definition of the general problem. The final requirements could only be defined after gathering empirical data, consisting of interviews and example configurations for 235 SMEs.

The CCS system was evaluated using empirical evidence to examine its validity, effectiveness and utility. The artefact should be considered *valid* if it enables the management of an SME to create a category configuration for his own business on his own. It should be considered *effective* if the quality of a category configuration produced with the help of the CCS system is higher than a configuration produced without its support. Following the definition of the specific problem, the artefact should be considered to have *utility* if it allows a manger to produce an effective category configuration on his own, at lower cost compared to the alternative solution of purchasing consulting support for the same task. The cost caused by the effort which the manager puts into creating a category configuration using the CCS system alone should be less than the consulting cost (consultant's configuration effort, plus consultant's margin, plus transaction cost, plus manager's effort for disclosing company information to the consultant).

To evaluate the validity, effectiveness and utility of the solution, it is therefore necessary to assess the quality of a category configuration created by a manager with the help of the CCS system in a defined time frame. These conditions can be met in the controlled environment of a laboratory experiment. The idea is to randomly assign a number of test persons to two groups, both of which are given the same time frame to produce a category configuration. The experimental group uses the CCS system for performing the configuration, while the control group uses the same user interface, but without displaying any of the configuration suggestions. To ensure comparable empirical evidence, all test persons have to configure the same company case, they need to have access to the same information about the company, and they need to have similar knowledge in the fields of management and information systems.

THE AUTOMATED CATEGORY CONFIGURATION SUPPORT SYSTEM

This section provides an overview of the CCS system. It implements the previously defined general requirements for an automated category configuration approach and was applied to the most important categories of ERP5. The general approach of the CCS system is to ask the manager of a small company a set of questions about the business and the improvements he expects from an ERP implementation. The answers are automatically compared to a set of interview examples from other companies. Configuration suggestions are made for each category based on similarity calculations.

Four main components make up the CCS system: the questionnaire system, the configuration user interface, the example and template store and the suggestion system. This section describes each component and how they together implement the previously defined requirements for automated category configuration support.

The Questionnaire System

A configuration process using the CCS system starts with filling out a questionnaire. The order in which the questions are displayed and the conditions under which a question is applied or omitted are defined using states and transitions. The implementation as a finite state machine allows representing questionnaires as graphs, which helps to manage many questions and complex dependencies. For the specific problem of ERP5 category configuration, two questionnaires have been created, a complete category configuration questionnaire and an ERP5 starter questionnaire.

The complete category configuration questionnaire is used for gathering example data and for creating a production-ready ERP5 category configuration. It currently consists of 90 questions. In line with the second general requirement (support continuous extension of explanatory variables), the questionnaire is continually extended with new questions resulting from new ERP5 implementation projects. Automatic consistency checking of existing example data after a questionnaire update is achieved using a questionnaire update workflow. The questionnaire follows a business process improvement ERP implementation approach. Instead of asking for lists of requirements, the questionnaire focusses on the business processes of the company and how they might be improved by implementing an ERP. Questions with textual, nominal and numerical answers are used. The questionnaire does not require any ERP5-specific knowledge to be filled out. It thus complies with the fourth general requirement (not require application system specific knowledge).

The ERP5 starter questionnaire is a short version of the questionnaire. It contains only the 15 most important questions, which are mostly answered as text. It thus omits any detail of operations but focusses on the general priorities for an ERP implementation. The objective is to create a basic ERP5 category configuration quickly for demonstration and training purposes. When using the ERP5 Starter questionnaire the suggestion system performs the similarity calculation based only on those 15 questions. Appendix I shows an excerpt of the questionnaire with the answers of a small software company.

The collection of interviews for 235 companies showed that the configuration questionnaire only requires knowledge typically possessed by the management of an SME. But, it also showed that the quality of text answers is often not good enough without any feedback. In response to this finding, a correction suggestion system based on machine learning has been created to semi-automatically correct text answers. It was evaluated through a Massive Open Online Course (MOOC) with 1500 students (Wölfel 2014). The correction system was used during the MOOC to support tutors to correct many interviews efficiently. For the production operation of the CCS system, it is meant to be used in self-assessment mode to automatically suggest possible mistakes in the answers directly to the manager who fills out the questionnaire.

The Configuration User Interface

Once the questionnaire has been completed, the answer set is sent to the suggestion system. The returned suggestion results are presented in the configuration user interface (Figure 2). The user interface consists of two areas: the configuration area on the left and the suggestion area on the right. In the *configuration area* the user edits his final category configuration. It behaves like any spreadsheet application. It consists of one table for each base category. The user can select the currently edited base category in the lower table bar of the configuration area. He can manually edit the categories in the configuration area,

Figure 2. The configuration user interface

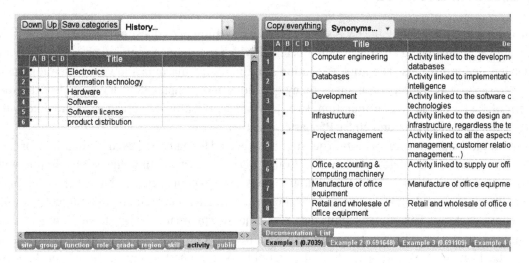

just as in a spreadsheet application. The first four columns define the path of a category in the category hierarchy. The further columns define title and description of each category.

The *suggestion area* displays suggested categories for the currently selected base category. Each time the user selects a different base category table in the configuration area on the left, the suggestion area on the right is reloaded to display the suggestions for the currently edited base category. To use suitable suggestions in his configuration, the user copies categories from the suggestion area into the configuration area, either by dragging single categories from right to left, or by using the "copy everything" button to copy a whole template or example table. A selection box in the top of the suggestion area displays synonyms for each category. When clicking on one synonym, the category in the corresponding line is replaced by the synonym.

Different types of suggestions are presented in three views: list view, example view and template view. The user can switch between views by selecting one of the tables in the bottom bar of the suggestion area. The *list view* displays in one table a list of suggested aggregated canonical categories corresponding to the base category which has been selected in the configuration area. The categories are provided by the suggestion system using similarity calculation and consolidation of categories from example data.

The *example view* shows five tables, each with a complete configuration of the selected base category from a company in the example data set which is identified as similar by the suggestion system. List view and example view are available for all base categories except site, group and nationality. Single companies in the example data store could be identified by displaying their site or group; therefore, the example-based approaches cannot be applied to these categories. For nationality, there are too few exceptions from the standard template to gain additional advantage from the example-based approaches.

The *template view* contains tables with predefined standard categories. Other than list view and example view, which are dynamically generated from example data, the tables in template view represent static configuration knowledge explicated as best-of-breed configurations. Two types of templates are differentiated: category templates and meta category templates. *Category templates* define a list of tables with predefined ready-to-use categories. They are particularly useful to support the configuration of function, role, grade, region and nationality. *Meta category templates* define a list of tables which each include a typical hierarchy of meta categories which are meant to be instantiated by the user; for example, site/continent, site/continent/country, site/continent/country/city. This approach is particularly useful for the categories of site and group, in which the actual categories are different for each company, but there are only a limited number of viable ways to structure the categories.

When the user finishes the category configuration, it can be exported from the CCS system and imported into an ERP5 instance. Optionally, it can be previously reviewed on-line by an ERP5 consultant. The answers to the questionnaire usually contain all information the consultant needs to verify the suitability of the configuration for the company. If the user agrees, his answer set and configuration again becomes part of the example data store. This way, the CCS system is improved with each application to a new company.

The Example and Template Data Store

All suggestions presented in the list view and example views of the configuration user interface originate from category configurations for real companies. Each configuration example is stored together with a corresponding interview in the example data store of the CCS system. For the specific problem of ERP5 category configuration, interviews and configurations for 563 SMEs have been created during the investigation. For quality assurance the example data store implements a review workflow. All answers and configurations are reviewed and eventually annotated with corrections using the correction suggestion system. After the review, the company is contacted again to submit a new version. Once the answer set and category configuration have no remaining corrections they are put into "released" state. Currently, 235 example data sets are released. Only those are taken into account by the suggestion system.

The structure of example data and how it is related to the rest of the CCS system is shown in an entity-relationship-model (Figure 3). Answers are related to the corresponding question and, optionally, to a correction line. Corrections are split into a general correction and a specific correction line.

Figure 3. Entity-Relationship-Model of the CCS System

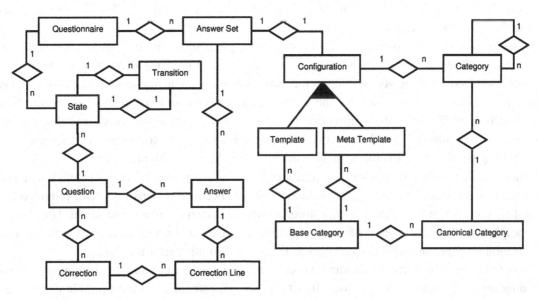

The general correction can be related to one or multiple questions. The correction line is related to the answer and adds a comment which describes the effect of the general correction to the specific case. Thanks to this indirection, one general correction can be applied to many answers which allows to use machine learning for the correction suggestion system.

A similar indirection can be found for questions which are related to questionnaires using a question state entity. This way, one question can be shared by different questionnaires. Since the questions of the category configuration questionnaire do not ask any ERP5-specific information, it is thus possible to clone the questionnaire, possibly adding a few questions and reusing it, including all of the collected machine learning data for correction suggestion to create an approach to configure the categories for a different ERP package than ERP5 in the same CCS system.

All answers corresponding to one interview are aggregated to an answer set which is related to one category configuration. A configuration defines for each base category (site, group, function, etc.) a hierarchy of categories. Through the clustering process of the suggestion system, categories are aggregated to canonical categories to provide the list view and the synonym list to the configuration user interface. Two particular specialisations of the category configuration entity are provided in the form of templates and meta templates. Other than usual configurations, they are not provided for a single company but define the categories and structures for the template and meta template views in the configuration user interface for a particular base category.

The Suggestion System

Once the configuration questionnaire is filled out completely, it is processed by the suggestion system to deliver category suggestions to the configuration user interface. The suggestion approach used in this latest iteration of the research process is based on the findings from creating configurations for 235 companies. For some categories, the data is not only high-dimensional (many possible values for a category), but also highly unbalanced (few exemplifications per category). A machine learning approach such as the prototype from the first research cycle (Wölfel & Smets, 2012) cannot give satisfying results under these conditions. This latest iteration of the suggestion system implements an approach based on similarities between the example data to propose suitable categories and consolidation of categories to decrease the solution space.

The suggestion system consists of a set of processes implemented with rapidminer. A preprocessing process first reads all answers from the example data store and aggregates all answers belonging to the same interview into a holistic vector. The vector consists of one dimension for each numerical and each Boolean answer and one dimension for the Term Frequency–Inverse Document Frequency (TF-IDF) value of each word. To create the word vector, the process aggregates all text answers belonging to the same interview into one string and converts it to lower case. The process tokenizes the string into words, filters out stop words and stems the remaining words using the Snowball algorithm.

Both, example view and list view of the configuration user interface rely on the calculation of a similarity measure. It is calculated using the Euclidean distance between the answer vector provided by the user and all vectors from the example data store. Similarity is derived from distance by 1/ln(distance). The *example view process* takes the five most similar examples and provides their complete category configuration (except site and group categories) to the configuration user interface.

The *list view process* aims at providing a combined view of the most suitable canonical categories corresponding to the answers of the user. In a first step, all categories in the example data store run through a consolidation process. The objectives are to identify similar categories, to group them together, to decrease the solution space and to be able to derive a similarity for each group of categories instead of a similarity per example. Three approaches were implemented and evaluated: clustering of n-grams, grouping by wordnet synonyms and an approach based on wikipedia redirects.

Using clustering of *n-grams,* groups of similar terms can be created, but it cannot provide a canonical form for a term. Therefore the implementation defined the most frequent category as the canonical form for all other categories in the group. The approach was discarded because no satisfying balance between enough synonyms and too many false positives could be found. Since it operates on the syntactical level, it is prone to wrongly suggesting homonyms as being similar categories.

Wordnet (Princeton University, 2010) is a lexical database of English. It defines lexical and semantic relations of terms. The implementation used the synonym relation provided by wordnet to group categories. Wordnet synonyms turned out to be too strict to reduce the number of categories to a satisfying amount. Using hyponym and hypernym relations on the other hand gave too many false positives. Wordnet also does not contain many compound terms typically used in categories such as "internet provider" or "marketing manager."

Best results were achieved using synonyms and canonical terms using *wikipedia redirects.* By analysing how wikipedia redirects a search term to the canonical title of an article, it is possible to identify a canonical term for a group of synonyms. The search terms "ISP" and "Internet provider" are for example both redirected to the canonical term "Internet Service Provider." All redirect relations are stored in the downloadable wikipedia database. An implementation of this idea exists in the form of a public web service (Ipeirotis, 2013). For the problem of category grouping, a process implemented in rapidminer reads all categories from the example store, queries the web service for their canonical terms and provides each canonical term together with all synonyms for the list view process and for the synonym list in the configuration user interface. Through this form of category consolidation, the solution space for category configuration can be decreased significantly. The number of different values for the activity configuration of 235 companies decreased from more than 7451 to 1276 (Figure 4).

The list view process fetches all categories from the 20 examples most similar to the user's answers, replaces them with their canonical terms and sums up the similarities for each occurrence of each consolidated category. For each base category, a new single consolidated category hierarchy is built level by level out of the 20 individual hierarchies. It selects the most similar first-level categories, then searches for the most similar second-level categories which fit into one of the selected first-level categories, and so on until the fourth hierarchy level. The same category can occur in different hierarchy levels. Depending on the company's view on industrial activities, it could define categories like retail/car, retail/bicycle or rather like car/retail, car/production. To build a homogeneous structure out of several examples, the canonical level is decided for each category based on the frequency of occurrence in the examples store.

To summarise, the CCS system implements the requirements for the general problem of automated category configuration support for the specific case of ERP5. It supports a large number of possible values for the target variables by using a similarity measure and by reducing the solution space through category consolidation based on wikipedia redirects. It supports continuous extension of explanatory variables through a questionnaire update workflow and by aggregating text answers into a single vector for similarity calculation. It supports textual, numerical and nominal answers using Euclidean distance between the user's answer vector and example data. The questionnaire does not require any application system specific knowledge but focusses on organisational knowledge and follows a business process improvement approach. The CCS system was applied to ERP5 by creating an example database of interviews

Figure 4. Comparison of activity growth with and without consolidation

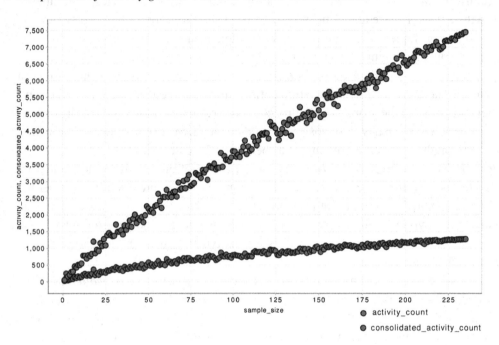

and ERP5 category configurations for 235 companies. The next section describes the empirical evaluation of the validity, effectiveness and utility of the CCS system and evaluation of the research process used.

EVALUATION

Evaluation Methodology

We used a laboratory experiment and a survey to evaluate the CCS system for its validity, effectiveness and utility. The laboratory experiment was conducted with one hundred bachelor and master students of information systems at TU Dresden. The test was performed under exam conditions: The students had 1:20 hours to read the information on the company and to complete the category configuration which they knew would be graded afterwards. To foster extrinsic motivation and create a complete and high quality category configuration, all students were offered to substitute one exercise on the final exam of the course with the grade reached in the test.

A thirty-point scheme was used to assess the quality of the category configuration for each student, with three points for each category: three points for a correctly configured category, two points in case of a minor error in content or structure, one point in case of a major error in content and structure, zero points in case of an unusable or undefined category. To compensate for the lesser experience level of students compared to company managers, the students received a general introduction to ERP packages and categories one week before the test. During the test, all students had full access to documentation related to ERP5 and category configuration. The information about the case was provided by the written answers from the management of the company to the same configuration questionnaire which is part of the CCS system.

To obtain an indication for the reliability of the approach, the configuration case chosen for the laboratory experiment should neither especially favour nor penalise the used example data set of 235 configurations. The approach of the CCS system is based on suggesting categories from similar examples. The similarity of one example to the next most similar example (neighbour similarity) can thus be defined as an indicator of how well the approach is expected to operate for one particular example compared to others. A case with an average neighbour similarity value would thus favour the generalizability of the test results. The requirements for choosing a configuration for the laboratory experiment were:

- The neighbour similarity of the case should be near the mean and the median of all neighbour similarities in the example database,
- The case should be an existing small company,
- The answers to the configuration questions should be available to the students in order to provide the information required for performing the category configuration, and
- The business domain of the company should be familiar to the students.

All requirements were met by the case of a small Canadian IT company which is part of the example data base. For the test, it was removed from the training data of the CCS system to not show the actual configuration as one of the suggested categories.

In addition to the laboratory experiment, a questionnaire assessed the *perception* of the configuration task and the *usage* and *perceived utility* of the CCS system. Both groups were asked in general, and for each category specifically, how difficult they perceived the configuration task to be and how confident they felt about their configuration being correct. The test persons in the experimental group, which performed the configuration with the help of the CCS system, were additionally asked for each category and for each support functionality if they used at least one of the proposed categories in their configuration and if the suggestions helped them to understand how to configure the respective category.

Evaluation of Validity, Effectiveness, and Utility

To evaluate the validity and effectiveness of the CCS System, the arithmetic mean of points achieved in the laboratory experiment by the experimental group using the CCS system consisting of 52 test persons was compared to the control group consisting of 46 test persons[1]. The mean value for the experimental group was 20.46154 points versus 17.10870 points for the control group. The Shapiro-Wilk normality test gives p-values of 0.1345 and 0.677, thus normality distribution can be assumed. Fisher's F-Test gives a p-value of 0.8563, so we assume homogeneity of variances. The T-Test for normally distributed independent samples gives a p-value of 0.001851 for checking the alternative hypothesis of values for the experimental group being greater than for the control group. Therefore, we can reject the null hypothesis and infer that the quality increase of 19,6% for the configurations created with the help of the CCS system compared to the configurations created without the suggestion functionalities is significant.

The questionnaire was filled out by 49 test persons from the experimental group and 43 test persons from the control group. The experimental group seemed to have perceived the configuration task as easier compared to the control group. The experimental group also seemed to be slightly more confident that their configurations were correct than the control group. Both results turned out not to be statistically significant, however.

The results regarding the usage of the different suggestion functions (templates, meta templates, list view and example view) for the respective base categories are clearer. All test persons from the experimental group used at least one of the suggested categories in their configuration. Where available, all different suggestion functionalities were used with similar frequency (Figure 5). The exception to this was the synonym function which was only used by three test persons. The reason is that the synonym list is meant as an expert tool to find out more specific categories for a displayed canonical category for experienced users. It is therefore not included in the remaining evaluation.

The base categories for which suggestions were used by the largest number of test persons were role (92%), function (88%) and grade (84%). This finding indicates that the CCS System is most useful when both types of suggestion approaches can be applied together, those based on example data and those based on templates. Region was the only category for which less than half of the test persons (49%) used at least one of the suggested categories. The reason is that the case used for the laboratory experiment required a particularly local regional configuration of the area around Montreal in Canada.

The test persons were asked for each suggestion functionality whether it helped them to understand the respective category. On a scale from 1 (do not agree at all) to 6 (totally agree) for each suggestion function and for each category, more than half of the test persons agreed at least slightly. The perceived contribution of each function to understanding category configuration was aggregated over all categories where the respective function was available (Figure 6). The contributions of templates and meta templates to understanding category configuration were most widely agreed upon, but these functions are only applicable to those categories with few possible values which are easier to configure anyway.

To summarise, empirical evaluation indicates that the CCS system is *valid*. During the laboratory experiment, test persons actively used the proposed categories to create an ERP5 category configuration for a small company. They perceived the suggestion functionalities as being helpful to better understanding how to configure the respective categories. The evaluation of the laboratory experiment indicates

Figure 5. Usage per category and per suggestion function

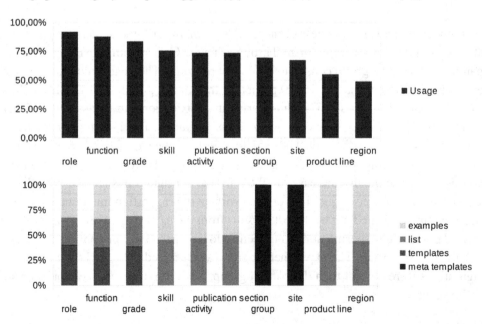

Figure 6. Perceived contribution of each functionality to understanding categories

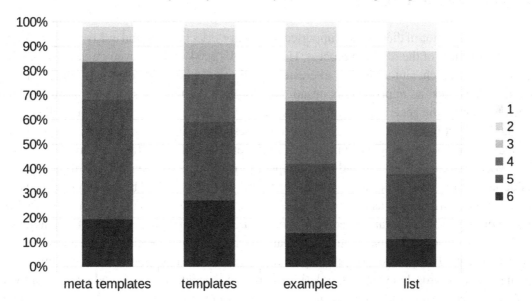

that the CCS System is *effective* because the quality of the configurations created with the help of the CCS system is on average 19,6% higher compared to the configurations created without the suggestion functionalities. The difference in quality was proved to be statistically significant.

The CCS system is argued to have *utility* for the management of a small company willing to adopt an ERP. The laboratory experiment showed that the CCS System enables a person who is not a consultant but has basic management knowledge to create an effective category configuration for a small company on his own in 1:20 hours. This duration is similar to what it would take a consultant to interview the management of a small company and create the category configuration. Adding transaction costs and the margin of the consultant, it is argued that by using the CCS system it is possible for the manager to create an effective category configuration at lower cost compared to the alternative solution of purchasing consulting support for the same task.

The evaluation of the questionnaire indicates that the CCS System has utility for teaching ERP implementation because it helps students to better understand category configuration. The CCS System is argued to have utility for researchers because it shows how different approaches based on templates and example data can be used to create an effective solution for automated category configuration support, a problem which exists in general across different ERP packages. The solution was proven to solve the problem for the specific case of ERP5 effectively. The CCS System can be extended to create different questionnaires for the configuration of different ERP packages. All source code of the CCS System is open source. Since ERP5's categories are semantically strictly defined, it is even possible to use the current example data and create rules to automatically convert the returned suggestions into categories for other ERP packages such as OpenERP.

Evaluation of Research

The empirical evaluation of the artefact supported its validity, effectiveness and utility. This section evaluates the effectiveness of the research process. Hevner et al. (2004) define seven guidelines for effective design-science research. Guideline 1 is to create a viable and innovative construct, model, method, or instantiation to address an important organisational problem. The CCS System is an instantiation of an approach to address the general problem of automating ERP category configuration applied to ERP5. The created artefact is innovative, because it is to the best of the author's knowledge the first and only automated solution to the category configuration problem. It is also the first solution which uses text analysis, vocabulary consolidation and meta templates to automate ERP package configuration.

Guideline 2 is to create a solution to a relevant and heretofore unsolved business problem. The problem of category configuration as part of the ERP implementation process is relevant to SMEs because consulting efforts, which can far exceed license costs, are a financial burden for SMEs (Janssens et al., 2007). This paper discussed existing automation approaches to support ERP package configuration, but none of them tackled the problem of category configuration which has been unresolved until this study. Guideline 3 is to rigorously evaluate the designed artefact through well-executed evaluation methods. The validity, effectiveness and utility of the CCS system were evaluated empirically through a laboratory experiment and a survey. The methodology and results of the evaluation have been outlined in the previous sections.

Guideline 4 requires the design science research to provide clear and verifiable contributions. The evaluation indicates that the CCS system enables a person who is not an ERP consultant but has basic management knowledge to create a category configuration on his own in reasonable time with higher quality. It also showed that the CCS system helps to better understand category configuration. The successful application of a suggestion approach based on similarity of text answers to ERP5 shows the applicability of this innovative approach to ERP package configuration. Guideline 5 is to apply rigorous methods to the design and evaluation of the artefact. The information required to design the CCS system was gathered through expert interviews with ERP5 consultants, analysis of previous ERP5 configuration cases and a review of literature on prior configuration approaches. The process for designing the CCS system followed the seven activities of the soft design science methodology (Baskerville et al., 2009). The evaluation of the laboratory experiment and the questionnaire used descriptive statistics and significance tests.

Guideline 6 is to design the artefact through an iterative search for an effective solution. A first iteration of the CCS system produced a prototype based on machine learning and knowledge engineering (Wölfel & Smets, 2012). The analysis of 235 configuration cases showed that a suggestion approach based on similarity measures would be more effective for the high-dimensional and highly unbalanced configuration data. This finding led to the latest iteration of the research process presented in this paper. The different approaches for category consolidation were created iteratively until the most suitable one based on wikipedia redirects was found. Similarly, the correction suggestion system for the configuration questionnaire was designed through many iterations of category configuration courses with students (Wölfel, 2014).

Guideline 7 demands to communicate design-science research to management- and technology-oriented audiences. The knowledge about category configuration gathered during the research process was taught to more than 1500 students of technical and management degrees, as well as 28 tutors, through the One Student One ERP (OSOE) project which also publishes all learning material online under creative commons license (OSOE Project, 2015). During the project, the gathered knowledge was also transferred to managerial technicians of SMEs in Cameroon, Germany and Romania, which participated as project partners and example clients for ERP5 Starter. Technical information was shared in conferences in Brazil, France and Germany and in collaboration with French universities. All source code of the CCS system is developed in a publicly git repository under an open source license (Nexedi SA, 2015).

CONCLUSION

Contributions to Theory

This study argues to be an important contribution to information systems theory. It is, to the knowledge of the author, the first investigation that precisely defines category configuration as a general ERP implementation problem. The investigation shows through the examples of ERP5, OpenERP and SAP that categories are a general concept shared across different ERP packages and across different business areas.

While previous approaches to automate ERP package configuration focussed on a particular ERP package or a particular business process, the approaches followed in this investigation and implemented in the CCS system are generally applicable to other ERP packages, not only to ERP5. The questionnaire does not contain any ERP5-specific questions. The category suggestions can be converted into categories of other ERP packages. The design of the CCS system presented in this paper therefore contributes to the general understanding of automating category configuration, not only to the specific case of ERP5.

The analysis of configuration data collected from 235 companies showed that category configuration is often characterized by high-dimensional and highly unbalanced data. This finding is useful for further research because it implies that rule-based and machine-learning based approaches face challenges to giving satisfying results with reasonable effort. The designed solution alternative, based on similarity measure, category consolidation, templates and meta templates, was applied successfully to ERP5. The evaluation of the CCS System showed that a suggestion approach based on similarities can produce satisfying results even when the number of possible values is much higher than the number of examples.

The search process for a satisfying solution for automated category consolidation resulted in the finding that wikipedia redirection information is most effective for consolidating the kind of vocabulary found in ERP category configuration. The effectiveness of this approach is supported by the consolidation of the category "activity" from 7451 original categories to 1276 consolidated categories. This finding contributes to information systems research because it shows that the semantic information explicated in wikipedia redirects is suitable for effective consolidation of large vocabularies in the domain of business information systems.

Implications for Practice

The main practical implication of the CCS system is that it can reduce the financial burden of ERP implementation for SMEs. It streamlines part of the ERP package configuration process by enabling the management of a small business to create an effective ERP category configuration on its own. The questionnaire focusses on business process improvements and does not require any technical or ERP-specific knowledge. The evaluation of the CCS system indicates that, with its help, the management of a small business can achieve category configuration at lower cost compared to the alternative solution of purchasing consulting support for the same task.

Used together with configuration wizards such as ERP5 Configurator, the CCS system allows for an alternative ERP implementation process in which a basic ERP configuration is first created by the management of an SME on its own. Further tailoring options with higher impact on the ERP system cannot be automated easily and therefore require a transfer of ERP implementation knowledge to the SME. ERP5 Starter (Wölfel, 2012) accomplishes this through a standardised consulting process and mass customization of ERP implementation documentation.

The second implication of the CCS system is for teaching of ERP implementation. In courses such as "ERP: Theory, Practice and Configuration" (OSOE Project, 2014), students perform an initial consulting process for an ERP implementation for a real small company. They interview the management and create a basic ERP package configuration for the company. The results of the evaluation indicate that by using the CCS system in an ERP implementation course, students better understand ERP category configuration and achieve more effective results.

LIMITATIONS AND FUTURE RESEARCH

The CCS System supports continuous extension of explanatory variables by aggregating the answers of all text questions into one. The similarity calculation is implemented generally independently from the actual questions on the questionnaire. In this way it is possible to extend the questionnaire without having to adapt the existing example data or the similarity calculation processes. This requirement was defined because in category configuration the explanatory variables which influence the suitability of certain category values for a particular configuration case are not entirely known in advance. Now that the current questionnaire has been proven to be complete enough to give satisfying results, it could be considered to drop the requirement for future research. Then, it would be possible to define a custom process for each base category which explicitly uses only a subset of the whole questionnaire for similarity calculation.

The CCS System was formally evaluated by a laboratory experiment with one hundred university students. Bachelor and master students of information systems were chosen to approximate knowledge in the fields of management and information systems possessed by managers of small businesses. The company for the experiment was chosen from the example data store based on the requirements that it should neither especially favour nor penalise the gathered example data set of 235 companies, and that the business domain should be familiar to the students. Future research could consider repeating the empirical evaluation with other companies to better assess the reliability of the artefact. In addition to empirical evaluation, qualitative evaluation using case studies can be considered. It will be interesting to observe SMEs which use the CCS system to create their category configuration on their own and evaluate how many changes need to be performed on the initial category configuration after defined time intervals.

ACKNOWLEDGMENT

This work was accomplished as a part of the Cloud Consulting project of the Eureka Eurostars innovation program (project A1107003E). Thanks to all project partners, especially Jingjing Xu from Nexedi for the quality review of the example data store and Marco Mariani from Nexedi for the programming of the configuration user interface. Thanks to BEIA for the contribution of many configuration cases and to RapidMiner GmbH for the implementation of the find-similar process and individual advice which made it possible to finish the similarity calculation and rapidminer integration. The author would also like to thank the anonymous reviewers and editor for their insightful comments and suggestions.

REFERENCES

Adam, F., & ODoherty, P. (2000). Lessons from enterprise resource planning implementations in Ireland - towards smaller and shorter ERP projects. *Journal of Information Technology*, *15*(4), 305–316. doi:10.1080/02683960010008953

Balint, B. (2015). Obtaining Value from the Customization of Packaged Business Software: A Model and Simulation. *International Journal of Enterprise Information Systems*, *11*(1), 33–49. doi:10.4018/ijeis.2015010103

Baskerville, R., Pries-Heje, J., & Venable, J. (2009). Soft design science methodology. In *Proceedings of the 4th international conference on design science research in information systems and technology* (p. 9). ACM.

Brehm, L., Heinzl, A., & Markus, M. L. (2001). Tailoring ERP Systems: A Spectrum Of Choices And Their Implications. In *Proceedings of the 34th Annual Hawaii International Conference on System Sciences*. New York, NY: Institute of Electrical and Electronics Engineers. doi:10.1109/HICSS.2001.927130

Bucher, D., & Meissner, J. (2010). *Automatic Parameter Configuration for Inventory Management in SAP ERP/APO* (Working Paper). The Department of Management Science.

Campos, R., Carvalho, R. A., & Rodrigues, J. S. (2007). Enterprise Modeling for Development Processes of Open-Source ERP. *18th Production and Operation Management Society Conference*.

Deep, A., Guttridge, P., Dani, S., & Burns, N. (2008). Investigating factors affecting ERP selection in made-to-order SME sector. *Journal of Manufacturing Technology Management*, *19*(4), 430–446. doi:10.1108/17410380810869905

Dreibelbis, A., Hechler, E., Milman, I., Oberhofer, M., van Run, P., & Wolfson, D. (2008). *Enterprise Master Data Management: An SOA Approach to Managing Core Information*. Pearson Education.

Gregor, S., & Hevner, A. R. (2013). Positioning and Presenting Design Science Research for Maximum Impact. *Management Information Systems Quarterly*, *37*(2), 337–A6.

Hevner, A. R., March, S. T., Park, J., & Ram, S. (2004). Design science in information systems research. *MIS Quarterly, 28*(1), 75–105.

Hofmann, P. (2008). ERP is Dead, Long Live ERP. *IEEE Internet Computing*, *12*(4), 84–88. doi:10.1109/MIC.2008.78

Hufgard, A. (1994). *Betriebswirtschaftliche Softwarebibliotheken und Adaption: empirischer Befund, Produkte, Methoden, Werkzeuge, Dienstleistungen und ein Modell zur Planung und Realisierung im Unternehmen*. München: Vahlen.

Ipeirotis, P. (2013, February 25). *WikiSynonyms: Find synonyms using Wikipedia redirects*. Retrieved from http://www.behind-the-enemy-lines.com/2013/02/ wikisynonyms- find- synonyms-using.html

Janssens, G., Kusters, R. J., & Heemstra, F. (2007). Clustering ERP Implementation Project Activities: A Foundation for Project Size Definition. In S. Sadiq, M. Reichert, K. Schulz, J. Trienekens, C. Moller, & R. J. Kusters (Eds.), *Proceedings of the 1st International Joint Workshop on Technologies for Collaborative Business Processes and Management of Enterprise Information Systems*, (pp. 23–32). Institute for Systems and Technologies of Information.

Kinni, T. B. (1995). Process improvement, part 2. *Industry Week/IW, 244*(4), 45.

Koch, S., & Mitteregger, K. (2014). Linking customisation of ERP systems to support effort: an empirical study. *Enterprise Information Systems*, 1–27. http://doi.org/<ALIGNMENT.qj></ALIGNMENT>10.1080/17517575.2014.917705

Koh, S. C. L., & Simpson, M. (2007). Could enterprise resource planning create a competitive advantage for small businesses? *Benchmarking: An International Journal*, *14*(1), 59–76. doi:10.1108/14635770710730937

Morabito, V., Pace, S., & Previtali, P. (2005). ERP marketing and Italian SMEs. *European Management Journal*, *23*(5), 590–598. doi:10.1016/j.emj.2005.09.014

Nah, F. F. H., Lau, J. L. S., & Kuang, J. (2001). Critical factors for successful implementation of enterprise systems. *Business Process Management Journal*, *7*(3), 285–296. doi:10.1108/14637150110392782

Negi, T., & Bansal, V. (2013). A Methodology to Bridge Information Gap in ERP Implementation Life Cycle. *International Journal of Enterprise Information Systems*, *9*(2), 70–82. doi:10.4018/jeis.2013040104

Nexedi, S. A. (2014). *How to fill the Category Spreadsheet*. Retrieved January 28, 2014, from http://www.erp5.com/P-CLOUDIA-Category.Spreadsheet.HowTo

Nexedi, S. A. (2015). *The cloud-consulting git repository*. Retrieved February 19, 2015, from http://git.erp5.org/gitweb/cloud-consulting.git?js=1

Ng, C. S. (2013). Exploring Relationships in Tailoring Option, Task Category, and Effort in ERP Software Maintenance. *International Journal of Enterprise Information Systems*, *9*(2), 83–105. doi:10.4018/jeis.2013040105

Offermann, P., Levina, O., Schönherr, M., & Bub, U. (2009). Outline of a design science research process. In *Proceedings of the 4th International Conference on Design Science Research in Information Systems and Technology* (*Vol. 7*, pp. 1–11). New York, NY: ACM. http://doi.org/ doi:10.1145/1555619.1555629

OpenERP SA. (2014). *Managing your Customers*. Retrieved January 27, 2014, from https://doc.openerp. com/book/2/3_CRM_Contacts/contacts/#categorizing-your-partners

OSOE Project. (2014). *ERP: Theory, Practice and Configuration*. Retrieved February 22, 2014, from http://www.osoe-project.org/lesson/osoe-Lecture.ERP.Configuration. Introduction

OSOE Project. (2015). *OSOE Meetings*. Retrieved February 19, 2014, from http://www.osoe-project. org/meeting

Pries-Heje, L. (2008). Time, Attitude, and User Participation: How Prior Events Determine User Attitudes in ERP Implementation.[IJEIS]. *International Journal of Enterprise Information Systems*, *4*(3), 48–65. doi:10.4018/jeis.2008070104

Princeton University. (2010). *About WordNet*. Retrieved February 13, 2014, from http://wordnet.princeton.edu

SAP AG. (2014). *Territory Hierarchy*. Retrieved January 28, 2014, from http://help.sap.com/saphelp_crm70/helpdata/en/de/d2fab855024f8d936fea84e9b9b551/content.htm

Sebastiani, F. (2002). Machine learning in automated text categorization. *ACM Computing Surveys*, *34*(1), 1-47.

Snider, B., Da Silveira, G., & Balakrishnan, J. (2009). ERP implementation at SMEs: Analysis of five Canadian cases. *International Journal of Operations & Production Management*, *29*(1), 4–29. doi:10.1108/01443570910925343

Thome, R., & Hufgard, A. (2006). *Continuous system engineering: discovering the organizational potential of standard software*. Munich: OXYGON.

Timbrell, G., & Gable, G. (2002). The SAP ecosystem: a knowledge perspective. In *Proceedings of the Information Resources Management Association International Conference* (pp. 1115–1118). Hershey, PA: Information Resources Management Association.

Tsoi, S. K., Cheung, C. F., & Lee, W. B. (2003). Knowledge-based customization of enterprise applications. *Expert Systems with Applications*, *25*(1), 123–132. doi:10.1016/S0957-4174(03)00012-5

Van Velsen, L., Huijs, C., & Van der Geest, T. (2008). Eliciting User Input for Requirements on Personalization: The Case of a Dutch ERP System. *International Journal of Enterprise Information Systems*, *4*(4), 34–46. doi:10.4018/jeis.2008100103

Wölfel, K. (2012). ERP5 Starter: Open-Source-ERP-Einführung durch standardisierte Beratung. *HMD - Praxis der Wirtschaftsinformatik, 283*, 58–67.

Wölfel, K. (2014). Suggestion-based Correction Support for MOOCs. In Tagungsband der Multikonferenz Wirtschaftsinformatik (MKWI), Paderborn, Deutschland.

Wölfel, K., & Smets, J.-P. (2012). Tailoring FOS-ERP Packages: Automation as an Opportunity for Small Businesses. In Free and Open Source Enterprise Resource Planning: Systems and Strategies (pp. 116–133). IGI Global.

Zach, O., Munkvold, B. E., & Olsen, D. H. (2014). ERP system implementation in SMEs: Exploring the influences of the SME context. *Enterprise Information Systems*, *8*(2), 309–335. doi:10.1080/1751 7575.2012.702358

KEY TERMS AND DEFINITIONS

Category Configuration: Defining taxonomies to model the structure of a company and the company's view of the world in an ERP system.

Category Templates: Predefined hierarchies of standard categories which represent static configuration knowledge explicated as best-of-breed configurations.

Design-Science: A research approach based on designing, applying and evaluating innovative artefacts.

Enterprise Resource Planning (ERP) System: An integrated software solution which enables an organisation to manage its resources an business processes.

ERP Configuration: Adapting an ERP package to the specific needs of an organisation by setting parameters and changing the master data of the ERP system. Configuration is distinguished from more heavy forms of ERP Tailoring such as changing the source code of the ERP or programming additional workflows, forms or reports.

Meta Category Templates: Predefined hierarchies of meta categories which explicate general concepts meant to be instantiated by the user.

Massive Open Online Course (MOOC): An internet based course which aims to transfer knowledge to a great number of learners and is open to anyone.

Term Frequency–Inverse Document Frequency (TF-IDF): Measure used to rate the relevance of a term in a document collection.

ENDNOTE

[1]   The control group originally consisted of 48 students, but two of them left the experiment early with zero and one point, respectively, so they were not taken into account in the evaluation.

APPENDIX I: CASE STUDY QUESTIONNAIRE

In the following the most important questions of the configuration questionnaire are listed together with the answers from a small software company. The category configuration of this company is shown in Appendix II.

Identity of the Implementation Field

Nature: (ex. corporation, non profit organisation, agency) Corporation.
Name: Aurora Systems GmbH.
Country: Germany.
Number of Employee or of Permanent Staff: 2 (+1 occasionally for marketing material design).
Number of Sites: 2.

Activity of the Implementation Field

What Does the Implementation Field Sell, Offer or Produce?

Aurora Systems sells Kallimachos, a library management software. The program is highly specialized for use in school libraries, so the target marked is quite narrow. The software is sold as school wide licenses and update licenses. The price depends on the extent of needed functionality. Accompanying Kallimachos, hardware (barcode scanners), expandable items (barcode labels, protective film) and services (support, custom function programming) are sold.

Aurora Systems offers a second product line, called meine-schulbibliothek.de Under this brand Kallimachos hosting services are rented on a yearly basis, also accompanied by above mentioned products and services.

What Does the Implementation Field Purchase, Recycle, Receives or Uses?

Aurora systems purchases hardware in form of barcode scanners and adapters, which are configured and sold for use with the Kallimachos software. Further, expendable items like labels, transparent film, CDs and office material are purchased regularly. The company uses computers, office printers and a special barcode printer.

Who Are the Contacts of the Implementation Field?

Aurora System's clients are all kind of non-academic schools. The contacts are professors, secretaries (education → agent) and school directors (education → manager). Sometimes regional public administrations or towns can be clients too, if they by licenses for many of their schools together. On the supplier side, contacts are sales agents.

The most important contacts are public Länder administration organisations, like the Bavarian state institute for education research or the Bavarian state library which advise schools and highly influence their decision on which library management software to buy. These organisations usually have many satellite offices distributed above Bavarian cities. The agents in these offices are important "multipliers" because their opinion about library software largely influences the schools in their region.

What Are the Typical Skills and Initial Training of the Staff?

The most important skills are IT skills, management skills and "sales and distribution skills". IT skills are needed in the areas of programming (application- web, and system programming, languages), system and web administration. Management skills are most important in the areas of marketing and especially communication which requires deep knowledge about our software and what the different stakeholder demand. Sales and distribution skills are rather specific to our sales and distribution process. It's required to know enough about our products to advise a client and demands the ability to configure our software and a barcode scanner and to use the label printer. The "user support" skill is product specific and requires only little IT knowledge (system administration support is apart from general user support) Soft skills are also required for marketing and communication, English language skills for software development.

Management of the Implementation Field

Please provide an example of management area or of business process which the implementation field is handling in a way which it considers itself as being good or successful. Explain what reasons make this business process or business area successful.

A successful business process of Aurora Systems is the sale order and distribution process, which is quite streamlined and quick and at the same time highly flexible. It's based on the distinction between standardized and flexible workflow components. Standardized parts in the sales process are conducted by the sale agent at Höchberg site. It consists in barcode scanner configuration, label printing, and product packaging. Some sale orders are purely standardized like a barcode label sale order and are only treated by Höchberg site. The client-advising and software configuration part is conducted by the Dresden site and very flexible. There is a highly detailed order form and clients are supported in their decision of what functionality to buy, so the software can be afforded by very small primary school libraries (200 books) as well as serve the need of big high school libraries (20.000 books) Custom function programming and foreign data integration can be included in the software configuration. The configured software is then packaged and sent by Höchberg site.

Please provide an example of management area or of business process which the implementation field is handling in a way which it considers itself as being poor or wrong, and which could be improved according to him or her. Explain from what point of view the management area or business process is currently not well implemented.

The CRM and pre sale process is still very poor. There is no management of leads and prospects. Prospects are either not contacted again, if the initial contact doesn't lead to a sale or they're only contacted on an irregular basis. Customers are not informed about product updates regularly and not asked, whether the product is used successfully. The market is well defined, and it is possible to get contact information about all our leads, but marketing instruments are not used methodically. Communication with "multipliers" which influence the opinion of our leads is not managed and far too irregular.

Explain what the implementation field expects from an ERP as 1st priority to improve its own management?

Most important for Aurora Systems is the standardization of communication with clients, prospects, leads and multipliers to improve our poor CRM and pre sale communication processes. Already managing all our contacts as persons and organisation in an ERP and defining clients, leads, prospects and multipliers and registering each contact and campaign will help a lot in this area.

Explain what the implementation field expects from an ERP as 2nd priority to improve its own management?

Using an ERP, it would be possible to fully automate the sale order process of our new meine-schul-bibliothek.de hosting service. The client would only fill in a subscription form and the client instance would be created automatically. After the test period is over, if the client accepts, an invoice would be generated automatically every year.

Explain what the implementation field expects from an ERP as 3rd priority to improve its own management?

The standardization of sale and purchase orders in a common database as wall as stock management of our sold hardware and expandable items would further improve our sale order and distribution process of our physical and license-based products.

APPENDIX II: CASE STUDY CATEGORY CONFIGURATION

The tables on the following pages show the category configuration of a small software company. The configuration questionnaire filled by the manager of this company can be found in appendix I.

For each base category a list or hierarchy of categories is defined in a table. The column *Path* defines the level in the hierarchy. The column *ID* is for the internal identification of the category, *Title* defines how the category is displayed in the ERP system, *Short Title* is for displaying the category in tables or selection list and *Description* contains a detailed definition of the category. The following tables show the configuration of the categories site, group, function, role, grade, region, skill, activity, publication section and product line.

Site defines the physical structure of an organization. The category is structured as a tree of sites with children sites.

Group defines the juridical structure of an organization with its subsidiaries and business units. Group categories can also define departments / sub-departments or divisions / sub-divisions, even if they are part of the same "juridical group". The category is structured by the concept of subordination.

Function describes the functional structure of the adopting organization and of organizations that it is doing business with. Functions of organizations are the nodes in the function tree, for example "factory", "warehouse", or "factory / warehouse". Functions of persons are represented by the leaves, for example "factory / manager" or "lab / director".

Role defines a categorization of all persons and organizations that are stakeholder of the company. Examples are staff, clients, potential clients, suppliers, or media. Clients might be further divided into direct clients and distributors, media may have subscribers and associations have members.

Grade describes the position in an organization from an honorific point of view. Salary is also usually based on grade, rather than on function.

Table 3. Site

Path	ID	Title	Short Title	Description
*	hoechberg	Höchberg	Höchberg	Office in Höchberg
*	dresden	Dresden	Dresden	Office in Dresden

Table 4. Group

Path				ID	Title	Short Title	Description
*				aurorasystems	Aurora Systems	Aurora	Aurora Systems is a small IT company specialised in the development of administration software for school libraries
	*			sales	Sales and Distribution	Sales	Sales department is in charge of distribution, marketing, sales as well as administrative work
*				germany	Administrations in Germany	Germany	German administration, governmental organisations and public insitutes
	*			bavaria	Administrations in Bavaria	Bavaria	Bavarian administration, governmental organisations and public insitutes
		*		education	Bavarian ministry of education and science	Education	The Bavarian ministry of education and science
			*	bsb	Bayerische Staatsbibliothek	BSB	The Bavarian state library has various satallite stations in Bavaria (Nürnberg, Würzburg, München, Regensburg) which advise schools in their region
			*	isb	Institut für Bildungsforschung	ISB	The Institut für Bildungsforschung is divided into various departements, some of which advise schools about library software
		*		würzburg	Administrations in Würzburg	Würzburg	Würzburg administration organisations
		*		munich	Administrations in Munich	Munich	Munich administration organisations

Table 5. Function

Path			ID	Title	Short Title	Description
*			sales	Sales and Distribution	Sales	An entity in charge of Sales and Distribution
	*		agent	Sales Agent	Agent	A person in charge of executing sale orders, packaging and distribution
*			marketing	Marketing	Marketing	An entity in charge of Marketing
	*		agent	Marketing Agent	Agent	A person in charge of designing marketing material like flyers etc.
*			company	Company	Company	A company is a legal entity which has been registered at a commerce registry and which has full autonomy.
	*		executive	Company Executive	Executive	A company executive has broad decision power and broad access to confidential information of the company.
	*		agent	Company Agent	Agent	A company agent is a regular staff of the company in charge of operations. He or she has little or no decision power.
*			education	Education	Education	An educational organisation such as a school
	*		manager	Education Manager	Manager	A manager in an educational organisation such as a school director
	*		agent	Education Agent	Agent	An agent in an educational organisation such as a school secretary
	*		professor	Professor	Professor	A professor in an educational organisation
*			admin	Public Administration and institutes	Administration	Public administration and istitutes like the education departement of a city, the Bavarian institute of the bavarian state library
	*		manager	Public Administration Manager	Manager	A public administration manager has decision power
	*		agent	Public Administraton Agent	Agent	An public administration agent is regular staff of the public administration in charge of operations

Table 6. Role

Path		ID	Title	Short Title	Description
*		multiplier	Multiplier	Multiplier	A multiplier is somone who influences the opinion of our prospects and leads. For example someone part of an organization which advises schools about library products
*		internal	Staff	Staff	Corporate staff
*		client	Client	Client	Client
*		supplier	Supplier	Supplier	Supplier
*		admin	Administration	Administration	Public administration, tax office
*		user	User	User	A registered user of meine-schulbibliothek.de
*		lead	Sales Lead	Lead	A person or an organisation that is potentially interested in purchasing a product or service from our compagny group (first stage in sales process)
*		prospect	Sales Prospect	Prospect	A person or an organisation that is interested in purchasing a product or service from our compagny group (qualified sales lead)

Table 7. Grade

Path		ID	Title	Short Title	Description
*		employee	Employee	Employee	Full time or part time employee
*		trainee	Trainee	Trainee	Trainee
*		associate	Associate	Associate	Associate or owner of the company

Table 8. Region

Path				ID	Title	Short Title	Description
*				germany	Germany	Germany	Germany is our main marked. The most important distinction is between differen Bundesländer Beacause there are different school laws and schools adminstrations in each Bundesland
	*			bavaria	Bavaria	Bavaria	Most of our schools are located in Bavaria, so we further distinguish between different Regierungsbezirke as its important to our clients to know how many other Kallimachos Schools are located in ther nearest region
		*		unterfranken	Unterfranken	Unterfranken	Schools in Unterfranken
		*		oberfranken	Oberfranken	Oberfranken	Schools in Oberfranken
		*		mittelfranken	Mittelfranken	Mittelfranken	Schools in Mittelfranken
		*		oberpfalz	Oberpfalz	Oberpfalz	Schools in Oberpfalz
		*		schwaben	Schwaben	Schwaben	Schools in Schwaben
		*		oberbayern	Oberbayern	Oberbayern	Schools in Oberbayern
		*		niederbayern	Niederbayern	Niederbayern	Schools in Niederbayern
		*		munich	München	München	Schools in Munic (Also Munic is a city, it's a Regierungsbezirk of its own)
	*			baden-wuerttemberg	Baden-Württemberg	Baden-Württemberg	Schools in the Bundesland Baden-Württemberg
	*			hessen	Hessen	Hessen	Schools in the Bundesland Hessen
	*			niedersachsen	Niedersachsen	Niedersachsen	Schools in the Bundesland Niedersachsen
	*			berlin	Berlin	Berlin	Schools in the Bundesland Berlin
*				luxemburg	Luxemburg	Luxemburg	Interested schools in Luxemburg
*				suisse	Switzerland	Switzerland	Interested schools in Switzerland

Table 9. Skill

Path				ID	Title	Short Title	Description
*				management	Management		Management skills
	*			marketing	Marketing	Marketing	Ability to create marketing materials and marketing concepts
	*			communication	Communication	Communicatio n	Ability to establish and maintain commination with "multipliers" and public administration for advertising
*				sales	Sales and Distribution	Sales	Skills related to sales and distribution
	*			advise	Advise clients	Advise	Ability to advise a client about what functionality he needs in the event of selling a kallimachos license or meine-schulbibliothek.de contract
	*			distribution	Distribution	Distribution	Skills related to distribution and packaging of our products
		*		configuration	Kallimachos Configuration	Configuration	Ability to configure the Kallimachos library Program according to a sale order
		*		scanner	Adjusting Scanner	Scanner	Ability to correctly adjust a barcode scanner for sale
		*		barcode	Printing Barcode Labels	Barcode	Ability to use the lable printer and software to print custom barcode labels for our clients
*				support	User Support	Suport	Ability to support Kallimachos and meine-schulbibliothek.de users
*				design	Design	Design	Multimedia design skills
	*			graphic	Graphic Design	Graphic	Ability to design graphics, logos, layouts, etc.
*				admin	Administration	Administration	Business administration skills
	*			accounting	Accounting	Accounting	Ability to book keep accounting transactions
*				it	Information Technology	IT	Information Technology skills
	*			sysadmin	System Administration	Sysadmin	System administration skills
		*		linux	Linux System Administration	Linux	Ability to administer a Linux System
		*		macos	MacOS System Administration	MacOS	Ability to administer a MacOS System
		*		windows	Windows System Administration	Windows	Ability to administer a Windows System
	*			webadmin	Website Administration	Website	Ability to administer a website
	*			programming	Programming	Programming	Skills related to programming
		*		lang	Programming Languages	Languages	Knowledge of programming languages
			*	python	Python	Python	Ability to programme in Python
		*		system	System Programming	System	Ability to programmatically interface with an OS
			*	linux	Linux System Programming	Linux	Ability to programmatically interface with a linux system
			*	macos	MacOS System Programming	MacOS	Ability to programmatically interface with a MacOS system
			*	windows	Windows System Programming	Windows	Ability to programmatically interface with a Windows system
		*		application	Application Programming	Application	Application programming skills
		*		web	Web Application Programming	Web	Web application programming skills
*				lang	Language	Language	Ability to work in a given language
	*			en	English	English	Ability to work in English
	*			de	German	German	Ability to work in German
*				soft	Softskills	Softskills	Skills which are not really technical and not really taught at university
	*			presentation	Presentations	Presentations	Ability to create stunning presentations
	*			speech	Give Presentation	Speech	Ability to give convincing presentations
	*			formatting	Document Formatting	Formatting	Ability to create well formatted documents
*				library	Library Management	Library	Librarian and library management skills

Region defines sales areas from a geographic-political point of view. The category is used to record the location of Organizations and Persons and to generate reports where sales and clients

Skills are assigned to persons and are part of the human resource management functionalities. They can also be assigned to people outside the adopting organization to record skills that for example consultants provide to the organization. Some skills can be defined universally, like languages or drivers licenses. Others are organization-specific, like the ability to control a specific machine.

Activity defines all relevant industrial activities for an organisation and is used to categorize clients and suppliers.

Publication Section is used to categorize documents by document types, for example contracts, press releases or project reports.

Product Line defines the hierarchy of products and services for purchase and sales. It is also used to categorize clients by product interest.

Table 10. Activity

Path				ID	Title	Short Title	Description
*				education	Education	Education	Education
	*			school	School	School	Any kind of non-academic school (primary, high school, professional school)
	*			university	University	University	Universities and higher education (ex. Kyoto University, Lille3, Telecom Lille1, Université de Dakar, MIT)
*				industry	Industry	Industry	Industry and services
	*			banking	Banking and Finance	Banking	Banking and finance (ex. HSBC, BNP Paribas, City bank)
	*			logistic	Logistic	Logistic	Logistics (ex. UPS, CGM)
	*			it	Information Technology	IT	Information technology (ex. IBM, Bull, NEC)
		*		expendable	Expendable items	Expendable	Expendable items used in conjunction wit it, like barcode labels
		*		hardware	Hardware	Hardware	Provider of hardware such as servers, laptops, routers (ex. Asus, Dell, Supermicro)
		*		consulting	IT Consulting	Consulting	Provider of consulting services for network, applications, security (ex. IBM Global Services)
		*		webagency	Web Agency	Web Agency	Provider of web site design and implementation (ex. Quadra)
		*		software	Software (Proprietary)	Software	Proprietary software publisher (ex. Microsoft)
		*		floss	Open Source - Free Software	FLOSS	Open Source software publisher and service provider
*				nonprofit	Non-profit	Non-profit	Non-profit organisations (NGO)
	*			association	Non-profit Association	Association	Not for profit associations (ex. April, AFUL, MSF)
	*			foundation	Non-profit Foundation	Foundation	Foundations (ex. FSF, Fondation de France)
*				government	Government	Government	Government organisations
	*			town	City	City	Towns and cities (ex. Paris City, Tokyo City, Dakar City, Campos City)
	*			regional	Regional Government	Regional Government	Regional government (ex. California Government, Bavaria Länder, Catalonia Generalitat, Lorrain Region)
		*		agency	Regional Agency	Agency	For example regional eductaion agencies
*				professional	Professional Organisation	Professional	Professional organisations (for profit or not for profit)
	*			chamber	Chamber of Commerce	Chamber	Chambers of commerce, business registries

Table 11. Publication Section

Path		ID	Title	Short Title	Description
*		marketing	Marketing	Marketing	Marketing documents including web site, presentations, leaflets
	*	kallimachos	Kallimachos	Kallimachos	Marketing Documents for Kallimachos
	*	msbde	meine-schulbibliothek.de	msbde	Marketing Documents for meine-schulbibliothek.de
*		news	Global News Feed	News	News about related to marketing, projects, operations, etc. It can be anything.
*		documentation	Documentation	Documentation	Kallimachos documentation for users and Aurora Systems staff.
*		process	Business Processes	Process	Documents related to core business processes
*		technology	Technology Library	Technologies	A collection of articles and links to technologies commonly used Aurora Systems or implemented In Kallimachos
*		template	Template	Template	Document templates of general use (ex. Offer, Letter, Fax.)
*		tax	Tax	Tax	Tax and social declarations
*		other	Other documents	Other	A place holder for documents which can not be categorised with the current categorisation. Based On the content of Other, new categories may be created to improve the categorisation system.

Table 12. Production Line

Path			ID	Title	Short Title	Description
*			kallimachos	Kallimachos	Kallimachos	Kallimachos library program licenses and services
	*		license	Licenses	License	Kallimachos Licenses with different kinds of functionality
	*		update	Update Licences	Update	Kallimachos update licenses
	*		support	Support Services	Support	Kallimachos support services
	*		programming	Custom Functions Programming	Programming	Kallimachos custom function programming services
*			msbde	meine-schulbibliothek.de	MSBDE	meine-schulbibliothek.de services
	*		hosting	Hosting Services	Hosting	meine-schulbibliothek.de hosting services
	*		support	Support Servies	Support	meine-schulbibliothek.de support services
	*		programming	Programming Services	Programming	meine-schulbibliothek.de custom function programming services
*			expendable	Expendable items	Expendable	Expendable items for library administration
	*		barcode	Barcode labels	Barcode	Barcode labels for books
	*		ink_ribbon	TT Ink Ribbon	Ink Ribbon	Thermo transfer ink ribbon to print barcode labels
	*		film	Protective film	Film	Protective film for barcode labels
*			hardware	Hardware	Hardware	Any hardware
	*		scanner	Barcode Scanners	Scanners	Barcode scanners for libraries
		*	ccd	CCD Scanners	CCD	Cheap CCD scanners
		*	laser	Laser Scanners	Laser	High quality laser scanners

Chapter 5
Continuous Assurance and Business Compliance in Enterprise Information Systems

Rui Pedro Marques
University of Aveiro, Portugal & University of Minho, Portugal

ABSTRACT

The increase of reliability and compliance of business processes is currently a major concern of organizations which simultaneously intend to achieve their organizational objectives and be compliant with external regulations. Thus, organizations are frequently looking for methods, tools and solutions which enable them to improve business compliance, and reduce the likelihood of situations that may jeopardize their operational performance and corporate image. This chapter aims to bring together a set of results and conclusions from a research project whose purpose was to conceptualize and validate an innovative solution which simultaneously monitors and audits organizational transactions executed in Enterprise Information Systems. A prototype was developed and deployed in a near-real environment. From the results, we conclude that the prototype offers Continuous Assurance services and is applicable to any organizational transaction, regardless of its type, dimension, business area or even its information system support technology. This independence is guaranteed by the abstraction level of an ontological model which is used to represent the organizational transaction we intend to monitor and audit. A case study enabled us to confirm the feasibility and effectiveness of the proposal in business compliance.

INTRODUCTION

Currently, organizations are living in a very regulated and competitive business environment. This, along with the challenges resulting from evolving business models pressured by factors as the new ICT (Information and Communication Technologies) trends and changing conditions in the environment, has forced organizations to reinvent themselves. Furthermore, the volume and complexity of business processes and the different threats and risks they are exposed to (Alan & Allen, 2005) have spurred or-

DOI: 10.4018/978-1-5225-2382-6.ch005

ganizations to look for solutions which enable them to control and monitor their transactions, evaluating and validating them in a comprehensive manner in order to meet current demands.

However, the traditional auditing, which occurs mostly after the completion of transactions, has proven inefficient, increasing the likelihood of errors and fraud not detected in time, and resulting in a negative impact for organizations (Askary, Goodwin & Lanis, 2012). See, for example, the current global financial crisis and successive well-known scandals in some organizations, such as Lehman Brothers, A-Tec, Madoff, Kaupthing Bank, WorldCom, Enron, Parmalat and Tyco cases and many others. Thereby, automatic mechanisms will make it possible to mitigate the risk associated to these issues (Bodoni, 2014; Markham, 2006). Furthermore, the continuous monitoring of the behavior of enterprise systems is becoming apparent, since it allows to detect problems in run-time and to solve them before they negatively affect business (Shuchih & Boris, 2008).

There are some regulatory requirements and risk control structures which help and encourage organizations to strengthen effectiveness of their risk management activities, ensuring an appropriate management of business risks and the effective operation of internal control systems (Pereira & Mira da Silva, 2012; Spies & Tabet, 2012). The most well-known regulation in this area is SOX (Sarbanes-Oxley Act). COSO (Committee of Sponsoring Organizations of the Treadway Commission) and COBIT (Control Objectives for Information and Related Technology) are the most used reference frameworks. In Europe measures for the statutory auditing were also taken by Directive 2006/43/CE of the European Parliament and of the Council of 17th May 2006, helping to improve the integrity and efficiency of financial statements and, accordingly, enhance the orderly functioning of markets.

It is necessary to find solutions which allow organizations to continuously evaluate, monitor and validate their transactions, preferably in a non-intrusive way concerning business operations. The optimization of the operational performance will also be possible if this auditing is done in real time (in the shortest time possible after any relevant event occurrence), reducing in this way the associated risks (Arnold & Sutton, 2007; Lech, 2011). Thus, the adoption of appropriate mechanisms to implement Continuous Assurance in accordance with applicable legislative and regulatory framework is crucial for organizations to be sufficiently prepared to survive, regardless of exposure and of the large number of risks they are subject to. Continuous Assurance can be defined as a set of services that using technology and data transactions produces audit results immediately or within a short period of time after the occurrence of relevant events (Vasarhelyi, Alles & Williams, 2010).

This chapter presents the results and conclusion of a research project (Marques, Santos & Santos, 2015) whose main objective was the development of real-time assurance services, having as support the organizational transactions according to an ontological model of organizational transactions. The use of an ontological model in this project was important because it helped to understand the essence of the organizational transactions and their relationships and characteristics, allowing the independence that is needed to make the project applicable to any organizational transaction, regardless of its type, dimension, business area or even its information system support technology. In parallel, even from a simpler business view, detachment from any ontological representation results in the inability to generate organizational knowledge (Filipowska, Hepp, Kaczmarek & Markovic, 2009).

The ontological model used in this project was the 'Enterprise Ontology', proposed by Dietz (2006). This model is adapted to represent the essential structure of the organizational transactions, with no significant complexities but simultaneously with: coherence (i.e. parts constituting an integral whole); consistency (there is no contradiction or irregularities); comprehension (all the important issues are handled); and concisely (i.e. model does not contain superfluous matters). Furthermore, this ontology has been successfully applied in some practical projects (Albani & Dietz, 2011).

This chapter is structured as follows: the next section presents the background on the chapter's subject, providing an overview of the fundamental topics for this work, and a summary of the most relevant related works; in the third section, a case study is briefly presented, namely its motivation, conceptualization, development and implementation; then results are presented, analyzed and discussed; finally, the last section presents the final remarks.

BACKGROUND

There are some topics on risk management and business compliance which address the aforementioned organizational concerns. BAM (Business Activity Monitoring) and BPM (Business Process Management) are two of them. BAM allows that events generated by various applications and systems of an organization, or by services of inter-organizational cooperation, can be processed in real time in order to identify critical situations in the performance indicators (Goomas, Smith & Ludwig, 2011). In turn, BPM enables the visualization, monitoring and management of events within the business process, and allows the highest-level visualization of the state of the execution of business processes, reducing the causes of the occurrences of exceptions (Goomas, Smith & Ludwig, 2011).

Aurora was a joint project from several universities (Abadi, Carney, Cetintemel, Cherniack, Convey, Lee, Stonebraker, Tatbul & Zdonik, 2003), whose objectives were to handle and manage a very large amount of data streams and to allow the creation of optimized queries, considering indexes and system inputs specified by the users. This was a precursor of other monitoring systems of data flow, e.g. Medusa and Borealis (Balazinska, Balakrishnan, Madden & Stonebraker, 2008; Balazinska, Balakrishnan & Stonebraker, 2004). Like Aurora, the project STREAM (Arasu, Babcock, Babu, Cieslewicz, Datar, Ito, Motwani, Srivastava & Widom, 2004) is a Data Stream Management System. STREAM supports a large number of declarative continuous queries over continuous data streams and/ or over traditional data repositories. The monitoring is done by controlling the results of queries made.

CEP (Complex Event Processing) is also a relevant topic because it includes methods, techniques and tools to process events in real time. It is capable of analyzing a series of data in real time with the aim to identify patterns and generate events that can be processed and treated (Balis, Kowalewski & Bubak, 2011). The work EasyCredit (Greiner, Duster, Pouatcha & Ammon, 2006) was successfully implemented in the banking sector. It is a system like BAM, using the concept of CEP and the pipeline used in the monitoring of credit transactions in real time. Within the works surveyed, one of them uses mining tools and CEP to analyze records of a database log in real time, and presents the sequence and the model of the transactions analyzed (Ferreira & Gillblad, 2009).

In addition, for some authors, continuous monitoring and the related continuous computing technologies are important sources to improve performance of enterprise information systems. Nijaz (2005), for example, developed a framework for implementation of continuous computing technologies. Furthermore, a new approach which aims to design mobile auditing assistance systems, allowing auditors to independently perform auditing tasks on a real-time basis, is emerging (Wen-Lung, 2014).

Finally, we must mention the concept of Continuous Assurance, because it addresses this problem domain thoroughly, since it is directly related to continuous monitoring, continuous auditing and continuous risk assessment of organizational transactions (Marques, 2017). In 1999, the term Continuous Assurance began to arouse much interest when a joint committee of the AICPA (American Institute of Certified Public Accountants) and the CICA (Canadian Institute of Chartered Accountants) took up the issue of Continuous Assurance and defined the term as a set of services which enables independent auditors to provide written assurance on a subject matter using a series of auditors' reports issued simultaneously with, or a short period of time after, the occurrence of events underlying the subject (Vasarhelyi, Alles & Williams, 2010).

Continuous Assurance is made up of three components: CCM (Continuous Controls Monitoring) to monitor the operation of internal control mechanisms; CDA (Continuous Data Assurance) to verify the integrity and validity of data; and CRMA (Continuous Risk Monitoring and Assessment) to estimate the risk (Vasarhelyi, Alles & Williams, 2010).

A recent survey on Continuous Assurance (Marques, 2017) allows to conclude that tools and solutions were recently made available in the market. Despite the fact that the vendors of these solutions call their products as Continuous Assurance solutions, these products focus more on the component CDA. The implementation of CCM solutions is very complex due to significant differences in the types of business objects, process configurations and controls and then it is not cost-effective. Thus, these solutions have developed some very specific CCM sub-routines targeted at specific enterprise systems. Although Continuous Assurance is maturing, both in practice and in research, the findings measured in the existing implementations are being used to improve future solutions (Vasarhelyi, Alles & Williams, 2010).

Guerreiro, Marques and Gaaloul (2016) presented a business transaction compliance solution using an enterprise information system environment to evaluate the impact of enforcing two distinct control schemas: feedforward and feedback. This solution presents feedforward control because it monitors and audits transactions in run-time, comparing their executions with execution patterns; and feedback control because it directly interferes in the enterprise information system when a negative situation happens. Furthermore, this solution enables an evolvable instantiation of the execution patterns. The authors also discuss the benefits of enforcing feedforward and feedback control schemas as a solution to guarantee the compliance of business processes execution.

CASE STUDY

This section summarizes the work of Marques, Santos and Santos (2015): a proposal which shows evidence of being effective in providing Continuous Assurance services. The motivation and the conceptual description of the prototype architecture are presented. Furthermore, the implementation which allowed to test the prototype and to collect data in order to validate the proposed solution is also described.

Motivation

The literature review upon this topic provides evidence that assurance services applied to organizational transactions constitute a research topic of interest, because it meets the current concerns of organizations and the recommendations of the recent regulations regarding the organizational auditing in order to mitigate the risks.

Thus, it is necessary to continuously monitor transactions in real time (closer to the occurrence), creating an additional layer of control which works with operational information systems and that ensures the compliance of the transactions execution, making it possible to estimate and assess potential risks. In the literature review some issues were noted with regard to the implementation of services of the three components of Continuous Assurance in information systems. It is to highlight the importance of presenting the possibility of providing information systems with full Continuous Assurance services for any transaction types. Thus, the information system is no longer specific to a particular ERP or organizational area, but adaptable and able to be parameterized to any organizational context.

The use of an ontological model capable of representing organizational transactions in a coherent, comprehensive, consistent and concise way can be the key to solve these issues. The ontological representation of each transaction becomes the object of the information system and is the requirement for parameterization and adaptation of the information system to organizational contexts. Therefore, the customization of algorithms for monitoring, analysis, auditing and risk assessment of specific transactions is eliminated.

The adoption of a model for ontological representation of organizational transactions supports the improvement of assessment and estimation of risk associated with the transactions execution, since the organizational transactions come to be represented by the events that compose them. These events are manageable parts which allow the construction of risk profiles of organizational transactions and subsequently the effective continuous identification of the risk associated with the execution of the transaction. In this context, risk profiles refer to the classification of different types of behavior that may occur in the execution of a transaction. In this work, two terms are considered to characterize risk profiles: negative profiles, which refer to all unwanted behaviors during the execution of transactions, for example incomplete or poorly executed operations, lack of crucial procedures, non-conformities, delays, incongruities and malfeasance; and positive profiles, which refer to all valid and appropriate events (Santos, 2009).

A solution with assurance services capable of monitoring organizational transactions supported by enterprise information systems with the level and detail that an ontological model provides is an innovative vision. Also considering that there may be different risk profiles for each organizational transaction, the development of a repository that contains and maintains the risk profiles of the transactions to monitor and audit, following the ontology, makes this challenge even greater in the theme of Continuous Assurance applied to organizational transactions. This view of monitoring, controlling and auditing organizational transactions is innovative since no reference to any implementation of risk profiles repository in the aforementioned way was evident in the literature review. Another innovative aspect of this view is the attempt to provide assurance services to organizational transactions following the structure of an ontology, which presents the transaction at a very low level, at its essence, contrary to what happens in most monitoring of transactions that occur at a high level (for example, compare whether a completed transaction followed a set of established procedures).

This chapter presents a new vision of organizational auditing focused on assurance services in transactions executed and supported exclusively in digital format, typically ERP systems, from the most elementary steps and actions which compose the essence of organizational transactions. Moreover, this work proves that it is feasible to develop information systems with continuous assurance services applicable to any organizational transaction represented by an ontological model and executed exclusively in digital format. The development of a prototype and the deployment of the case study, summarized in this chapter, allowed to reach this conclusion.

This work followed a quantitative approach, because the prototype deployment provided quantitative data which led to findings about the proposal and its feasibility (Myers, 1997; Patton, 2002). The research was conducted using the Design Science methodology, because this methodology is commonly associated with the problem-solving paradigm, and its main objective is the design and evaluation of

IT artifacts intended to solve an identified organizational problem (Hevner & Chatterjee, 2010; Peffers, Rothenberger, Tuunanen & Vaezi, 2012).

Conceptual Description of the Prototype

The solution conceptualization and the prototype development took into consideration a model for evaluating systems with Continuous Assurance services (Marques, Santos & Santos, 2013a; Marques, Santos & Santos, 2016), since it presents a set of characteristics that should be possessed by any information system with continuous assurance services. These characteristics are synthesized in Table 1. The requirements which serve as a basis for the solution's conceptualization and development are based on the aforementioned model and its characteristics.

The considered requirements are the following:

- **Req1:** The system should be able to record the operations which compose the organizational transactions and which are performed in the operational information system.
- **Req2:** The system should enable the instantiation of risk profiles associated with organizational transactions.
- **Req3:** The system should be capable of recognizing risk profiles, which were followed by the already concluded organizational transactions.
- **Req4:** The system should be capable of determining possible risk profiles, which are being followed or likely to be followed by organizational transactions still in progress.
- **Req5:** The system should provide the presentation of the executed operations, which were monitored.
- **Req6:** The system should provide the presentation of execution patterns, which are being followed or are likely to be followed.

Table 1. Dimensions of the model and their metrics

Dimensions	Characteristics
Monitoring (dimension)	− Real-time monitoring of operations − Real-time identification of irregular operations − Real-time verification of the processing of required operations at all previous steps − Real-time detection of lack of operations
Compliance (dimension)	− Recognition of execution patterns − Ascertaining of fulfilling of rules − Detection of potential errors − Verification of compliance of existing policies
Estimation (dimension)	− Estimation of possible results − Determination of possible execution patterns which are likely to be followed
Reporting (requirement)	− Real-time presentation of the executed operations which were monitored − Real-time presentation of execution patterns which are being followed or are likely to be followed − Real-time presentation of the compliance verification in transactions executions − Real-time presentation of the risk estimated on determining possible execution patterns − Real-time alert for irregular situations in monitoring, compliance verification and estimation of negative results

(Adapted from: Marques, Santos & Santos, 2016)

- **Req7:** The system should provide the presentation of results of the compliance verification in the execution of transactions.
- **Req8:** The system should provide the presentation of risk estimated on determining possible execution patterns.
- **Req9:** The system should be able to alert for irregular situations in monitoring, compliance verification and estimation of negative results.
- **Req10:** The system should provide its functionalities in real time.

The following considerations had to be taken into account in the conceptualization of the solution:

1. A layer of internal control mechanisms should be conceptualized in order to be incorporated in the operational information system (e.g. ERP), which supports the execution of transactions. These internal control mechanisms when embedded into operational information system must be aligned with the adopted ontological model. This consideration indirectly addresses Req1.

2. A repository - Real Online Transaction Repository - which is able to record, maintain and manage all the data derived from internal control mechanisms and that represents the transactional events occurring on-line must be conceptualized. This consideration addresses Req1.

3. A risk profiles repository should be able to maintain and manage the known negative and positive risk profiles of each transaction. These profiles must be modeled according to the ontological model. This consideration addresses Req2.

4. To address Req3 and Req4, another artifact must be conceptualized. This module should be capable of comparing the data from the internal control mechanisms with the records maintained in the risk profiles repository and then to be able to recognize the risk profile of every organizational transaction execution, which is already concluded or still in progress. The ability to recognize risk profiles also enables to:

    a. Determine which profile is being followed by running each transaction execution regardless of their state of completeness. Therefore, before the completion of the transaction execution, the risk profile or risk profiles, which are being followed by the transaction execution, are already possible to be estimated; however, if the transaction execution is following none of the risk profiles defined in the Risk Profile Repository, the system should present this execution as an unknown transaction;

    b. Estimate possible results, because on recognizing the possible risk profile of an organizational transaction still in progress, the system should qualitatively estimate the results. If the possible risk profiles associated with the transaction execution are positive, results without negative effects for organizations are predicted;

    c. Ascertain the fulfilling of rules and policies because on recognizing the risk profile, all policies and rules, which were defined in every risk profile, should be automatically checked;

    d. Detect potential errors, because on recognizing the possible risk profiles for every transaction execution, the system is assessing these possible risk profiles regarding their type (negative or positive). When the system identifies possible negative or unknown risk profiles, it is detecting potential error;

    e. Identify irregular operations because when the system is able to verify the non-fulfilling of rules; to detect potential errors; and to detect the compliance of existing policies, it should identify the irregular operation, which is causing the negative situation (e.g. delay in execution, unauthorized executor or unexpected operation);

f.   Detect the lack of operations, because this lack should be detected during the continuous comparison with the defined risk profiles in the Risk Profiles Repository. When there is lack of an operation, and this lack is safeguarded in a defined risk profile, this risk profile is automatically indicated and associated with this fault; and

g.   Verify the processing of required operations at all previous steps, because when a risk profile is identified for an organizational transaction execution, all performed operations, which compose it, are also checked, so that they may be validated regarding the definition of the risk profile of this transaction.

5.   The on-line results of the Transaction Comparator module should be presented to the users of the system through an interface and a report. This interface and report should contain the history of the results of the transaction auditing and monitoring and a picture of the current situation regarding the organizational transactions still in progress. Furthermore, notifications should be provided to the users when negative situations occur. This consideration addresses Req5, Req6, Req7, Req8 and Req9.

Figure 1 schematically represents the proposed conceptual architecture.

From the analysis of Figure 1, we perceive that the proposal is intended to be connected to the operational information system, i.e. internal control mechanisms should be incorporated in the operational information system in order to monitor the status of the various phases and stages (defined by the adopted

Figure 1. Conceptual architecture of the proposed solution
(Source: Marques, Santos & Santos, 2015)

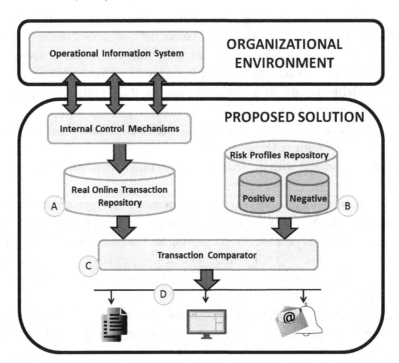

ontological model) of transactions according to the first specified requirement. These internal control mechanisms must provide data about the monitored operations to the Real Online Transaction Repository (component A), which manages and maintains this information referring to the various states of the transactions execution, as specified in Req1 and in the second consideration.

To meet the third consideration and Req2, the architecture has the component B, which illustrates the risk profiles repository of the organizational transactions to be monitored and audited. The component C is the module intended to be able to compare the various records in the risk profiles repository and to determine which profile is being followed by running each transaction, according to the information received by component A. It addresses Req3 and Req4 and the fourth consideration.

For the fifth consideration, and also for Req6, Req7, Req8 and Req9, the results of the organizational transactions monitoring carried out by comparison module (component C) are made available to the users of the system through different means (component D), enabling the viewing of the current state and the history of control of the audited transactions.

To meet the requirement about the real-time function (Req10), some aspects should be considered: the time and the rhythm of organizational transactions are variable and in different orders of greatness (transactions may have running times in the order of minutes, days or several months depending on the situation in question); a real-time system is one, where the correctness not only depends on the functionality but also on the timeliness of this functionality. Thus, because the purpose of the system is not to act in a direct and intrusive way on the execution of transactions, but rather to control, monitor, audit and then work with reporting functions, the real-time concept is defined within this work as the interval of time closer to the occurrence of an event. This interval of time may be variable but it is the time which allows the user of the system to effectively react in a corrective way, after being alerted of an anomaly. It is variable because it also depends on the pace and the rhythm of the transaction in question.

Solution Development

This section presents the aspects related to the development of the prototype. Technical issues are detailed, but at a high level in order to allow an easier understanding of the development process.

Regarding the internal control mechanisms, the use of triggers in operational databases was the option to develop them because it is a way of detecting events, since insertion, edition or deletion of a record or a record field means the occurrence of an event of a given organizational transaction. These mechanisms were developed in order to return data essential for this monitoring to the Real Online Transaction Repository, each time they are activated.

The data which derive from triggers were taken into consideration for the design and development of the Real Online Transaction Repository. Thus, the database structure needs entities to represent: the various triggers implemented in the database of the operational information system; the trigger types; every trigger occurrence; the data associated to each performed operation; the data associated to the precedent operation (when it exists); the users who are executors; and the user's roles.

The Risk Profiles Repository intends to address the issues of all models of the adopted ontology. The development of this repository follows the development of the database suggested by Marques, Santos and Santos (2013b), which ontologically represents organizational transactions. Thus, it needs entities to represent: all organizational transactions; the risk profiles, which are known for each transaction; the existing risk profile types in order to allow the classification of the profiles of each transaction; all the events that may be considered as part of the execution of organizational transactions; the different types of events which ontologically characterize an organizational transaction; and the user's roles.

The Transaction Comparator module was conceptualized in order to be able to compare the data from the internal control mechanisms with the records maintained in the Risk Profiles Repository and then to be able to recognize the risk profiles of the execution of organizational transactions. Simultaneously, it must provide information to the users about this processing and the respective results. It is composed of three layers:

1. Data access layer, which does not comprise data, but only the data access services, covering a business view of the access to data, and detaching the logical layer.
2. Logic layer, which is responsible for implementing the business rules associated with the problem being solved. It uses the services of the data access layer and returns the results to the presentation layer for dissemination. The logic layer is responsible for the key features of this module, because it assesses the operations performed in the operational information system (these data are contained in the Real Online Transaction Repository), comparing them with the execution patterns (risk profiles), defined in the Risk Profiles Repository.
3. Presentation layer, which is responsible for interaction with the users of the system, having all presentation logic and mechanisms, including the provision of the results derived from the logic layer. It refers to the process Loading Results of the flowchart depicted in Figure 2.

Figure 2 illustrates, in a general way, the function of the Transaction Comparator, from the perspective of the logic layer and, in its final stage, the presentation layer as well. The process Loading Risk Profiles intends to create an object that contains all risk profiles defined in the Risk Profiles Repository in order to be able to use them in the subsequent processes. After obtaining the list of risk profiles, the Transaction Comparator module continuously interacts, via data access layer, with the database of the Real Online Transaction Repository to determine whether operations were performed and detected by triggers in the operational information system (and recorded in the Real Online Transaction Repository) since the last interaction with this repository.

When a new operation is performed and detected in the operational information system, the flowchart indicates that a process called 'Loading sequences of related operations' runs. This process aims to aggregate operations which are related since they belong to the same transaction execution. Thus, a chronological sequence of execution of operations is possible to be established in order to allow the comparison with the sequence of events defined in the risk profiles of reference. After this process another one, designated as Classification of Sequences, runs. It is responsible for identifying possible risk profiles for each sequence of operations (transactions) in the list of sequences. Besides checking the compliance by chronological order of execution of operations, auditing the authorization of the executors, auditing the time in which the operations are performed, it is also responsible for the correct classification of the possible risk profiles as negative, positive or unknown, allowing to qualitatively estimate the risks associated to the execution of transactions.

The prototype of this solution includes three different means of disseminating results: interfaces so that the results of monitoring and auditing of organizational transactions can be visualized at run-time by users on a computer; reports in spreadsheet format to allow the users to visualize the results as well as manipulate them for other purposes, e.g. statistical objectives or to support the decision making; e-mail to alert users of high-risk situations.

Figure 2. Flowchart of the transaction comparator
(Source: Marques, Santos & Santos, 2015)

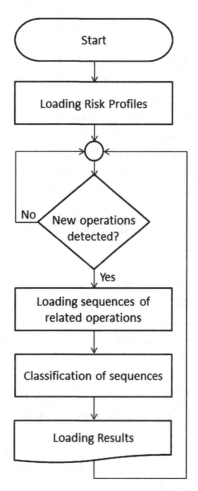

Implementation

This section presents the implementation of the proposed solution fully developed and prototyped in an organizational environment.

To validate the prototype it was necessary to implement it in an organizational environment, and to this end, we used the course 'Enterprise Simulation' of the degree in Accounting from the University of Aveiro (Portugal), because it yields a controlled environment, and also allows the application of the prototype in different organizational areas. This course, included in the last year of the degree, aims to simulate the organizational activities. The students create their own enterprise, develop its operations in the business during an operational period in accordance with the economic calendar and prepare and disseminate financial statements. The organizational transactions which are most executed in this course are the commercial and the accounting ones. However, those with the most occurrences are related to sales and the respective accounting entries, and therefore, this implementation gave more emphasis to these transactions (Silva, 2009).

The various risk profiles of the organizational transactions, which were used as object of study, were modeled. After this modeling, it was necessary to determine which of the possible events were monitored through the detection of insertion, modification or deletion of records in the ERP database. It was also necessary to determine the tables of the database which allow the detections of those events. And only then were we able to develop triggers on those tables that give monitoring data to the Real Online Transaction Repository. The choice of a trigger type depends solely on the type of operation which is intended to be monitored. But regardless of the trigger type (insert, update or delete), all of them have to return information about themselves and the operation they control.

The prototype was made available to three enterprises of the 'Enterprise Simulation' and the implementation lasted nearly three months. In order to collect data we used the reports produced by the system. The analysis of these reports was performed using a support file in which the researcher registered some indicators to subsequently have data for a more general analysis. These indicators had the purpose of:

- Telling how many risk profiles were actually followed by the transaction execution;
- Indicating the number of positive and negative risk profiles, which were followed by the transaction execution;
- Enabling to determine the success rate in the identification of risk profiles, showing the number of risk profiles which were correctly and incorrectly identified by the prototype; and the number of risk profiles which were not identified;
- Enabling to determine the rate of risk profiles which were correctly identified by type (positive and negative), presenting the number of risk profiles, positive and negative, which were correctly identified by the prototype;
- Enabling to determine the rate of risk profiles which were incorrectly identified by type, presenting the number of risk profiles, positive and negative, which were incorrectly identified by the prototype;
- Enabling to determine the rate of risk profiles which were not identified by type, presenting the number of risk profiles, positive and negative, which were not identified by the prototype;
- Enabling to determine the rate of false positives and false negatives as regards the classification of risk profiles which were correctly identified by type, showing: the number of risk profiles which were correctly and incorrectly classified as negative risk profiles out of a total of negative risk profiles which were identified by the prototype; and the number of risk profiles which were correctly and incorrectly classified as positive risk profiles out of a total of positive risk profiles;
- Enabling to determine the rate of false positives and false negatives as regards the evaluation of risk profiles which were correctly identified by the system concerning the completion of transaction executions (complete or incomplete), showing: the number of risk profiles which were correctly and incorrectly classified as complete out of a total of risk profiles which were correctly identified by the prototype; and the number of risk profiles which were correctly and incorrectly classified as incomplete out of a total of risk profiles which were correctly identified by the prototype;
- Enabling to determine the rate of false positives and false negatives as regards the auditing on user permission, presenting: the number of risk profiles which were correctly and incorrectly audited by the prototype regarding user's permission (authorized or unauthorized) in transaction executions in situations when all executors have an authorized role; and the number of risk profiles which were correctly and incorrectly audited in situations when at least one executor has an unauthorized role;

- Enabling to determine the rate of false positives and false negatives as regards the auditing on timing in which transactions were executed, presenting: the number of risk profiles which were correctly and incorrectly audited by the prototype in regard to timing (in time or delay) in transaction executions in situations when the transaction is executed in time; and the number of risk profiles which were correctly and incorrectly audited in situations when the transaction is executed with delay;
- Showing the result of observation of the operations which occurred in every transaction execution in order to determine whether we are facing a situation of alert (consider the transactions that followed an unknown risk profile and the transactions that followed only negative risk profiles, as alert situations);
- Indicating whether the prototype triggered alerts for every transaction execution with the aim to determine the rate of false positives and false negatives of alerts in risk situations;
- Indicating the date and time of: the occurrence responsible for the state of alert; the detection of the occurrence responsible for the state of alert; and the alert;
- Determining the time intervals between the occurrence and detection of events and the alert.

Besides these instruments, the participants (elements that managed the simulated enterprises) were asked to take notes on the operations which were being carried out and their execution date and time for later analysis, and to make it possible to evaluate whether all operations were monitored.

DISCUSSION OF RESULTS

From the three enterprises, we observe that 282 transactions, made up of the occurrence of 1129 operations, were executed. These transactions and operations imposed the performance of 2423 analyses supported by the reports generated by the prototype. The number of analyses corresponds to the number of possible risk profiles for the various transactions to be examined in all reports. The number of analyses is much higher than the number of transactions, because the identification of many possible risk profiles for an incomplete transaction execution may be common. Out of a total of 2423 analyses, 880 positive risk profiles, 1306 negative risk profiles and 237 unknown risk profiles were identified.

Furthermore, given the 2186 possible risk profiles, it was observed that 2115 were indicated as performed by users with authorized roles and the remaining 71 were indicated as performed by users with unauthorized roles; 1231 possible risk profiles were indicated as performed in time and the remaining 955 with delay.

Analyzing the indicators, we can conclude that the prototype was able to:

1. Monitor all operations which compose the organizational transactions and which are performed in the operational information system;
2. Correctly identify all possible risk profiles, positive and negative, for every transaction execution, regardless of their state of completion when the transaction execution followed one or more known risk profiles defined in the Risk Profiles Repository;
3. Correctly identify an unknown transaction, regardless of their state of completion when its execution did not follow any of the known risk profiles;

4. Correctly classify as positive risk profile or negative risk profile all possible positive risk profiles identified in transaction executions;

5. Correctly classify, as complete or incomplete, the transaction executions whose possible risk profile is respectively complete or incomplete;

6. Correctly audit all possible risk profiles identified in transaction executions as regards the transaction executors, both when they were performed by users with authorized roles and when they were performed by users with unauthorized roles;

7. Correctly classify, as performed in time, all possible risk profiles identified in the transaction executions regarding their time of execution, when all operations were carried out without delay;

8. Correctly classify, as performed with delay, all possible risk profiles identified in the transaction executions regarding their time of execution, when at least one operation was carried out with delay;

9. Correctly identify almost all situations that are not alert caused by the existence of transaction executions whose risk profiles are positive or because e-mail alerts were already sent in the past in alert situations, and therefore, the prototype does not send e-mail alerts. The percentage of not being e-mailed an alert is equal to or greater than 99.7%, with a significance level of 1%;

10. Correctly identify almost all situations that are alert caused by the existence of execution of transactions whose risk profiles are unknown, and therefore, the prototype sends e-mail alerts. The percentage of being e-mailed an alert is equal to or greater than 99.9%, with a significance level of 1%; and

11. Correctly identify all situations that are alert caused by the occurrence of transaction executions whose risk profiles are negative, and therefore, the prototype sends e-mail alerts. E-mail alerts were sent in all situations in which they must have been sent.

Moreover, also from the analyses of the indicators, we can observe that:

12. Half of the occurrences were detected in zero seconds, and only 25% of cases had detection time greater than one second (96.7% of the operations were detected by the prototype up to 1 second after their occurrence);

13. The overwhelming majority of e-mail alerts were sent up to 9 seconds after the detection of the operation which caused the alert situation; at least 75% of the e-mails were sent up to 6 seconds; at least half of the e-mail alerts were sent up to 5 seconds; and in only 25% of the situations the e-mails were sent up to 4 seconds, despite having been observed cases in which the alerts were sent up to 1 second;

14. The information in the reports and in the prototype interface allows us to conclude that the prototype provided the presentation of:

    a. The executed operations, which were monitored;

    b. Execution patterns which are being followed or are likely to be followed;

    c. Results of the compliance verification in the execution of transactions;

    d. Risk estimated on determining possible execution patterns; and

    e. Alerts for irregular situations in monitoring, compliance verification and estimation of negative results.

These results allow us to conclude that the initial requirements were met in full.

Validation of the Solution as a Provider of Continuous Assurance Services

The validation of the solution as an information system with Continuous Assurance services was carried out using the set of characteristics of the model of evaluation of information systems with Continuous Assurance services (Marques, Santos & Santos, 2013a; Marques, Santos & Santos, 2016). The authors of this model state that an information system with Continuous Assurance services should be evaluated by dimensions: 'monitoring', 'compliance', 'estimation' and 'reporting'. Thus, we ascertained that the results fit the following set of 15 characteristics identified in the evaluation model:

1. **Real-Time Monitoring of Operations (Dimension 'Monitoring'):** To evaluate this result, consider that real-time is defined within this work as the time interval closer to the occurrence of an event. According to result 12, we can conclude that the prototype is able to monitor operations in real time, because the time of detection is very inferior when compared, in common sense, with the time of execution of the operations associated with organizational transactions, due to the fact that the latter depends on the capacity and speed of execution by users of operational information systems, and therefore, the order of greatness of the running times of organizational transactions is much higher than the capacity of detection of the prototype. Another reason that leads us to this validation is result 1.

2. **Real-Time Identification of Irregular Operations (Dimension 'Monitoring'):** The results evaluated in the previous item are valid for both the regular operations and the irregular. However, the identification of an operation as irregular is only possible due to the coexistence of other characteristics pertaining to the dimension 'compliance'. When the prototype is able to verify the non-fulfilling of rules, to detect potential errors or to detect the compliance of existing policies, it is possible to identify which irregular operation is causing the negative situation.

3. **Real-Time Verification of the Processing of Required Operations at All Previous Steps (Dimension 'Monitoring'):** This characteristic is also checked, but it has to be analyzed in parallel with another characteristic: the capacity of recognizing execution patterns. When a risk profile is identified in an execution of organizational transactions by the prototype (results 2 and 4), the prototype ensures that the sequence of operations is being properly performed in accordance with this risk profile. Thus, when we validate that the prototype is able to correctly identify all risk profiles associated to a transaction execution, we are also validating this characteristic. Nevertheless, we cannot assertively come to the conclusion about the time required for this identification, because proper controls were not designed in order to collect these data. However, considering the intervals of time which were taken as indicators of the time to send e-mail alerts in negative situations, we are elucidated that the processing time for verification of the required processing of operations at all previous steps precedes that time. Although the method of measuring the time of sending e-mail alerts is not strict, this is indicative of its effectiveness. Being that the verification is performed before the alert (the alert is always a consequence), we can then conclude that this verification is processed in real time for the same reasons indicated in item 1.

4. **Real-Time Detection of Lack of Operations (Dimension 'Monitoring'):** This characteristic is also related to the capacity of recognizing execution patterns (dimension 'compliance'), because the lack of an operation in a sequence of operations of an organizational transaction is detected during the continuous comparison with the defined risk profiles. When there is lack of an operation, and this lack is safeguarded in a defined risk profile, this risk profile is automatically indicated and

associated with this fault. But if this lack is not safeguarded in any risk profile, this failure will be associated to a situation of unknown risk profile, which is cause of alarm by the prototype. Results 2, 3 and 4 and the real-time aspect (already commented in item 3) validate this characteristic.

5. **Recognition of Execution Patterns (Dimension 'Compliance'):** From results 2 and 3, we can affirm that the prototype is capable of recognizing execution patterns.

6. **Ascertaining of Fulfilling of Rules (Dimension 'Compliance'):** Some issues were addressed and parameterized as rules in the risk profiles: the sequence of operations (already validated in items 3, 4 and 5); the time at which each transaction was executed (validated by results 7 and 8); the authorization of users as executors (validated by result 6); and the state of completion of transaction executions (validated by result 5). Because the prototype reveals no deficiencies in these audits, this characteristic is also checked and validated.

7. **Detection of Potential Errors (Dimension 'Compliance'):** Based on results 2 and 3, if all negative risk profiles are correctly identified, as well as all transactions which follow unknown risk profiles, then we can say that the prototype detects potential errors.

8. **Verification of Compliance of Existing Policies (Dimension 'Compliance'):** This characteristic is validated for the same reasons which were presented in item 6. Rule and policy are not differentiated in this work, and their implementation is exactly the same, since their only difference lies in their origins. To be more specific, rule refers to all conditions imposed by national or international directives whereas policy refers to a set of procedures defined internally by each organization. In this work, this differentiation is not made, because the aim of the study is to validate the ability to audit guidelines, regardless of the fact they are rules or policies.

9. **Estimation of Possible Results (Dimension 'Estimation'):** This characteristic must be evaluated in combination with the next characteristic, which is also validated. If the prototype is able to determine possible risk profiles for a particular transaction which is not yet fully completed, it is possible to qualitatively estimate the result. We can validate this characteristic basing on results 2, 3 and 4.

10. **Determination of Possible Execution Patterns Which are Likely to be Followed (Dimension 'Estimation'):** This characteristic is validated because when a transaction is initiated, the prototype presents the possible risk profiles for this transaction execution regardless of their state of completeness. Therefore, before the completion of the transaction execution, the pattern or patterns that are being followed by the transaction execution are already possible to be estimated. The prototype does not show any deficiencies in the identification of risk profiles.

11. **Real-Time Presentation of the Executed Operations Which Were Monitored (Dimension 'Reporting'):** This and the following set of characteristics comprise the real-time concept which is assured and justified in item 3. The prototype allows the visualization of the performed operations by two means: consulting the report issued by the system and consulting the interface. Thus, this requirement is validated.

12. **Real-Time Presentation of Execution Patterns Which are Being Followed or are Likely to be Followed (Dimension 'Reporting'):** As in the previous item, this information is also provided both by the interface and by the report.

13. **Real-Time Presentation of the Compliance Verification in the Execution of Transactions (Dimension 'Reporting'):** The developed prototype enables to validate sequences of operations or execution patterns associated with each transaction, indicating if a transaction execution is positive, negative or unknown; audit the users who were executors regarding their authorization; monitor

the status of completion of organizational transactions; and control the time at which transactions are executed. Regarding the compliance verification, it can attest that results of the previously mentioned controls are reported and presented both in the report and in the interface of the system.

14. **Real-Time Presentation of the Risk Estimated on Determining Possible Execution Patterns (Dimension 'Reporting'):** This information is included in possible risk profiles which were identified for each transaction execution through their classification as positive or negative, i.e., the prototype allows a qualitative estimation of the risk of the transactions execution.

15. **Real-Time Alert for Irregular Situations in Monitoring, Compliance Verification and Estimation of Negative Results (Dimension 'Reporting'):** This characteristic is validated regarding results 9, 10, 11 and 13.

From the foregoing, we can conclude that the proposed system is indeed an information system with Continuous Assurance services because all characteristics were validated.

CONCLUSION AND FUTURE WORK

Concluding

1. A proposal of architecture for the development of an information system with continuous assurance services was made. This architecture was technologically deployed and the prototype was tested in simulated organizational environment;

2. The prototype is an information system with continuous assurance services because all characteristics considered essential and very important for an information system of this type were checked and confirmed in the prototype;

3. The use of an ontological model in the development and in the operationalization of the proposed system gives adaptability and flexibility to the system, since any organizational transactions which are represented by the adopted ontology can be monitored and audited by the prototype, because their ontological representation is object of parameterization of the system.

Therefore we can conclude that it is possible to develop information systems with continuous assurance services applicable to any organizational transactions which are represented by an ontological model and executed exclusively in digital format.

Finally, we can state that this work contributes to ensure the feasibility of development and the effective use of an information system with full continuous assurance services, having as support an ontological model, and which is considerably flexible and adaptable in order to be applicable to any organizational transaction. Moreover, this research contributes to a new vision of organizational auditing focused on assurance services in transactions executed and in digital format in compliance with the formalisms of a business ontological model of organizational transactions.

For future work we suggest the development of an additional module which allows the self-learning of risk profiles; in other words, the system should be able to suggest new risk profiles to the user based on information regarding the unknown risk profiles, which are constantly identified by the system. Approaches based on knowledge learning similar to those presented by Chen and Wang (2012) and by Sanin and Szczerbicki (2006) or data mining approaches may be possible ways to conceptualize this self-learning module.

REFERENCES

Abadi, D. J., Carney, D., Cetintemel, U., Cherniack, M., Convey, C., Lee, S., & Zdonik, S. et al. (2003). Aurora: A new model and architecture for data stream management. *The International Journal on Very Large Data Bases*, *12*(2), 120–139. doi:10.1007/s00778-003-0095-z

Alan, D. S., & Allen, R. L. (2005). Identity theft and e-fraud as critical crm concerns. *International Journal of Enterprise Information Systems*, *1*(2), 17–36. doi:10.4018/jeis.2005040102

Albani, A., & Dietz, J. L. G. (2011). Enterprise ontology based development of information systems. *International Journal of Internet and Enterprise Management*, *7*(1), 41–63. doi:10.1504/IJIEM.2011.038382

Arasu, A., Babcock, B., Babu, S., Cieslewicz, J., Datar, M., Ito, K., & Widom, J. et al. (2004). Stream: The stanford data stream management system. *A Quarterly Bulletin of the Computer Society of the IEEE Technical Committee on Data Engineering*, *26*(1), 19–26.

Arnold, V., & Sutton, S. G. (2007). The impact of enterprise systems on business and audit practice and the implications for university accounting education. *International Journal of Enterprise Information Systems*, *3*(4), 1–21. doi:10.4018/jeis.2007100101

Askary, S., Goodwin, D., & Lanis, R. (2012). Improvements in audit risks related to information technology frauds. *International Journal of Enterprise Information Systems*, *8*(2), 52–63. doi:10.4018/jeis.2012040104

Balazinska, M., Balakrishnan, H., Madden, S. R., & Stonebraker, M. (2008). Fault-tolerance in the borealis distributed stream processing system. *ACM Transactions on Database Systems*, *33*(1), 1–44. doi:10.1145/1331904.1331907

Balazinska, M., Balakrishnan, H., & Stonebraker, M. (2004). Load management and high availability in the medusa distributed stream processing system. In L. Liu (Ed.), *ACM SIGMOD International Conference on Management of Data*: (pp. 929-930). Paris, France: ACM. doi:10.1145/1007568.1007701

Balis, B., Kowalewski, B., & Bubak, M. (2011). Real-time grid monitoring based on complex event processing. *Future Generation Computer Systems*, *27*(8), 1103–1112. doi:10.1016/j.future.2011.04.005

Bodoni, S. (2014). Kaupthing creditors, madoff, a-tec, lehman brothers: Bankruptcy. *Bloomberg News*. Retrieved January 12, 2014, from http://www.bloomberg.com/news/2010-11-25/kaupthing-creditors-madoff-a-tec-lehman-brothers-bankruptcy.html

Chen, T., & Wang, Y.-C. (2012). An integrated project management system for facilitating knowledge learning. *International Journal of Enterprise Information Systems*, *8*(2), 30–51. doi:10.4018/jeis.2012040103

Dietz, J. L. G. (2006). *Enterprise ontology: Theory and methodology*. New York: Springer-Verlag Inc. doi:10.1007/3-540-33149-2

Ferreira, D., & Gillblad, D. (2009). Discovering process models from unlabelled event logs. In U. Dayal, J. Eder, J. Koehler, & H. Reijers (Eds.), *Business process management* (Vol. 5701, pp. 143–158). Heidelberg, Germany: Springer. doi:10.1007/978-3-642-03848-8_11

Filipowska, A., Hepp, M., Kaczmarek, M., & Markovic, I. (2009). Organisational ontology framework for semantic business process management. In W. Abramowicz (Ed.), *Business information systems* (Vol. 21, pp. 1–12). Heidelberg, Germany: Springer. doi:10.1007/978-3-642-01190-0_1

Goomas, D. T., Smith, S. M., & Ludwig, T. D. (2011). Business activity monitoring: Real-time group goals and feedback using an overhead scoreboard in a distribution center. *Journal of Organizational Behavior Management, 31*(3), 196–209. doi:10.1080/01608061.2011.589715

Greiner, T., Duster, W., Pouatcha, F., & Ammon, R. v. (2006). *Business activity monitoring of norisbank taking the example of the application easycredit and the future adoption of complex event processing.* Paper presented at the IEEE Services Computing Workshops, Chicago, IL.

Guerreiro, S., Marques, R. P., & Gaaloul, K. (2016). *Optimizing business processes compliance using an evolvable risk-based approach.* Paper presented at the Hawaii International Conference on System Sciences (HICSS-49), Kauai, HI. doi:10.1109/HICSS.2016.699

Hevner, A., & Chatterjee, S. (2010). Design science research in information systems. In *Design research in information systems* (Vol. 22, pp. 9–22). New York: Springer. doi:10.1007/978-1-4419-5653-8_2

Lankhorst, M. (2013). *Enterprise architecture at work: Modelling, communication and analysis.* Heidelberg, Germany: Springer. doi:10.1007/978-3-642-29651-2

Lech, P. (2011). Is it really so 'strategic'?: Motivational factors for investing in enterprise systems. *International Journal of Enterprise Information Systems, 7*(4), 13–22.

Markham, J. W. (2006). *Financial history of modern united states corporate scandals.* New York: M.E. Sharpe.

Marques, R. P. (2017). Continuous Assurance – The Use of Technology for Business Compliance. In M. Khosrow-Pour (Ed.), *Encyclopedia of Information Science and Technology* (4th ed.). Hershey, PA: IGI Global.

Marques, R. P., Santos, H., & Santos, C. (2013a). A conceptual model for evaluating systems with continuous assurance services. *Procedia Technology, 9,* 304–309. doi:10.1016/j.protcy.2013.12.034

Marques, R. P., Santos, H., & Santos, C. (2013b). *An enterprise ontology-based database for continuous monitoring application.* Paper presented at the IEEE 15th Conference on Business Informatics, Vienna, Austria. doi:10.1109/CBI.2013.10

Marques, R. P., Santos, H., & Santos, C. (2015). Monitoring organizational transactions in enterprise information systems with continuous assurance requirements. *International Journal of Enterprise Information Systems, 11*(1), 13–32. doi:10.4018/ijeis.2015010102

Marques, R. P., Santos, H., & Santos, C. (2016). Evaluating information systems with continuous assurance services. *International Journal of Information Systems in the Service Sector, 8*(3), 1–15. doi:10.4018/IJISSS.2016070101

Marques, R. P., Santos, H. M. D., & Santos, C. (2013c). Organizational transactions with real time monitoring and auditing. *The Learning Organization, 20*(6), 390–405. doi:10.1108/TLO-09-2013-0048

Myers, M. D. (1997). Qualitative research in information systems. *Management Information Systems Quarterly*, *21*(2), 241–242. doi:10.2307/249422

Nijaz, B. (2005). Continuous computing technologies for improving performances of enterprise information systems. *International Journal of Enterprise Information Systems*, *1*(4), 70–89. doi:10.4018/jeis.2005100105

Patton, M. Q. (2002). *Qualitative evaluation and research methods* (3rd ed.). Thousand Oaks, CA: Sage Publications Inc.

Peffers, K., Rothenberger, M., Tuunanen, T., & Vaezi, R. (2012). Design science research evaluation. In K. Peffers, M. Rothenberger, & B. Kuechler (Eds.), *Design science research in information systems. Advances in theory and practice* (Vol. 7286, pp. 398–410). Heidelberg, Germany: Springer. doi:10.1007/978-3-642-29863-9_29

Pereira, R., & Mira da Silva, M. (2012). Designing a new integrated it governance and it management framework based on both scientific and practitioner viewpoint. *International Journal of Enterprise Information Systems*, *8*(4), 1–43. doi:10.4018/jeis.2012100101

Sanin, C., & Szczerbicki, E. (2006). Using set of experience in the process of transforming information into knowledge. *International Journal of Enterprise Information Systems*, *2*(2), 45–62. doi:10.4018/jeis.2006040104

Santos, C. (2009). *Modelo conceptual para auditoria organizacional contínua com análise em tempo real*. Penafiel: Editorial Novembro.

Shuchih, E. C., & Boris, M. (2008). Monitoring enterprise applications and the future of self-healing applications. *International Journal of Enterprise Information Systems*, *4*(2), 54–66. doi:10.4018/jeis.2008040104

Silva, F. (2009). *As tecnologias da informação e comunicação e o ensino da contabilidade* (Master's degree dissertation). University of Aveiro, Portugal.

Spies, M., & Tabet, S. (2012). Emerging standards and protocols for governance, risk, and compliance management. In *Handbook of research on e-business standards and protocols: Documents, data and advanced web technologies* (pp. 768–790). Hershey, PA: IGI Global. doi:10.4018/978-1-4666-0146-8.ch035

Vasarhelyi, M., Alles, M., & Williams, K. T. (2010). *Continuous assurance for the now economy*. Sydney: Institute of Chartered Accountants in Australia.

Wen-Lung, S. (2014). Improving firm performance through a mobile auditing assistance system. *International Journal of Enterprise Information Systems*, *10*(4), 22–35. doi:10.4018/ijeis.2014100102

KEY TERMS AND DEFINITIONS

Business Compliance: Observance of all of the legal laws, regulations and policies in regards to how manage businesses.

Case Study: Research methodology that aims to test theoretical models by using them in real world situations.

Continuous Assurance: Set of services which, making use of technology, uses the information immediately and produces audit results simultaneously or within a short period of time after the occurrence of relevant events.

Continuous Auditing: Activities undertaken to assess the business compliance to rules, policies or legislation, providing warranty and credibility to operations.

Continuous Monitoring: Process responsible for the management of internal control mechanisms in order to ensure their effectiveness, allowing to obtain timely information about transactions.

Enterprise Information System: System which aims to improve the functions of enterprise business processes by integration.

Prototype: An original model on which something is patterned.

Risk Profiles: Classification of different types of behavior that may occur in the execution of a transaction.

Chapter 6
Contemporary Issues in Enterprise Information Systems:
A Critical Review of CSFs in ERP Implementations

Ebru E. Saygili
Yasar University, Turkey

Arikan Tarik Saygili
Izmir University of Economics, Turkey

ABSTRACT

The widespread usage of enterprise information systems (EIS) by various companies operating in different countries has led to digitalization of inter and intra-organizational business functions like customer relationship management (CRM) and supply chain management (SCM). This study considers current issues in EIS implementations in the context of enterprise resource planning (ERP) systems in different countries, industries and companies. Due to the increasing demands and varying needs of different parties, ERP implementations are getting more complex, which means considering a greater number and variety of critical success factors (CSFs). This study therefore reviews the current literature related to CSFs and their classifications before introducing a new conceptual model of 40 CSFs for successful EIS implementations.

INTRODUCTION

Over the last two decades, researchers and practitioners have conducted a number of studies of enterprise information systems (EIS). Due to the need to automate systems for processing vast amounts of data and also resolve timing and planning problems, early EISs were accounting information systems (Deschmukh, 2006), material requirements planning (MRP) systems and manufacturing resource planning (MRP II) systems (Umble et al., 2003; Al-Mashari et al., 2003). Enterprise Resource Planning (ERP)

DOI: 10.4018/978-1-5225-2382-6.ch006

systems were developed as a more advanced business solution (Davenport, 2000) to integrate business functions (Klaus et al., 2000) and to promote inter-organizational coordination Grabski et al., 2011).

ERP systems necessitate more collaboration between different enterprises and across different departments within the same enterprise, which has stimulated more and deeper research for understanding inter-organizational relations (e.g. Alimazighi and Bouhmadi, 2011; Daneva and Wieringa, 2006; Eckartz et al., 2010; Pigni et al., 2005). A majority of EIS studies concern ERP, specifically exploring critical success factors (CSFs). These play an important role in EIS implementations by reducing costs and set up times as well as increasing user satisfaction. This study discusses current issues and recently defined CSFs in ERP implementations to highlight the challenges facing EISs as they move into second-wave value propositions. The first section discusses contemporary issues in EIS while the following sections describe this study's methodology, results and a proposed conceptual model for CSFs in ERP implementations. The final section evaluates the study's contribution and suggests future research.

CONTEMPORARY ISSUES IN ENTERPRISE INFORMATION SYSTEMS

Having moved beyond initial ERP implementation, companies are now looking for ways to optimize their investment by extending the functionality of their ERP systems. These second wave implementations include data warehousing, customer relationship management (CRM), supplier relationship management (SRM) or advanced planning and optimization (Hawking et al. 2004). The newer implementations of ERP enable companies to move towards extended EISs that include supply chain management and provide extra tools such as real-time transaction tracking and internal process integration (Kelle and Akbulut, 2005). Because digitalization of business functions requires re-evaluation of the traditional vertically integrated business model, ERP software vendors have started to provide the users with more advanced decision support tools, known as new ERP software extensions. Some of the most popular versions of these new tools are: Advanced Planning and Scheduling (APS), Demand Planning and Revenue Management (DPRM), Customer Relationship Management (CRM), Sales Force Automation (SFA), and Supply Chain Management (SCM) (Kelle and Akbulut, 2005).

ERP systems have significantly changed the way operations take place within a company and business practices between different partners, leading to digitalization and automation of business functions. For instance, digital accounting systems in ERP speed up recording, classifying, summarizing and reporting desired accounting information, provide financial data and reports in electronic format across all accounting cycles, and promote communication of related data to interested partners. Digital accounting is based on a coherent information system ensured by ERP-type systems and the use of internet for transmitting information generated by the system both within and outside the company. Figure 1 summarizes these changes, including the operations and technologies or systems involved in acquisition, sales, payment and receipt processes, and also how they interact with the ERP system in digital accounting (Genete and Tugui, 2008).

The last decade has seen an increase in studies in the CSFs research stream, covering different countries, industries and companies. Various developing countries have been studied, including Taiwan (Liu, 2011), India (Garg and Agarwal, 2014), Iran (Amid et al., 2012), China (Srivastava et al., 2009; Zhang et al., 2005; Zhu et al., 2010), Poland (Ziemba & Oblak, 2013) and Saudi Arabia (Aldayel et al., 2011; Ullah et al. 2013). Whereas early studies were conducted in large manufacturing companies, recent studies explore the CSFs for ERP implementations in a range of industries and sectors, like oil and gas

Figure 1. Acquisition and sales operations in digital accounting

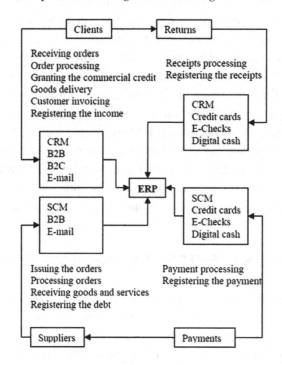

(Gajic et al., 2014), higher education (ALdayel et al., 2011; Ullah et al. 2013; Le Duc, 2014), health (Garg and Agarwal, 2014), high tech (Liu, 2011), project-based engineering and construction (Kwak et al. 2012), and public administration (Ziemba and Oblak, 2013; Mengistie et al. 2013). Other studies have investigated small and medium enterprises (SMEs) (Ahmad & Cuenca, 2013; Chang et al., 2010, Malhotra & Temponi, 2010; Doom et al., 2010).

It has been argued that because ERP systems have now reached a level of maturity where the required resources for implementation are understood by both vendors and organizations, configuration should be relatively easy and require only short implementation cycles (Jacobs, 2007). Morton and Hu (2008) developed a set of propositions based on structural contingency theory and Mintzberg's (1979) ideal structural types of organization about the relationships between the characteristics of ERP systems and the dimensions of organizational structure. They suggest that ERP systems are a good fit with some organization types but a poor fit with others. Organizations whose structures fit better with ERP systems are more likely to implement them successfully. More specifically, Gattiker and Goodhue (2004) proposed that the organizational structure of machine bureaucracies fits more closely with ERP systems than professional bureaucracies, adhocracies or divisionalized forms. High interdependence among organizational sub-units, contributes to ERP-related benefits because ERPs help coordinate activities and facilitate information flows. However, when differentiation among sub-units is high, organizations may incur ERP-related compromise or design costs (Gattiker and Goodhue, 2004). One case study of a university (Wagner and Newell, 2004) reveals that where you have diverse user groups, with different work practices and epistemic cultures, and with different levels of background experience, a single industry solution is not going to be 'best' from all perspectives, making it inappropriate to impose homogeneous work practices.

Amoako-Gyampah (2007) found that users' perceptions of perceived usefulness, ease of use of the technology, and level of intrinsic involvement all affect their intention to use ERP technology. This suggests that managerial efforts to increase users' perceptions of the usefulness and personal relevance of the technology will help make implementation successful.

METHODOLOGY

For this study, a comprehensive search through the most cited 17 relevant articles published between 1999 and 2013 was conducted to identify which CSFs most affect ERP implementations. Table 1 lists the studies, applied methodology and number of CSFs. Most of the researchers used a literature review and case studies to identify and classify CSFs. Some researchers, such as Somers and Nelson (2001), Ehie and Madsen (2005), and Ahmad and Cuenca (2013), conducted empirical field studies in various organizations in different parts of the world in order to identify and analyze more closely the factors affecting successful ERP implementations. Some of the studies that identified and classified significant CSFs identified are mentioned in the results section below.

The number of CSFs identified by the studies listed in Table 1 varied greatly, from only 9 (Umble et al., 2003) to 34 (Ehie and Madsen, 2005).

Previous research has suggested various ways to classify CSFs for practical and strategic reasons. This study comprehensively reviewed these CSF categorizations, as presented in the next section in Table 3. In light of previous research about CSF categories, we propose the conceptual model in Figure 2, which groups CSFs under four inter-related categories: Administration, Project and Team Management, ERP Software and Organization. The list of CSFs under each category is presented in Table 2. The categories are inter-related through bridging CSFs. For instance, senior management can monitor ERP implementation by appointing an executive level individual as project champion with direct responsibility for the project's outcome. A project management structure with a steering committee enables senior management to directly monitor the project team's decision making process. Dedicated resources determine decisions about ERP software. The ERP implementation strategy affects project and team management. ERP software decisions are made according to the existing business and legacy systems of organizations. The selected ERP package changes business processes in the organization. Administrative bodies have to manage culture change while the project team manages the expectations of the organization regarding ERP software. User acceptance provides organizational feedback for management. Some CSFs are related with external parties like consultants, vendors, country specific regulations, customers (CRM) and suppliers (SRM).

RESULTS

Tables 2 and 3 present the results of our comprehensive review of studies identifying and classifying CSFs. Our conceptual model in Figure 2 re-categorizes 40 CSFs identified by the previous studies listed in Table 2 in 4 new categories: Administration (CSFs 1-8), Project and Team Management (9-22), ERP Software (23-33) and Organization (34-40).

Table 1. Most cited studies related to CSFs

Author (s)	Number of CSFs identified	Methodology
Holland and Light (1999)	13	Multiple case studies
Bingi et al. (1999)	10	Multiple case studies
Brown and Vessey (1999)	12	Case study, literature review
Sumner (1999)	10	Multiple case studies
Somers and Nelson (2001)	22	Survey
Nah et al. (2001)	11	Literature review
Al-Mashari et al. (2003)	12	Literature review
Umble et al. (2003)	9	Case study
Ehie and Madsen (2005)	34	Survey
Gargeya and Brady (2005)	20	Literature review and content analysis
Finney and Corbett (2007)	26	Literature review and content analysis
Basoglu et al. (2007)	14	Literature review
Bradley (2008)	10	Multiple case studies
Ngai et al. (2008)	18	Literature review and multiple case studies
Dezdar and Sulaiman (2009)	17	Literature review and content analysis
Ghosh and Skiniewski (2010)	22	Literature review
Ahmad and Cuenca (2013)	33	Literature review and survey

Figure 2. A conceptual model for ERP implementation success

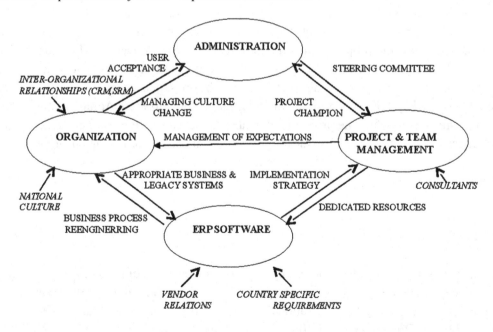

Table 2. Previously identified CSFs Categorized according to Proposed Conceptual Model

CSF No.	CSFs	Authors
CSFs Related to Administration		
1.	Business Plan and Vision	Holland and Light (1999); Nah et al. (2001); Dezdar and Sulaiman (2009)
2.	Top management support	Holland and Light (1999); Basoglu et al. (2007); Ghosh and Skiniewski (2010)
3.	Effective communication	Holland and Light (1999); Gargeya and Brady (2005); Ghosh and Skiniewski (2010)
4.	Project champion	Nah et al. (2001); Bradley (2008); Dezdar and Sulaiman (2009); Ahmad and Cuenca (2013)
5.	Interdepartmental cooperation	Somers and Nelson (2001); Ehie and Madsen (2005); Ahmad and Cuenca (2013)
6.	Change management	Al-Mashari et al. (2003); Ngai et al. (2008); Dezdar and Sulaiman (2009)
7.	Managing cultural change	Nah et al. (2001); Bradley (2008); Ngai et al. (2008); Ahmad and Cuenca (2013)
8.	Monitoring and evaluation of performance	Holland and Light (1999); Ehie and Madsen (2005); Al-Mashari et al. (2003)
CSFs Related to Project and Team Management		
9.	Steering committee	Somers and Nelson (2001); Bradley (2008); Ngai et al. (2008); Ahmad and Cuenca (2013)
10.	Use of consultants	Sumner (1999); Brown and Vessey (1999); Gargeya and Brady (2005); Ahmad and Cuenca (2013)
11.	Employee/team morale and motivation	Bingi et al. (1999); Finney and Corbett (2007); Ngai et al. (2008)
12.	Project team competence and composition	Ngai et al. (2008); Ghosh and Skiniewski (2010); Ahmad and Cuenca (2013)
13.	Empowered decision makers	Finney and Corbett (2007); Ghosh and Skiniewski (2010); Ahmad and Cuenca (2013)
14.	ERP team work	Nah et al. (2001); Umble et al. (2003); Dezdar and Sulaiman (2009); Ahmad and Cuenca (2013)
15.	Project management	Holland and Light (1999); Al-Mashari et al. (2003); Dezdar and Sulaiman (2009)
16.	Management of expectations	Somers and Nelson (2001); Ngai et al. (2008); Bradley (2008); Ahmad and Cuenca (2013)
17.	Dedicated resources	Gargeya and Brady (2005); Ghosh and Skiniewski (2010); Ahmad and Cuenca (2013)
18.	Implementation costs	Ehie and Madsen (2005); Finney and Corbett (2007); Ghosh and Skiniewski (2010)
19.	Implementation time	Ghosh and Skiniewski (2010); Bingi et al. (1999); Gargeya and Brady (2005); Bradley (2008)
20.	Clear goals and objectives	Gargeya and Brady (2005); Bradley (2008); Ngai et al. (2008); Ahmad and Cuenca (2013)
21.	Define scope and vision based performance	Umble et al. (2003); Ehie and Madsen (2005); Gargeya and Brady (2005)
22.	Feasibility of ERP project	Gargeya and Brady (2005); Ehie and Madsen (2005); Ahmad and Cuenca (2013)
CSFs Related to ERP Software		
23.	Ongoing vendor support	Somers and Nelson (2001); Ngai et al. (2008); Bradley (2008); Ahmad and Cuenca (2013)
24.	Vendor development tools	Somers and Nelson (2001); Ngai et al. (2008); Bradley (2008); Ahmad and Cuenca (2013)
25.	Business process reengineering	Holland and Light (1999); Al-Mashari et al. (2003); Ahmad and Cuenca (2013)
26.	Minimal customization	Dezdar and Sulaiman (2009); Ghosh and Skiniewski (2010); Ahmad and Cuenca (2013)
27.	Data accuracy	Ehie and Madsen (2005); Umble et al. (2003); Ngai et al. (2008)
28.	Data conversion and integration	Al-Mashari et al. (2003); Ehie and Madsen (2005); Ahmad and Cuenca (2013)
29.	ERP package selection	Bingi et al. (1999); Ngai et al. (2008); Dezdar and Sulaiman (2009); Ahmad and Cuenca (2013)

continued on next page

Table 2. Continued

CSF No.	CSFs	Authors
CSFs Related to Administration		
30.	Implementation strategies	Holland and Light (1999); Ngai et al. (2008); Ghosh and Skiniewski (2010)
31.	Software configuration:	Holland and Light (1999); Finney and Corbett (2007); Ahmad and Cuenca (2013)
32.	Software testing and troubleshooting	Holland and Light (1999); Al-Mashari et al. (2003); Ngai et al. (2008)
33.	Country related functional requirements	Ngai et al. (2008)
CSFs Related to Organization		
34.	Organizational characteristics	Brown and Vessey (1999); Gargeya and Brady (2005); Ngai et al. (2008)
35.	IT infrastructure	Ehie and Madsen (2005); Finney and Corbett (2007); Ngai et al. (2008)
36.	Appropriate business and legacy systems	Holland and Light (1999); Al-Mashari et al. (2003); Ahmad and Cuenca (2013)
37.	User training and education:	Basoglu et al. (2007); Dezdar and Sulaiman (2009); Ahmad and Cuenca (2013)
38.	Education on new business processes	Ghosh and Skiniewski (2010); Ahmad and Cuenca (2013)
39.	Interdepartmental communication	Ngai et al. (2008); Ghosh and Skiniewski (2010); Ahmad and Cuenca (2013)
40.	User acceptance	Finney and Corbett (2007); Basoglu et al. (2007)

Table 3. Classifications of CSFs in previous ERP literature

CSF No.	CSFs	Nah et al. (2001)	Al Mashari et al. (2003)	Ehie and Madsen (2005)	Gargeya and Brady (2005)	Finney and Corbett (2007)	Ngai et al. (2008)	Bradley (2008)	Ahmad and Cuenca (2013)
CSFs Related to Administration									
1.	**Business Plan and Vision**	Chartering	Setting up			Strategic	Business plan,vision, goal justification	Planning	
2.	**Top management support**	Chartering	Setting up	Top management support	Success factor	Strategic	Top management support	Leading	Organizational
3.	**Effective communication**	Chartering	Implementation	Top management support	Success factor	Tactical	Communication	Leading	
4.	**Project champion**	Chartering				Strategic	Project champion	Leading	Organizational
5.	**Interdepartmental cooperation**			Top management support			Project management		Neutral
6.	**Change management**	Project	Implementation	Human resources development		Strategic	Change management, culture and programme	Leading	
7.	**Managing cultural change**	Project	Implementation			Strategic	Change management, culture and programme	Leading	Organizational

continued on next page

Table 3. Continued

CSF No.	CSFs	Nah et al. (2001)	Al Mashari et al. (2003)	Ehie and Madsen (2005)	Gargeya and Brady (2005)	Finney and Corbett (2007)	Ngai et al. (2008)	Bradley (2008)	Ahmad and Cuenca (2013)
CSFs Related to Administration									
8.	Monitoring and evaluation of performance	Shakedown	Evaluation	Cost / budget		Tactical	Monitoring and evaluation of performance	Controlling	Organizational
CSFs Related to Project Team and Management									
9.	Steering committee						ERP teamwork and composition	Controlling	Operational
10.	Use of consultants			Consulting services	Success factor	Tactical	ERP teamwork and composition	Staffing	Organizational
11.	Employee/team morale and motivation					Tactical	ERP teamwork and composition		
12.	Project team competence and composition	Chartering		Project management	Success factor	Tactical	ERP teamwork and composition	Staffing	Organizational
13.	Empowered decision makers			Project management	Success factor	Tactical	ERP teamwork and composition	Staffing	Operational
14.	ERP team work	Chartering		Project management		Tactical		Staffing	
15.	Project management	Chartering	Implementation	Project management	Success factor	Strategic	Project management	Organizing	Organizational
16.	Management of expectations						Project management	Leading	Operational
17.	Dedicated resources				Success factor		Project management		Operational
18.	Implementation costs			Cost / budget	Failure factor	Tactical	Project management	Organizing	
19.	Implementation time			Evaluation of ERP project	Failure factor	Strategic	Project management	Organizing	
20.	Clear goals and objectives			Evaluation of ERP project	Success factor		Project management	Planning	Organizational
21.	Define scope and vision based performance			Evaluation of ERP project	Failure factor				
22.	Feasibility of ERP project			Evaluation of ERP project	Failure factor				Organizational
CSFs Related to ERP Software									
23.	Ongoing vendor support						ERP Vendor	Staffing	Operational
24.	Vendor development tools						ERP Vendor	Staffing	Operational
25.	Business process reengineering		Implementation	Process reengineering	Success factor	Tactical	Business process reengineering	Other	Organizational
26.	Minimal customization				Success factor		Business process reengineering	Other	

continued on next page

Table 3. Continued

CSF No.	CSFs	Nah et al. (2001)	Al Mashari et al. (2003)	Ehie and Madsen (2005)	Gargeya and Brady (2005)	Finney and Corbett (2007)	Ngai et al. (2008)	Bradley (2008)	Ahmad and Cuenca (2013)
CSFs Related to Administration									
27.	Data accuracy			Process reengineering			Data management		
28.	Data conversion and integration		Implementation	Process reengineering		Tactical	Data management		Operational
29.	ERP package selection		Implementation	Process reengineering		Tactical	ERP strategy and implementation strategy	Other	Organizational
30.	Implementation strategies			Process reengineering	Success factor	Strategic	ERP strategy and implementation strategy		Organizational
31.	Software configuration					Tactical	Software development, testing and troubleshooting		Operational
32.	Software testing and troubleshooting		Implementation		Failure factor	Tactical	Software development, testing and troubleshooting	Leading	Organizational
33.	Country related functional requirements						Country related functional requirements		
CSFs Related to Organization									
34.	Organizational characteristics				Success factor		Organizational characteristics		
35.	IT infrastructure			IT infrastructure		Tactical	Organizational characteristics		
36.	Appropriate business and legacy systems	Chartering	Implementation			Tactical	Appropriate business and legacy systems	Other	
37.	User training and education		Implementation	Human resources development	Failure factor	Tactical	Change management, culture and programme	Staffing	Organizational
38.	Education on new business processes			Project management	Failure factor	Tactical	Change management, culture and programme		Operational
39.	Interdepartmental communication						Communication		Organizational
40.	User acceptance				Failure factor				

From our thorough review of previous studies, we found that the most frequently mentioned 40 CSFs were defined and categorized in various ways, as shown in Table 3. This indicates that a general consensus is lacking on which set of factors are most important for successful ERP implementations. For example, Nah et al. (2001) identified 11 CSFs after carefully reviewing 10 articles in the information systems field. They also classified these factors according to the ERP life cycle model of Markus and Tanis (2000). This model consists of four phases:

- **Chartering:** Decisions defining the business case and solution constraints.
- **Project:** Getting system and end users up and running.
- **Shakedown:** Stabilizing, eliminating bugs', getting to normal operations.
- **Onward and Upward Phases:** Maintaining systems, supporting users, getting results, upgrading, system extensions.

Preparation, analysis and design of ERP implementations take place in the chartering phase while the project and shakedown phases involve implementation activities and the onward and upward phase includes maintenance activities. What makes Nah et al.'s study valuable is the inclusion of a schedule showing when and for how long each CRF affects the ERP implementation process. For example, the influence of some CSFs continues throughout the ERP life cycle while others only start in the project or shakedown phases before continuing for the rest of the cycle. According to this schedule, ERP Teamwork and Composition, Top Management Support, Effective Communication, Project Management, and Project Champion are CSFs that affect the whole ERP cycle; therefore, they are considered the most important of the factors identified by Nah et al.

Al-Mashari et al. (2003) argue that the technical and organizational aspects of implementing an ERP system must be very well understood and harmonized if the system is to produce tangible and intangible benefits. They proposed three phases for their taxonomy of CSFs:

- **Setting-Up:** Emphasizing the importance of managerial and leadership styles and approaches (top management support) as well as organizational vision and plans on successful ERP applications.
- **Implementation:** Emphasizing critical factors such as software selection, training, effective communication and ability of organizational change and adaptation while installing and operating ERP systems
- **Evaluation Phases:** Emphasizing the importance of careful monitoring and evaluating feedbacks periodically as well as management support once, as it should be evident from beginning till the end.

Al-Mashari et al. claim that the most important ingredient in successful ERP implementation is leadership and commitment as part of the first phase. They also found that that careful auditing of the system and organizational changes in order to harmonize them through rational benchmarking contributes to successful implementation. Their taxonomy provides a clear vision and well-designed business directory for ERP success.

Ehie and Madsen (2005) conducted both a thorough literature review of factors leading to success or failure of ERP systems and extensive interviews with ERP experts and consultants in order to develop a questionnaire exploring almost every aspect of ERP-related issues, which also asked users to rate ERP implementation in their companies. The questionnaire were pre-tested by ERP users before being sent to 200 companies identified as either users or in the process of implementing an ERP system out of 689 Midwestern US companies. Although the response rate was low (36%) due to confidentiality constraints, the results were statistically reliable. Ehie and Madsen identified 34 critical ERP-related success attributes that they categorized under the following eight CSFs:

- Project management principles,
- Feasibility/evaluation of ERP project,
- Human resource development,
- Process re-engineering,
- Top management support,
- Cost/budget,
- IT infrastructure, and
- Consulting services.

They also found strongly significant correlations between 6 of the 8 CSF categories and the success of ERP implementation, with only Human Resource Development and IT Infrastructure having insignificant correlations.

Gargeya and Brady (2005) performed a content analysis covering articles published about 44 companies using SAP systems. They identified six critical factors for success or failure of ERP implementation, which they ranked for the importance of their effects as follows:

- Working with SAP functionality/maintained scope,
- Project team/management support/consultants,
- Internal readiness/training,
- Dealing with organizational diversity,
- Planning/development/budgeting, and
- Adequate testing.

Gargeya and Brady found that success factors were not necessarily the same ones that cause failure in implementing ERP systems, suggesting that practitioners should consider two distinct sets of factors in ERP implementation: one set to ensure success, and another to avoid failure. The most important critical success factors were top management support and vision, while factors such as not considering internal readiness, resistance to change and inadequate time to plan and to get used to the idea of change were the most important critical failure factors.

Finney and Corbett (2007) content analyzed 45 carefully selected articles were to identify and classify strategic and tactical CSFs. They categorized factors as strategic if they were important elements in the process of efficient and effective ERP implementations. They found that top management support, visioning and proper planning, managing cultural change, effective change management were among the most important strategic critical factors. They found that similar factors were responsible for success or failure as Gargeya and Brady did. However, Finney and Corbett also claimed that change management is the most critical strategic factor for successful ERP implementations. They defined tactical critical success factors as those methodological elements required for successful ERP implementations, such as keeping up team morale and motivation, selection of ERP software, consulting clients, establishing an effective communication plan and post implementation evaluation. Both Gargeya and Brady and Finney and Corbett mentioned that relying on secondary sources limited their ability to gain more reliable data. Finney and Corbett also emphasize that stakeholders' perspectives is one of the most important yet ignored elements while determining CSFs.

Ngai et al. (2008) conducted one of the broadest literature reviews, covering books, articles, doctoral dissertations and conference papers from 10 different countries. They identified 18 CSFs that were similar to previous studies. These included establishing an appropriate business and IT system, proper planning, clearly defined visions, goals and objectives, change management and company culture, effective communication, forming an effective ERP team, selection of ERP software, monitoring the whole process. Their research revealed the importance of top management support and training and education, in other words convincing, motivating and educating ERP system users at every level in order to eliminate doubts, uncertainty and resistance to change company-wide for successful ERP implementation.

ERP systems are usually thought to be employed by large-scale enterprises. However, Ahmad and Cuenca (2013) analyzed successful ERP implementations in SMEs to identify CSFs from the perspectives of smaller scale users. Their study is also valuable for its categorization of CSFs as operational, organizational and neutral, and their analysis of the interrelationships of the critical issues involved in ERP implementation in SMEs. Ahmad and Cuenca identified CSFs before analyzing interactions between them. Finally, they determined which factors made the greatest impact at each significant stage of ERP implementations. To do this reliably and develop an acceptable ERP model to apply successfully to SMEs, they critically reviewed 50 relevant articles and interviewed ERP experts. The identified significant CSF impacts through industry surveys before testing the applicability of these significant CSFs to SMEs.

They identified 33 CSFs through their literature review and discovered that CSFs classified as organizational have the greatest impact on ERP implementations. These include top management support and commitment, selection of proper ERP software, effective management and eliminating resistance to change throughout the organization, effective planning and implementing the process. These were also the most significant CSFs in similar studies. However, the operational factors defined by Ahmad and Cuenca include more specific explanations of organizational CSFs, such as having good project scope management, vendor support, education and training on new business processes and applications. Interestingly, Ahmad and Cuenca found that software customization and interdepartmental cooperation neutral elements, which contradicted other similar studies. This may be because interdepartmental cooperation is not as important or difficult in SMEs as in large enterprises; similarly, software customization for successful ERP implementations is also not as difficult so not a major issue for SMEs as it is for larger scale enterprises.

DISCUSSION

In this section, we consider our classification of CSFs according to the proposed model in Figure 2. The 8 CSFs (1-8) in the administration category concern a wide range of business functions: business planning, project management, top management support, communication, change management, human resources, cost and budget, monitoring and evaluating performance. This category included 2 success factors but no failure factor. Business planning and vision is the first CSF introduced in planning/chartering phase, followed by top management support, effective communication and project champion in the chartering/setting up phase, although they all have influence throughout the implementation. Change management and managing cultural change were only effective from the project/implementation phase while monitoring and evaluation appeared in the shakedown/evaluation phase. Overall, CSFs in this category prominently featured leadership, management, and strategic and organizational features.

Our project and team management category includes 14 CSFs (9-24), with the majority being tactical and related to ERP teamwork, project management and evaluation. As project teams are cross-functional this category includes both success and failure factors characterized by controlling, staffing, organizing, planning or leading. There were operational CSFs as well as organizational CSFs.

The third category includes 11 CSFs (23-33) related to ERP software. All are success factors for the implementation phase except for software testing and troubleshooting, and all are tactical factors except for implementation strategies. Both operational and organizational factors appear, concerning business process reengineering, data management, software development, testing and troubleshooting, country related functional requirements, and ERP vendor and implementation strategy. Ongoing vendor support and vendor development tools are classified as staffing factors whereas software testing and troubleshooting is a leading factor.

The organization category consists of 7 CSFs (34-40): organizational characteristics, appropriate business and legacy systems, communication, human resources development, IT infrastructure, project management change management culture and programme. All are tactical and implementation failure factors, except for organizational characteristics. User training and education are classified as organizational whereas education on new business processes is operational.

CONCLUSION

While ERP systems provide valuable benefits to users if successfully adopted, their implementation is very complex, causing many enthusiastic adopters to experience serious problems during setting up and implementation. In many cases, the disappointed adopters report that ERP implementations fail and are therefore cancelled due to cost and time overruns and organizational and/or structural mismatches (Ngai et al., 2008). To better identify and understand which CSFs promote successful installation and implementation of ERP systems, many studies have been conducted during the last decade. These have identified various success factors and classified them in different ways. The results of this research is extremely valuable for designing and implementing ERP systems so that they successfully benefit the users as intended.

This study identified and then re-categorized the CSFs from previous studies in order to provide a more comprehensive framework for analyzing and using the valuable existing data and contributions to the field. The CSFs we identified were presented in Tables 2 and 3 while Figure 2 presented our conceptual model grouping these CSFs for ERP implementations in four inter-related categories: Administration, Project Management, ERP Software and Organization.

The main limitation in this study was the difficulty in conducting empirical research by accessing primary data due to justified confidentiality issues raised by private enterprises. Nevertheless, we agree with Finney and Corbett (2007) that exploring CSFs empirically from stakeholders' perspectives will provide valuable insights that will lead to more successful ERP implementations.

REFERENCES

Ahmad, M. M., & Cuenca, R. P. (2013). Critical success factors for ERP implementation in SMEs. *Robotics and Computer-integrated Manufacturing, 29*(3), 104–111. doi:10.1016/j.rcim.2012.04.019

Al-Mashari, M., Al-Mudimigh, A., & Zairi, M. (2003). Enterprise resource planning: Taxonomy of critical factors. *European Journal of Operational Research, 146*(2), 352–364. doi:10.1016/S0377-2217(02)00554-4

ALdayel, A. I., Aldayel, M. S., & Al-Mudimigh, A. S. (2011). The Critical Success Factors of ERP implementation in Higher Education in Saudi Arabia: A Case Study. *Journal of Information Technology & Economic Development, 2*(2).

Alimazighi, Z., & Bouhmadi, A. (2011) Adapting goal oriented approaches in requirement engineering of Inter-Organizational Information System. *Proceedings of Fifth International Conference on Research Challenges in Information Science*, 1-7. doi:10.1109/RCIS.2011.6006847

Amid, A., Moalagh, M., & Ravasan, A. Z. (2012). Identification and classification of ERP critical failure factors in Iranian industries. *Information Systems, 37*(3), 227–237. doi:10.1016/j.is.2011.10.010

Amoako-Gyampah, K. (2007). Perceived usefulness, user involvement and behavioral intention: An empirical study of ERP implementation. *Computers in Human Behavior, 23*(3), 1232–1248. doi:10.1016/j.chb.2004.12.002

Basoglu, N., Daim, T., & Kerimoglu, O. (2007). Organizational adoption of enterprise resource planning systems: A conceptual framework. *The Journal of High Technology Management Research, 18*(1), 73–97. doi:10.1016/j.hitech.2007.03.005

Bingi, P., Sharma, M. K., & Godla, J. K. (1999). Critical issues affecting an ERP implementation. *IS Management, 16*(3), 7–14.

Botta-Genoulaz, V., & Millet, P. A. (2005). A classification for better use of ERP systems. *Computers in Industry, 56*(6), 573–587. doi:10.1016/j.compind.2005.02.007

Bradley, J. (2008). Management based critical success factors in the implementation of enterprise resource planning systems. *International Journal of Accounting Information Systems, 9*(3), 175–200. doi:10.1016/j.accinf.2008.04.001

Brown, C., & Vessey, I. (1999, January). ERP implementation approaches: toward a contingency framework. In *Proceedings of the 20th international conference on Information Systems* (pp. 411-416). Association for Information Systems.

Daneva, M., & Wieringa, R. J. (2006). A requirements engineering framework for cross-organizational ERP systems. *Requirements Engineering, 11*(3), 194–204. doi:10.1007/s00766-006-0034-9

Davenport, T. H. (2000). *Mission critical: Realizing the promise of enterprise systems*. Harvard Business Press.

Deshmukh, A. (2006). *Digital accounting: The effects of the internet and ERP on accounting*. IGI Global. doi:10.4018/978-1-59140-738-6

Dezdar, S., & Ainin, S. (2011). The influence of organizational factors on successful ERP implementation. *Management Decision, 49*(6), 911–926. doi:10.1108/00251741111143603

Dezdar, S., & Sulaiman, A. (2009). Successful enterprise resource planning implementation: Taxonomy of critical factors. *Industrial Management & Data Systems, 109*(8), 1037–1052. doi:10.1108/02635570910991283

Eckartz, S., Katsma, C., & Daneva, M. (2010). Inter-organizational Business Case in ES Implementations: Exploring the Impact of Coordination Structures and Their Properties. *ENTERprise Information Systems: Communications in Computer and Information Science Series, 10*, 188–197. doi:10.1007/978-3-642-16419-4_19

Ehie, I. C., & Madsen, M. (2005). Identifying critical issues in enterprise resource planning (ERP) implementation. *Computers in Industry, 56*(6), 545–557. doi:10.1016/j.compind.2005.02.006

Finney, S., & Corbett, M. (2007). ERP implementation: A compilation and analysis of critical success factors. *Business Process Management Journal, 13*(3), 329–347. doi:10.1108/14637150710752272

Gajic, G., Stankovski, S., Ostojic, G., Tesic, Z., & Miladinovic, L. (2014). Method of evaluating the impact of ERP implementation critical success factors–a case study in oil and gas industries. *Enterprise Information Systems, 8*(1), 84–106. doi:10.1080/17517575.2012.690105

Garg, P., & Agarwal, D. (2014). Critical success factors for ERP implementation in a Fortis hospital: An empirical investigation. *Journal of Enterprise Information Management, 27*(4), 402–423. doi:10.1108/JEIM-06-2012-0027

Gargeya, V. B., & Brady, C. (2005). Success and failure factors of adopting SAP in ERP system implementation. *Business Process Management Journal, 11*(5), 501–516. doi:10.1108/14637150510619858

Gattiker, T. F., & Goodhue, D. L. (2004). Understanding the local-level costs and benefits of ERP through organizational information processing theory. *Information & Management, 41*(4), 431–443. doi:10.1016/S0378-7206(03)00082-X

Genete, L. D., & Tugui, A. (2008). From ERP Systems to Digital Accounting in Relations with Customers and Suppliers. *Selected Papers from the WSEAS Conferences in Spain September 2008*, 57-63.

Ghosh, S., & Skibniewski, M. J. (2010). Enterprise resource planning systems implementation as a complex project: a conceptual framework. *Journal of Business Economics and Management*, (4), 533-549.

Grabski, S. V., Leech, S. A., & Schmidt, P. J. (2011). A review of ERP research: A future agenda for accounting information systems. *Journal of Information Systems, 25*(1), 37–78. doi:10.2308/jis.2011.25.1.37

Hawking, P., Stein, A., & Foster, S. (2004, January). Revisiting ERP systems: benefit realization. In *System Sciences, 2004.Proceedings of the 37th Annual Hawaii International Conference on* (pp. 8-pp). IEEE.

Holland, C. P., & Light, B. (1999). A critical success factors model for ERP implementation. *IEEE Software, 16*(3), 30–36. doi:10.1109/52.765784

Jacobs, F. R. (2007). Enterprise resource planning (ERP)—A brief history. *Journal of Operations Management, 25*(2), 357–363. doi:10.1016/j.jom.2006.11.005

Kelle, P., & Akbulut, A. (2005). The role of ERP tools in supply chain information sharing, cooperation, and cost optimization. *International Journal of Production Economics*, *93*, 41–52. doi:10.1016/j.ijpe.2004.06.004

Klaus, H., Rosemann, M., & Gable, G. G. (2000). What is ERP? *Information Systems Frontiers*, *2*(2), 141–162. doi:10.1023/A:1026543906354

Kwak, Y. H., Park, J., Chung, B. Y., & Ghosh, S. (2012). Understanding end-users' acceptance of enterprise resource planning (ERP) system in project-based sectors. *Engineering Management. IEEE Transactions on*, *59*(2), 266–277.

Le Duc, M. (2014). Critical success factors for implementing ERP in the curriculum of university business education: A case study.*Proceedings of the 8th European Conference on Information Management and Evaluation, ECIME 2014*, 128-135.

Liu, P. L. (2011). Empirical study on influence of critical success factors on ERP knowledge management on management performance in high-tech industries in Taiwan. *Expert Systems with Applications*, *38*(8), 10696–10704. doi:10.1016/j.eswa.2011.02.045

Markus, M. L., & Tanis, C. (2000). The enterprise systems experience-from adoption to success. *Framing the domains of IT research: Glimpsing the future through the past, 173*, 207-173.

Mengistie, A. A., Heaton, D. P., & Rainforth, M. (2013). Analysis of the critical success factors for ERP systems implementation in U.S. federal offices. *Lecture Notes in Information Systems and Organisation*, *4*, 183–198. doi:10.1007/978-3-642-37021-2_15

Nah, F. F. H., Lau, J. L. S., & Kuang, J. (2001). Critical factors for successful implementation of enterprise systems. *Business Process Management Journal*, *7*(3), 285–296. doi:10.1108/14637150110392782

Ngai, E. W., Law, C. C., & Wat, F. K. (2008). Examining the critical success factors in the adoption of enterprise resource planning. *Computers in Industry*, *59*(6), 548–564. doi:10.1016/j.compind.2007.12.001

Pigni, F., Ravarini, A., Sciuto, D., Zanaboni, C. A., & Burn, J. (2005). Business Associations as Hubs of Inter-Organizational Information Systems for SMEs – The 2Cities Portal. In S. B. Eom (Ed.), *Inter-organizational Information Systems in the Internet Age* (pp. 134–168). doi:10.4018/978-1-59140-318-0.ch006

Somers, T. M., & Nelson, K. (2001, January). The impact of critical success factors across the stages of enterprise resource planning implementations. In *System Sciences, 2001.Proceedings of the 34th Annual Hawaii International Conference on*. IEEE. doi:10.1109/HICSS.2001.927129

Srivastava, M., & Gips, B. J. (2009). Chinese cultural implications for ERP implementation. *Journal of Technology Management & Innovation*, *4*(1), 105–113. doi:10.4067/S0718-27242009000100009

Sumner, M. (2000). Risk factors in enterprise-wide/ERP projects. *Journal of Information Technology*, *15*(4), 317–327. doi:10.1080/02683960010009079

Ullah, Z., Al-Mudimigh, A. S., Al-Ghamdi, A. A. M., & Saleem, F. (2013). Critical Success Factors of ERP Implementation at Higher Education Institutes: A Brief Case Study. International Information Institute Information, 16(10), 7369.

Umble, E. J., Haft, R. R., & Umble, M. M. (2003). Enterprise resource planning: Implementation procedures and critical success factors. *European Journal of Operational Research*, *146*(2), 241–257. doi:10.1016/S0377-2217(02)00547-7

Wagner, E. L., & Newell, S. (2004). Best for whom? The tension between best practice ERP packages and diverse epistemic cultures in a university context. *The Journal of Strategic Information Systems*, *13*(4), 305–328. doi:10.1016/j.jsis.2004.11.002

Zhang, Z., Lee, M. K., Huang, P., Zhang, L., & Huang, X. (2005). A framework of ERP systems implementation success in China: An empirical study. *International Journal of Production Economics*, *98*(1), 56–80. doi:10.1016/j.ijpe.2004.09.004

Zhu, Y., Li, Y., Wang, W., & Chen, J. (2010). What leads to post-implementation success of ERP? An empirical study of the Chinese retail industry. *International Journal of Information Management*, *30*(3), 265–276. doi:10.1016/j.ijinfomgt.2009.09.007

Ziemba, E., & Oblak, I. (2013, July). Critical success factors for ERP systems implementation in public administration. *Proceedings of the Informing Science and Information Technology Education Conference*, 1-19.

KEY TERMS AND DEFINITIONS

Business Process Reengineering: Restructuring business processes adjusted to the ERP system.

Change Management: Using change management tools to resolve conflicts and resistance problems which occur in ERP implementations.

Critical Success Factors (CSFs): A number of factors related with a wide arrange of issues like ERP project, top management, organization, information technologies and end users which enhance success in ERP implementations.

Customization: Modifications in ERP software according to existing business processes when necessary.

Effective Communication: Top management should provide effective communication with employees and other participants in ERP implementations.

Enterprise Resource Planning (ERP) Systems: Generic software packages providing digital business applications.

ERP Implementation: Installation process of ERP systems in organizations.

ERP Team: ERP implementation team constitutes of competent members from different departments.

Project Champion: Project champion performs crucial functions in ERP team like leadership, facilitation and marketing the ERP project to users.

Project Management: Project management strategies applied in ERP projects through detailed planning and control to avoid duration and budget overruns.

Steering Committee: A group of departmental and project managers enabling senior management to monitor project team decisions.

Vendor: Supplier of ERP system.

Chapter 7
Extending IMPLEMENT Framework for Enterprise Information Systems Implementation to Information System Innovation

Aparna Raman
Management Development Institute, India

D. P. Goyal
Management Development Institute, India

ABSTRACT

Enterprise Information systems implementation is one of the most challenging parts of IT strategy for an organization, since implementation brings in efficiency in the system and justifies the investments made. Therefore, it becomes increasingly important to study the perspectives of implementation to understand the current dynamics. The purpose of this paper is twofold, first is to explore the type of literature that exists in information system implementation and secondly to determine the research methodologies incorporated therein for the information system field's implementation in specific. The basic content analysis is done to review the articles on information system implementation. A total of 47 articles were selected from peer reviewed journals and conferences. The study was conducted to assess the methodology used, the strategies followed along with the issues and challenges faced in the implementation. It presents an arena of the studies done in information system implementation in past 20 years (typically 1993 to 2013). The IMPLEMENT framework has been proposed to synthesize the literature finding for smooth functioning of IS implementation process. The factors influencing the adoption of information system innovation are described. The comprehensive framework for information innovation process is developed. This framework is then mapped to IMPLEMENT framework. This study would encourage the practitioners in the information systems domain to improve upon their organizational capability and incorporate other best practices.

DOI: 10.4018/978-1-5225-2382-6.ch007

INTRODUCTION

Information system implementation involves the design of the framework and model, the management's role and strategies. The user's involvement in information system implementation is one of the critical aspects of information system since; it can point us to where the system can fail. Top management and training are the two most important organizational factors that are known to effect information system implementation (Hwang, Lin & Lin, 2012).

Information system implementation has been a pioneer study in the field of information systems. There has been literature on debate between the technical aspects vis-à-vis human behavioural aspects. Some authors (Keen & Scott-Morton 1978) mention that implementation is an intuitive skill and the best way to deal with implementation is to be technically competent. Whereas others (Hirschheim, 1985:158, Friedman & Cornford, 1989) mention that implementation depends on user involvement, how the prototyping is done, the information analysis done and the change agents. Implementation stage is one of the most risky stages of the information systems lifecycle. There is resistance from users and hence the role of team and the management becomes extremely important.

Some models that define IT implementation is diffusion models (Cooper & Zmud, 1990) which states that in a user community, it's an organizational effect that works towards diffusing the appropriate information technology. The other model is the Lewinian model which discusses implementation as a process of innovation and implementation brings in change for which unfreeze and freeze models would work to an extent. Pinto, J. & Millet I, 1999, mention that human processes and behavioural components are important for success of information systems. They also mention that how project prioritization, communication among people and techniques on planning and scheduling can help in dealing with the change control pressures and also deal with the system development lifecycle politics. Cross functional teams are the key according to them.

The previous studies included situational normativism philosophy (Shakun, 1975), process theory of implementation (Zand & Sorensen, 1975), theory based on user influence (Lucas, 1974), theory of implementation (Debrabander & Edstrom, 1977) and documentation as a success factor (Neal & Radnor, 1973). Some other studies are the paradigm of organization information system (Van Gigch & Le Moigne, 1990), idealized design methodology (R.L. Ackoff, 1981) and systematic enterprise theory (Eriksson, 2004). Kolb Frohman model of information system implementation was widely used in the seventies. It facilitated budget making process of the government.

This study lays its focus on core information systems implementation. Overall a diverse view is adopted by the researchers over the period of years. The earlier studies focused on the social technical aspect and organization bit as a whole, whereas, the dynamism of the environment is taken care in the recent studies.

OBJECTIVES OF THE STUDY

The major objectives of this study are:

1. To study the literature of the information system implementation and understand the main perspectives and findings by them.
2. To understand the research methodologies used by authors and understand what kind of research has been appreciated the most.
3. To understand what shape the future research can take from the existing research.
4. To understand how the research can be extended in context of information systems innovation.

RESEARCH METHODOLOGY

A simple content analysis was conducted on research articles and articles in international journals. Search was conducted using the search databases, Proquest, EBSCO, Emerald, INFORMS, JSTOR, IGIGLOBAL for finding articles on information systems implementation. A total of 47 articles were retrieved from various top journals are mentioned in the Table 1. The research paper was examined from

Table 1. Journals list

Sno.	Journals	No. of Studies (References)
1	Information Systems Research	1
2	International Journal of Accounting Information Systems	2
3	International Journal of Enterprise Information Systems	16
4	European Management Journal	1
5	International Journal of Information Management	4
6	Databases for advances in IS	1
7	BPM Journal	2
8	Information & Management	6
9	Journal of Management Information Systems	1
10	MIS Quarterly	2
11	Management Science	2
12	Journal of Strategic Information Systems	2
13	International Journal of Project Management	1
14	Administrative science quarterly	1
15	IT & People	1
16	Journal of achievement in MME	1
17	Journal of biomedical information	1
18	Scandinavian Journal of Management	1

the perspective of understanding the finding and the gaps and future recommendations. The assessment matrix was consolidated on the basis of research methodology used (See Table 7 and 8).

ANALYSIS OF INFORMATION SYSTEM IMPLEMENTATION STUDIES

Information system implementation literature ranges from information methodologies, organization change and structure, business process re-engineering and user satisfaction. (Boahene, 1999; Dawson, 2001; Groth, 1999; Larsen & Myers 1997). The studies analyzed below first touches upon the methodology and models and then strategy, management support, the success factors and implementation issues are studied further.

Model, Framework Development and Methodology in IS Implementation

Models and frameworks provide blueprints for information system implementation in most organizations. The applicability of the framework depends on case to case, but new theories are evolving out of base theories which indicate how the alignment of the implementation to the business goals is important to achieve success in information systems implementation. The main findings are that implementation should align with goals of the organization and corrective actions should be taken to make better implementation decisions. (Rita Kukafka et al., 2003, Hee woong Kim & Shan L Pan, 2006). Different approaches to study implementations have been considered such as frame based research, social representations approach and social work practice model. (Bijan Azad, Samer Faraj, 2011; Uri Gal, Nicholas Berente, 2008; Drake, Melinda Geremillo, 2000). Detailed research should be carried out on different approaches. Also, there exists scope for detailed research and the limitations related to case based research apply to the studies (See Table 2).

IS Implementation Strategy

The authors have considered different approaches and perspectives as important for the information system implementation. (MG Ward and D Bawden, 1997; Finn Borum, John K. Christiansen, 2006; Kai R. T. Larsen, 2003; James Y. L. et al., 1994; Joe Nandhakumar,2005, Muscatello & Chen, 2008). The impediments and challenges also further affect the IT implementation (Rong-Ruey Duh et.al, 2006; Uday Apte et al 1990). Detailed empirical study should be done on studies. The limitations of case studies exist in the studies involving detailed case studies. Longitudinal studies should be done in studies considering cross sectional view (See Table 3).

Management Support in IS Implementation

Managerial interaction, task interdependence and high quality external support is key links to successful IS implementation. (Randolph B et al, 1990; Rajeev Sharma et al, 2003; James Y. L. Thong et al, 1996). Continuous feedback and a great charismatic leadership styles elevate project performance (Linying Dong, 2008; Eric Wang et al, 2005). Longitudinal studies with sufficient sample size should be considered for further research in studies and detailed empirical analysis on research could be considered in studies (See Table 4).

Success Factors in IS Implementation

The critical success factors as a tool was devised by Rockart, 1979 to determine what an organization can do to succeed. Lai (2006) discussed the 26 critical success factors for FOCUS implementation models (which are business objective, rapid, supported, self directed). Further the five dimensions of Chinese culture and their dependence on CSF has been discussed. The implementation management techniques are a must for success (Bradley, 2008). The critical success factors are difficult to determine at the early stage of product lifecycle (Koh et al, 2011). The top management support, and other personal characteristic and competencies are significantly associated with the successful implementation of information systems (Aziz et al, 2011). Country wise study like for Malaysia, Slovenia, Tehran, Oman, Bahrain, Pakistan and China has been carried out (Aziz et al, 2011; Hinai et al, 2013; Khattak et al, 2013, Zarei et al, 2010; Sternad et al,2009; Kamhawi, 2007).Further research should be carried out in identifying and combining the critical success factors in studies in different cultures and scenarios. Also literature could be further explored for building strong theoretical base in studies (See Table 5).

IS Implementation Issues

Decision making and dynamic environment for technology, change resistance, individual information system expertise and training are the key issues in IS implementation (Pan et al, 2008; Beaumaster, 1999). The various factors that impact ERP implementation are: language, culture, politics, government regulations, management style, and labor skills and strategies can prevent IS issues. (Sheu et al, 2004; Mandal et al., 2003). Detailed empirical study should be done on studies. The limitations of case studies exist in the studies involving detailed case studies (See Table 6).

THE IMPLEMENT FRAMEWORK

The above literature synthesis leads us to a comprehensive framework which entails the factors that affect the information system implementation. Therefore, if the managers or the stakeholders would keep in mind the specific factors which needs to be kept in mind during the IS implementation then the implementation would emerge with lesser issues.

Figure 1 lists down the following *nine* factors.

Issue Diagnosing and Understanding

The issues related to language, culture, politics, government regulations, management style, system expertise, training and labor issues should be diagnosed, understood and mitigated. (Pan et al, 2008 ; Beaumaster, 1999, Sheu et al, 2004 & Mandal et al., 2003). Bramorski, 2003 further mentions that the organization needs to understand the pitfalls in the current scenario, including the slowness or dysfunctional factors, missing customer focus, deficiency in business structures and operation systems or IT systems. Further the customer expectations should be understood. The improvement opportunities must be understood. The future process visions, targets and goals must be set. Certain roadblocks such as difficulty in migration from old to new system, unavailability of skilled project people, turnover of key project persons, high costs of implementation, difficulty in project requirement estimation, resistance

Figure 1. IMPLEMENT framework

from staff, unclear strategic directions, knowledge gap between implementer and uses, coordination between functional groups, bugs in software's and support and training should be clearly diagnosed and understood (Kumar et al, 2003). Kim et al 2005 mention that the critical impediments to ERP implementation are human resources and capabilities, cross functional coordination, systems development, change management and organizational learning.

Measure Success Factors

The critical success factors should be measured at all stages of the implementation from the beginning to end to estimate what needs to be repeated and what needs to be curbed (Koh et al, 2011 & Aziz et al, 2011). A lot of studies focus on determining the critical success factors for enterprise information system implementations. Nour and Mouakket (2011) mention that success factor could be categorized according to the pre-implementation, main implementation and post implementation. The success factors could be based on change management, usability, information quality, resources, performance, strategic impact, maintenance, technical skill requirements, management commitment, process, culture, structure, IT infrastructure, reputation and service (Nour & Mouakket, 2011). Motwani et al, 2005 mention the classification of ERP literature on the basis of conceptual building and theory testing and further mention that the success factors for an organization could be strategic initiatives, learning capacity, cultural readiness, IT leveragability and knowledge sharing, network relationships, change management and process management.

Predictive Capability Development

The different factors of IS implementation influence each other and hence they should be studied in tandem. Also, the issues in information system implementation can be reversed (Kim et al 2006). Therefore predictive capability is a must to assess both the influence of factors as well as reversal of information system implementation. Developing organizational capabilities (Lee et al, 2007) and IT capabilities are extremely important to manage the enterprise information systems. Lee et al 2007, further mention that the training availability, technical expertise and knowledge levels aid in predictive capability development. The knowledge management including knowledge acquisition, knowledge application and sharing has an important role to play.

Launch Guidelines for IS Implementation

The clear guidelines for the IS implementation should be set at every milestone defined for the project. This would assist in the smooth movement of implementation process specially for mass implementation (Hansen et al, 1995). Boddy and Mcbeth (2000) mention that guidelines help in providing some consistency, hence similar grouping of them and then further working on the personal insights of the top management and the people working on the projects, help in providing significant difference.

Emerge with Strategies to Implement

The various strategies that need to be adopted during implementation should emerge out clearly. For eg: the user centered approach (Ward et al, 1997), perspectives (administrative, political and network) (Borum et al, 2006), Organizational power and intentionality (Larsen 2003), consultant vendor approach (Thong et al, 1994) and reusability based strategy (Apte et al, 1990) and more. Task interdependence plays an important role in management helping to implement enterprise information systems (Sharma & Yetton, 2003). Further the strategies that should affect the enterprise information system could be i) resource information ii) user involvement iii) organization analysis iv) anticipated changes in the environment v) solution to resistance during implementation vi) information technology as per business requirement vii) responsiveness and responsibility viii) clarity of documentation (Gottschalk, 1999).

Management Support

Feedback, leadership styles, size dependency, management rationality are some of the important aspects of the management support. The management support plays an important role for the project to take direction and also on decision making aspects. Top management beliefs and participation are said to have a great impact on assimilation of enterprise systems. Top management beliefs are the subjective psychological state of the top management whereas top management participation refers to the behaviour and actions performed for ERP assimilation (Liang et al, 2007).

Explore the Behavioural and Social Issues

The socio-cognitive processes, the behaviours and human issues and work practices (micro and macro) should be explored and remedial steps should be taken when required (Gal et al, 2008 & Drake et al,

2001). Motwani et al mention that the cooperative, interpersonal and group behaviour results in superior implementation and therefore, it becomes important to address the human resource management issues. The technology acceptance and the organizational culture, leadership and change issues should be dealt properly (Ke & Wei, 2008).

Needs and Goals Focus

The needs and goals focus are important for the developers involved in the IS implementation to achieve success (Kukafka et al., 2003). Brown, 1999 mention that explicit measurable activities are important to ensure knowledge transfer from partner to internal employees who are key to value chain as well as project success. Further process innovation with an aggressive time schedule and pilot phase in strategy are associated with initial project success.

Technology Understanding

The technology understanding is critical for IS implementation as it could help potentially in a smooth implementation process. Lack of technology understanding can pave way for issues uncalled for. The studies on technology acceptance including the perceived usefulness and perceived ease of use on behavioural intentions have concluded that communication and training help in technology acceptance (Gyampah, 2007). Technology understanding and acceptance play an important role in the resources and behavioural management.

EXTENDING THE IMPLEMENT FRAMEWORK TO INFORMATION SYSTEM INNOVATION

What is Information System Innovation?

Information technology has been continuously studied as a positive influence in creating market differentiation and competitive advantage (Porter and Millar, 1985). Information System Innovation (IS Innovation) can be defined as "*an architectural innovation originating in what they call the 'information technology base'*" (Lyytinen& Rose, 2003). Some of the examples of IS innovations are world wide web (Agarwal et al, 2000), EDI (Niederman, 1998), DBMS (Grover & Teng, 1992), DSS (Sauter, 1996), IT outsourcing (Loh, 1992), GSS (Chin et al, 1995) and teleconferencing (Grover et al, 1997). Davis (1986), mentioned different roles of organization in innovation which can be extended to information systems innovation: organization as user of innovation, inventor of innovation, both user and inventor of innovation, as a vehicle of innovation and the organization as innovation.

The information systems innovation studies have studied the different phenomenon of the innovations and discussed the various methodologies, the competencies, the processes, organizational alignment, types of innovation, the adoption factors, challenges and the different genres it is being applied in. The table below shows the different themes and the corresponding studies. The detailed studies and their impact are shown in the Table 9.

Factors Affecting the Overall Information Systems Innovation Process

The information systems innovation is a multi-stage process and it is predominantly affected by the level of IS investment in an organization (Kleis et al, 2012). The institutional factors such as regulation to govern supply push and demand pull approaches, account for the institutional interventions (King et al, 1994). Reality checks and promoting credibility are also other such instruments which contribute to innovative IT climate and further facilitate the process throughout (Watts et al, 2006).

Information Systems Investment

Investments reap benefits in case of IS innovations and traditionally innovation knowledge management, innovation production and external innovation collaboration contributes to knowledge production and further innovation output. (Kleis et al, 2012)

Institutional Factors

King et al. discuss that government authorities, international agencies, professional and trade industry organizations, research oriented higher education institute, trend setting corporations, the multinational corporations, the financial corporations, labour organizations and the religious organizations are the institutions influencing IT innovation. The influence and the regulation have also been discussed further.

Innovative IT Climate

The IT innovative climates in context of IT management has been studied earlier (Boynton et al, 1994). IT knowledge and absorptive capacity leads to further clear mission, planning commitment, sharing of the information and decision making. Certain other factors, like peer relation and networking, support and motivation are other factors which contribute to Innovative IT climate (Watts et al.2006)

IS Innovation Process

A five step process has been devised to understand IS innovation:

- **Creation of IS Innovation:** Literature exists in the architectural knowledge, community learning, IT based knowledge capabilities, technology, disruptive innovation systems, mindful front end innovations, which help in creation of IS innovation.
- **Organizing Vision:** Interpretation, legitimating and mobilization are three factors that contribute to organizing vision for an organization that confirms a need to adopt an IS innovation. (Swanson & Ram miller, 1997)
- **Adoption & Diffusion of IS Innovation:** There are numerous studies on adoption and diffusion of innovation (Jones et al (2001), Zmud (1982), Chatman (1986), Mustonen-Ollila et al (2003), Kamal (2006), Jeyraj et al (2006), Moore& Benbasat (1991), Grover et al (1997) and Gu et al (2012)). A list of constructs that affect IS innovation can be drawn from these studies.

- **IS Innovation Implementation:** Once, the adoption and diffusion of innovation takes place, IS implementation involves handling the barriers (strategic, structural, cultural and behavioural) (Bartoli et al, 2004) and further discussing, should there be an implementation delay, how is that handled.
- **Value to Organizations and Performance:** There have been studies which measure the IT affecting Innovation which further helps improve the firm's performance. Such studies will be taken into concern here. (Huang et al, 2005 & Ismail et al, 2012)

Extending IMPLEMENT Framework to Information System Innovation

The initiation of the Information Systems innovation takes place after analysis of *issue diagnosis* and understanding. This process starts with the pressure to change an existing system and therefore necessitates the creation of disruptive system. Further, based on the sense of urgency to make the change, and after understanding and *measuring success factors*, the vision can be organized. After coming to an agreement that the new solution can be implemented, the adoption process begins with *top management support* and *Predictive Capability Development*. The *behavioural and social issues* are also taken into consideration before implementation of the innovation.

The implementation of the information system innovation begins with *Launch Guidelines for IS implementation*. Further, good subsystem integration with *technological understanding* and full partnership helps in smooth implementation. The value to organizations and performance can be ensured mapping the performance to the need and goal focus of the innovation. Therefore the IMPLEMENT framework can be extended to the information system innovation.

Figure 2. Comprehensive information systems innovation framework

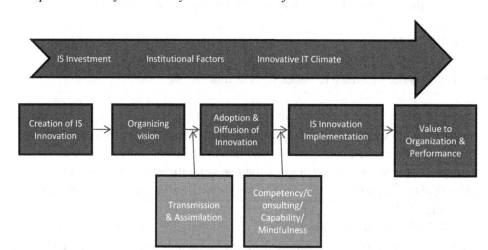

LIMITATIONS AND RECOMMENDATIONS

The limitation of this research is that the implementation is dependent on the basic assumptions that each industry follows. Therefore, most of the studies are case based and specific in nature. There is a huge scope for further empirical development and creating a guideline for practicing managers. Limited numbers of research articles were studied for a certain period and therefore, the scope is indicative of the papers published in the period and not exhaustive.

With the changing information technology, the adoption of implementation will differ according to the needs of the systems. It is always important to report the findings of the previous studies such that both the research and practitioner community benefit and there is further scope of expansion of knowledge. Therefore, a further this framework could be studied empirically which would indicate how the implementation will incorporate situational problem planning, evaluating and incorporating a better mechanism in itself. The basic theories will still apply to the core implementation issues.

CONCLUSION

Information system implementation is a vast arena, wherein implementation techniques vary from case per case but the basic theories and principle remains the same. The pragmatism provided by managers these days has a penultimate bearing on the success of the project. Further research should be conducted on the information systems implementation with an interpretivist approach. By applying the right mix to the socio technical system in the organization, we can bring in a lot of improvement in the implementation projects. This study would benefit the researchers, academicians as well as practitioners.

The researchers would find a comprehensive list of studies done to aid their progressive research path. The academicians would find the case based studies a guideline to teach the students the issues and other technicalities of implementation. The practitioners would get an overview of the different implementation scenarios, issues and they would find it convenient to make decisions based on these discussions. Therefore, this study will emerge as a link to guide a wide variety of audience. The framework would enable them to implement the information systems in a more systematic and penetrative way.

The study deduces a research framework which shows the IS innovation process from the creation of IS innovation till how it provides values to the organization and performance of the organizations. This framework can serve as an aid both to the researchers and the managers. The researchers can further prove this model empirically, whereas the managers can understand the IS innovation process in an organization. This IS innovation process framework is mapped to the IMPLEMENT framework to understand how innovation can be facilitated through implementation framework.

ACKNOWLEDGMENT

The authors would like to thank the anonymous reviewers and the editor for their insightful comments and suggestions. The authors would also like to thank the other authors who have provided understanding of their work.

REFERENCES

Ackoff, R. L. (1981). *Creating the Corporate Future*. New York: John Wiley & Sons.

Agarwal, R., & Karahanna, E. (2000). Time flies when youre having fun: Cognitive absorption and beliefs about information technology usage. *Management Information Systems Quarterly*, *24*(4), 665–694. doi:10.2307/3250951

Al-Hinai, H. S., Edwards, H. M., & Humphries, L. (2013). The Changing Importance of Critical Success Factors During ERP Implementation: An Empirical Study from Oman. *International Journal of Enterprise Information Systems*, *9*(3), 1–21. doi:10.4018/jeis.2013070101

Apte, U., Sankar, C. S., Thakur, M., & Turner, J. E. (1990, December). Reusability-Based Strategy for Development of Information Systems: Implementation Experience of a Bank. *Management Information Systems Quarterly*, *14*(4), 421–433. doi:10.2307/249791

Azad, B. & Faraz, S. (2011). Using signature matrix to analyze conflicting frames during the IS implementation process. *International Journal of Accounting Information Systems*.

Bartoli, A., & Phillipe, H. (2004). Managing change and innovation in IT implementation process. *Journal of Manufacturing Technology Management*, *15*(5), 5. doi:10.1108/17410380410540417

Beaumaster, S. (1999). *Information Technology Implementation Issues: An Analysis* (Thesis). Virginia Polytechnic Institute and State University.

Bhatti, T. R. (2005). Critical success factors for the implementation of enterprise resource planning (ERP): empirical validation. *The Second International Conference on Innovation in Information Technology (IIT'05)*.

Boahene, M. (1999). Information Systems Development Methodologies: Are you being served?. *Proceedings of the 10th Australasian Conference on Information Systems*, 88-99.

Bondarouk, T., & Rue, H. (2008). HRM systems for successful information technology implementation: Evidence from three case studies. *European Management Journal*, *26*(3), 153–165. doi:10.1016/j.emj.2008.02.001

Borum, F., & Christiansen, J. (2006). Actors and structure in IS projects: What makes implementation happen? *Scandinavian Journal of Management*, *22*(3), 213–237. doi:10.1016/j.scaman.2006.10.006

Boynton, A. C., Zmud, R. W., & Jacobs, G. C. (1994). The influence of IT management practice on IT use in large organizations. *Management Information Systems Quarterly*, *18*(3), 299–318. doi:10.2307/249620

Bradley, J. (2008). Management based critical success factors in the implementation of Enterprise Resource Planning systems. *International Journal of Accounting Information Systems*, 9(3), 175–200. doi:10.1016/j.accinf.2008.04.001

Bramorski, T. (2003, August). A Case Study of ERP Implementation Issues. *ICEB Second International Conference on Electronic Business*.

Brown, C., & Vessey, I. (1999, January). ERP implementation approaches: toward a contingency framework. In *Proceedings of the 20th international conference on Information Systems* (pp. 411-416). Association for Information Systems.

Chatzoglou, P., & Diamantidis, A. (2009, April). IT/IS implementation risks and their impact on firm performance. *International Journal of Information Management*, 29(2), 119–128. doi:10.1016/j.ijinfomgt.2008.04.008

Chin, W. W., Gopal, A., & Salisbury, W. D. (1997). Advancing the theory of adaptive structuration: The development of a scale to measure faithfulness of appropriation. *Information Systems Research*, 8(4), 342–367. doi:10.1287/isre.8.4.342

Cohen, J. E., Lemley, M. A., & Lemleyt, M. A. (2012). Patent Scope and Innovation in the Software Industry. *California Law Review, 89*(1), 1-57.

Cooper, R., & Zmud, R. (1990, February). Information Technology Implementation Research: A Technological Diffusion Approach. *Management Science*, 36(2), 123–139. doi:10.1287/mnsc.36.2.123

Davis, F. (1989). Perceived Usefulness, Perceived Ease of Use, and User Acceptance of Information Technology. *MIS Quarterly, 13*(3), 319-340.

Dawson, J., & Owens, J. (2008). Critical success factors in the chartering phase: A case study of an ERP implementation. *International Journal of Enterprise Information Systems*, 4(3), 9–24. doi:10.4018/jeis.2008070102

Dawson, P. (2001). Organizational Change. In B. Millett & R. Wiesner (Eds.), *Management and Organizational Behavior* (pp. 211–223). Brisbane: John Wiley.

Dhillon, G. (2004). Dimensions of power and IS implementation, Information & Management. *Information & Management*, 41(5), 635–644. doi:10.1016/j.im.2003.02.001

Dhillon, G. (2005). Gaining benefits from IS/IT implementation: Interpretations from case studies. *International Journal of Information Management*, 25(6), 502–515. doi:10.1016/j.ijinfomgt.2005.08.004

Dhillon, G., Caldeira, M., & Wenger, M. (2011). Intentionality and power interplay in IS implementation: The case of an asset management firm. *The Journal of Strategic Information Systems*, 20(4), 438–448. doi:10.1016/j.jsis.2011.09.003

Dong, L. (2008). Exploring the impact of top management support of enterprise systems implementations outcomes: Two cases. *Business Process Management Journal*, 14(2), 204–218. doi:10.1108/14637150810864934

Duh, R., Chow, C. W., & Chen, H. (2006). Strategy, IT applications for planning and control, and firm performance: The impact of impediments to IT implementation. *Information & Management, 43*(8), 939–949. doi:10.1016/j.im.2006.08.007

Erikkson. (2008). *Ten Guidelines for the Implementation of Information Systems: Research in Progress.* IRIS31: The 31st Information Systems Research Seminar in Scandinavia, Are, Sweden.

Farzaneh, M., Vanani, I. R., & Sohrabi, B. (2013). A Survey Study of Influential Factors in the Implementation of Enterprise Resource Planning Systems. *International Journal of Enterprise Information Systems, 9*(1), 76–96. doi:10.4018/jeis.2013010105

Friedman, A. L., & Cornford, D. C. (1989). *Computer Systems Development: History, Organization and Implementation.* Chichester, UK: Wiley.

Gal, U., & Berente, N. (2008). A social representations perspective on information systems implementation: Rethinking the concept of frames. *Information Technology & People, 21*(2), 133–154. doi:10.1108/09593840810881051

Geremillo, M. (2000). *Information systems implementation: A social worker's perspective.* University of Sarasota.

Groth, L. (1999). *Future Organizational Design: The Scope for the IT-based Enterprise.* Brisbane: John Wiley.

Grover, V., Fiedler, K., & Teng, J. (1997). Evidence on Swansons Empirical Model of Information Systems Tri-Core Innovation. *Information Systems Research, 8*(3), 273–287. doi:10.1287/isre.8.3.273

Grover, V., & Teng, J. T. (1992). An examination of DBMS adoption and success in American organizations. *Information & Management, 23*(5), 239–248. doi:10.1016/0378-7206(92)90055-K

Gu, V. C., Cao, Q., & Duan, W. (2012). Unified Modeling Language (UML) IT adoption — A holistic model of organizational capabilities perspective. *Decision Support Systems, 54*(1), 257–269. doi:10.1016/j.dss.2012.05.034

Haider, A. (2008). Information systems implementation in production environments. *Journal of Achievements in Materials and Manufacturing Engineering, 31*(2).

Hanafizadeh, P., Gholami, R., Dadbin, S., & Standage, N. (2010). The core critical success factors in implementation of enterprise resource planning systems. *International Journal of Enterprise Information Systems, 6*(2), 82–111. doi:10.4018/jeis.2010040105

Hansen, H. (1995). Conceptual framework and guidelines for the implementation of mass information systems. *Information & Management, 28*(2), 125–142. doi:10.1016/0378-7206(95)94021-4

Hirschheim, R. A. (1985). *Office Automation: A Social and Organizational Perspective.* Chichester, UK: Wiley.

Huang, C. J., & Liu, C. J. (2005). Exploration for the relationship between innovation, IT and performance. *Journal of Intellectual Capital, 6*(2), 237–252. doi:10.1108/14691930510592825

Hwang, M., & Lin, J. (2012). Organizational factors for successful implementation of information systems: Disentangling the effect of top management support and training. *Proceedings of the Southern Association for Information Systems Conference*.

Ismail, Z., Doostdar, S., & Harun, Z. (2012). Factors influencing the implementation of a safety management system for construction sites. *Safety Science*, *50*(3), 418–423. doi:10.1016/j.ssci.2011.10.001

Janssens, G., Kusters, R., & Heemstra, F. (2008). Sizing ERP implementation projects: An activity-based approach. *International Journal of Enterprise Information Systems*, *4*(3), 25–47. doi:10.4018/jeis.2008070103

Jeyaraj, A., Rottman, J. W., & Lacity, M. C. (2006). A review of the predictors, linkages, and biases in IT innovation adoption research. *Journal of Information Technology*, *21*(1), 1–23. doi:10.1057/palgrave.jit.2000056

Jones, N., Myers, M., & Jones, N. D. (2001). Assessing Three Theories of Information Systems Innovation: An Interpretive Case Study of a Funds Management Company. *PACIS 2001 Proceedings*.

Kai, R. T., & Larsen. (2003). Development of the Information Systems Implementation Research Method. *Proceedings of the 36th Hawaii International Conference on System Sciences*.

Kamal, M.M. (2006). IT innovation adoption in the government sector : identifying the critical success factors. *Journal of Enterprise Information Management, 19*(1/2).

Kamhawi, E. M. (2007). Critical factors for implementation success of ERP systems: An empirical investigation from Bahrain. *International Journal of Enterprise Information Systems*, *3*(2), 34–49. doi:10.4018/jeis.2007040103

Keen, P. G. W., & Scott-Morton, M. S. (1978). *Decision Support Systems: An Organizational Perspective*. Reading, MA: Addison-Wesley.

Khattak, M. A. O., She, Y., Memon, Z. A., Syed, N., Hussain, S., & Irfan, M. (2013). Investigating Critical Success Factors Affecting ERP Implementation in Chinese and Pakistani Enterprises. *International Journal of Enterprise Information Systems*, *9*(3), 39–76. doi:10.4018/jeis.2013070103

Kim, H., & Pan, S. (2006). Towards a Process Model of Information Systems Implementation: The Case of Customer Relationship Management, Database for Advances in Information Systems; Winter 2006. *The Data Base for Advances in Information Systems*, (Winter), 2006.

King, J. L., Gurbaxani, V., Kraemer, K. L., McFarlan, F. W., Raman, K. S., & Yap, C. S. (1994). Institutional factors in information technology innovation. *Information Systems Research*, *5*(2), 139–169. doi:10.1287/isre.5.2.139

Kini, R. B., & Basaviah, S. (2013). Critical Success Factors in the Implementation of Enterprise Resource Planning Systems in Small and Midsize Businesses: Microsoft Navision Implementation. *International Journal of Enterprise Information Systems*, *9*(1), 97–117. doi:10.4018/jeis.2013010106

Kleis, L., Chwelos, P., Ramirez, R. V., & Cockburn, I. (2012). Information Technology and Intangible Output: The Impact of IT Investment on Innovation Productivity. *Information Systems Research*, *23*(1), 42–59. doi:10.1287/isre.1100.0338

Kukafka, R., Johnson, S., & Allegrantec, J. (2003). Grounding a new information technology implementation framework in behavioral science: A systematic analysis of the literature on IT use. *Journal of Biomedical Informatics*, *36*(3), 218–227. doi:10.1016/j.jbi.2003.09.002 PMID:14615230

Lai, I. K. (2006). The critical success factors across ERP implementation models: An empirical study in China. *International Journal of Enterprise Information Systems*, *2*(3), 24–42. doi:10.4018/jeis.2006070103

Lai, V., & Mahapatra, R. (1997). Exploring the research in information technology implementation. *Information & Management*, *32*(4), 187–201. doi:10.1016/S0378-7206(97)00022-0

Larsen, M. A., & Myers, M. D. (1997). BPR Success or Failure? A Business Process Reengineering Project in the Financial Services Industry. *Proceedings of the 18th International Conference on Information Systems*, 367-382.

Loh, L., & Venkatraman, N. (1992). Determinants of information technology outsourcing: A cross-sectional analysis. *Journal of Management Information Systems*, *9*(1), 7–24. doi:10.1080/07421222.1992.11517945

Lucas, H. (1981). *Implementation: The Key to Successful Information Systems*. Columbia university press.

Lucas, H., et al. (1990). *Information Systems Implementation: Testing a Structural Model*. Alex Publishing Corporations.

Lyytinen, K., & Rose, G. M. (2003). Disruptive information system innovation: The case of internet computing. *Information Systems Journal*, *13*(4), 301–330. doi:10.1046/j.1365-2575.2003.00155.x

Marble, R. (2003). A system implementation study: Management commitment to project management. *Information & Management*, *41*(1), 111–123. doi:10.1016/S0378-7206(03)00031-4

Melvin, F. (1975, October). Policy Making Under Discontinuous Change: The Situational Normativism Approach. *Management Science*, *22*(2), 226–235. doi:10.1287/mnsc.22.2.226

Moore, G. C., & Benbasat, I. (1991). Development of an instrument to measure the perceptions of adopting an information technology innovation. *Information Systems Research*, *2*(3), 192–222. doi:10.1287/isre.2.3.192

Muscatello, J. R., & Chen, I. J. (2008). Enterprise resource planning (ERP) implementations: Theory and practice. *International Journal of Enterprise Information Systems*, *4*(1), 63–83. doi:10.4018/jeis.2008010105

Mustonen-Ollila, E., & Lyytinen, K. (2003). Why organizations adopt information system process innovations: A longitudinal study using Diffusion of Innovation theory. *Information Systems Journal*, *13*(3), 275–297. doi:10.1046/j.1365-2575.2003.00141.x

Nah, F. F. H., Lau, J. L. S., & Kuang, J. (2001). Critical factors for successful implementation of enterprise systems. *Business Process Management Journal*, *7*(3), 285–296. doi:10.1108/14637150110392782

Nandhakumar, J., Rossi, M., & Talvinen, J. (2005). The dynamics of contextual forces of ERP implementation. *The Journal of Strategic Information Systems*, *14*(2), 221–242. doi:10.1016/j.jsis.2005.04.002

Niederman, F. (2001). Global information systems and human resource management: A research agenda. *Global Perspective of Information Technology Management*, 30.

Nour, M. A., & Mouakket, S. (2011). A classification framework of critical success factors for erp systems implementation: A multi-stakeholder perspective. *International Journal of Enterprise Information Systems*, *7*(1), 56–71. doi:10.4018/jeis.2011010104

OReilly, C. A., & Chatman, J. (1986). Organizational commitment and psychological attachment: The effects of compliance, identification, and internalization on prosocial behavior. *The Journal of Applied Psychology*, *71*(3), 492–499. doi:10.1037/0021-9010.71.3.492

Pan, G., Hackney, R., & Pan, S. (2008). Information Systems implementation failure: Insights from prism. *International Journal of Information Management*, *28*(4), 259–269. doi:10.1016/j.ijinfomgt.2007.07.001

Pinto, J., & Millet, I. (1999). *Successful Information Systems Implementation*. Project Management Institute.

Porter, M. E., & Millar, V. E. (1985). *How information gives you competitive advantage*. Academic Press.

Sankar, C. S. (2010). Factors that improve ERP implementation strategies in an organization. *International Journal of Enterprise Information Systems*, *6*(2), 15–34. doi:10.4018/jeis.2010040102

Sauter, V. L. (2005). Competitive intelligence systems: Qualitative DSS for strategic decision making. *ACM SIGMIS Database*, *36*(2), 43–57. doi:10.1145/1066149.1066154

Sharma, R., & Yetton, P. (2003). The contingent effects of management support and task interdependence on successful information systems implementation. *MIS Quarterly, 27*(4), 533-555.

Sternad, S., Bobek, S., Dezelak, Z., & Lampret, A. (2009). Critical success factors (CSFs) for enterprise resource planning (ERP) solution implementation in SMEs: What does matter for business integration. *International Journal of Enterprise Information Systems*, *5*(3), 27–46. doi:10.4018/jeis.2009070103

Swanson, E. B., & Ramiller, N. C. (1997). The Organizing Vision in Information Systems Innovation. *Organization Science*, *8*(5), 458–474. doi:10.1287/orsc.8.5.458

Thong, J., Yap, C.-S., & Raman, K. S. (1994, Fall). Engagement of External Expertise in Information Systems Implementation. *Journal of Management Information Systems*, *11*(2), 209–231. doi:10.1080/07421222.1994.11518046

Thong, J., Yap, C.-S., & Raman, K. S. (1996, June). Yap Chee-sing & Raman K.S (1996), Top Management Support, External Expertise and Information Systems Implementation in Small Businesses. *Information Systems Research*, *7*(2), 248–267. doi:10.1287/isre.7.2.248

van Gigch, J. P., & Moigne, J. L. L. (1990). The design of an organization information system: Intelligent artifacts for complex organizations. *Information & Management*, *19*(5), 325–331. doi:10.1016/0378-7206(90)90046-K

Wang, E., Chou, H. W., & Jiang, J. (2005). The impacts of charismatic leadership style on team cohesiveness and overall performance during ERP implementation. *International Journal of Project Management*, *23*(3), 173–180. doi:10.1016/j.ijproman.2004.09.003

Ward, M. G., & Bawden, D. (1997). User-centered and User-sensitive Implementation of, and Training for, Information Systems: A Case Study. *International Journal of Information Management, 17*(I), 55–71. doi:10.1016/S0268-4012(96)00042-4

Watts, S., & Henderson, J. C. (2006). Innovative IT climates: CIO perspectives. *The Journal of Strategic Information Systems, 15*(2), 125–151. doi:10.1016/j.jsis.2005.08.001

Wenrich, K., & Ahmad, N. (2009). Lessons learned during a decade of ERP experience: A case study. *International Journal of Enterprise Information Systems, 5*(1), 55–73. doi:10.4018/jeis.2009010105

Yeoh, W., Koronios, A., & Gao, J. (2008). Managing the implementation of business intelligence systems: A critical success factors framework. *International Journal of Enterprise Information Systems, 4*(3), 79–94. doi:10.4018/jeis.2008070106

Zand, D. E., & Sorenson, R. E. (1975). Theory of change and the effective use of management science. *Administrative Science Quarterly, 20*(4), 532–545. doi:10.2307/2392021

Zantow. (2009). *Understanding user attitudes in IS implementation through technological frames An interpretive, ethnographic case study* (Thesis). Department of Management Birkbeck, University of London.

Zarei, B., & Naeli, M. (2010). Critical Success Factors in Enterprise Resource Planning Implementation A Case-Study Approach. *International Journal of Enterprise Information Systems, 6*(3), 48–58. doi:10.4018/jeis.2010070104

Zmud, R. W. (2012). Diffusion of Modern Software Practices: Influence of Centralization and Formalization. *Management Science, 28*(12), 1421–1431.

KEY TERMS AND DEFINITIONS

IMPLEMENT Framework: An information system implementation framework comprising of Issue Diagnosing and understanding, Measure success factors, Predictive Capability Development, Launch Guidelines for IS implementation, Emerge with Strategies to Implement, Management Support, Explore the behavioural and social issues, Needs and goals focus and Technology Understanding.

Implementation: The process of installing and maintaining a new system to establish a predefined goal.

Information Management Strategy: The guidance on how the information systems activities should be run by the organization is done by the information management strategies. The IM strategy analyzes the relationship of the IS strategy with the organizational strategies.

Information System Innovation: Information System Innovation (IS Innovation) can be defined as "an architectural innovation originating in what they call the 'information technology base."

Information Systems: An information system is a system which helps in organizing and analysing data. This makes it possible to answer questions and solve problems relevant to the mission of an organization.

Information Technology Strategy: The IT strategy mainly consists of the technology policies. It is a matrix of computing, communication, data and application and it mainly deals with the supply side of IS strategy.

Innovation Strategy: Organizations which find newer ways of doing business attract a lot of customer base and if the services match customer expectations then customer retention and loyalty can generate huge profits. One such example is of Amazon, where innovation was the core strategy.

Key Success Factors: Key Success Factors are those activities or business process and practices which are defined by the market and are critical to the vendor/customer relationship.

Project Management: Project management is the discipline of initiating, planning, executing, controlling, and closing the predefined goal established by a team (small or large) to achieve specific goals and meet specific success criteria.

Top Management Support: The degree to which senior management understands the importance of the IS function and the extent to which it is involved in IS activities.

APPENDIX

Table 2. Model, frameworks and methodology

S.no.	Authors	Objectives	Findings
1	Hans Robert Hansen (1995)	• Conceptual framework Development • Implementation guidelines for mass information systems	• Framework of mass IS implementation developed • decisions of mass IS: Where to offer mass IS and what is the right time to introduce mass IS
2	Rita Kukafka et al. (2003)	Conceptual framework Building used by health planners accounting for the multiple determinants of behavior.	The analysis indicates the necessity for developers to focus on the needs and goals of the organization.
3	Hee woong Kim, Shan L Pan (2006)	• explaining how factors of IS implementation influence each other • propose model as to how IS failures can be reversed.	• Predictive capability for IS implementation should be measured. • For any course in IS project, corrective action or alternate paths can be taken.
4	Bijan Azad, Samer Faraj (2011)	• Introduction to research methodology for situations where there is a diversity of stakeholder perspectives and • Where IS implementation research has difficulty accommodating the variety of views theoretically and empirically.	• Usage of frame elements signature matrix method IS research • The paper has contributed to the methodological aspects of frame-based research by highlighting a method of frames analysis
5	Uri Gal, Nicholas Berente (2008)	"social representations" approach to the study of socio-cognitive processes during information systems (IS) implementation as an alternative to the technological frames framework.	• Technological frames framework is overly technologically centered, temporally bounded, and individually focused, it may lead to symptomatic explanations of IS implementation. • Alternatively, using the theory of social representations can offer more fundamental causal explanations of IS implementation processes.
6	Drake, Melinda Geremillo (2000)	Examination of the difference between the two levels of social work practice: micro and macro as the difference relates to IT in social work. Development of model that could address the factors that affects IT in social work.	Information systems should be designed with micro users in mind and the system should be designed to address the work but not to fit the technology.
7	Nour and Mouakket (2011)	The authors investigate the current literature of CSF if ERP implementation and then map CSF to three different stages of ERP system project lifecycle.	The ERP CSF scheme as per the author included the stakeholders as end users, top management, IS department, project team, organization and vendor. They were assessed for different phases in ERP lifecycle. They are pre-implementation, main implementation, and post implementation.

Table 3. IS implementation strategy

S.No.	Authors	Objectives	Findings
1	MG Ward and D Bawden (1997)	To study the implementation of a new personal computer operating environment within an accountancy/consulting firm and investigating a 'user-sensitive' style of training	The easily understandable information to users at all stages of the implementation process is encouraged by the user-centred approach to implementation. Also training is important
2	Finn Borum,, John K. Christiansen (2006)	To analyze an attempt at change linked to efforts to introduce an information system.	The administrative perspective, the political perspective and the network perspective is identified in information system
3	Kai R. T. Larsen (2003)	The paper examines the use of ISI-RM on a single case study.	Different independent variables such as individual variables, task variables, structure variables, technology variables, process variables, interorganizational variables and environmental variables
4	Gurpreet S. Dhillon, Mário Caldeira, Mitchell R. Wenger (2011)	The interplay between intentionality of stakeholders, organizational power and information systems (IS) implementation in the context of an European firm implementing an Enterprise Resource Planning system is studied.	The study contributes to the literature by providing insights into the systemic nature of organizational power regarding IS implementations and how it relates to individual intentions
5	James Y. L. Thong, Chee-Sing Yap and K. S. Raman (1994)	This paper compares the information systems (IS) effectiveness of a group of small businesses that engage separate consultants and vendors (consultant- vendor approach) with that of another group of small businesses that engage vendors who also provide consultancy service (vendor-only approach)	The small businesses that adopt the vendor-only approach have more effective information systems than small businesses that adopt the consultant-vendor approach
6	Rong-Ruey Duh, Chee W. Chow, Hueiling Chen (2006)	To examine the association among strategy, the extent of IT applications to 12 planning and control functions, and firm performance.	The relationship between strategy and the extent of IT applications, and between the latter and firm performance were both stronger when the level of impediments to IT implementation was low.
7	Uday Apte, Chetan S. Sankar, Meru Thakur, Joel E. Turner (1990)	This study describes the experience of a large bank in designing and implementing an information systems strategy that is based on the concept Of reusability.	The major challenges in implementing the reusability-based strategy are managerial, not technical.

continued on next page

Table 3. Continued

S.No.	Authors	Objectives	Findings
8	Joe Nandhakumar, Matti Rossi, Jari Talvinen (2005)	To explore the process of a large-scale ERP implementation project and the contextual issues that shaped the process	This paper finds that by taking account of managers' intentions, the technology affordance and the power/cultural context (social structure), we can explain the triggers of technology drift associated with ERP system, as well as the consequences of these drifts.
9	Janssens, G., Kusters, R., & Heemstra, F. (2008)	The research aims to define a metric that can define the size of ERP project based on predicting the effort required to complete an ERP project. 21 logical clusters have been derived from 405 ERP implementation activities.	The clusters were grouped under selection, project configuration, project management, organizational and system design, configuration and installation, customization, infrastructure, reorganization, system implementation, Training, Set up maintenance, training and set up maintenance.
10	Sankar, C. S. (2010)	The research aims to study a list of factors that could improve ERP implementations	The strategic factors were identified as large resource commitment to project, adoption of corporate standards that promote process harmonization, making decisions that are irreversible and top management support.
11	Muscatello, J. R., & Chen, I. J. (2008)	The research aims to provide fresh insights into current practices of ERP implementation	The strategic initiatives such as decision making at cross functional level along with executive commitment, human resources, project management, IT, business process, training, project support and communication yields results.

Table 4. Management support

S.no.	Authors	Objectives	Findings
1	Robert P. Marble (2003)	To compare ERP initiatives and experiences as implemented by manufacturing industry	The companies of different sizes approach ERP implementations differently across a range of issues.
2	Randolph B. Cooper and Robert W. Zmud (1990)	This paper studies the interaction of managerial tasks with the information technology and the resulting effect on the adoption and infusion of that technology.	The identification of the importance of positioning managerial Rationality appropriately in the IT implementation research.
3	James Y. L. Thong, Chee-Sing Yap and K. S. Raman(1996)	To reexamine the role of top management support in IS implementation in small businesses.	While top management support is essential for IS effectiveness, high quality external IS expertise is even more critical for small businesses operating in an environment of resource poverty.
4	Mark I. Hwang,Cindy T. Lin,Jerry W. Lin (2012)	To investigate different models of top management support and training using data collected from an extensive list of prior studies.	Although top management support and training have generally been recognized as critical success factors, their positive effects are not always borne out in empirical data.
5	Rajeev Sharma, Phillip yetton (2003)	The effect of management support on implementation success	The effect of management support on implementation success is a positive function of task interdependence. This study has identified task Interdependence as a key variable that differentiates between implementation contexts.
6	Linying Dong (2008)	To compare the applicability of the three perspectives to enrich the understanding of TMS under the context of enterprise systems (ES) implementation.	Top managers need to constantly obtain feedback from users, and adjust their supportive actions and the level of these supportive actions accordingly.
7	Eric Wang, Huey-Wen Chou, James Jiang (2005)	The purpose of this study is to examine the influence of project managers charismatic leadership styles on project teams cohesiveness and thus the teams overall performance during ERP implementation in Taiwan.	ERP project leaders charismatic leadership style significantly influences the level of team cohesiveness, which, in turn, affects the overall project team performance

Table 5. Success factors in IS implementation

	Authors	Objectives	Findings
1	Joseph Bradley (2008)	To examine critical success factors for implementing Enterprise Resource Planning systems using the framework of classical management theory.	Implementation management techniques used at successful firms, but used less or not at all at unsuccessful firms.
2	S.C.L. Koh, A. Gunasekaran, T. Goodman (2011)	The aim of this research is to capitalize on the opportunities presented by gaps in the existing literature on ERPII. The research aims to gather primary evidence from all four respondent types and compare and contrast these outlooks against existing literature where possible.	The results did not find any relationships between ERPII CSFs and the four research perspectives. This underlines the difficulty in distinguishing ERPII CSFs at this early stage in its product lifecycle.
3	Sangjae Lee, Gyoo Gun Lim (2003)	The main purpose is to study how partnership attributes affect EDI implementation and performance.	Companies that plan to adopt EDI can decide whether their partner relationship is appropriate for EDI implementation.
4	Aziz, Nur Mardhiyah and Salleh,Hafez (2011)	This research paper seeks to identify the CSFs that influence the successful implementation of IT/IS in construction industry in Malaysia.	The results of this study reveal that top management support, and other personal characteristic and competencies are significantly associated with the successful implementations of IT/IS.
5	Hanafizadeh, P., Gholami, R., Dadbin, S., & Standage, N. (2010)	This research identifies the core critical success factors, by studying 62 papers using content analysis and entropy method.	Five companies were reviewed to reinforce the critical success factors. The organization culture has a major impact on the overall outcome.
6	Lai, I. K. (2006)	This research aims to identify the key factors across ERP implementation models. The study is conducted in two phases: A questionnaire survey among experienced ERP consultants and interview to examine the importance of these factors.	The results suggest that the implementation is more successful if the implementation challenges and leverages are addressed.
7	Al-Hinai, H. S., Edwards, H. M., & Humphries, L. (2013).	This research aims to study the critical success factors in ERP implementation in Oman. Four Hypothesis were suggested. Individual CSF's vary in importance across ERP implementation lifecycle. Secondly, number of the critical success factors that are important increases across ERP implementation lifecycle. Thirdly, categories of CSF vary in importance across ERP implementation lifecycle. Finally, technical CSF's are of less importance than other CSF's for successful ERP implementation.	The three hypotheses were proved true by the study and the last hypothesis was rejected.
8	Yeoh, W., Koronios, A., & Gao, J. (2008)	Delphi Method, three rounds of study with 15 BI experts. The CSF are committed management support and sponsorship, business user-oriented change management, clear business vision and well-established case, business-driven methodology and project management, business-centric championship and balanced project team composition, strategic and extensible technical framework, and sustainable data quality and governance framework.	Trend of multidimensional factors contributing towards business intelligence was recognized.
9	Nah, F. F. H., Lau, J. L. S., & Kuang, J. (2001)	A process theory approach (Markus & Tannis, 2000) who identified four phases in ERP lifecycle: chartering, project, shakedown, upward and downward and further classified the CSF based on those phases.	11 CSF were identified. ERP teamwork and composition, top management support, business plan and vision, project management, project champion, appropriate business and legacy systems, change management program and culture, business process re-engineering and minimum customization, software development, testing and troubleshooting and monitoring and evaluation of performance.
10	Farzaneh, M., Vanani, I. R., & Sohrabi, B. (2013)	The authors aim to study a list of potential success factors of ERP which are identified critical and complementary to ERP projects.	The critical success factors were divided into social factors (project management, employee, organization factors and vendor capability), Technical factor (Functional and non functional requirements), and intellectual; factors (requirement management, change management and environment)

continued on next page

Table 5. Continued

	Authors	Objectives	Findings
11	Khattak, M. A. O., She, Y., Memon, Z. A., Syed, N., Hussain, S., & Irfan, M. (2013)	The CSF of projects are identified by validating responses from 12 organizations using questionnaire survey approach and comparison is done for China and Pakistani enterprises	Quality and quantity of training and education of personnel/users, role and effectiveness of management in reducing the users' resistance, use of steering committee for control purpose, top management support or involvement, clearly specified goals/objectives/scope regarding ERP system, ease of system's use and users' acceptance, vendor's support, project management, effective communication among the organizational members and a balanced team for ERP implementation are practically considered by the successful enterprises in China
12	Dawson, J., & Owens, J. (2008)	The research aims at finding the factors resulting in failure of ERP at company X in chartering phase of development.	The factors identified are project champion, project management, business vision and, top management support, ERP team and composition, effective communication, appropriate business and legacy systems, commitment to change and a vanilla ERP approach
13	Kini, R. B., & Basaviah, S. (2013)	The research aims to study CSF of various ERP implementation and delve into real life experiences of SMB who have installed Microsoft Dynamics Navision (NAV)	In Bahrain, the user did not find top management support, training and change management impactful in project success, whereas organization size, internal IT capabilities, and competitive pressure significantly influence ERP implementation.
14	Zarei, B., & Naeli, M. (2010)	The research aims to study the CSF from a case study involving Esfahan Steel company, which started ERP implementation in 2002.	Five CSF have been studied in detail: Project Management, Top management Support, Business Process Re-engineering, change management and Training
15	Sternad, S., Bobek, S., Dezelak, Z., & Lampret, A. (2009)	The research aims to survey SME's in Slovenia and pay attention to strategies, methods and CSF from SME point of view.	Clear goals, objectives, scope and planning; project team competence and organization and top management support and involvement were found as the most important CSF for the SME's in Slovenia
16	Kamhawi, E. M. (2007)	The research aims to study CSF for ERP in a developing country, Bahrain	Project planning, organizational resistance, and ease of use had impact, whereas no significant impact was found on top-management support, technical fit, training, competitive pressure, and strategic fit on both project and business success

Table 6. IS implementation issues

	Authors	Objectives	Findings
1	Gary Pan, Ray Hackney,, Shan L. Pan(2008)	To diagnose the issues surrounding IS development and devise useful management strategies for any future system implementation	Sequences of decision mistakes may accelerate to project failure
2	Suzanne Beaumaster(1999)	To study issues facing local government executives with regard to IT implementation	Issues identified were: Training · Rapidly Changing Technology · Resistance to Change · Individual IT Expertise
3	Purnendu Mandal, A. Gunasekaran (2003)	To study: A) specific information needs at the operational and managerial levels for various functional areas B) How will the proposed ERP system integrate with the existing information systems C) What is the schedule for adaptation of the new system?	It was found that repair was not cost effective and replacement was the only option. Success of SAP was due to closely following pre-implementation, implementation, and post-implementation strategies
4	Chwen Sheu; Bongsug Chae, Chen-Lung Yang(2004)	The primary purpose was to investigate the dimensions of national differences and how they select ERP implementation practices across nations.	Findings suggest that language, culture, politics, government regulations, management style, and labor skills impact various ERP implementation practices at different countries.
5	Wenrich, K., & Ahmad, N. (2009)	This paper aims at positive and negative consequences of decision making during a decade of ERP experience	The behaviours to avoid are mentioned as categorizing ERP implementation as an IT exercise and source code customization. The impediments to success are mentioned as inconsistent requirement, understaffing project teams, expecting to move in identical manner and capabilities management.

Table 7. Assessment matrix of IS implementation research

S.No.	Authors	Qualitative (Case Based or Interviews)	Quantitative	User Focus	Extensive Literature Review
	**Model, Framework Development and Methodology**				
1.	Hans Robert Hansen (1995)		✓		
2.	Rita Kukafka et al. (2003)	✓		✓	
3.	Hee woong Kim, Shan L Pan (2006)	✓			
4.	Bijan Azad, Samer Faraj (2011)	✓			
5.	Uri Gal, Nicholas Berente (2008)				✓
6.	Drake, Melinda Geremillo (2000)		✓	✓	✓
7.	Nour and Mouakket (2011)			✓	✓
	**Management Support**				
8.	Robert P. Marble (2003)		✓	✓	
9.	Randolph B. Cooper and Robert W. Zmud (1990)		✓	✓	
10.	James Y. L. Thong, Chee-Sing Yap and K. S. Raman(1996)		✓	✓	
11.	Mark I. Hwang,Cindy T. Lin,Jerry W. Lin (2012)		✓	✓	
12.	Rajeev Sharma, Phillip yetton (2003)		✓	✓	✓
13.	Linying Dong (2008)	✓		✓	
14.	Eric Wang, Huey-Wen Chou, James Jiang (2005)		✓		
	**Success Factors in IS Implementation**				
15.	Joseph Bradley (2008)	✓		✓	✓
16.	S.C.L. Koh, A. Gunasekaran, T. Goodman (2011)	✓		✓	✓
17.	Sangjae Lee, Gyoo Gun Lim (2003)		✓	✓	✓
18.	Aziz, Nur Mardhiyah and Salleh,Hafez (2011)	✓		✓	✓
19.	Hanafizadeh, P., Gholami, R., Dadbin, S., & Standage, N. (2010)		✓	✓	✓
20.	Lai, I. K. (2006)	✓		✓	
21.	Al-Hinai, H. S., Edwards, H. M., & Humphries, L. (2013).		✓		
22.	Yeoh, W., Koronios, A., & Gao, J. (2008)	✓	✓		
23.	Nah, F. F. H., Lau, J. L. S., & Kuang, J. (2001)				✓
24.	Farzaneh, M., Vanani, I. R., & Sohrabi, B. (2013)		✓		
25.	Khattak, M. A. O., She, Y., Memon, Z. A., Syed, N., Hussain, S., & Irfan, M. (2013)	✓			
26.	Dawson, J., & Owens, J. (2008)	✓			

continued on next page

Extending IMPLEMENT Framework

Table 7. Continued

	Model, Framework Development and Methodology				
27.	Kini, R. B., & Basaviah, S. (2013)				✓
28.	Zarei, B., & Naeli, M. (2010)	✓			
29.	Sternad, S., Bobek, S., Dezelak, Z., & Lampret, A. (2009)		✓		
30.	Kamhawi, E. M. (2007)		✓		
	IS Implementation Strategy				
31.	MG Ward and D Bawden (1997)	✓		✓	
32.	Finn Borum,, John K. Christiansen (2006)	✓		✓	✓
33.	Kai R. T. Larsen (2003)				✓
34.	Gurpreet S. Dhillon, Mário Caldeira, Mitchell R. Wenger (2011)	✓		✓	✓
35.	James Y. L. Thong, Chee-Sing Yap and K. S. Raman (1994)		✓	✓	✓
36.	Rong-Ruey Duh, Chee W. Chow, Hueiling Chen (2006)		✓	✓	✓
37.	Uday Apte, Chetan S. Sankar, Meru Thakur, Joel E. Turner (1990)		✓		✓
38.	Joe Nandhakumar, Matti Rossi, Jari Talvinen (2005)	✓			
39.	Janssens, G., Kusters, R., & Heemstra, F. (2008)				✓
40.	Sankar, C. S. (2010)	✓			
41.	Muscatello, J. R., & Chen, I. J. (2008)		✓		
	IS Implementation Issues				
42.	Gary Pan, Ray Hackney,, Shan L. Pan(2008)	✓			✓
43.	Suzanne Beaumaster(1999)	✓			✓
44.	Purnendu Mandal, A. Gunasekaran (2003)	✓			
45.	Chwen Sheu; Bongsug Chae, Chen-Lung Yang(2004)	✓		✓	✓
46.	Harold G. Levine and Don Rossmoore (1993)	✓			
47.	Wenrich, K., & Ahmad, N. (2009)	✓		✓	

Table 8. Research methodology matrix

Methodology	Sr. number of articles studied	Total Items
Qualitative (Case Based or interview)	2,3,4,13,15,16,18,20,22,25,28,31,32,34,38,40, 42,43,44,45,46,47	22
Quantitative	1,6,8,9,10,11,12,13,14,17,19,21,22,24,29,30,35,36,37,41	20
User focus	2,6,7,8,9,10,11,12,13,15,16,17,18,19,20, 31,32,34,35,36,45,47	22
Extensive Literature Review	5,6,7,12,15,16,17,18,19, 23,27,32,33,34,35,36,37,39,42,43, 45	21

Table 9. Themes in the information systems innovation studies

Themes in IS studies	Subthemes and Authors
Methodologies	• Design Science (Wastell et,al., 2009) • Going Beyond dominant paradigm of IS research (Fichman, 2004)
Competencies	• Architectural Knowledge (Andersson et al., 2008) • Consultancies and Capabilities (E. Burton Swanson, 2010) • Competitive Intelligence (Nemutanzhela & Iyamu, 2011) • Innovating Mindfully (E. Burton Swanson and Neil C. Ramiller, 2004) • Influence of IS competencies on Process Innovation (Monideepa Tarafdar a, Steven R. Gordon, 2007) • Manager's guide to innovation waves (E. Burton Swanson, 2012) • IT Investment on Innovation Productivity (Kleis, L., Chwelos, P., Ramirez, R. V., & Cockburn, I., 2012)
Processes	• Innovation in Information Infrastructures (Bendik Bygstad, 2010) • Innovation and Knowledge Creation (Silvio Popadiuka,Chun Wei Choob. 2006) • Managing change and innovation in IT implementation process (Bartoli, A., & Hermel, P., 2004) • Swanson's Tri-Core Model of Information Systems Innovation (Grover, V., Fiedler, K., & Teng, J., 1997) • IT-intensive value innovation in the electronic economy (Sawy, El et. al, 1999) • Embedding new information technology artifacts into innovative design practices (Baxter et. al, 2010) • Continuous Innovation Through IT-Enabled Knowledge Capabilities (Joshi et al, 2010)
Organizational Alignment	• Community Learning (Wang et al, 2009) • Deploying IT for organizational Innovation (Jaka Lindic et al, 2011) • Centralization and Formalization (Zmud, 1982) • Relation between Innovation, IT and performance (Huang, Cheng Jen;Liu, Chun Ju, 2005) • IT Innovation in SME's (Dibrell, Clay;Davis, Peter S;Craig, Justin, 2008) • Innovative IT Climates (Stephanie Watts, John C. Henderson, 2006) • Institutional Factors in IT innovation (John Leslie King, Vijay Gurbaxani, Kenneth L. Kraemer, F. Warren McFarlan, K. S.Raman and C. S. Yap, 1994) • Institutional Influences on IS security Innovation (Carol Hsu, Jae-Nam Lee,Detmar W. Straub,2012) • Organizing Vision for IS innovation (Swanson, E. B., & Ramiller, N. C., 1997) • Measurement of IT related organizational innovation (Fichman, R. G., 2001) • Organizational mechanisms for enhancing user innovation in information technology (Nambisan, S., Agarwal, R., & Tanniru, M., 1999)
Types of Innovation	• Disruptive Innovation (Kalle Lyytinen & Gregory M. Rose, 2003) • Technological Innovation (Kelly & Kranzberg, 1978) • Process Innovation (Davenport, 2013) • Market Facing Innovation (Vargo et al, 2008)
Adoption Factors	• Adoption of IS process Innovation (Erja Mustonen-Ollila & Kalle Lyytinen, 2003) • predictors, linkages, and biases in IT innovation adoption research (Anand Jeyaraj, Joseph W Rottman, Mary C Lacity, 2006) • Measure the Perceptions of Adopting an Information Technology Innovation (Moore, G. C., & Benbasat, I., 1991) • SMEs & IS innovations adoption (Ramdani et al., 2007) • IT adoption — A holistic model of organizational capabilities perspective (Gu et al, 2012)
Challenges	• Challenges in front-end of innovation (Lea Hannola & Paivi Ovaska, 2011) • Organizational Challenges for innovation of IT systems (Chandan, H. C., & Urhuogo, I., 2012) • Organizational challenges for innovation in information systems (Chandan et al, 2012) • Reactions to Implementation Delays in IS innovation (Livingstone et al, 2002)
Genres	• IT Enabled Innovation as a paradigm (Colin Ashursta, Alison Freerb, Jessica Ekdahlc, Chris Gibbons, 2012) • Supply chain Management (Kim, Daekwan; Cavusgil, S Tamer;Calantone, Roger J, 2006) • Environmental Sustainability (Nigel P. Melville, 2010) • IT innovation adoption in government sector (Kamal, M M, 2006) • Information Systems Innovation in the Humanitarian Sector (Tsuime, 2011)

Table 10. List of studies on information systems innovations

Sno.	Studies	Objective	Type	Findings	Implication
1.	Design Science in IS innovation (Wastell et al., 2009)	to argue the case of design science adoption in IS innovation	Laboratory Experimental Study	Design science should draw more on the proven methods of "good design" to create its own praxis. Ecologically designed feedback, embodying a strong mapping between task goals and system status, produces superior task Performance. Second, that predictive decision aids provide clear benefits over other forms of user support, such as advisory systems	This study takes a different approach of practical adoption of technology with knowledge, which is different from the inherent behavorial studies on innovation.
2.	Architectural knowledge in inter-organizational IT innovation (Andersson et al., 2008)	front-end process of inter-organizational IT innovation theoretical model of architectural knowledge development in inter-organizational IT innovation	Action Research	The four dimensions are technology capability awareness, Use context sensitivity, business model understanding, and boundary-spanning competence.	
3.	Community learning in information technology innovation (Wang et al, 2009)	The learning cycle model is extended using the IT innovation literature. The dependence of the dependence of community learning on organizational Learning is then measured empirically.	Literature Review: Discourse Analysis	First, it initiates discussion about the possibility of learning at a level that transcends and encompasses the organizational level. Second, we promote learning-about as the complement of the more familiar learning-by-doing. Learning-about is crucial in the diffusion and adoption of IT innovations, because it is the means by which organizations tap into and make use of the knowledge embedded in the community discourse. Third, the paper continues the development and application of work on the general characterization of knowledge in IT innovation, specifically the distinctions among know-what, know-why, and know-how.	
4.	Consultancies and capabilities in innovating with IT E. Burton Swanson (2010)	examine the consultancy's capabilities and contributions both to the client (within an engagement) and to the broader support of the innovation (across and beyond engagements).	Literature review	Consulting Specializations: business strategy, technology assessment, business process improvement, systems integration, business support services	
5.	Deploying information technologies for organizational innovation: Lessons from case studies Jaka Lindic et al (2011)	how leading organizations are using emerging technologies to enable novel forms of ideation that can radically increase the sheer volume of ideas they explore. In	Case Study	Firstly, research is needed that explores how we might better engage users in the design of creative technologies to solve local innovation challenges. Second, research is needed to systematically evaluate the costs and benefits of technologies as they pertain to innovation. Third, research is needed on the actual design process, especially how are emergent technical solutions, to address challenges with managing ideas within the organization.	

continued on next page

Table 10. Continued

Sno.	Studies	Objective	Type	Findings	Implication
6.	Diffusion of Modern Software Practices: Influence of Centralization and Formalization (Zmud, 1982)	a study which examines the influence of centralization and formaliza-tion on organizational innovation	Survey method	necessity of tightly bounding the scope of variables, such as centralization and formalization, whose operationalization is dependent on the organizational locations of the individuals whose behavior is being influenced	
7.	Disruptive information system innovation: the case of internet computing(Kalle Lyytinen* & Gregory M. Rose, 2003)	how modalities of applying ICT technologies in their form and scope exhibit radical breaks, which are introduced herein as 'disruptive IS innovations'.	Literature based	Quad-core model of IS innovation. First, on a theoretical plane, we formulate the concept of a disruptive IS innovation and illustrate its applicability by analysing internet computing and its impact on the IS field. Second, we recommend expanding IS innovation studies from studying instances of IS innovation to the study of innovation types and their interactions. Third, we expand Swanson's (1994) innovation model in order that the resulting model is more Suitable to analyzing long-term changes in the IS field. IT innovation sets (IT base, systems development, services)	Managers and ISD specialists can use the disruptive IS innovation model to evaluate to what extent they should organize and plan for the inevitable change ('the wave') that is going to occur next in light of risks, benefits and opportunity costs.
8.	A Framework for Enhancing the Information Systems Innovation: Using Competitive Intelligences (Nemutanzhela& Iyamu, 2011)	This study was conducted with the primary aim to understand the impact of Competitive Intelligence (CI) on Information systems (IS) innovation products and services in organisations	Case Study Method	Knowledge sharing is critical to Information System Innovation in the organisation that deploys it, making it very useful for competitive advantage. The study helps managers to gain better understanding of how knowledge sharing influences products and services in the organisations.	
9.	Exploration for the relationship between innovation, IT and performance Huang, Cheng Jen;Liu, Chun Ju (2005)	This study aims to ask two important research questions: " DO the investments of innovation capital and information technology (IT) capital have a non linear relationship with firm performance ? and "Does the interaction between innovation capital and IT capital have synergy effects on firm performance>	Multiple regression models	Innovation capital has a non linear relationship (inverted U shape) with firm performance and IT capital has no significant impact on firm performance.	
10.	Exploring IT-enabled innovation: A new paradigm? Colin Ashursta, Alison Freerb, Jessica Ekdahlc, Chris Gibbonsc (2012)	This paper reports on findings from 10 case studies of successful IT-enabled innovation covering a wide range of organizations and projects.	Case Study	third IT paradigm, different from previous paradigms of technology implementation and a planned approach to benefits realization. Further work is required to explore this paradigm and how organizations can make the 'paradigm shift' required.	

continued on next page

Table 10. Continued

Sno.	Studies	Objective	Type	Findings	Implication
11.	Challenging front-end-of-innovation in information systems (2011) Lea Hannola & Paivi Ovaska	The objective of the IS development project is to develop and modify systems that satisfy customers and users need on schedule and within a budget	Literature Analysis	A conceptual model discloses the challenges in front end, such as inadequate processes, shortage of resources, poor communications and changing understanding of requirements. As a practical contribution, IS organizations should focus more on agile and innovative approaches concerning the requirements process instead of traditional requirements engineering approach.	
12.	Fueling Innovation through Information Technology in SMEs (Dibrell, Clay;Davis, Peter S;Craig, Justin, 2008)	The paper describes a study that investigates the mediating effects of information technology on relationships among product and process innovations and firm performance	Quantitative: Structured Equation modeling	There is evidence that a) increases on the strategic emphasis placed on innovation, both product and process positively impact the prominence managers place on IT 2) the impact of innovation on performance is primarily indirect felt via the mechanism of importance managers place on IT 3) an increased emphasis on IT assets managers perception of their firms performance as compared with that observed among peer firms.	
13.	Generative mechanisms for innovation in information infrastructures (Bendik Bygstad, 2010)	This paper investigates innovation in information infrastructures	Case Study	From the analysis it is proposed that there are two self-reinforcing mechanisms in information infrastructures. The first is the innovation mechanism, resulting in a new service. The second is the service mechanism, resulting in more users and profits. The two mechanisms feed on each other.	
14.	Information System Innovations and Supply Chain Management: Channel Relationships and Firm Performance(Kim, Daekwan;Cavusgil, S Tamer;Calantone, Roger J, 2006)	This study explores how innovation surrounding supply chain communication (SCCS) affect channel relationship and market performance.	Quantitative: Structured Equation modeling	The influence of applied technological innovation for SCCS is not strong enough to affect either responsiveness of the partnership or firm performance whereas administrative innovations for SCCS affect both.	

continued on next page

Table 10. Continued

Sno.	Studies	Objective	Type	Findings	Implication
15.	Information systems innovation for environmental sustainability (Nigel P. Melville, 2010)	examine questions spanning organizations and the natural environment but have largely omitted the information systems perspective.	Literature Review	We develop a research agenda on information systems innovation for environmental sustainability that demonstrates the critical role that IS can play in shaping beliefs about the environment, in enabling and transforming sustainable processes and practices in organizations, and in improving environmental and economic performance.	Other examples of IS research areas that might inform and be informed by environmental sustainability issues include (1) the role of the CIO in driving sustainability issues and influencing other business functions (Enns et al. 2003); (2) trust and privacy of individual and organizational resource data (Smith et al. 1996); and (3) the role of information systems agility in enabling expeditious changes to business processes congenial to environmental sustainability (Goodhue et al. 2009).
16.	Why organizations adopt information system process innovations: a longitudinal study using Diffusion of Innovation theory(Erja Mustonen-Ollila* & Kalle Lyytinen)	This paper identifies factors that affected over 200 information system (IS) process innovation adoption decisions in three organizational environments over a period that spanned four decades. The analysis is based on Rogers's (1995) theory of Diffusion of Innovations (DOI)	Multisite Case approach	The results show that several DOI factors strongly affect IS process innovation adoption. These include user need recognition, availability of technological infrastructure, past experience, own trials, autonomous work, ease of use, learning by doing and standards. Yet, a large number of IS process innovation adoptions followed no discernible pattern.	
17.	Innovating Mindfully with Information Technology (E. Burton Swanson and Neil C. Ramiller), 2004	Mindful firm is contrasted with mindless innovation. One of our primary goals has been to raise questions about (1) what itm eans to be mindful in innovating with IT, (2) when organizations should be mindful, and (3) how organizations can be mindful.	Literature Review	Conceptualization for use in IT research: first, recognizing the institutionally embedded nature of the IT innovation, and second, specifying a process model for organizational innovation that takes cognizance of the larger institutional context. With	

continued on next page

Table 10. Continued

Sno.	Studies	Objective	Type	Findings	Implication
18.	Innovation and knowledge creation: How are these concepts related? Silvio Popadiuka,_, Chun Wei Choob. 2006	This paper reviews the important theoretical work in both streams of research, highlighting the fundamental similarities and differences. Four major models of innovation are compared, and the distinction between radical and incremental innovation is examined.	Literature review	In the first quadrant, the firm creates new knowledge through exploration that is based on tacit knowledge, and commercializes this knowledge by making use of new market knowledge.	
19.	Innovative IT climates: CIO perspectives (Stephanie Watts *, John C. Henderson 1, 2006)	This research investigates innovative CIOs in the context of their organizational climate theory.	Qualitative Analysis: Interviews	We identify and characterize four dimensions of innovative IT climates using a theoretical model based on the climate literature. Inductive grounded-theoretic methods are then utilized to develop two additional dimensions of innovative IT climates - reality-checking and promoting credibility.	
20.	Institutional Factors in Information Technology Innovation (John Leslie King, Vijay Gurbaxani, Kenneth L. Kraemer, F. Warren McFarlan, K. S.Raman and C. S. Yap, 1994)	This paper makes three points. First, long-established intellectual perspectives on inno vation from neoclassical economics and organization theory are inadequate to explain the dynamics of actual innovative change in the IT domain. A broader view adopted from economic history and the new institutionalism in sociology provides a stronger base for understanding the role of institutions in IT innovation. Second, institutional intervention in IT innovation can be constructed at the intersection of the influence and regulatory powers of institutions and the ideologies of supply-push and demand-pull models of innovation. Examples of such analysis are provided. Third, institutional pol icy formation regarding IT innovation is facilitated by an understanding of the multifaceted role of institutions in the innovative process, and on the contingencies governing any given institution/innovation mix.	Literature review	The institutional power to influence and regulate can be linked to ideologies governing supply-push and demand pull approaches to innovation in an effort to account for possible institutional interventions.	

continued on next page

Table 10. Continued

Sno.	Studies	Objective	Type	Findings	Implication
21.	How organizations adopt information system process innovations: a longitudinal analysis (Erja Mustonen-Ollila1 and Kalle Lyytinen2,2004)	Four distinct periods that roughly follow Friedman's and Cornford's categorization of IS development eras are analysed in terms of the rate and distribution of ISPI adoptions. We analyse for each era the rate of adopting different types of ISPIs, identify who made adoption decisions for those ISPI types and determine whether these ISPIs originated internally or externally.	Qualitative case studies	The variation in ISPI adoptions can thus be partly explained by development environments, the types of IS involved and attention bias.	
22.	Institutional Influences on Information Systems Security Innovations(Carol Hsu, Jac-Nam Lee,Detmar W. Straub,2012)	This research investigates information security management as an administrative innovation	Mixed research methods approach	Drawing from neo-institutional theory and the innovation diffusion literature, this study proposes an integrative framework of the adoption and assimilation of information security management. Furthermore, the field study findings offer empirical support for the moderating effects of economic and organizational capability in the presence of coercive and mimetic isomorphism. From a theoretical perspective, it provides a good starting point for theoretical refinements on the institutionalization of information security management. It also provides an analytical tool that can be used for managerial intervention in the diffusion of information security management in organizations.	implications for research in the area of organizational theory and the information security management literature, and for practices regarding how managers can factor into their information security planning the key implementation variables discovered in this study. The
23.	Understanding the influence of information systems competencies on process innovation: A resource-based view(Monideepa Tarafdar a,*,1, Steven R. Gordon b,2, 2007)	The resource based view of firms is used to explore how information system (IS) competencies affect process innovation in an organization	Case study	The findings illustrate how six IS competencies – Knowledge Management, Collaboration, Project Management, Ambidexterity, IT/Innovation Governance, Business-IS Linkages – can differentially affect the conception, development and implementation of process innovations.	
24.	IT innovation adoption in the government sector: identifying the critical success factors Kamal, M M (2006)	The purpose of this paper is to see how IT is adopted in government organizations and explore what factors impact its adoption	Case Study	The author has identified 42 critical success factors for IT innovation adoption which provides sufficient understanding of their importance	

continued on next page

Table 10. Continued

Sno.	Studies	Objective	Type	Findings	Implication
25.	A review of the predictors, linkages, and biases in IT innovation adoption research Anand Jeyaraj, Joseph W Rottman, Mary C Lacity	review and analysis of the rich body of research on the adoption and diffusion of IT-based innovations by individuals and organizations	Literature Review	The authors give ten areas for further exploration: 1. Continue to use the best predictors of individual adoption. 2. Continue to examine promising predictors of individual adoption. 3. Continue to use the best predictors of organizational adoption. 4. Continue to examine promising predictors of organizational adoption5. Use individual characteristics in organizational adoption studies6. Use environmental characteristics in individual adoption research7. Increase the study of Rate of Adoption as a dependent variable in individual adoption research. 8. Increase the study of outcomes as a dependent variable in both individual and organizational adoption research to overcome the pro-innovation bias9. Increase the study of actual system use as a dependent variable in both individual and organizational adoption research to overcome the self-reporting bias. 10. Increase the study of non-adopters to overcome the adopter bias in individual adoption studies	
26.	The Manager's Guide to IT Innovation Waves, E. Burton Swanson	How should managers understand this apparent IT wave phenomenon and come to terms with it?	Article	1. Breaking the Surface 2. Sending Out Ripples3. Causing a Squawk4. Building the Swell5. Riding the CrestInnovating Mindfully — Rather Than Mindlessly	
27.	Information Technology and Intangible Output: The Impact of IT Investment on Innovation Productivity (Landon Kleis et al)	we contribute to the literature by comprehensively examining the contribution of IT to innovation production across multiple contexts using a quality-based measure of innovation output.	Quantitative	importance of IT in creating value at an intermediate stage of production, through improved innovation productivity.	

continued on next page

Table 10. Continued

Sno.	Studies	Objective	Type	Findings	Implication
28.	Going Beyond the Dominant Paradigm for Information Technology Innovation Research: Emerging Concepts and Methods(Robert G. Fichman)	This essay suggests that the dominant paradigm may be reaching the point of diminishing returns as a framework for supporting ground-breaking research, and urges researchers to adopt a more innovative approach to the study of IT innovation itself.	Literature review	Innovation Configurations: Which holistic combinations of factors explain IT innovation outcomes on large-scale deployment efforts? • Social Contagion: When are the forces of social contagion the strongest and what variables carry the contagion effect? • Management Fashion: What triggers the emergence of IT fashions and determines whether a fashion will be transient or become an enduring institution? • Innovation Mindfulness: What characterizes more mindful organizations, and how do their innovation outcomes differ from less mindful organizations? • Technology Destiny: How do the determinants of the rate/extent of innovation implementation vary depending on a technology's destiny? • Quality of Innovation: What characterizes organizations that exhibit greater quality of innovation, and how does this quality relate to innovation impacts? • Performance Impacts: Under what contextual conditions are the performance impacts of innovative IT the greatest?	
29.	Managing change and innovation in IT implementation process (Bartoli, Annie;Hermel, Philippe)	Strategically controlling the change induced by technology innovations in order to benefit from contribution of IT tools.	Literature	The quality of design and implementation of innovation appears with IT, which can generate consequently non quality in overall operation of company.	

continued on next page

Table 10. Continued

Sno.	Studies	Objective	Type	Findings	Implication
30.	Development of an Instrument to Measure the Perceptions of Adopting an InformationTechnology InnovationAuthor(s): Gary C. Moore and Izak Benbasat	This paper reports on the development of an instrument designed to measure the various perceptions that an individual may have of adopting an information technology (IT) innovation.	Field Test	The instrument development research described here offers several contributions. The most obvious is the creation of an overall instrument to measure various perceptions of using an information technology innovation. The creation process included surveying known existing instruments, choosing appropriate items, creating new items as necessary, and then undertaking an extensive scale development process. It is believed that the method of developing the scales provides a high degree of confidence in their content and constructs validity. The result is a parsimonious, 34-item instrument, comprising seven scales, all with acceptable levels of reliability. This instrument can now be used to investigate how perceptions affect individuals' actual use of information technology as well as other innovations.	
31.	Organizational challenges for innovation in information systems	examine the organizational challenges for innovation in information systems in each of the three areas of this model	Literature	innovation in information systems needs to be managed like any other corporate function, e.g. marketing or sales.	
32.	The Organizing Vision in Information Systems Innovation, E. Burton Swanson and Neil C. Ramiller	Introduce the notion of organizing vision and explain how a collective, cognitive view of new technologies enables success in information systems innovation both within and across firms	Literature	Specifically, we have proposed in this essay that early adoption and diffusion take place in the context of, indeed depend upon, essential institutional proc-esses that manifest themselves in the creation of a collective image of the innovation. We call this image an ''organizing vision.''	
33.	The Role of Aggregation in the Measurement of IT-Related Organizational InnovationAuthor(s): Robert G. Fichman	This article begins with a conceptual analysis that identifies the circumstances when these tradeoffs are most likely to favor aggregated measures	Emperical analysis	It is found that aggregation should be favorable when: (1) the researcher's interest is in general innovation or a model that generalizes to a class of innovations, (2) antecedents have effects in the same direction in all assimilation stages, (3) characteristicso f organizationsc an be treated as constant across the innovations in the study, (4) characteristicso f innovationsc an not be treated as constant across organizations in the study, (5) the set of innovations being aggregated includes substitutes or moderate complements, and (6) sources of noise in the measurement of innovation may be present.	

continued on next page

Table 10. Continued

Sno.	Studies	Objective	Type	Findings	Implication
34.	Empirical Evidence on Swanson's Tri-Core Model of Information Systems InnovationAuthor(s): Varun Grover, Kirk Fiedler and James Teng	The authors present Swanson's tri-core model of IS innovation along with preliminary data to test aspects of the model proposed by Swanson.	Cox's Regression	We would suggest that while there is room and need for further theoretical refinement, elaboration, and ex tension of the model, the pattern of results indicates that there are systemic differences in IS innovation types.	
35.	Organizational mechanisms for enhancing user innovation in information technology, Nambisan. Agarwal, & Tanniru	This paper argues that deliberate organizational design actions in the form of mechanisms can enhance technology users' propensity to innovate in information technology	Emperical Study: Multivariate Analysis	The theory of mechanism effects presented here is admittedly modest and in need of further extension. For example, it might be possible to identify additional categories of knowledge that are relevant to IT innovation and, hence, to propose a more comprehensive taxonomy. The empirical study focused on mechanisms that have been discussed in prior literature	
36.	Constructing a framework for it-enabled innovations (Watad, M.et al, 2009)	This paper introduces a new conceptual framework of IT-enabled innovations. The framework conceptualizes the innovation process as an open system and builds on recent trends in the business and computing environments	Literature	It conceptualizes the innovation process as an open system with a feedback loop. The central part of the framework consists of four main constructs: managerial activities, organizational context, IT availability, and the knowledge base of the organization. The dynamics of these constructs influences the effectiveness of IT-enabled innovations.	
37.	IT-intensive value innovation in the electronic economy: Insights from Marshall industries (Sawy, El et. Al, 1999)	This article focuses on providing a framework for guiding enterprise as it transforms into function more effectively in electronics industry.	Case based	The article provides a staged junction box model for guiding the transformation and also articulates the elements of the new value logic for enterprises in electronic economy.	
38.	The process of embedding new information technology artifacts into innovative design practices (Baxter et. Al, 2010)	To explore the challenges associated with such migration, we develop the concept of embeddedness of IT artifacts by drawing on research that highlights the critical role of representational artifacts in knowledge, design, and distributed cognition	Case based	we identify four relevant themes associated with embedding new artifacts into knowledge-creating practice: (1) motivating the new artifact; (2) anchoring the new artifact in the old; (3) experimenting with the new artifact; and (4) confidence in using the newartifact.	
39.	Organizational challenges for innovation in information systems (chandan et al, 2012)	In this paper, using the governance, resources and processes model for an organization, we examine the organizational challenges for innovation in information systems in each of the three areas of this model.	Literature	In summary, innovation in information systems needs to be managed like any other corporate function, e.g. marketing or sales.	

continued on next page

Table 10. Continued

Sno.	Studies	Objective	Type	Findings	Implication
40.	Patent Scope and Innovation in the Software Industry (Cohen et al, 2001)	We argue that patent law needs some refinement if it is to promote rather than impede the growth of this new market, which is characterized by rapid sequential innovation, reuse and re-combination of components, and strong network effects that privilege interoperable com-ponents and products. In particular, we argue for two sorts of new rules in software patent cases	Literature	Exploration of the consequences of patent protection for innovation in the software industry is just beginning. Here, w e have tried t o suggest some of the pitfalls that existing patent doctrine may create for software developers throughout the research and development process	
41.	SMEs & IS innovations adoption: A review & assessment of previous research (Ramdani et al., 2007)	this paper critically reviews the IS innovations adoption research in general, and in SMEs (Small to Medium-sized Enterprises) context in particular	Literature	From a critical review of IS innovations adoption literature, it can be argued that theories used to study IS innovations adoption in small business context have served its purpose to a great extent to explain IS acceptance form different perspectives	
42.	Unified Modeling Language (UML) IT adoption — A holistic model of organizational capabilities perspective (Gu et al, 2012)	This study develops an integrated research model to examine various factors affecting the IT adoption in the context of the Unified Modeling Language (UML).	Quantitative	This study has identified a comprehensive IT adoption model from the organizational capabilities perspective and has explored the relationship between seven organizational related constructs (i.e., IT characteristics, organization technology, environment, organization structure, organization process, organization culture, and project culture) and the UML adoption process.	
43.	Changing the Competitive Landscape: Continuous Innovation Through IT-Enabled Knowledge Capabilities (Joshi et al, 2010)	Invoking absorptive capacity (ACAP) theory, we introduce and develop the concepts of three types of IT-enabled knowledge capabilities	Quantitative	This study makes important contributions to research, methodology, and practice in IS, competitive dynamics, and firm innovation. From a theoretical standpoint, first, this study contributes to the IS literature by empirically establishing the link between IT and innovation.	
44.	Diffusion Theory: A Review and Test of a Conceptual Model in Information Diffusion (1986)	The purpose of this study was to test diffusion theory in study of awareness, use and diffusion of innovation in job environment of working poor	Literature	Time was seen as a crucial element in diffusion of information. The nature of innovation, the job information, affected its diffusion through channels.	

continued on next page

Table 10. Continued

Sno.	Studies	Objective	Type	Findings	Implication
45.	ICT Innovation in Contemporary India: Three Emerging Narratives (Rai et al, 2011)	This paper discusses ICT innovation in India using a narrative framework. We argue that ICT innovation has not been a subject sufficiently researched in information systems from the perspective of innovation in developing countries	Literature	We see our paper here as contributing on two fronts. One, it provides a deeper insight into the phenomenon of complex technological innovation in India. It reveals three distinct narratives of such innovation. The second important contribution of this paper is to highlight the evolution of this process over time. In our data analysis, we find that the narratives are evolving from one stage to another.	
46.	Information Systems Innovation in the Humanitarian Sector (Tsuiime, 2011)	IS innovation in the context of the humanitarian sector highlights the need for contextbased approaches to innovation. In this article, we explore the process of the improvement, development, and implementation of an international development organization's logistics and supply chain system in Chad.	Case based	Using an ANT conceptualization of innovation, the translation process was greatly constrained and shaped by the context. Innovation in rural and remote settings with no public infrastructure (power and communication) is not easy. WFP had to set up its own infrastructure (power generators, radio and satellite communication networks, etc.) and related IT hardware and software.	
47.	Changes in Attitudes Toward an Information Systems Innovation: Reactions to Implementation Delays (Livingstone et al, 2002)	Our research team experienced the delay phenomenon while in the midst of a research project in a large university library in the U.S. The intent of the original research project was to examine individual adjustment to new computing technologies in a longitudinal study.	Case based	This research project examined changes in employee attitudes toward change and toward working with computers related to a delay in the implementation of an organization's information systems innovation. Attitudes toward change and attitudes toward working with computers became more positive following the delay, contrary to expectations.	
48.	Innovation Systems in India's IT Industry: An Empirical Investigation (Taganas et al, 2006)	There is a need to direct policy to address this systemic failure and bring in industry-wide innovation	Article	the study concludes that although India's software sectors internationally competitive, the system of innovation has generally been weak to spur innovation within the industry	
49.	Innovation and knowledge creation: How are these concepts related? (Popadiuk et. Al (2006))	This paper reviews the important theoretical work in both streams of research, highlighting the fundamental similarities and differences.	Literature	Our discussion here suggests that knowledge creation is focused on the generation and application of knowledge that leads to new capabilities for the firm. Innovation, on the other hand, is also concerned with how these new capabilities may be turned into products and services that have economic value in markets.	

Chapter 8
Investigating Impact of Inter–Organizational Factors in Measuring ERP Systems Success:
Bruneian Perspectives

Afzaal H. Seyal
Universiti Tecknologi Brunei, Brunei

Mohd Noah A. Rahman
Universiti Tecknologi Brunei, Brunei

ABSTRACT

The cardinal aim of this study is to assess the success of an Enterprise Resource Planning (ERP) system in investigating the role played by the top management and government support, external expertise, perceived benefits and the impact of business vision. This is a quantitative field study conducted on 150 business firms randomly selected from the Brunei Yellow Pages. In this study, 30% of the companies had practiced the ERP for more than one year. A statistical software package PSW-18 was used to analyse the data. The majority of the previous findings which include all contextual variables used were significant with an exception to the top management support which proved insignificant. Those results were compared with existing studies. The practical implications are discussed and a conclusion is drawn.

INTRODUCTION

The Enterprise Resource Planning (ERP) systems is an information systems (IS) that is used by multifunctional companies working in different regions (Umble *et al.,* 2003).The system is large, complex and difficult to implement (Gupta, 2000). In order to ensure its successful implementation, it requires careful planning and execution.

DOI: 10.4018/978-1-5225-2382-6.ch008

An ERP system enjoys its popularity because of its apparent capacity to improve business efficacy and operational efficiency (Chou & Chang, 2008). ERP system is evolving and it integrates many advanced applications which include the supply chain management (SCM), customer relationship management (CRM) and electronic procurement (Aydin & Tunali, 2007). Furthermore, adopting an ERP systems as a primary platform to share and exchange of organization information and provide access through internet technology which is considered as a hall marks of leading edge organizations (Davenport, 2000).

The ERP system differs from other form of information technology (IT) implementation because it provides a real opportunity for modern organizations to integrate all their business functions and processes (Martin, 1998).

The widespread use of Information and Communication Technologies (ICT) for efficient and effective business functions has changed the working operations of businesses around the globe. Majority of the organizations are relying on the cutting-edge technologies that can cut down the costs and bring benefits to businesses. In this regard, business organizations are investing in the e-business option, in order to gain more benefits and to improve on how their businesses function. Enterprise Resource Planning (ERP) systems are information systems (IS) used by multifunctional companies working in different regions (Umble *et al.*, 2003). By implementing ERP, organizations will have better control over their business operations. According to Gupta (2000), the system is complex, large and difficult to implement. It requires careful planning and execution in order to ensure its successful implementation. Furthermore, the ERP system is different from other information technology implementation, therefore, they provide real opportunity for modern organizations to integrate their business processes and functions (Martin, 1998).

The ERP system is becoming popular worldwide and gaining competitive and strategic advantages. In fact, adopting ERP system as the primary platform for sharing and exchanging of organizational information and providing access to it through internet technology which is considered a hall marks of leading organizations (Davenport, 2000). ERP system enjoys its present popularity because of its apparent capacity to improve operational efficiency and business efficacy (Chou & Chang, 2008). Whereas, Aydin and Tunali, (2007) suggest that ERP system is evolving and integrating many advanced applications including supply chain management (SCM), customer relationship management (CRM) and e-Procurement.

In today's uncertain economic climate, organizations require suitable IT-enabled systems that provide significant reduction in operational costs and improvement in the efficency of business processes. ERP is a very useful integrated software that streamlines business processes and corporates functions (Wee, 2000). Broadly speaking, the business ERP comes under the domain of organizational broad base supply chain management system (SCM). In addition, ERP can be defined as an information system that is designed to improve global management of operations in accounting, financing, production, logistic, human resources, sales and supplies (Chen, 2001). It deals with better integration of different departments' information needs (Gupta *et al.*, 1986). In multinational companies, transactions' data go through the entire information system of the logistics chain that includes information pertaining to suppliers and customer orders of goods or services from any place in the world (Sheu *et al.*, 2004).

ERP system facilitates the integration of information linking a set of suppliers, distributors and clients through geographic restrictions (Jacob &Whybark, 2000; Soh *et al.*, 2000; Hammer & Stanton, 1999; Davenport, 1998). Information about the supply and the demand of products and services is shared in real time and in an accurate and homogeneous manner (Chen & Popovich, 2003). The strategic purpose of implementing an ERP system varies across companies (Willcock & Sykes, 2000). It involves perceived advantages both tangible and intangible, of this ERP system which is difficult to define (Hsu and Chen, 2004). In international systems of the logistic chain, information that is managed with ERP system provides competitive advantage (Akkermans *et al.,* 2003). ERP system and SCM are the basis for a better oganizational performance and competative advantage (Bergstrom and Stehn, 2005).

From the above discussion, it is evident that implementing ERP has become an important option for many businesses across the globe. This gives competitive advantage as well as to enhance productivity. Based on recent evidence from industry reports and IS studies, there are now more business enterprises implementing ERP to enhance business processes and to gain both tangible and intangible benefits (Mabert, *et al.,* 2003; AMR Research, 2005). In 2009, AMR cited in its report that ERP has grown into US$64.8 billion market worldwide. (www.amrresearch.com/Content/view.asp?pmillid=18789).

The increased use of these new technologies has resulted in more studies dealing with issues pertaining to adoption, implementation as well as evaluation of critical success factors and implementation methodologies (Hong & Kim, 2002; Wei *et al.,* 2007; Seethmraju and Seethmraju, 2008; Petter *et al.,* 2008; Abdalghaffar, 2012). However, the researchers' focus had been shifted towards these dimensions on studies to evaluate the impact of ERP systems, measure the success of ERP and/or assess its effectiveness (Law and Ngai. 2007). Researchers faced a big challenge in conducting the studies due to lack of knowledge regarding issues pertaining to IS success (Gable *et al.,* 2003; Iivari, 2005). Other researches in areas dealing with ERP systems, measurement, evaluation or assessment is the recent phenomenon (Tan and Pan, 2002; Gable *et al.,* 2003; We & Wang, 2005; Ifinedo & Davidrajah, 2005; Ifinedo & Nahar, 2006; Ifinedo, 2008).

Shanks *et al.,* (2000) explained that ERP implementation 'comes after the adoption decision and is considered' as a time where a company must concentrate and evaluate its processes in detail'. Firms generally start with a planning for the ERP system then move towards different project phases to implement it. This procedure is followed by large number of business organizations adopting the ERP system. However, as Cragg and Mitchell, (2000) reported that 75% of these projects was regarded as failure. Failure rate is very high because of ERP implementation process is very expensive. Several researchers had studied the critical success factors of organizations in order to reduce failure rate in the implementation of the ERP system (Rajapakse and Seddon, 2003). Kim *et al.,* (2005) identified three reasons for failure of ERP project, namely: (1) complexity of the implementation process, (2) misfit between ERP and organizational business processes, and project management, and, (3) incompetent consultants. Davenport (2000) and Klaus *et al.,* (2000) stated that to assess the success of ERP system in implementing organizations was difficult because of its complex nature. In addition, some organizations failed to evaluate the benefits or success factors in measuring their ERP system success (Ifinedo, 2005). Furthermore, Robbins-Gioia, (2006) reported in their industry survey that 46% of the participants noted that even though their organizations had an ERP system implemented, they failed to use the system to improve the way they conduct business (www.robbinsgioia.com/nextevents/012802_esp.aspx). Beside that, researchers have identified several reasons of ERP project failures, where majority of ERP implementing firms did not know the extent to which technology could enable them to realize organizational goals. Thus by elimating or minimizing them at the firm-level, could increase the propensity of ERP success (Umble *et al.,* 2003).

On the other hand, Shanks *et al.,* (2000) identified various critical success factors for ERP implementation such as top management support, vendor/customer partnership, selection of softwares/consultants, vendor supports and business process reengineering (Al-Mashari & Zairi, 2000; Umble, 2003; Sedera & Tan, 2005).

Lack of knowledge in assessing ERP successfully had led to do this pioneering research study in Brunei Darussalam. The major motivation of this study, nevertheless, stemmed from the theoretical concerned that majority of the previous researches which were undertaken in the developed world and there is the contextual difference between developing and developed countries and their implication for IS success have been totally different (Heeks, 2002, 2003). Higgo, (2003) further stated that information system was influenced by both the organizational context in term of strucutre, policies, politics and culture as well as an understanding of the context in which IS being embedded. This is important and due consideration should be given to these factors that influenced the success and failure of IS (Kelegai, 2005). Therefore, it is imperative to conduct studies on the success of various IS in the developing countries in differet regional and geoographical setting. Since the studies on the ERP brings multi-dimensionality and explores the topic from different perspective, we therefore believe that the results of the current study may add to the body of knowledge which not only from organizational and practioners' point of view but may also contribute to the theory which itself especially in ASEAN context.

Within this context before discussing the review of literature in the next section, we discuss an overiew of the Brunei Government efforts in promoting ICT through various developments programs and building the necessary infrastructure in meeting the ICT capacity.

*Brunei Government's initiative towards ICT*Brunei Darussalam is small tiny South East Asian Sultanate with a population of 405,938 (CIA World report, 2011). Brunei Darussalam is situated on the northwestern edge of the island of Borneo, an island which is also a part of Indonesia and Malaysia. It is located on the equator and at the tip of Borneo between Sabah and Sarawak of Malaysia. Its economy is based on oil and gas. Brunei is third largest oil producer in Southeast Asia with an average production of 180,000 barrels per day. Brunei Darussalam enjoys a high quality of life with an estimated US$31,000 per capita income, the second highest in ASEAN (www.bt.com.bn) with GDP of US$12.37 billion (2010) (www.worldbank.com).

Brunei Darussalam globally, is a member of the Association of South East Asian Nations (ASEAN), Asia-Pacific Economic Council (APEC) and World Trade Organization (WTO). Brunei government is committed to diversifying from oil/gas-based economy to other non-oil industries and is determined to support the ICT-based businesses. The government has allocated B$7.3 millions for ICT development-Infrastructure for e-government projects in the 8th National Development Plan. Brunei Darussalam IT (BIT) Council has been set up and has given funds to promote e-business program within the kingdom under the e-government framework. For the last two years the Ministry of Development, Brunei Economic Development Board (BEDB) and Ministry of Industry and Primary Resources (MIRP) were heavily spending to achieve e-business activities including eCommerce and Brunei vision in order to transform Brunei Darussalam to a more knowlegeable, thoughtful, multi-skilled, and paperless economy by year 2035. This is known as "Wawasan 2035" in local language-Malay, meaning "vision 2035".

The National Development Plan encourages growth of SMEs to generate employment and revenue by replacing government-funded development programs with private-funded ones, putting the government in a stronger position in balancing the national budget while ensuring long-term support for local businesses. In an effort to develop a more coherent approach that encourages positive growth and development the BEBD; has formulated several effective and promising local business development programs and initiatives through a framework that emphasizes capability, capital and connectivity. With this aim, several of initiatives have been introduced such as setting up an iCenter-a Brunei's first ICT incubation center that focuses on nurturing ICT entrepreneurs to develop Made-in-Brunei products and applications through a well structured and effective incubation program. It also included the establishment of Knowledge or K-Hub to serve as a technology-based research and development (R&D) center by setting up Brunei Telecom (TelBru) ICT center for Leadership & Management; TechOne-Global/microsoft Experience Center; UBD/IBM partnership for developing a climate modelling research center and the Ministry of Defense for National Modelling and Simulation Center. The K-hub is Brunei's first commercial green building utilizing solar power generation and energy-efficient technologies to meet its energy requirement. (www.bedb.com.bn)

From an academic perspective, studies have been conducted among SMEs and large businesses especially in the areas of e-commerce (Seyal & Rahman, 2002, 2003; Looi, 2005; Seyal *et al.* 2007) but there is dreath of studies in regard to adoption of other ebusiness domains such as EDI and e-Procurement and no prior work had been undertaken especially in the area of ERP. We believe that there are some success stories among the businesses regarding implementation of ERP. This pioneering study was conducted in Feb 2013, focused on ERP success factors among the Bruneian business organizations that have implemented the ERP software for the past two-years and measure their success are included as sampling frame regardless of the classification of small, medium and large organizations. The present study is confined to the Bruneian context and has several reasons for that: (1) Because of the massive campaigning of various governmental bodies such as Brunei IT Council, Ministry of Industry and Primary Resources, the use of the technology by the businesses are increasing and its now time to conduct studies to monitor and guage the benefits. (2) the few existing researches address the ERP in developing countries such as Zhang *et al.* (2005) in China; Koh *et al.* (2006) in Greece; Nah *et al.* (2007) in Malaysia; Kamhawi (2007) in Bahrin; Maldonado and Sierra (2013) in Latin America has brought contradicting success and failure outcome that has brought the researchers and practitioners on board and they become incresingly interested in analyzing ERP adoption in various regions. (3) Srite *et al.* (2008) sugests that it is imperative to evaluate IT adoptions in every local context and not merely adopt previous findings from other regions. At the time of this study and up to our knowledge no prior research was found addressing explicitly the Bruneian experience within Bruneian context.

The study therefore has the following specific objectives:

1. To understand the ERP success factor among Bruneian businesses, by assessing the validity of ERP success model of Ifinedo & Nehar (2006) within the context of Brunei Darussalam.
2. To study the various internal and external factors (business vision, top management support, external expertise, government support and perceived benefits) by contributing to the success of ERP system.

REVIEW OF RELEVANT LITERATURE

The present study utilizes the various framework of IS success model in general and ERP success model in particular. It sought to establish a link between several contextural variables in order to find out their suitability in the ERP systems in Bruneian businesses.

The literature tends to fall into a number of categories with regard to a business setting. Most studies focused on the business managers' and business owners' attitudes toward technology in relation to its adoption and utilization. In addition, some researchers have studied the small business owners' dominating role in Information Technology implementation (Cragg & King, 1993; Doukidis *et al.*, 1994; Julien & Raymond, 1994; Thong & Yap, 1995). Several studies have also been conducted to identify various technological and environmental factors for ERP implementation in developed countries and identified how environmental or technical factors had influenced its success. Thong *et al.*, (1996) and Bajwa *et al.*, (1998) identified a wide range of contingency factors that positively influenced the success of IT systems, namely: the organization's size, organizational culture and structure, internal IT support, top management support, government support, and, external expertise (quality vendor/consultant). While, previous research has provided information regarding the effects of some of these contextural variables on IT project success, as it is fair to generalize that top management support and engagement of quality vendors and consultants are among the most widely cited positive influences in the adoption of various IT systems (Bajwa *et al.*, 1998; Wang & Chen, 2006). Abdulghaffar (2012) studied the environmental and organizational factors which affected the success of ERP implementation in developing country e.g., Egypt. He found out that government regulations, ICT infrastructure, and other organizational factors were related to success of ERP implementation.

It is apparent from the undergoing discussion that research on ERP implementation was conducted from different perspective Noudoostbeni *et al.* (2009) noted ten critical success factors and all of them were internal such as project management variable, top management support, clear goals, well defined objectives and communications. Peslak (2012) discussed about the various industry variables affecting ERP success that are external to the organization. Farzaneh *et al.* (2013) studied the influential factors in the implementation of ERP systems. They proposed and discussed three main factors for evaluating the success of ERP implementation that were social, intellectual and technical factors. Rajendran and Elangovan (2012) extensively examined the role of external pressure on ERP adoption and success. Maldonado and Sierra (2013) identified ten factors that was identified by the Latin America experts prior to their study and that included top management support, external consultants, ERP user satisfaction, user training and business vision and strategy are the five main factors.

However, their study investigated different set of variables such as ERP ease of use (EOU), project implementation success and formal communication program with measuring user satisfaction as surrogate variable to measure ERP business improvement success and found significant relationship between EOU and project implementation success and user satisfaction that in turn predict the business improvement success. Similarly, Mexas *et al.* (2013) conducted a literature search and reported various criteria for selecting an ERP system in Brazil. Hanafzadeh *et al.*, (2010) studied the various factors that determine the success or failure of ERP implementation. Cartman and Salazar (2011) found high level of ERP adoption with large size companies. Another study noted the high failure rate of ERP implementation on the basis of demographical variables (Nour & Mouakket 2011). From a small firm's perspective, Abdel-Kader and Nguyen (2011) conducted a study to investigate the implementation process from success achieved and problem faced.

Measuring ERP Success: Theoretical Perspective

In the present context ERP success is the dependent variable. As Ifinedo and Nahar (2007) affirm, there are several perspectives of the success of ERP adoptions but as Estevez (2009) pointed out, measuring it should be oriented at gauging the business benefits ERP provides to the organization. Accordingly, he focused on the missing bridge between IT adoption and the benefits it brings to the organizations (Estevez, 2009). Considering its importance, we need to examine it in details. Success of IT system has been discussed using different attributes of "quality" and "impact"(DeLone & McLean, 1992; Myers *et al.* 1997) that led to the classifications to measure the dependent variable. DeLone and McLean (1992) developed an integrated, multidimensional model to measure the success. Delone and McLean's IS Success Model (1992) has become a standard for the specification and justification of the measurement in information system research. The McLean' IS success model identified six interrelated dimensions of IS success.

The model suggested that success can be measured by success dimensions, namely: system quality, the output information quality, the use of the output, user's satisfaction, the effect of the IS on the behavior of the user (individual impact); and organizational impact. Delone and McLean revised the model and stated that although the success dimensions and measurements should be selected based on empirical study and objectives, it was preferable to use tested and proven measures. As the model needed further validation, Delone and McLean, (2003) proposed an updated model for their E-commerce study in 2003 by adding a service quality components, i.e., the measure for user's attitude i.e. intention to use. Organizational and individual impact failures as well as net benefits were then identified.

Research Model and Development of Hypotheses

Based on the above mentioned discussion and on the basis of contigency theory (Lawrence and Lorsch, 1967) who proposed that more and more internal and external factors to be included in the organizational structure that can handle the uncertainities in the environment effectively. Similarly,a wide range of contingency factors that positively influence the success of IT systems has been identified (Ein-Dor and Segev, 1978; Thong *et al.*, 1996; Bajwa *et al.*, 1998). Therefore a theoretical model was prepared that not only include the variables from the existing study (Ifinedo, 2008) but also included the two new variables that "perceived benefits" and "government support" to test their suitability for large businesses. This is shown in Figure 1 as below.

Measuring the ERP success has passed through various stages: firstly, measuring ERP system success was considered similiar to measuring IS success or effectiveness (Thong *et al.* 1996); at later stages, it was re-evaluated and defined to include utilization of the system to enhance organizational goal (Gable *et al.*, 2003). from researchers perspectives. Whereas, the researchers like Martin, (1998); Markus and Tanis, 2000 and Yu, 2005 excluded the technical issues for measuring the success. Other researchers discussed the value, benefits and financial indicators which were included to measure the ERP system success vis-a-vis organizational performance (Poston & Grabski, 2001; Nicolaou, 2004).

The framework for ERP success was modified by Ifinedo (2008) it was by excluding the financial parameter in his study; he then declared that ERP systems were to be a different class of IT system. He stressed the importance of a specialized success measurement framework or model for measuring the success of such a system. He challenged the model developed by Gable *et al.*, (2003) to measure the success of ERP and redefined some of the of work dimension cited by Delone and McLean (1992). Gable *et al.*, (2003) had eliminated through rigid data collection and analysis the user's satisfaction dimension of DeLone and McLean's (1992) framework. Ifinedo and Nahr (2006) proposed an extended ERP system success model that included workgroup impact, i.e., the workgroup as the functional department of an organization. Researchers like Devenport, (2000) and Klaus *et al.* (2000) noticed that the inclusion of workgroup dimension were adopted to enhance efficient cross functioning operation.

In conclusion, we adapted the model after Ifinedo, (2008), and used the same instrument to measure the ERP success. However, the model was then modified and extended by including two additional variables such as; 'governmental support' and 'perceived benefits'. These variables were previously studied by Seyal and Rahman (2002) in their Brunei-based study on e-commerce adoption among SMEs and were found significant. Although these variables were used in different context, however, the inclusion of these for large businesses might bring some interesting findings to show their relevancy for the large organizations.

This was considered the most utilized and cited model for IS evaluation research. Measuring the ERP success has passed through various stages: firstly, measuring ERP system success was considered similiar to measuring IS success or effectiveness (Thong *et al.* 1996); at later stages, it was re-evaluated and definedto include utilization of the system to enhance organizational goal (Gable *et al.* 2003). from researchers perspectives. Whereas, the researchers like Martin, (1998); Markus and Tanis, 2000 and Yu, 2005 excluded the technical issues for measuring the success. Other researchers also discussed the value, benefits and financial indicators which were included to measure the ERP system success vis-a-vis organizational performance (Poston and Grabski, 2001; Nicolaou, 2004).

There is no existing literature about ERP success in Brunei due to its small market size, thus, creating an information gap as to the success of ERP systems in its businesses in the ASEAN context. As shown in Figure 1, this study was designed to fill in this gap using Ifinedo's (2008) model. Relevent hypotheses supporting the inclusion of the research variables were postulated to provide the insight of this research.

Business Vision

Business vision is the general expression of the organization which reflects the expectations and values of the major stakeholders of the business organizations (Johnson and Scholes, 1999). The issue of business vision is directly related to the strategic management so several business organizations tend to adopt to ERP system to meet their organizational objectives including business vision (Davenport, 1998, 2000; Bingi *et al.*, 1999). The most important reason for ERP adoption is gaining strategic advantage and improving customer service (Davenport, 2000). Researchers (Markus and Tanis, 2000; Yu, 2005) have stressed that an ERP is more than just another IT system for the adopting firm and business. Therefore, it must have a clear understanding of how the ERP system will support their business vision. Ifinedo's (2008) study also supported the inclusion of the variable. Thus it is hypothesized:

H1: The business vision of the organization is positively associated with the ERP system success.

Figure 1.
(modified model adapted after Ifinedo,2008)

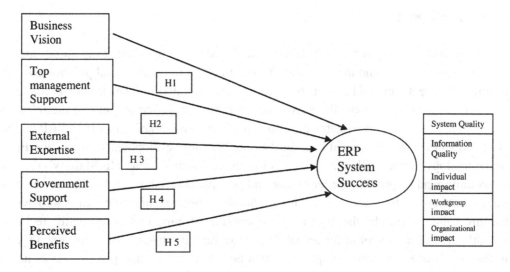

Top Management Support

Top management suport refers to the extent of which top managers in the organization provide direction, have the authority, and resources during and after the acquisitions of various IT systems at the organizational level. Conventionally, when the top management supported an IT project, the members of the organizations acted positively. For instance, when the executives at ELF-Atochem adopted the ERP system, it ensured positive outcomes (Davenport, 1998). In addition, a large body of literature affirmed the view that support coming from the top management was critical for its successful implementation (Davenport, 1998; Bingi *et al.*, 1999; Somers and Nelson, 2004). In fact, top management support was relevant for the overall success of the software application (Ifinedo, 2006). Hong and Kim (2002) and Somers and Nelson (2004) as well as Ifinedo (2008) also noted the the crucial nature of securing top management support and comittment so as to ensure the success of ERP projects in any organizations. On the basis, we propose our second hypotheses:

H2: The top management support is positively associated with the ERP system success.

External Expertise

External expertise refers to the extent to which external mediating agencies such as vendors and consultants provide knowledge, training, maintenance and other technical supports to the adopting organization. For the purpose of this study, both the vendor and the consultant were grouped as external expertise (Bajwa *et al.* 1998). According to Markus and Tanis, (2000) and Wang and Chen (2006), competent providers of ERP system did not only train clients during the system'implementations but also guide and nurture the adoptrd organizations through a wealth of experience. During ERP adoption, these organizations expected heavily on the transfer of knowledge and support as well as having cooperative, trustworthy and credible partners. Ifinedo, (2008) has found the importance of the support of the external expertise on ERP success. Thus it is hypothesized:

H3: The role of external expertise support is positively associated with the ERP system success.

Government Support

The role of the government support has been was considered very important at the initial stage of new information systems adoption and implementation. The impact of governmental policies and initiative has been shown to have direct and indirect stimulation to the supply of information that produces faster technology. For many organizations, the government has been a source of funding the infrastructure (Kettinger, 1994). This study investigates government's involvement and support in ERP adoption in SMEs. By establishing a governmental body in its infrastructure development, namely, the Brunei Information Technology Council (BIT Council), Ministry of Communications, His Majesty's Government has shown commitment by providing a legitimate and positive leadership role to digitize its economy.

Several researchers in the recent years have studied the governmental role. Ang and Pavri (1994) stated that direct intervention by the government is considered important in promoting technological innovation although the degree of influence on firms may vary among countries. Seah and Fjermestad (1997) in their study of EC adoption emphasized that both government and private sectors had played vital roles in supporting the pillars of EC framework. An understanding of the roles of the government as the facilitator for EC would promote the strategic framework for EC. Papazafeiropoulou and Pouloudi (2000) argued that the government should recognize the unique qualities of the Internet and new EC environments and should treat the different groups of stakeholders differently according to their specific need. Utomo and Dodgson (2001) in their IT diffusion among Indonesian SMEs have further confirmed that government could play an effective role as facilitator in providing assistance to SMEs that have limited IT resources.

In several Singapore-based studies, researchers Yap *et al.* (1994) examined the impact of government incentive program on IT in forty small businesses. Evidence has shown that governmental incentive in the form of economic, financial and technological support had lowered the barrier of IT adoption. Goh (1995) suggested that government could play a leadership role in the diffusion of innovation. Tan and Teo (1998); Teo and Tan, (2000) have discussed the government role and support for the Internet adoption studies. Scupola (2003) showed that SMEs desired governmental intervention both in term of influence and regulation; such intervention should concentrate on knowledge deployment, subsidies and mobilization. This governmental support was measured in this study by using a construct created by Tan and Teo (abid) for their Singapore-based study. It was evident that researchers for the various IS-based studies used the government support as a variable. However, the use of the same method for the ERP research has not been reported especially in ASEAN context, thus, it is hypothesized:

H4: The role of government support is positively associated with the ERP system success.

Perceived Benefits

This variable had studied together with several others researchers in technological innovation researches (Saunders and Clark, 1992; Premkumar and Ramamurthy, 1995; Moore and Benbasat, 1996). The E-businesses that have adopted the ERP system with the inclusion of perceived benefits showed that it was one of the significant contributing factors for success (Chau and Turner, 2002; Drew, 2003; Abid, 2010). Chwelos *et al.* (2001) studied the variable for developing an EDI adoption model and concluded, (in addition to other findings) that higher perceived benefits would lead to greater intent to adopt the EDI. For a successful business it was considered as one of the prime criteria of ERP implementation and adoption, i.e., to gain benefits from existing ways of doing things. Therefore, in order for organizations to measure success of ERP system, it had to be evaluated on the basis of perceived benefits (We *et al.* 2009) such as cost reduction; better flow of information, reduction in processing time; and better coordinations of business processes (Ramirez and Garcia, 2005). According to Yi-fen and Yang (2010), although the ERP implementation were complex and costly, business organizations might engage in ERP implementation if the perceived benefits exceeded perceive risks and costs. Similarly, Shiau *et al.* (2009) noted in their study that with the ERP implementation the organizations gained benefits such as improved customer services, better production schedulings and reduced manufacturing costs.

H5: The perceived ERP benefits are positive when associated with the ERP system success.

METHODOLOGY

Design of the Instrument

From the review of the literature and on the basis of the model developed that ful-fill the research objectives, the questionnaire was modified and edited. The questionnaire was further tested to asses the reliablity and validity. On the basis of face and content validity, it was revised and refined before administrating the survey. The multidimensional instrument was developed in three parts to capture the information. Part 1 contained demographic and organizational data, consisting of questions pertaining to data with nominal and ordinal measurements. Part 2 captured the information on external as well as inter-organizational factors on 5-point Likert scale (1-strongly disagrees to 5 for strongly agree). Part 3 captured responses on ERP success on five-point Likert scale. ERP success referred to how the adoption of an ERP system in the organization which enhanced effectiveness. This was measured with a twenty-five item questionnaire using the 5-point Likert scale. The instrument was adapted from Ifinedo, (2008). Table 2 provides details of the sources of constructs and the number of items used in this study.

Data Collection

In view of the the small market size, a random sampling of around 150 business organizations were selected from the Yellow pages of Brunei Telecom directory (2010). Techniques like step-wise sample size determiniation as suggested by Simon and Burstein (1985) was used to justify the sample size, i.e., not be less than 100. Business organizations were approached personally by field staff recreuited for this purpose. From observations from previous Brunei-based studies revealed that with small trade volume and local culture, Bruneian managers were approached personally in order to increase the response rate. In the past, all other methods such as mail survey, telephonic or online or Web-based survey had poor response rate. The sampling frame included both priviate and public sector organizations. Whereas, the unit of analysis for this study was on the firm-level so the key personnels such as functional managers, senior managers and/or deputy directors of ICT were approached to fill-in the questionnaire.

The Sample

One hundred and fifty questionnaires were sent to the various business organizations in the Brunei-Muara district (capital area). Out of them, 87 questionnaires were received. On the closer examination, only forty-five were retained for the study. The reasons were some of the business organizations started only using the ERP system for the past three to six months, while some of the questionnaires were not filled-in, by the first level managers so they were dropped from this study. This made the response rate to 30% that would not be considered as very attractive. However, it was in line with the minimum recommended rate of 30% for survey research (Johnson and Owens, 2003). The basic statistics and reliability coefficient are provided in the Table 2.

Response bias is a type of cognitive bias which can affect the results of statistical survey especially in the case when respondents answer the question in the way not reflecting their true beliefs. This may happen when the respondents wish to please the questioner by answering what: appears to be the "morally right" answer. This occurs often in the wording of the questionnaire (Lee, 2001). This was dealt by improving the face validity of the questionnaire by having the expert opinion on all the items of question-naire and by physically examining the questionnaire by our survey team at the time of data collection.

Controlling Non-Response Bias: Non-response bias was checked following the suggestion given by Armstrong and Overton (1977), where characteristics of non-respondents were assumed to be similar to late respondent. Non-response bias was found to be not existent based on independent samples t-tests with none of the demographics being statistically significant (p > 0.05, two-tailed tests).

RESULTS

Data obtained from the survey were analysed using descriptive statistics, factor analysis as well as cor-relation and regression analysis, using SPSS- 18.

Background Profile

The background data of participating managers, as well as their organizational profile is summarized in Table 1. The Table 1 describes the characteristics of respondents. Majority is relatively young male executives within age group of 25-35 years (40%).

Validity and Reliability

In order to assess the validity and reliability, tests were performed in this study. For getting the reliability of the questionnaire the coefficient of Cronbach's alpha (1951) was taken into account. Minimum Cron-bach's alpha values are greater than 0.70 indicates reliability of the instrument (Nunnally, 1978). During the initial screening of conducting reliability tests some items were dropped because of low corrected-item total correlation which was less than 0.40, i.e., the cut-off value suggested (Hair *et al.* 1998). The remaining items were applied the factor analysis subjected to principal component analysis using varimax rotation, in addition to considering Kaiser-Normalization as techniques of rotation to examine both the individual items and the relationship among them (Hair *et al.* 1998). All the items that were loaded on more than one factor at cut-off value of 0.40 were eliminated from the constructs (The result of the factor analysis is not attached to avoid the unnecessary length of the paper. In addition, two types of validity were assessed to validate: convergent and discriminant validities. Churchill, (1979) has suggested that convergent and discriminant validities should be examined for construct validity. Therefore, convergent validity was assessed by examining composite reliability (CR) and average variance extracted (AVE) from the five constructs (Hair *et al.* 1998).

CR is calculated by squaring the sum of loadings, and then dividing it by the sum of squared loadings, plus the sun of the measurement error whereas, the AVE measures the variance captured by the indicators relative to measurement error. Table 2 provides the quality control; statistics with internal consistency and CR values. The CR values for all five constructs were between the suggested minimum of 0.70 (Hair *et al.*, 1998). Table 3 shows the inter-constructs correlation and values shown diagonally represent the variance. The average variance of 0.50 suggested need for further evidence for convergent validity (Fornell and Larcker, 1981) These AVE values could also be used to assess discriminant validity which occur when the AVE exceed the square pair wise correlation between the construct (Espinoza, 1999).

Table 1. Demographical and organizational data

Variable	Description	Percentage
Gender	Male	64%
	Female	36%
Age	Between 25-35	40%
	Between 36-40	35%
	Above 40	25%
Position	Managers/Supervisors	58%
	Deputy Directors/Deputy Managers	28%
	Directors/Senior Executives	14%
Participating Organizations	Wholesale/retailers	20%
	Trading	25%
	Shipping	10%
	Construction	15%
	Petroleum/Natural Gas	8%
	Manufacturing	12%
	Electrical	10%
Major tasks accomplished with ERP Systems	Customer services	15%
	Order entry	20%
	Order tracking	20%
	Billing	25%
	Sales/Marketing	20%
	Planning/Scheduling	13%
	HR	12%
Types of ERP Systems in use	Microsoft	67%
	Oracle E-business	61%
	Oracle People soft	50%
	SAP business 1	62%
	SAP R/3	46%
	EPICOR	64%
	In-house	40%

Common Method Variance

The data on all constructs in this study is self-reported and collected from single respondents which are liable to this common method variance problem. It is because of this reason that the correlation or part of them does not occur to actual relationship between variables as they are measured by the same method (Podsakoff *et al.* 2003). A common method variance will tend to inflate the correlation between the variables (Bagozzi and Yi, 1998). To examine the common method variance we conducted a Harman's single factor test (Podsakoff *et al.* 2003) by using SPSS factor analysis. The result has indicated that

Table 2. Reliability and quality control statistics

	Mean	Std. dev	CronbachAlpha (α)	Original items	CR	Source
Business Vision	3.74	0.74	.70	2	.75	Davenport (2000), Deloitte Consulting (2000)
Top management support	3.15	0.54	.74	4	.72	Krumbholz & Maiden, (2001)
External experts role	3.83	0.54	.73	5	.76	Thong *et al.* (1996)
Government support	3.59	0.76	.96	3	.70	Tan and Teo 1998
Perceived Benefits	3.86	0.55	.71	4	.74	Chwelos *et al.* (2001)
ERP success	3.40	0.58	.74	25	.72	Gable *et al.* (2003), Ifinedo, (2006)

largest variance explained by an individual factor is 36%. It may seem high but still is below 50% of the cut-out limit. Therefore, we believe that there is no significant problem with common method variance.

Correlation Analysis

As shown in Table 3, zero order correlation is made between the various independent variables prior to regression analysis. The correlation provides directional support for the predicted relationship and shows that co-linearity among the independent variables are within acceptable range (Hair *et al.* 1998). The Table 3 indicates the AVE that is bold and diagonal and the square root should be larger than off-diagonal elements and is further evident from the Table data where no case has been noticed and none of the correlation between the construct is greater than square root of AVE (diagonal).

Regression Analysis

Regression analysis is conducted not only to find out the relationship between the five independent variables on the ERP system success but also to find the predictive indicators of the ERP success among the surveyed business organizations in Brunei. In line with the principles of multivariate data analysis, data is screened for outliers. Cases with standard deviation greater than 2 and cases with missing values are removed. The result of regression analysis is presented in Table 4. The model has statistically significant F-ratio and model possesses sufficient explanatory power as indicated by R^2 coefficient that shows

Table 3. Showing Inter-constructs correlation

Constructs	1	2	3	4	5	6
Business vision (1)	**0.58**					
Top management support (2)	.45*	**0.60**				
External expertise support (3)	.11	.05	**0.55**			
Government support(4)	.19	.29*	.38*	**0.83**		
Perceived benefits (5)	.18	.23*	.55*	.30*	**0.53**	
ERP success (6)	.48*	.18	.46*	.29*	.37*	

Diagonal represents the total variance explained. * shows significant values at p< 0.05

Table 4. Showing regression analysis

Variables	Beta	t-value	p-value	Result	Remarks
Business Vision	.512	5.09	.000	**Significant**	**H1 supported**
Top management support	.075	.719	.474	Not Significant	H2 not supported
Role of external expertise	.207	2.483	.015	**Significant**	**H3 supported**
Role of government support	.256	2.750	.007	**Significant**	**H4 supported**
Perceived benefits	.401	4.407	.000	**Significant**	**H5 supported**

Dependent variable: ERP systems success

R^2 = 52%, Adjusted R^2= .49, F=15.88, -statistically significant (p<0.00)

52% of the variance in the ERP success is explained by the business vision, top management support, governmental support, external expertise role and the perceived benefits. From the Table 4, it is further evident that four out of five variables are significant predictors of the ERP system success.

In addition, the adjusted R^2 of 0.46 (46%) is used to incorporate the effect of including additional independent variable in a multiple regression equation indicating further that there is some inflation in the R^2 value (Hair *et al.* 1998).

Beta coefficients are the coefficients of the independent variables when all the variables are expressed in standardized form. They were used here to compare the relative importance of each independent variable directly in relation to the dependent variable. The highest beta coefficient of 0.512 among the five attributes showed that 'business vision' was the most important variable in measuring the ERP success. This business vision was followed by 'perceived benefits' (coefficient = 0.401), 'government support' (coefficient= 0.256) followed by 'role of external expertise' (coefficient= 0.207).

DISCUSSION

This pioneering study explored the ERP implementation process among various Bruneian business organizations along with the factors that contributed towards the ERP success. Study results revealed that 51% of the businesses had implemented the ERP system in the past. The results showed that four (4) out of five (5) inter-organizational and external factors contributed significantly towards ERP success among the surveyed organizations. Other findings also showed a positive relationship among the variables proving evidence to establish positive relationship between these variables. It also showed that the result model supported the findings, i.e., statistically significant in measuring ERP system success with greater than 50% variation. This model possessed a better explanatory power than various previous researches in the area of e-commerce in Singapore and Brunei ranging from 0.36, 0.41, 0.65 (Kendall *et al.* 2001; Seyal and Rahman, 2002; Looi 2005). However, in Ifinedo, (2008) study, the measured ERP success in Finland was found to be 17% of the variance and mostly contributed by three external variables (Table 5). Therefore, this study has fulfilled both of its objectives.

The study concluded that this business vision had contributed significantly towards the ERP success. This further being illustrated that the business vision of an organization could impact on the overall success of the ERP software; when ERP implementation supports the organizational goals and mission, the success level of ERP system inclined to be high. In other words when successful organizations have clear objectives of its ERP implementation as part of the overall firm's strategic plan, the business specifically gains from this investment as compared to those wherein the same objectives are not embedded in the firm's strategic directions. This leads to the first hypotheses (H1) as true. The results support the prior work of Davenport (2000); Chwelos *et al.* (2001) and Ifinedo (2008) who believed that success level of IT systems including ERP remains low if it is not properly linked with the firm's overall objectives. In other words, when firms articulate the linkage between ERP acquisition and implantation with business vision, positive outcome and overall success of software system tend to be high (Ifinedo, 2008).The findings support the previous studies, i.e., when ERP adoption supports the mission and organizational goals, success level of ERP systems remains high (Jafari *et al.* 2006; Ifinedo, 2008; Ngai *et al.* 2008; Mirbagheri and Marthandan, 2012).

Previous studies have strongly emphasized on the role of top management role in promoting the technology especially those within the context of E-businesses among SMEs. Evidence from literature affirms that top management awareness and support are important and significant criteria for technology adoption (Mirbagheri and Marthandan, 2012). Top management can provide smoother environment with support and commitment. Awareness of top management while implementing ERP brings better results to obtain cooperation of staff and coordination. While assessing the success of ERP, Ifinedo, (2008) noticed that overall benefits of ERP systems may be low in situations where top management support is either low or non-existent. Unfortunately, in this study we could not find support for the role of top management as one of the success factor of ERP. Contrary to studies done by DeLone and McLean, (1992); Davenport, (1998); Bingi, *et al.* (1999); Somers and Nelson, (2004); Nandhakumar *et al.* (2005) and Ifinedo, (2008), the results of this study does not confirm with their findings. It might be due to the plausible reasons, as stated in the literature. The literature, IS research strands ERP studies have generally viewed top management support as the most important factor for ERP implementation success (Somers & Nelson, 2004).

A typical view was that ERP implementation project 'completely hinges' on the strong and sustained commitment of the top management (Al-Mudimigh *et al.* 2001) and in all stages of ERP implementation (Plant and Willcock, 2007). In many researches the failures of ERP system, had been generally linked with the absence of top management which caused the failure of project (Sarkar & Lee, 2003). They stated that during the implementation of ERP system, any changes like; the acquisition of the company by other; the CEO leaving the company; a new CEO being appointed; and the new CEO's agenda being 'dominated by other concern'. Nevertheless, the researcher straight forwardly linked the failure of top management to a lack of committed leadership. Akkerman and Van-Helden (2002) also suggested that any top management support is closely related and, hence, changes in any of them will ripple through in all the others, as they reinforce each other in the same direction which leads to virtuous and vicious cycles of ERP. Nevertheless, Neufeld *et al.* (2007) suggested that top management support construct has not been sufficiently integrated into existing user adoption theories nor has literature defined specific top management behaviour that is associated with technology implementation success.

On the other hand, results supported that of Bajwa's *et al.* (1998); results showed no direct relationship between top management support and EIS success. While the result contradicted the findings of all above mentioned studies the plausible reason might be due to the decision process that had affected by exogenous reasons than business-related factors or based on internally important factors (Lee & Lee, 2004) especially when they related to ERP implementation. This aspect needed to be investigated accordingly. The hypotheses H2 therefore, could not be accepted.

Furthermore, the study provided detailed data as to how the role of external expertise could have the impact on the overall success of ERP system, data analysis which revealed a strong relationship between them. Literature has further supported that the quality of external expertise is very important measurement of ERP success during project acquisition and implementation. Study results also indicated that impact of external expertise in the organization remained high and significant when quality external expertise, i.e., vendor and/or consultants, were hired. The results supported the prior work of Gefen, (2004); Ko *et al.* (2005); and Ifinedo, (2008). Thus our hypothesis H3 is accepted.

In addition, the results showed that the role of the government support was found to be significant in determining ERP success. According to Teo and Tan, (1998), the impact of government policies and initiatives were shown to have direct and indirect effects to making information readily accessible, thus, producing faster technology diffusion, such as, government efforts to establish a national information infrastructure in US, Singapore or in Malaysia. It has shown where the government has provided a legitimate and positive leadership role in developing the information infrastructure in its efforts to promote technological support to the businesses (Kettinger, 1994; Tan & Teo, 1998; Irefin *et al.*, 2012).

In several Brunei-based studies within the context of technology adoption in SMEs, it was reported by Seyal & Rahman, (2000, 2003) that the government support remained crucial for promoting the technology not only for SMEs but also for the large scale businesses. Therefore, the results supported all prior studies by Yap *et al.*, (1994); Tan and Teo (1998); Teo and Tan (2000); Utomo and Dodgson (2001); and Scupola (2003). Thus the hypothesis H4 is accepted.

Perceived benefits are found to be an important predictor of ERP success within the context of Bruneian businesses. Our results supported the findings of Seyal and Rahman (2000), i.e., where perceived benefits were important pre-requisites to technology implementation (e-commerce) especially in medium sized organizations. In addition, it was also concluded that the factor "perceived benefits" were related to the size of the business; for small organizations the significance of this factor for the adoption of the technology remained ineffective. The results further supported Moore and Benbasat, (1996); Chwelos *et al.*, (2001) and Abid (2010) that perceived benefits were the most influential determinants of the technology usage. Thus the hypothesis H5 is accepted.

Finally we draw comparison of this study with the study of Ifinedo (2008) as shown in Table 5.

The above comparison showed similarities and dissimilarities especially in terms of measuring ERP success as a descriptive variable. The reliability coefficient in this study (0.74) was less than in Ifinedo's work (0.89) but a little higher than the specified criteria of (0.70) as stated by Hair *et al.* (1998). It is interesting to note that in this study, ERP success was measured on a 10-items construct clustered into three sets: four (4) items for system quality; four (4) items for information quality, and, two (2) items for organizational impact. The items measuring individual and workgroup impact were excluded from the ERP success construct because of low factor loading that is indicative of the insignificant nature of this construct among Bruneian businesses. Finally, the addition of two contextual variables in our study has increased the R^2 value in regard to Ifinedo's work.

CONCLUSION AND PRACTICAL IMPLICATIONS

The primary purpose of this study was threefold, namely: (1) to identify the use of ERP among the Bruneian Businesses; (2) to measure the success of ERP; and, (3) to find out the role of five contextual variables in determining the ERP success. At an outset, the study revealed that almost half of the

Table 5. Showing comparative analysis of two studies

Parameters	This Study	Ifinedo, (2008)
Year	2013	2008
Where	Brunei Darussalam (SE-Asia)	Finland, Estonia (North-Europe)
Sample size	45	44
Response rate	30%	9.5%
Independent variables	Business vision, top management support, external expertise, government support and perceived benefits	Business vision, top management support and external expertise
Dependent variables	ERP success factor measured on 25-item scale only 10 items were retained with system quality, information quality and organizational impact	ERP success factors measured on 25-item scale divided into five constructs: system quality, information quality, individual impact, workgroup impact and organizational impact
Cronbach alpha	.74	.89
R^2	57%	17%
Statistical Analysis	Correlation & Regression	PLS-graph
Findings	4 out of 5 hypotheses supported	3 out of 3 were supported

surveyed organizations have implemented the ERP system with a mean success of 3.40. Secondly, the instrument used to assess the ERP success was adapted from the previous studies. The original instrument consists of a 25-items questionnaire; this study used a modified version with 10-items instead of 25. Fifteen items were deleted because of low corrected item total and after varimax rotation of factor analysis. Finally, four (4) out of five (5) variables used for the study excluding the role of top management were supported. Surprisingly, these findings did not agree in general, with previous studies and in particular, with studies conducted in Brunei, suggesting that this matter must be addressed accordingly.

Limitations

As in most researches using survey methodology, this study has its weaknesses. Several limitations of this study qualify the findings and suggest direction for future research. The study is limited to its small sample size and controllable variables. By readdressing the research design, study could further be improved.

Practical Implications

Results of this study provided interesting implications for practitioners and for those in public offices who are responsible for promoting or speeding up the ERP implementation process among the Bruneian businesses. The success of ERP systems was measured through the standard instrument modified by Ifinedo and Nahar (2006) in his work in Finland & Estonia in 2008; this instrument consisted of a 25-item questionnaire clustered under five constructs, as mentioned earlier. In this study, ERP success among Bruneian businesses was measured using a Likert scale, 10-items questionnaire, and grouped under three construct, namely: system quality, information quality and organizational impact. This provided an insight on e-business practices among the business organizations. Participating organizations focused more on the benefits of the ERP system such as information quality and organizational impact brought about by the use of this software. Nevertheless, the success model proposed by Gable *et al.* (2003) measuring individual impact, and, that of Ifinedo and Nahar (2006) measuring workgroup impact, could not be supported. Their inclusion was made with basic assumption to enhance efficient cross-functional operation in the various sub-units could not be supported. In sum, any future endeavour to measure the success of software application should focus mainly on the following: (1) system itself; (2) information quality; and (3) its impact on the organization.

The significance of four (4) contextual variables in this study provided valuable insights on how businesses find them relevant in measuring ERP success. The business owners and regulatory authorities should focus on these and highlight them in planning seminars and road shows so that the organizations that are in the process of considering the ERP systems should consider it during the implementation phase as well. Nevertheless, it is also good to explore why governmental intervention, e.g., supporting top management, is not significant in implementing the technology in large scale organizations.

REFERENCES

Abdel-Kader, M., & Nguyen, T. P. (2011). An investigation of enterprise resource planning implementation in a small firm: A study of problems encountered and successes achieved. *International Journal of Enterprise Information Systems*, 7(1), 18–40. doi:10.4018/jeis.2011010102

Abdelghaffar, H. (2012). Success factors for ERP implementation in large organizations: The case of Egypt. *Electronic Journal of Information Systems in Developing Countries*, 52(4), 1–13.

Abid, A. A. (2010). *Perceived impacts and barriers to e-Business technology adoption: A preliminary study* (Unpublished Master's Dissertation). Caulfield School of IT, Monash University, Melbourne, Australia.

Agarwal, R., & Prasad, J. (1997). The role of innovation characteristics and perceived voluntaries in the acceptance of information technology. *Decision Sciences*, 28(3), 557–582. doi:10.1111/j.1540-5915.1997.tb01322.x

Akkermans, H. A., Bogerd, P., Yu, C. E. V., & Wassenhove, L. N. (2003). The impact of ERP on supply chain management: Exploratory findings from a European Delphi study. *European Journal of Operational Research*, 146(2), 284–301. doi:10.1016/S0377-2217(02)00550-7

Al-Mashari, M., & Zairi, M. (2000). Information and business process equality: The case of SAP R/3 implementation. *Electronic Journal of Information Systems in Developing Countries*, 2(4), 1–15.

Ang, J., & Pavri, F. (1994). A survey and critique of the impact of information technology. *International Journal of Information Management*, 17(3), 122–130. doi:10.1016/0268-4012(94)90031-0

Aydin, A. O., & Tunali, S. (2007). Intelligent agent technologies promise in emerging arena: Mass customization. *Proceedings of the 6th WSEAS International Conference on Artificial Intelligent, Knowledge Engineering and Data Bases*.

Bajwa, D., Rai, A., & Brennan, I. (1998). Key antecedents of executive information system success: A path analytic approach. *Decision Support Systems*, 22(1), 31–43. doi:10.1016/S0167-9236(97)00032-8

Bergstrom, M., & Stehn, L. (2005). Matching industrialised timber frame housing needs and enterprise resource planning: A change process. *International Journal of Production Economics, 97*(2), 172–184. doi:10.1016/j.ijpe.2004.06.052

Bingi, P., Sharma, M., & Godla, J. (1999). Critical issues affecting an ERP implementation. *Information Systems Management, 16*(3), 7–14. doi:10.1201/1078/43197.16.3.19990601/31310.2

Cartman, C., & Salazar, A. (2011). The influence of organizational size, internal IT capabilities and competitive and vendor pressure on ERP adoption in SMEs. *International Journal of Enterprise Information Systems, 7*(3), 68–92. doi:10.4018/jeis.2011070104

Chau, S. B., & Turner, P. (2002). A framework for analyzing factors influencing small to medium sized enterprises: Ability to derive benefits from the conduct of Web-based electronic commerce (EC).*Proceedings of Xth European Conference on Information Systems.*

Chen, I. J. (2001). Planning for ERP systems: Analysis and future trends. *Supply Chain Management Review, 7*(5), 374–386.

Chen, I. J., & Popovich, K. (2003). Understanding customer relationship management. *Business Process Management Journal, 9*(5), 672–688. doi:10.1108/14637150310496758

Chou, S. W., & Chang, Y. L. (2008). The Implementation Factors that Influence the ERP Benefits. *Decision Support Systems, 46*(1), 149–157. doi:10.1016/j.dss.2008.06.003

Churchill, G. A. J. (1979). A paradigm for developing better measures of marketing constructs. *JMR, Journal of Marketing Research, 15*(1), 64–73. doi:10.2307/3150876

Chwelos, P., Benbasat, I., & Dexter, A. S. (2001). Empirical test on EDI adoption model. *Information Systems Research, 12*(1), 304–321. doi:10.1287/isre.12.3.304.9708

CIA World Fact Book. (2010). *Country Report*. Retrieved from www.cia.gov/cia/publications

Cragg, P. B., & King, M. (1993). Small-firm computing: Motivators and inhibitors. *Management Information Systems Quarterly, 17*(1), 47–60. doi:10.2307/249509

Cragg, P. B., and Mitchell, E. (2000). Benchmarking IT practices in small firms. *Proceedings of ACIS.*

Cronbach, L. J. (1951). Coefficient alpha and the internal structure of test. *Psychometrika, 16*(3), 297–334. doi:10.1007/BF02310555

Davenport, T. (1998). Putting the enterprise into the enterprise system. *Harvard Business Review, 76*(4), 121–131. PMID:10181586

Davenport, T. (2000). *Mission Critical*. Boston, MA: Harvard Business School Press.

Deloitte-Consulting. (2000). *ERP's second wave: Maximizing the value of ERP-enabled processes*. Available at: www.dc.com/Insight/research

DeLone, W. H., & McLean, E. R. (1992). Information systems success: The quest for the dependent variable. *Information Systems Research, 3*(1), 60–69. doi:10.1287/isre.3.1.60

DeLone, W. H., & McLean, E. R. (2003). The DeLone and McLean model of information systems success: A ten-year update. *Journal of Management Information Systems*, *19*(4), 9–30.

Doukidis, G. I., Smithson, S., & Lybereas, T. (1994). Trends in information technology in small business. *Journal of End User Computing*, *6*, 15–25.

Drew, S. (2003). Strategic use of e-Commerce by SMEs in the east of England. *European Management Journal*, *21*(1), 79–88. doi:10.1016/S0263-2373(02)00148-2

Ein-Dor, P., & Segev, E. (1978). Organizational context and the success of management information systems. *Management Science*, *24*(10), 1064–1077. doi:10.1287/mnsc.24.10.1064

Espinoza, M. M. (1999). Assessing the cross-cultural applicability of a service quality measure: A comparative study between Quebec and Peru. *International Journal of Service Industry Management*, *10*(5), 449–468. doi:10.1108/09564239910288987

Farzaneh, M., Vanani, I. R., & Sohrabi, B. (2013). A survey study of influential factors in the implementation of enterprise resource planning systems. *International Journal of Enterprise Information Systems*, *9*(1), 76–96. doi:10.4018/jeis.2013010105

Fornell, C., & Larcker, D. F. (1981). Evaluating structural equation models with unobservable variables and measurement error. *JMR, Journal of Marketing Research*, *18*(10), 39–50. doi:10.2307/3151312

Gable, G. G., Sedera, D., & Chan, T. (2003). Measuring Enterprise Systems Success: A preliminary model. *Proceedings of the 9th AMCIS Conference*, 576-591.

Gefen, D. (2004). What makes an ERP implementation relationship worthwhile: Linking trust, mechanism and ERP usefulness? *Journal of Management Information Systems*, *21*(1), 263–288.

Goh, H. P. (1995). The diffusion of Internet in Singapore: A Content analytic approach. Faculty of Business Administration, National University of Singapore.

Gupta, A. (2000). Enterprise Resource Planning: The emerging organizational value systems. *Industrial Management & System*, *100*(3), 114–118. doi:10.1108/02635570010286131

Gupta, A. K., Raj, S. P., & Wilemon, D. (1986). A Model for Studying RID-Marketing Interface: The Product Innovation Process. *Journal of Marketing*, *50*(2), 7–17. doi:10.2307/1251596

Hair, J. F., Anderson, R. E., Tatham, R. L., & Black, W. C. (1998). *Multivariate Data Analysis* (5th ed.). Englewood Cliff, NJ: Prentice-Hall.

Hammer, M., & Santon, S. (1999). How process enterprises really work? *Harvard Business Review*, *77*(6), 108–118. PMID:10662000

Hanafzadeh, P., Gholami, R., Dadbin, S., & Standage, N. (2010). The core critical success factors in implementations of Enterprise resource planning systems. *International Journal of Enterprise Information Systems*, *6*(2), 82–111. doi:10.4018/jeis.2010040105

Hong, K., & Kim, Y. (2002). The critical success factors for ERP implementation: An organizational fit perspective. *Information & Management*, *40*(1), 25–40. doi:10.1016/S0378-7206(01)00134-3

Hsu, L. L., & Chen, M. (2004). Impacts of ERP systems on the integrated-interaction performance of manufacturing and marketing. *Industrial Management & Data Systems, 104*(1/2), 42–55. doi:10.1108/02635570410514089

Ifinedo, P. (2006). *Enterprise resource planning system success assessment: An integrative framework* (Unpublished doctoral dissertation). Department of Computer Science and Information Systems, University of Jyvaskyla, Jyvaskyla, Finland.

Ifinedo, P. (2008). Impact of business vision, top management support and external expertise on ERP success. *Business Process Management Journal, 14*(4), 551–568. doi:10.1108/14637150810888073

Ifinedo, P., & Davidrajuh, R. (2005). Digital divide in Europe: Assessing and comparing the e-readiness of a developed and an emerging economy in the Nordic region. *Electronic Government: An International Journal, 2*(2), 111–133. doi:10.1504/EG.2005.007090

Ifinedo, P., & Nahar, N. (2006). Quality, impact and success of ERP systems: A study involving some firms in the Nordic-Baltic region. *Journal of Information Technology Impact, 6*(1), 19–46.

Iivari, J. (2003). An empirical test of DeLone-McLean model of information systems success. *The Data Base for Advances in Information Systems, 36*(2), 8–27. doi:10.1145/1066149.1066152

Irefin, I. A., Abdul-Azeez, I. A., & Tijani, A. A. (2012). An investigative study of the factors affecting the adoption of ICT in SME in Nigeria. *Australian Journal of Business and Management Research, 2*(2), 1–9.

Jacobs, F. R., & Whybark, D. C. (2000). *Why ERP a Premier on SAP Implementation?* New York: Irwin/McGraw-Hill.

Jafari, S. M., Osman, R. M., Yusuff, & Tang, S. H. (2006). ERP implementation in Malaysia: The importance of critical success factor. *International Journal of Engineering & Technology, 3*(1), 125-131.

Johnson, G., & Scholes, K. (1999). *Exploring corporate strategy: text & cases*. London: Prentice-Hall.

Johnson, T., & Owens, L. (2003). *Survey response rate reporting in the professional literature*. Paper presented at the 58th Annual Meeting of the American Association for Public Opinion Research, Nashville, TN. Retrieved from www.sel.uic.edu/publist/Conference/rr_reporting.pdf

Julien, P. and Raymond, L. (1994, Summer). Factors of new technology adoption in the retail sector. *Entrepreneurship Theory and Practice*, 79-90.

Kamhawi, E. (2007). Critical factors in implementation success of ERP system: An empirical investigation from Bahrain. *International Journal of Enterprise Information Systems, 3*(2), 34–49. doi:10.4018/jeis.2007040103

Kandall, J. D., Tung, L. L., Chua, K. H., Ng, C. H. D., & Tan, S. M. (2001). Receptivity of Singapore SMEs to e-commerce adoption. *The Journal of Strategic Information Systems, 10*(3), 223–242. doi:10.1016/S0963-8687(01)00048-8

Kettinger, J. (1994). National infrastructure diffusion and US information super highway. *Information & Management, 27*(6), 357–369. doi:10.1016/0378-7206(94)90016-7

Kim, Y., Lee, Z., & Gosain, S. (2005). Impediments to successful ERP implementation process. *Business Process Management Journal, 11*(2), 158–170. doi:10.1108/14637150510591156

Klaus, H., Rosemann, M., & Gable, G. G. (2000). What is ERP? *Information Systems Frontiers, 2*(2), 141–162. doi:10.1023/A:1026543906354

Ko, D., Kirsch, J. L., & King, W. R. (2005). Antecedents of knowledge transfer from consultants to clients in enterprise system implementations. *Management Information Systems Quarterly, 29*(1), 59–85.

Krumbholz. M., and Maiden, N. (2001). The implementation of enterprise resource planning packages in different organizational and national cultures. *Information Systems, 26*(30), 185-204.

Law, C. C. H., & Ngai, E. W. T. (2007). ERP systems adoption: An exploratory study of the organizational factors and impacts of ERP success. *Information & Management, 44*(4), 418–432. doi:10.1016/j.im.2007.03.004

Lee, S. C., & Lee, H. G. (2004). The importance of change management after ERP implementation: An information capability perspective.*Proceedings of the 25th International Conference on Information Systems*.

Looi, H. C. (2005). E-commerce adoption in Brunei Darussalam: A quantitative analysis of factors influencing its adoption. *Communications of the AIS, 15*, 61–81.

Mabert, V., Soni, A., & Venkataramanan, M. (2003). Enterprise resource planning: Managing the implication process. *European Journal of Operational Research, 146*(2), 302–314. doi:10.1016/S0377-2217(02)00551-9

Maldonado, M., & Sierra, V. (2013). User satisfaction as the foundation of the success following an ERP adoption: An empirical study from Latin America. *International Journal of Enterprise Information Systems, 9*(3), 77–99. doi:10.4018/jeis.2013070104

Markus, L., & Tanis, C. (2000). The enterprise systems experience from adoption to success. In R. W. Zmud (Ed.), *Framing the Domains of IT Research: Glimpsing the Future through the Past*. Cincinnati, OH: Pinnaflex Educational Resources, Inc.

Markus, L., Tanis, P. C., & Van, F. (2000). Multi-site ERP implementation. *Communications of the ACM, 43*(4), 42–46. doi:10.1145/332051.332068

Martin, M. (1998). Enterprise Resource Planning. *Fortune, 137*(2), 149–151.

Mexas, M. P., Quelhas, G. O. L., Costa, H. G., & Lameira, V. (2013). A set of criteria for selection of enterprise resource planning (ERP). *International Journal of Enterprise Information Systems, 9*(2), 44–69. doi:10.4018/jeis.2013040103

Mirbagheri, F. A., & Marthandan, G. (2012). Success factors of ERP implementation in SMEs in Malaysia. *International Journal of Computing & Corporate Research, 2*(6). Retrieved from www.ijccr.com

Moore, G. C., & Benbasat, I. (1996). Development of an instrument to measure the perceptions of adopting an information technology innovation. *Information Systems Research, 2*(3), 192–222. doi:10.1287/isre.2.3.192

Nandhakumar, J., Rossi, M., & Talvinen, J. (2005). The dynamics of contextual forces of ERP implementation. *The Journal of Strategic Information Systems, 18*(2), 79–105.

Ngai, E. W. T., Law, C. C. H., & Wat, F. K. T. (2008). Examining the critical success factors in the adoption of enterprise resource planning. *Computers in Industry,* 1–17. doi:10.1016/j.compnd.2007.12.001]

Nicolaou, A. I. (2004). Firms performance effects in relation to the implementation and use of ERP system. *Journal of Information Systems, 18*(2), 79–105. doi:10.2308/jis.2004.18.2.79

Nour, M. A., & Mouakket, S. (2011). A classification framework of critical success factor for ERP Systems implementation: A multi-stakeholder perspective. *International Journal of Enterprise Information Systems, 7*(1), 56–71. doi:10.4018/jeis.2011010104

Nunnally, J. C. (1978). *Psychometric Theory.* McGraw-Hill.

Papazafeiropoulou, A., & Pouloudi. (2000). The government role in improving EC adoption. *Proceedings of European Conference on Information Systems,* 709-716.

Peslak, A. R. (2012). Industry variables affecting ERP success and Status. *International Journal of Enterprise Information Systems, 8*(3), 15–30. doi:10.4018/jeis.2012070102

Petter, S., DeLone, W., & McLean, E. (2008). Measuring information systems success: Model, dimensions, measures and interrelationship. *European Journal of Information Systems, 17*(3), 236–263. doi:10.1057/ejis.2008.15

Plant, R., & Willcocks, L. (2007). Critical success factor in international ERP implementation: A case research approach. *Journal of Computer Information Systems, 47*(3), 60–70.

Podsakoff, P., MacKenzie, S., Lee, J., & Podsakoff, N. (2003). Common method biases in behavioural research: A critical review of the literature and recommended remedies. *The Journal of Applied Psychology, 88*(5), 879–890. doi:10.1037/0021-9010.88.5.879 PMID:14516251

Poston, R., & Grabski, S. (2001). Financial impacts of enterprise resource planning implementation. *International Journal of AIS, 2*(4), 271–294.

Premkumar, G., & Ramamurthy, K. (1995). The role of inter-organizational and organizational factors on the decision mode for adoption of inter-organizational systems. *Decision Sciences, 26*(3), 303–336. doi:10.1111/j.1540-5915.1995.tb01431.x

Rajapakse, J., & Seddon, P. (2005). Why ERP may not suitable for organizations in developing countries?*Proceedings of PACIS.*

Rajendran, R., & Elangovan, N. (2012). Response of small enterprise to the pressure of ERP adoption. *International Journal of Enterprise, 8*(1), 28–50. doi:10.4018/jeis.2012010103

Ramirez, P., & Garcia, R. (2005). Successful ERP in Chile: An empirical study. *Proceedings of European, Mediterranean and Middle Eastern Conference on Information System.*

Research, A. M. R. (2005). *The steady stream of ERP investment.* Retrieved from www.amrresearch.com

Robbins-Gioia, L. L. C. (2006). *ERP survey result: Point to need for higher implementation success.* Retrieved from http://www.robbinsgioia.com/news_events/012802_esp.aspx.march

Saunders, C. S., & Clark, S. (1992). EDI adoption and implementation: A focus on inter-organizational linkages. *Information Resources Management Journal, 5*(1), 9–19. doi:10.4018/irmj.1992010102

Scupola, A. (2003). Government intervention in SMEs e-Commerce adoption: An institutional approach. *Proceedings of 7th Pacific Asia Conference on Information Systems,* 184-195.

Seah, T. S., & Fjermestad, J. (1997). *Roles of government and the private sector: Electronic Commerce in Singapore.* Retrieved from http://www.hsb.baylor.edu/ramsower/ais.ac.97/papers/seah.htm

Sedra, D., & Tan, F. (2005). User Satisfaction: an overarching measure of enterprise systems success. Proceedings of the PACIS.

Seethmraju, R., & Seethmraju, J. (2008). Adoption of ERP in a middle-sized enterprise: A case Study. *Proceedings of 19th Australasian Conference on Information Systems.*

Seyal, A. H., & Rahman, M. N. (2002). *Research report on Electronic Commerce adoption in small and medium enterprises in Brunei Darussalam.* Institut Teknologi Brunei.

Seyal, A. H., & Rahman, M. N. (2003). A preliminary investigation of E-Commerce adoption in small and medium enterprises in Brunei. *Journal of Global Information Technology Management, 6*(2), 6–26. doi:10.1080/1097198X.2003.10856347

Scyal, A. H., Rahman, M. N., & Mohamad, H. A. Y. (2007). A Quantitative analysis of factors contributing towards EDI adoption among Bruneian SMEs: A pilot study. *Business Process Management Journal, 3*(5), 728–746. doi:10.1108/14637150710823183

Shank, G., Parr, A., Hu, B., Corbitt, B., Thanasankit, T., & Seddon, P. (2000). Difference in critical success factors in ERP systems implementation in Australia and China: A cultural analysis.*Proceedings of the 8th European Conference on Information Systems*, 537-549.

Sheu, C., Chae, C., & Yang, C. (2004). National differences in ERP implementations: Issues and challenges. *Omega, 32*(5), 61–371. doi:10.1016/j.omega.2004.02.001

Shieu, W. L., Hsu, P. Y., & Wang, J. Z. (2009). Development of measures to assess the ERP adoption of small and medium enterprises. *Journal of Enterprise Information Management, 22*(1/2), 99–118. doi:10.1108/17410390910922859

Simon, J. L., & Burstein, P. (1985). *Basic research methods in social science* (3rd ed.). New York: Random House.

Sims, R. R. (2002). Organizational Success through Effective HRM. Retrieved from www.books.goggle.com/books

Soh, C. K., & Tay-Yap, J. (2000). Cultural its and misfits: Is ERP a universal solution? *Communications of the ACM, 43*(4), 47–51. doi:10.1145/332051.332070

Somers, T. M., & Nelson, K. G. (2004). A taxonomy of players and activities across the ERP project life cycle. *Information & Management, 41*(3), 57–78. doi:10.1016/S0378-7206(03)00023-5

Srite, M., Bennett, J., & Galy, E. (2008). Does within culture matter? An empirical study of computer usage. *Journal of Global Information Management*, *16*(1), 1–25. doi:10.4018/jgim.2008010101

Tan, C. W., & Pan, S. L. (2002). ERP success: The search for a comprehensive framework.*Proceedings of 8th Americas Conference on Information Systems*.

Tan, N., & Teo, T. S. H. (1998). Factors influencing the adoption of the Internet. *International Journal of Electronic Commerce*, *2*(3), 5–18. doi:10.1080/10864415.1998.11518312

Teo, T. S. H., & Tan, M. (2000). Factors influencing the adoption of Internet banking. *Journal of the Association for Information Systems*, *1*(5), 36.

Thong, J. Y. L., & Yap, C. S. (1995). CEO characteristics, organizational characteristics and information technology adoption in small business. *Omega*, *23*(4), 429–442. doi:10.1016/0305-0483(95)00017-I

Thong, J. Y. L., Yap, C. S., & Raman, K. S. (1996). Top management support, external expertise and information systems implementation in small businesses. *Information Systems Research*, *7*(2), 248–267. doi:10.1287/isre.7.2.248

Umble, E. J., Haft, R. R., & Umble, M. M. (2003). Enterprise resource planning: Implementation, procedures, and critical success factors. *European Journal of Operational Research*, *146*(2), 241–253. doi:10.1016/S0377-2217(02)00547-7

Utomo, H., & Dodgson, M. (2001). Contributing factors to the diffusion of IT within small and medium sized firms in Indonesia. *Journal of Global Information Technology Management*, *4*(2), 22–37. doi:10.1080/1097198X.2001.10856300

Wang, E. T. G., & Chen, J. H. F. (2006). Effect of internal support and consultant quality on the consulting process and ERP system quality. *Decision Support Systems*, *42*(2), 1029–1041. doi:10.1016/j.dss.2005.08.005

We, J., & Wang, S. (2005). What drives mobile commerce: An empirical evaluation of the revised technology acceptance model? *Information & Management*, *42*, 719–729.

We, K. S., Loong, A. C. Y., Leong, Y. M., & Ooi, K. B. (2009). Measuring ERP systems success: A re-specification of the DeLone and McLean's IS success model.*Symposium on progress in Information and Communication Technologies*.

Wee, S. (2000). Juggling toward ERP success: Keep key success factors high. *ERP News*. Retrieved from http://www.erpnews.com/erpnews/erp904/02get.html

Willcock, L. P., & Sykes, R. (2000). The role of the CIO and it functions in ERP. *Communications of the ACM*, *43*(4), 32–38. doi:10.1145/332051.332065

Yap, C. S., Thong, J. Y. L., & Raman, K. S. (1994). Effect of government incentive in computerization in small business. *European Journal of Information Systems*, *3*(3), 191–200. doi:10.1057/ejis.1994.20

Yi-fen, S., & Yang, C. (2010). Why are enterprise resources planning systems indispensable to supply chain management? *European Journal of Operational Research*, *203*(1), 81–94. doi:10.1016/j.ejor.2009.07.003

Yu, C. S. (2005). Causes influencing the effectiveness of the post-implementation ERP system. *Industrial Management & Data Systems*, *105*(1), 15–32. doi:10.1108/02635570510575225

Zhang, Z., Lee, M. K., Huang, P., & Eiang, H. X. (2005). A framework of ERP systems implementation success in China: An empirical study. *International Journal of Production Economics*, *98*(1), 56–80. doi:10.1016/j.ijpe.2004.09.004

KEY TERMS AND DEFINITIONS

Average Variance Extracted: It is calculated as a measurement of variance captured by the indicators relative to measurement errors.

Beta Coefficient: The coefficients of the independent variables when all the variables are expressed in standardized form.

Business Vision: The general expression of the organization which reflects the expectations and values of the major stakeholders of the business organizations.

Composite Reliability: It is calculated by squaring the sum of loadings, and then dividing it by the square of loadings, plus the sum of the measurement errors.

ERP: Enterprise Resource Planning is an information system that is designed to improve global management of operations in accounting, finance, production, logistic, human resources, sales and supplies.

External Expertise: The extent to which external mediating agencies such as vendors and consultants provide knowledge, training, maintenance and other technical supports to the adopting organization.

Kaiser-Normalization: It is a technique of rotation to examine both the individual items and the relationship between them.

Response Bias: It is a type of cognitive bias which can affect the results of statistical survey especially in the case when respondents answer the question in the way not reflecting their true beliefs.

Top Management Support: The extent to which top managers in the organization provide direction, have the authority, and resources and after the acquisitions of various IT systems at the organizational level.

Chapter 9
Re-Thinking the Challenges of Enterprise Architecture Implementation

Mark Dale
Swinburne University of Technology, Australia

ABSTRACT

Enterprise architecture (EA) has provided organizations with powerful frameworks with which to plan, manage, model and coordinate the alignment of organizational IS/ IT portfolios with organizational strategy. However, for the benefits of EA to be realized, it needs to also contribute to the process of implementing the specified systems and platforms. Whilst implementation was seen by early authors as an integral aspect of the EA process, it has since generally been ignored by authors, or investigated through an ontological lens of discreet technical architecture activities that does not account for the social context of an EA implementation (EAI). Drawing on an actual case study of an EAI in a large Australian financial services organization, I examine the importance of the EAI process to the delivery of the systems and platforms specified in the EA plans and highlight an alternative perspective that has the potential to sensitize scholars and practitioners appreciate to the social context of an EAI.

CASE STUDY DESCRIPTION

Bank1 is a large Australian bank and operates internationally. The EA process was initiated by the architects in response to a change in strategic direction of the organization. In Bank1, the architects are structurally differentiated from the business and are situated in the technology function. They are also structurally differentiated from other technology units due to their strategic and IS/ IT portfolio design focus (as distinct from operational support and project delivery focus. Once the EA plans were approved by the executives of the business and technology, the architects began to select the hardware and software products that would realize the changes to the IS/ IT portfolio specified in the EA plans and to develop an implementation schedule for the delivery of those products into operation. As the architects owned the EA process, they were responsible for building support and commitment for the selected technol-

DOI: 10.4018/978-1-5225-2382-6.ch009

ogy products with business and technology stakeholders. All technology projects at Bank1 are funded by the business and are staffed by specialist technology staff. It was therefore critical that the architects build connections with stakeholders from both the business and technology in order to realize the IS/IT portfolio improvements described in the EA plans.

The architects at Bank1 viewed their EAI role in technical terms and their objectives were to select new systems and develop implementation plans to deliver those systems into operation. The practices of the architects effectively created an impermeable boundary around them and made it difficult for information to flow into and out from the architecture team. When selecting the software and hardware products, the architects mapped key architectural objectives to available commercial- off-the-shelf (COTS) software and hardware products. Working amongst themselves, they developed evaluation templates and criteria to help them assess the suitability of various COTs products. The criteria emphasized architectural and performance goals (i.e. strategy alignment, flexibility, scalability, interoperability) which represented important improvements to the existing architecture of Bank1's technology portfolio. However, business and technology staff were not involved in the design of the evaluation criteria and whilst these criteria may have reflected the values and concerns of the architects, they represent a partial understanding of requirements since they take little account of what is important to the business, especially when selecting new software and hardware products (cost versus benefit, manage costs, continue to make a profit, etc.). The architects also paid little attention to the concerns and information needs of technology and technology project staff and did not engage with them. They would not discuss the selected technology products with technology project staff which meant that the business and technology were potentially investing in and implementing technology products that would be replaced by the EAI. The architects also made it difficult for people to engage with them as their preferred method of communication was via a wiki. The architects were virtually inaccessible to technology staff and gave little consideration to their expert understanding of the existing architecture and its technology components.

When the architects presented the plans for the selected hardware and software products and the programs of work to the senior executives of the business divisions for approval, these executives were reluctant to commit to funding the hardware and software products and the programs of work specified by the architects, and eventually the implementation of the EA was abandoned altogether. Consequently, there was no overarching technology vision at Bank1 and the business divisions developed and implemented their own architectures for their own particular needs rather than the requirements of the organization.

Scenarios such as this one reflect the difficulty that organizations have in transitioning from the development of their EA plans to the implementation of those plans. Though the need for EA appears to be well accepted and many organizations have adopted EA, many organizations are unable to build and exploit their EA plans (Roeleven, 2008). Researchers have addressed many of the factors associated with EAI failure such as the technical expertise and training of architects (Aier & Schelp, 2009), governance processes and structures (Buchanan & Soley, 2002; Ross, 2003) and the efficacy of frameworks, methods and modelling tools (Jonkers et al., 2003; Lankhorst et al., 2005), but despite the efforts of researchers to address the problem of EAI failure, the EAI failure rate continues to be high. There are concerns that the failure rate of EA initiatives is higher in comparison to other technology projects (Sidorova & Kappelman, 2010). Many business and IT practitioners, as reported in some surveys, have little confidence in EA being successful and anticipate EA projects to fail (Shaw, 2010). The high failure rate of EAI initiatives raises interesting questions for scholars - how to make sense of the continued failure of EAI initiatives and the inability of organizations to transition from the development of their EA plans to the implementation of those plans. What existing theoretical perspectives might be usefully drawn on by

EA researchers to do so, what new or alternative perspectives might be more relevant, and what are the implications of choosing certain perspectives over others in accounting for and articulating particular issues and insights associated with EAI failure?

In what follows, I will examine the treatment of EAI by authors and the dominant positivist perspective of EAI that authors have adopted. My purpose is to highlight the motivations for EA, its development in government and industry as they attempted to the deal with the challenges and opportunities of new technologies and the limited attention that early EA authors gave to implementation. I also examine the rationalist assumptions underlying EAI thinking and contrast these assumptions with the problems of EAI identified in the case study. I suggest alternative perspectives of EAI that may be helpful in making sense of the sorts of challenges that architects face when attempting to build support for and commitment to the selected systems and programs of work required to implement their EA plans.

THE TREATMENT OF EAI IN THE EA LITERATURE

The origins of EA date back to the 1960s to IBM's Business Systems Planning (BSP) methodology (Kerner, 1979). BSP clearly shows that IBM was exploring ways to align the technology portfolio of an organization with data and business process requirements, though in a partitioned or stovepiped way (Carlson, 1979; Zachman, 1982). In the 1980s, with the increasing convergence of information technologies including office automation, word processing, data processing and data communications technologies organizations needed to understand how they could oversee the acquisition and evolution of information technologies. This need is captured in a series of three contemporaneous articles published in the Harvard Business Review under the title The Information Archipelago (McKenney & McFarlan, 1982; McFarlan et al., 1983; McFarlan et al., 1983; Harrel, 2011). BSP resembled EA as it provided a method for identifying not only what systems to integrate, but the role these systems should play and how they should be implemented.

Early authors recognized that the success of an EA initiative was dependent on the successful implementation of the EA plans and that some organizations had difficulty in successfully implementing their EA plans. The term 'architecture', as it is applied in an IT context, first appeared around 1986, when PRISM published *Dispersion and Interconnection: Approaches to Distributed Systems Architecture*. In this paper, the authors argued there was a compelling perception in many organizations that there existed "problems which can only be addressed by the development of an architecture" (Hammer et al., 1986). Interestingly, the PRISM report mentions that whilst architecture projects can be successful, most architecture projects fail because of: 1) the perceived irrelevance of architecture planning documentation, 2) completed architecture projects failing to address relevant problems, 3) waning interest in the architecture effort, and 4) architecture projects taking so long to complete they were obsolete by the time they were delivered (Hammer et al., 1986, p. 2).

After an initial interest in the challenges of successfully implementing an EA, later authors have tended to focus of the technical challenges of producing and organizing EA plans and have paid little attention to implementation. In 1987, Zachman introduced his Framework for Information Systems Architecture (Zachman, 1987), which drew on the business systems planning (BSP)[1] approach and emphasis on the alignment of data, business processes and technology (See Figure 1). Zachman's original framework is a high level architecture information taxonomy based on viewpoints represented by the Ballpark View, Owner's View, Designer's View, Builder's View, Out- of-context View, and Actual System rows of the

Figure 1. The original Zachman framework for information systems architecture
(Zachman, 1987)

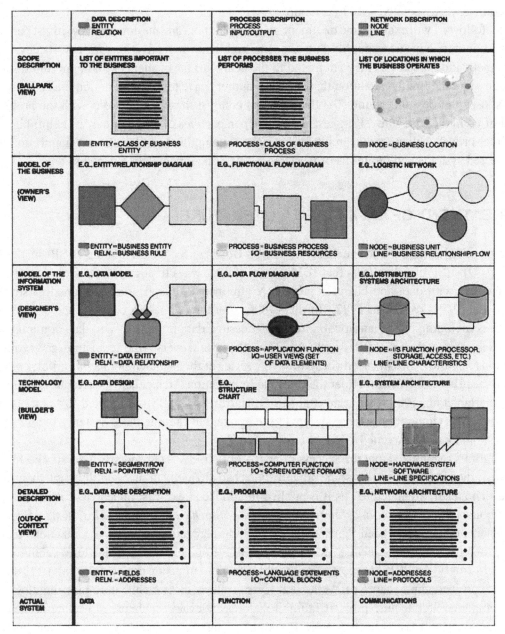

matrix and the contexts are represented by the Data Description, Process Description and Network Description columns. Although the framework provides a structure for EA information management and serves to guide the practitioner on what to consider and how to organize EA information, it does not address how an information systems architecture is implemented and the reader is left to work through that problem themselves.

Figure 2. The expanded Zachman framework for information systems architecture
(Sowa and Zachman, 1992)

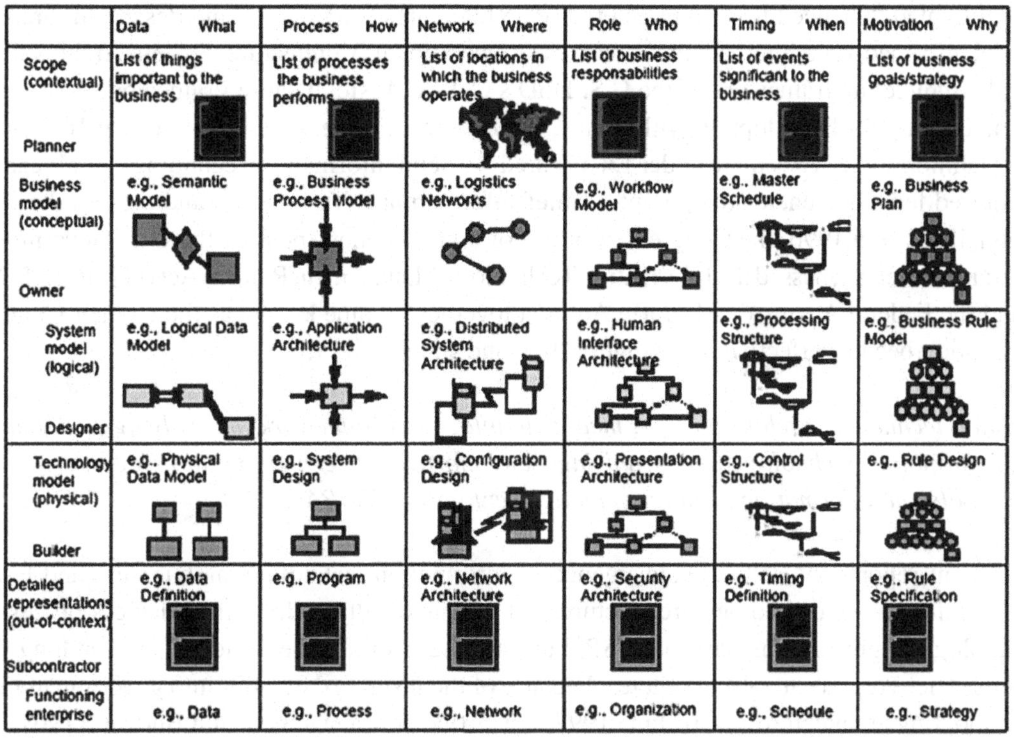

In 1992, Sowa and Zachman extended the original version of the Zachman Framework for Information Systems Architecture (See Figure 2) and the concept of an 'enterprise-wide' focus began to crystallise. While the word 'enterprise' only appeared twice in (Zachman, 1987), it appears more than 40 times in Sowa's and Zachman's 1992 paper (Sowa and Zachman, 1992), although the expression "enterprise architecture," does not appear in these papers. Sowa and Zachman (1992), treat implementation as part of EA plan development and 'implementation models' represent the technically most detailed models of all the artefacts associated with an EA (See Functioning Systems row). In the context of the expanded Zachman framework (Sowa and Zachman, 1992), the challenge of implementation is seen to be in providing an appropriate and actionable level of architectural information, which can be handed over to a developer to execute. How architects interact with business staff and developers to produce these models and how they are able to build support for and commitment to fund the specified systems are seen not to be relevant.

After 1992, interest in EA discipline grew rapidly, with many frameworks, methodologies, model representations, definition languages, description languages, tools and styles being produced. This interest in EA is reflective of the proliferation of network technologies, the opportunities and disruptive change they brought to organizations who sought to adopt them and the drive toward the inter-connection of business processes and functions. The Internet was opened to the public in 1989 and the commercial application of the World Wide Web emerged in 1994. Both developments made it possible for systems to be accessible across organizations and around the world. It was at this time that governments, in particular the United States Government, became interested in EA. In 1994, a Defense Science Board report highlighted the need for EA within the Department of Defense (U.S. DoD) (U.S. DoD, 1994). This report highlighted "the need for a joint enterprise architectures framework" and described three views of data and information architecture that became the Operational Architecture, System Architecture and Technical Architecture framework of the U.S. DoD's C4ISR14 Architecture Framework.

The motivation for EA adoption within the U.S Government intensified in 1996. On 16 July 1996, President Clinton signed Executive Order 13011 titled "Federal Information Technology." This executive order required federal agencies to appoint a Chief Information Officer (CIO) and created the Federal CIO Council. Also in 1996, the Congress, mindful of all the money spent by the U.S. Government on information technology, passed the Information Technology Management Reform Act (ITMRA) (ITMRA, 1996) and the Federal Acquisition Reform Act that together became known as the Clinger-Cohen Act. This legislation became effective on 8 August 1996 and states in part:

'Information technology architecture', ... means an integrated framework for evolving or maintaining existing information technology and acquiring new information technology to achieve the agency's strategic goals and information resources management goals (ITMRA, 1996).

Subsequent reports showed the convergence of information technology architecture and EA. The concept of information technology architecture still fundamentally reflects the business process, data and technology alignment emphases of BSP, but now incorporates the notion of overarching design constraints. These reports are also of interest because of the insights they offer into government motivations for adopting architecture. On 16 June 1997, the Office of Management and Budget (OMB) issued a memorandum for the heads of executive departments and agencies of the U.S. Government with the subject of Information Technology Architectures (OMB, 1997) that stated:

The Information Technology Architecture (ITA) describes the relationships among the work the agency does, the information the agency uses, and the information technology that the agency needs. It includes standards that guide the design of new systems. An ITA makes it easier to share information internally (e.g. agency-wide e-mail) and to reduce the number of information systems that perform similar functions. The ITA provides the technology vision to guide resource decisions that reduce costs and improve mission performance (OMB, 1997).

In this memo (OMB, 1997), the OMB broadened the scope of information technology architecture stating that it must also include an EA. It goes on to define EA as:

The explicit description of the current and desired relationships among business and management processes and information technology. It describes the "target" situation, which the agency wishes to create and maintain by managing its IT portfolio (OMB, 1997).

Whilst many of these frameworks and tools addressed the technical challenges of developing EA plans such as modelling and visualizing the different data and systems dimensions of an EA, they did not address the types of implementation problems raised in the PRISM report (Hammer et al., 1986) and authors tended to assume that if architectural artefacts were technically competent, they would be implemented. The implementation of an EA, as it is characterized in the government architecture documentation at this time, is treated as part of the modelling activities associated with EA plan development. The transition from the creation of the EA plans to the implementation of those plans does not attract the attention of authors, since the underlying assumption is that whatever is planned is done.

Outside of government EA efforts, interest in EA continued in the late 1980s and 1990s and interest in EA research resulted in a number of EA frameworks at this time. Since PRISM first introduced the 'architecture' concept, there has been a growing body of published works on EA frameworks. Some EA frameworks and methodologies clearly evolved from software architecture and systems architecture frameworks and methods, while others emerged from fresh perspectives (Hammer et al., 1986; Zachman, 1987; Sowa & Zachman, 1992; Spewak, 1992; Luftman et al., 1993; Boar, 1998; Armour et al., 1999a; Armour et al., 1999b; Perks & Beveridge, 2003; The Open Group, 2003; Bernard, 2005; Schekkerman, 2004; Carlock & Lane, 2006; Ross et al., 2006; Sage & Biemer, 2007, The Open Group, 2009). In these frameworks, implementation is generally conceptualized as a technical architecture activity and results from the production of technically competent artefacts. Implementation is understood in terms of technical artefacts that are defined and socially produced through the interactions between architects and their stakeholders, but how architects negotiate and reconcile the concerns and objectives of stakeholders with their own understanding of the problem at hand is not addressed. The Open Group Architecture Framework (TOGAF, 2003) for example, describes the implementation of an EA as a series of technical architecture activities, but does not explain how architects build support for and commitment to the required platforms and systems.

Since 2000, professional organizations have also played a role in trying to build a consistent definition and body of knowledge associated with EA, but in general have paid little attention to the challenges of successfully implementing an EA. Organizations such as the Centre for the Advancement of the Enterprise Architecture Profession (CAEAP) have sought to promote the EA profession distinguishing it from other professions and seek to promote the professional development

of architects through the certification of EA standards. Other organizations such as the Institute for Enterprise Architecture Developments (IFEAD) and the Association of Enterprise Architects (AEA) seek to promote EA research and the exchange of EA knowledge within the EA community. The Guide to the (Evolving) Enterprise Architecture Body of Knowledge (EABOK Draft) (Hagan, 2004) provides a competency framework for the professional development of architects based around key knowledge areas associated with EA practice. Whilst the EABOK specifically acknowledges EAI as a 'transitional process that involves the implementation of new systems' (Hagan, 2004, p.12), it deliberately avoids the area of implementation. Though the guide provides important information for practitioners about the processes for developing EA plans and modelling methods for business process, data, infrastructure and security, the practitioner is left to work through the challenges of transitioning from the creation of the EA plans to the implementation of those plans for themselves. Due to the general absence of formal tertiary degree programs in EA, professional organizations such as CAEAP, IFEAD, and materials such as the EABOK have filled an important gap in building knowledge about EA. However, a characteristic of these organizations and materials is that they continue to emphasize tools, methodologies, and documentation, and offer comparatively little assistance for dealing with the practical realities and difficulties that architects seem to face when transitioning from the creation of their EA plans to the implementation of those plans.

Nearly three decades after PRISM's architecture framework, authors have generally not accounted for the problems of EAI, as identified in the PRISM report. EA is well accepted and many organizations have spent significant amounts of money establishing EA functions and developing EA plans. However, many of these organizations are unable to realize the benefits they expected from their EA plans because they are unable to implement them (Roeleven, 2008).

CHALLENGES OF SUCCESSFULLY IMPLEMENTING EA

Despite the efforts of researchers to address the problem of EAI failure, the EAI failure rate continues to be high and is a cause of concern. A relatively recent survey of eighty-nine organizations revealed that sixty-six per cent of EAI efforts fail because of insufficient awareness about the benefits to be delivered, differences in perspectives and expectations amongst stakeholders and architects, and organizational politics (Roeleven, 2008). Many business and IT practitioners, as reported in some surveys, have little confidence in EA being successful and anticipate EA projects to fail (Shaw, 2010). A U.S. Department of Defense briefing (Harrel, 2011) on a relatively recent EA effort highlights the disappointments and frustrations associated with EAI failure.

We have invested over $400 million developing architecture since 2001. There has been value created in this effort, but none of that value is recognized due to a lack of tangible program output. There is a strong opinion among oversight bodies, and within the business organizations, that the effort has been one of developing architecture in the absence of any plans for implementation. Architecture development has too many "constructs", too many models, too little recognizable links to business processes and outcomes with business missions (Harrell, 2011, 61).

Cost is also seen as a principal determinant of implementation failure (DeMarco, 1995). The collective, integrated set of architectures can become unaffordable when applied across the organization and potentially the architect will not be able to demonstrate any positive return on investment in the short to medium term. The following comments of an architect practitioner illustrate how insufficient funding for an EAI effort can affect the realization of EA goals.

In my consulting practice I see one organization after another engender an architecture group because they realize that architecture is the key to product family reuse, and thus a desirable goal. But then the architecture group is funded only as a part of the first implementation project, and that project's budget is set in the usual fashion for our industry, i.e., in the mid-range between Impossible and Highly Unlikely. In other words, the architecture group is a sham. It has a charter, but no funding. After a momentary digression on reuse, it is treated as an adjunct to the project and driven by the same dynamic as all the rest of the project, getting the product out the door as quickly and cheaply as possible. It is no surprise that no useful architecture ever comes out of such a group. Organizations that pay the cost of architecture get what they pay for and organizations that don't get [nothing]. My experience is that the enormous majority of architectural efforts in our industry are in this latter category (DeMarco, 1995).

The difficulty that organizations have in developing an architecture competence is a possible factor that causes stakeholders to lose interest in the EA effort. The empirical research of Ross et al., (2006) indicates that enterprises develop their EA competence very slowly and as a consequence the success rate for EA efforts is often much lower than expected. Some enterprises greatly scale back or abandoned their EA efforts while others seek alternative enterprise architecting strategies because the ones they have employed previously have not delivered the expected benefits within the expected timeframe (Harrell, 2011).

The difficulty of establishing business requirements and the conflicting and multiple perspectives of stakeholders are also factors affecting EAI failure. For some time, researchers have been aware that the failure of EAI initiatives can be rooted in the gap between what is designed by architects and the requirements of stakeholders (Goodhue et al., 1992). Architects and their stakeholders have difficulty understanding one another (van der Raadt et al., 2008). The failure of architects to identify and incorporate into their EA plans critical business requirements is viewed as a driver of EAI failure (Roeleven, 2008). Part of the issue is that the objectives of stakeholders may not help to meet organizational objectives (van der Raadt et al., 2008) and as such have been characterized as 'wicked' because they are not amenable to a single problem formulation or solution, have no well-defined set of potential solutions and can be considered symptoms of other problems (Harrel, 2011). In spite of the contradictory, competing and 'wicked' nature of stakeholder objectives, each stakeholder expects the EA to meet their needs and the extent to which stakeholders see the EA as meeting their objectives will determine their level of interest in and support for the implementation of the EA plans (van der Raadt et al., 2008).

DOMINANT APPROACHES TO THE PROBLEMS OF EAI

Over the last decade, the problems of EAI failure have attracted the attention of researchers and practitioners. In examining this area, authors have tended to use a positivist paradigm (Kornak & Distefano, 2002) and focused on the different roles of frameworks, methodologies and modelling techniques (Jonkers et al., 2003; Lankhorst et al., 2005), the technical expertise and training of architects (Aier & Schelp, 2009), change management processes (Josey et al., 2009; Janssen & Klievink, 2010), and governance processes and structures (Buchanan & Soley, 2002; Ross, 2003). There have been several attempts at categorizing the reasons why EA initiatives do not deliver their expected benefits (see Table 1). Most research has focused on identifying technical factors that cause EAI failure and consequently reflects a rationalist assumption that if an architect deals with these factors, EAI failure can be avoided.

More recently, researchers have focused on dedicated EA management functions within organizations and situate the execution of EAI projects within those functions (Schmidt & Buxman, 2011). These functions have oversight of the organization's IT environments and provide continuous and long-term management of the EA. Whilst EA functions may provide benefits to organizations in helping them to remain flexible and able to respond to market opportunities, there is a need for further research exploring links between the implementation effectiveness of such functions and relations between the architects and their stakeholders.

Although researchers' focus on EA frameworks, tools and techniques has been questioned (Ross et al., 2006), this focus is indicative of some of the problems with EA initiatives and has resulted in significant contributions to knowledge in areas of EA management, planning, design, and modelling methods (Simon et al., 2013). However, in the socio-technical context of an EAI, Smolander et al. (2008) proposed there is too much emphasis on the technical aspects of EAI and not enough on the social aspects. For example, in Zachman's Framework for Information Systems Architecture (Zachman, 1987), the emphasis is on the organization of architectural artefacts and the individual artefacts displayed in each cell of the framework

Table 1. Conceptualizations of EAI failure

Conceptualization of EAI Failure	Reference
Process failure	Poutanen, 2012; Richardson et al., 1990; Boster et al., 2000; Van der Raadt et al., 2008, 2010; Hjort-Madsen, 2006; Martin, 2012
Design failure, Alignment failure	Bradley et al., 2012; Bruls et al., 2011; Boh and Yellin, 2006; Roeleven, 2008; Gregor et al., 2007
Framework failure	Peristeras and Tarabanis, 2000
Management failure, Benefits failure	Simon et al., 2013; Schmidt and Buxman, 2011; Ross et al., 2006; Ross, 2003; Kettinger et, al., 2010
Project failure (time and budget)	Roeleven, 2008; Boster et al., 2000; Armour et al., 1999b
Partner/ Vendor Failure	Ross and Beath, 2006
Organizational learning failure	Poutanen, 2012

represent architectural 'facts'. Whilst the framework adds to our knowledge of how EA artefacts may be organized, it does not advance our understanding of the social context of an EAI or how the competing and contradictory objectives of stakeholders may be managed.

Other frameworks characterize the development and implementation of EA plans as a ready-made and structured process that can be reproduced at will. The development of an EA, in terms of the TOGAF (Josey et al., 2009), includes four architectural plans: a data architecture plan, application architecture plan, technology architecture plan and business architecture plan. These architectures interlink through predefined inputs and outputs and architectural modelling activities. The assumption underlying the structured tasks associated with implementing architectures is that if you get the technical aspects of the architecture right, the human and relational aspects will fall into place. This view could be said to convey a somewhat simplified and abstracted perspective that reveals little of what might be required in actual practice. For example, the selection of technology components is seen as a two-step sequence 1) defining the application functionality required, and 2) mapping the required functionality to available commercial-off-the-shelf (COTS) and open source products. The emphasis here is on describing a decision-making process and such a view fails to highlight the different perspectives and objectives that stakeholders may have, the trade-offs that architects may be expected to make and the negotiation that may occur between architects and their stakeholders.

AN ALTERNATIVE APPROACH: THE IMPORTANCE OF UNDERSTANDING THE SOCIAL AND RELATIONAL ASPECTS OF EAI

As an EA scholar and practitioner, I am sensitive to the relevance of EAI research to the EA practitioner community. In relation to EAI research, researchers have argued for more practically oriented EA planning methods and frameworks (Simon et al., 2013) and others have argued for research that balances the current narrow technical focus of existing research with a focus on the multiple perspectives on EA (Rozanski & Woods, 2007). Whilst existing approaches may have served a technically oriented audience well, they have resulted in a lack of research and skills in the social processes associated with an EAI. Recent research does indicate that architecture represents design trade-offs among properties such as cost, usability, maintainability and performance and these represent the explicit commitment of a particular group toward a particular objective or course of action (Smolander et al., 2008). Architecture is the product of a process of decision making and negotiation for resources needed for building the systems, including personnel, expert skills and funding (Bass et al., 2003). Likewise, a successful EAI can be considered as something that emerges from the cooperation amongst stakeholders whilst taking into consideration situational constraints of monetary resources, legacy systems, available technology and the skills and experience of staff.

A potential outcome of the limited research into the social processes associated with EAI may be that EA researchers are in the main not addressing topics of interest and concern to practitioners. This could be interpreted as indicating that EA researchers fail to appreciate the sorts of implementation concerns that trouble practitioners and do not fully appreciate or understand the implementation of an EA or the EAI role that architects are required to fulfil. Research suggests that published EA research and the published writing and research of EA practitioners focus on quite different areas and this inhibits the training and education of architects (Simon et al., 2013). An investigation into how the roles and practices of architects influence support for and commitment to an EAI would help tertiary institutions to be more effective in preparing future architecture practitioners (Simon et al., 2013).

Research suggests that the disappointing outcomes associated with EAI are not related to the development of the EA plans, but are related to the social aspects of EA (Smolander et al., 2008). For example, there are problems with the working styles of architects, which do not encourage effective interaction, and communication with stakeholders (Poutanen, 2012). Authors have pointed out that architects and stakeholders have difficulty communicating with each other and in working together (Poutanen, 2012), architects do not understand the different perspectives of stakeholders (Smolander et al., 2008; Smolander & Rossi, 2008) and the reclusive personalities of some architects causes difficulties in their interaction with stakeholders (Van der Raadt et al., 2008). EAI failure is seen as the failure of architects to develop an 'empathetic' understanding of their stakeholders, to 'walk in the shoes' of their stakeholders and appreciate the 'world' from the perspectives and concerns of those stakeholders (Seppänen, 2009) and to bridge the intellectual and organizational boundaries between themselves and their stakeholders (Poutanen, 2012).

The social problems of EAI are not dissimilar to those found in the information systems literature. For several decades, IS researchers have argued against the neglect of social issues in understanding IS project requirements for the sake of more technical requirements (Goguen, 1993). User requirements are viewed as coming from the social system of the workplace rather than from the minds of the users (Goguen, 1993) and this explains why some scholars have encouraged the use of anthropological approaches in understanding IS project requirements (Hughes and Wood-Harper et. al., 1999). Research highlights that not only are IS project requirements grounded in the social context of the participants, but the process of requirements analysis is itself social (Goguen, 1993). For example, it is argued that one needs to be aware of whose world view is being imposed during requirements analysis when different stakeholders are involved in the same project (Goguen, 1993; Goguen, 1994). This research takes the view that useful insights can be derived into the problems of EAI by understanding the social context of an EAI and that approaches which sensitize practitioners to the organizational context of an EAI can supplement existing technical frameworks, methods and tools.

In a large organization, architects will interact with a number of stakeholders in the course of an EAI (IEEE, 2000). Broadly speaking, the major stakeholder groups involved in an EAI include: business and technology executives and general management, business and technology teams, end users of different lines of business, systems development and operations staff, technology project teams and external partners (e.g. vendors) (Schmidt & Buxman, 2011). In relation to the literature, two observations can be made: firstly, no studies investigated the different perspectives and objectives amongst business and technology stakeholders. Whilst van der Raadt et al., (2008) examine stakeholders' perceptions of an EA, they focus on technology stakeholders and do not consider business stakeholders. Secondly, many EA studies do not consistently adopt the same labels for the stakeholders involved in an EA. For example, in some EA literature business and technology stakeholders are undifferentiated. Kettinger et al., (2010) refer to the business and technology stakeholders involved in an EA as general managers. In Ross and Beath (2006), all people involved in an EA initiative are managers. In a few studies, researchers refer specifically to individual groups such as senior management, program and project managers (van der Raadt et al., 2008, Schmidt and Buxman, 2011). In general, however, there is a lack of clarity about the participants referred to in the studies and this raises questions as to whether the different stakeholders involved in an EAI and their objectives and concerns are appropriately differentiated for understanding the nature of their involvement and the nature of their interaction with architects.

An important research direction to pursue would be one that focuses on the practices of architects and the extent to which these practices influence the interactions between architects and their stakeholders. The findings of such research would have implications for our understanding of the extent to which the practices of architects influence their capacity to build support for and commitment to the systems and platforms specified in their EAI plans. The findings may have implications for the extent to which technical specialization is required in the architecture role. These findings may provide an improved understanding of whether architects need to be technical specialists as well as relationally competent, or can architecture subject matter expertise alone make individuals suitable for the architecture role? The knowledge areas and competencies prescribed in the materials produced by professional organizations could also be reviewed in light of these findings, providing an improved understanding to aspiring architects about knowledge areas and competencies that they would need to be effective in their EAI work.

CONCLUSION

Based on the gaps in our knowledge of the social aspects of EAI and the emphasis on the technical aspects of EAI found in existing research, we need to improve our understanding of the practices of architects, including the relationships they build with their stakeholders and how this may affect the transition from the development of the EA plans to the implementation of those plans. In addition to being technology focused, the success of EAI is influenced by the role of stakeholders and interactions between architects and stakeholders. Architects' expertise in linking multiple domains of architecture into an integrated and coherent view of an organization's technology portfolio may be useful for planning the technology selection and coordinating the programs of implementation work, but the efficacy of such work will largely depend on how well architects are able to assimilate in to their planning and analysis the perspectives and concerns of stakeholders.

ACKNOWLEDGMENT

The author would like to thank the anonymous reviewers and the editor for their insightful comments and suggestions.

REFERENCES

Aier, S., & Schelp, J. (2009). A reassessment of enterprise architecture implementation. In *Proceedings of the 2009 International Conference on Service-Oriented Computing* (pp. 35-47). Berlin: Springer-Verlag.

Armour, F. J., & Kaisler, S. H. (2001, November/ December). Enterprise architecture: Agile transition and implementation. *IT Pro*, 30-37.

Armour, F. J., Kaisler, S. H., & Liu, S. Y. (1999a, January). A big-picture look at enterprise architectures. *IEEE IT Professional*, *1*(1), 35–42. doi:10.1109/6294.774792

Armour, F. J., Kaisler, S. H., & Liu, S. Y. (1999b, July/August). Building an enterprise architecture step by step. *IT Pro*, 31-39.

Bass, L., Clements, P., & Kazman, R. (2003). *Software Architecture in Practice* (2nd ed.). Boston: Addison-Wesley.

Bernard, S. A. (2005). *Introduction to Enterprise Architecture*. AuthorHouse.

Boar, B. H. (1998). *Constructing Blueprints for Enterprise IT Architectures*. New York: John Wiley & Sons.

Boh, W., & Yellin, D. (2006). Using enterprise architecture standards in managing information technology. *Journal of Management Information Systems*, *23*(3), 163–207. doi:10.2753/MIS0742-1222230307

Boster, M., Liu, S., & Thomas, R. (2000, July/August). Getting the most from your enterprise architecture. *IEEE - IT Pro*. Retrieved from http://app.search.lib.unimelb.edu.au/

Bradley, R. V., Pratt, R. M. E., Byrd, T. A., Outlay, C. N., & Wynn, D. E. Jnr. (2012). Enterprise architecture, IT effectiveness and the mediating role of IT alignment in US hospitals. *Information Systems Journal*, *22*(2), 97–127. doi:10.1111/j.1365-2575.2011.00379.x

Bruls, W. A., van Steenbergen, M., Foothuis, R. M., Bos, B., & Brinkemper, S. (2010). Domain architectures as an instrument to refine architecture. *Communications of the Association for Information Systems*, *27*, 517–540.

Buchanan, R. D., & Soley, R. M. (2002). *Aligning enterprise architecture and IT investments with corporate goals*. Object Management Group.

Carlock, P. G., & Fenton, R. E. (2001). System of systems (SoS) enterprise systems engineering for information- intensive organizations. *Systems Engineering*, *4*(4), 242–261. doi:10.1002/sys.1021

Carlson, W. M. (1979). Business information analysis and integration technique (BIAIT) - The new horizon. *Database*, *10*(4), 3–9.

Goguen, J. A. (1993). Social issues in requirements engineering. *Proceedings of IEEE International Symposium on Requirements Engineering*. Retrieved from http://ieeexplore.ieee.org/xpl/mostRecentIssue. jsp?punumber=896&filter%3DAND%28p_IS_Number%3A7734%29&pageNumber=2

Goguen, J. A. (1994). Requirements Engineering as the Reconciliation of Social and Technical Issues. In M. Jirotka & J. A. Goguen (Eds.), *Requirements Engineering* (pp. 165–199). Academic Press Professional, Inc.

Goodhue, D. L., Kirsch, L. J., Quillard, J. A., & Wybo, M. D. (1992). Strategic data planning: Lessons from the field. *Management Information Systems Quarterly*, *16*(1), 11–34. doi:10.2307/249699

Gregor, S., Hart, D., & Martin, N. (2007). Enterprise architectures: Enablers of business strategy and IS/IT alignment in government. *Information Technology & People*, *20*(2), 96–120. doi:10.1108/09593840710758031

Hagan, P. J. (Ed.). (2004). *Guide to the (evolving) enterprise architecture body of knowledge* (Draft). Retrieved from http://www.mitre.org/work/tech_papers/tech_papers_04/04_0104/index.html

Hammer, M., Champy, J., & Davenport, D. (1986, June). *Dispersion and Interconnection: Approaches to Distributed Systems Architecture*. Partnership for Research in Information Systems Management (PRISM). Retrieved from https://c.ymcdn.com/sites/www.globalaea.org/resource/collection/EAAC3D6C-D447-451C- AC5F-6E1DC7788D42/PRISM_Report.pdf

Harrel, J. M. (2011). *Developing Enterprise Architectures to Address the Enterprise Dilemma Of Deciding What Should Be Sustained Versus What Should Be Changed* (PhD Thesis). George Mason University, Fairfax, VA.

Hjort-Madsen, K. (2006). Enterprise architecture implementation and management: A case study. *Proceedings of the 39th Hawaii International Conference on System Sciences*, 1-10. Retrieved from http:// ieeexplore. ieee.org/xpl/login.jsp?tp=&arnumber=1579432&url=http%3A%2F%2Fieeexplore.ieee. org%2Fxpls%2Fabs_all. jsp%3Farnumber%3D1579432

Hughes, J., & Wood-Harper, T. (1999). Addressing organisational issues in requirements engineering practice: Lessons from action cases. *Australasian Journal of Information Systems*, *6*(2), 64–74. doi:10.3127/ajis.v6i2.293

Information Technology Management Reform Act of. 1996, Sections 5001-5142. (1996). Retrieved from http:// govinfo.library.unt.edu/npr/library/misc/s1124.html

Institute of Electrical and Electronics Engineers. (2000). *1471-2000 - IEEE Recommended Practice for Architectural Description for Software-Intensive Systems*. IEEE Computer Society. Retrieved from http:// www.enterprise-architecture.info/Images/Documents/IEEE%201471-2000.pdf

Janssen, M., & Klievink, B. (2010). ICT-project failure in public administration: The need to include risk management in enterprise architectures. *Proceedings of the 11th Annual International Conference on Digital Government Research on Public Administration Online: Challenges and Opportunities*, 147-152.

Jonkers, H., Lankhorst, M., van Burren, R., Hoppenbrouwers, S., & Bonsangue, M. (2003). Concepts for modelling enterprise architecture. *Via Nova Architectura*. Retrieved from http://www.via-nova-architectura. org/ proceedings/lac-2003/concepts-for-modeling-enterprise-architectures-2.html

Josey, A., Harrison, R., Homan, P., Rouse, M. F., van Sante, T., Turner, M., & van der Merwe, P. (2009). *TOGAF version 9 – A pocket guide*. Reading, UK: The Open Group.

Kerner, D. (1979). Business information characterization study. *Database, 10*(4), 10–17.

Kettinger, W. J., Marchland, D. A., & Davis, J. M. (2010). Designing enterprise IT architectures to optimize flexibility and standardization in global business. *MIS Quarterly Executive, 9*(2), 95–113.

Kornak, A., & Distefano, J. (2002). *Cap Gemini Ernst & Young Guide to Wireless Enterprise Application Architecture*. New York: John Wiley & Sons.

Lankhorst, M. M., Iacob, M. E., & Jonkers, H. (2005). *Enterprise architecture at work: modelling, communication and analysis*. Berlin: Springer-Verlag.

Luftman, J. N., Lewis, P. R., & Oldach, S. H. (1993). Transforming the enterprise: The alignment of business and information technology strategies. *IBM Systems Journal, 32*(1), 198–221. doi:10.1147/ sj.321.0198

Martin, A. (2012). Enterprise IT architecture in large federated organizations: The art of the possible. *Information Systems Management, 29*(2), 137–147. doi:10.1080/10580530.2012.662103

McFarlan, F. W., McKenney, J., & Pyburn, P. (1983). The information archipelago - plotting a course. *Harvard Business Review, 61*(1), 145–156. PMID:10299000

McFarlan, F. W., & McKenney, J. L. (1983). The information archipelago - governing the new world. *Harvard Business Review, 61*(4), 91–99.

McKenny, J. L., & McFarlan, F. W. (1979). The information archipelago - maps and bridges. *Harvard Business Review, 60*(5), 109–114.

Office of Management and Budget. (1997). *Memorandum for the Heads of Executive Departments and Agencies, M-97-16, 18 June*. Retrieved from http://www.whitehouse.gov/omb/memoranda_m97-16/

Peristeras, V., & Tarabanis, K. (2000). Towards an enterprise architecture for public administration using a top- down approach. *European Journal of Information Systems, 9*(4), 252–260. doi:10.1057/ palgrave.ejis.3000378

Perks, C., & Beveridge, T. (2003). *A guide to enterprise architecture*. Berlin: Springer-Verlag.

Poutanen, J. (2012). The social dimension of enterprise architecture in government. *Journal of Enterprise Architecture, 8*(2), 19–29.

Richardson, G., Jackson, B., & Dickson, G. (1990). A principles-based enterprise architecture: Lessons from Texaco and Star Enterprise. *Management Information Systems Quarterly, 14*(4), 385–403. doi:10.2307/249787

Roeleven, S. (2008). *Why two thirds of enterprise architecture projects fail* [Electronic version]. ARIS Expert Paper. Retrieved from http://www.softwareag.com

Ross, J. (2003). Creating a strategic IT architecture competency: Learning in stages. *MIS Quarterly Executive, 2*(1), 31–43.

Ross, J., Weill, P., & Robertson, D. (2006). *Enterprise architecture as strategy: Creating a foundation for execution*. Boston: Harvard Business School Press.

Ross, J. W., & Beath, C. M. (2006). Sustainable IT outsourcing success: Let enterprise architecture be your guide. *MIS Quarterly Executive, 5*(4), 181–192.

Rozanski, N., & Woods, E. (2007). *Software systems architecture – Working with stakeholders using viewpoints and perspectives*. Upper Saddle River, NJ: Addison-Wesley.

Sage, A. P., & Biemer, S. M. (2007, September). Processes for system family architecting, design, and integration. *IEEE Systems Journal, 1*(1).

Schekkerman, J. (2004b). *Trends in enterprise architecture: How are organizations progressing?* Amersfoort, Netherlands: Institute for Enterprise Architecture Developments.

Schmidt, C., & Buxman, P. (2011). Outcomes and success factors of enterprise IT architecture management: Empirical insight from the international financial services industry. *European Journal of Information Systems, 20*(2), 168–185. doi:10.1057/ejis.2010.68

Seppänen, V. (2009). *Experiences on enterprise architecture work in government administration*. Retrieved from www.vm.fi/vm/en/04_publications_and_documents/01_publications/04_public_management/20090121Experi/ name.jsp

Shaw, B. (2010). *Enterprise architecture – Will yours fail?* Retrieved from http://www.itprojecttemplates.com/ WP_EA_Will_Yours_Fail.htm

Sidorova, A., & Kappelman, L. A. (2010). Enterprise architecture as politics: An actor-network theory perspective. In L. A. Kappelman (Ed.), *The SIM guide to enterprise architecture*. Boca Raton, FL: CRC Press.

Simon, D., Fischbach, K., & Schoder, D. (2013). An exploration of enterprise architecture research. *Communications of the Association for Information Systems, 32*, 1–72.

Smolander, K., & Rossi, M. (2008). Conflicts, compromises, and political decisions: Methodological challenges of enterprise-wide e-business architecture creation. *Journal of Database Management, 19*(1), 19–40. doi:10.4018/jdm.2008010102

Sowa, J. F., & Zachman, J. (1992). Extending and formalizing the framework for information systems architecture. *IBM Systems, 31*(3), 590–616. doi:10.1147/sj.313.0590

Spewak, S. H. (1992). *Enterprise architecture planning: Developing a blueprint for data, applications and technology*. New York: John Wiley and Sons.

The Open Group. (2003). *TOGAF (The open group architecture framework) version 8.1*. Retrieved from www. opengroup.org/architecture/togaf8/ downloads.htm

The Open Group. (2009). *TOGAF version 9 enterprise edition*. Zaltbommel, Netherlands: Van Haren Publishing.

U.S. Department of Defense, Defense Science Board. (1994). *Report of the Defense Science Board Summer Study Task Force on Information Architecture for the Battlefield (October)*. Retrieved from https://www.google.com.au/webhp?sourceid=chrome-instant&ion=1&espv=2&ie=UTF-8#q=report%20of%20the%20defense%20science%20board%20summer%20study%20task%20force%20on%20information%20architecture%20for%20the%20battlefield

Van der Raadt, B., Bonnet, M., Schouten, S., & van Vliet, H. (2010). The relation between EA effectiveness and stakeholder satisfaction. *Journal of Systems and Software*, *83*(10), 1954–1969. doi:10.1016/j.jss.2010.05.076

Van der Raadt, B., Schouten, S., & van Vliet, H. (2008). Stakeholder perceptions of enterprise architecture, software architecture. In *Software Architecture, LNCS* (Vol. 5292, pp. 19–34). Berlin: Springer-Verlag. doi:10.1007/978-3-540-88030-1_4

Zachman, J. (1987). A framework for information systems architecture. *IBM Systems Journal*, *26*(3), 276–292. doi:10.1147/sj.263.0276

Zachman, J. A. (1982). Business systems planning and business information control study: A comparison. *IBM Systems Journal*, *21*(1), 31–53. doi:10.1147/sj.211.0031

KEY TERMS AND DEFINITIONS

Enterprise Architecture Implementation: The architectural processes and tasks associated with the identification of the specific systems and platforms (i.e. products) to deliver the enterprise architecture into operation and the development of the implementation plans to schedule and coordinate the delivery of those systems into operation.

Positivist: Researchers who take a positivist position assume that the world, including the social world exists independently of consciousness and experience and is made up of hard objective phenomena which can be explained by 'empirically testable theories that can be verified and falsified'.

Rational: Researchers who adopt a rationalist perspective assume that there is a 'one-best-way' and that if architects adopt a particular architectural framework or modelling approach, for instance, then failure can be avoided.

Relational Competence: Architects who demonstrate relational competence are able to take into consideration the perspectives and concerns of others to reveal the complexity of the task at hand and align their own responses to that task with the enhanced interpretation.

Social: This term, as it is used in this paper, refers to interactions between architects and also between architects and their stakeholders and includes the different perspectives, concerns, priorities and values that architects and their stakeholders may hold.

This work was previously published in the International Journal of Enterprise Information Systems (IJEIS) Vol. 12, Issue 2, April –June 2016 edited by M Tavana, pp. 14-25, copyright 2009 by IGI Publishing (an imprint of IGI Global).

Chapter 10
Developing an Effective Strategy for Organizational Business Intelligence

Paul Hawking
Victoria University, Australia

Carmine Sellitto
Victoria University, Australia

ABSTRACT

Business Intelligence has been adopted across numerous industry sectors where the commensurate benefits have been reported as being significant to those that fall short of expectations. Indeed, an effective strategy that aligns company objectives and Business Intelligence has been shown to be an important factor in firm realizing organizational benefits. Using a case study approach, the paper documents the salient aspects of an energy company's Business Intelligence strategy that directly enhanced informational requirements. The firm's strategy embodied the adherence to certain guiding principles ensuring that the introduction of Business Intelligence directly addressed the company's needs. The paper presents a novel description of a company's Business Intelligence strategy that will provide valuable lessons for not only researchers, but also industry practitioners.

INTRODUCTION

Companies today have come to realize the importance of providing accurate, relevant and timely information— information that allows their organisational personnel to engage in effective decision-making practices (Isik et al, 2013). Traditionally the information required as input for decision making resided in a plethora of transaction processing systems. As the number and diversity of these systems increased so did the issues associated with the extraction and integration of the associated data required to support decisions. To overcome these integration issues many companies implemented an Enterprise Resource Planning (ERP). These systems enabled companies to gain efficiencies in their business processes and associated transactions through the high degree of integration of their company-wide business processes,

DOI: 10.4018/978-1-5225-2382-6.ch010

and the standardisation of the associated data (Davenport et al, 2003). ERP systems are an essential element of the corporate information systems infrastructure allowing businesses to be competitive in today's world, as well as providing foundation for future growth (Chou et al, 2005).

Although companies have implemented an ERP system there are still issues associated with the analysis of data. One reason is that the implemented ERP system replaces many of the legacy systems however a number of legacy systems are still used. This either due to the lack of equivalent functionality in the ERP systems, budgetary constraints or a future replacement. No matter what the reasons for their existence these legacy systems contain data which contribute to decision making. Often this data needs to be integrated and with the ERP systems data to provide a complete and relevant data for analysis. Another issue is type of reporting available in the ERP system. The Online Transaction Processing (OLTP) environment which underpins the ERP systems limits the types of reports that can be generated and thus the level analysis and insight that can be achieved.

The increased informational requirements of companies and the availability of appropriate computing technology resulted in the evolution of existing IT systems and the emergence of new solutions. These included Knowledge Management (KM), Data Mining (DM), Collaborative Systems (CS), Corporate Performance Management (CPM), Knowledge Discovery (KD) and Analytics, with the term Business Intelligence (BI) tending to be used to encompass all (Gibson et al, 2004; Olszak & Ziemba, 2007).

Business Intelligence (BI) for many companies was implemented as an extension of their ERP Systems in order to gain greater insight into their business processes and associated transactions as well as integrating other data sources. According to Howson (2007, p.2) Business Intelligence is a process that "...allows people at all levels of an organization to access, interact with, and analyse data to manage the business, improve performance, discover opportunities, and operate efficiently". The analysis of corporate data allows a firm to improve productivity and achieve competitive advantage over other firms that may not have the same capabilities (Luftman & Ben-Tvi, 2010; Watson & Wixom, 2007). Indeed, the effective use of Business Intelligence is considered an essential factor in the competiveness of a company especially in changing markets (Luftman & Ben-Tvi, 2010; Watson & Wixom, 2007).

One industry experiencing considerable change is the electrical power utilities industry sector. This sector has been impacted by increased competition, changing regulatory frameworks, renewable energy and the introduction of new technologies. This dynamic environment has increased the needs for firm's to have cohesive decision-making processes to respond to these competitive pressures (Nasir et al, 2013). There has been limited research on the adoption and use of Business Intelligence in this industry sector, particularly in regards to having a strategy to support organisational decision making. Hence, the research contribution of this paper centres on the documenting of the Business Intelligence use and strategy development by a large Australian energy company. The strategic approach reported could be usefully adopted by of companies in the energy sector or even other industry groups.

LITERATURE REVIEW

Davenport et al (2003) focused on 163 executives working in large enterprises around the world to identify how companies were using Enterprise Resource Planning (ERP) systems to improve business performance and the specific practices that resulted in sustained value creation. They identified that the implementation of an ERP system resulted in sustained value creation however, some corporations realized far more comparable benefits than others. These benefits were directly related to the actions of management in regards to the on-going development and evolution of their ERP system. Furthermore, Davenport et al (2003) identified three major evolutionary stages in regards to grouping the types of benefits that could be realized through the adoption of ERP systems. These stages related to the firm's processes being integrated and optimized, which in turn facilitated the information flows across the various functional areas of the business. The premise underling of each stage was for firms to:

- **Integrate:** This stage reflects the unification and standardisation of data and processes. ERP systems can be used to better integrate business processes and the associated organizational units.
- **Optimize:** Reflects a stage that aligns the business processes to the overall corporate strategy through the utilisation of embedded "best practice" processes which are enacted when an ERP system is adopted.
- **Informate:** Reflects a stage were the information generated by the ERP system is used to transform work practices. This involves transforming the ERP systems data into context rich information to support effective decision making.

These stages tend to be evolutionary and are reflective of a company's ERP systems maturity level. The concept of maturity is often used to describe the advancement of both people and organisations. Implicit in this notion is that with increasing maturity there are improvements in quantitative or qualitative firm capabilities. Accordingly the more mature a company is in regard to their ERP system the more value they realize from the system. Notably, in recent times, the use of Business Intelligence has been an important aspect of underpinned organisational decision making activities (Hawking & Sellitto, 2010).

Harris and Davenport (2006) in a study of 450 executives across 370 globally located companies identified the factors that underpinned the value of ERP systems, as well as how companies used these systems to enhance their competitiveness and differentiation. One of the key findings from this study was that improved decision making was the most sought out and realized benefit. While most ERP systems were originally justified on the basis of Information Technology (IT) and operational cost savings, senior management's underlying objective was to improve the quality and transparency of information. Top performing companies were able to achieve this by implementing their ERP systems extensively throughout their organizations across a broad range of business functions. This provided an increased level of integration. Harris and Davenport (2006) also found that top performing companies were more likely to integrate their business processes across organizational boundaries with suppliers and customers.

Related to the desired benefit of improved decision making, top performing companies aggressively used information and analytics to improve decision making (Harris and Davenport, 2006; Hawking and Sellitto, 2010). These findings are supported by Gartner, a leading business analyst firm, who conducted a worldwide survey of 2,000 Chief Information Officers and identified Business Intelligence as the number one technology priority for companies (Gartner, 2013). This is supported by another survey which found that 83 percent of Chief Information Officers identified Business Intelligence as one of the tools to enhance competitiveness (IBM, 2010)[1]. It is estimated that the worldwide revenue for Business Intelligence software will reach $US17.1 billion by 2017 (Gartner, 2012). Arguably, the increased expenditure on Business Intelligence applications reflects the level of impact these systems can potentially have on a company's performance.

Williams and Williams (2006) identified a number of companies that gained a significant return on investment (ROI) from their Business Intelligence initiatives. The Data Warehousing Institute (TDWI, 2005) reported that the use of Business Intelligence in a number of organisations such as Hewlett Packard and the US Army had a significantly positive impact on their performance. Hewlett Packard's Business Intelligence initiative resulted in an increase in the value of worker productivity of approximately USD$10.6 million, whilst the company's reporting costs were reduced by some USD$8.6 million. The US Army found that as a result of their Business Intelligence implementation, 10 trained analysts could complete as much work as 200 traditional analysts. In another example of the value of Business Intelligence, Cincinnati Zoo believe that they have achieved significant cost savings and increased visits by 50,000 in 2011 resulting in a 25 percent increase in food sales and 7.5 percent increase in retail sales. Overall they believe they have achieved an annual ROI of 411 percent (IBM, 2013). This level of ROI is not unusual with a crop technology company, Becker Underwoord, reporting that they achieved a ROI of 311 percent over a 3 month period (Nucleus Research, 2011). MoneyGram International used Businesses Intelligence to prevent $37.7million in fraud and reduce customer fraud complaint by 72 percent (IBM, 2014).

Although Business Intelligence is seen as a priority for many companies to survive in a competitive market there is uncertainty as to the path to follow. Researchers have identified that companies utilise Business Intelligence in different ways, with varying levels of success. A review of the literature indicates that companies often fail to realize the expected benefits associated with Business Intelligence and sometimes consider the project to be a failure in itself (Chenoweth et. al., 2006; Hwang et al., 2004; Johnson, 2004; Arte 2003; Adelman and Moss 2002). Some have noted that in Business Intelligence projects the information that is generated is inaccurate or irrelevant to the user's needs or indeed, delivered too late to be useful. Indeed, a high proportional of top global companies tend to not make appropriate decisions in response to major competitive changes (Biere, 2011). Researchers have attempted to map Business Intelligence usage and best practices to provide a roadmap for companies to move forward and maximise the benefits of their Business Intelligence initiatives (Grublješič and Jaklič, 2014). A common approach by researchers to improve the effectiveness of Business Intelligence is the identification of Critical Success Factors (Harrison, 2012; Hawking and Sellitto, 2010; Yeoh et al., 2008). An alternative approach has been the development of Business Intelligence Maturity Models (Watson et al, 2001; McDonald, 2004; Hamer, 2005; Eckerson, 2007, ASUG, 2007; Hewlett Packard, 2007, Gartner cited Hostmann, 2007). The purpose of these models is to provide companies with directives to improve the management of their corporate data, as well as maximise the benefits obtained from Business Intelligence.

Raber et al (2013) analysed different Business Intelligence Maturity Models and found that a Business Intelligence strategy that focuses on the organization's processes and technology was an important indicator of more mature companies. Lahrmann et al (2011) highlighted the importance of an effective Business Intelligence strategy however, were surprised that many of the maturity models examined did not actually include a Business Intelligence strategy. A Business Intelligence strategy should focus on formalising business needs, aligning business partners and then implementing a comprehensive Business Intelligence solution with defined processes for the collection, integration, processing and analysis of information to facilitate effective enterprise wide decision making (Boyer et al, 2010; Pant, 2009). For many companies, a contributing factor to their Business Intelligence initiatives not achieving the goals can be a lack of an effective Business Intelligence strategy (Boyer at al 2010).

In examining the literature there is a lack of reporting of how different companies develop and implement their Business Intelligence strategies. It is important that different approaches are documented enabling researchers and practitioners to gain a better understanding of the factors that need to be considered to achieve effective Business Intelligence.

RESEARCH METHOD

This research investigated the development and implementation of a Business Intelligence strategy by a large energy firm using a case study approach. Meyers (2013: p. 78) defines case study research as one that "…uses empirical evidence from one or more organisations where an attempt is made to study the subject matter in context. Multiple sources of evidence are used, although most of the evidence comes from interviews and documents". Yin (2014) suggests the importance of studying information systems in "real life" contexts to better understand them. Irani and Love (2008) strongly support the use of case studies to investigate different aspects of information systems. A number of researchers have used the case study approach to investigate different aspects of Business Intelligence adoption, implementation and subsequent use (McBride, 2014; Spruit et al, 2014; Alekh et al, 2013; Vuksic, 2013; Sammon and Finnegan; 2000).

The data collection for this research draws from multiple sources and included the examination of existing documents, content analysis of industry presentations and interviews of company stakeholders. The inclusion of a diverse range of data sources in research has been referred to as meaningful matter by allowing researchers to draw conclusions or inferences about a particular phenomenon (Krippendorf, 2004). The conducting of interviews with company stakeholders used the responsive interview (Rubin and Rubin, 2005) approach. This approach involved people being selected to be interviewed due their specialised knowledge about the research issue or problem. The interviewer adopted a semi-structured interview style and then developed further questions based on the interviewee's answers. This continued until the interviewer had gained deep responses to questions posed and also understood the issues raised from interviewee's point of view. This approach allowed the conversations to flow and move from one topic to the next. This gave the interviewee some ability to direct the conversation. The questions enabled the researcher to seek certain information if it had not been covered in the conversation. As such, the case study is presented as a summary of interview highlighting the important aspects of the research issue being investigated.

CASE STUDY

Company A is an Australian energy company that specialises in infrastructure maintenance and electricity distribution in the State of Victoria. The company supplies electricity to approximately 800,000 customers in regional and rural areas across the central and western districts of the state. The company is also responsible for the supplying of electricity to more than 330,000 customers in the State's central business district and inner areas. The company had a revenue stream of just over AUD$1 billion in 2012 and employed some 2,000 employees.

The company owns extensive infrastructure to enable the supply of electricity. This infrastructure includes approximately 590,000 electricity poles carrying 90,000 kilometres of cable over a supply area more than 146,000 square kilometres. In recent times the company has been a leader in installing advanced meter technology (smart meters) which allows them to achieve important efficiency gains.

Background

In the early 1990's, the company continually faced challenges in the provision of electricity to customers via an infrastructure network that required continual maintenance. It had numerous information systems in place that supported their infrastructure maintenance programs and assisted with keeping costs in check. However, this became more and more difficult as the company had numerous disparate information systems that hindered the integration of company-wide business processes, which in turn impacted on timely access to important information. The integration of business processes was also a major issue as they lacked standardisation. Over time the number of supporting information technology systems and their associated costs increased significantly. There was also the impending problem of Year 2000 approaching which may have required many of these systems to be re-implemented.

In the late 1990s, the decision was made to implement SAP's ERP system's Enterprise Asset Management (EAM) functionality to address many of the issues. To further support the company's needs, additional functionality was subsequently introduced through the expansion of the ERP system with modules that included Works and Asset Management, Resource Planning and Scheduling, Logistics, Accounting and Human Resources. Furthermore, the SAP ERP system was configured to best support the requirements of the electricity utility business. Significant benefits were identified in terms of employee productivity improvements, reductions in inventory and enhanced management decision making. Another unexpected benefit was the ability to sell the SAP "best practice" template (Works and Asset Management) which the firm created, and were subsequently adopted by other utility companies. Indeed, the firm's template has been successfully deployed to three electricity utilities and a gas distribution utility in the United Kingdom.

Even though the company had implemented the SAP ERP system they were still finding it difficult to retrieve information for reporting to support decision making. The reason for this was that the ERP system had not replaced all of their existing systems. The information from the remaining legacy systems was required to be integrated with the information from the ERP system for reporting purposes. Hence, the company invested in two different Business Intelligence environments, SAP and Business Objects to address this problem.

These two systems, although providing some improvements, also caused a number of issues. One manger elaborates on the initial investment:

We wanted Business Objects to provide the reporting layer of our Business Intelligence. But we purchased Business Objects before SAP subsequently purchased the company— so the systems were not easily integrated. (Business Intelligence Manager)

Another issue related to employees needing to retrieve reports from both Business Intelligence environments where there was limited integration of information between the two. This resulted in monthly key performance indicator reports being developed and reported via spread sheets. It soon became evident that many of the Business Intelligence reports were not strategically aligned to support executive decision making.

The Development of an Information Management Strategy

In 2008 the company decided to develop what they termed was an Information Management Strategy which was directly underpinned by Business Intelligence. The main goals of the strategy were to:

- Implement a single Enterprise Data Warehouse to facilitate the storage and analysis of both operational and strategic operations. This would enable a "single version of the truth" to be achieved.
- Strategically align reporting to ensure that only relevant and intelligent data was reported.
- Improve financial information and data to support consolidation, planning and forecasting.
- Ensure that the right information was provided to the right people at the right time through web-based portals.
- Retire Business Objects to consolidate report environments and reduce IT costs.

The Information Management Strategy had six key components that accommodated important inter-related elements and included information hierarchy; strategies that addressed reporting, technology and application level issues; a governance model and the Business Intelligence architecture itself. The components and issues associated with the company's Information Management Strategy are now further described.

Information Hierarchy

The Information Hierarchy was designed to determine the information requirements of the organisational stakeholders. This was achieved through a top-down approach where the information required was strategically aligned with a person's level of management and included performance measures. The identified performance measures would enhance visibility and accountability, subsequently influencing and changing behaviour. There were two aspects to the information definitions requirements; Performance Management information (Grow the Business) and Decision and Operation Support information (Manage the Business). The Performance Management information related to performance measures supporting value-based management that utilised a Balance Scorecard approach. Accordingly, the key performance measures were related to financial and non-financial performance (Financial, Assets, Customers, Processes and People). Notably, the information required was aggregated information used to support high-level management decision making.

The Decision and Operation Support information was focussed on operational efficiency. This information reflected business processes and was associated with transactions. These transactions were supported by SAP and non-SAP systems. The Business Intelligence Manager indicated that:

There was an important requirement for the information to be real time and detailed.

One of the expected benefits from the identification of these informational requirements was the creation of a shared common data source. This provided more efficient access to information and reports, which in turn facilitated effective decision making.

The company identified a number of dependent factors that were associated with Information Hierarchy requirements. These factors were concerned with gaining buy-in or support from people at the performance management and operations management level. It was considered essential that all levels of management were supportive of the proposed information hierarchy to ensure its adoption across the company.

Another factor was the use of the performance measures, which were dependent on the availability and reliability of data used to calculate these measures. This was to be achieved by the creation of a central repository that stored organizational data by subject area. To ensure there was a change in corporate behaviour, business processes and supporting technology needed to be aligned to the firm's strategic objectives. A change management process was implemented to ensure staff understood these expectations, an issue that was reinforced through staff appraisal and compensation schemes.

Reporting Strategy

The Reporting Strategy provided guiding principles and processes for the development and delivery of information to end users. The strategy had three aspects: Enterprise Requirements, Efficiency and Preferences, and Technical Requirements. The Enterprise Requirements provided guidelines for the priority/criteria associated with report development. Criteria were aligned with business justification and the relationship to performance measures. A pertinent comment on this issue by Business Intelligence personnel was that:

It was important that the reports developed were not clones of the reports in the old system.

It was perceived important to manage the information requirements of users in an endeavour to promote the new reporting system. The Efficiency and Preference aspect of the Reporting Strategy was related to report design and distribution. This involved the level of information detail in each report and the level of interactivity required for analysis. Report design and visualisation guidelines were developed to assist with standardisation and facilitated end user learning. The frequency of when the information was required was also determined. This influenced how the report was distributed and when the information needed to be updated. The Technical Requirements were related identifying and defining the technical infrastructure needed to support the Reporting Strategy.

A key requirement of the Reporting Strategy was the development and distribution of strategically aligned reports to the appropriate decision makers. By using the Information Hierarchy as a reference, the performance measures were able to be identified for the different end users. This initially required a combination of information technology and business staff to be involved in the project:

The business people on the team were seen as the reporting experts. (Business Intelligence Manager)

The involvement of end users in the report design process was crucial to the implementation of the new reports and the resultant business process changes.

Governance Model

The Governance Model identified the information governance roles and responsibilities within the company. It tended to further enhance the link between business units and information technology. The roles within the Governance Model included; Business Process Champions, SAP Business Intelligence Technicians, Business Analysts and external Implementation Partners when required.

The company identified the need for a formal structure to ensure the success of the Governance model:

The Business Intelligence Steering Committee is responsible for the data governance process and associated business rules. (Business Analyst)

It was also considered important to provide training for users in Business Intelligence analysis processes. One of the responsibilities of the governance team was to develop a process to evaluate the reports needed by end users and management. This required extensive user involvement.

To act as reference for the evaluation of reports an information template that reflected end user needs was deemed essential. Alternatively, it was also deemed important to document when reporting was not undertaken, and the reasons for this shortcoming. These shortcomings were considered in the design of future reports.

Application Strategy

The Application Strategy was responsible for providing the Business Intelligence environment so as to deliver consistent and high quality data to IT applications and the subsequent information to users. This included the implementation of an Enterprise Data Warehouse (EDW) to store data that supported the various business units. This ensured information integrity across the various data repositories that could be accessed by user friendly reporting tools. The repository environment ensured consistency of information and data quality across the reporting tools. All these reporting tools could be accessed through a single common environment:

We decided to that to provide this single environment we stopped using Business Objects reporting tools. (Business Intelligence Manager)

Furthermore, executive information access through dashboards enabled users to drill down to greater levels of business detail. The EDW provided a standardised Business Intelligence environment which reduced duplicate processes while minimising the handling of data and improved overall data integrity. It enabled those previously responsible for collecting and transforming the data to spend more time on data analysis. There was also a reduction in costs associated with only needing to use a reporting system with a standardised interface environment. Part of this standardisation was achieved through the use of SAP's pre-configured Business Content function.

Business Intelligence Architecture

The Business Intelligence architecture was designed on the principles of scalability and reusable architecture to facilitate future business needs such as mergers and acquisitions. It was considered essential to avoid future performance issues.

The implementation of the architecture was designed from a top down perspective and adopted a phased incremental approach. Although there were long term goals, there were also a number of "quick wins" identified. The company acknowledged that unknown reporting requirements existed and these would evolve over time. An initial priority was the establishment of the Subject Area Repositories to provide a "single version of the truth". A longer term priority was the implementation financial budgeting, planning and consolidation functionality.

The company now has a Business Intelligence environment that stores 5 terabytes of data which is extracted from 14 sources systems and it accessed by 630 users. The company is also concerned about the growth of their Business Intelligence environment especially with the upcoming additional load of storing data from smart meters. They have recently purchased an in-memory data processing solution to provide a Business intelligence environment to allow them to accommodate the vast amount of data being collected from smart meters and new infrastructure installations.

As part of the interview the respondent was asked to identify any factors that he considered critical to the success of their Information Management Strategy. The Information Management Strategy was made up of a number of components (Information Hierarchy, Reporting Strategy, Governance Model, Application Strategy, and Business Intelligence Architecture). The interview revealed that each one of these components had factors which contributed to their success or were considered dependencies. Table 1 lists the success factors for each component.

Each component of the Information Management Strategy had a differed focus and therefore it would not have been unrealistic to expect that the relevance of different success factors would vary between each component. The interviewee (the manager) was asked to identify the factors which contributed to their success in regards to Business Intelligence. He indicated that a Business Intelligence *Strategy* is extremely importance to focus people's efforts and underpin associated decisions. The strategy needs to have executive management buy-in and sponsorship. He also identified the importance of a flexible and scalable technology landscape to support the reporting requirements of the company. Associated with this is the quality of the source systems where the Business Intelligence information is extracted from. A number of examples were provided of the negative impact of poor quality source systems have on Business Intelligence.

Table 1. Information management strategy components success factors identified from interview

Component	Success Factor
Information Hierarchy	Management Support; Strategic Alignment; Identification of Key Performance Indicators Change Management
Report Strategy	Strategic Alignment; Identification of Key Performance Indicators; Involvement of Business and Technical Personnel; User Participation
Governance Model	Training; User Participation
Application Strategy	Data Quality ; Business Content
Business Intelligence Architecture	Performance

The only reference in the interview specifically to the Business Intelligence implementation was the importance of the availability of appropriate technical resources. The interviewee specified that having Business Intelligence resources, Administration resource, SQL resource, and Subject Matter resources contributed to the success of the project.

CASE STUDY SUMMARY

The company had initially implemented an ERP system to standardize data structures and integrate its business processes. Over a period of time they refined their business processes and the supporting functionality with the assistance of their ERP system. This reflects the integrate and optimize stages that companies undertake in regard to their Enterprise Systems as proposed by Davenport et al (2003). The last stage of the journey reflects an Informate stage. In the case study, the Informate stage is associated with the company implementing Business Intelligence to improve information delivery and analysis in an endeavour to support decision making.

The company has been using Business Intelligence for more than a decade. Originally, the ad hoc approach to Business Intelligence resulted in limited benefits. Key performance indicators (KPI's) were identified but not well used, and there was a slow effort to formalise standards and processes. Indeed, many of the Business Intelligence maturity models suggest that companies start with an ad hoc approach to Business Intelligence. This is characterised by a range of different Business Intelligence solutions, poor data quality, departmental rather than firm-wide approach, a lack of standards, and poorly defined key metrics (ASUG, 2007; Hewlett Packard, 2007). These issues tend to contribute to companies not achieving their expected benefits from their initially Business Intelligence initiatives as reflected in the case study. The lack of benefit realization often results in companies revisiting their Business Intelligence initiatives (Hawking and Rowley, 2012). The way Business Intelligence was implemented and used was characteristic of an early stage of Business Intelligence maturity (Information Anarchy) according to the ASUG Business Intelligence Maturity Model (2007).

The company, in identifying the short-comings of their initial Business Intelligence implementation, developed an Information Management Strategy to provide some overarching guiding principles for the implementation and use of Business Intelligence to ensure a closer alignment with company's needs. The Information Management Strategy was multi-faceted when conceptualised and applied, reflecting an understanding of the different aspects of Business intelligence that needed to be considered when wishing to successfully implement such a system. The strategy included:

1. The required information to support decision making with the company (Information Hierarchy).
2. The presentation and delivery of information to support decision making (Reporting Strategy).
3. The software solutions and underlying technologies to sourcing, storage, analysis and presentation of information (Application Strategy/Business Intelligence Architecture).
4. The implementation and management of effective Business Intelligence (Governance Model).

One important component of the strategy was to adopt an enterprise approach to the use of Business Intelligence. Initially this was achieved through the consolidation of existing Business Intelligence technologies and the implementation of an Enterprise Data Warehouse (EDW). The desire to move to a single environment by the discontinuance of the Business Objects environment was facilitated by SAP acquiring Business Objects in 2007. These actions would be considered as an improvement in Business Intelligence Maturity and would be consistent with the Information Collaboration stage of the ASUG Business Intelligence Maturity Model (2007).

CONCLUSION

The case study documented in this paper provides an example of a Business Intelligence strategy developed for a utilities company. This strategic approach could be equally applied to companies in other industry sectors. The Business Intelligence history of the company demonstrates the iterative approach companies experience as they mature and identify the short comings of their existing Business Intelligence approaches.

Since conducting the initial interviews there have been further developments on the requirements of the company's Business Intelligence needs to support. These requirements are associated with the storage and analysis of large disparate data sets (Big Data). Victoria in 2011 introduced smart metering to households throughout the state. The implication of this is that the case study company collects readings for approximately 800,000 metres every half hour. This data needs to be stored, analysed and made available to consumers. The company is implementing SAP's in-memory database (HANA) to assist with this analysis.

As a result of the Victorian Government Bushfire Royal Commission recommended that the transmission infrastructure is monitored and maintained. To document this maintenance photographic evidence is required to be collected and stored on a regular basis for all rural infrastructure. The company is investigating how they can effectively store and analyse these large volume photographic data.

ACKNOWLEDGMENT

The authors wish to thank the academics that reviewed the paper. The feedback received assisted us in updating and improving the paper's value to readers.

REFERENCES

Adelman, S., & Moss, L. T. (2002). *Data Warehouse Project Management*. Boston: Addison Wesley.

Alekh, D., Maheshwari, N., & Kalicharan, S. (2013). A Business Intelligence Technique for Forecasting the Automobile Sales using Adaptive Intelligent Systems (ANFIS and ANN). *International Journal of Computers and Applications, 74*(1), 7–13.

ASUG. (2007). *ASUG/SAP Benchmarking Initiative: Business Intelligence/Analytics*. Presentation at American SAP User Group Conference, Atlanta, GA.

Atre, S. (2003). *The Top 10 Critical Challenges For Business Intelligence Success*. C. C. Publishing. Retrieved from http://www.computerworld.com/computerworld/records/images/pdf/BusIntellWPonline.pdf

Ballou, D. P., & Tayi, G. K. (1999). Enhancing data quality in data warehouse environments. *Communications of the ACM*, *42*(1), 73–78. doi:10.1145/291469.291471

Biere, M. (2011). *The New Era of Enterprise Business Intelligence*. IBM Press.

Boyer, J., Frank, B., Green, B., Harris, T., & van De Vanter, K. (2010). *Business Intelligence Strategy: A Practical Guide for Achieving BI Excellence*. MC Press.

Chenoweth, T., Corral, K., & Demirkan, H. (2006). Seven key interventions for data warehouse success. *Communications of the ACM*, *49*(1), 114–119. doi:10.1145/1107458.1107464

Chou, D. C., Tripuramallu, H. B., & Chou, A. Y. (2005). BI and ERP integration. *Information Management & Computer Security*, *13*(5), 340–349. doi:10.1108/09685220510627241

Davenport, T., Harris, J., & Cantrell, S. (2003). *The Return of Enterprise Solutions: The Director's Cut*. Accenture.

Dresner, H. J., Buytendijk, F., Linden, A., Friedman, T., Strange, K. H., Knox, M., & Camm, M. (2002), The Business Intelligence Competency Center: An Essential Business Strategy. Gartner Research, ID R-15-2248.

Eckerson, W. (2007). *Performance Dashboards: Measuring, Monitoring, and Managing Your Business*. Published by Wiley-Interscience.

Evans, P., & Wurster, T. (1997). Strategy and the new economics of information. *Harvard Business Review*, (September-October), 70–82. PMID:10170332

Gartner. (2012). *Gartner Forecasts Global Business Intelligence Market to Grow*. Available at www.Gartner.com

Gartner. (2013). *Gartner Executive Program Survey of More Than 2,000 CIOs Shows Digital Technologies Are Top Priorities in 2013*. Available at http://www.gartner.com/newsroom/id/2304615

Golfarelli, M., Rizzi, S., & Cella, I. (2004), Beyond Data Warehousing: What's next in Business Intelligence?*Proceedings of the 7th ACM international workshop on Data warehousing and OLAP*, 1-6. doi:10.1145/1031763.1031765

Grublješič, T., & Jaklič, J. (2014). Three Dimensions of Business Intelligence Systems Use Behavior. *International Journal of Enterprise Information Systems*, *10*(3), 62–76. doi:10.4018/ijeis.2014070105

Harison, E. (2012). Critical Success Factors of Business Intelligence System Implementations: Evidence from the Energy Sector. *International Journal of Enterprise Information Systems*, *8*(2), 1–13. doi:10.4018/jeis.2012040101

Harris, J., & Davenport, T. (2006). *New Growth From Enterprise Systems*. Accenture.

Hawking, P., & Rowley, C. (2012). *Tetra Pak's Journey to Business Intelligence Maturity. In Effective Strategy Execution: Improving Performance with Business Intelligence*. Springer.

Hawking, P., & Sellitto, C. (2010). Business Intelligence (BI) Critical Success Factors *ACIS 2010 Proceedings*. Retrieved from http://aisel.aisnet.org/acis2010/4

Hewlett-Packard. (2007). *The HP Business Intelligence Maturity Model: describing the BI journey*. Hewlett-Packard.

Hindriks, C. (2007). Towards chain wide Business Intelligence. University of Twente.

Hostmann, B., (2007, November). BI Competency Centres: Bringing Intelligence to the Business. *Business Performance Management*.

Hwang, H.-G., Ku, C.-Y., Yen, D. C., & Cheng, C. C. (2004). Critical factors influencing the adoption of data warehouse technology: A study of the banking industry in Taiwan. *Decision Support Systems, 37*(1), 1–21. doi:10.1016/S0167-9236(02)00191-4

IBM. (2013). *The Case for Business Analytics in Midsize Firms*. Retrieved from http://www-03.ibm.com/innovation/us/engines/assets/ibm-business-analytics-case-study-1-22-13.pdf

IBM. (2014). *Better business outcomes with IBM Big Data & Analytics*. Retrieved from http://www-935.ibm.com/services/multimedia/59898_Better_Business_Outcomes_White_Paper_Final_NIW03048-USEN-00_Final_Jan21_14.pdf

IDC. (1996). *Financial Impact of Data Warehousing*. International Data Corporation.

Irani, Z., & Love, P. (2008). *Evaluating Information Systems in The Public and Private Sectors*. Oxford, UK: Elsevier.

Isik, O., Jones, M., & Sidorova, A. (2013). Business intelligence success: The roles of BI capabilities and decision environments. *Information & Management, 50*(1), 13–23. doi:10.1016/j.im.2012.12.001

Johnson, L.K. (2004). Strategies for Data Warehousing. *MIT Sloan Management Review, 45*(3), 9.

Krippendorff, K. (2004). *Content Analysis: An Introduction to its Methodology*. Beverly Hills, CA: Sage Publications.

Lahrmann, G., Marx, F., Winter, R., & Wortmann, F. (2011). Business Intelligence Maturity: Development and Evaluation of a Theoretical Model. Proceedings of HICSS.

Luftman, J., & Ben-Tvi, T. (2010). Key issues for IT executives 2010: Judicious IT investments continue post-recession. *MISQ Executive, 9*(4), 263–273.

Lyons, D. (2004). Too much information. *Forbes*, 110–115.

McBride, N. (2014, February). Business intelligence in magazine distribution. *International Journal of Information Management, 34*(1), 58–62. doi:10.1016/j.ijinfomgt.2013.09.006

McDonald, K. (2004). *Is SAP the Right Infrastructure for your Enterprise Analytics.* Presentation at American SAP User Group Conference, Atlanta, GA.

Morris, H. (2003). The Financial Impact of Business Analytics: Build vs. Buy. *DM Review, 13*(1), 40-41.

Myers, M. D. (2013). *Qualitative Research in Business and Management* (2nd ed.). London: Sage.

Nasir, A., Ruiz, F., & Palacios, M. (2013). Organisational learning, strategic rigidity and technology adoption: Implications for electric utilities and renewable energy firms. *Renewable & Sustainable Energy Reviews, 22,* 438–445. doi:10.1016/j.rser.2013.01.039

Nucleus Research. (2011). *IBM ROI Case Study: Becker Underwood.* Retrieved from http://www.nucle-usresearch.com/research/roi-case-studies/ibm-roicase-study-becker-underwood/Becker%20Underwoo

Pant, P. (2009). *Business Intelligence: How to build successful BI strategy.* Deloitte Consulting. Available at http://www.deloitte.com/assets/Dcom-SouthAfrica/Local%20Assets/Documents/Business%20 intelligence%20that%20aligns%20with%20enterprise%20goals.pdf

Raber, D., Wortmann, F., & Winter, R. (2013). Towards The Measurement Of Business Intelligence Maturity. Proceedings of ECIS 2013.

Rubin, H. J., & Rubin, I. S. (2005). *Qualitative interviewing: The art of hearing data* (2nd ed.). Thousand Oaks, CA: Sage. doi:10.4135/9781452226651

Sammon, D., & Finnegan, P. (2000). The ten commandments of data warehousing. *ACM SIGMIS Database, 31*(4), 82–91. doi:10.1145/506760.506767

Spruit, M., Vroon, R., & Batenburg, R. (2014). Towards healthcare business intelligence in long-term care: An explorative case study in the Netherlands. *Computers in Human Behavior, 30,* 698–707. doi:10.1016/j.chb.2013.07.038

Vuksic, V., Bach, M., & Popovic, A. (2013). Supporting performance management with business process management and business intelligence: A case analysis of integration and orchestration. *International Journal of Information Management, 33*(4), 613–619. doi:10.1016/j.ijinfomgt.2013.03.008

Watson, H., Ariyachandra, T., & Matyska, J. Jr. (2001). Data Warehousing Stages Of Growth. *Information Systems Management, 18*(3), 41–50. doi:10.1201/1078/43196.18.3.20010601/31289.6

Watson, H. J., & Wixom, H. (2007). Enterprise agility and mature BI capabilities. *Business Intelligence Journal, 12*(3), 13–28.

Williams, S., & Williams, N. (2006). *The Profit Impact of Business Intelligence.* New York: Morgan Kaufmann.

Yeoh, W., Koronios, A., & Gao, J. (2008). Managing the Implementation of Business Intelligence Systems: A Critical Success Factors Framework. *International Journal of Enterprise Information Systems, 4*(3), 79–94. doi:10.4018/jeis.2008070106

Yin, R. (1994). *Case Study Research, Design and Methods* (5th ed.). Newbury Park, CA: Sage Publications.

KEY TERMS AND DEFINITIONS

Business Intelligence: A solution that allows people at all levels of an organization to access, interact with, and analyse data to manage the business, improve performance, discover opportunities, and operate efficiently.

Business Intelligence Strategy: A plan of action to maximise the impact of Business Intelligence on an organisation.

Business Objects: One of the leading Business Intelligence vendors which was acquired by SAP.

Critical Success Factors: Factors that need to be identified and managed to ensure the success of a project.

Enterprise Resource Planning (ERP) Systems: A real time modular information system responsible for automating and managing transactions associated with a company's core business processes.

Maturity Model: A business tool to assess the capabilities of an organisation in regards to a particular phenomenon.

Online Transaction Processing (OLTP): Information systems responsible for transaction processing.

SAP: A leading vendor of ERP systems and Business Intelligence.

ENDNOTE

[1]   The Essential CIO: Insights from the Global Chief Information Officer Study, IBM Institute for Business Value, 2010

Chapter 11
To Code or Not to Code:
Obtaining Value From the Customization of Packaged Application Software

Bryon Balint
Belmont University, USA

ABSTRACT

Businesses that purchase packaged application software – for example, an Enterprise Resource Planning system – must make choices about customization. Software vendors, anecdotal evidence, and practitioner-oriented research all recommend that organizations should customize software as little as possible, and instead adapt their processes to meet the "best practices" of the software. However, businesses continue to exceed their budgets on implementing and maintaining customized software, often to a significant extent. This suggests that either these organizations are making poor decisions, or that the conventional wisdom about customization is incorrect. In this paper we model the primary factors in the customization decision: "fit" between the desired business process and the packaged software; costs related to development, maintenance, integration, and performance; and benefits related to increased fit, integration, performance, and user acceptance. We use simulation techniques to illustrate the conditions under which customization is likely to provide value to the organization, as well as conditions under which customization should be avoided.

INTRODUCTION

Enterprise Resource Planning (ERP) systems are the most complex category of Enterprise Information Systems. While ERP adoption has progressed into some service industries, the vast majority of the ERP user base continues to be large manufacturing firms (META Group, 2004). Firms make the decision to implement ERP systems for many reasons, sometimes technical (Y2K or the obsolescence of old systems, for example) but predominantly to meet operational business requirements. One reason that many firms choose to implement ERP is in order to achieve competitive advantage over other firms in the same industry (Jafarnejad, Ansari, Youshanlouei, & Mood, 2012). The logic is that by following the business processes prescribed by the functionality and structure of the ERP system, business units (BU's) within

DOI: 10.4018/978-1-5225-2382-6.ch011

a firm will be collectively more efficient because they will be able to share data effortlessly (Ravasan & Rouhani, 2014). ERP systems have been shown to give firms an advantage over their competitors on several performance dimensions including profit margin, return on assets, and inventory turnover (Hitt, Wu & Zhou, 2002; Tang & Marthandan, 2011). However, many companies decide to implement an ERP system after some of their competitors have already implemented or started implementing the same ERP system. For example, General Motors, Ford, Volvo and BMW all use SAP, the ERP market leader (SAP, 2014).

One way in which companies seek to extract additional gains from an ERP systems and other packaged software is to tailor it using custom development that meets business-specific needs. For example, a publisher may have a complex royalty structure that is not handled within the standard accounting functionality of an ERP package. Given this situation, the publisher can either choose to simplify its royalty process or to modify the ERP package with custom development in order to handle its existing process. Most ERP vendors provide a mechanism for custom development but warn against it. One advertised benefit of ERP systems is the "best practices" that are embedded in the software; custom development may be incongruent with these practices, or may interfere with their use. Custom development may also affect the integration of data across different areas, another important benefit of ERP systems. In addition, all custom development must be maintained over time, and custom development that is done poorly may slow down system performance (Ng, 2013).

In spite of these potential issues, many firms in the publisher's situation would choose to customize the package. A responsible implementation project manager would conduct some form of cost-benefit analysis to decide which pieces of custom development to create. Unfortunately, not all of these analyses are complete or accurate. Benefits from customization may be overstated, and software development costs are notoriously underestimated (Harter, Krishnan, & Slaughter, 2000). As a result, firms may not derive the value from custom development that they expect; in fact, custom development may decrease the overall value of the system. However, ERP project managers that fully understand the costs and benefits of custom development should be able to make more knowledgeable decisions about it.

In this paper we present a model of custom development in the context of packaged application software. The model is most relevant to large-scale business software such as ERP systems, but can be generalizable to any business application software. We then use simulation techniques to model different conditions under which custom development may occur. As a result, we are able to describe and interpret the optimal conditions for the custom development related to packaged software. Implications and limitations of our model are also discussed.

LITERATURE REVIEW

A firm that implements a business software application package is naturally going to encounter some "gaps" between the functionality that the package provides and the business requirements. In these cases, a firm may choose to either adapt its processes to conform to the software package, or it may choose to customize the package itself (Soffer, Boaz, & Dov, 2005; Zarei & Naeli, 2010). Because most ERP packages are designed to be general, i.e. to be used by a wide range of businesses in different industries, they usually have some degree of customization or "configuration" built in that does not involve custom development (Chand, Hachey, Hunton, Owhoso, & Vasudevan, 2005; Negi & Bansal, 2013). Light (2005) looked at the qualities of custom development in the ERP environment in terms of context, content and process. Reasons for customization included the filling of functional gaps, making the system more appealing and acceptable to users, increasing efficiency, and facilitating a smoother implementation. Light concluded that, as with any software development, the reasons for performing custom development were not perfectly rational. In particular, some of the reasons for doing custom development were political in nature, such as justifying the existence of either in-house personnel or consultants, or compensating for misunderstandings about the package when it was selected. This suggests that custom development for ERP may not always serve the same goals as the ERP implementation itself. Data conversion from legacy systems to the ERP system is an important step that is often customized; however, it is not always technically possible or feasible within the scope of the implementation (Umble, Haft, & Umble, 2003; Grossman & Walsh, 2004). Organizations must strike a balance between their own ability to adapt to ERP practices and the possible adaptations associated with various types of customization, as well as their costs (Luo & Strong, 2004; Parthasarathy & Anbazhagan, 2007).

Assessing the value or impact of an ERP system is a difficult task, largely because of the reach and complexity of ERP systems. Chand et al. (2005) have demonstrated a balanced scorecard approach, including process-driven, customer-driven, finance-driven, and innovation-driven measures. Son-Yu (2005) also suggested a qualitative approach for evaluating the effectiveness of an ERP system in the post-implementation environment, when many of the costs stemming from custom development should be realized. Gefen and Ragowsky (2005) have suggested a process-driven approach, evaluating ERP benefits on a module-by-module basis. Standard financial measures of performance like ROI are often inapplicable because the financial benefits of ERP may not materialize for 5 years or more (Dowlatshahi, 2004). However, Hitt et al (2002) analyzed data from over 350 firms that implemented SAP and found positive impacts on many financial measures such as labor productivity, return on assets, profit margin, and even market value. Others have shown that ERP can have a positive impact on operational measures such as time to order and inventory turnover (Coteller & Bendoly, 2006; Kamhawi, 2007; Goeke & Faley, 2010). ERP implementations have also been shown to moderate factors that affect job satisfaction, such as skill variety and autonomy (Morris & Venkatesh, 2010). Finally, ERP investments have been shown to change industry dynamics – for example, creating more concentrated markets or greater churn among rivals in an industry. ERP systems often embody efficient or "best-practice" business processes, and the centralized nature of the technology makes it easy to propagate those practices throughout the entire organization (McAfee & Brynjolffson, 2008).

In short, research to date only describes qualitative differences related to the impact of custom development on the ERP environment. To the best of our knowledge, there has been no attempt to directly link the impact of custom development on performance measures that are typically used with ERP. In addition, there needs to be a deeper understanding of the different categories of development and the impact that they may have, as well as the costs and benefits associated with ERP development.

MODEL OF CUSTOM DEVELOPMENT

First, we will specify the different benefit and cost categories associated with custom development of packaged application software. Our overarching assumption is that custom development is undertaken to improve the "fit" of the packaged software to the organization, broadly construed. "Fit" primarily indicates the degree of match between the organization's business requirements and the procedures embedded in the software. These requirements may be encapsulated in the packaged software itself, or may involve integration with other information systems the organization is using (Méxas, Quelhas, Costa, & Lameira, 2013). It may also include features that increase the ease of use or performance of the software, leading to greater user acceptance.

Packaged application software will have some degree of fit "out of the box". Organizations typically go through a lengthy evaluation process when choosing a package to ensure that the software meets as many requirements as possible without the need for custom development (Karaarslan & Gundogar, 2009). We refer to this as the *starting fit*. Starting fit is important for two reasons. First, the greater the starting fit, the greater the likelihood that the ending fit will be higher. Second, the starting fit provides a boundary for the amount of custom development that may be undertaken; if the starting fit is very high, a large amount of custom development is simply unnecessary. We refer to the degree of fit after custom development has taken place as the *ending fit*. The ending fit can be interpreted as the overall value of the system to the organization; the higher the ending fit, the more value the organization will be able to obtain. We model the ending fit E as a continuous variable ranging from 0 (no fit) to 1 (perfect fit). Starting fit f is modeled as a discrete variable uniformly distributed between 0.5 and 0.9. The minimum boundary of 0.5 is intuitive; with so many packaged applications available, an organization would not choose an application that did not initially fit at least half of its requirements. We chose a maximum boundary of 0.9 to allow room for us to isolate the impact of custom development.

The difference between the starting fit and the maximum ending fit of 1 represents the amount of room available for improvement via custom development. Thus, custom development time d is logically bounded between 0 and $|1 - f|$. For example if $f = 0.6$, d would have a maximum value of 0.4, indicating that the organization wished to close the gap as much as possible through custom development. A minimum value of $d = 0.04$ would indicate that the organization accepts the gap in fit and wishes to do a minimal amount of custom development. We specify categories of benefits from custom development as well as costs in the following sections.

Benefits of Custom Development

We group the benefits of custom development into four categories. The first and most important is custom development that directly addresses the gap in fit. In the publisher example, this would include custom development that handles the unique royalty structure from an accounting perspective. We refer to this as *change in fit* development. Theoretically this category h is bounded between 0 and d, but we model this variable as bounded between $0.9 \times d$ and $0.1 \times d$. Intuitively, in most cases we expect that this category would encompass the majority of custom development time (Light, 2005; Van Velsen, Huijs, & Van der Geest, 2008).

The second category is the amount of time spent on development that facilitates *user acceptance*. Research has shown that a lack of user acceptance can single-handedly derail an ERP implementation effort (Sumner, 2000; Ravasan & Mansouri, 2014). Executive involvement and change management activities can increase the degree of user acceptance (Kontoghiorges, 2005) but custom development can also help (Pries-Heje, 2008). Frequently, packaged software that makes work easier in one BU may increase work in another BU (Seddon, Calvert & Yang, 2010). For example, a new process for procurement may increase the amount of data needed to create a purchase order, which would also increase the amount of required entry time (Balint, 2011). This increased data may make work easier for the accounting department and the organization as a whole, but the purchasing department could be worse off. Custom development – for example, a custom screen that facilitates data entry for the purchasing department – may help to increase the purchasing department's ultimate acceptance of the system without increasing the objective fit of the system to business requirements (Maldonado & Sierra, 2013). Formally, development that facilitates user acceptance a is bounded by $| d - h |$. We model user acceptance by varying a between $0.8 \times | d - h |$ and $0.1 \times | d - h |$.

The third category of custom development is development that facilitates *integration*. One of the primary benefits of ERP systems in particular is the integration of data across BU's (Isikdag, Underwood, Kuruoglu, & Acikalin, 2013). In the aforementioned publishing and purchasing examples, care must be taken to ensure that integration of data across areas is maintained. This is less easy than it may seem; integration points among the different modules of ERP systems are not always intuitive. Furthermore, integration points may change as the application software is maintained and updated. In addition, custom development may be needed to ensure that integration is maintained across multiple systems (Srinivasan, 2010). An organization with a Service Oriented Architecture philosophy may wish to use a separate information system for a specific function like an online storefront, for example. Custom development may be needed to ensure that the packaged software works with the outside system.

We model development that facilitates integration i using a negative linear term and a positive quadratic term. The negative linear term reflects the fact that integration by itself does not increase fit; rather, custom development that ensures integration is necessary merely to ensure that integration is maintained. Therefore, integration development can be conceived as a necessary by-product of other kinds of custom development. Theoretically, i is bounded by $| d - [h + a] |$. We model i as bounded between $.9 \times | d - [h + a] |$ and $.5 \times | d - [h + a] |$.

The final category of custom development is development that improves *system performance*. Packaged application software is developed by software development professionals who can tunc and optimize the software package to deliver maximum performance. Individuals who perform custom development will be less likely to be able to deliver the same level of performance due to lack of knowledge or experience. In addition, custom developers will not have the same level of knowledge about the base package as the original developers do. Similar to i, we model custom development related to performance p with a negative linear term and a positive quadratic term. Development related to performance by itself does not increase fit, but some amount of development is necessary to make sure that acceptable performance levels are maintained. Performance-related custom development can also be conceived as a by-product of other categories of development. In our model, we model p as $d - [h + a + i]$. In other words, p consumes the amount of available development time after development related to fit, user acceptance and integration is performed. In a complementary fashion, we could also model i as $d - [h + a + p]$; in other words, custom development related to integration and custom development related to performance are expected to affect the ending fit in a similar way.

Costs of Custom Development

The costs associated with the custom development of packaged software are straightforward. With ERP implementations contractors are often used for custom development, and they must be paid an hourly wage. When full-time employees are used, salary and benefits are necessary costs. In either case there are overhead expenses: project management and administration costs, office space, etc. The costs associated with custom development have been shown to comprise up to 60% of an ERP implementation budget (Francalanci, 2001).

We model the costs of custom development in two ways. First, we model the direct initial development costs using a cost parameter λ. This parameter is continuous and theoretically could range between 0 and 1. In our model, we bind λ to take values between 0.1 (the minimum proportion of development costs to total costs) and 0.5 (the maximum proportion of development costs to total costs). Stated more simply, higher values of λ indicate more expensive custom development. In our analysis we vary λ in 10% increments between 0.1 and 0.5.

The second cost component is the amount of *maintenance* required for the custom development. Software maintenance costs are frequently underestimated but may constitute a significant proportion of overall development costs (Gable, Chan, & Tan, 2001). We model maintenance costs m as a proportion of initial development costs λ. Formally m could take any value – maintenance costs over time could even exceed initial development costs (Ng, 2012). In our model we bound m between 0.1 and 0.5. We model m as a direct proportion of λ for simplicity; in practice, there could be an inverse relationship between initial development costs and maintenance costs. For example, more effort put initial requirements gathering and testing during the initial development phase may drastically reduce the amount of maintenance required long-term (Harter et al, 2000).

In summary, our overall cost / benefit model may be depicted as follows:

$$E = f + h + a - i + i^2 - p + p^2 - d\lambda - dm\lambda \tag{1}$$

Where:

E is the ending fit of the packaged application,
f is the starting fit of the packaged application,
h is the custom development designed to directly improve the fit,
a is the custom development designed to improve user acceptance,
i is the custom development designed to improve integration,
p is the custom development designed to improve system performance,
d is the total initial custom development time,
m is the total custom development maintenance time, and
λ is the custom development cost parameter.

Equation (1) indicates the overall fit of the system after custom development has taken place. Another way to evaluate the model is through the inequality:

$$h + a - i + i^2 - p + p^2 > d\lambda - dm\lambda \tag{2}$$

The left side of equation (2) indicates the overall benefit from custom development, while the right side indicates the overall cost. Thus if equation (2) is true then we should undertake custom development; otherwise, we should not. We will refer to the sum of the above variables as the *net value* of custom development, or N.

RESEARCH METHOD

We use a Monte Carlo-type simulation to generate data for analysis. Monte Carlo simulation techniques are typically used to generate many random instances of a stochastic process (Kennedy, 2003). To generate the Monte Carlo simulation, we programmed Model (1) into Stata and then generated a total of 450,000 observations using Stata's *simulate* function (Cameron & Trivedi, 2010). Results were analyzed using Stata and Microsoft Excel.

RESULTS

Descriptive data and correlations are reported in Tables 1 and 2. Other results from the simulation are depicted in Tables 3 through 8.

To ensure that the model has external validity, we first examine the relationship between development costs λ and two measures: the overall value of the system or ending fit E, and the net value of custom development N. Table 3 depicts the mean values of E and N at various levels of λ. As λ decreases, E and N both increase. The interpretation is straightforward: As the cost of development relative to fit decreases, custom development becomes more cost-effective.

Proposition 1: As the cost of development decreases, the net value of custom development and the overall value of the system increase.

We next examine the role of starting fit f. Table 4 shows values of E and N at various levels of λ and f. For all values of λ, as starting fit increases the average value of the system increases at an increasing rate. This suggests that the starting fit is the primary determinant of the overall value of the system. While the gap in fit can be shrunk by custom development, it cannot be shrunk 100% due to gaps in integration, performance, and maintenance costs. More simply, a better initial fit will always trump custom development.

Proposition 2a: As starting fit increases, the overall value of the system increases for all levels of development cost.
Proposition 2b: As starting fit increases, the overall value of the system increases at an increasing rate for all levels of development cost.

The relationship between starting fit and the net value of custom development is not as straightforward. For higher values of λ, the net value of custom development is negative but becomes more positive as the starting fit increases. But for lower values of λ, the net value of custom development is positive but becomes more negative as starting fit increases. The inflection point appears around $\lambda = 0.352$. The interpretation is that for development costs above the inflection point, development is more expensive. As the starting fit increases the potential for custom development decreases, so the net value of custom development increases (i.e., becomes less costly). For development costs below the inflection point, development is less costly. But as the starting fit increases the potential for custom development decreases, reducing its net value.

Proposition 3a: Above the inflection point ($\lambda > 0.352$), as the starting fit increases, the net value of custom development increases.

Proposition 3b: Below the inflection point ($\lambda < 0.352$), as the starting fit increases, the net value of custom development decreases.

To illustrate these propositions further, Table 5 depicts some results where the level of development increases for different levels of λ and f. For levels of λ above the inflection point and a given level of starting fit, E and N decrease as the amount of development increases. For levels of λ below the inflection point and a given level of starting fit, E and N increase as the level of development increases.

We now examine the behavior of the model at the inflection point $\lambda = 0.352$. At the inflection point, as starting fit increases the net value of custom development first decreases, then increases. We can further identify these changes with different levels of custom development. For any given level of starting fit, as the level of custom development increases N first decreases, then increases. Table 6 illustrates this phenomenon with some sample values. This has an interesting implication. At the inflection point it appears that the lower the level of starting fit, the greater the net value that can be attained through custom development. However, a significant amount of development must occur before the net value becomes positive. Presumably this is because custom development that is allocated toward increasing fit must be large enough to overcome the negative effects of custom development on integration and performance.

Proposition 4: At the inflection point ($\lambda = 0.352$), the lower the starting fit the larger the benefit that can be obtained from custom development.

We now examine the individual components of custom development. The first and most important component is custom development designed to directly improve fit, h in our model. The simulation illustrates that increases in h directly increase both the ending fit of the system and the net value of custom development. Importantly, this finding is robust to all levels of development costs, starting fit and total time spent on custom development. Table 7 illustrates some of these results. The interpretation is fairly intuitive: As the amount of time spent on custom development that improves fit increases, the ending fit increases. Nevertheless, knowing that this result holds across so many conditions is useful.

Proposition 5: As the amount of development time spent on improving fit increases, the overall value of the system increases.

The second component of custom development we examine is development designed to improve user acceptance, or u in our model. Similar to development designed to improve fit, increases in u directly increase both the ending fit of the system and the net value of custom development. In addition, this finding applies for all levels of development costs, starting fit and total time spent on custom development. Table 8 illustrates some of these results. While this finding is straightforward it is not intuitive as the previous one; development designed to increase user acceptance also has a robust positive impact on ending fit.

Proposition 6: As the amount of development time spent on improving user acceptance increases, the overall value of the system increases.

Finally, we examine custom development related to improving either system performance (p) or system integration (i). Mathematically these are treated the same in our initial model, so the same results hold for each. Our model shows that generally, as i increases the ending fit and the net value of custom development both decrease. This finding holds for all levels of λ and f. However, the changes in E and N are not smooth as i increases; there is a little variation. This is best illustrated in Figures 1 and 2. Figure 1 is a scatterplot of all observations of N for values of i between the 10th and 90th percentiles, and Figure 2 is a scatterplot of all observations of E over the same values of i. In both graphs, the blue markers represent observations with a starting fit of 0.5 through 0.6, and the green markers represent observations with a starting fit of 0.8 through 0.9. A downward trend is visible in both of these graphs for both ranges of starting fit. Therefore, increases in i (or p) are detrimental to the net value of custom development and the overall fit of the system.

Proposition 7: As the amount of development time spent on improving system integration increases, the net value of custom development and the overall value of the system decrease.

Proposition 8: As the amount of development time spent on improving system performance increases, the net value of custom development and the overall value of the system decrease.

DISCUSSION

The goal of our model is to shed light on some of the conditions that make the custom development of packaged software more cost-effective. Obviously, the per-unit cost of development (λ) is an important factor, perhaps the most important. The relationship between development cost and net value is linear and straightforward. Apart from this factor, the critical distinction appears to lie in the starting fit of the system, which puts a boundary on the necessary amount of development. As the starting fit increases the average value of the system increases at an increasing rate, regardless of the cost of custom development.

Figure 1. Impact of development related to system integration on net value of custom development

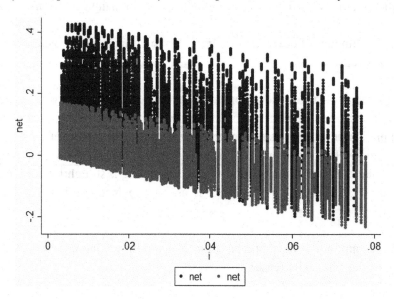

Figure 2. Impact of development related to system integration on ending value of system

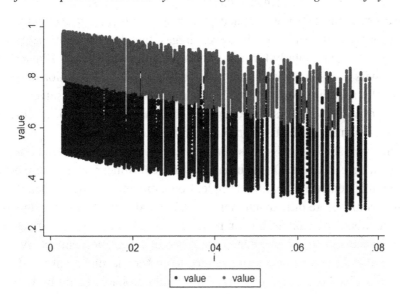

This suggests that choosing the system with the highest starting fit should be of the utmost importance to organizations, and that even organizations with a high amount of custom development experience should not depend solely on custom development to achieve a higher degree of fit. At the same time, understanding the optimal amount of custom development given a particular unit development cost is important in determining its net value. For development costs above the inflection point ($\lambda = 0.352$ in our model), custom development seldom generates a positive net value, no matter the starting fit. For development costs below the inflection point, custom development has a positive net value but that value decreases as starting fit increases. In other words, even when custom development is relatively cheap an organization should try to do as little as possible by choosing a high starting fit. For simplicity, our model assigns all custom development the same value. In reality, this result suggests that custom development should first target gaps in fit that may be conceived as "low-hanging fruit" where the benefit is more likely to be realized (Nair, Reddy, & Samuel, 2014). Beyond those instances, the cost-effectiveness of custom development is less assured.

For a given level of starting fit, we can make some other generalizations. First, with unit development costs below the inflection point, more development is better for a given level of starting fit. This is mixed news for software developers. A higher amount of development provides more value, meaning more work; however, net value is only provided at lower rates. For organizations, this result indicates that value can be obtained from custom development, but not as much value as can be obtained from a higher starting fit. Interestingly, at the inflection point for cost it also appears that more custom development is better. As the starting fit decreases, more development becomes feasible, and the net value of development increases. At the same time the ending fit of the system decreases, because custom development cannot completely address the gap in fit.

Lastly, we look at the different categories of custom development. Naturally, custom development that is designed to increase fit is effective at increasing fit. However, custom development that is designed to increase user acceptance is equally effective at increasing the overall value of the system. In a typical implementation, increasing fit is the primary reason for performing custom development (Light, 2005). In our model, the average time spent on user acceptance development is less than half of the time spent on development to increase fit. Our results however suggest that development spent on user acceptance may be equally important, particularly for important user groups (Sudevan, Bhasi, & Pramod, 2014). Finally, the effectiveness of custom development in increasing system integration or system performance is mixed, but generally negative. Performance and integration are not themselves directly tied to how well a system fits an organization. This result suggests that custom development allocated to increasing performance or integration should be used only in extreme circumstances.

Like any model, ours rests on a series of assumptions and simplifications. One criticism of our model might be the independence of terms. One could argue for a curvilinear relationship between overall development time and maintenance time, for example. Low amounts of development time could indicate little development, and therefore little maintenance; or, it could indicate a larger amount of low-quality development, which would precipitate higher maintenance. One could also argue for a relationship between user acceptance and fit, or between some types of integration and fit. Another variation on our model might be to make some of the terms related to custom development non-linear. With custom development related to fit in particular, organizations would probably begin by first writing code that addresses the largest and most important gaps in fit. This would suggest that the benefit from this type of development would be higher at first, and then would taper off as the less important gaps are tackled. This reasoning could also be extended to development designed to increase user acceptance or system performance.

CONCLUSION

This study presented a model of custom development in the context of packaged business software. We used Monte Carlo simulations to generate data, and then examine the results of the model while varying three groups of variables: development costs, the starting fit of the system, and different categories of development. Our key finding is that increases in starting fit outweigh any gains that may be obtained through custom development. For a given level of starting fit, the net value of system development is largely determined by development costs. Finally, Benefits are larger when the custom development time is spent implementing changes that either increase fit or user acceptance of the system.

REFERENCES

Balint, B. (2011). Difficulties in enterprise system implementation: The case of Millicent Homes. *Journal of Information Technology Case and Applications Research*, 13(3), 72–84. doi:10.1080/1522 8053.2011.10856213

Cameron, A. C., & Trivedi, P. K. (2010). *Microeconometrics using Stata*. College Station, TX: Stata Press.

Chand, D., Hachey, G., Hunton, J., Owhoso, V., & Vasudevan, S. (2005). A balanced scorecard based framework for assessing the strategic impacts of ERP systems. *Computers in Industry*, 56(6), 558–572. doi:10.1016/j.compind.2005.02.011

Cotteleer, M. J., & Bendoly, E. (2006). Order Lead-Time Improvement Following Enterprise Information Technology Implementation: An Empirical Study. *Management Information Systems Quarterly*, *30*(3), 643–660.

Dowlatshahi, S. (2005). Strategic Success Factors in Enterprise Resource Planning Design and Implementation: A Case-study Approach. *International Journal of Production Research*, *43*(18), 3745–3771. doi:10.1080/00207540500140864

Francalanci, C. (2001). Predicting the implementation effort of ERP projects: Empirical evidence on SAP/R3. *Journal of Information Technology*, *16*(1), 33–48. doi:10.1080/02683960010035943

Gable, G. G., Chan, T., & Tan, W. (2001). Large packaged application software maintenance: A research framework. *Journal of Software Maintenance & Evolution: Research & Practice*, *13*(6), 351–371. doi:10.1002/smr.237

Gefen, D., & Ragowsky, A. (2005). A Multi-Level approach to Measuring the Benefits of an ERP system in Manufacturing Firms. *Information Systems Management*, *22*(Winter), 18–25. doi:10.1201/1078/449 12.22.1.20051201/85735.3

Goeke, R. J., & Faley, R. H. (2009). Do SAP Successes Outperform Themselves and Their Competitors? *Communications of the ACM*, *52*(10), 113–117. doi:10.1145/1562764.1562793

Grossman, T., & Walsh, J. (2004). Avoiding the Pitfalls of ERP System Implementation. *Information Systems Management*, *21*(2), 38–42. doi:10.1201/1078/44118.21.2.20040301/80420.6

Harter, D., Krishnan, M. S., & Slaughter, S. A. (2000). Effects of Process Maturity on Quality, Cycle Time, and Effort in Software Product Development. *Management Science*, *46*(4), 451–466. doi:10.1287/mnsc.46.4.451.12056

Hitt, L. M., Wu, D. J., & Zhou, X. (2002). Investment in Enterprise Resource Planning: Business Impact and Productivity Measures. *Journal of Management Information Systems*, *19*(1), 71–98.

Isikdag, U., Underwood, J., Kuruoglu, M., & Acikalin, U. (2013). Data Integration Capability Evaluation of ERP Systems: A Construction Industry Perspective. *International Journal of Enterprise Information Systems*, *9*(3), 113–129. doi:10.4018/jeis.2013070106

Jafarnejad, A., Ansari, M., Youshanlouei, H. R., & Mood, M. (2012). A Hybrid MCDM Approach for Solving the ERP System Selection Problem with Application to Steel Industry. *International Journal of Enterprise Information Systems*, *8*(3), 54–73. doi:10.4018/jeis.2012070104

Kamhawi, E. M. (2007). Critical Factors for Implementation Success of ERP Systems: An Empirical Investigation from Bahrain. *International Journal of Enterprise Information Systems*, *3*(2), 34–49. doi:10.4018/jeis.2007040103

Karaarslan, N., & Gundogar, E. (2009). An application for modular capability-based ERP software selection using AHP method. *International Journal of Advanced Manufacturing Technology*, *42*(10), 1025–1033. doi:10.1007/s00170-008-1522-5

Kennedy, P. (2003). *A Guide to Econometrics* (5th ed.). Cambridge, MA: The MIT Press.

Kontoghiorges, C. (2005). Key Organizational and HR Factors for Rapid Technology Assimilation. *Organization Development Journal, 23*(1), 26–39.

Light, B. (2005). Going Beyond Misfit as a Reason for ERP Package Customization. *Computers in Industry, 56*(6), 606–619. doi:10.1016/j.compind.2005.02.008

Lucas, H., Walton, E., & Ginzberg, M. (1988). Implementing packaged software. *Management Information Systems Quarterly, 12*(4), 537–549. doi:10.2307/249129

Luo, W., & Strong, D. M. (2004). A Framework for Evaluating ERP Implementation Choices. *IEEE Transactions on Engineering Management, 51*(3), 322–333. doi:10.1109/TEM.2004.830862

Mabert, V. M., Soni, A., & Venkataraman, M. A. (2000). Enterprise Resource Planning Survey of US Manufacturing Firms. *Production and Inventory Management Journal, 41*(20), 52–58.

Maldonado, M., & Sierra, V. (2013). User Satisfaction as the Foundation of the Success Following an ERP Adoption: An Empirical Study from Latin America. *International Journal of Enterprise Information Systems, 9*(3), 77–99. doi:10.4018/jeis.2013070104

Markus, M. L., Tanis, C., & Ven Fenema, P. C. (2000). Multisite ERP Implementations. *Communications of the ACM, 43*(4), 42–46. doi:10.1145/332051.332068

McAfee, A., & Brynjolfsson, E. (2008). Investing in the IT that makes a competitive difference. *Harvard Business Review, 86*(7), 98–107. PMID:18271321

META Group. (2004). *Market Research: The State of ERP Services*. Stamford, CT: META Group, Inc.

Méxas, M. P., Quelhas, O. L., Costa, H. G., & Lameira, V. D. (2013). A Set of Criteria for Selection of Enterprise Resource Planning (ERP). *International Journal of Enterprise Information Systems, 9*(2), 44–69. doi:10.4018/jeis.2013040103

Morris, M. G., & Venkatesh, V. (2010). Job Characteristics and Job Satisfaction: Understanding the Role of Enterprise Resource Planning System Implementation. *Management Information Systems Quarterly, 34*(1), 143–161.

Nair, J., Reddy, D. B., & Samuel, A. A. (2014). Conceptualizing Dimensions of Enterprise Resource Planning Systems Success: A SocioTechnical Perspective. *International Journal of Enterprise Information Systems, 10*(1), 53–75. doi:10.4018/ijeis.2014010104

Negi, T., & Bansal, V. (2013). A Methodology to Bridge Information Gap in ERP Implementation Life Cycle. *International Journal of Enterprise Information Systems, 9*(2), 70–82. doi:10.4018/jeis.2013040104

Ng, C. S. (2012). A Case on ERP Custom Add-On in Taiwan: Implications to System Fit, Acceptance and Maintenance Costs. *International Journal of Enterprise Information Systems, 8*(4), 44–62. doi:10.4018/jeis.2012100102

Ng, C. S. (2013). Exploring Relationships in Tailoring Option, Task Category, and Effort in ERP Software Maintenance. *International Journal of Enterprise Information Systems, 9*(2), 83–105. doi:10.4018/jeis.2013040105

Parthasarathy, S., & Anbazhagan, N. (2007). Evaluating ERP Implementation Choices Using AHP. *International Journal of Enterprise Information Systems*, *3*(3), 52–65. doi:10.4018/jeis.2007070104

Pries-Heje, L. (2008). Time, Attitude, and User Participation: How Prior Events Determine User Attitudes in ERP Implementation. *International Journal of Enterprise Information Systems*, *4*(3), 48–65. doi:10.4018/jeis.2008070104

Ravasan, A. Z., & Mansouri, T. (2014). A FCM-Based Dynamic Modeling of ERP Implementation Critical Failure Factors. *International Journal of Enterprise Information Systems*, *10*(1), 32–52. doi:10.4018/ijeis.2014010103

Ravasan, A. Z., & Rouhani, S. (2014). An Expert System for Predicting ERP Post-Implementation Benefits Using Artificial Neural Network. *International Journal of Enterprise Information Systems*, *10*(3), 24–45. doi:10.4018/ijeis.2014070103

SAP. (2014). *Regional information and user groups*. Retrieved October 14, 2014 from https://websmp107.sap-ag.de/public/usergroups/list

Seddon, P. B., Calvert, C., & Yong, S. (2010). A multi-project model of key factors affecting organizational benefits from enterprise systems. *Management Information Systems Quarterly*, *34*(2), 305–328.

Soffer, P., Boaz, G., & Dov, D. (2005). Aligning an ERP System with Enterprise Requirements: An Object-Process Based Approach. *Computers in Industry*, *56*(6), 639–662. doi:10.1016/j.compind.2005.03.002

Son-Yu, C. (2005). Causes Influencing the Effectiveness of the Post-Implementation ERP system. *Industrial Management & Data Systems*, *105*(1), 115–132. doi:10.1108/02635570510575225

Srinivasan, M. (2010). E-Business and ERP: A Conceptual Framework toward the Business Transformation to an Integrated E-Supply Chain. *International Journal of Enterprise Information Systems*, *6*(4), 1–19. doi:10.4018/jeis.2010100101

Sudevan, S., Bhasi, M., & Pramod, K. (2014). Distinct Stakeholder Roles Across the ERP Implementation Lifecycle: A Case Study. *International Journal of Enterprise Information Systems*, *10*(4), 59–72. doi:10.4018/ijeis.2014100104

Sumner, M. (2000). Risk factors in enterprise-wide / ERP projects. *Journal of Information Technology*, *15*(4), 317–327. doi:10.1080/02683960010009079

Tang, C. M., & Marthandan, G. (2011). An Analytical Model to Measure IS-Enabled Organizational Effectiveness. *International Journal of Enterprise Information Systems*, *7*(2), 50–65. doi:10.4018/jeis.2011040104

Umble, E. J., Haft, R. R., & Umble, M. M. (2003). Enterprise Resource Planning: Implementation Procedures and Critical Success Factors. *European Journal of Operational Research*, *146*(2), 241–257. doi:10.1016/S0377-2217(02)00547-7

Van Velsen, L., Huijs, C., & Van der Geest, T. (2008). Eliciting User Input for Requirements on Personalization: The Case of a Dutch ERP System. *International Journal of Enterprise Information Systems*, *4*(4), 34–46. doi:10.4018/jeis.2008100103

Worley, J. H., Chatha, K. A., Weston, R. H., Aguirre, O., & Grabot, B. (2005). Implementation and Optimization of ERP Systems: A Better Integration of Processes, Roles, Knowledge and User Competencies. *Computers in Industry*, *56*(6), 620–638. doi:10.1016/j.compind.2005.03.006

Zarei, B., & Naeli, M. (2010). Critical Success Factors in Enterprise Resource Planning Implementation A Case-Study Approach. *International Journal of Enterprise Information Systems*, *6*(3), 48–58. doi:10.4018/jeis.2010070104

KEY TERMS AND DEFINITIONS

Customization: The process of making changes to packaged software, either by changing or adding to the existing software code.

Enterprise Resource Planning (ERP): A category of software that is used to manage multiple business units within an enterprise. ERP systems are particularly popular in manufacturing environments.

Fit: The degree to which packaged software meets the needs of a particular enterprise.

Gap: A functional requirement within an enterprise that is not fulfilled by packaged software. Can be interpreted as the opposite of fit.

Integration: The degree to which the procedures and data within a software application work together seamlessly.

Monte Carlo: A process by which numerical results may be generated from mathematical models. Typically uses repeated random sampling of variable within a defined range of values.

Packaged Software: Software that is purchased as a finished product rather than created anew.

System Performance: The processing speed, reliability and consistency of a software application.

User Acceptance: The degree to which the users of a software application are ready and willing to use it. Often defined as a function of perceived usefulness and perceived ease-of-use.

APPENDIX

Table 1. Descriptive data

Variable	Mean	Std Dev	Min	Max
starting fit (f)	0.7000	0.1414	0.5000	0.9000
development time (d)	0.1650	0.1230	0.0100	0.5000
change in fit development time (h)	0.0825	0.0813	0.0010	0.4500
user acceptance development time (a)	0.0371	0.0452	0.0001	0.3600
system integration development time (i)	0.0318	0.0377	0.0001	0.3645
system performance development time (p)	0.0154	0.0218	0.0000	0.2430
development cost (λ)	0.3000	0.1414	0.1000	0.5000
maintenance (m)	0.3000	0.1414	0.1000	0.5000
net value of custom development (N)	0.0112	0.0850	-0.6479	0.4251
value of system / ending fit (E)	0.7112	0.1596	-0.1479	0.9850

Table 2. Correlations

	f	d	h	a	i	p	λ	N	E
f	1.000								
d	-0.633*	1.000*							
h	-0.479*	0.757*	1.000						
a	-0.387*	0.612*	0.117*	1.000					
i	-0.398*	0.628*	0.121*	0.383*	1.000				
p	-0.333*	0.527*	0.101*	0.321*	0.643*	1.000			
λ	0.000	0.000	0.000	0.000	0.000	0.000	1.000		
N	-0.073*	0.118*	0.517*	0.070*	-0.561*	-0.508*	-0.357*	1.000	
E	0.847*	-0.498*	-0.149*	-0.306*	-0.651*	-0.566*	-0.190*	0.468*	1.000

* $p < .05$

Table 3. Custom development costs and value

Cost of Development	Mean Ending Fit	Mean Net Value of Custom Development
$\lambda = 0.500$	0.668	-0.032
$\lambda = 0.400$	0.689	-0.010
$\lambda = 0.352$	0.700	0.000
$\lambda = 0.300$	0.711	0.011
$\lambda = 0.200$	0.733	0.033
$\lambda = 0.100$	0.754	0.054

Table 4. Starting fit and value

Cost of Development	Starting Fit	Mean Ending Fit	Net Value of Custom Development
λ = 0.500	0.500	0.449	-0.0509
	0.600	0.558	-0.0418
	0.700	0.668	-0.0322
	0.800	0.778	-0.0221
	0.900	0.889	-0.0113
λ = 0.400	0.500	0.485	-0.0151
	0.600	0.587	-0.0132
	0.700	0.689	-0.0108
	0.800	0.792	-0.0078
	0.900	0.896	-0.0042
λ = 0.200	0.500	0.556	0.0564
	0.600	0.643	0.0440
	0.700	0.732	0.0321
	0.800	0.821	0.0208
	0.900	0.910	0.0101
λ = 0.100	0.500	0.592	0.0921
	0.600	0.673	0.0726
	0.700	0.754	0.0536
	0.800	0.835	0.0351
	0.900	0.917	0.0173

Table 5. Amount and value of custom development

Cost of Development	Starting Fit	Amount of Custom Development	Mean Ending Fit	Net Value of Custom Development
λ = 0.400	f = 0.600	0.080	0.5940	-0.0060
		0.160	0.5889	-0.0111
		0.240	0.5848	-0.0152
		0.320	0.5817	-0.0183
		0.400	0.5795	-0.0205
	f = 0.800	0.040	0.7969	-0.0031
		0.080	0.7940	-0.0060
		0.120	0.7913	-0.0087
		0.160	0.7889	-0.0111
		0.200	0.7868	-0.0132
λ = 0.200	f = 0.600	0.080	0.6148	0.0148
		0.160	0.6305	0.0305
		0.240	0.6472	0.0472
		0.320	0.6649	0.0649
		0.400	0.6835	0.0835
	f = 0.800	0.040	0.8073	0.0073
		0.080	0.8148	0.0148
		0.120	0.8225	0.0225
		0.160	0.8305	0.0305
		0.200	0.8388	0.0388

Table 6. Amount and value of custom development at inflection point

Starting Fit	Amount of Custom Development	Mean Ending Fit	Net Value of Custom Development
f = 0.600	0.080	0.5990	-0.0010
	0.160	0.5989	-0.0011
	0.240	0.5997	-0.0003
	0.320	0.6015	-0.0015
	0.400	0.6043	-0.0043
f = 0.800	0.040	0.7994	-0.0006
	0.080	0.7990	-0.0010
	0.120	0.7988	-0.0012
	0.160	0.7989	-0.0011
	0.200	0.7992	-0.0008

Table 7. Amount and value of custom development dedicated to improving fit

Cost of Development	Starting Fit	Amount of Custom Development Related to Improving Fit	Mean Ending Fit	Net Value of Custom Development
λ = 0.400	$f = 0.600$ $d = 0.200$	0.020	0.5016	-0.0984
		0.060	0.5435	-0.0565
		0.100	0.5861	-0.0139
		0.140	0.6295	0.0295
		0.180	0.6737	0.0737
	$f = 0.800$ $d = 0.100$	0.010	0.7489	-0.0511
		0.030	0.7706	-0.0294
		0.050	0.7925	-0.0075
		0.070	0.8146	0.0146
		0.090	0.8368	0.0368
λ = 0.200	$f = 0.600$ $d = 0.200$	0.020	0.5536	-0.0464
		0.060	0.5955	-0.0045
		0.100	0.6381	0.0381
		0.140	0.6815	0.0815
		0.180	0.7257	0.1257
	$f = 0.800$ $d = 0.100$	0.010	0.7749	-0.0251
		0.030	0.7966	-0.0034
		0.050	0.8185	0.0185
		0.070	0.8406	0.0406
		0.090	0.8628	0.0628

Table 8. Amount and value of custom development dedicated to improving user acceptance

Cost of Development	Starting Fit	Amount of Custom Development Related to Improving Fit	Mean Ending Fit	Net Value of Custom Development
$\lambda = 0.400$	$f = 0.600$ $d = 0.200$ $h = 0.100$	0.020	0.5370	-0.0630
		0.040	0.5760	-0.0240
		0.060	0.6155	0.0155
		0.080	0.6555	0.0555
	$f = 0.800$ $d = 0.100$ $h = 0.050$	0.010	0.7675	-0.0325
		0.020	0.7874	-0.0126
		0.030	0.8075	0.0075
		0.040	0.8277	0.0277
$\lambda = 0.200$	$f = 0.600$ $d = 0.200$ $h = 0.100$	0.020	0.5890	-0.0110
		0.040	0.6280	0.0280
		0.060	0.6675	0.0675
		0.080	0.7075	0.1075
	$f = 0.800$ $d = 0.100$ $h = 0.050$	0.010	0.7935	-0.0065
		0.020	0.8134	0.0134
		0.030	0.8335	0.0335
		0.040	0.8537	0.0537

Chapter 12
Decoding Success Factors of Innovation Culture

Stephen Burdon
University of Technology Sydney, Australia

Kyeong Kang
University of Technology Sydney, Australia

Grant Mooney
University of Technology Sydney, Australia

ABSTRACT

This chapter presents the results and findings of a research project on innovation culture in Australian information technology sector organisations. The primary objective of this study was to establish the determinants of a successful enterprise innovation culture in organisations with a strong industry reputation for radical innovation initiatives. We obtained 244 responses from 102 member organisations of the Australian Information Industry Association (AIIA). The survey explored the internal and external characteristics of a successful innovative organisation. Both employees' and competitors' perspectives on "what makes a particular organisation a successful innovator" were the main focus. Our findings indicated that the absence of a successful innovation culture is a serious impediment to growth and success. However, preferences for the key innovation culture attributes varied significantly by executive functions, size of the organization and type of ownership structure. Thus, a mix of key innovation attributes should be deployed and tailored to each organisation, based on their industry and strategic objectives.

INTRODUCTION

Establishing an enterprise innovation culture is critical for enabling agile processes, product and service development to be successful in a competitive business environment. Unfortunately, many senior business leaders remain focused on digital advancement to achieve their performance goals (McKinsey, 2014). While digital advancement is an innovation enabler, fostering an enterprise innovation culture geared towards growth should be a complementary organisational endeavor for sustained business growth and

DOI: 10.4018/978-1-5225-2382-6.ch012

competitive advantage. This is a challenging feat; unique approaches are required for different types of businesses, and it will be necessary to nurture cultural traits of individuals towards achieving a collaborative and successful innovation culture.

An objective analysis of the organisation is the first step. Individuals and communities typically tweak a few procedural issues that may deliver gains that are difficult to measure. Identifying the real change agents is the key to value creation and nurturing innovation culture within a given organisational setting. This study looked at external and internal characteristics of innovative organisations, using a targeted survey to define cultural traits for successful innovation. Both employees' and competitors' perspectives on, "what makes a particular organisation a successful innovator" were also explored. The primary objective of this study was to establish the determinants of a successful enterprise innovation culture with a strong industry reputation for radical innovation initiatives.

The survey was designed to tease out organisational cultural traits according to employees' roles, organisation type and size. It also considered the importance of specific attributes, such as organizational size, definition of strategic intent and commitment of resources to successful innovation.

The survey was distributed to the commercial members' executives of the Australian Information Industry Association (AIIA). We chose to research the AIIA members because most of them were from the information technology and services sectors. Other members include technology-oriented companies from other sectors such as retail banking, airlines and universities. 244 responses were received from 102 member organisations. The survey responses were analysed to derive measures for innovation attributes.

RELATED LITERATURE

Innovation Culture

Historically, as a business grows and achieves leadership position in its market, barriers of entry for competitors are high for a limited period of time. As other players strive to catch up, over time more competitors increase their market share. However, fast moving competitive business environments today face a stream of emerging technologies, with new products and services requiring agility and constant adaptation by all players in the market. Innovative ability is critical for an early entrant in the market and also a primary reason for growth and success (Schein, 2010; Xiao and Dasgupta, 2005, Kang, 2010).

Many organisations are aware that they need to establish certain cultural traits to achieve successful innovation. However, executives mistakenly tend to focus on advancing workplace digitalisation in the quest for achieving innovation – this alone rarely creates enterprise innovation culture. It has been reported that up to 5% of current business costs are being invested towards organisation digital advancement at any point of time. However, this is just one of the enablers for innovation and by no means, the only one (McKinsey, 2014). Market expansion may be achieved through digitalisation because of greater customer engagement, but in order to achieve and nurture innovation culture, a balance of human cultural attributes, adoption of new technologies and successful business strategies needs to be finetuned and pursued.

Consider the fact that, the larger organisation, the more likelihood there is that an individual may come up with a creative idea. It is unlikely that the end product or service will be an outcome of the individual alone; rather a successful outcome will be due to teamwork enabled by cultural attributes of the organisation, collaboration enabled by technology and harnessing this idea towards fulfillment of a business strategy (Manz et al, 2009; Manz et al, 2009; Koen et al, 2011). A sustained generation of ideas and successful business outcomes will be viewed as successful innovation, both internally and externally. These ideas could be new procedures, products or services that generate value to the organisation in the form of growth and returning superior financial metrics.

"Culture" is a self-sustaining pattern of behavior, thinking, beliefs, and feelings in a given organisational environment (Saunlere, 2013). A superior enterprise innovation culture enables promotion of an honest transfer of executive leaderships' vision or business strategies to non-executives' perception, ensuring a rapid feedback, development and refinement of ideas followed by action through collaboration. The collaboration may be enabled by digital technologies, while actions lead to growth and superior financial metrics. This process of sustained translation of ideas into action is perceived both internally and externally as successful innovation. Innovation includes new ideas in processes, products and services yielding significant benefits to individuals throughout the organisation and externally. Successful action and collaboration fosters learning, attitudes and an organisational culture that enables the innovation processes to repeat sustainably, and the greater outcome for the organization is that, it allows executives to see beyond current issues and gleam into future prospects (Mohammadisadr et. al, 2012; Chesbrough, 2010Dobni, 2008; Schein, 2004; Helriegel and Woodman, 2001).

Organisational Culture and Innovation Success

Organisational culture comprises both shared understanding of issues and shared perceptions of its members. Organisational culture also helps individuals to differentiate between acceptable and unacceptable behaviors within a given context, and it also governs the ways in which an organisation deals with individual performance issues such as failure, mishaps, success and rewards, as a system (Pearce et al, 2009; Schein 2010; Remneland-Wikhamn, 2011). Further, organisational culture plays an important role in day-to-day actions undertaken by individuals and in decision-making, such as, "what magnitude of risk is acceptable", "expectations for reward" and "effective teamwork".

Some organisational traits identified by Shaker et al, (2004) for innovation success were cultural orientation of employees, decentralisation of processes, higher use of strategic controls and a lower emphasis on financial controls. These traits enabled employees to make mistakes and learn effectively from their environment under management-controlled conditions. Christensen and Anthony (2005) took a similar view, labelling these traits as "continuous innovation support". Other organisational culture studies in innovation success have further identified role, organisational structure, task and resources as contributors to its success (Prahalad and Ramaswamy, 2004; Mortara et al, 2010; Pheysey, 1993; Katzenbach et al, 2014)). When roles, organisational structure, tasks and resources align favorably in an organisation, it leads to innovation success. In addition to these internal attributes, innovation success is further influenced by external factors, such as maturity of industry sector and overall economic conditions. To a large extent, it is a perception both externally and internally, with higher profit margins, superior financial metrics, high morale and recognition from peers and competitors, representing clear measurable outcomes (Burdon et al, 2013; Faems et al, 2005; Foster and Kaplan, 2001). However, the absence of one or more of these outcomes doesn't necessarily means that an organisation is not innovative. In many cases, small successes and innovations in the current time may yield higher returns in the future, when market and economic conditions improve. Others, take the view that innovation can be supported by use of management tools to enable collaboration, control risk taking, convert ideas into action and provide incentives to individuals satisfying innovation targets (Saunlere, 2013, Mooney, 2009; Faems et al, 2005; Gumnusluolu and Ilsev, 2008).

Many researchers are of the opinion that management approaches and processes can be implemented to foster favourable social and cultural settings to encourage innovation, leading the organisation towards measurable success with improved financial metrics (Damonpore, 2002, Chesbrough, 2010; Christine et al, 2002; Druker, 2000). Such approaches can succeed, particularly in larger organisations. It is universally accepted that the right 'social settings' and 'organisational culture' ensure that, not only, new and improved products and services are delivered to the customers, but also sustained improvements in service provisions, better business processes, an evolving business model, recognised organisational brand and improved communications at all levels (Christensen et al, 2005; Henderson; 2006; Vermeulen, 2010; Jaruzelski et al, 2011). Further, these achievements are not possible without a purposeful search for opportunities, the successful outcomes of which we recognise as innovation (Drucker, 2000; Grabher et al, 2008; Hamel, 2009; Vaccaro, 20010; Remneland-Wikhamn, 2011).

Innovation can be described as radical or incremental innovations, requiring different processes, knowledge, resources, and personnel performance. Radical innovation creates changes and upheavals either in the market or in the mainstream (Davila et al, 2005; Henriques, 2009; Jaruzelski et al, 2011; Saunière,, 2013). Incremental innovation on the other hand is described as continuous improvements in a stable market. It is highly dependent on the size of the organisation. Usually small companies empower managers to find the key 'person or persons', combining this with internal 'activities'. The selected key person(s) and activity enables rapid implementation of risky ideas that lead to radical innovation. In large companies, where processes, knowledge, resources and personnel are much more structured, organisational aspects such as structure, size, business processes and more specialised functions are significant factors in regulating activities and slowing the pace of innovation (McKinsey, 2014; Chandan and Urhuogo, 2012). It should be noted that these are generalisations rather than the rules. There are always exceptions and it is possible that large organisations may be more successful in innovation and small organisations more bureaucratic. Organisational culture is the key to successful innovation and helps in shaping executives' decisions, such as encouraging others, even in the face of adversity, to persist with efforts in risky situations to yield longer term outcomes that can be seen as innovation.

At a higher level, there are four major necessary components in an innovation framework: individual entrepreneurs, a cohort (a group of similarly trained professionals), organisational culture and national policy. These components provide social and technical conditions that foster creativity, invention and rapid development of ideas. Critically, the culture as determined by individuals and as a group, leads to transformation of creative ideas, rapid implementation and eventually results in innovation success.

APPROACH

In the context of this study, the greater the gap between a 'new idea' and the 'current state of the technology', the more natural it is for executives to dismiss that the idea is irrelevant when considering the risk of implementation (Swanson and Ramiler, 2004). Taking on the risk and persisting with implementation leads to success, termed as innovation; and the greater the gap between the idea and the state of current technology, the more radical is the innovation. In the initial stages of innovation, there are no measurable outcomes, but perceptions of achievements within and about the organisation do exist. Hence, discovering different perceptions within and about the organidation is likely to lead to indications of future innovation success. Thus, in this chapter, we explored how executives and external entities viewed "innovation" in an organisation presently, and foreseeable future innovation success.

We conducted a survey exploring innovation indicators and applied quantitative and qualitative methods to analyse the survey results. Executives from the information industry sector were asked to score the attributes of their own organisation culture and also that of competing organisations. This enabled us to explore the executives' personal views about how successful their own organisation was relative to their competitors in regards to innovation. We were also able to understand their levels of organisational achievements through overall ratings, perceived levels of achievements, organisational structure, business turnover, etc., relate them to commercial success and at what level their innovation was perceived to be. We explored different factors such as ownership types and roles related these to organisational culture leading to innovation success (Figure 1). The qualitative approach further enabled us to correlate key attributes and characteristics of successful innovation culture.

DATA COLLECTION AND MEASUREMENTS

A questionnaire was designed for executives in the information industry to explore the level of innovation in their own organisation and perceptions of their competitors. The nine survey questions were a mix of demographic questions for use in categorising the respondents' roles and defining the size of their organisation, apart from questions for gauging perceptions of innovation attributes. The respondents were provided with multiple-choice options and open-ended questions. The online survey was sent to the Australian Information Industry Association (AIIA) commercial members' executives in the last quarter of 2013. We received 244 responses from 102 organizations.

Each respondent was asked to nominate the top three most innovative organisations in their industry sector, with reasons for their ranking, and compare their own organisation to industry leaders. An earlier research by AON Hewitt (McKinsey, 2012) covered a wider range of industries in Australia. Their results indicated that only 25% of organisations judged themselves as innovative, compared to a figure of 78% information industry organisations. This was a clear indicator that compared with Australian businesses across all industries, the information industry sector organisations were viewed as successful innovators with enterprise cultures that fostered innovation.

Figure 1. Key innovation attributes by different roles and ownerships

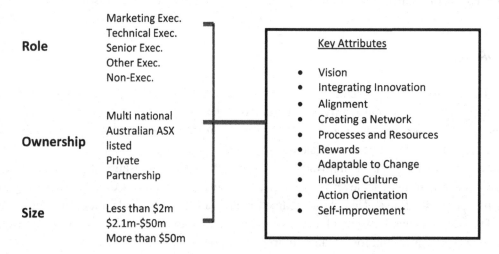

The survey also explored key cultural attributes thought to be essential for innovation in organisations (McKinsey, 2012). The respondents were asked to assess their own organisations' ability to meet ten attributes as outlined in Table 1.

Ratings for responses to questions corresponding to different innovation attributes were correlated with various segments of the survey to examine different aspects of innovation culture.

Findings

How Innovative are the Organisations According to Different Executive Functions?

Survey respondents assessed their own organisations' enterprise culture, and when these scores were correlated with the organisational growth rate (as a surrogate for success), even for organisations that were not growing, 62.1% of the respondents thought they had innovation culture. Over 85% of respondents from growing organisations believed their organisation had an innovation culture. As long as organisations are growing, growth rate itself seems to be irrelevant as an indicator for successful innovation (Mooney, 2009). However, these results also strongly indicate that the absence of innovation culture is a serious impediment to growth and innovation success. Organisations viewed as innovative, both externally and internally, returned superior financial performance with average net profit margin of 20%.

Figure 2 illustrates how the different functional executive roles had varying perceptions about the key innovation attributes within their organisations. Technical executives on average gave the lowest ratings for the ten innovation attributes. In comparison, non-technical executives gave higher scores, particularly the senior executives and non-executives.

Table 1. Ten key attributes for enterprise culture

Key Attributes	Questions
Vision	My organisation has a well-defined vision, goals and strategic intent.
Integrating Innovation	My organisation has been successful in weaving innovation achievement into the fabric of the business.
Alignment	My organisation is successful in communicating and aligning employee activities to the strategic plan.
Creating a network	My organisation has built a network of innovation resources internally and externally.
Processes & Resources	My organisation provides processes, time and/or funds for innovative projects.
Rewards	My organisation actively encourages and rewards people who generate and/or drive new ideas.
Adaptable to Change	My organisation is adaptable and easily embraces change.
Inclusive Culture	People in my organisation see themselves as an interlinked community, not just a company of employees.
Action Orientation	My organisation values 'doing', taking risks and experimenting, over detailed and methodical planning.
Self-Improvement	My organisation encourages learning and self-improvement in its people and allows sufficient freedom for this.

(McKinsey, 2012)

Figure 2. Perceptions of innovation ability by executive function

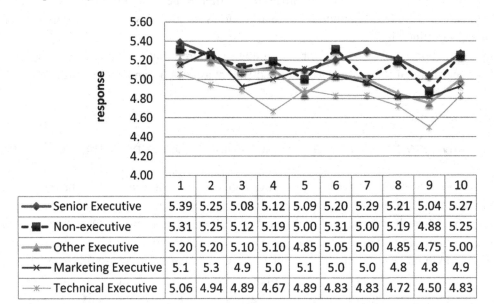

	1	2	3	4	5	6	7	8	9	10
Senior Executive	5.39	5.25	5.08	5.12	5.09	5.20	5.29	5.21	5.04	5.27
Non-executive	5.31	5.25	5.12	5.19	5.00	5.31	5.00	5.19	4.88	5.25
Other Executive	5.20	5.20	5.10	5.10	4.85	5.05	5.00	4.85	4.75	5.00
Marketing Executive	5.1	5.3	4.9	5.0	5.1	5.0	5.0	4.8	4.8	4.9
Technical Executive	5.06	4.94	4.89	4.67	4.89	4.83	4.83	4.72	4.50	4.83

How Innovative are the Organisations by Ownership Structure?

Privately-owned Australian organisations scored well on innovation, closely followed by the multi-national companies. Overall, Australian partnership organisations scored highest on the innovation attributes, followed by Australian private organisations, then Multinationals with an Australian presence, and lastly, Australian ASX-listed organisations. The differences between the highest- and lowest-scored categories by ownership structure were large – over 10%. The attributes with the largest differences were the 'ability of the organisation to communicate and align employee activities to the strategic plan', followed by 'ability to create an inclusive interlinked culture', and their 'ability to encourage learning and self-improvement in its people'.

Australian partnerships' average scores were highest at 5.26, while AXS-listed companies were worst with only 4.50. Average scores across all ownership types was 5.08 (see Figure 3).

Australian partnerships scored high on attribute 3 'alignment' and attribute 8 'inclusive culture' compared to other types of organisations. Australian private companies scored well for attribute 5 'process and resources', attribute 6 'rewards' and attribute 7 'adaptable to change'. ASX-listed companies scored poorly for attribute 4 'creating a network' and attribute 5 'process and resources' – this contributed towards their rating as lowest amongst all the types of organisations.

The ratings indicated that overall, Australian partnerships took innovation more seriously than the other business structures, while Australian ASX-listed organisations were the least focused on innovation.

Innovation Attributes by Organisation Structure

Self-improvement was the highest-rated innovation attribute in partnership organisations, which were rated as most innovative overall. We postulate this is most likely due to their flat structures of close-knit professionals. Partnerships also tend to be agile at adapting to changing market conditions. Highly-moti-

Figure 3. Perceptions of innovation ability by ownership structure

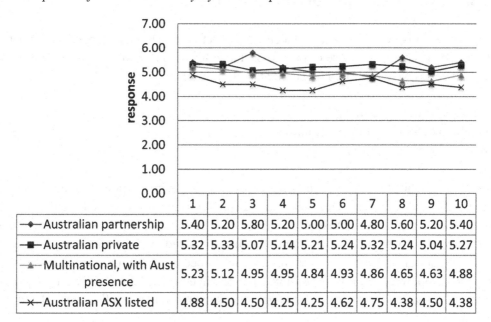

	1	2	3	4	5	6	7	8	9	10
Australian partnership	5.40	5.20	5.80	5.20	5.00	5.00	4.80	5.60	5.20	5.40
Australian private	5.32	5.33	5.07	5.14	5.21	5.24	5.32	5.24	5.04	5.27
Multinational, with Aust presence	5.23	5.12	4.95	4.95	4.84	4.93	4.86	4.65	4.63	4.88
Australian ASX listed	4.88	4.50	4.50	4.25	4.25	4.62	4.75	4.38	4.50	4.38

vated individuals across a flat structure support an innovation culture that evolves naturally and enables the development of new ideas in rapid succession, without needing approvals from other layers. Larger companies scored significantly lower in all key innovation attributes; by implication, the culture in these organisations is less conducive to innovation. Multinationals were found to be better than ASX-listed companies. Figure 3 summarises the differences in scores for innovation attributes. Smaller companies on average have superior engagement. Partnership structures were more successful at innovation than other privately-owned companies. The leadership within these smaller private companies is usually more entrepreneurial and open to seeking radical innovation.

Multinationals and ASX-listed companies focus on development, execution and implementation of great ideas. In contrast, partnerships and privately-owned companies believed they were high achievers in the area of being growth-focused proactive organisation. Private companies and Partnerships strongly believed in development of ideas, engagement of talent and were more growth focused. In contrast to public companies, privately-owned companies achieved higher innovation outcomes from great ideas. Privately-owned companies also focused strongly on employees' individual capabilities critical for forming cohesive innovation team cultures.

In summary, there was a significant difference between the scores for both Australian private and partnership organisations compared with that of the multinationals and ASX-listed organisations. Private and partnership organisations scored significantly higher across the board, and their employees had much more positive views of their innovation culture. There was a 20% difference in the scores for inclusive culture of multinationals and ASX-listed organisations.

Comparisons between multinationals and ASX-listed organisations were also interesting. There was over a 10% difference in scores for the two attributes 'creating a network' and 'processes & resources', with ASX-listed organisations scoring poorly. It appears that multinationals have established a culture that mitigates some of the inherent disadvantages of size and innovate effectively compared to their ASX-listed counterparts.

Innovation Attributes by Size of Organisations

The structure of the Australia-New Zealand technology sector has a higher proportion of what could be called smaller organisations. Because of this, to enable comparison between organisations of different sizes, three categories were drawn up based on annual turnover:

- Less than $2.0 million (small).
- $2.1 million to $50.0 million (medium).
- More than $50.0 million (large).

The small organisations achieved the highest scores in six of the innovation attributes, while medium-sized organisations did so in four. The 'self-improvement' attribute were scored highly by both small- and medium-sized organisations. 'Vision', 'processes and resources', 'rewards', 'adaptable to change' and 'self-improvement' were also scored highly by medium-sized organisations. In general small- and medium-sized organisations had a higher requirement for 'processes & resources' and 'rewards', possibly to motivate their employees towards innovation activities. In contrast, large organisations scored higher for 'processes & resources'; it could be that large organisations are more well-resourced and structured for innovation.

Executive Functions: Impact on Innovation

Senior executives in general gave higher scores for their own innovation culture, over and above the other executives in their organisation (Figure 2). They rated the attributes of "Adaptable to change" and "Self-improvement" as the highest priority. This suggests that senior executives take more responsibility for innovation, have a better sense of the consequences of changes and possess a broader view of

Figure 4. Perceptions of innovation ability by size of annual turnover

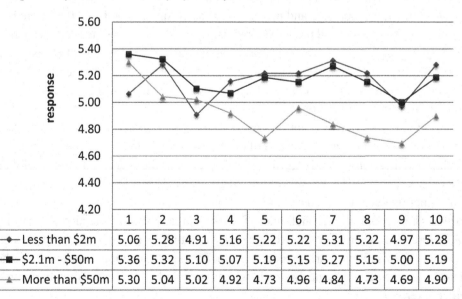

	1	2	3	4	5	6	7	8	9	10
◆ Less than $2m	5.06	5.28	4.91	5.16	5.22	5.22	5.31	5.22	4.97	5.28
■ $2.1m - $50m	5.36	5.32	5.10	5.07	5.19	5.15	5.27	5.15	5.00	5.19
▲ More than $50m	5.30	5.04	5.02	4.92	4.73	4.96	4.84	4.73	4.69	4.90

innovation. Contrary to our expectations, technical executives rated the attribute of "action orientation" lower, compared to senior and marketing executives. Technical executives were also more pessimistic about innovation levels in their organisation. The key strengths of successful organisations appear to be their executives' ability to harness internal talent for developing new ideas, and having 'procedures & resources' in place to execute these ideas well.

DISCUSSIONS

Perspectives and Key Attributes of Innovation

Our findings suggest that organisations would do well to engage with the innovation attribute of 'Vision'; all executives scored this attribute highly for innovation culture. However, marketing and other executives preferred 'Integrating innovation' while technical executives preferred 'Reward' as a vehicle to deliver innovation and gave it an equal importance as 'Vision' (see Figure 5). The survey also indicated that most executives prefer to have a process in place for radical innovation. Australian private and partnership organisations focused more on 'integration' and 'alignment'. The private organisations preferred weaving innovation into the fabric of their businesses, while partnerships focused on communication and alignment of employee activities with their strategic plans.

Large organisations focused more on 'Vision'. The findings clearly indicated that different sized organisations chose to adapt different vehicles for innovation culture. Smaller organisations preferred to be objective, and innovate through adaptability and easily embracing change. This preference can constrain the organisation's innovation strategy, if it moves on before the benefits of innovation are realised.

Figure 5. Perspectives and key attributes of innovation by role, ownership structure and size of annual turnover

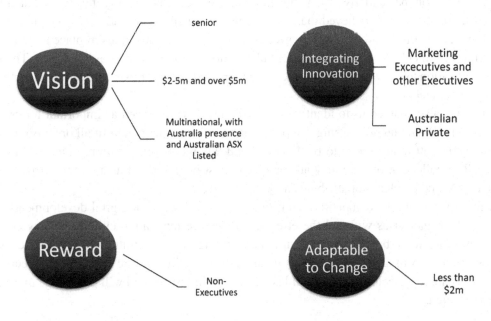

Nomination From Contributors for Being Innovative

Only one large organisation, Google, stood out for being nominated by its competitors as the most innovative organisation. Many well-known leading organisations in the retail banking, telecommunications and airlines sectors received surprisingly low scores for being innovative from their professional peers. Respondents chose Google because of its success in the attributes of 'Development of great ideas' (25%), and 'Execution and implementation of great ideas' (22%).

Multinationals and Australian ASX-listed organisations achieved markedly lower nominations for being innovative than their smaller private and partnership counterparts. These results lend credence to the hypothesis that larger organisations have to work harder to build innovation cultures and management processes to support these cultures. Both segments however, got lower scores for 'Creating a network' and 'Processes & resources'. The multinationals with an Australian presence received higher scores on average than Australian ASX-listed organisations. This suggests that the primarily USA-owned multinationals have a better innovation culture. Interestingly, they were given higher ratings by respondents from other organisations for growth and success.

The findings also indicated that organisations that promoted 'self-improvement' and had an 'Inclusive Culture' were much likely to have well-developed innovation cultures, and were recognised for this both internally and amongst other companies externally. The third most important attribute for innovation success nominated by respondents was the organisation's ability to 'engage talent'.

CONCLUSION

Our study has shown that the absence of successful innovation culture is a serious impediment to growth and success. Preferences for requirements for some key innovation attributes for innovation culture varied significantly by executive functions, size of the organization and type of ownership structure.

This study also confirmed that Australian technology organisations are highly innovative and focused on radical innovation, particularly of new products and services, even in organisations that showed no growth. Participants strongly believed that their employer organisations had very good innovation cultures with both executives and employees agreeing that there were processes in place to be innovative. A strong innovation culture was seen as essential for success in the technology industry. The need for continual innovation for new products was clearly understood and established, together with a high level of urgency in the technology sector's work culture.

The findings also enabled us to identify key attributes that were seen as important for creating innovation culture. We found no one single approach to innovation that would fit all organisations. A mix of key innovation attributes needs to be deployed and tailored to organisation, industry and strategic objectives. The collection of these key attributes can best be described as a toolbox, from which the appropriate mix and emphasis of attributes may be selected.

With intensifying global competition and rapid waves of change in digital developments, increasingly many more industries will feel the effects, and require innovation cultures to stay competitive and relevant. In addition, businesses need an understanding of digital initiatives that are necessary for innovation success. Although this study has examined innovation culture from the perspective of the information technology sector, it has useful lessons for all industries and will encourage more research input into this area.

ACKNOWLEDGMENT

The authors would like to express thanks and gratitude to the reviewers for their timely review and their constructive and helpful comments.

The authors would like to thank Australian Information Industry Association for supporting this research.

REFERENCES

Burdon, S. W., Al-Kilidar, H., & Mooney, G. R. (2013). Evaluating an Organizations Cultural Readiness for Innovation. *International Journal of Business Innovation and Research*, 7(5), 572–589. doi:10.1504/IJBIR.2013.056179

Chandan, H. C., & Urhuogo, I. (2012). Organizational Challenges for Innovation in Information Systems. *SAIS 2012 Proceedings*.

Chesbrough, H. (2010). *Business model Innovation: Opportunities and barriers*. Elsevier.

Christensen, C., & Anthony, S. (2005). *Building Your Internal Growth Engine*. HBR, Strategy & Innovation, Jan/Feb.

Christensen, C., & Raynor, M. (2003). *The Innovator's Solution*. HBSP.

Davila, T., Estein, M., & Sheldon, R. (2005). Making Innovation work: How to make it, measure it and profit from it. Prentice Hall.

Drucker, P. (2000). *The Discipline of Innovation, HBR*. Financial Data.

Faems, D., Looy, B. V., & Debackere, K. (2005). Interorganizational collaboration and innovation: Toward a portfolio approach. *Journal of Product Innovation Management*, 22(3), 238–250. doi:10.1111/j.0737-6782.2005.00120.x

Foster, R., & Kaplan, S. (2001). *Creative Destruction*. New York: Doubleday Publishing.

Gottlieb, J., & Willmott, P. (2014). *The digital tipping point*. McKinsey & Company.

Grabher, G., Ibert, O., & Flohr, S. (2008). The neglected king: The customer in the new knowledge ecology of innovation. *Economic Geography*, 84(3), 253–280. doi:10.1111/j.1944-8287.2008.tb00365.x

Gumusluoglu, L., & Ilsev, A. (2009). Transformational leadership, creativity and organizational innovation. *Journal of Business Research*, 62(4), 461–473. doi:10.1016/j.jbusres.2007.07.032

Hamel, G. (2009). Moon Shots for Management. *Harvard Business Review*, 87(2), 91–98. PMID:19266704

Henderson, R. (2006). The innovators dilemma as a problem of organizational competence. *Product Innovation Management*, 23(1), 5–11. doi:10.1111/j.1540-5885.2005.00175.x

Henriques, A. (2009). *When radical innovation is not plausible*. Available at http://innovomics.wordpress.com/tag/innovation/page/4/

Jaruzelski, B., Loehr, J., & Holman, R. (2011). Global innovation 1000: why culture is key. *Strategy + Business, 65*. Available at http://www.strategybusiness.com/article/11404

Kang, K. (2010). Considering Culture in Designing Web Based E-commerce. In E-Commerce. In-Tech.

Katzenbach, J., von Post, R., & Thomas, J. (2014). The critical few: Components of a truly effective culture. *Strategy+Business, 74*, 1-9.

Koen, A., Bertels, H. M., & Elsum, I. (2011). The three faces of business model innovation: Challenges for established firms. *Research-Technology Management, 54*(3), 52–59. doi:10.5437/08953608X5403009

Lewrick, M., & Raeside, R. (2010). Transformation and change process in innovation models: Start-up and mature companies. *International Journal of Business Innovation and Research, 4*(6), 515–534. doi:10.1504/IJBIR.2010.035711

Manz, C. C., Pearce, C. L., & Sims, H. P. Jr. (2009). The Ins and Outs of Leading Teams: An Overview. *Organizational Dynamics, 38*(3), 179–182. doi:10.1016/j.orgdyn.2009.04.005

Manz, C. C., Pearce, C. L., & Sims, H. P. Jr. (2009). The Ins and Outs of Leading Teams: An Overview. *Organizational Dynamics, 38*(3), 179–182. doi:10.1016/j.orgdyn.2009.04.005

McKinsey. (2012). *Global Survey: Making Innovation Structures Work*. McKinsey & Company, McKinsey Insight. Available at: http://www.mckinsey.com/insights/organization

McKinsey. (2014). *McKinsey Global Survey results: The Digital Tipping Point*. McKinsey & Company.

Mooney, G. R. (2009). *Enterprise Creativity and innovation, 1*. Berlin, Germany: Lambert Academic Publishing.

Mortara. L, Slacik. I, Napp. J. J, Minshall. T. (2010). Implementing open innovation: cultural issues. *Int. J. Entrepreneurship and Innovation Management, 11*(4).

Newman, I., Ridenore, C. S., & Ridenore, C. (1998). *Qualitative-Quantitative Research Methodology: Exploring the Interactive Continuum* (1st ed.). Southern Illinois University Press.

Pearce, C. L., Manz, C. C., & Sims, H. P. Jr. (2009). Where Do We Go From Here?: Is Shared Leadership the Key to Team Success? *Organizational Dynamics, 38*(3), 234–238. doi:10.1016/j.orgdyn.2009.04.008

Pheysey, D. C. (1993). *Organizational Cultures: Types and Transformation*. New York: Rutledge. doi:10.4324/9780203028568

Prahalad, C. K., & Ramaswamy, V. (2004b). Co-creation experiences: The next practice in value creation. *Journal of Interactive Marketing, 18*(3), 5–14. doi:10.1002/dir.20015

Remneland-Wikhamn, B. (2011). Path dependence as a barrier for Soft and Open innovation. *International Journal of Business Innovation and Research, 5*(6), 714–730. doi:10.1504/IJBIR.2011.043207

Saunière, J.-C. (2013). Innovation that counts. PriceWaterhouseCoopers.

Schein, E. H. (2010). Organizational culture and Leadership (4th ed.). John Wiley & Sons.

Shaker, Xahar, & Hayton. (2004, Summer). Entrepreneurship in Family vs. Non-Family Companies. *Entrepreneurship Theory & Practice*.

Vaccaro, A., Parente, R., & Veloso, F. M. (2010). Knowledge management tools, inter organizational relationships, innovation and firm performance. *Technological Forecasting and Social Change*, *77*(7), 1076–1089. doi:10.1016/j.techfore.2010.02.006

Vermeulen, F., Puranam, P., & Gulati, R. (2010). Change for change's sake. *Harvard Business Review*, *88*(6), 70–76.

KEY TERMS AND DEFINITIONS

Australian Information Industry Association (AIIA): A national non-profit organization representing the information technology and telecommunications industry sectors, and a network for collaboration and providing a voice of influence to the industry grouping.

AXS-Listed: Australian Securities Exchange (AXS) Ltd, or ASX Limited, is an Australian public company that operates in Australia's primary securities exchange, the Australian Securities Exchange.

Innovation Ability: Individual skills befitting innovative activities.

Innovation Attributes: key attributes of enterprise culture that promotes innovation. These attributes are usually referred to those ten key attributes mentioned in the McKinsey report.

Innovation Culture: A work environment that supports creative ideas and innovation.

Innovation Success: Organizational benefits from innovation through enabling management process, strategic and financial controls.

Multinational Organization: An organization operating in several countries.

Organisation Culture: A system of individual and team values and believes that governs how people behave, share and influence people in an organization.

Ownership Structure: Structure of the organization to communicate and align employee activities.

Size of Organizations: A major determinant of the organization size is the number of employees. However, in some cases it may also refer to the magnitude of the turnover.

Chapter 13
Benefits of Customer Relationship Management on Customer Satisfaction:
An Empirical Study

Nastaran Mohammadhossein
Universiti Teknologi Malaysia, Malaysia

Mohammad Nazir Ahmad
Universiti Teknologi Malaysia, Malaysia

Nor Hidayati Zakaria
Universiti Teknologi Malaysia, Malaysia

ABSTRACT

The purpose of this study is to investigate the efficacy of customer relationship management (CRM) benefits for customers in relation to customer satisfaction. A model has been developed and empirically tested through data collected from a survey of 150 customers of three Malaysian companies. The results indicate that the benefits of CRM for customers have had a significant positive effect on their satisfaction towards marketing companies. Personalized services, responsiveness to customers' needs, customer segmentation, customization of marketing, multichannel integration, time-saving and improving customer knowledge are the benefits that we proposed would affect customer satisfaction and significantly improve marketing performance. Additionally, the results reveal that all the benefits found, with the exception of time-saving, enhanced customer satisfaction. This paper contributes to the existing literature by incorporating the benefits of CRM for customers, and the relationships of these benefits with their satisfaction in the proposed model.

DOI: 10.4018/978-1-5225-2382-6.ch013

INTRODUCTION

In recent years, the world has undergone rapid changes due to technological advances. In order to be a winner in this race, firms and companies should be more active and powerful. It is important for organizations to keep existing customers and simultaneously target new customers. CRM can help in discovering and attracting new customers. This research is an effort to find out some of the benefits of CRM for customers and determine how this impacts their satisfaction. The implementation of CRM is an effort to find solutions that assist organizations to develop customer relationships with a high rate of satisfaction.

CRM is a vital factor for an organization to provide a customer-centric business and retain effective marketing, sales and service processes (Carolyn, Melissa, & Chandana, 2003). In addition, CRM aims to record and evaluate customer connections, which is a vital aspect for companies to be successful in a dynamic market (Sarvari & Alp Ustundag, 2016).

The information gathered from current customers can be used to attract new customers. CRM can help to identify applicants and potential partners, and mix current customer information with potential customer requirements. By using this information, a company can distinguish its products and services to offer unrivalled services to new customer groups (Tiwana, 2001).

A number of organizational benefits will help companies benefit by using CRM to have a closer approach to customers, increasing customer satisfaction and customer retention. CRM systems enable communications that aid in simplifying a long-term relationship structure between a company and its customers (Hendricks, 2007).

Over the past decades, many organizations of varying sizes and types have realized the advantages of providing customer satisfaction, since preserving existing customers is cheaper than attracting new ones. The powerful relationship between customer satisfaction and profit-making has been approved, so increasing customer satisfaction then becomes an important goal for companies (Ahrari & Amirusefi, 2012). Customer satisfaction is an important measure for companies in developing, checking, and evaluating products and service contributions, in addition to inspiring and motivating employees. Customer satisfaction and customer orientation are vital competitive benefits in all areas of production (Kotler, 2000). Hence, it would be helpful for companies to understand how the implementation of CRM can increase the rate of satisfaction among their customers.

Since CRM can be related to the satisfaction of customer needs, there are some research studies that have examined the impact of customer satisfaction and retention with CRM (Mithas, Krishnan, & Fornell, 2005; Verhoef, 2003; Zikmund, Raymond McLeod, & Gilbert, 2003; Carter & Yeo, 2016). Some information systems researchers have developed studies and theories relating to the effect of CRM systems. The study around CRM and its critical factors shows that there is inadequate knowledge about the effect of CRM and its benefits for a company's customer satisfaction level. However, previous research does not clarify why CRM applications affect customer satisfaction (Mithas, Krishnan, & Fornell, 2005). Through having a good background on CRM benefits for customers, it is essential to discover how the relationship with them can help companies determine how to improve their customer satisfaction levels by implementing CRM.

It is hoped that this research will help the researcher to find the importance of CRM for improving customer satisfaction. Moreover, we have gathered information from past studies which have researched CRM benefits from a customer perspective so as to help future researchers gain a beneficial background. Providing a model that clarifies the relationship between CRM benefits and customer satisfaction would also be beneficial for future studies. This study will assist companies and top managers to have a complete view about the impact of CRM on their customers, and to find a better way to manage their relationships with customers. Nowadays, methods of finding new customers for a company need to be different from its business competitors.

This paper is organized as follows; Following section deals with literature review and definitions. We discuss the lack of the study in existing literature relating to CRM benefits for customers, customer satisfaction and the relationship between CRM and customer satisfaction. Then we explain the methods employed in this research. Afterward we explain the research model and hypothesis. Then analysis and results are drawn. Finall part gives some conclusions reached and remarks on future work.

LITERATURE REVIEW

Customer Relationship Management

Customers have always been the key, as well as a major concern for businesses all around the world. They are considered to be fundamental for an organization's activities that can enable it to participate in a marketing competition with other companies. The significance of this importance has caused an increased requirement for organizations to integrate knowledge for building close collaboration and partnering relationships with customers (Parvatiyar & Sheth, 2001).Therefore, companies gradually affiliated themselves with the changing environment to become more innovative in replying to the changes of customers' requirements and needs (Prabhaker, 2001; Tseng, 2016). In recent years, companies are emphasising more on products that are based on customer-centric factors. CRM can play a vital role in this change, which is underpinned by information and communication (Ryals & Knox, 2001). Hence, implementing CRM as an information system has become increasingly common (Zgener & I'raz, 2006).

CRM has been defined in a range of different ways. According to Buttle (Buttle, 2004), CRM means different things to different people. In some definitions, CRM is a way to find, acquire, and retain customers. For others, it is an approach of automating the front office functions of sales, marketing, and customer service. For some vendors, whatever their current product may be, that is CRM. (Hashemi, 2012).

According to the Gartner group (2008):

Customer relationship management (CRM) is an IT-enabled business strategy, the outcome of which optimizes profitability, revenue and customer satisfaction by organizing around customer segments, fostering customers- satisfying behaviour and implementing a customer centric process.

In addition, certain studies look at CRM more holistically, explaining CRM through its relationship with technology and as a business strategy (Bose 2002; Buttle, 2004; Goodhue, 2002; Sathish, 2002). CRM systems control all customer activities, from first contact to continuing services and repeating sales; and in turn receiving value from every step. By managing these steps, companies can ensure that customer information, needs and attributes are all working in a well-organized way. Therefore, it provides a complete consideration of customer interests, needs and plans (Rushforth, 2007). Companies can remove the confusion which exists in productivity, efficiency and control of every level through appropriate use of CRM (Rushforth, 2007). Consequently, by looking towards the CRM definition, it is clear that satisfying the needs and requirements of the customer is a significant part of CRM, and it has a vital impact on changing the strategies of an organization in its relationship with customers and clients.

Customer Relationship Management Benefits

Results in a cross-cultural and multi-industry study of CRM, which was completed by Thomas and Kumar (2004), implies the idea that desired CRM benefits do not differ through industries or cultures as predetermined by earlier thoughts. Therefore, through successful CRM implementation it is in fact rational to obtain the desired benefits. In this part, we will have a quick review of the general benefits of CRM for companies; and in the next part we will then specifically focus on these benefits for the customers.

According to Gray and Byun (2001), CRM benefits have namely: enhanced the capability of organizations to retain and obtain customers, increased customers' respective lifetimes, and obtained better service at lower costs. With CRM systems, customers are served better on a day to day basis; and, with more reliable information to hand, they demand less of these services. Therefore, if there is less need to contact the company for different problems, the customer satisfaction level increases (Leach, 2003).

Companies also achieve significant benefits from CRM (Swift, 2001). Swift states that benefits are usually found in one or more of the following areas:

1. Decreased costs of recruiting customers.
2. No need to have a great deal of customers to protect a stable volume of business.
3. Lower costs of sales.
4. Higher customer profitability.
5. Increased customer retention and loyalty.

Since the CRM system's focus is on customers, it can help to recognize those customers who are paying higher margins. Once those customers are identified, it becomes simple to analyse their condition and recognize what other procedures or product attributes can help them. Finally, this process helps companies to surpass their competitors while they are negotiating with customers. They can do this by cost reduction strategies that are provided by the company offerings (Nasershariati & Khan, 2011). Also, the CRM system helps to find those customers which are not paying "fair" margins (Leach, 2003). CRM systems thereby become a central part of business processes, and can provide a better use of inventory if customer needs are known (Nasershariati & Khan, 2011) .

In general, 20 percent of the customers of each company provide 80 percent of the revenue and income (McKim, 2000). Therefore, a company must recognize its important and valued customers and take good care of them. On the other hand, the other customers, who make up the remaining 20 percent of the income, must be evaluated for further confirmation. Beside this, there is a group of customers generating no profit which the company can seek to change into valued customers. CRM can also help to build up sufficient data on each customer's business patterns. This will then help a company to know the customer's mind better, and find out how to behave with these particular customers during the buying process (Bose 2002). In addition, a company can use this information to incorporate marketing arrangements into its campaigns while it gets to know the present customers.

We conclude from the above that the agreed version of finding the true customer is to investigate the important benefits that CRM can bring to companies and customers alike (Dyché, 2002). An innovative and customer-focused knowledge organization can be created from the adoption of the right customer-centric organization and efficient use of CRM.

Satisfaction

Organizations must be capable of satisfying their customer needs and requirements in order to achieve customer satisfaction. This is crucial since customers' needs shape the perceived disappointment of a customer (Kotler, 2000). Customers' needs are related to the form of human desires which are shaped by culture and individual personality (Kotler, 2000). According to a study by Hoyer and MacInnis (2001), satisfied customers shape the establishment of each successful business, since customer satisfaction is a guide to the replication of a purchase, brand loyalty, and optimistic word of mouth. The consequences of not satisfying customers can have a negative impact on productivity of organizations and companies. In accordance with Hoyer and Macinnis (Hoyer, 2001), displeased consumers can come to a decision to:

- Stop purchasing the goods or services.
- Complain to the organization or to competitors and maybe return the item.
- Engage in negative word-of-mouth communication.

Satisfaction refers to a person's feeling of either happiness or disappointment arising from comparing a product's recognized performance according to his or her expectation. Similarly, customer satisfaction is an indicator of the future financial success of the company (Kotler, 2000). It also shows the level of happiness provided by the products or services. By conducting a review about the concept of customer satisfaction, it is clear that there are many definitions related to this topic. Companies make use of customer satisfaction increasingly as a standard, when assessing the quality of products and services. Besides, it is normally used as a part of the employee bonus system. Customer satisfaction impacts cash flows, increases productivity, and improves both profits and strategic implications. Customer satisfaction relating to goods and services may be received from diverse areas or may be influenced by different factors. Thus, it should be measured as a separate and individual circumstance (Veloutsou, 2005).

Customer Satisfaction and Its Measurement

According to Kim (2003), customer satisfaction is a reaction that a product or service can provide based on customer needs, and can determine if the purchaser will become a stable customer or not. Customer satisfaction is a very significant ability of a service supplier to construct a high degree of satisfaction for product differentiation. This will be an invaluable aid in developing a good relationship with customers in today's tough business world (Deng, 2009). Measuring customer satisfaction offers an instant, significant and objective criticism concerning customer preferences and expectations (Mihelis & Malandrakis, 2001). In developing satisfaction among customers, companies need to be more careful regarding the type of customer services that they offer.

Achieving customer focus requires leveraging existing customer information in order to gain a deeper insight into the relationships with customers. It is also necessary to improve customer service-related processes so as to provide services which are quick, error free and convenient for customers. From customer responses, a company would be able to evaluate the satisfaction level of customers (Hadzagas, 2011). A firm can conduct a survey on customer satisfaction once a year using a satisfaction index provided by an outside consultancy to measure services, personnel, and treatments.

According to Delone and McLean (2003), "user satisfaction is one of the most vital dependent variables used in measuring the success of the system because of the non-volitional condition of majority of the systems".

According to Delone and McLean (2003), system utilization may lead to user satisfaction. The procedure here is obvious; if a user does not use the system, he or she cannot be either pleased or unhappy. There must be a contact with the system to outline a reaction about the system. In this model repeat purchases, repeat visits and user surveys are the measures which can be used as a gauge to ascertain the reaction of the user to the system. We will use repeat purchases and repeat visits as a measure by which to recognize customer satisfaction as an indirect user with CRM systems.

Customer Relationship Management and Customer Satisfaction

In recent years, the domain of a customer's decision has increased by the use of banking, broadcasting, telecommunication, and many other scopes of business. In this new changing environment, companies feel the need to have a strong relationship with their customers much more keenly than before. This has led to the arrival of customer relationship management and customer satisfaction measurement, and has finally come to the point where CRM and CSM are merging.

The final aim of CRM is customer satisfaction (Kim, Suh, & Hwang, 2003). Measuring customer satisfaction is difficult as it is hard to quantify the satisfaction level. It means that quality in enterprises and organizations is represented by customer satisfaction. Similarly, customer satisfaction will also provide an approach to provide a customer-focused management in companies.

According to Karimi and Somers (2001), appropriate CRM practices can directly impact customer satisfaction ratings, thereby leading to increased customer retention. As we mentioned above, the concept of CRM is focused on its ability to retain customers so as to increase the profits of a business.

Companies must focus on obtaining customer satisfaction while at the same time trying to rationalize the costs. The right technology can help them to improve customer benefits, which then results in satisfied customers. The basic standards of customer satisfaction are represented by satisfied customers who tend to be loyal, as well as more likely to recommend the business services to others. Thus, it will help to both acquire new customers and retain current customers to increase competitive advantages, which is the most important goal of CRM.

We have ascertained the benefits of CRM for customers from previous literature studies. In Next part, we aim to measure and realize the relationship and effect of these benefits upon customer satisfaction.

THE RESEARCH MODEL

Consistent with the literature reviewed above, we demonstrate the seven benefits of CRM for customers which was gathered from a previous study. These are namely: improve personalized service, responsiveness to customers' needs, customer segmentation, improve customization of marketing, multichannel integration, time saving, and improve customer knowledge. All of these qualities have a positive relationship with customer satisfaction. We have proposed a model which has seven constructs that will have an effect on customer satisfaction. In addition, there are also two constructs for measuring satisfaction, namely: repeat purchases and repeat visits.

Figure 1 is a basic model for this research. There may be some limitations or problems, which will be determined according to the data and the relationship between the hypotheses. These will be discussed later in this study. In the section concerning hypothesis development, we will discuss the relationship of CRM benefits with customers and customer satisfaction. We will show this relation by the hypotheses.

HYPOTHESIS DEVELOPMENT

According to the previous discussions in this research, we found seven benefits of CRM from the customer's point of view. We will discuss about the relationship between these benefits and customer satisfaction in the following parts. Each relation will be shown in a hypothesis to clarify the relationship between the benefits of CRM and customer satisfaction.

Personalized Services and Customer Satisfaction

With personalized services, a company can focus on what a customer wants to buy rather than what the company wants to sell. Therefore, providing one-to-one services is a strategy designed to meet customers' needs and help them to become happy.

There are many ways to apply the principles of one-to-one services, improving customer satisfaction and the effectiveness of the relationship. CRM has a huge impact on the provision of personalized services for customers and facilitates the way in which companies wish to increase their individualized

Figure 1. A basic model for this research

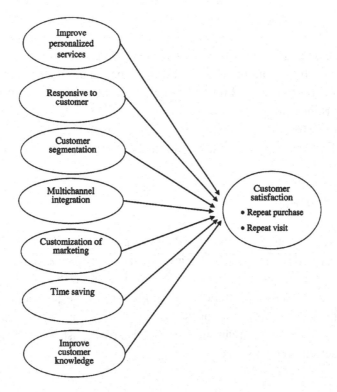

services. In some organizations, CRM is known to have been designed for one-to-one (Peppers, 1999) customer communications (Injazz J. Chen, 2003).

According to Dwayne Ball (2006):

The rationale makes common sense: personalization should produce a more satisfactory transaction, and over time, a more satisfactory relationship. Personalized service should simply be better service than routine service that does not take the individual's needs into account.

Based on the importance of personalized services to customers and the ability of CRM to help in developing this benefit for customers, CRM will result in increased customer satisfaction. Thus, we believe that offering more personalized services through CRM affects customer satisfaction positively.

H1: There will be a positive relationship between CRM personalized services and customer satisfaction.

Improving Customer Knowledge and Customer Satisfaction

In recent times, marketing and information systems researchers have improved theories about the result of CRM applications, with some development towards empirical validations (Jayachandran, Satish, Kelly Hewett, & Kaufman, 2004; Reinartz, Krafft, & Hoyer, 2004; Romano & Fjermestad, 2003; Srinivasan, Anderson, & Ponnavolu, 2002). However, there is still incomplete knowledge about the impact of CRM applications on customer knowledge and customer satisfaction. Customer knowledge can also benefit customers through enabling the company to respond to their needs based on their purchasing behaviour and their suitable services. By this reason discovering a customer's taste and personalizing products can be the result of customer knowledge.

Customer knowledge provides customer satisfaction because companies can change their offerings to suit customers' requirements. Jayachandran, Hewett, and Kaufman (2004) provide empirical evidence that customer knowledge processes improve the speed and efficiency of a company's customer response. Better knowledge of customer behaviour helps firms manage customers so as to raise the perceived value of the firm's contribution for customers and increase the chance of retaining customer loyalty (Sunil Mithas, 2005). Therefore, better customer knowledge provided by CRM enables a firm to increase its customer satisfaction.

H2: There will be a positive relationship between improving customer knowledge with CRM and customer satisfaction

Customer Segmentation and Customer Satisfaction

Segmentation, or target marketing, shifted a company's attention to adjusting products and marketing efforts according to customer needs. Changing customer needs and preferences require firms to define slighter and smaller segments (Injazz J. Chen, 2003).

According to Speed and Smith (1992), use of segmentation is a way to enhance customer satisfaction, customer loyalty and customer retention. Market segmentation may be a helpful instrument for companies which continually search for alternative ways to advance the level of satisfaction among their customers (Epetimehin, 2011).

Therefore, customers can be segmented into groups based on age, gender, demographics, etc. CRM will provide companies the capability to categorize their customers into similar groups according to their various requirements. CRM applications facilitate the process of segmentation. For example, customer segmentation will help companies to introduce their new products to the right groups. It can also help customers to have easier access to the products and services through placing them in an accurate group. Therefore, by presenting appropriate products and services to customers, their satisfaction levels will increase and they will become more pleased. Here, we will find the relationship between customer segmentation and their satisfaction as a hypothesis.

H3: There will be a positive relationship between CRM customer segmentation and customer satisfaction.

Multic Channel Integration and Customer Satisfaction

When efficiently executed in a company, a multichannel advance will smooth the association between a customer and a company. It can help the management to leverage all customer touch points to increase revenue, strengthen customer satisfaction, and streamline sales and service costs (Peterson, Gröne, Kammer, & Kirscheneder, 2009).

According to Wallace, Giese and Johnson (2004):

Results show that multiple channel retail strategies enhance the portfolio of service outputs provided to the customer, thus enhancing customer satisfaction and ultimately customer retailer loyalty. These results suggest that multiple channel retailing can be a useful strategy for building customer retailer loyalty.

Use of electronic channels such as emails, websites, as well as technologies like e-mobile or SMS can be other channels of communications, which can be controlled through CRM. CRM facilities will help companies to maintain contact with their customers by different channels and improve their relationships. There are growing numbers of channels by which a company can interact with its customers. Through an iterative process, Payne & Frow (2004) categorized many channel options into six categories, namely: sales force, outlets, telephone marketing, direct marketing, e-commerce and m-commerce.

According to the report of GoToAssist (2009), the benefits of multichannel integration is that of enhancing customer experience and increased satisfaction. Eventually, we believe that multichannel integration has a positive impact on customer satisfaction. The approach of companies using multichannel integration should be supple enough to regulate changes in customer expectations. So, here we will examine the relationship between multichannel integration and customer satisfaction.

H4: There will be a positive relationship between CRM multi-channel integration and customer satisfaction.

Customization of Marketing and Customer Satisfaction

The purpose of customization is to increase customer satisfaction, and the loyalty that is exhibited by customers (Adele Berndt, 2005). Customization of marketing and customer satisfaction by themselves are significant metrics for tracking the success of CRM systems.

Customization enhances the involvement of customers and staff, creates more academic inputs, as well as creating a competitive edge. Thus it is clear that without proper knowledge and information of customer expectations and requirements, it is almost impossible to produce customer satisfaction (Anwar, Gulzar, & Ayesha Anwar, 2011). CRM applications can provide a good source of knowledge about customers and their past needs. It can also help companies to track customers' purchases and obtain their needs to provide more customized products and services for each of them.

Customization will provide facilities for users to clearly specify their preferences and tailor products and services based on these preferences in internet-based services (Lam, Chan, Fang, & Brzenzinski, 2005). Customization provides users with apparent control, that is, a more successful way to obtain customer satisfaction (Johansson, Ba, & Chase, 2001). Consequently, an online service or e-commerce site may obtain better satisfaction when the site enables users to control their selections for products and services (Lam et al., 2005).

From a theoretical viewpoint, it is important to know whether or not the association of CRM applications with improvement in customer satisfaction is mediated by the customization of marketing. We therefore believe that there is a direct relationship between CRM customization of marketing and customer satisfaction.

H5: There will be a positive relationship between CRM customization of marketing and customer satisfaction.

Time Saving with CRM and Customer Satisfaction

According to Garcia (2012) concrete time plays a significant role, but has little role in customer time satisfaction. Some results show that, by giving the customer more quality time, customer satisfaction with time can be gained.

Moreover, companies need to be conscious about the importance of contact time to a customer relationship. A CRM application is a good tool to manage the time of contact with customers. Managing customers' time and decreasing wasted time can also lead to customer satisfaction. Time satisfaction might be influenced by how satisfying the whole service experience is perceived by the customer (Garcia et al., 2012).

The CRM system will proceed the process of interacting with customers by using member logins in the online purchase or using member cards in stores or companies. This will enable the customer to connect to the system without any need to input their information again. These facilities will serve to decrease the actual amount of time spent in making a purchase. In addition, it will help the sales person or employee of the company to have a more complete knowledge and information about each customer. Also, they can provide assistance to customers by finding their desired product or service based on their background. Reduction in time spent and time-saving has a positive relationship to customer satisfaction (Kohli, 2004; Lee, 2003).

H6: There will be a positive relationship between time-saving with CRM and customer satisfaction.

Responsiveness to Customers and Customer Satisfaction

It is the right of each customer to want companies to foresee what will bring value to them through finding and addressing their unknown wants and needs. Further, these unknown wants and needs must be changed into new products and services. For this reason, CRM is a significant tool that will help companies to know and find out the needs of their customers, and be responsible when dealing with them (Chen & Chen, 2004; Kim, Suh, & Hwang, 2003; Mark Xu, 2005).

Response to customer enquiries and their needs is a driver of customer satisfaction. Therefore, customer satisfaction is no longer the benchmark, since many marketers have coined the term "customer delight" (i.e. delivering quality service ahead of customer expectations) (Pandey & Devasagayam, 2010).

As CRM uses a significant database, all the information and records of each customer will be stored. This will enable customers to track their requests and needs faster than before. All of this will result in customer satisfaction. Customers can find better service quality if the company can address their needs.

H7: There will be a positive relationship between CRM responsiveness and customer satisfaction.

RESEARCH METHOD

Data Collection and Analysis Tool

A structured questionnaire survey is adopted as being the most suitable research method. It is adopted because this is the most appropriate way to collect relevant primary data from a high proportion of customers in busy leading companies. This enables them to analyse the expressed relatedness between the 7 aforementioned CRM benefits in the proposed model and customer satisfaction.

The Questionnaire is comprised of three different sections. Three questions relate to personal information concerning the respondents. The purpose of the questionnaire was to prepare empirical evidence in relation to CRM customer benefits and customer satisfaction.

The questionnaire comprises of the following sections:

- Personal information (gender, age, education).
- Customers' repeat purchases and visits (frequency of purchases and visits).
- CRM benefits for customers (a predefined list of 7 categories of CRM benefits).

The core of the questionnaire consists of the aspects of CRM benefits. For every aspect, we ask customers to designate the importance of that aspect, and finally, we ask about their satisfaction in that respect.

The respondent was asked to fill out their degree of agreement via a five-point Likert scale (with 5 = completely agree, to 1 = completely disagree).

To establish the content validity of the questionnaire, questions regarding the measurement of dimensions were posed during an interview with three doctors and four practitioners in CRM and marketing, to change, reduce and refine those items that are not valid. The last questionnaire contained 25 questions. Pre-testing and pilot testing of the actions were done by choosing users from the CRM field, in addition to experts in the area. Only two items were modified in this level.

For analysing data resulting from questionnaires, the Partial Least Squares (PLS) procedure has been used and the software used is SmartPLS. PLS facilitates simultaneous analysis of the association between dimensions and their equivalent constructs, and the empirical associations between model constructs.

Population and Sample Size

In this study the research location should be selected from organizations or companies who used CRM applications for their transactions with customers. Therefore, three companies (AEON, Tesco, and PETRONAS) in the Skudai area of Malaysia were selected as the locations for this study. The main reasons for this selection were the limitation of time and access to study in a wider research area.

To provide accuracy and precision of the analysis, a sample of 150 respondents was used. Therefore, 150 questionnaires have been disseminated between customers randomly. Of 150 respondents; 15 people were under high school graduation, 12 persons were high school graduates, 70 people held a diploma, 36 held a bachelor degree, 12 people possessed a master degree, and five of the respondents held a PhD degree. The ages of the respondents were namely: 19% between 18 to 24, 55% between 25 and 34, while 26% of the respondents were more than 35-years-old.

Reliability and Validity

For preparing the reliability of the research, the Cronbach's Alpha method has been used (Jamshidi, Rasli, & Yusof, 2012). Every construct shows Cronbach's alpha readings of suitable values above 0.60 (Nunnally, 1970). The Cronbach's alpha score for each construct represents the reliability of the overall scale. The Cronbach's alpha for each construct is prepared in Table 1. For each benefit of CRM, three items measure the performance; and for the satisfaction construct, there are two items for each measurement (repeat purchases, repeat visits) with the aim of measuring customer satisfaction.

In addition, we can determine the composite reliability through investigating the loadings of the obvious variables with their individual dimensions. A usually correct threshold value for composite reliability is 0.7 or greater, even though values below 0.7 have been considered acceptable (0.6) (Hair, Anderson, Tatham, & Black, 1998). Convergent validity is measured by factor loading and composite reliability measures (Hair et al., 1998). For composite reliability outcomes, a threshold value of 0.5 was situated for testing the convergent validity (Sridharan, Deng, Kirk, & Corbitt, 2010). In addition, all the item loadings indicated significant t-values, suggesting convergent validity was achieved.

Table 1. Cronbach's alpha and Composite Reliability final measurement models

Dimension/construct		Number of Items	Cronbach's alpha/ Correlation coefficient	Composite Reliability	Result
Personalized service		3	0.641906	0.796251	Accept
Customer knowledge		3	0.848916	0.884453	Accept
Customer segmentation		3	0.772063	0.866645	Accept
Multichannel integration		3	0.659953	0.814854	Accept
Customization of marketing		3	0.696526	0.831535	Accept
Time saving		3	0.699239	0.898820	Accept
Responsiveness to customers		3	0.836840	0.901491	Accept
Satisfaction	Repeat purchase	2	0.908943	0.936203	Accept
	Repeat visit	2			

From the confirmatory factor analysis consequence in Table 2, we observed that the factor loadings of all items are larger than 0.65. The factor loadings or regression assessment of the latent to the experiential variable should be more than 0.50 (Hair, Black, Babin, Anderson, & Tatham, 2006). It shows that all the constructs are according to the construct and convergent validity tests (Kamariah & Sentosa, 2008).

Discriminant validity is measured by comparing the association between the construct and the square root of average variance extracted (AVE). AVE shows the general amount of variance in the indicators accounted for by the latent construct. The square root of AVE should be more than the correlations among the constructs for acceptable discriminant validity (Gefen & Straub, 2005; Wixom & Todd, 2005). Table 3 represents a satisfactory discriminant validity between every pair of constructs, with all AVE square roots being more than the correlation among the constructs.

Table 2. Measure factor loading

Dimension/Construct		Item	Factor Loadings	t-value
Personalized service		PS1	0.762359	13.740563
		PS2	0.826739	19.855423
		PS3	0.662153	6.420360
Customer knowledge		CK1	0.744326	15.832029
		CK2	0.878389	28.543776
		CK3	0.913333	52.106244
Customer segmentation		CS1	0.875018	27.862106
		CS2	0.826147	19.967519
		CS3	0.778340	9.829638
Multichannel Integration		MI1	0.812332	22.329634
		MI2	0.743068	7.176410
		MI2	0.756984	11.380571
Customization of marketing		C1	0.811286	11.937025
		C2	0.776544	12.236112
		C3	0.777822	14.398471
Time saving		T1	0.899783	3.631372
		T2	0.856576	3.404293
		T3	0.836562	2.872915
Responsiveness to customers		R1	0.911797	19.365749
		R2	0.846020	11.096687
		R3	0.844361	8.501831
Satisfaction	Repeat purchase	RP1	0.882499	31.177079
		RP2	0.858813	21.993322
	Repeat visit	RV1	0.924861	38.029722
		RV2	0.878631	52.832055

PS= Personalized service, R= Responsiveness to customers, CS= Customer segmentation, MI= Multichannel Integration, C= Customization of marketing, T= Time saving, CK= Customer knowledge, RP= Repeat purchase, RV=Repeat Visit.

Table 3. AVE Square roots and inter-correlation

Constructs	CK	C	MI	PS	R	SAT	CS	T
CK	0.848482							
C	0.585661	0.788714						
MI	0.673913	0.510649	0.771374					
PS	0.616394	0.512427	0.599733	0.753466				
R	-0.368426	-0.420472	-0.345524	-0.406899	0.867961			
SAT	0.695106	0.627043	0.669145	0.607820	-0.244443	0.886526		
CS	0.486074	0.271390	0.478989	0.462505	0.468203	-0.506445	0.827443	
T	0.041551	0.071087	0.159278	0.057753	-0.188542	-0.037001	-0.087411	0.864709

PS= Personalized service, R= Responsiveness to customers, CS= Customer segmentation, MI= Multichannel Integration, C= Customization of marketing, T= Time saving, CK= Customer knowledge, SAT=Satisfaction.

Structural Model Testing

Hypothesis and moderating effects are examined by testing the standardized beta coefficient (std. β). Beside this, the squared multiple correlation coefficient (R^2) in the model is assessed as an implication of the overall predictive power of the proposed model. Figure 2 shows the structural model with path coefficient (β) between CRM benefits and customer satisfaction; R^2 for customer satisfaction, computed t-values and path loadings for all CRM benefits.

RESULTS

The results of the hypothesis test are summarized in Table 4, which shows the results of the proposed relationships.

Figure 2 shows the structural model with path coefficient (β) between CRM benefits and customer satisfaction; R^2 for customer satisfaction, computed t-values, and path loadings for all CRM benefits.

The results in the provided model test the positive relationship between CRM benefits for customers and customer satisfaction. This shows that, since the level of hypothesis is higher in CRM, the level of customer satisfaction would also be higher. This research affords quantitative, empirical confirmation of a significant, positive relationship existing between the hypothesis with CRM and satisfaction. The squared multiple correlation coefficients (R^2) of 0.67 shows that there is a statistically considerable, positive relationship between the hypotheses in this study.

Supporting the overall hypothesis, results show that CRM benefits for customers are associated with customer satisfaction. The path coefficient (β) = 0.143, p < 0.005, t = 1.944 between personalized services and customer satisfaction proves the extensive positive relationship, supporting H1.

Specifically, we find a positive relationship between customer knowledge and customer satisfaction (β = 0.223, p < 0.005, t = 2.767), supporting H2. Customer segmentation also had significant positive relationships with customer satisfaction (β = 0.221, p < 0.005, t = 2.317), confirming H3. In addition, the perceived usefulness of multichannel integration (β = 0.238, p < 0.005, t = 2.249), bolstered H4.

Figure 2. Relationship between CRM benefits for customers and customer satisfaction
PS= Personalized service, R= Responsiveness to customers, CS= Customer segmentation, MI= Multichannel Integration, C=
Customization of marketing, T= Time saving, CK= Customer knowledge, SAT= Satisfaction.

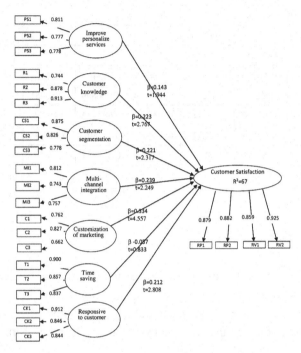

Table 4. Hypothesis results

	Hypothesized path	**Coefficient (t-value)**	**Result**
H1	PS→SAT	0.143(1.944)	Accept
H2	CK→SAT	0.223(2.767)	Accept
H3	CS→SAT	0.221(2.317)	Accept
H4	MI→SAT	0.238(2.249)	Accept
H5	C→SAT	0.334(4.557)	Accept
H6	T→SAT	-0.057(0.833)	Reject
H7	R→SAT	0.212(2.808)	Accept

PS= Personalized service, R= Responsiveness to customers, CS= Customer segmentation, MI= Multichannel Integration, C= Customization of marketing, T= Time saving, CK= Customer knowledge, SAT= Satisfaction.

As predicted by H5, the perceived usefulness of customization of marketing had a significant and positive relationship to customer satisfaction ($\beta = 0.334$, $p < 0.005$, t =4. 557).

Hypothesis H6 is concerned with the relationship of time saving in CRM with customer satisfaction. The path coefficient (β) = -0.057, $p < 0.005$, t = 0.833 between time-saving for customers through CRM implementation and their satisfaction did not present a positive relationship with the proposed model. This result is in line with Garcia (2012) who also found that concrete time has a significant role, but only plays a minor role in customer time satisfaction. It should be considered that there are a lot of other factors that have an impact on time-saving, namely: waiting time, contact time, feedback time, etc. In this study, the questionnaire has been distributed among customers of companies who do most of their purchasing by membership cards. However, the customers who did not have any cards were shopping the same way. Thus, there was no significant difference between the loyal fixed customers and the others who were not members. Purchasing through websites and online shopping can help customers utilize their time more appropriately. Shopping on the internet takes less time than purchasing in traditional retail outlets, due to the many time-consuming actions associated with the latter (Rohm Andrew J, 2004). As many customers find it difficult to estimate the economic value of their time against the amount of money saved, they prefer to save time and money through shopping online (John, 2008). One of the limitations of this study was related to the lack of measuring customer satisfaction through online purchases. Therefore, saving time was not completely clear and recognized for customers who were purchasing from traditional retail outlets.

Finally, as predicted by H7, we found a significant relationship between improving responsibility by CRM and customer satisfaction($(\beta) = 0.212$, $p < 0.005$, $t=2.808$).

DISCUSSIONS

As mentioned above, the objectives of the paper are to find the benefits of CRM for customers and present a model which shows the exploration of the relationship among CRM customers and how it assists with customer satisfaction.

The findings shown above contribute to the relevant literature by recognizing the benefits of CRM for customers which have been previously established. These are namely: personalized service, responsiveness to customer needs, customer segmentation, customization of marketing, multichannel integration, time, and customer knowledge.

In order to address the importance of these benefits for companies, we proposed a model which focuses on the relationship of these benefits to improve customer satisfaction. The empirical data was collected from three Malaysian companies who have implemented CRM. It is evident from the results that six benefits of CRM, namely: personalized service, responsiveness to customer needs, customer segmentation, customization of marketing, multichannel integration, and customer knowledge significantly affect customer satisfaction. However, the impact of time on customer satisfaction does not have a significant effect. This result is in line with previous studies which have focused on the relationship of each of these benefits with satisfaction (Adele Berndt, 2005; Chen & Chen, 2004; Dwayne Ball, Coelho, & Vilares, 2006; Speed & Smith, 1992; Wallace, Giese, & Johnson, 2004).

Saving time for customers by CRM was not found to affect customer satisfaction significantly in traditional retail outlets, since the greatest impact of saving time through CRM can be obtained through online shopping. Another explanation of why time-saving aspects of the model have not had positive results might be related to the limitation of the sample size. It was limited to three Malaysian companies which do not have any online shopping facilities.

This paper contributes to the research in two important areas and three interesting points to the practice. In terms of research, firstly, our study is one of the few attempts to build a model to investigate the relationship between CRM benefits for customers and satisfaction. The findings presented in this research have important implications for CRM researchers. Accordingly, there are still limitations in this area. Second, to the best of our knowledge, a probable research direction is to evaluate the generalizability of our results in other business contexts. For example, this could be conducted in namely: consumer markets, online markets and/or in other countries. Third, these findings not only imply that the CRM area is still tactical for majority of research studies to improve customer satisfaction, but also provides clues to explain the causality between customers and CRM.

In terms of practice, this model can firstly be considered as a plan for companies which will lead to improve revenue in marketing and facilitate organizational success. Second, we have found empirical evidence supporting the favourable impacts of these benefits on customer satisfaction that can have a huge impact on organizational performance. Consequently, for the companies and organizations who have implemented CRM in order to improve customer satisfaction, it is advisable to concentrate on understanding and satisfying these benefits of CRM through customer-centric management by adopting a suitable CRM technology and obtaining a CRM outlook on customer-facing processes. Third, the significant result of this model is perhaps the one that managers should focus on. CRM also provides additional benefits for customers, namely, those benefits which will occur inside the companies through the implementation of CRM, if rapid positive results are targeted.

According to the findings of this study, it should be considered that with all research, the results of this study are subject to certain limitations and these limitations should be considered throughout the explanation of the results. On the other hand, it should also be borne in mind that some of these limitations point to scopes for future research. The study was performed in three companies. Customer satisfaction results in these companies could be an avenue for further research since specific conditions of the companies could have had effects on the measurements of customer satisfaction and behaviours.

CONCLUSION

To sum up, this article proposed the incorporation of CRM customer benefits with customer satisfaction in a model. The findings have broken ground for a new methodology in the field of research on customer satisfaction and also CRM.

The proposed model has demonstrated that six benefits of CRM for customers have direct influence on increasing customer satisfaction. It does so by using a well-structured process and procedure, aimed at making a contribution in both the research community and the practical world of business. The importance of CRM is thus established, and it is suggested that, in the future, CRM benefits for customers will be more widely considered.

REFERENCES

Adele Berndt, F. H., & Roux. (2005). Implementing a customer relationship management programme in an emerging market. *Journal of Global Business and Technology*, *1*(2).

Adrian Payne, P. F. (2004). The role of multichannel integration in customer relationship management. *Industrial Marketing Management*, 33.

Ahrari, M., & Amirusefi, R. (2012). Survey relationship between service quality and customer relationship management. *Journal of American Science*, *8*(9).

Anwar, A., Gulzar, A., & Anwar. (2011). Impact of Self-Designed Products on Customer Satisfaction. *Contemporary Research in Business*.

Ball, D., Coelho, P. S., & Vilares, M. J. (2006). Service Personalization and Loyalty. *Services Marketing, 20*(6), 391-403.

Bose, R. (2002). Customer relationship management, key component for IT success. *Industrial Management & Data Systems, 102*(2), 89–97. doi:10.1108/02635570210419636

Buttle, F. (2004). *Customer relationship management: Concepts and tools*. Sydney: Elsevier.

Carolyn, C. Y., Melissa, D., & Chandana, U. (2003). *Organizational Transformation through CRM Implementation: a descriptive case study*. Working papers-series, School of Information Systems.

Carter, S., & Yeo, A. C.-M. (2016). Students-as-customers satisfaction, predictive retention with marketing implications: The case of Malaysian higher education business students. *International Journal of Educational Management, 30*(5), 635–652. doi:10.1108/IJEM-09-2014-0129

Chen, Q., & Chen, H. (2004). Exploring the success factors of eCRM strategies in practice. *Database Marketing and Customer Strategy Management, 11*(4), 333–343. doi:10.1057/palgrave.dbm.3240232

Delone, & McLean. (2003). The DeLone and McLean Model of Information Systems Success: A Ten-Year Update. *Journal of Management Information Systems, 19*(4).

Deng, Z., Lu, Y., Wei, K. K., & Zhang, J. (2009). Understanding customer satisfaction and loyalty: An empirical study of mobile instant messages in China. *International Journal of Information Management, 30*.

Dyché, J. (2002). *The CRM handbook: A business guide to customer relationship management*. Academic Press.

Epetimehin, F. M. (2011). Market Segmentation: A Tool for Improving Customer Satisfaction and Retention in Insurance Service Delivery. *Journal of Emerging Trends in Economics and Management Sciences, 2*(1).

Garcia, D., Archer, T., Moradi, S., & Ghiabi, B. (2012). Waiting in Vain: Managing Time and Customer Satisfaction at Call Centers. *SciRes., 3*(2).

Gefen, D., & Straub, D. (2005). A Practical Guide to Factorial Validity Using PLS-Graph: Tutorial and Annotated Example. *Communications of the Association for Information Systems, 16*, 91–103.

Goodhue, D. L., Wixom, B. H., & Watson, H. J. (2002). Realizing business benefits through CRM: Hitting the right target in the right way. *MIS Quarterly Executive, 1*(2), 79–94.

GoToAssist. (2009). *Developing A True Multi-Channel Contact Center*. Author.

Gray, P., & Byun, J. (2001). *Customer Relationship Management. Center for Research on Information Technology and Organisations*. University of California.

Group, G. (2008). Magic Quadrant for CRM Services Providers. G. R. C. Research.

Hadzagas, C. (2011). Applying Customer Relationship Management Systems for Customer Satisfaction: An Empirical Approach for Small-and-Medium-Sized Companies. *European Journal of Economics, Finance and Administrative Sciences,* (40).

Hair, A., Tatham, & Black. (1998). Multivariate data analysis Englewood Cliffs, NJ: Printice-Hall Inc.

Hair, Black, Babin, Anderson, & Tatham. (2006). *Multivariate Data Analysis.* Upper Saddle River, NJ: Prentice-Hall.

Hashemi, K. (2012). Customer Retention Strategies on Internet (e-CRM); Features and Principles. *Journal of American Science, 8*(2).

Hendricks, K. B., Singhal, V. R., & Stratman, J. K. (2007). The impact of enterprise systems on corporate performance: A study of ERP, SCM, and CRM system implementations. *Journal of Operations Management, 25*(1), 65–82. doi:10.1016/j.jom.2006.02.002

Hoyer, W. D., & MacInnis, D. J. (2001). *Consumer Behavior.* Boston: Houghton Mifflin Company.

Injazz, J., & Chen, K. P. (2003). Understanding customer relationship management (CRM):People, process and technology. *Business Process Management Journal, 19*(5).

Jamshidi, Rasli, & Yusof. (2012). Essential Competencies for the Supervisors of Oil and Gas Industrial Companies. *Procedia: Social and Behavioral Sciences,* 40.

Jayachandran, , & Hewett, , & Kaufman, P. (2004). Customer Response Capability in a Sense-and-Respond Era. The Role of Customer Knowledge Process. *Journal of the Academy of Marketing Science,* 32.

Johansson, W., Ba, S., & Chase, R. (2001). Virtual customer satisfaction: A service management perspective.*Proceedings of the Seventh Americas Conference on Information System,* 857-866.

Kamariah, N. M., & Sentosa, I. (2008). *The Integration of Technology Acceptance Model and Technology of Puchasing Behavior (A Structural Equation Modeling Approach).* Paper presented at the the Proceeding of Asia Pacific Conference on Management of Technology and Technology Entrepreneurship, Melaka, Malaysia.

Karimi, J., Somers, T. M., & Gupta, Y. P. (2001). Impact of Information Technology Management Practices on Customer Service. *Journal of Management Information Systems, 17,* 125–158.

Kim, Suh, & Hwang. (2003). A model for evaluating the effectiveness of CRM using the balanced scorecard. *Interactive Marketing, 17*(2).

Kohli, R., Devaraj, S., & Mahmood, A. M. (2004). Understanding Determinants of Online Customer Satisfaction:A Decision Process Perspective. *Journal of Management Information Systems, 21*(1).

Kotler, P. (2000). *Marketing Management.* Upper Saddle River, NJ: Academic Press.

Lam, C. F., & Brzenzinski. (2005). The Effects of Customization on Satisfaction with Mobile Systems. Idea Group Publishing.

Leach, B. (2003). Success of CRM systems hinges on establishment of measureable benefits. *Pulp & Paper, 77*(6), 48.

Lee, J., Pi, S., Kwok, R. C., & Huynh, M. Q. (2003). The Contribution of Commitment Value in Internet Commerce: An Empirical Investigation. *Journal of the Association for Information Systems, 4.*

Mark Xu, J. W. (2005). Gaining customer knowledge through analytical CRM. *Industrial Management & Data Systems, 105*(7).

McKim, B. (2000). How to measure CRM success. *Target Marketing, 23*(10), 138.

Mihelis, G., Grigoroudis, E., Siskos, Y., Politis, Y., & Malandrakis, Y. (2001). Customer Satisfaction Measurement in the Private Bank Sector. *European Journal of Operational Research*, 130.

Mithas, S., Krishnan, M. S., & Fornell, C. (2005). Why Do Customer Relationship Management Applications Affect Customer Satisfaction? *Journal of Marketing, 69*(4), 201–209. doi:10.1509/jmkg.2005.69.4.201

Nasershariati, F., & Khan, A. (2011). *CRM system benefits A case study of the banking sector.* Malardalen University.

Nunnally, J. C. (1970). *Introduction to Psychological Measurement.* New York: McGraw-Hill.

Pandey, D. S. K., & Devasagayam, D. R. (2010). *Responsiveness as Antecedent of Satisfaction and Referrals in Financial Services Marketing.* Paper presented at the 10th Global Conference on Business & Economics.

Parvatiyar, A., & Sheth, J. N. (2001). Conceptual framework of customer relationship management. In *Customer Relationship Management* (pp. 3–25). Emerging Concepts, Tools and Applications.

Peppers, D., & Rogers, M. (1999). *The One to One Manager: Real-World Lessons in Customer Relationship Management.* Academic Press.

Peterson, D. M., Gröne, D. F., Kammer, D. K., & Kirscheneder, J. (2009). *Multi-Channel Customer Management Delighting Consumers, Driving Efficiency.* Information Technology, Marketing & Sales.

Prabhaker, P. (2001). Integrating Marketing-manufacturing Strategies. *Journal of Business and Industrial Marketing, 16*(2), 113–128. doi:10.1108/08858620110384141

Reinartz, W., Krafft, M., & Hoyer, W. D. (2004). The Customer Relationship Management Process: Its measurement and impact on performance. *JMR, Journal of Marketing Research, 41*(3), 293–305. doi:10.1509/jmkr.41.3.293.35991

Rohm Andrew, J, S. V. (2004). A typology of online shoppers based on shopping motivations. *Journal of Business Research, 57*(7).

Romano, & Fjermestad. (2003). Electronic commerce customer relationship management. *Information Technology and Management, 4*(2-3), 233-258.

Rushforth, J. A. (2007). *Maximizing relationship value with CRM systems: why commercial banks need to move beyond contact management to true customer relationship management.* Retrieved 10/30/2012, 2012, from http://www.accessmylibrary.com/article-1G1-158960824/maximizing-relationship-value-crm.html

Ryals, & Knox. (2001). Cross-Functional Issues in the Implementation of Relationship Marketing Through Customer Relationship Management. *European Management Journal, 19*, 534-542.

Sarvari, P. A., Ustundag, A., & Takci, H. (2016). Performance evaluation of different customer segmentation approaches based on RFM and demographics analysi. *Kybernetes*, *45*(7), 1129–1157. doi:10.1108/K-07-2015-0180

Sathish, S., Pan, S. L., & Raman, K. S. (2002). *Customer relationship management (CRM) network: A new approach to studying CRM*. Paper presented at the Eighth Americas Conference on Information Systems (AMCIS), Dallas, TX.

Speed, R., & Smith, G. (1992). Retailing financial services segmentation. *The Service Industries, 12*.

Sridharan, B., Deng, H., Kirk, J., & Corbitt, B. (2010). Structural equation modelling for evaluating the user perceptions of e-learning effectiveness in higher education.*18th European Conference on Information Systems*.

Srinivasan, S. S., Anderson, R., & Ponnavolu, K. (2002). Customer loyalty in e-commerce: An exploration of its antecedents and consequences. *Journal of Retailing*, *78*(1), 41–50. doi:10.1016/S0022-4359(01)00065-3

Sunil Mithas, M. S. K. (2005). Why Do Customer Relationship Management Applications Affect Customer Satisfaction? *Journal of Marketing*, *69*(4), 201–209. doi:10.1509/jmkg.2005.69.4.201

Swift, R. (2001). *Accelerating Customer Relationship Management: Using CRM and Relationship Technologies*. Academic Press.

Thomas, J. S., & Kumar, R. (2004). Getting the most out of all of your customers. *Harvard Business Review*, 116–123. PMID:15241958

Tiwana, A. (2001). The essential guide to knowledge management. *E-Business and CRM Applications*.

Tseng, S.-M. (2016). Knowledge management capability, customer relationship management, and service quality.*Journal of Enterprise Information Management*,*29*(2), 202–221. doi:10.1108/JEIM-04-2014-0042

Veloutsou, C., Gilbert, R.G., Moutinho, L.A. and Good, M. M. (2005). Measuring transactionspecific satisfaction in services. *European Journal of Marketing, 39*(5-6), 606-628.

Verhoef, P. (2003). Understanding the effect of customer relationship management efforts on customer retention and customer share development. *Journal of Marketing*, *67*(4), 30–45. doi:10.1509/jmkg.67.4.30.18685

Wallace, D. W., Giese, J. L., & Johnson, J. L. (2004). Customer retailer loyalty in the context of multiple channel strategies. *Journal of Retailing*, 80.

Wixom, B. H., & Todd, P. A. (2005). A theorectical integration of user satisfaction and technology acceptance. *Information Systems Research*, *16*(1), 85–102. doi:10.1287/isre.1050.0042

Zgener, S.-O., & I˙raz, R. (2006). Customer relationship management in small–medium enterprises: The case of Turkish tourism industry. *Tourism Management*, 27.

Zikmund, McLeod, & Gilbert. (2003). *Customer Relationship Management, Integrating marketing strategy and information technology*. Academic Press.

KEY TERMS AND DEFINITIONS

Customer Relationship Management: Customer relationship management (CRM) refers to practices, strategies and technologies that companies use to manage and examine customer interactions and data during the customer lifecycle, with the goal of refining business relationships with customers, supporting in customer retention and achiving sales growth.

Customer Satisfaction: Customer satisfaction (often abbreviated as CSAT, more correctly CSat) is a dimension regularly used in marketing. It is a measure of how products and services provided by a company meet or surpass customer expectation.

Integration: The end result of a process that purposes to stitch together diverse and disparate subsystems, so that the data contained in each becomes part of a larger, more widespread system which when needed ideally, rapidly and simply shares data. Frequently it requires that companies build a customized architecture or construction of applications to associate new or existing hardware, software and other infrastructures.

Knowledge: Knowledge is understanding, awareness or considering of someone or something, such as evidences, information, descriptions, or abilities, which is attained through experience or education by observing, determining, or learning.

Knowledge Management: Process of producing, distributing, using and organizing the knowledge and information of an organization. It refers to a multi-disciplinary approach to achieving managerial objectives by making the best use of knowledge.

Multichannel Integration: The practice by which companies interrelate with customers through several channels, both direct and indirect, with the purpose of selling them goods and services.

Personal Service: Intellectual or manual work performed by a service provider in serving a customer.

Responsibility: A duty or obligation to achieve or complete a duty satisfactory that one must accomplish which assigned by someone, or created by one's own promise or conditions.

Segmentation: Dividing the marketplace into parts, or segments, which are definable, available, actionable, and profitable and have a growth potential are considered as segmentation. In other words, a company would find it impossible to target the entire market, because of time, cost and effort limitations.

Chapter 14
Information Technology Paraphernalia for Supply Chain Management Decisions

Chandra Sekhar Patro
GVP College of Engineering (Autonomous), India

K. Madhu Kishore Raghunath
National Institute of Technology, Warangal, India

ABSTRACT

Technology and world around have always been advancing time to time. One can speak of diverse areas to show how important IT is in daily business life, and of much Supply chain is one such area with more scope for Information Technology (IT) and has become a determinant of competitive advantage across the organizations. In order to survive in today's competitive environment the firms need to manage the future supply chain. In order to deliver quality information to the decision-maker at the right time and in order to automate the process of data collection, collation and refinement, the companies have to make IT an ally, harness its full potential and use it in the best possible means. IT is beneficial for cooperation and integration within the stakeholders of the supply chain. The chapter throw a light upon the stature of various technology based Tools in Supply Chain Management (SCM). The study also highlights the contribution of technology in helping to restructure the entire supply chain process to achieve higher service levels, lower inventory and the supply chain costs.

INTRODUCTION

Supply Chain Management (SCM) is managing the network of interconnected businesses involved in the ultimate provision of product and service packages required by end customers (Harland, 1996). Supply Chain Management spans all movement and storage of raw materials, work-in-process inventory, and finished goods from point-of-origin to point-of consumption. Supply Chain encompasses the planning and management of all activities involved in sourcing, procurement, conversion, and logistics management activities. Supply chain management is defined as the integration of key business processes from

DOI: 10.4018/978-1-5225-2382-6.ch014

end user through original suppliers that provides products, services, and information and hence, adds value for customers and other stakeholders (Lambert, Cooper, and Pagh, 1998). Supply chain management is increasingly applied operations paradigm for enhancing overall organizational competitiveness. Supply chain management is a set of approaches utilized to effectively integrate suppliers, manufacturers, warehouses, and stores, so that merchandise is produced and distributed at the right quantities, to the right locations, and at the right time, in order to minimize system wide cost while satisfying service level requirements (Simchi-Levi, Kaminsky, & Simchi-Levi, 2000).

Information Technology is revolutionizing the way in which the individuals live and work. This is changing all the aspects of peoples' life style. The digital revolution has given mankind the ability to treat information with mathematical precision, to transmit it with high accuracy and to manipulate it. These capabilities are bringing into being, a whole world within and around the physical world. The Internet increases the richness of communications through greater interactivity between the firm and the customer (Watson, Akelsen, and Pitt, 1998). Internet is playing an essential role in building commercially viable supply chains in order to meet the challenges of virtual enterprises Graham and Hardaker (2000). Armstrong and Hagel (1996) argue that there is beginning of an evolution in supply chain towards online business communities. Supply chain management emphasizes the overall and long-term benefit of all parties on the chain through co-operation and information sharing. This signifies the importance of communication and the application of information technology in Supply chain management (Yu, Yan, & Cheng, 2001).

Today, Information and Technology must be conceived of broadly to encompass the information that businesses create and use as well as a wide spectrum of increasingly convergent and linked technologies that process the information with the emergence of the personal computer, optical fiber networks, the explosion of the Internet and the World Wide Web. The cost and availability of information resources allow easy linkages and eliminate information-related time delays in any supply chain network. This means that organizations are moving toward a concept known as Electronic Commerce, where transactions are completed via a variety of electronic media, including electronic data interchange (EDI), electronic funds transfer (EFT), bar codes, fax, automated voice mail, CD-ROM catalogs, and a variety of others as the old paper type transactions are becoming increasingly obsolete (Patro & Raghunath, 2015).

The complexity of Supply chain management has also forced companies to go for online communication systems. Companies need to invest large amount of money for redesigning internal organizational and technical processes, changing traditional and fundamental product distribution channels and customer service procedure and training staff to achieve IT-enabled supply chain (Motwani, Madan, & Gunasekaran, 2000). In order to meet the demands organizations are trying to make their supply chains more agile and form virtual enterprises (Gunasekaran and Ngai, 2004). In the supply chain management field it therefore becomes ever more important to collaborate and integrate with business partners in order to deliver the best possible end product to the customer (Cooper, Lambert, & Pagh, 1997; Pereira, 2009; Subramani, 2004). Li, Yang, Sun, & Sohal (2009) considering the high demands for integration and collaboration it is logical that IT has become increasingly important in the various positions in the supply chain. Interest in research has therefore also shifted towards the role of IT in SCM and by implication also some focus on the conditions that make it possible for IT to support SCM. Jharkharia & Shankar (2004) use in this regard the term enablers since the question focuses on things that make it possible for IT to support SCM. The companies need to put emphasis on developing a framework that would help in implementing a successful and cost effective IT system for achieving an effective Supply chain management.

BACKGROUND

The literature is primarily aimed at helping the practitioners in implementing a successful Information Technology system for achieving an effective Supply Chain Management. According to Chopra and Meindl (2007), the objective for every supply chain should be to maximize the overall value generated. Effective and efficient supply chain involves the management of supply chain assets, products, information and funds in order to maximize profitability. They identified different positions in the supply chain: supplier, manufacturer, distributor, retailer and customer. Dedrick, Gurbaxani, and Kraemer (2003), identified that information technology have a positive and significant impact on labour productivity and economic growth. In supply chain the investments in information technology may turn against business parties if those information technology investments are not used by the people that constitute an organization. If employees do not use new tools of information technology in their work processes then the investments should not be made. According to Jharkharia & Shankar (2004) consensus among the partners is of great importance for an effective supply chain. In this context consensus among partners should be reached about what enablers are important in order for IT to be able to support the supply chain and strive for enhancement of integration and collaboration.

Prasad (2007) identified the various tools of IT, which helps to make optimum decision at every stage of a supply chain. The whole supply chain has been divided into five modules, namely, source, make, store, distribute, and market. The study shows how IT helps to manage its supply chain in reducing the costs, having better relationship with both its suppliers/vendors and customers, and give better product and services to its customers. Gunasekaran and Ngai (2004) proposed a classification scheme for the role of IT in supply chain management and identified six major categories that focus on developing an IT-enabled SCM. The model consists of the six defined categories: Strategic Planning, Virtual Enterprise, Infrastructure, Knowledge and IT Management, Implementation of Technology. Iskandar, Kurokawa, and LeBlanc (2001) identified that adoption of Electronic Data Interchange (EDI) has a significant difference between the first and second tier automotive suppliers, signaling the possibility that different level of importance are ascribed to IT enablers in different positions in the supply chain.

Salo and Karjaluoto (2006) highlighted the importance of integrating both internal and external systems in the supply chain to make the coordination of activities easier. Not all available information needs to be shared but the relevant information only to be shared, as too much confuses people. Chu and Lee (2006) states that exchange of information is the foundation for collaboration in supply chain and with the increase of new practices, such as vendor managed inventory, information sharing is becoming even more important. Mehdi, Farzad and Kamal (2008) emphasized that the importance of technology on supply chain is much larger as it facilitates inter organizational communication and in turn reduces cycle times and develops collaborative work. IT provides opportunities for an organization to expand their markets worldwide. Lin, Kuei, Madu, and Winch (2010) presented a framework on supply chain excellence, emphasizing two distinct paths of knowledge acquisition that is qualitative and quantitative inquiry for which four factors are considered as the antecedents of supply chain excellence, such as collaboration, organizational conditions, technology adoption, and operations.

Ajmal and Kristianto (2010) elucidated that knowledge sharing in supply chain by developing analytical models to minimize knowledge sharing uncertainty. With enhanced understanding, managers can spotlight their actions, increasing their firms' competitiveness. Pathak and Vidyarthi (2011) stressed that one of the critical enablers for an efficient and effective supply chain is timely planning and information processing across the entire value-added chain. Selecting the right mix of analytical software and hardware alternatives at various planning and execution levels of an organization is essential to remain competitive in a supply chain system. Radhakrishnan, David, Hales, & Sridharan (2011) argued that to sustain integration partner firms must establish a formal system to evaluate supply chain-wide performance. Barratt (2004) states that the exchange of information is the foundation of collaboration in the supply chain and with the increase of new practices, such as vendor managed inventory, information sharing is becoming even more important (Chu & Lee, 2006). Subramani (2004) found that the role of IT in supply chain is reducing costs, provide decision making support and improve customer service. The need for increased flexibility is also mentioned (Zhang, Vonderembse, & Lim, 2005).

Brookman, Smit, and Silvius (2012) in the study reported that a significant difference for the enabler 'Funds for IT enablement' is found between the supplier position and other positions. The main reason for perceiving a factor as important can be found on the dividing line between 'processes and collaboration' and 'benefits and collaboration'. Das and Dellana (2013) proposed a Supplier Quality Affiliation (SQA) approach that is integrated into a mixed integer programming Strategic Supply Chain Management (SSCM) model for overall improvement of the supply chain business process. The outcome of the SQA model is then integrated into the SSCM model for ensuring input quality while providing several options for overall business gains of the supply chain members, which include suppliers, manufacturers and retailers. Gyanendra, Rajeev, & Vivek (2014) focused on the emerging trends of supply chain in current scenario, and conclude that it provides broader awareness of SCM concepts. Managing the supply chain by making use of IT services has paved a new way of confiscating the uncertainty and enhancing the customer service and thus creating a competitive edge. Patro and Raghunath (2015) found that most of the employees are satisfied with the emerging new trends in contrast to existing trends that are practiced in the organizations. The study concluded that though the emerging trends are gaining importance in the modern era, the existing age old techniques should also be carried on like a coin which has both head and tail to create a balance within SCM in the modern era.

METHODOLOGY

The methodology of the study includes a theoretical analysis of literature related to IT trends in Supply Chain Management and an empirical study on productivity by use of IT tools. A survey was conducted in different private sector manufacturing organizations of Andhra Pradesh, India. A sample size of 140 respondents was considered to know the satisfaction level of the employees at various level of the organization. A simple random sampling technique was adopted for the study. The Executives, Supervisors, Clerks, Office Managers, and Technical Staff of different manufacturing organizations in private sector are asked whether they are satisfied with the various IT based SCM trends practiced in their organizations. The data was collected from both primary and secondary sources. The Primary data was gathered from the respondents i.e. employees through personal interaction, direct personal observation and also gathered information by evaluating opinions of employees in different private sector organizations. The secondary data was collected from the various organizations websites, libraries, annual reports, magazines, conference proceedings, journals and newspaper publications to add more materiality to the study.

ROLE OF INFORMATION TECHNOLOGY IN SCM

Recently with the development of Information Technology, the concepts of supply chain design and management have become a popular operations paradigm. The complexity of supply chain management has also forced the companies to go for online communication systems (Fasanghari, Roudsari, & Chaharsooghi, 2008). The role of Information Technology in Supply Chain Management that integrates capabilities as outlined by Auramo, Kauremaa, & Tanskanen (2005) in to three essential functions is shown in Figure 1.

Transaction Execution

The processing of transactions is essential for the use of Information Technology in increasing the efficiency of repetitive information exchanges between supply chain partners. The use of information technology in exchanging the information is typically related to the tasks such as order processing, billing, delivery verification, generating and sending dispatch advices, and producing order quotes (Cross, 2000). The drivers of transaction execution are referred as reduction of costs, volume of transactions, speeding up information transfer, and elimination of human errors (Auramo, Kauremaa, & Tanskanen, 2005).

Collaboration and Coordination

The aspect of collaboration and coordination represents the use of Information Technology for sharing planning-related information such as demand forecasts and other demand information, inventory information, and production capacity information, with the intention of increasing the effectiveness of the supply chain (Lee and Whang, 1997). It also supports the monitoring of individual orders or shipments, which may consist of components or final products, with the aim of coordinating their delivery or conveying timely information of their location. The drivers supporting supply chain management are unpredictable and logistically demanding environment (Auramo, Kauremaa, & Tanskanen, 2005).

Figure 1. Functional Roles of IT in SCM

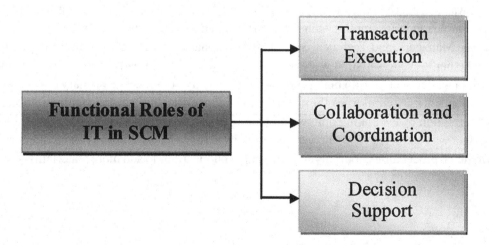

Decision Support Systems

The used of decision support systems in supply chain management increase the speed of decision making, which will help to increase the supply chain's flexibility and adaptability, and help organizations cope with the uncertainties of the operating environment (Simchi-Levi, Kaminsky, & Simchi-Levi, 2003). In this case, the analytical power of computers is used to provide assistance to managerial decisions. The drivers of decision support systems are project-orientation of the business, and in-transit delivery consolidation (Swaminathan & Tayur, 2003).

This functional system enables to handle day-to-day transactions and electronic commerce across the supply chain and thus help align supply and demand by sharing information on orders, daily scheduling, planning and decision making, supporting the demand, shipment planning. It further enables strategic analysis by providing tools, such as an integrated network model to help managers evaluate plants, distribution centers, suppliers, and third-party service alternatives.

APPLICATIONOF IT PARAPHERNALIA IN SCM

There is always a gap between traditional supply chain management and IT based supply chain management. Therefore, the views regarding the existing trends and emerging trends under IT based SCM are put forth which bridges this gap.

Existing Information Technology Trends

The application of existing information technology based trends for effective functioning of the supply chain management system in the enterprises is discussed as shown in Figure 2.

Figure 2. Information Technology Trends in SCM

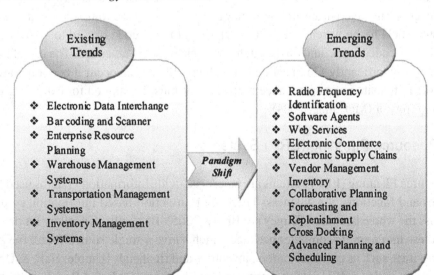

Electronic Data Interchange (EDI)

Electronic Data Interchange has been widely used by the enterprises in supply chains to facilitate transactions and information exchanges. EDI is used by supply chain partners to exchange essential information necessary for the effective running of their businesses (Rushton, Oxley & Croucher, 2000). EDI limits the flexibility of suppliers who are connected to more than one customer since they are required to support specific technologies for each (Golden & Powell, 1999). For instance, EDI is used for sending invoices, bills of lading, confirmation of dispatch, shipping details and any information that the linked organizations choose to exchange. The benefits of EDI are quick process to information, better customer service, reduced paper work, increased productivity, improved tracing and expediting, cost efficiency and improved billing (Ngai & Gunasekaran, 2004).

The development of Internet EDI with its lower initial costs, allows more medium and smaller sized firms entry to the EDI network. It allows small and medium sized companies to engage in automatic data sharing and brings them lower cost and increased business benefits. Thus, businesses will initiate Internet EDI quicker, and the importance of the 'readiness for EDI' factor will increase (Williamson, Harrison, & Jordan, 2004). Through the use of EDI supply chain partners can overcome the distortions and exaggeration in supply and demand information by improving technologies to facilitate real time sharing of actual demand and supply information.

Bar Coding and Scanner

Bar Codes are the representation of a number or code in a form suitable for reading by machines. Bar codes are widely used throughout the supply chain to identify and track goods at all stages in the process. Bar codes are a series of different width lines that may be presented in a horizontal order, called ladder orientation, or a vertical order, called picket fence orientation. The use of bar codes can speed up operations significantly (Rushton, Oxley and Croucher, 2000). Scanners are most visible in the checkout counter of super markets and hyper markets. This code specifies the name of a product and its manufacturer. Other applications are tracking the moving items such as components in PC assembly operations, automobiles in assembly plants (Denolf, Trienekens, Wognuma, van der Vorst, & Omta, 2015).

For instance, goods received in a warehouse may be identified by the warehouse management system and added to stock held in the warehouse. When put away, the bar code is used to associate the storage location with the bar-coded stock, and on dispatch the stock record is amended. The use of bar codes can speed up operations significantly. On the other hand, the problems can occur if bar codes are defaced or the labels fall off in transit. The maintenance management must be applied for extending the long-life period of this equipment (McCathie, 2004).

Enterprise Resource Planning (ERP) Systems

Enterprise Resource Planning (ERP) systems are enterprise-wide information systems used for automating all activities and functions of a business. These are transaction-based information systems that are integrated across the whole business (Gargeya & Brady, 2005). Basically, they allow for data capture for the whole business into a single computer package which's give a single source for all the key business information activities, such as customer orders, inventory and financials (Umble, Haft, & Umble, 2003). Many companies now view ERP systems from vendors like Baan, SAP and People soft as the core of their IT infrastructure. ERP systems have become enterprise-wide transaction processing tools which capture the data and reduce the manual activities and task associated with processing financial, inventory and customer order information (Denolf, Trienekens, Wognuma, van der Vorst, & Omta, 2015).

ERP system achieve a high level of integration by utilizing a single data model, developing a common understanding of what the shared data represents and establishing a set of rules for accessing data. In addition to the huge costs that are involved in procuring an ERP application, installation of such systems will entail widespread change within the organization. It will have implications in terms of Business Process Reengineering (BPR), changes in organizational structure, people and change management (Finney and Corbett, 2007). Many companies have benefited from using this system whilst some have experienced severe problems with their application. Generally, they also require a lot of customization and training for each user.

Warehouse Management Systems

Warehouse management systems are systems that control all the traditional activities of warehouse operations. Areas covered usually include receipt of goods, allocation or recording of storage locations, replenishment of picking locations, production of picking instructions or lists, order picking, order assembly and stock rotation. Some systems are used in conjunction with radio frequency (RF) communication equipment. This equipment can be mounted on fork-lift trucks. The warehouse management system communicates with the RF system and directs the activities of the warehouse staff (Patterson, Grimm, & Corsi, 2003).

There are highly sophisticated systems that control the operations of fully automated warehouses. This may include automated storage and retrieval systems (AS/RS), automated guided vehicles (AGVs), and the many other devices that are relatively common in today's modern warehouse such as, conveyors, carousels, sortation systems, etc. A number of computer models have now been developed to assist in the planning of warehouse design and configuration (McCathie, 2004). These are generally very sophisticated 3D simulation models that provide a graphic, moving illustration on the computer screen of the layout of the warehouse.

Transportation Management Systems

Transportation Management Systems provide more visibility into shipments and orders. Scheduling issues are also addressed on time. Multiple transportation options can be explored as a result of earlier visibility into the supply chain. Timely communication and status reports can also be obtained. By having control on its supply chain, businesses can make efficient routing decisions (McCathie, 2004).

An example of such a system is developed by Target Corporation and NTE. Initially Target was making transportation requests manually for inbound shipments. There was limited visibility for shipments and as a result of this; there were more number of less-than-truckloads, which was not cost-effective. Implementation of the new system resulted in target vendors submitting the relevant freight information electronically with increased speed and efficiency. The new system resulted in improved cost controls, better labour planning and reduced administrative overheads (Singh, Arora, & Mishra, 2014).

Inventory Management Systems

During the mid to late 1990s, retailers began implementing modern inventory management systems, made possible in large part by advances in computer and software technology. The systems work in a circular process, from purchase tracking to inventory monitoring to re-ordering and back around again. Inventory management systems are the rule for such enterprises, but smaller businesses and vendors use them, too. The systems ensure customers always have enough of what they want and balance that goal against a retailer's financial need to maintain as little stock as possible. Mismanaged inventory means disappointed customers, too much cash tied up in warehouses and slower sales (Singh, Arora, & Mishra, 2014). Factors such as quicker production cycles, a proliferation of products, multi-national production contracts and the nature of the big-box store make them a necessity.

Modern inventory management systems must have the ability to track sales and available inventory, communicate with suppliers in near real-time and receive and incorporate other data, such as seasonal demand. They also must be flexible, allowing for a merchant's intuition. And, they must tell a storeowner when it's time to reorder and how much to purchase.

Emerging Information Technology Trends in SCM

The emerging information technology trends which support the supply chain management decision process as shown in Figure 2. are discussed as follows:

Radio Frequency Identification (RFID)

The need to minimize operating costs and employed assets has resulted in the adoption of radio frequency technology to track inventories within a supply chain down to the item level, thus reducing channel volume and enhancing forecasting and planning capabilities (D'Avanzo, Starr, & Von Lewinski, 2004). Radio Frequency Identification (RFID) is a type of automatic identification system. The purpose of an RFID system is to enable data to be transmitted by a portable device, called a tag, which is read by an RFID reader and processed according to the needs of a particular application. The data transmitted by the tag may provide identification or location information, or specifics about the product tagged, such as price, colour, date of purchase, etc. The tag is a microchip connected to a small antenna. The chip can capture a certain amount of data (EPIC, 2016).

The impact of RFID from a supply chain perspective includes: supply chain inversion, pressure on inventory, increased regulation and legislation, cost control, connectivity and visibility. Supply chain inversion concerns shifting from a push system to a pull system. In terms of increased regulation and legislation, government regulation has led to more product information and safety requirements. RFID has been used for traceability and visibility of products. In terms of cost cutting, RFID is used to reduce labour costs. Other practical applications of RFID include authentication (Coronado, Lyons, Michaelides, & Kehoe, 2004) and shrink prevention. In terms of authentication, the use of electronic sealing through RF tags can warrant the authenticity and origin of a product. RF tags can be used to prevent non-malicious and malicious shrinks. Non-malicious shrink is associated with product handling. Original equipment manufacturers (OEM's), retailers and suppliers benefit equally from tracking inventories. In the view of Schneider (2003), retailers are very interested in turning the supply chain management industry into an

RFID-dependent business as long as it is cost efficient. The drinks sector has been using RFID to track and manage its inventory to decrease product losses and increase revenues.

Software Agents

Artificial Intelligence emerged into the paradigm of software agents with the application area of multi-agent systems. A software agent is a software system, which has attributes of intelligence, autonomy, perception or acting on behalf of a user. Agents can behave autonomously or proactively. The intelligence of an agent refers to its ability of performing tasks or actions using relevant information gathered as part of different problem-solving techniques such as influencing, reasoning and application specific knowledge (Coronado, Lyons, Michaelides, & Kehoe, 2004). Java has been the most common tool for building such intelligent agents which are increasingly becoming mobile. The classification of agents given by Haag, Cummings, & Philips (2006) suggests that there are four essential types of intelligent software agents:

1. Buyer agents or shopping bots work very efficiently for commodity products such as CDs, books, electronic components, and other one-size fits-all products.
2. Monitoring and Surveillance Agents are used to observe and report on equipment, usually computer systems. The agents may keep track of company inventory levels, observe competitors' prices and relay them back to the company, watch stock manipulation by insider trading and rumors, etc.
3. User agents or personal agents perform tasks like checking e-mail and sorting it according to the user's order of preference, and alert when important emails arrive.
4. Data mining agents uses information technology to find trends and patterns in an abundance of information from many different sources. The user can sort through this information in order to find whatever information they are seeking.

Decision Support Systems

Decision Support Systems (DSS) are a specific class of computerized information systems that supports business and organizational decision-making activities. A properly designed DSS is an interactive software-based system intended to help decision makers compile useful information from raw data, documents, personal knowledge, and/or business models to identify and solve problems and make decisions (Coronado, Lyons, Michaelides, & Kehoe, 2004). Typical information that a decision support application might gather and present would be: an inventory of all current information assets (including legacy and relational data sources, cubes, data warehouses, and data marts); comparative sales figures between one week and the other week; projected revenue figures based on new product sales assumptions; and the consequences of different decision alternatives, given past experience in a context that is described (Patro and Raghunath, 2015).

In SCM, there is always a likelihood of having disagreements among parties for a certain decision making process. This phenomenon gets worse, when the business environment becomes more competitive and turbulent. Accordingly, Decision Support Systems (DSS) have been integrating in various areas like logistics, inventory management, facility design, sales analysis etc. (Lee, Lee, & Han, 1999).

Web Services

Web services are application interfaces accessible via Internet standards that use XML and that employ at least one of the following standards: Simple Object Access Protocol (SOAP), Web Services Description Language (WSDL) or Universal Description, Discovery and Integration (UDDI). These standards, and the next generation standards that are being built on them, are defining the way that forward-thinking enterprise manage lightweight integration tasks. In the view of Sun Microsystems (2004), web services interoperability for supply chain management is being used to support business-to-customer models. The computing giant provided an example where retailers offer electronic goods to consumers. To fulfill orders, the retailer has to manage stock levels in warehouses (Coronado, Lyons, Michaelides, & Kehoe, 2004).

A typical business-to-business model is used when an item in stock falls below a certain threshold. In that case the retailer must restock the item from the relevant manufacturer's inventory. In order to fulfill a retailer's request, a manufacturer may have to execute a production run to build the finished goods. In reality, a manufacturer would have to order the component parts from its suppliers and that may be a manual process which is supported through the use of fax (Singh, Arora, & Mishra, 2014).

Electronic Commerce

Electronic commerce refers to the wide range of tools and techniques utilized to conduct business in a paperless environment. Electronic commerce therefore includes electronic data interchange, e-mail, electronic fund transfers, electronic publishing, image processing, electronic bulletin boards, shared databases and magnetic/optical data capture. Companies are able to automate the process of moving documents electronically between suppliers and customers. This system provides access to customers all over the world and thus eliminates geographical limitations (Singh, Arora, & Mishra, 2014). Some of the E-commerce applications with applications in B2C (Business to Consumer) and B2B (Business to Business) space, which are changing the dynamics of Supply Chain Management include: E-tailing, E-Procurement, and E-Auctions.

Electronic Supply Chains

Electronic Supply Chains (ESC) refers to those supply chains that are electronically facilitated between or among participating firms. Also called Virtual Supply Chains, these are realized in two forms, EDI-based or Internet based. EDI generally connects firms through proprietary Value Added Networks (VAN), whereas the Internet generally connects firms through open networks which use standard protocols. The ESC links trading partners to allow them to buy, sell and move products, services and cash (Sammon and Hanley, 2007). Due to the low implementation costs, the introduction of the Internet has brought about opportunities that allow firms to transact with other enterprises electronically.

The e-supply chain also envisages use of internet-based applications to transact and exchange information like product and inventory information with their downstream or upstream trading partners. Supply Chain initiatives like Collaborative Planning, Forecasting and Replenishment (CPFR), Vendor Managed Inventory (VMI), Efficient Customer Response (ECR) and Quick Response have been increasingly facilitated in the new e-supply chain paradigm. Information sharing among suppliers, manufacturers, distributors and retailers are greatly improved. American-On-Line and lastminute.com have achieved innovative results using ESCs (Gunasekharan & Ngai, 2004).

Vendor Management Inventory (VMI)

Vendor Management Inventory is a distribution channel operating system whereby the inventory at the distributor/retailer is monitored and managed by the manufacturer vendor. It is a family of business model in which buyer of a product provides certain information to the supplier of that product and the supplier takes full responsibility for maintaining an agreed inventory of the material, usually at the buyer's consumption location. It includes several activities including determining appropriate order quantities, managing proper product mixes (Singh, Arora, & Mishra, 2014). The vendor's computer acquires data electronically; no manual data entry is required at the recipient's end which helps in reducing the lead time and in eliminating the vendors recording errors (Patterson, Grimm, & Corsi, 2003).

Collaborative Planning Forecasting and Replenishment (CPFR)

CPFR can be defined as a collaboration where two or more parties in the supply chain jointly plan a number of promotional activities and work on synchronized forecasts, on the basis of which production and replenishment processes are determined. The term CPFR was first introduced in 1995, in connection with a pilot project between Wal-Mart. Warner-Lambert, Benchmarking partners, SAP and Manugistics. The objective of CPFR is to better align supply and demand through trading partner data interchange exception based management and structured collaboration in order to eliminate issues and constraints in fulfilling consumer expectations (Patterson, Grimm, & Corsi, 2003). CPFR is a business practice that reduces inventory costs while improving product availability across the supply chain. The CPFR process begins with an agreement between the trading partners to share information with each other and to collaborate on planning with the ultimate goal of delivering products based on true market demand (Singh, Arora, & Mishra, 2014).

Cross Docking

Cross docking is a practice in Logistics of unloading materials from an incoming semi-trailer, truck or rail, car and loading this material directly into outbound trucks, trailers, or rail cars, With little or no storage between them. It is a function of warehouses or distribution centers, which was introduced by Wal Mart. Cross docking, is a system in which the vendor's ship merchandise to a distribution centres in pre packed quantities required by each store. The merchandise is delivered to one side of the distribution centre; the floor ready merchandise is then transferred to the other side of distribution centre for delivery to a store (Patterson, Grimm, & Corsi, 2003). Cross docking is a process by which products are aptly room the inbound dock to the outbound dock, avoiding the need to store and prepare order replenishment. It either picked or moved directly from the inbound dock to the outbound dock, avoiding the need to store and prepare order replenishment. It not only reduces material handling but also reduces the need to store the products in the warehouse (Singh, Arora, & Mishra, 2014).

Advanced Planning and Scheduling (APS)

Advanced Planning and Scheduling is also referred to as Advanced Manufacturing. It refers to a manufacturing management process by which raw materials and production capacity are optimally allocated to meet the demand. APS is especially well suited to environments where simpler planning methods cannot adequately address complex trade-offs between competing priorities. Traditional planning system utilize a stepwise procedure to allocate material and production capacity. This approach is simple but cumbersome, and does not readily adapt to changes in demand, resource capacity or material availability (Patro and Raghunath, 2015). APS has commonly been applied where one or more of the following conditions are present i.e., Make to order manufacturing; Capital intensive production processes, where plant capacity is constrained; and Products that require a large number of components or manufacturing tasks. Advanced planning and scheduling software enables manufacturing scheduling and advanced scheduling optimization within these environments (Singh, Arora, & Mishra, 2014).

DATA ANALYSIS AND DISCUSSION

An analysis based on the personal interaction with the employees and through observations was made to know their satisfaction level on the information technology based supply chain management trends practiced in their organizations. In the process of collecting the information employees were informed to draw an inference within the four important decisions of Supply Chain Management (SCM) i.e. Location decisions, Inventory decisions, Production decisions and Transport/Distribution decisions, which are imperative for effective implementation of SCM system in the organization. The information collected from various sources are carefully computed, tabulated, analyzed and interpreted. The statistical technique used for analyzing the data collected from the tabulated data would be analyzed with tables and charts wherever necessary, so as to draw inferences based on findings, suggestions and conclusions.

Location Decisions

Location decision is one of the important decisions to be taken in Supply Chain Management, as every organization from the point of establishing its layout in the right place till the point of reaching its customer in the right time. Location decisions play a significant role in the implementation of technology based supply chain management system in the organizations. The satisfaction level of the employees regarding the IT tools used in Location decisions is shown in Table 1.

The respondents opinion on the emerging and existing trends followed by their companies show that in the case of existing trends 35 per cent employees are satisfied with the location decision, 40 per cent of the employees are not satisfied with the existing trends because of their traditional makeover, whereas 25 per cent employees are having a neutral opinion as they find it feasible in some area and vice versa. Emerging trends are the upcoming trends with a touch of technology enhancement of the effectiveness in the activities seeing through the opinion of employees with regard to emerging trends 56 per cent of employees are satisfied with the new and advanced techniques because of their technological superiority, 18 per cent of the employees were not satisfied as they found the change was difficult to adapt, whereas 26 per cent of employees were of mixed opinion regarding the use of emerging techniques in the supply chain management system of the organization.

Inventory Decisions

Inventory decisions all together holds an important substance for every organization, planning of inventory has become the major factor in a country like India. Demand plays an influential role and thus

Table 1. Respondents opinion on IT based location decisions

S. No.	Company	No. of Employees		Existing Trends			Emerging Trends		
				Satisfied	Not Satisfied	Neutral	Satisfied	Not Satisfied	Neutral
1	A	32	#	9	16	7	15	8	9
			%	28	50	22	47	25	28
2	B	25	#	9	10	6	14	4	7
			%	36	40	24	56	16	28
3	C	20	#	7	7	6	12	3	5
			%	35	35	30	60	15	25
4	D	24	#	8	10	6	14	4	6
			%	33	42	25	58	17	25
5	E	18	#	8	6	4	11	3	4
			%	44	33	22	61	17	22
6	F	21	#	8	7	6	12	3	6
			%	38	33	29	57	14	29
Total		140	#	49	56	35	78	25	37
			%	35	40	25	56	18	26

inventory decision like buffering, smoothing and rationing of stock levels has to be kept in check and we have made an effort to see the efficiency levels in these decisions using existing and emerging trends. The responses of the employees regarding the use of IT based supply chain tools used in Inventory decisions is shown in Table 2.

The inventory decision analysis depicts that 43 per cent of respondents are satisfied with the existing trends pertained in their organizations because of its simple methodology, 31 per cent of respondents are not satisfied as they view it as a old methodology in new generation, and the respondents holding mixed ideas are 26 per cent. In the view of emerging trends practiced by the companies, the satisfaction percentage of the respondents have increased to 56 per cent because of its modern methodology but as everything has a other side 22 per cent of respondents are not satisfied and 21 percent of respondents are holding neutral view on the implementation of the IT based inventory decisions in their organizations.

Production Decisions

Production refers to the conversion of raw materials into finished product and to make this process effective production decision has to be accurate, as any wrong estimation will put the company into trouble. The production decisions are imperative while implementing technology based supply chain management system. The satisfaction level of the respondents regarding the IT based SCM tools used in Production decisions is shown in Table 3.

The production decision deals with what, how and when questions of production and coming to review of the existing and emerging trends of production the following is the outcome, 39 per cent of employees are satisfied with the existing trends and 30 per cent find it not so up to the mark as production

Table 2. Respondents opinion on IT based inventory decisions

S. No.	Company	No. of Employees		Existing Trends			Emerging Trends		
				Satisfied	Not Satisfied	Neutral	Satisfied	Not Satisfied	Neutral
1	A	32	#	12	9	11	18	7	7
			%	38	28	34	56	22	22
2	B	25	#	11	8	6	14	5	6
			%	44	32	24	56	20	24
3	C	20	#	9	7	4	11	6	3
			%	45	35	20	55	30	15
4	D	24	#	10	8	6	14	6	4
			%	42	33	25	58	25	17
5	E	18	#	8	6	4	10	3	5
			%	44	33	22	56	17	28
6	F	21	#	10	6	5	12	4	5
			%	48	29	24	57	19	24
Total		140	#	60	44	36	79	31	30
			%	43	31	26	56	22	21

Table 3. Respondents opinion on IT based production decisions

S. No.	Company	No. of Employees		Existing Trends			Emerging Trends		
				Satisfied	Not Satisfied	Neutral	Satisfied	Not Satisfied	Neutral
1	A	32	#	12	10	10	17	9	6
			%	38	31	31	53	28	19
2	B	25	#	9	8	8	12	3	10
			%	36	32	32	48	12	40
3	C	20	#	8	6	6	10	3	7
			%	40	30	30	50	15	35
4	D	24	#	10	9	5	12	4	8
			%	42	38	21	50	17	33
5	E	18	#	7	5	6	10	3	5
			%	39	28	33	56	17	28
6	F	21	#	9	4	8	12	4	5
			%	43	19	38	57	19	24
Total		140	#	55	42	43	73	26	41
			%	39	30	31	52	19	29

analysis using existing methods become difficult and people holding mixed reviews include 31 per cent who find it both satisfactory and vice-versa. Emerging trends are however, an upgrade to the existing trends and the companies can expect an hike in percentage of satisfaction as it is true in the given case as the satisfaction percentage is 52 and the dissatisfaction level has decreased to 19 per cent and people with mixed review are 29 per cent.

Transport/Distribution Decisions

Transport and distribution is the core for every organization. As once production decision has been taken and implemented the transport or distribution decisions have to be planned and are important for meeting the demand effectively. In a country like India, where demand is continuously increasing with increasing population and thus these decisions help us in reaching the final customer in time a without any delay. A small delay now a day's shifts the demand of a company to another company. The satisfaction level of the employees regarding the IT tools used in Transport/Distribution decisions is shown in Table 4.

The views of employees with regard to existing trends and emerging trends on the distribution system is, 41 per cent of employees are satisfied with the existing trends though the other side has 44 per cent showing more dissatisfaction because of the lean transportation and distribution structure of organization without much use of technology and thus people holding mixed opinion account for 16 per cent. Emerging trends in Transport and distribution has started to show their impact on organizational effectiveness and this is evident by 56 per cent of satisfaction levels in employees against 39 per cent of dissatisfaction and the mixed review accounts for 55 per cent showing a complete dominance of emerging trend on existing trends of Transport and distribution decision.

Table 4. Respondents opinion on IT based transport/distribution decisions

S. No.	Company	No. of Employees		Existing Trends			Emerging Trends		
				Satisfied	Not Satisfied	Neutral	Satisfied	Not Satisfied	Neutral
1	A	32	#	11	14	7	16	13	3
			%	34	44	22	50	41	9
2	B	25	#	8	12	5	13	11	1
			%	32	48	20	52	44	4
3	C	20	#	8	9	3	11	7	2
			%	40	45	15	55	35	10
4	D	24	#	10	12	2	13	11	0
			%	42	50	8	54	46	0
5	E	18	#	9	6	3	12	5	1
			%	50	33	17	67	28	6
6	F	21	#	11	8	2	14	7	0
			%	52	38	10	67	33	0
Total		140	#	57	61	22	79	54	7
			%	41	44	16	56	39	5

The overall comparison of the satisfaction level of the employees of different private sector manufacturing organizations and Information Technology based Supply Chain Management decisions is shown in Table 5.

The analysis shows that most of the employees are satisfied with the emerging new trends in contrast to existing trends that are practiced in the organizations. Based on the comments and suggestions of the employees, it can be concluded that though the emerging trends are gaining importance in the modern era, the existing age old techniques should also be carried on like a coin which have both head and tail to create a balance within Supply Chain Management in the modern era.

CHALLENGES IN IMPLEMENTING INFORMATION TECHNOLOGY IN SCM

Any company that has undertaken the mission of implementing an integrated supply chain management strategy with the use of IT tools knows that one of the greatest challenges it faces is the significant change in internal culture that is required to make the supply chain redesign successful (Macleod, 1994; Towill, 1997). However, it may be difficult to accomplish but change can be implemented successfully when directed by a strong and knowledgeable leader, who understands the tools available for achieving positive change, as well as their role in initiating and sustaining these changes (Auramo, Kauremaa, & Tanskanen, 2005; Oldenborgh, 2004). Knowing some of the top supply chain technology mistakes and challenges can help make the implementation process run smoother.

1. **Failure to Secure Top Management Sponsorship and Leadership:** Since supply chain processes impact so much of a company's mission, vision and critical value-chain that securing top management nod and leadership is herculean task for cross-functional commitment, deriving hierarchical accountability, or allocating proper resources to ensure a successful adaptation and implementation.
2. **Wrong Process and Worst Practice:** Prior to an implementation process, it is vital for companies to conduct research ensuring the new technology is supported by the right process and is in ground with cross-industry best practices related to that process. The ultimate benefits of a technology is best gained by consulting existing IT powered enterprises who have successfully implemented

Table 5. Overall comparison of the IT based SCM decisions

SCM Decisions		Existing Trends			Emerging Trends		
		Satisfied	Not Satisfied	Neutral	Satisfied	Not Satisfied	Neutral
Location Decisions	#	49	56	35	78	25	37
	%	35	40	25	56	18	26
Production Decisions	#	55	42	43	73	26	41
	%	39	30	31	52	19	29
Inventory Decisions	#	60	44	36	79	31	30
	%	43	31	26	56	22	21
Transport/ Distribution Decisions	#	57	61	22	79	54	7
	%	41	44	16	56	39	5

such technology within their supply chains. Hence, wrong practices should be avoided by seeking referrals from companies that have gained significant benefits in utilizing the technology.

3. **Inaccurate and Obsolete Information:** There is a thin gap being on the top of the list or at the bottom that is timely and accurate information supplied to the process hence Before implementing any new software, the implementation team must first dedicate efforts to make sure that all data related in any way to the application is clean and accurate.

4. **No Cross-Functional Representation:** A broad-based team that is empowered to make decisions about planning and implementation will ensure a successful supply chain deployment. This team should include the ultimate stakeholders in use of the new technology, and all those who will benefit with improved process flow and information. Systems integration is a critical requirement in most supply chain technology. It is essential that the implementation team have IT representation to lead the systems integration effort and address needs for inbound and outbound data or new integration and information reporting needs, which is seldom seen.

5. **Broad Scope:** While a long-term end-state is the goal, do not attempt to implement everything at once. Focus on core needs of the process being automated and on scope that can deliver the initial benefits of an implementation. Celebrate short-term wins and incremental benefits. A limited focus on quick initial benefits from the implementation and sustaining value in subsequent future functionality releases can help in obtaining longer-term commitment to automation and change.

IMPACT OF IT IN SUPPLY CHAIN MANAGEMENT

In general, application of Information Technology trends in Supply Chain Management enables great opportunities ranging from direct operational benefits to the creation of strategic advantage (McFarlan, 1984; Benjamin, Rockart, Scott Morton, & Wyman, 1985; Gunasekharan and Ngai, 2004; Singh, Arora, & Mishra, 2014). Porter and Millar (1985) advocated that IT changes the industry structures and rules of competition, creates competitive advantage, and also creates new business opportunities. In the supply chain context, Bowersox and Daugherty (1995) outlined that IT is key in supporting companies creating strategic advantage by enabling centralized strategic planning with day-to-day centralized operations.

Information Technology has a profound impact on managing supply chains. Kemppainen and Vepsäläinen (2003) argue that IT is alongside specialization, outsourcing, and a key precondition for networking of organizations. Golicic, Davis, McCarthy, & Mentzer (2002) intended that because of information technologies, supply chains become less integrated and more market oriented. Williams, Esper, & Ozment (2002) suggest that electronic SCM combines the structural benefits of SCM with the efficiency benefits of an arms length approach, enabling, for example, lower cost through possibilities of selecting from a larger supplier base. Malone, Yates, & Benjamin (1987) proposes that the value offerings through IT are electronic communication (speed of communication), electronic brokerage (by IT providing a 'lean', automated intermediary for resolving market transactions), and electronic integration (coupling of processes). IT seems to be particularly important in fast clock speed industries (Guimaraes, Cook, & Natarajan, 2002) or when flexibility and agility are needed (Sanders & Premus, 2002). Levary (2000) suggest that IT in SCM provides reduction of cycle time, reduction of inventories, minimization of bullwhip effect, and improvement of effectiveness of distribution channels.

Finally, with regard to the impact and benefits of IT, the controversial phenomenon, productivity paradox of IT (Loveman, 1991) cannot be avoided. Devaraj and Kohli (2003) argued that the conceptual problem relating to the productivity paradox of IT is that only IT investment is considered and its actual usage is not considered. The use of IT was positively and statistically significantly related to revenue and quality improvements with a specified time lag; while the investment in IT, as such, with the same data, was not (Patro and Raghunath, 2015). In addition, David (1990) suggested that this innovation did not first affect productivity, and argues that there are common problems with the introduction of new technology, which may realize productivity gains only after a considerable time lag.

BENEFITS OF E-BUSINESS TECHNOLOGIES IN SCM

The evolution of Information Technology (IT) practices and techniques is a factor that enabled the integration of supply chains into value systems. In order to assess the competitive value of IT techniques and methods for SCM, Therefore, maximizing IT investment could lead firms to higher profitability and effectiveness.

Improving Customer Service Elements

Customer service is commonly an essential part of company's strategy, but views of its contents vary. In logistics it means making the products available for the customer. This involves, however, much more than just delivering the products when ordered. Christoper (1998) discusses logistical customer service using the classification into pre-transaction, transaction and post-transaction elements. Good pre-transaction customer service means that customers understands what the company is able to supply, the company is easy to contact, and the company can adapt delivery systems to particular customer needs. The transaction elements of customer service are between order and delivery, for example order cycle time, delivery preciseness and order status information. The post-transaction elements refer to issues after the customer has received the original product, for example availability of spares and correct billing.

Improves Information Quality

Informational benefits of IT are generally broken into information access, information flexibility, and information quality (Mirani and Lederer, 1998). Information access benefits provide supply chain decision makers with faster and/or easier access to internal and external information. Information flexibility benefits allow decision makers to easily manipulate the content and format of retrieved information. Information quality benefits make the available information more useful, accurate, and reliable. It improves the usefulness of information for strategic planning and operational control.

Planning Collaboration Improve Agility of the Supply Network

Agility is a key capability for companies in an environment of rapid and unpredictable change. Christopher and Towill (2000) define agility as "a business-wide capability that embraces organizational structures, information systems, logistics processes and, in particular, mindsets." They state that agile supply chain is market sensitive, which means capability to respond to real demand in volatile markets. Bruce and Daly (2004) stated that sharing of information between the supply network partners is essential for reaching agility.

Strategic Benefits Coupled with Process Re-design

As noted in the literature review, IT is suggested to have strategic impact on companies and supply chain management. To receive strategic benefits with IT, supply chain processes have to be changed and that some companies have been able to do this. In extant literature, business process re-engineering (BPR) authors hold that the link of IT use and simultaneous design of business processes is a vital ingredient to benefit from development efforts notably (Venkatraman 1994; Hammer, 1990; Davenport & Short 1990).

Thus, the benefits of IT in SCM are manifold and can vary from the implementation method. Moreover, the use of IT is closely related to process changes and as such, SCM can be viewed as a process change that is helped or enabled by IT. This makes it difficult, or even in many cases a profane academic exercise, to separate the origin of the benefit, whether derived from IT, process change, or both.

CONCLUSION

World is shrinking day by day with advancement of information technology. Customers' expectations are also increasing and companies are prone to more and more uncertain environment. Companies will find that their conventional supply chain integration will have to be expanded beyond their peripheries. The strategic and technological innovations in supply chain will impact on how organizations transact in future. However clear vision, strong planning and technical insight into the transformational capabilities would be necessary to ensure that organizations maximize the technological potential for better supply chain management and ultimately improved competitiveness.

Internet technology, World Wide Web, Electronic commerce, etc., will change the way an organization does business. The organizations must realize that they must harness the power of technology to collaborate with their business partners, that means using a new breed of SCM application, the Internet and other networking links to observe past performance and historical trends to determine how much output should be made as well finding the best and cost effective method. Recent technological developments and trends in the current business environment suggest that the information technology has become critical for a supply chain to function. The business environment continues to emphasize more variety, better quality, greater reliability and quicker response to a dynamic, customer driven market place. One of the best ways to serve this demanding market is to develop supply chain management information systems through the use of information technology and related tools to impart the information at the right time and right place to the ultimate user.

ACKNOWLEDGMENT

The authors would like to thank the anonymous reviewers and the editor for their insightful comments and suggestions.

REFERENCES

Ajmal, M. M., & Kristianto, Y. (2010). Knowledge Sharing in Supply Chain. *International Journal of Strategic Decision Sciences*, *1*(4), 44–55. doi:10.4018/jsds.2010100103

Armstrong, A., & Hagel, J. III. (1996). The real value of online communities. *Harvard Business Review*, (May/June), 134–140.

Auramo, J., Kauremaa, J., & Tanskanen, K. (2005). Benefits of IT in Supply Chain Management: An explorative study of progressive companies. *International Journal of Physical Distribution & Logistics Management*, *35*(2), 82–100. doi:10.1108/09600030510590282

Barratt, M. (2004). Understanding the meaning of collaboration in the supply chain. *Supply Chain Management: An International Journal*, *9*(1), 30–42. doi:10.1108/13598540410517566

Barua, A., Konana, P., Whinston, A. B., & Yin, F. (2004). An empirical investigation of net-enabled business value: An exploratory investigation. *Management Information Systems Quarterly*, *28*(4), 585–620.

Benjamin, R. I., Rockart, J. F., Scott Morton, M. S., & Wyman, J. (1984). Information Technology: A Strategic Opportunity. *Sloan Management Review*, *25*(3), 3–10.

Bowersox, D. J., & Daugherty, P. J. (1995). Logistics paradigms: The impact of information technology. *Journal of Business Logistics*, *16*(1), 65–80.

Brookman, F., Smit, J., & Silvius, A. J. G. (2012). Perception of Information Technology Enablers for Supply Chain Management. *Communications of the IIMA*, *12*(2), 51–64.

Brown, S. A. (1997). *Revolution at the Checkout Counter: the explosion of the bar code*. London: Harvard University Press.

Bruce, M., Daly, L., & Towers, N. (2004). Lean or agile, a solution for supply chain management in the textiles and clothing industry? *International Journal of Operations & Production Management*, *24*(2), 151–170. doi:10.1108/01443570410514867

Chopra, S., & Meindl, P. (2001). *Supply Chain Management: Strategy, Planning, and Operation*. Upper Saddle River, NJ: Prentice Hall.

Chopra, S., & Meindl, P. (2007). *Supply chain management: Strategy planning, and operation* (3rd ed.). Upper Saddle River, NJ: Pearson Prentice Hall.

Christopher, M. (1998). *Logistics and Supply Chain Management Strategies for Reducing Cost and Improving service*. London, UK: Pittman Publishing.

Christopher, M., & Towill, D. (2000). Supply chain migration from lean and functional to agile and customized. *Supply Chain Management: An International Journal*, *5*(4), 206–213. doi:10.1108/13598540010347334

Chu, W. H. J., & Lee, C. C. (2006). Strategic information sharing in a supply chain. *European Journal of Operational Research*, *174*(3), 1567–1579. doi:10.1016/j.ejor.2005.02.053

Cooper, M. C., Lambert, D. M., & Pagh, J. D. (1997). Supply chain management: More than a new name for logistics. *The International Journal of Logistics Management*, *8*(1), 1–14. doi:10.1108/09574099710805556

Coronado, A. E., Lyons, A. C., Michaelides, Z., & Kehoe, D. F. (2004). *Automotive supply chain models and technologies: A review of some latest developments*. Retrieved from, www.emeraldinsight. com/1741-0398.htm

Cross, G. J. (2000). How e-business is transforming supply chain management. *The Journal of Business Strategy*, *21*(2), 36–39. doi:10.1108/eb040073

D'Avanzo, R., Starr, E., & Von Lewinski, H. (2004). Supply chain and the bottom line: A critical link. *Outlook: Accenture*, *1*, 39–45.

Das, K., & Dellana, S. A. (2013). A Quality and Partnering-Based Model for Improving Supply Chain Performance. *International Journal of Strategic Decision Sciences*, *4*(3), 1–31. doi:10.4018/jsds.2013070101

Davenport, T. H., & Short, J. E. (1990). The New Industrial Engineering: Information Technology and Business Process Redesign. *Sloan Management Review*, *31*(4), 11–27.

David, P. A. (1990). The Dynamo and the Computer: An historical Perspective on the Modern Productivity Paradox. *The American Economic Review*, *80*(2), 355–361.

Dedrick, J., Gurbaxani, V., & Kraemer, K. (2003). Information Technology and Economic Performance: A Critical Review of the Empirical Evidence. *ACM Computing Surveys*, *35*(1), 1–28. doi:10.1145/641865.641866

Denolf, J. M., Trienekens, J. H., Wognuma, P. M., van der Vorst, J. G. A. J., & Omta, S. W. F. (2015). Towards a framework of critical success factors for implementing supply chain information systems. *Computers in Industry*, *68*, 16–26. doi:10.1016/j.compind.2014.12.012

Devaraj, S., & Kohli, R. (2003). Performance Impacts of Information Technology: Is Actual Usage the Missing Link. *Management Science*, *49*(3), 273–289. doi:10.1287/mnsc.49.3.273.12736

EPIC. (2016). *Radio Frequency Identification*. Retrieved 12 December, 2016, from http://www.epic. org/privacy/rfid/

Fasanghari, M., Roudsari, F. H., & Chaharsooghi, S. K. (2008). Assessing the Impact of Information Technology on Supply Chain Management. *World Applied Sciences Journal*, *4*(1), 87–93.

Finney, S., & Corbett, M. (2007). ERP implementation: A compilation and analysis of critical success factors. *Business Process Management Journal*, *13*(3), 329–347. doi:10.1108/14637150710752272

Gargeya, V. B., & Brady, C. (2005). Success and failure factors of adopting SAP in ERP system implementation. *Business Process Management Journal*, *11*(5), 501–516. doi:10.1108/14637150510619858

Golden, W., & Powell, P. (1999). Exploring inter-organisational systems and flexibility in Ireland: A case of two value chains. *International Journal of Agile Management Systems*, *1*(3), 169–184. doi:10.1108/14654659910296544

Golicic, S. L., Davis, D. F., McCarthy, T. M., & Mentzer, J. T. (2002). The impact of e-commerce on supply chain relationships. *International Journal of Physical Distribution & Logistics Management*, *32*(10), 851–871. doi:10.1108/09600030210455447

Graham, G., & Hardaker, G. (2000). Supply Chain management across the Internet. *International Journal of Physical Distribution & Logistics Management*, *30*(3/4), 286–295. doi:10.1108/09600030010326055

Guimaraes, T., Cook, D., & Natarajan, N. (2002). Exploring the Importance of Business Clockspeed as a Moderator for Determinants of Supplier Network Performance. *Decision Sciences*, *33*(4), 629–644. doi:10.1111/j.1540-5915.2002.tb01659.x

Gunasekaran, A., & Ngai, E. W. T. (2004). Information systems in supply chain integration and management. *European Journal of Operational Research*, *159*(2), 269–295. doi:10.1016/j.ejor.2003.08.016

Gunasekharan, A., & Ngai, E. W. T. (2004). Virtual Supply Chain Management. *Production Planning and Control*, *15*(6), 584–595. doi:10.1080/09537280412331283955

Gyanendra, S., Rajeev, A., & Vivek, M. (2014). Emerging Trends in Supply Chain Management. *International Journal of Research in Engineering and Technology*, *3*(10), 100–103.

Haag, S., Cummings, M., & Philips, A. (2006). *Management Information Systems for the Information Age*. McGraw Hill College.

Hammer, M. (1990). Reengineering Work: Don't Automate, Obliterate. *Harvard Business Review*, *68*(4), 104–112.

Harland, C. M. (1996). Supply chain management: Relationships, chains, and networks. *British Journal of Management*, *7*(s1), 63–80. doi:10.1111/j.1467-8551.1996.tb00148.x

Himanshu, S. M., Murty, J. S., Senapati, S. K., & Khuntia, K. (2011). Importance of Information Technology for Effective Supply Chain Management. *International Journal of Modern Engineering Research*, *1*(2), 747–751.

Iskandar, B. Y., Kurokawa, S., & LeBlanc, L. J. (2001). Business-to-business electronic commerce from first- and second-tier automotive suppliers perspectives: A preliminary analysis for hypotheses generation. *Technovation*, *21*(11), 719–731. doi:10.1016/S0166-4972(01)00053-0

Jaana, A., Kauremaa, J., & Tanskanen, K. (2005). Benefits of IT in supply chain management: An explorative study of progressive companies. *International Journal of Physical Distribution & Logistics Management*, *35*(2), 82–100. doi:10.1108/09600030510590282

Jharkharia, S., & Shankar, R. (2004). IT enablement of supply chains: Modeling the enablers. *International Journal of Productivity and Performance Management*, *53*(8), 700–712. doi:10.1108/17410400410569116

Kemppainen, K., & Vepsäläinen, A. P. J. (2003). Trends in industrial supply chains and networks. *International Journal of Physical Distribution & Logistics Management, 33*(8), 701–719. doi:10.1108/09600030310502885

Kopczak, L. (1997). Logistics partnership and supply chain restructuration: Survey results from the U.S. computer industry. *Production and Operations Management, 6*(3), 226–247. doi:10.1111/j.1937-5956.1997. tb00428.x

Lambert, D. M., Cooper, M. C., & Pagh, J. D. (1998). Supply chain management: Implementation issues and research opportunities. *International Journal of Logistics Management, 9*(2), 1–19. doi:10.1108/09574099810805807

Lee, C., Lee, K. C., & Han, J. (1999). A Web-based Decision Support System for Logistics Decision-Making. *Proceedings of the Academy of Information and Management Sciences, 3*(1).

Lee, H. L., & Whang, S. (1997). Bullwhip Effect in Supply Chains. *Sloan Management Review, 38*(3), 93–102.

Levary, R. R. (2000). Better Supply Chains through Information Technology. *Industrial Management (Des Plaines), 42*(3), 24–30.

Li, G., Yang, H., Sun, L., & Sohal, A. S. (2009). The impact of IT implementation on supply chain integration and performance. *International Journal of Production Economics, 120*(1), 125–138. doi:10.1016/j. ijpe.2008.07.017

Lin, C., Kuei, C., Madu, C. N., & Winch, J. (2010). Identifying Critical Success Factors for Supply Chain Excellence. *International Journal of Strategic Decision Sciences, 1*(3), 49–70. doi:10.4018/ jsds.2010070104

Loveman, G. (1991). Cash drain, no gain. *Computerworld, 25*(47), 69–70.

Macleod, M. (1994, July). What's new in supply chain software?. *Purchasing & Supply Management,* 22-25.

Malone, T. W., Yates, J., & Benjamin, R. I. (1987). Electronic markets and electronic hierarchies. *Communications of the ACM, 30*(6), 484–497. doi:10.1145/214762.214766

McCathie, L. (2004). *The advantages and disadvantages of barcodes and radio frequency identification in supply chain management.* School of Information Technology and Computer Science, Bachelor of Information and Communication Technology (Honours), University of Wollongong. Retrieved from http://www.ro.uow.edu.au/thesesinfo/9

McFarlan, F. W. (1984). Information technology changes the way you compete. *Harvard Business Review, 62*(3), 98–103.

Mehdi, F., Farzad, H. R., & Kamal, C. S. (2008). Assessing the Impact of Information Technology on Supply Chain Management. *World Applied Sciences Journal, 4*(1), 87–93.

Mirani, R., & Lederer, A. L. (1998). An Instrument for assessing the organizational benefits of IS projects. *Decision Sciences, 29*(4), 803–838. doi:10.1111/j.1540-5915.1998.tb00878.x

Motwani, J., Madan, M., & Gunasekaran, A. (2000). Information technology in managing supply chains. *Logistics Information Management, 13*(5), 320–327. doi:10.1108/09576050010378540

Nagarjuna, B., & Siddaiah, T. (2012). Impact of information Technology – Paradigm shifts in SCM. *Journal of Exclusive Management Science, 1*(3), 1–7.

Ngai, E. W., & Gunasekaran, A. (2004). Implementation of EDI in Hong Kong: An empirical analysis. *Industrial Management & Data Systems, 104*(1), 88–100. doi:10.1108/02635570410514124

Oldenborgh, M. V. (1994). Distribution superhighway. *International Business, 7*(6), 80–84.

Palmer, R. C. (1995). *The Bar Code Book: Reading, Printing and Specification of Bar Code Symbols* (3rd ed.). Helmers Publishing Inc.

Pathak, J., & Vidyarthi, N. (2011). Cost Framework for Evaluation of Information Technology Alternatives in Supply Chain. *International Journal of Strategic Decision Sciences, 2*(1), 66–84. doi:10.4018/jsds.2011010104

Patro, C. S., & Raghunath, K. M. K. (2015). Impetus to Supply Chain Decisions with IT Tools: An Empirical Study. *International Journal of Enterprise Information Systems, 11*(3), 52–67. doi:10.4018/IJEIS.2015070104

Patterson, K. A., Grimm, C. M., & Corsi, T. M. (2003). Adopting new technologies for supply chain management. *Transportation Research Part E, Logistics and Transportation Review, 39*(2), 95–121. doi:10.1016/S1366-5545(02)00041-8

Pereira, J. V. (2009). The new supply chains frontier: Information management. *International Journal of Information Management, 29*(5), 372–379. doi:10.1016/j.ijinfomgt.2009.02.001

Porter, M. E., & Millar, V. E. (1985). How information gives you competitive advantage. *Harvard Business Review, 63*(4), 149–160.

Prasad, R. (2007). IT Enabled Supply Chain Management. *Serbian Journal of Management, 2*(1), 47–56.

Radhakrishnan, A., David, D., Hales, D., & Sridharan, V. S. (2011). Mapping the Critical Links between Supply Chain Evaluation System and Supply Chain Integration Sustainability: An Empirical Study. *International Journal of Strategic Decision Sciences, 2*(1), 44–65. doi:10.4018/jsds.2011010103

Rai, A., Patnayakuni, R., & Patnayakuni, N. (2006). Firm performance impacts of digitally enabled supply chain integration capabilities. *Management Information Systems Quarterly, 30*(2), 225–246.

Rushton, A., Oxley, J., & Croucher, P. (2000). *IT in the supply chain. The Handbook of Logistics and Distribution Management.* Bell & Bain Ltd., Glasgow.

Sahay, B. (2002). *Supply Chain Management in the Twenty First Century.* Macmillan Publishers.

Salo, J., & Karjaluoto, H. (2006). IT-Enabled Supply Chain Management. *Contemporary Management Research, 2*(1), 17–30. doi:10.7903/cmr.76

Sammon, D., & Hanley, P. (2007). Case Study: Becoming a 100 per cent e-corporation: benefits of pursuing an e-supply chain strategy. *Supply Chain Management, 12*(4), 297–303. doi:10.1108/13598540710759817

Sanders, N. R., & Premus, R. (2002). IT applications in supply chain organizations: A link between competitive priorities and organizational benefits. *Journal of Business Logistics*, *23*(1), 65–83. doi:10.1002/j.2158-1592.2002.tb00016.x

Schneider, M. (2003). *Radio Frequency Identification (RFID) Technology and its Applications in the Commercial Construction Industry* (Thesis). University of Kentucky.

Simchi-Levi, D., Kaminsky, P., & Simchi-Levi, E. (2000). *Designing and Managing the Supply Chain: Concepts, Strategies and Case Studies* (International Edition). Singapore: McGraw-Hill.

Simchi-Levi, D., Kaminsky, P., & Simchi-Levi, E. (2003). *Designing and Managing the Supply Chain: Concepts, Strategies, and Case Studies*. New York: McGraw-Hill.

Singh, G., Arora, R., & Mishra, V. (2014). Emerging Trends in Supply Chain Management. *International Journal of Research in Engineering and Technology*, *3*(10), 100–103.

Subramani, M. (2004). How do suppliers benefit from information technology use in supply chain relationships? *Management Information Systems Quarterly*, *28*(1), 45–73.

SunMicrosystems. (2004). *Web Services*. Retrieved 12 December, 2016, http://www.java.sun.com/webservices/docs/1.3/wsi-sampleapp/

Swaminathan, J. M., & Tayur, S. R. (2003). Models for Supply Chains in E-Business. *Management Science*, *49*(10), 1387–1406. doi:10.1287/mnsc.49.10.1387.17309

Thongchattu, C., & Buranajarukorn, P. (2007). The Utilisation of e-Tools of Information Technology towards Thorough Supply Chain Management.*Naresuan University Research Conference*.

Towill, D. (1997). The seamless supply chain - the predators strategic advantage. *International Journal of Technology Management*, *13*(1), 37–56. doi:10.1504/IJTM.1997.001649

Umble, E. J., Haft, R. R., & Umble, M. M. (2003). Enterprise resource planning: Implementation procedures and critical success factors. *European Journal of Operational Research*, *146*(2), 241–257. doi:10.1016/S0377-2217(02)00547-7

Venkatraman, N. (1994). IT-Enabled Business Transformation: From Automation to Business Scope Redefinition. *Sloan Management Review*, *35*(2), 73–87.

Watson, R. T., Akelsen, S., & Pitt, L. F. (1998). Building mountains in that flat landscape of the World Wide Web. *California Management Review*, *40*(2), 36–56. doi:10.2307/41165932

Williams, L. R., Esper, T. L., & Ozment, J. (2002). The electronic supply chain. *International Journal of Physical Distribution & Logistics Management*, *32*(8), 703–719. doi:10.1108/09600030210444935

Williamson, E. A., Harrison, D. K., & Jordan, M. (2004). Information systems development within supply chain management. *International Journal of Information Management*, *24*(5), 375–385. doi:10.1016/j.ijinfomgt.2004.06.002

Yu, Z., Yan, H., & Cheng, T. C. E. (2001). Benefits of information sharing with supply chain partnerships. *Industrial Management & Data Systems*, *101*(3), 114–119. doi:10.1108/02635570110386625

Zhang, Q., Vonderembse, M. A., & Lim, J. S. (2005). Logistics flexibility and its impact on customer satisfaction. *The International Journal of Logistics Management*, *16*(1), 71–95. doi:10.1108/09574090510617367

KEY TERMS AND DEFINITIONS

Asset Management: A systematic process of deploying, operating, maintaining, upgrading, and disposing of assets cost-effectively.

E-Auctions: Refer to the sites on the web which run conventional auctions.

E-Procurement: Refers to purchase of goods and services which are not directly used in the main business of a company.

E-Tailing: Refers to using the Internet for selling goods over the internet.

Electronic Supply Chain Management: E-SCM is an optimization of business processes and business value in every corner of the extended enterprise - right from the supplier's supplier to the customer's customer.

Information Technology (IT): Information technology is a term that encompasses all forms of technology utilized to create, capture, manipulate, communicate, exchange, present, and use information in its various forms.

Logistics: It refers to planning, execution, and control of the procurement, movement, and stationing of personnel, material, and other resources to achieve the objectives of a SCM.

Strategic Sourcing: It is a component of supply chain management for improving and re-evaluating the purchasing activities.

Supply Chain: It is referred as the sequence of processes involved in the production and distribution of a commodity.

Supply Chain Strategy: It is an iterative process that evaluates the cost- benefit trade-offs of operational components.

Chapter 15
Data Envelopment Analysis for Measuring and Evaluating Efficiency on IT Outsourcing Operations

João Correia dos Santos
Instituto Superior Técnico, Portugal

Miguel Mira da Silva
Instituto Superior Técnico, Portugal

ABSTRACT

During the last decades, the IT service sector has been one of the fastest growing segment in the global economy, consequently, Information Technology (IT) outsourcing providers face several challenges: contracts are based on a multi-service configuration; high degree of variance between clients; market dynamism through rivalry, accelerated innovation, client requisites and relationship management. As a result, service providers employ several tools and methods to find the best fit between standardization (mainly for productivity increase) and customization (primarily for client satisfaction), because IT outsourcing operational context display a multi-input and multi-output set of variables that need to be known and managed, thus efficiency measurement is essential to delivery optimised IT operations. The purpose of this work is to identify, describe, evaluate and present a model based on Data Envelopment Analysis (DEA), which is a linear programming technique able to manipulate multiple inputs and outputs. DEA allows the identification of the most efficient operation that enables providers to set the best operational strategy to follow. To develop our research, design science research was applied, and eighteen contracts were used to evaluate our model's utility the results show the importance of quantitative measures in a dynamic business environment like IT outsourcing. This work is a major contribution for measuring efficiency in IT outsourcing operations.

DOI: 10.4018/978-1-5225-2382-6.ch015

INTRODUCTION

Inside Information Technology (IT) service sector, (IT) outsourcing has been one of the most studied subjects in the IT academic area (Lacity & Hirschheim, 1993; Quinn & Hilmer, 1994; Dibbern & all, 2004; Brown & Wilson, 2005; Cullen, 2009) offering a considerable body of knowledge. Consequently, like in other business areas, performance evaluation is a core concern for management (Schaffnit, Rosen, & Paradi, 1997; Gronroos & Ojasalo, 2004).

While in the manufacturing sector, efficiency measurement is well established, in which, efficiency is defined as a ratio of the production outputs to its inputs. In contrast, measuring service efficiency is still evolving, as services are configurations of people, technology, processes and stakeholders all connected by value propositions and shared information, thus simply transferring the traditional concept of productivity and efficiency from manufacturing to services is bound to fail because of the immateriality and intangibility of services.

Even though efficiency and productivity are used, generally, in the same meaning, they were defined by Abbott (Abbott, 2006) differently. While efficiency can be described as being the degree to which resources are being used in an optimal fashion to produce outputs of a given quantity, productivity is a measure of the physical output produced from the use of a given quantity of inputs.

Therefore, IT outsourcing providers face two main challenges: firstly, the balance between standardization (in order to obtain productivity gains) and customization (for client satisfaction). Secondly, efficiency measurement so as to record, analyse and optimize operations, regardless of the level of standardization or customization.

Therefore, our main research goal is to identify a set of common service dimensions feasible to characterize IT outsourcing operations and identify input and output variables to calculate efficiency ratios and facilitate comparisons between service operations in order to select the best practices and standardize those same practices, which will allow operations and costs optimization.

In this study the authors try to explore what variables can be used to determine the efficiency in IT outsourcing contracts. A nonparametric method based on mathematical programming technique, Data Envelopment Analysis (DEA) (Charnes, Cooper, & Rhodes, 1978) was used.

DEA compares each unit in terms of its abilities to convert inputs into outputs with all other units and computes (through linear programming) an efficiency score based on the ratio of outputs and inputs, establishing a rank among the contracts as well as discovering which dimension (the less performing one) has to be improved. The DEA method offers many opportunities for an inefficient unit (underperforming contracts) to become efficient regarding its reference set of efficient units (Charnes & al, 1994). DEA has already proven its usefulness in several service sectors and industries, but no study investigating their applicability in IT outsourcing performance measurement has so far been reported. It is, therefore, worthwhile to extend the traditional DEA models into IT outsourcing efficiency, a topic for academic and organizational enrichment.

This research was conducted using Design Science Research Methodology (DSRM) that aims at creating and evaluating artifacts to solve relevant organizational problems (Hevner A., March, Park, & Ram, 2004). The steps of DSRM are reflected in the sections of this research.

The paper proceeds as follows. Section 2 presents the related work. Section 3 presents the research problem. Section 4 details the research methodology. Section 5 explains in detail the developed artifact. Section 6 presents the artifact demonstration. Section 7 describes the evaluation. Finally, in Section 8 the conclusions that emerge from the present research work are presented as well as future research.

RELATED WORK

For IT outsourcing providers, each contract has unique aspects that are difficult to measure. Some clients keep their own on-site staff, equipment ownership and responsibility for part of the services, while others totally rely on service providers (Cullen, Seddon, & Willcocks, 2005).

Given the range of possibilities, it is not usually simple to identify the variables and cost drivers to be measured during an IT outsourcing life cycle, in order to have standard performance indicators across different IT outsourcing contracts.

The existing research, although complete, is not clear about which service dimensions and service items to consider when configuring a service operation that serve multiple clients through the use of complex service systems composed of people, technology, and information.

Therefore, in order to search for those constructs, the authors have researched on the existing service operations literature that give a helpful insight into the ways services are produced and consumed; for instance, Lynn Shostack (1987) identified both complexity and divergence as concepts that are employed as a service scale. Silvestro (1992) studied service classifications based on volume, e.g. the number of customers processed per day in a specific service dimension. Johnston (2008) correlated high-capability and high-commodity processes, and attempted to present an effective area for service delivery. Glushko (2010) completed research on the types of service encounters (person-to-person and system-to-person) and proposed a service model framework to increase service customization through the use of technology.

On IT outsourcing literature, the authors found some frameworks and approaches that provide a helpful insight into service items search as well as performance measurement.

The history of IT outsourcing goes back to the 1960s (Hirschheim, George, & Wong, 2004), since then, the decision to use external entities to manage internal information systems and the people that operate them represent an option for many organizations to optimize costs and operations. According to Willcocks and Lacity (1998) *"Handing over to third-party management of IT/IS assets, resources and/ or activities for a required result"*. As indicated by Hancox and Hackney (2000), *"precise definitions of information technology (IT) outsourcing differ in the literature, but there is general agreement that it is the carrying out of IT functions by third parties"*.

Therefore, the appeal for outsourcing is simple, organizations want to reduce operational costs, obtain higher efficiency standards and enhance operational flexibility, enabling them to respond to ever-changing market conditions. In this sense, IT outsourcing service providers must ensure that they have all the necessary tools to delivery services according to client specificity and that are committed to the value co-creation by exploring the benefits and mitigating the risks of an IT outsourcing arrangement, since IT is part of the organization business strategy (Ward & Griffits, 1996).

However, in IT outsourcing services, there is no "one size fits all" approach, since each contract reflects the idiosyncrasies of the relation created between provider that applies a competence and a client that integrates the applied competences with other resources, co-creating value (Spohrer, Vargo, Caswell, & Maglio, 2008).

According to Stern (Stern & Deimler, 2006), *"One of the primary tactical decisions a manager must make is how performance will be measured."* Performance measurement can be defined as the process of quantifying the efficiency and effectiveness of actions. Thus, the measurement function is to develop a method for generating a class of information (metrics) that will be useful in a variety of problems and situations (Neely, Gregory, & Platts, 2005).

One of the most known methods for performance measurement in organizations is the balanced scorecard (Kaplan & Cooper, 1998), which allows performance measure and reporting.

In IT outsourcing, Domberger (2000) measured performance in two fronts, the desired performance (client expectation of service quality prior to awarding a contract) and the realized performance (that can be referred to as effective performance). Necessarily, contract management involves realized performance assessment.

Cullen (2009) developed the IT outsourcing contract scorecard based on four vectors (quality, finance, relationship and strategy) to measure contract success through a set of key performance indicators based on accomplished goals and descriptive statistics.

Thus, in IT outsourcing literature, performance and efficiency measurement focuses on the post-contract management reporting, in which a report is delivered by the provider when problems are detected in contract execution (mainly at the operational level). This guarantees that communication to senior management is done in a quick and efficient manner (Matthew, 1996), using IT service management (ITSM) frameworks, like ITIL (Addy, 2007).

Frameworks like ITIL provide broad guidelines to reach the highest number of practitioners and to allow organizations to adapt to their own reality. However, IT services efficiency measurement in ITIL is generally based on a set of performance indicators expressed as ratios, like the ratio of an output over an input, as presented in (1).

$$Efficiency = \frac{Output}{Input} \qquad (1)$$

For instance, through the ratio of the number of servers divided by the number of technicians, the number of technicians per server is obtained. Other examples are unit cost per output (total cost divided by units produced); labour productivity (number of completed transactions divided by number of labour hours); cycle time (number of days to complete job orders divided by number of job orders completed).

This type of efficiency ratios are found in IT management literature (Keyes, 2005; Alison Cartlidge, 2007; Axelos, 2011),

When there are multiple inputs and outputs, it becomes difficult to use formula (1). Therefore, in the presence of multiple inputs and outputs, the efficiency score can be calculated using the "weighted cost approach" given by (2).

$$Efficiency = \frac{Weighted\,Sum\,of\,Outputs}{Weighted\,Sum\,of\,Inputs} \qquad (2)$$

However, this type of ratio provides limited analysis, since it assumes that all weights are uniform, which is not true as many times there is a complex relationship and tradeoffs between inputs and outputs (Sherman & Zhu, 2006).

According to Sherman, *Ratios can provide very useful managerial information about efficiency; however, they are incapable of accommodating multiple inputs and outputs when accurate objective relative weights for inputs and outputs are not known* (Sherman & Zhu, 2006, p. 57).

To mitigate this limitation, Farrell (1957) introduced a new measure for (technical) efficiency, which employs the concept of the efficient production function. This method measures the relative efficiency of the individual units known as decision making units (DMUs), which can be an organization, a contract, or a store. Each of these has a number of inputs used to produce several outputs and consists in comparing that entity with a hypothetically perfectly efficient entity represented by the production function.

The efficient production function is some postulated standard of perfect efficiency and is defined as the output that a perfectly efficient entity could obtain from any given combination of inputs.

The first step in calculating the technical efficiency through this method is to determine the efficient production function, which can be done in two ways: via a theoretical function or via an empirical function. On the one hand, the problem of using a theoretical function is that it is very difficult to define a realistic theoretical function for a complex process. On the other, the empirical production function is estimated from inputs and outputs observations of a number of entities. Therefore, it is easier to compare performances to the best actually achieved (the empirical production function) than to compare them to some unattainable ideal (the theoretical function) (Mishra, 2012). Consequently, when there are multiple inputs and outputs to be considered, efficiency measurement can be done through the Data Envelopment Analysis (DEA) developed by Charnes et al (1978) that is based on Farrell's work.

Thnassoulis (1996) compared DEA to ratio analysis as alternative tools for assessing the performance of organisational units that use one or more resources (inputs) to obtain one or more outputs whereas the inputs and/or outputs are possibly unequal. The comparison focuses on how well the two methods agree on the performance of units. Thnassoulis concludes that the suitability of both methods depends on the way inputs, outputs and ratios are combined into a summary of performance indicators of individual units.

Additionally, the use of standard ratios does not provide any target suggestion for input variables while DEA models do because of their linear programming structure.

DEA has been successfully applied as a major tool for efficiency measurement in several business operations (Charnes & al, 1994; Zhu, 2000; Sherman & Zhu, 2006; Mishra, 2012) but has never been used in the IT outsourcing literature.

RESEARCH PROBLEM

The aim of this paper is to solve a real problem faced by IT outsourcing providers. An IT outsourcing contract can be based on one IT service (single service contract) or in many IT services (multi-service contract), therefore providers need to know the set of service items feasible to use in service configuration and the corresponding set of input and output variables in order to achieve efficiency.

Therefore, efficiency measurement must be done through methods capable of dealing with several inputs and outputs. Yet, the most used technique to calculate efficiency in IT services is based on simple ratios as presented in (1) and (2) (Keyes, 2005, p. 45; Addy, 2007; Axelos, 2011). Thus, an approach suitable to deal with multiple input and output variables is Data Envelopment Analysis (DEA) (Charnes, Cooper, & Rhodes, 1978).

Consequently, this research is based on investigating what service items can be used to configure an IT outsourcing operation and research the applicability of DEA to IT outsourcing performance measurement so as to research what new data can be obtained for management enrichment.

RESEARCH METHODOLOGY

This research was conducted using Design Science Research Methodology (DSRM) that aims to create and evaluate IT artifacts intended to solve identified organizational problems. These artifacts include constructs (vocabulary and symbols), models (abstractions and representations), methods (algorithms and practices) and instantiations (implemented and prototype systems) (Hevner A., March, Park, & Ram, 2004). The steps of DSRM are: problem identification and motivation; objectives of a solution definition; design and development; demonstration; evaluation; and communication (Peffers, Tuunanen, Rothenberger, & Chatterjee, 2007).

This research approach, following Peffers (2007) guide for DSRM includes the following phases: problem identification, objectives definition, design and development, demonstration, evaluation and communication. Figure 1 depicts DSRM methodology that was employed to address the particular characteristics of this research. This cycle can be repeated as many times as necessary to achieve the research goal.

Therefore, this methodology has been chosen because DSRM is appropriate to researches that seek to extend the boundaries of human and organizational capabilities by creating new and innovative artifacts, enabling the solution of relevant problems.

PROPOSAL

According to DSRM, this section is used to present the proposed model and its components in order to answer the research problem. Therefore, the following subsections present the variables, assumptions and functions that constitute our model.

The challenge for service efficiency is that productivity and perceived quality are seen as an inseparable phenomenon. Therefore, it is often claimed that quality and productivity cannot be improved at

Figure 1. Design Science Research Methodology (DSRM) process model
(Peffers, Tuunanen, Rothenberger, & Chatterjee, 2007)

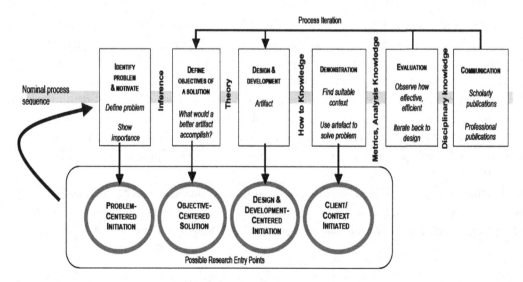

same time. Thus delivering services to clients in minimal time and maximal reliability has been found to be the most critical factor influencing service quality perceptions and satisfaction (Parasuraman, Zeithaml, & Berry, 1988).

Therefore, in order to have standard performance indicators, across different IT outsourcing contracts providers must know the set of service dimensions and service items that contribute for service configuration.

Consequently, those service items will have a set of input and output variables, allowing building a model to assess service efficiency. This model allows identifying what cost should be minimized, what contracts presents higher divergence, (in human resources and processes), and what contract is generating more revenue. To achieve these goals the authors, propose to use Data Envelopment Analysis (DEA).

In the following sections, the authors present the several service items that were considered relevant in an IT outsourcing operation; grouped by service dimensions, followed by the input and output variables framed within DEA approach.

IT Outsourcing Service Dimensions and Service Items

The next sections detail the service items existent in an IT outsourcing operation grouped by the following service dimensions: a) *Service interactions*, in which people and systems integrate the value created in the different service contexts and interactions; b) *Demand and workload variance*, provides the data for capacity management in order to ensure a constant service delivery; c) *Service delivery variance*, must be used with the ability to adapt to market changes and client requirements; d) *Service data*, summarizes the logical means necessary to deliver the services, like databases, meta-data and records all relevant data about the client and service; e) *The service package*, summarizes the physical means necessary to deliver the services; f) *Service quality*, encloses the methodologies and techniques used by the provider to guarantee service quality, for instance the standard ISO20000; g) *Service financials*, is the dimension, in which, providers manage service cost and service price.

In the next sub sections, these dimensions and the respective service items are detailed.

Service Interaction

Considering that the customer is part of the service production process, providers need to account for and map all the touch points and variance related to customer interaction, therefore, the authors present customer interaction as a dimension with the following service items:

1. **Service Interface:** The interface type between customer and supplier (From Automated to Human). This item links the highest human intervention for customization and the highest automation possible for standardization. Today, thanks to technology, it is possible to use mass customization.
2. **Service Communication:** This has the purpose of managing all types of communications between provider and client; in this case, the authors intend to refer to the tags given to service communication, such as incident, change request, new request, broadcast information, segmented information, client information.
3. **Type of Site:** This item intends to identify which type of site is covered by the service, allowing the provider to identify if all client sites have the same treatment and SLA or if, inside the client scope, different sites can have different treatment, e.g. a central building versus a branch.

4. **Contact Time Per Interaction:** Generally, higher times of client contact happens in customized contracts, in which, the client has a dedicated service manager. On the other hand, with standardized contracts, the client only takes up the provider's time in case of need. This amount of time is measured in a specific unit of time (seconds, minutes, hours) per interaction.

Demand and Workload Variance

A frequent problem for providers is the difficulty in managing flexible demand. According to Kotler and Armstrong (2009), market analysis is always necessary to estimate capacity, so as to analyze the evolution of the customer's business and to evaluate how stable the volume of demand will be.

Providers can manage demand by trying to shape the behavior of users, for instance, by offering tools and guidance to help them solve problems by themselves, e.g. an IT knowledge base or service desk platform, which will register for future analysis the sources of demand and problems.

This dimension was found on (Shostack, 1987; Chase & Aquilano, 1992; Silvestro, Fitzgerald, Johnston, & Voss, 1992; Cullen, Seddon, & Willcocks, 2005; Johnston & Graham, 2008; Fitzsimmons & Fitzsimmons, 2010), and is related to the amount of work necessary to perform a certain task relating to human or machinery labor. For his dimension, the authors propose the following service items:

1. **Volume for Service Requests:** Which represent the estimated value that the provider predict for service delivery, based on data gathered or provided by client.
2. **Volume for Service Incidents:** Which represent the estimated value that the provider predict for incidents during a certain period of service delivery, based on statistical data.
3. **Service Team Workload:** Represents the human resources necessary for service execution during the several phases of an IT outsourcing contract.
4. **Service Infrastructure/Machinery Workload:** Represents the physical resources necessary for service execution during the several phases of an IT outsourcing contract, i.e. servers, routers, LAN, desktops, among other resources.
5. **Contract Duration:** This item influences directly the volume of resources used since it represents the service delivery period.

Service Delivery Variance

The service delivery variance is related to how and when a service changes between clients and between service deliveries. The variance level can affect the effort in adapting processes, people and infrastructure (Shostack, 1987; Schmenner, 1986; Johnston & Graham, 2008; Fitzsimmons & Fitzsimmons, 2010). This dimension leads to two service items:

1. **Client Requisites Variance:** How predictable the changes in client requirements are? Leading to provider process variance;
2. **Service Delivery Variance:** How predictable the changes in service deliveries are? Service deliveries are all equal? or exist internal/ or external factors that change the service delivery?

In order to mitigate the risk associated to variance, service providers can mitigate variance by cross-training employees in several technologies, in order to create a more flexible work force (Fitzsimmons & Fitzsimmons, 2010).

Another approach to follow is hardware standardization, as less diversity and higher stability in hardware use (using the same model of hardware over a long period of time) allows for better repair times and logistic operations optimization. One example is the use of pre-configured assets for field-force teams for incident repair. The drawback of this type of standardization, which can be based on technology, maker or market segment, is that it forces the provider to reduce its hardware portfolio, affecting the idiosyncrasies of certain clients.

Service Data

This dimension is related to the use of data, during service delivery, therefore, this service item, *the service record*, allows for the recording of all client data and interactions for posterior customer relationship management and analytics. This item is central in any of today's service systems, and can be the base of a customer-relationship management (CRM) system or an operational component based on incident management and service requests, supported by a management database (MDB) or configuration management database (CMDB).

Service Package

The Service package dimension is related to the resources that are used to deliver the service. For the provider, each service operation has unique characteristics. Some customers keep their own on-site staff, equipment ownership and responsibility for part of the services, while others rely totally on the provider.

Given the range of possibilities, it is not usually simple to identify the exact service configuration, thus, the following service items are proposed:

1. **Supporting Facilities (SF):** The facilities needed for service execution in the front office (FO) or in the back office (BO). This item can have the following values: totally shared; partially shared or totally dedicated (Fitzsimmons & Fitzsimmons, 2010).
2. **Facilitating Goods (FG):** These are objects that allow or facilitate service execution. They may belong to the vendor or to the client, and may allow greater customization. This item can have the following values: all provided by provider; partially provided; partially owned by client; or all provided by client (Fitzsimmons & Fitzsimmons, 2010).
3. **Asset Ownership:** This item identifies who owns the asset used in service execution.
4. **Asset Specificity (AS):** This item identifies a certain specificity for service execution (e.g. INTEL Server, IBM AS400, Unix).
5. **The Service Portfolio:** This item is related to the provider's service offering and identifies whether a service works alone or is based on other provider services. (Addy, 2007; Fitzsimmons & Fitzsimmons, 2010; Cullen, Seddon, & Willcocks, 2005).

Service Quality

The work of Parasuraman is essential for service quality analysis, thus delivering services to clients in minimal time and maximal reliability has been found to be the most critical factor influencing service quality (Parasuraman, Zeithaml, & Berry, 1988; Parasuraman & Zeithaml, 2002; Parasuraman, Zeithaml, & Malhotra, 2005). However, quality in IT outsourcing services has other variables that need to be know and managed. Therefore, for this dimension, several items were studied and identified.

1. **ITIL Service Level Agreement (SLA) Framework:** Which has three levels (service based SLA; multi-level service based SLA and customer based SLA) (Axelos, 2011), SLAs also contribute to service and cost variance because they vary among contracts and operations. Thus, the use of incident templates for known incidents and the normalization of the client's infrastructure is a best-practice approach, in order to allow the provider to execute the service efficiently. Such examples are normalized hardware, a platform for remote monitoring, and a platform for hardware operation among others.

2. **Service Penalties:** In any service contract, a penalty schedule exists (Cullen, 2009). As a result, penalties are also negotiated and adapted to exist in a service operation (e.g. standard repair time in next business day vs. tailored repair time in four hours) (Addy, 2007; Taylor & et-all, 2007).

3. **Governance Model:** A relevant service item in IT managed contracts, namely IT outsourcing. Thus general law often regulates the standard contracts, and tailored governance models are used in customized contracts (Cullen, 2009).

4. **Innovation:** A distinctive item in service operations with benefits for clients (Willcocks & Lacity, 2012) and it is also possible to specifically determine if something is a standardized innovation, based on a company's general rules, or if it is a tailored innovation for a specific contract.

5. **Service Catalogue:** This item identifies whether a service catalogue covers the full contract scope or only part of it. For instance, in a multi-service contract for help-desk, field support and server administration, the existing standard service catalogue can be only applicable for help-desk requests, and for the remaining services a specific service catalogue is created (Taylor & et-all, 2007). Thus, to both types of service catalogue we call respectively "Service catalogue" and "Contract catalogue".

6. **Supplier or Third-Party Dependence:** Dependence on third parties for service delivery is an operational risk (Fitzsimmons & Fitzsimmons, 2010); therefore, the goal of this item is to identify the presence of external suppliers. The authors have assumed that the higher the level of customization, the higher the dependence on external entities. One way providers can analyze this dependence is by taking the number of services provided by external providers and dividing it by the total number of services delivered to the final client.

Service Financials

A financial service dimension was included in the set of service dimensions and comprises two service items; cost and price, both of which contribute to the main purpose in private business organizations, which is to be profitable (Jensen & Meckling, 1976), consequently the following service items are presented:

1. **Service Costing:** This item is important, as a well-chosen cost-accounting method can allow for a better service sustainability. For instance service provider can use one of the following methods: Resource Cost Accounting (RCA), a suitable approach for standardization, followed by the Time driven ABC (T-ABC) and Activity Based Costing (ABC) (Kaplan & Cooper, 1998), and then the standard cost allocation for the highest level of customization.
2. **Service Pricing:** This item is essential for service revenue. In IT outsourcing contracts several price types can be used (Correia dos Santos & Mira da Silva, 2015).

The importance of the above items is that they allow several levels of configuration, giving providers the ability to manage customization and standardization according to provider goals and customer requirements.

To resume the first part of our proposal, the authors have summarized the service dimensions and service items proposed in Figure 2.

The constructs here found that all are bound by the fact that there is no right or wrong way to configure a service operation, as different organizations will have different preferences and approaches (Maglio, Kieliszewski, & Spohrer, 2010).

For instance, banking industry is urging the clients to use the internet to take care of regular bank transactions instead of coming to a bank in person. Insurance companies are establishing call centers for customer service, so that customers should interact over the telephone. Then, if customers perceive that they get the same quality or better quality than before, these changes have been successful.

Figure 2. Service dimensions and service items proposed

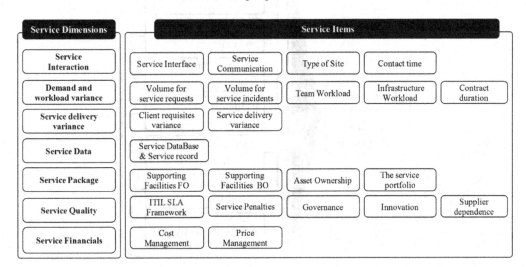

Therefore, providers must configure services, according to client requisites and their own goals that can lead to a more standardized or more customized service, since; each contract can have a different configuration. Consequently, process efficiency control to ensure that service operations are under control is essential, thus to achieve that the DEA technique is used.

Efficiency Measurement Through Data Envelopment Analysis

The DEA technique is used to find the set of coefficients that will give the maximum possible efficiency ratio of outputs to inputs for the organizational unit under evaluation. Since DEA solutions are sensitive to inaccuracies in the data, the adequateness of DMUs' inputs and outputs are essential for success (Sherman & Zhu, 2006). The proposed DEA model for IT outsourcing performance measurement follows the steps illustrated in Figure 3.

In the following paragraphs the several steps proposed are described considering their use in IT outsourcing operations.

Select Meaningful Decision Making Units (DMUs)

The selection of DMUs is based on the identification of particular characteristics of the problem under analysis. A DMU needs to be sufficiently similar so that the comparison makes sense. If DMUs are not comparable, then a separate analysis should be performed for each different set (Charnes & al, 1994).

For an IT outsourcing operation, which in some cases is based on a multi-service contract, some difficulties arise when choosing the right DMU, mainly due to the fact that some services are interrelated and difficult to split. For instance, in a multiservice-contract, a first line support for help-desk component

Figure 3. DEA modelling steps based on (Charnes & al, 1994)

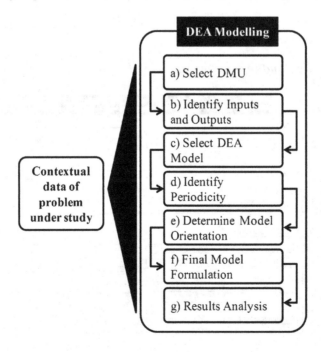

can provide shared support to several IT services allowing resources optimization, like end-user Support, printing and application support. On the other hand, in single service contracts, like end-user support that needs a first line support, optimization and scale effects are lower.

Consequently, this proposal is based on two possible approaches: a) The IT outsourcing operation is treated as a unique DMU for the several service types included; b) The DMU is based only on one IT service type (e.g. Printing or Telco, or end-user support), avoiding the risk of comparing different IT services. Both approaches can aggregate several inputs and outputs. This way, practitioners must select the DMU according the type of IT service to compare, meaning that inputs and outputs of multi-service contracts must be summed up. Single service contracts, to be comparable, must be based on the same type of IT service.

Identify Adequate Inputs and Outputs

In IT outsourcing operations the set of inputs and outputs selected should be inter-correlated. However, in some cases input variables may not be under management direct control. For example, an input variable such as; fixed expenditures (rent of facilities, amortization value of investments) could not be proportionally reduced as would be the case for variable expenditures, such as human resources (HR), energy consumption, or service platforms based on cloud computing infrastructure.

As a result, it is important to identify the variables that are discretionary (variable costs) versus non-discretionary (fixed costs), in order to evaluate them between DMUs. As stated by Sherman, "*when more than one input and/or output are involved in the production process, inefficiencies can also be due to the mix of inputs used to produce the mix of outputs, which is referred to as allocative efficiency*" (Sherman & Zhu, 2006, p. 55).

For input variables, which are fixed (such as a fixed cost), an input constraint must be entered to prevent input data reduction on the fixed value by the linear program, since if it is fixed, it must stay so.

Another attribute with impact on variables is weighting. In the absence of previous knowledge about the weights (*vi, ur*) associated with inputs *i* and outputs *r*, the DEA model allows each DMU to choose "freely" the weights of its inputs and outputs in order to maximize its own efficiency score, which will force DEA to assume those values as baseline.

On the other hand, in those IT service contracts that have a predetermined baseline, for instance for the number of human resources (HR) in the service team, the weighting can be used to establish the limit of reduction or increase. However, this facility should not be over-used, or the analysis will have its scope for optimisation severely reduced.

In addition, a different attribute of the variables is the level of control that organizations have over the occurrence of that variable (Banker & Morey, 1986), which can be controllable (hours worked) or uncontrollable (incidents occurred).

Knowing these basic rules for DEA variables selection, practitioners must understand the intrinsic characteristics of the variables to select. Five types of input and two types of output were chosen as candidates for the analysis performed in this study (Figure 4).

In Table 1, the variables used (inputs and outputs) to characterize an IT outsourcing operation are summarized. The subsequent paragraphs explain the variable selection.

Figure 4. The conceptual input-output framework proposed

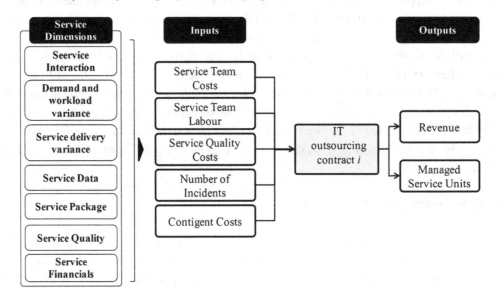

Input Variables Justification

Human Resources

In any type of service, service delivery and service quality require resource allocation and resource planning (Li, Field, Jiang, He, & Pang, 2015). Consequently, for IT outsourcing services the human workforce is essential.

Therefore, the HR variable is an input variable. HR labour can be measured in several ways, so some assumptions have to be made.

Firstly, total HR costs reported (wages, extra labour, fringe benefits) can be misleading because, in IT services, labour salaries are heterogeneous, and can vary according date of hiring and/ or on skill set; for instance, a specialised call centre technician is more expensive than a field support technician; thus this difference will create problems if wages are the only measure. Furthermore, even in the presence of cost minimization and identical production functions for all units, total labour cost will vary across DMUs.

Secondly, the use of team size as the only measure of HR would result in poor analysis of cost/benefit.

Thirdly, another possible approach would be to use a composed input, which would be the total wages multiplied by total service team per DMU. However, this means the DEA analysis would be limited and, consequently, if data are not well decomposed, they can jeopardize the results obtained.

Finally, the authors decided to use two input variables related to HR: *Service Team Costs (STC)*, which is the total HR costs, and *Service Team Labour (STL)*, which is a composed variable based on service team size multiplied by the total of hours worked.

This way deeper analysis of efficiency is possible, due to existence of a variable cost and a variable volume, both associated to HR, which is a central dimension in IT outsourcing operations.

Table 1. Proposed inputs and outputs

DMU	Type of Data	Variable	Measured as	Unit	Controllable/ Uncontrollable	Weighting
IT Service	Inputs	Service Team Costs (STC)	These costs include all the costs associated with the labour necessary to manage client solution.	Monetary unit	Controllable	Free
		Service Team Labour (STL)	Labour of service team, obtained by the number of hours of effective work of people, per contract per month.	Man-hour	Controllable	Free
		Service Quality Costs (SQC)	Costs of service quality to be compliant with client requirements: service levels and reporting (governance, service levels, Innovation). Costs with the service infrastructure.	Monetary unit	Controllable	Free
		Number of Incidents (NI)	The volume of incidents occurred in a specific period of time.	Total of occurrences	Uncontrollable	Free
		Contingent Costs (CC)	The costs occurred (service penalties) due to service outage.	Monetary unit	Uncontrollable	Free
	Outputs	Revenue (R)	Total revenue per DMU (IT service). Sum of all IT Services (1 to N) in which service item price has an essential role.	Monetary unit	Controllable	
		Managed Service Units (MSU)	Total of managed service units related to the DMU (IT service) under analysis.	Total of units managed	Controllable	

Infrastructure and Quality

After selecting HR input related variables, other input variables were identified, mainly associated to service infrastructure and service quality: *Service Quality Costs (SQC)*. These include contract governance, service levels achievement through a dedicated or shared service platform, and reporting.

The other two variables proposed are: *Number of Incidents (NI)*, the volume of incidents that occurred in a specific period of time; and *Contingent Costs (CC)*, the costs occurred due to service outage and service penalties.

Generally quality variables are assigned to overhead accounts rather than to a specific contract. Notwithstanding, in our research the objective was to identify these variables per DMU, since usually a DMU with a high number of incidents and high contingent costs is prone to efficiency increase.

Output Variables Justification

Revenue

For output variables two variables were selected. *Revenue (R)*, which is a variable, used in many DEA studies. However, if revenue is based on a fixed price, this factor can turn inefficient contracts into efficient ones. This is not wrong or bad if we intend to analyse costs and incomes, but it can lead to erroneous analysis related solely with operational efficiency, which will be demonstrated in the following section.

Managed Service Units

Therefore, in order to analyse only operational efficiency with accurate metrics, a different variable was used: the number of *Managed Service Units (MSU)*, which can be the total number of users, servers, routers, workstations, and any other applicable unit. These units are managed by the service team identified in the input variables and are framed in the quality thresholds defined. By using this output, it is possible to analyse which team is more efficient, and which contract has fewer incidents, and like so identify, disseminate and standardize best practices.

1. **Select the Type of DEA Model to Use:** According to Charnes et al (1994) practitioners should select the most appropriate type of DEA model for the problem under analysis. In outsourcing deals, economies of scale, derived from TCE theory (Williamson, 1985), are a major argument used by providers to enhance outsourcing virtues. As a result, the BCC model (Banker, Charnes, & Cooper, 1984) with variable returns of scale (VRS) was the one chosen for our proposal seeing as it allows the use of economies of scale for operational efficiency. This model allows the maximization of outputs and the minimization of inputs.
2. **Periodicity of DMU Observations**: In many cases DMUs are observed only once, like in a benchmarking study (Homburg, 2001). Nevertheless, observations for DMUs are frequently available over multiple time periods also named as windows analysis (time series data) (Golany & Storbeck, 1999). IT outsourcing contracts occur in a multi-year period, and it is important to perform an analysis where changes in efficiency over time can be identified, since providers tend to optimize operations. To answer this particularity using DEA and keeping our formulation over time by using a moving average analogue, each different period is treated as if it were a "different" DMU. Thus,

a DMU performance in a particular period is contrasted with its performance in other periods, in addition to the performance of other DMUs. This approach was first suggested by (Charnes & al, 1994).

3. **Model Orientation:** To decide if a model orientation is for Maximization or Minimization, simple questions can be made. For example: given the level of outputs that a DMU produces, how much could their use of inputs have been reduced while maintaining their current level of outputs? The answer to this question tells us this is an input minimization model. On the other hand, given the level of inputs used by a DMU, what level of outputs should they have achieved? The answer to this question tells us that this is an output maximization orientation. Therefore, the resolution of a DEA model can be done by minimizing inputs, by maximizing outputs, or both through an additive model (Charnes & al, 1994, p. 427). In IT outsourcing contracts, generally there are two types of outputs: financial (revenue) and the volume of managed service units (managed equipments, servers, users). Given that DEA works with observable data, and an IT outsourcing contract is a long-term relationship in which the price (revenue) is mainly fixed (Cullen, Seddon, & Willcocks, 2005), our proposed model is input oriented. Consequently, it will have as its main purpose to minimize inputs for the same level of outputs.

4. **Final Model Formulation:** Based on previous assumptions, the DMU's scores were calculated using the formulations presented below:

j = number of DMUs being evaluated in the DEA analysis (3).

SU_j = service unit number j.

θ = efficiency rating of the service unit being evaluated by DEA.

y_{rj} = amount of output r used by service unit j.

x_{ij} = amount of input i used by service unit j.

i = number of inputs used by the DMUs.

r = number of outputs generated by the DMUs.

u_r = coefficient or weight assigned by DEA to output r.

v_i = coefficient or weight assigned by DEA to input i.

After (3) in which the variables notation is presented, the proposed DEA model is based on a cycle that is executed j times to evaluate the relative efficiency score of a set of j DMUs, with each *DMUj* (j = 1,. . .,n). If we consider using i inputs $x_{ij} (i = 1,. . .,m)$, generating r outputs $y_{rj} (r = 1,. . ., s)$, then the weight v_i and u_r associated with inputs i and outputs r will be optimally determined by maximizing or minimizing (in our case it will be minimizing) the efficiency score of the targeted *DMUj*.

An efficiency score of one indicates that the targeted DMU is efficient when compared to another DMU and so lies on the efficiency frontier, which is composed by the set of efficient DMUs. An efficiency score of less than one indicates the targeted DMU is inefficient, and consequently prone to improvement.

As stated before, the major argument for adhering to IT outsourcing is that customers have access to the provider's economies of scale. The CCR model assumes the constant return to scale (CRS) characteristic, which is not coincident with economies of scale. Thus, to mitigate this issue, the BCC model developed by Banker et al. (1984), must be used, since it uses variable returns to scale (VRS) characteristic.

The BCC model adds an additional variable $u\theta$ to identify the returns of scale of the targeted DMU.

The difference between the CCR model and the BCC model present in (4) is the $»_i$ variable that is restricted to summing one, so the VRS is identical to the CRS with an additional constraint added to the LP problem. These results in the removal of the constraint in the CCR model that dictates DMUs must be scale efficient.

Consequently, the BCC model allows variable returns to scale and measures only technical efficiency for each DMU. That is, for a DMU to be considered as CCR efficient, it must be both scale and technically efficient. For a DMU to be considered BCC efficient, it only needs to be technically efficient. The BCC linear programming model is presented in formula (4).

Min θ The BCC Model (4)

$$\sum_{i=1}^{n} \lambda_i x_j - \theta x_{j0} \leq 0, \quad \forall j$$

$$\sum_{i=1}^{n} \lambda_i y_j - y_{j0} \geq 0, \quad \forall k$$

$$\lambda_j \geq 0 \qquad \qquad \forall i$$

$$\sum_i \lambda_i = 1$$

Where θ = *Efficiency Score*

λ_i = *Dual Variable*

5. **Results Analysis:** After model formulation, its execution produces a set of results that need to be interpreted to decide actions to take (Mahgary & Lahdelma, 1995).

The first analysis to be made is the number of DMUs to be included, since it needs to be sufficiently large so that discrimination between units is possible. The selection of input and output items is crucial for the successful application of DEA. Therefore, the process of selecting a small set of input and output items at the beginning and gradually enlarging the set to observe the effects of the added items is generally recommended (Sherman & Zhu, 2006).

If the number of DMUs (*j*) is less than the combined number of inputs and outputs, a large portion of the DMUs will be identified as efficient, and efficiency discrimination among DMUs is lost.

Hence, it is desirable that *j* exceeds the sum of *i* and *r* by several times as higher units to *input/output* ratio provide better results (Sherman & Zhu, 2006).

Secondly, the time frame under analysis must be as a long as possible, since the time period may hide important changes taking place, and a time period too small may not give a complete assessment of the DMUs' performance.

Thirdly, the use of BCC model allows the use of the VRS characteristic, which in turn allows the calculation of Technical Efficiency (TE), avoiding Scale Efficiency (SE) effects. Thus, SE (5) can be calculated by estimating both the CRS and VRS models and by looking at the difference in scores. The TE scores are identical under CRS models, but they can differ under VRS.

$$SE_j = TE_{CRS} / TE_{VRS} \tag{5}$$

Finally, after DMUs efficiency identification, targets can be set for the inefficient contracts to enable them to reach 100% relative efficiency. Since DMUs operate under similar circumstances, to use the best performance as input target is a realistic assumption (Mishra, 2012).

Thus, the input target (6) for an inefficient unit is the amount of input used by that DMU to produce the same level of output so as to make the DMU efficient.

$$Input\,Target_j = Actual\,Input_j * Efficiency_j \tag{6}$$

For inefficient DMUs, the input target will be smaller than the actual input. The difference between actual input and input target is the input slack. The input slack for an inefficient DMU is presented in (7).

$$Input\,Slack_j = Actual\,Input_j - Input\,Target_j \tag{7}$$

The proposed model in this work intends to calculate the minimal values that input variables can assume to generate the same level of outputs. The proposed variables represent the managed services component present in all types of IT outsourcing contracts.

The variables related to asset acquisition or renting were left out of our model, since we assumed that all contracts share the same type of infrastructure. The proposed model will be demonstrated in the next section.

Demonstration

This section corresponds to the demonstration step of DSRM, in which we validate that our proposal can be used to solve one or more instances of the stated problem. A sample constituted by 18 (eighteen) IT outsourcing service contracts was used. The data was gathered and assembled according to our proposed model in order to measure IT outsourcing operations efficiency. The data used is presented in Table 2.

The technical efficiency score has been calculated using Variable Return to Scale (VRS) so a BCC DEA model was executed. The periodicity studied was based on a single period due to the lack of historical data available in the format requested by our model. The tool used was Excel solver, following guidelines published in Sherman and Zhu (2006). Other software tools available could be used, namely: Frontier analysis, GAMS, or MATLAB.

Using all the data from Table 2, the first DEA simulation was executed, obtaining the efficiency scores for the 18 DMUs. Nine DMUs were identified with a (100%) score of technical efficiency, which means they operate at the most productive scale size. However, other nine DMUs still have potential for efficiency improvement.

The technical efficiency average score obtained through VRS model was (0.9311), indicating scope for improvement, which implies that on average DMUs could have used (6,89%) fewer resources to produce the same amount of output.

Nonetheless, a deeper results analysis is possible since several DMUs are inefficient, thus scoring between (1.0) and (0.9)DMU7, DMU8, and DMU17. Scoring more than (0.8): DMU1, DMU3, DMU14, DMU15. Scoring more than (0.7) DMU4, DMU5. Results from the first simulation can be analysed in Table 3.

Additionally, to test the stability of the results obtained, a standard procedure in DEA analysis was performed. A few efficient DMUs were deleted, namely (13, 16, 18), and again efficiency scores were computed and the results found to be stable.

Table 2. Quantities of inputs and outputs for each DMU

		Inputs					Outputs
Contracts - (DMUs)	Service Team-cost (STC)	Service Team- labour (STL)	Service quality-cost	Number of incidents (NI)	Contingent costs (CC)	Revenue (R)	Managed Serv. Units (MSU)
DMU 1	16.119,00	1.176	1.785,70	230	1.611,90	19.600,00	850
DMU 2	103.000,00	5.544	12.438,00	640	4.120,00	127.000,00	5.500
DMU 3	4.400,00	336	488,00	170	308,00	5.600,00	400
DMU 4	5.800,00	336	682,30	80	580,00	8.300,00	380
DMU 5	5.400,00	336	607,00	60	540,00	7.100,00	220
DMU 6	3.373,00	168	330,00	30	236,11	5.840,00	360
DMU 7	3.495,00	168	300,00	35	349,50	5.700,00	340
DMU 8	10.800,00	1.008	1.200,00	113	1.080,00	13.500,00	540
DMU 9	3.495,00	336	350,00	29	244,65	4.900,00	280
DMU 10	4.400,00	840	700,00	40	440,00	7.200,00	420
DMU 11	7.200,00	3.024	1.600,00	128	288,00	10.400,00	800
DMU 12	7.350,00	504	914,00	133	514,50	14.800,00	450
DMU 13	13.000,00	2.856	1.020,00	158	1.300,00	19.300,00	540
DMU 14	4.700,00	504	400,00	60	188,00	6.700,00	380
DMU 15	3.495,00	336	345,00	45	244,65	5.500,00	120
DMU 16	1.700,00	54	120,00	35	68,00	3.700,00	80
DMU 17	3.400,00	336	560,00	68	238,00	5.600,00	300
DMU 18	6.800,00	1.008	432,00	80	272,00	9.050,00	640
MEDIAN	5.050,00	420,00	583,50	74,00	328,75	7.150,00	390,00
AVERAGE	11.551,50	1.048,33	1.348,44	118,56	701,30	15.543,89	700,00
STD	23.124,70	1.406,30	2.804,58	141,97	948,95	28.223,14	1.215,00

Table 3. DMUs efficiency score, first and second simulation

	DEA First Simulation Outputs used: Revenue and Managed Service Units			DEA Second Simulation Outputs used: Managed Service Units	
DMUs	**Efficiency Score**	**DMUs Relative Position, Ascending Order (from inefficient to efficient)**	**Efficiency Score**	**DMUs Relative Position, Ascending Order (from inefficient to efficient)**	
DMU 1	0,82559	3	0,75219	7	
DMU 2	1,00000	16	1,00000	16	
DMU 3	0,87637	6	0,87637	9	
DMU 4	0,77271	2	0,63334	4	
DMU 5	0,73612	1	0,52406	2	
DMU 6	1,00000	12	1,00000	12	
DMU 7	0,99239	9	0,99133	11	
DMU 8	0,94646	8	0,58494	3	
DMU 9	1,00000	18	1,00000	18	
DMU 10	1,00000	17	1,00000	17	
DMU 11	1,00000	14	1,00000	14	
DMU 12	1,00000	10	0,66095	5	
DMU 13	1,00000	13	0,41150	1	
DMU 14	0,85752	5	0,80490	8	
DMU 15	0,84015	4	0,71773	6	
DMU 16	1,00000	11	1,00000	13	
DMU 17	0,91335	7	0,88662	10	
DMU 18	1,00000	15	1,00000	15	

Thus, the existence of a high number of efficient DMUs does not mean that no further analysis is necessary, or that it is already good enough, since some variables (input or output) can be working for results' distortion.

Therefore, we looked for which of the Output variables could disturb the final results. By observation we assumed that the Output variable "Revenue" could be influencing the final results, because the value of those variables is related to a subjective negotiation occurred between parties and often there is not a direct relation with operational efficiency. As a result, the output variable "Revenue" was deleted from our data and another simulation was performed with only one output variable: the "Managed Service Units."

Consequently, out of 18 DMUs, 7 obtained a relatively efficient result. DMU 12 and DMU 13 lost their efficiency, compared to the first simulation. The other inefficient DMUs obtained lower results than in simulation 1. The results obtained can be observed in Table 3, in the columns under the heading "DEA Second Simulation."

These results confirm that the output variable "Revenue" makes a significant contribution to the analysis of technical efficiency. However, since revenue in Outsourcing contracts is dependent on negotiations, it is a variable that can add bias to final efficiency results. Consequently, the data obtained in the second simulation, without the "Revenue" variable, provides different results concerning operational efficiency.

Other analysis that can be made is to compare DMU's evolution. Figure 3, presents a set of DMUs, namely: 1, 12, 13, 14 and 16, which are followed across the three analysed stages. Firstly, ordered by financial margin (given by: Revenue divided by Total Cost that is formed by adding service team cost to service quality cost and contingent cost). Secondly, ordered by efficiency score obtained from first simulation that includes both output variables. Finally, the second and last simulation presents the efficiency score calculated only with the output variable managed service units.

From Figure 5 analysis, it is possible to observe that the worst margin contract is DMU 1 (with a margin of 0, 43%), however is not the worst DMU in the efficiency score, obtaining the seventh place in second simulation.

On the other hand, the DMU 13(with a margin of 25, 98%) jumps for the worst efficiency score on the second simulation with a value of (0, 41%).

The DMU 12, (with a margin of 68, 59%) on first simulation obtain an efficiency score of 1, 00, however on second simulation jumps for the fifth place on efficiency score with a value of (0, 66%).

The DMU 16, which is the contract with the lowest Total Contract Value (TCV), presents the highest margin (95, 97%) and presents an efficiency score in all simulations.

The next step was to use DEA to establish targets for input variables, in order to obtain the same level of output for the variable "Managed Service Units". The variable Revenue was ignored in this calculation.

Table 4. presents the proposed targets for input variables, and the efficiency score obtained for each DMU. Out of 18 DMUs, 12 are relatively efficient while the remaining 6 DMUs have efficiency scores higher than (0.9), which mean that even though efficiency results improved, it is not possible to obtain (100%) efficiency for all DMUs.

In Table 5 we demonstrate with greater detail the potential for efficiency improvement for two selected DMUs, DMU 1 and DMU 14.

Figure 5. DMU's evolution between simulations

Contracts - (DMUs)	Total Cost	Revenue	Margin %		1st simulation			2nd simulation	
					Contracts - (DMUs)	Efficiency Score		Contracts - (DMUs)	Efficiency Score
1	19.516,60	19.600,00	0,43%		5	0,73612		13	0,41150
8	13.080,00	13.500,00	3,21%		4	0,77271		5	0,52406
2	119.558,00	127.000,00	6,22%		1	0,82559		8	0,58494
3	5.196,00	5.600,00	7,78%		15	0,84015		4	0,63334
5	6.547,00	7.100,00	8,45%		14	0,85752		12	0,66095
11	9.088,00	10.400,00	14,44%		3	0,87637		15	0,71773
4	7.062,30	8.300,00	17,53%		17	0,91335		1	0,75219
9	4.089,65	4.900,00	19,81%		8	0,94646		14	0,80490
18	7.504,00	9.050,00	20,60%		7	0,99239		3	0,87637
13	15.320,00	19.300,00	25,98%		18	1,00000		17	0,88662
14	5.288,00	6.700,00	26,70%		16	1,00000		7	0,99133
10	5.540,00	7.200,00	29,96%		6	1,00000		18	1,00000
17	4.198,00	5.600,00	33,40%		13	1,00000		11	1,00000
15	4.084,65	5.500,00	34,65%		11	1,00000		10	1,00000
7	4.144,50	5.700,00	37,53%		12	1,00000		16	1,00000
6	3.939,11	5.840,00	48,26%		2	1,00000		6	1,00000
12	8.778,50	14.800,00	68,59%		9	1,00000		2	1,00000
16	1.888,00	3.700,00	95,97%		10	1,00000		9	1,00000

Table 4. Input targets for potential improvements for inefficient DMUs.

DMUs	Service Team cost (STC)	Service Team Labour (STL)	Service Quality-cost (SQC)	Number of Incidents (NI)	Contingent Costs (CC)	Revenue (R)	Managed Serv. Units (MSU)	Efficiency Score
	Target Inputs					**Outputs**		
DMU 1	12.124,50	884,57	1.343,18	173	1212,45	N/A	850	1,000000
DMU 2	103.000,00	5.544,00	12.438,00	640	4120	N/A	5500	1,000000
DMU 3	3.856,02	294,46	427,67	148,98	269,92	N/A	400	0,999999
DMU 4	3.673,35	212,80	432,13	50,67	367,33	N/A	380	1,000000
DMU 5	2.829,90	176,08	318,10	31,44	282,99	N/A	220	1,000000
DMU 6	3.373,00	168,00	330,00	30	236,11	N/A	360	1,000000
DMU 7	3.464,70	166,54	297,40	34,7	346,47	N/A	340	0,996146
DMU 8	6.317,36	589,62	701,93	66,29	631,74	N/A	540	1,000000
DMU 9	3.495,00	336,00	350,00	29	244,65	N/A	280	1,000000
DMU 10	4.400,00	840,00	700,00	40	440	N/A	420	1,000000
DMU 11	7.200,00	3.024,00	1.600,00	128,33	288	N/A	800	1,000000
DMU 12	4.857,95	333,12	604,10	88,13	340,06	N/A	450	0,999998
DMU 13	5.349,47	1.175,24	419,73	65,02	534,95	N/A	540	0,999971
DMU 14	3.783,04	405,67	321,96	48,29	151,32	N/A	380	0,959991
DMU 15	2.508,45	241,16	247,62	32,3	175,59	N/A	120	0,999942
DMU 16	1.700,00	53,76	120,00	35	68	N/A	80	1,000000
DMU 17	3.014,50	297,90	496,51	60,29	211,01	N/A	300	1,000000
DMU 18	6.800,00	1.008,00	432,00	80	272	N/A	640	1,000000

Table 5. DMU1 and DMU14 target analysis

Inputs/ Outputs	DMU 1			DMU 14		
	Actual Data	Target	Potential Improvements	Actual Data	Target	Potential Improvements
Inputs						
Service Team-cost (STC)	16.119,00	12.124,50	-3.994, 50 (24, 78%)	4.700,00	3.783,04	-916, 96 (19, 51%)
Service Team-labor (STL)	1.176	884,57	-291,43 (24, 78%)	504	405,67	-98,33 (19, 51%)
Service quality-cost (SQC)	1.786	1.343,18	-442,52 (24, 78%)	400	321,96	-78,04 (19, 51%)
Number of incidents (NI)	230	173	-57,00 (24, 78%)	60	48,29	-11,71 (19, 51%)
Contingent costs (CC)	1.612	1212,45	-399,45 (24, 78%)	188	151,32	-36,68 (19, 51%)
Outputs						
Managed Serv. Units (MSU)	850	850	0,00	380	380	0,00

In terms of quantity of improvements as the two examples depicted in Table 5 show, DMU 1 should save the monthly service team labour capacity by 291 hours while DMU 14 should reduce the monthly service quality costs from 400 to 321,96. These improvements will allow inputs reduction but keep the same level of output.

Practitioners can do so by weighting some factors more heavily than others. For example, DMU 1 should save on STL and, subsequently, reduce on service team costs, while DMU 14, by reducing on monthly SQC, exist the risk of incident increase and consequently the contingent costs augment, which are undesired consequences. Moreover, some of the modification actions must be well planned.

In order to fulfil the last step of our proposed model – Data Analysis – we must refer that Scale Efficiency (SE) was the only analysis that was not possible to execute since we did not use the CRS (Constant Return to Scale) model, and the periodicity studied was based on a single period. All the other data analysis was demonstrated.

Evaluation

This section corresponds to the evaluation step of DSRM, in which the authors compare the results obtained from the demonstration to the objectives of the solution. In order to explain the evaluation, the framework proposed in (Pries-Heje, Richard, & Venable, Strategies for Design Science Research Evaluation, 2008) was used. This framework identifies what is actually evaluated, how it is evaluated, and when the evaluation takes place.

The main artifact evaluated is the proposed DEA efficiency model; for IT outsourcing contracts that is supported on the set of service dimensions and service items necessary for service process configuration.

The authors designed the artifact based on the main literature of the area, which provided a strong theoretical perspective. In order to provide some practitioner viewpoint, later the authors evaluated the proposal by performing interviews with IT service managers (with responsibilities in service delivery). With this evaluation, the authors aim to know which service items really matter to service providers; their opinions are useful since they interact with a wide range of clients.

This step represents a naturalistic evaluation since it was conducted using a real artifact in a real organization with real data facing real problems. By testing the proposed model in a real environment and comparing results, the authors were able to validate model usefulness.

The artifact was evaluated ex post (after it was developed and after the demonstration). The evaluation was done by comparing the results obtained through the proposed model and the results obtained by provider methods in use, based on efficiency standard ratios, like the ones presented in formulation (1).

Finally, practitioners' feedback was useful to evaluate our model's utility and results. The results obtained show that our model suggests minimization of inefficient input variables, which can lead providers to follow one of the following courses of action:

1. Margin increase (by cost reduction) or;
2. Market increase (by reducing final price and obtaining more customers) or;
3. Service quality improvement (by using the extra value obtained for customer care).

This way, a practitioner can choose between: better service for customers, or profit increase. For Druker (1956) the main responsibility of a business organization is to serve its customers while profit is an essential condition for the company's continued existence and sustainability. For Jensen (1976) the main purpose of a private business organization is to be profitable.

When asked about their preference, practitioners referred that their main responsibility was to serve customers while revenue and pricing were the responsibility of other departments. However, the importance of having a profitable operation is paramount and demanded by the board management.

Therefore, after analysing our proposal, practitioners referred they have always used financial ratios and standard average ratios and that all decisions were made based on that information.

After our demonstration, practitioners realized the limitations of the ratios used, and when asked about the use of our model to measure efficiency, they referred it would be a good leverage for IT outsourcing management and that the use of DEA would encourage some discipline in assembling data about contracts, allowing a richer analysis in the future.

Thus, practitioners mentioned that the success of our model is based on three essential steps: variables selection and setting; use the correct DEA model; and proper results interpretation.

Practitioners argued that:

the use of known ratios is simple and straightforward and avoids the inherent risk of wrong model formulation. I assume that when correctly formulated, DEA gives richer information. However, when badly used, it can lead to erroneous results with higher risk than only using simple ratios.

For instance the method for calculating the total working hours can change between contracts, giving data a different meaning; this statement is also argued by (Thanassoulis, Boussofiane, & Dyson, 1996; Sherman & Zhu, 2006).

In addition, in the service design phase, services must be designed for infrastructure sharing among customers, even in IT outsourcing, since the implementation of multiplexing gains through the use of shared platforms and shared teams would have a major impact. However, often IT outsourcing contracts are tailored, difficult to standardize and the use of dedicated teams and a dedicated infrastructure jeopardizes savings. Consequently, economies of scale and price elasticity do not exist, so profit maximization will be harder.

Furthermore, size makes metrics worse, because it is assumed that large contracts benefit from scale effect, but in general they are also more complex, which increases management time and costs.

Another major theme with impact in data quality and argued by the practitioners is the quantity of the service level agreements (SLA) offered in an IT outsourcing contract, since the higher the quantity of metrics, the more variability can be expected in costs. Often SLAs are defined according to the client's purpose and goals while the provider has to accept them and design the contract as agreed with the client.

As stated by the practitioners:

In one Help-desk contract, the main metric can be phone calls answered in less than 15 seconds and in another contract it can be the number of incidents solved at first contact. This operational difference forces changes in IT outsourcing configuration of human resources and service platforms.

Therefore, the findings obtained strongly establish the importance of understanding the different types of variables (inputs and outputs) that contribute to variance in IT outsourcing contracts, seeing as each customer's environment has unique aspects that can be more difficult to measure and standardize than others.

For the provider, each IT outsourcing contract has unique aspects, which are difficult to measure, and the service delivery phase requires resource allocation and resource planning (Li, Field, Jiang, He, & Pang, 2015).

Some customers keep their own on-site staff, equipment ownership and responsibility for part of the services so as to support organization business (Cullen, Seddon, & Willcocks, 2005) while others totally rely on the provider.

Given the range of possibilities, it is not easy to identify a set of close variables or cost drivers to measure all IT outsourcing contract types in order to have a standard performance indicator across different IT outsourcing contracts.

In this study, the authors tried to identify the variables that are always used in IT outsourcing contracts, which guarantee a common operational structure grounded on direct and indirect costs that are dimensioned for each contract based on scope and duration. Thus, practitioners' feedback was rather positive and homogenous, as the authors were able to validate the research problem's importance, and demonstrations showed our proposal's versatility for single and multiple services contracts

All interviewees believed that there is the need for better service understanding and that our proposal was a good tool to be used, and that all the proposed dimensions and items were seen as useful, and their use was seen as innovative, given that no equivalent solution is available for IT managed services.

The evaluation's main goal was to validate our model and assess if it is adapted to providers' use. Bearing that in mind, authors observed that practitioners were interested in the model and wanted to use it in more detail, even if some were uneasy about their ability to manipulate and understand DEA model and results.

CONCLUSION

The authors propose a model for measuring IT outsourcing efficiency, based on the BCC DEA approach, in which contracts were considered DMUs according to DEA terminology. A single relative-efficiency score characterises DMUs, allowing specific projections for improvements based on observable data (inputs and outputs).

The proposed model identifies and discusses the variables that generally describe IT outsourcing operations and is based on the following inputs (service team costs, service team labour, service quality costs, number of incidents, contingent costs) and two outputs (revenue and the number of managed units).

DEA differs from a simple efficiency ratio in that it accommodates multiple inputs and outputs and provides significant additional information through which efficiency improvements can be achieved. Consequently, quantitative techniques gain a wider role in managers' actions, since only with quantitative techniques it is possible to gather and process all the data available, in order to transform it into information for decision aiding.

Thus, the main contribution of this paper is an approach for efficiency measurement in IT outsourcing contracts in order to identify potential sources of inefficiency, recognizing best-practice DMUs for subsequent standardization of operations.

The discussed demonstration showed that by removing the output variable "Revenue", the operational results could be improved since that variable can have a high degree of subjectivity in IT outsourcing contracts.

The proposed DEA model is a tool for practitioners' use that can be extended to include other inputs and/or outputs and a greater number of DMUs.

The limitations of this study are related to the data available. The results obtained thereof shall be seen as an indication of how DEA could be applied to analyse performance in IT outsourcing operations. A total number of 18 contracts have been analysed, this limited number may result in an out-of-proportion importance given to outliers. Better results may be obtained by analysing a larger number of DMUs, where the effect of outliers is softened by a bigger group.

This study has empirically tested DEA in the context of IT outsourcing contracts. Our results, while limited by the data, are consistent with DEA principles. For academics, our results represent a significant first step towards testing DEA within IT outsourcing, and should provide encouragement to other research initiatives aimed at testing DEA implications in other outsourcing contracting contexts.

For future work, several paths are suggested. The first one should be testing the proposed model over multiple time periods also named as windows analysis (time series data) to validate our variables and results. Secondly, researchers could work on the generalization of our proposed model for service efficiency in general, depicted from IT outsourcing idiosyncrasies, since the proposed artifact has a comprehensive structure to be tested in other service sectors.

Finally, the nomination of the seven service dimensions and 23 service items can be considered excessive or minimalist depending on the research problem and service configuration. However, according to this research, the authors found it adequately complete, broad and capable of fitting in most scenarios of IT outsourcing operations. However, deeper research can be done on service item configuration and how those can be transformed in a scale for IT outsourcing service configuration optimisation.

REFERENCES

Abbott, M. (2006). The Productivity and Efficiency of the Australian Electricity Supply Industry. *Energy Economics*, *28*(4), 444–454. doi:10.1016/j.eneco.2005.10.007

Addy, R. (2007). *Effective IT Service Management*. Berlin: Springer.

Alison Cartlidge, e. a. (2007). *An introductory overview of ITIL v3*. UK Chapter of the itSMF.

Axelos. (2011). *ITIL Service Design*. TSO (The Stationery Office).

Banker, R., Charnes, A., & Cooper, W. (1984). Some Models for Estimating Technical and Scale Inefficiencies in Data Envelopment Analysis. *Management Science*, *30*(9), 1078–1092. doi:10.1287/mnsc.30.9.1078

Banker, R., & Morey, R. (1986). Efficiency analysis for exogenously fixed inputs and outputs. *Operations Research*, *34*(4), 513–521. doi:10.1287/opre.34.4.513

Brown, D., & Wilson, S. (2005). *The Black Book of Outsourcing. How to manage the changes, challenges and opportunities*. John Wiley & Sons Inc.

Charnes, A. (1994). *Data Envelopment Analysis, theory, methodology and applications*. Kluwer Academic Publishers.

Charnes, A., Cooper, W., & Rhodes, E. (1978, November). Measuring the Efficiency of Decision Making Units. *European Journal of Operations Research,* 429-444.

Chase, R. B., & Aquilano, N. J. (1992). A Matrix for linking Marketing and Production Variables in Service System Design. In *Production and operations management* (6th ed.). Homewood, IL: Irwin.

Correia dos Santos, J., & Mira da Silva, M. (2012). *Cost Management in IT Outsourcing contracts: The path to standardization. 19th International Business Information Management Association (IBIMA).* Barcelona: Ibima.

Correia dos Santos, J., & Mira da Silva, M. (2015). Mapping Critical Success Factors for IT Outsourcing: The Providers Perspective. *International Journal of Enterprise Information Systems, 11*(1), 62–84. doi:10.4018/ijeis.2015010105

Correia dos Santos, J., & Mira da Silva, M. (2015). Price management in IT outsourcing contracts. The path to flexibility. *Journal of Revenue and Pricing Management,* 1-23.

Costa, P., Santos, J., & Mira da Silva, M. (2013). Evaluation Criteria for Cloud Services. *IEEE 6th International Conference on Cloud Computing.* Santa Clara, CA: IEEE.

Cullen, S. (2009). *The Contract Scorecard: Successful Outsourcing by design.* England, UK: Gower Publishing Limited.

Cullen, S., Seddon, P., & Willcocks, L. (2005). IT Outsourcing configuration: Research into defining and designing outsourcing arrangements. *The Journal of Strategic Information Systems, 14*(4), 357–387. doi:10.1016/j.jsis.2005.07.001

Cullen, S., Seddon, P., & Willcocks, L. (2005, March). Managing Outsourcing: The Lifecycle Imperative. *MIS Quarterly Executive, 4*(1).

Dibbern, J., Goles, T., Hirschheim, R., & Jayatilaka, B. (2004). Information Systems Outsourcing: A survey and analysis of the literature. *The Data Base for Advances in Information Systems, 35*(4), 6–102. doi:10.1145/1035233.1035236

Domberger, S., Fernandez, P., & Fiebig, D. (2000). Modelling the price, performance and contract characteristics of IT outsourcing. *Journal of Information Technology, 15*(2), 107–118. doi:10.1080/026839600344302

Druker, P. F. (1956). *The Practice of Management.* Academic Press.

Fitzsimmons, J., & Fitzsimmons, M. (2010). *Service Management: Operations, Strategy, and Information Technology* (7th ed.). Singapore: McGraw-Hill.

Frei, F. X. (2006). Breaking the trade-Off Between Efficiency and Service. *Harvard Business Review,* (November), 1–12. PMID:17131566

Glushko, R. J. (2010). Seven Contexts for Service System Design. In P. Maglio, C. Kieliszewski, & J. Spohrer (Eds.), *Handbook of service science* (pp. 219–249). New York: Springer. doi:10.1007/978-1-4419-1628-0_11

Golany, B., & Storbeck, J. (1999). A Data Envelopment Analysis of the Operational Efficiency of Bank Branches. *Interfaces, 29*(3), 14–26. doi:10.1287/inte.29.3.14

Gronroos, C., & Ojasalo, K. (2004). Service productivity. Towards a conceptualization of the transformation of inputs into economic results in services. *Journal of Business Research*, 414–423.

Hancox, M., & Hackney, R. (2000). IT Outsourcing: Frameworks for conceptualizing Practice and Perception. *Information Systems Journal*, *10*(3), 217–237. doi:10.1046/j.1365-2575.2000.00082.x

Hevner, A., March, S., Park, J., & Ram, S. (2004). Design Science in Information Systems Research. *Management Information Systems Quarterly*, *28*(1), 75–105.

Hevner, A., March, S., Park, J., & Ram, S. (2004). Design Science in Information Systems Research. *Management Information Systems Quarterly*, *28*(1), 75–105.

Hirschheim, R., George, B., & Wong, S. (2004). Information Technology Outsourcing. The move towards offshoring. *Indian Journal of Economics and Business*.

Homburg, C. (2001). Using data envelopment analysis to benchmark activities. *International Journal of Production Economics*, *73*(1), 51–58. doi:10.1016/S0925-5273(01)00194-3

Horngren, C., Foster, G., & Datar, S. (2000). Cost Accounting a managerial emphasis (6th ed.). Prentice-Hall International, Inc.

Jensen, M. C., & Meckling, W. H. (1976). Theory of the Firm: Managerial Behaviour, Agency Costs and Ownership Structure. *Journal of Financial Economics*, *3*(4), 305–360. doi:10.1016/0304-405X(76)90026-X

Joha, A., & Janssen, M. (2014). Factors influencing the shaping of shared services business models: Balancing customization and standardization. *Strategic Outsourcing: An International Journal*, *7*(1), 47–65. doi:10.1108/SO-10-2013-0018

Johnston, R., & Graham, C. (2008). *Service Operations Management, Improving Service Delivery* (3rd ed.). London, UK: Prentice Hall, Financial Times (UK).

Kaplan, R. S., & Cooper, R. (1998). *Cost & Effect, using integrated cost systems to drive profitability and performance*. Boston: Harvard Business School Press.

Keyes, J. (2005). *Implementing the IT blanced scorecard: aligning IT with corporate strategy*. Boca Raton, FL: Taylor & Francis Group. doi:10.1201/9781420031348

Kotler, P., & Armstrong, G. (2009). Principles of Marketing (13th ed.). Englewood Cliffs, NJ: Prentice-Hall Inc.

Lacity, M., & Fox, J. (2008). Creating global shared services: Lessons from Reuters. *MIS Quarterly Executive*, *7*, 17–32.

Lacity, M., & Hirschheim, R. (1993). *Information Systems Outsourcing: Myths, Methaphors and Realities*. Chichester, UK: Wiley.

Lampel, J., & Mintzberg, H. (1996). Customizing Customization. *Sloan Management Review*, *38*(1), 21–30.

Langer, N., Mani, D., & Srikanth, K. (2014). Client Satisfaction Versus Profitability: An Empirical Analysis of the Impact of Formal Controls in Strategic Outsourcing Contracts. In A. H. Rudy Hirschheim (Ed.), Information Systems Outsourcing (pp. 67-88). Springer Berlin Heidelberg.

Lee, J. N., & Kim, Y. G. (1999). Effect of Partnership Quality on IS Outsourcing Sucess: Conceptual Framework and Empirical Validation. *Journal of Management Information Systems*, *15*(4), 29–61. doi :10.1080/07421222.1999.11518221

Li, G., Field, J. M., Jiang, H., He, T., & Pang, Y. (2015). Decision Models for Workforce and Technology Planning in. *Service Science*, *7*(1), 29–47. doi:10.1287/serv.2015.0094

Maglio, P., Kieliszewski, C., & Spohrer, J. (2010). *Handook of Service Science*. New York: Springer Verlag. doi:10.1007/978-1-4419-1628-0

Maglio, P., & Spohrer, J. (2008). Fundamentals of service science. *Journal of the Academy of Marketing Science*, *36*(I), 18–20. doi:10.1007/s11747-007-0058-9

Mahgary, S., & Lahdelma, R. (1995). Data envelopment analysis:Visualising the results. *European Journal of Operational Research*, *85*(3), 700–710. doi:10.1016/0377-2217(94)00303-T

Manes, A. T. (2003). *Web Services a managers guide*. Boston: Addison-Wesley.

Matthew, L. (1996). IT outsourcing contracts: Practical issues for management. *Industrial Management & Data Systems*, *96*(1), 15–20. doi:10.1108/02635579610107684

Mendes, C., & Mira da Silva, M. (2012). DEMO-based Service Level Agreements. *3rd International Conference on Exploring Service Science*.

Mishra, R. K. (2012). Measuring Supply Chain Efficiency: A Dea Approach. *Journal of Operations and Supply Chain Management*, *5*(1), 45–68.

Neely, A., Gregory, M., & Platts, K. (2005). Performance measurement system design. *International Journal of Operations & Production Management*, *25*(12), 1228–1263.

Oliva, R., & Kallenberg, R. (2003). Managing the transition from products to services. *International Journal of Service Industry Management*, *14*(2), 160–172. doi:10.1108/09564230310474138

Österle, H., Becker, J., Fank, U., Hess, T., Karagiannis, D., Krcmar, H., & Sinz, E. et al. (2010). Memorandum on design-oriented information systems research. *Journal of Information Systems*, *20*(1), 7–10. doi:10.1057/ejis.2010.55

Parasuraman, A., & Zeithaml, V. (2002). Measuring and Improving Service Quality:A Literature Reviewand Research Agenda. In B. Weitz (Ed.), *Handbook of Marketing*. Thousand Oaks, CA: Sage. doi:10.4135/9781848608283.n15

Parasuraman, A., Zeithaml, V., & Berry, L. (1988). SERVQUAL: A multiple-item scale for measuring consumer perceptions of service quality. *Journal of Retailing*, *64*(1), 12–40.

Parasuraman, A., Zeithaml, V., & Malhotra, A. (2005). E-S-Qual. A multiple-item Sclae for Assessing Electronic Service Quality. *Journal of Service Research*, 1–21.

Peffers, K., Tuunanen, T., Rothenberger, M., & Chatterjee, S. (2007). A Design Science Research Methodology for Information Systems Research. *Journal of Management Information Systems*, *24*(3), 45–77. doi:10.2753/MIS0742-1222240302

Prat, N., Comyn-Wattiau, I., & Akoka, J. (2014). Artifact Evaluation in Informtion Systems Design-Science Research–A Holistic View. *18th Pacific Asia Conference on Information Systems*.

Pries-Heje, J., Richard, B., & Venable, J. (2008). *Strategies for Design Science Research Evaluation*. ECIS.

Quinn, J., & Hilmer, F. (1994). Strategic Outsourcing. *Sloan Management Review*, 43–45.

Schaffnit, C., Rosen, D., & Paradi, G. (1997). Best Practice Analysis of Bank Branches: An Application of DEA in a Large Canadian Bank. *European Journal of Operational Research*, *98*(2), 269–289. doi:10.1016/S0377-2217(96)00347-5

Schmenner, R. (1986). How can services businesses Survive and prosper? *Sloan Management Review*, *27*(3), 21–32. PMID:10300742

Sherman, H., & Zhu, J. (2006). *Improving Service Performance using Data Envelopment Analysis (DEA)*. Springer.

Shostack, L. (1987). Service Positioning through Structural Change. *Journal of Marketing*, *51*(1), 34. doi:10.2307/1251142

Silvestro, R., Fitzgerald, L., Johnston, R., & Voss, C. (1992). Towards a Classification of Service Processes. *International Journal of Service Industry Management*, *3*(3), 62–75. doi:10.1108/09564239210015175

Smith, S., & Albaum, G. (2013). *Basic Marketing Research – Building Your Survey*. Qualtrics Labs, Inc.

Spohrer, J., Vargo, S., Caswell, N., & Maglio, P. (2008). The Service System Is the Basic Abstraction of Service Science. *41st Annual Hawaii International Conference on System Sciences (HICCS)*, *7*(4), 104-116. doi:10.1109/HICSS.2008.451

Stern, C., & Deimler, M. (2006). *The Boston Consulting Group on Strategy, classic concepts and new perspectives* (2nd ed.). John Wilcy & Sons Inc.

Swaminathan, J. (2001). Enabling Customization Using Standardized Operations. *California Management Review*, *43*(3), 125–135. doi:10.2307/41166092

Tan, C., & Sia, S. (2006). Managing Flexibility in Outsourcing. *Journal of the Association for Information Systems*, *7*(4), 179–206.

Taylor, S. (2007). *ITIL Service Design*. London: TSO, Office of Government Commerce.

Thanassoulis, E., Boussofiane, A., & Dyson, R. (1996). A Comparison of Data Envelopment Analysis and Ratio Analysis as Tools for Performance Assessment. *Omega*, *3*(3), 229–244. doi:10.1016/0305-0483(95)00060-7

Thenent, N., Settanni, E., Parry, G., Goh, Y., & Newnes, L. (2014). Cutting Cost in Service Systems: Are You Running with Scissors? *Journal of Strategic Change: Briefings in Entrepreneurial Finance*, *23*, 341–357.

Ward, J., & Griffits, P. (1996). *Strategic Planning for Information Systems* (2nd ed.). London: John Wiley & Sons Inc.

Wemmerlöv, U. (1990). A Taxonomy for Service Processes and its Implications for System Design. *International Journal of Service Industry Management, 1*(3), 20–40. doi:10.1108/09564239010002126

Willcocks, L., Cullen, S., & Craig, A. (2010). *The Outsourcing Enterprise: From Cost Management to Collaborative Innovation (Technology, Work and Globalization)*. Palgrave.

Willcocks, L., & Lacity, M. (1998). The sourcing and outsourcing of IS: Shock of the new. In L. Willcocks & M. Lacity (Eds.), *Strategic Sourcing of Information Technology: Perspectives and Practices* (pp. 1–41). Chichester, UK: Wiley.

Willcocks, L., & Lacity, M. (2012). *The New IT Outsourcing Landscape: From Innovation to Cloud Services*. Palgrave Macmillan. doi:10.1057/9781137012296

Williamson, O. E. (1985). *The Economic Institutions of Capitalism*. New York: Free Press.

Zhu, J. (2000). Multi-factor performance measure model with an application to fortune 500 companies. *European Journal of Operational Research, 123*(1), 105–124. doi:10.1016/S0377-2217(99)00096-X

KEY TERMS AND DEFINITIONS

DEA – Data Envelopment Analysis: A linear programming technique able to manipulate multiple inputs and outputs. The DEA technique is used to find the set of coefficients that will give the maximum possible efficiency ratio of outputs to inputs for the organizational unit under evaluation. DEA allows the identification of the most efficient operation that enables providers to set the best operational strategy to follow.

Decision Making Units (DMUs): A DMU is a specific characterization of the entities under investigation. The DMUs selection is based on the identification of particular characteristics of the problem under analysis. A DMU needs to be sufficiently similar so that the comparison makes sense. If DMUs are not comparable, then a separate analysis should be performed for each different set.

Design Science Research Methodology (DSRM): DSRM aims to create and evaluate IT artifacts intended to solve identified organizational problems. These artifacts include constructs (vocabulary and symbols), models (abstractions and representations), methods (algorithms and practices) and instantiations (implemented and prototype systems). The steps of DSR are: problem identification and motivation; objectives of a solution definition; design and development; demonstration; evaluation; and communication.

IT Outsourcing: IT outsourcing can be seen as the handing over to third-party management of IT/IS assets, resources and activities for a required result. The appeal for outsourcing is simple, organizations want to reduce operational costs, obtain higher efficiency standards and enhance operational flexibility, enabling them to respond to ever-changing market conditions.

IT Outsourcing Service Configuration: The set of steps necessary to configure an IT outsourcing operation, in which, the service items and their variables can assume different values according client requisites.

Performance Measurement: Performance measurement can be defined as the process of quantifying the efficiency and effectiveness of actions towards goals. Performance can be measured in two fronts, the desired performance (client expectation of service quality) and the realized performance (that can be referred to as effective performance). Thus, the measurement function is to develop a method for generating a class of information (metrics) that will be useful in a variety of problems and situations. One of the most known methods for performance measurement in organizations is the balanced scorecard, which allows performance measure and reporting.

Service Customization: Service customization allows providers to delivery their services tailored to client requisites, resulting in complex exchanges of information. Thus, customization is important for client satisfaction, since meeting individual client needs is a strategy that creates and delivers superior value, for which some clients are available to pay extra money, allowing both to differentiate from competitors.

Service Standardization: Service standardization can be described as the set of processes that have as its main purpose controlling the output activity and service quality whilst minimizing the risks and costs associated with the human factor and process divergence, delivering services to customers in minimal time, with minimal cost and with maximal reliability.

Chapter 16
Knowledge–Based Systems for Data Modelling:
Review and Challenges

Sabrina Šuman
Polytechnic of Rijeka, Croatia

Alen Jakupović
Polytechnic of Rijeka, Croatia

Mile Pavlić
University of Rijeka, Croatia

ABSTRACT

Data modelling is a complex process that depends on the knowledge and experience of the designers who carry it out. The lack of designers' expertise in that process negatively affects the quality of created models which has a significant impact on the quality of successive phases of information systems development. This chapter provides an overview of data modelling, especially the entity relationship method, main actors in the modelling process, and highlights the main problems and challenges in this field. Knowledge based system for data modelling support has a potential to minimize and prevent most of the problems that occur in modelling process. Therefore, a systematic review of the existing KB systems, methods, and tools for the data modelling process is made. By summarizing their main characteristics, some important desirable features of the new KB system for data modelling support are identified. With this in mind, a new KB system for data modelling support is proposed, which applies formal language theory (particularly translation) during the process of conceptual modelling.

DOI: 10.4018/978-1-5225-2382-6.ch016

INTRODUCTION

The information systems development process consists of the following phases: strategic planning, analysis, design, implementation, maintenance, and evaluation. As part of the information system design and implementation, the database structure has been developed. It serves to satisfy the information needs of information system users. This includes conceptual and logical database design (based on collected and analysed requirements), physical database design and database implementation (Elmasri & Navathe, 2011). This chapter is focused on the conceptual and logical database design in data modelling process that occurs in the design phase of information systems development.

Conceptual and logical database design (conceptual data modelling or data modelling) is an activity that is performed in the early stages of information systems development. Based on the user requirements, the process of the data modelling identifies the fundamental concepts and relationships of the observed reality and represents them in the conceptual schema form (Batini, Ceri & Navathe, 1992).

One of the main data modelling problems is the creation of a complete, easy-to-use, understandable and semantically correct conceptual schema. This process is knowledge intensive, complex and difficult (Teorey, 1999). Data modelling is critical in the development of information systems and errors committed in this stage are reflected in the poor quality of the database and incorrect query results Batini, Ceri, & Navathe, 1992; Martin & Leben, 1995).

Various Knowledge Based (KB) systems are developed to support data modelling in the development of the information system. KB system is a computer system that uses the methods and techniques of artificial intelligence to solve problems. The general structure of the KB system includes: knowledge base inference engine, self-learning, explanation and reasoning and user interface (Sajja & Akerkar, 2010).

KB system for data modelling can help users to develop better data models (Batini, Ceri, & Navathe, 1992). It can intervene, propose design choice, identify errors in the data model, and advise users to correct the model. The information system design process itself is appropriate for a problem domain for the KB system approach, because it is a non-algorithmic, non-trivial, and not completely deterministic problem (Lo & Choobineh, 2002).

The final goal of the authors' main research is the development of a KB system for the data modelling process using finite state transducers from formal language theory (i.e. translation). A conceptual proposal of that system is given in fifth section of the chapter. The other chapters' sections are organized in the following manner: the second section presents the data modelling process including its main actors and the entity relationship method, the third section deals with problems and challenges in the data modelling process, while a review of existing KB systems, tools and methods is given in the fourth section. The chapter ends with a conclusion, showing further directions of the author's research.

DATA MODELLING

During the analysis phase of information systems development user requirements are specified. The analysis identifies the need of a business organization for information. After the analysis phase, follows the design phase – the process that (based on user requirements specified in the analysis phase) results in a set of basic components of the information system, and formal representation of their relations which are independent of information systems implementation. The design phase consists of data relationship identification and design, database design and architectural design of the software product. The first two parts of the design phase are called data modelling. The data modelling method specifies the process of identification and representation of information objects and their relationship (Pavlić, 2011).

The result of a specific data method (e.g. the entity-relationship method) in the data modelling process is the data model (e.g. the entity-relationship model). The data model is constructed by information system designers, and validated by the end users. Its purpose is a formal representation of the data components of the information system and their relationships. The data model is the basis for the database creation and definition of software architecture. It contains three important concepts: entities, attributes of entities (properties, characteristics) and relationships between the entities (Pavlić, 2011).

The data model describes a static information structure through the entities and their relationships. The conceptual, logical and physical data model represents the three evolutionary stages of data modelling where each phase upgrades the previous data model with new details, optimizing it for implementation. The data model is often represented graphically with entity-relationship diagrams (ERD) or UML class diagrams (Merson, 2009).

ER Model

Each modelling method uses a small set of constructs (method vocabulary) and syntax rules (Siau, Wand, & Benbasat, 1996). Constructs are graphically or non-graphically expressed concepts whose purpose is to organize and present the knowledge of the interest domain. In the entity-relationship method (the most used method in data modelling), the main constructs are entities, relationships, and attributes (Siau & Rossi, 2011; Shoval & Shiran, 1997).

The entity-relationship method (ER method) graphically represents the data structure of the observed system. It has semantically rich and easily understandable concepts that represent the entities and their relationships. The method naturally describes a business organization, and its result (a data model diagram) is easy to understand and allows communication between the designer and the user. The ER method is used in many methodologies (e.g. CASE *Method, MIRIS, SSADM, IE). The result of the ER method application, developed by Peter Chen, (Chen, 1976), is the data model diagram (conceptual database schema) called entity relationship diagram – ERD (Pavlić, 2009). ERD is an image which shows the information that is created, stored, and used by a business system.

The entity-relationship method was designed as a means of getting a quick idea of the database structure. It is used for information system data modelling and design of its database. Together with a data flow diagram (the result of the process modelling), ER diagram gives the designer alternative logical views of the information system (Data Modelling, from https://www.liberty.edu).

The authors in the literature related to the field of software development, database design and CASE tools use different ERD notation, which creates difficulties in acquiring knowledge and skills necessary for novice designers. For the same reason, the transfer and comprehension of a particular ERD between designers and team members in separate locations are hindered. The use of a CASE tool and integrated data modelling method is dependent on the designer's knowledge of the method and the skill.

After analysing ten data modelling methods with different concepts and notations, the authors in Song, et al. (1995) found that the ERD notations differ in the following points:

- N-ary relationships are allowed or not allowed;
- Representation mode of limitations related to entities – the cardinality and optionality; notation for the minimum and maximum number of entity occurrences in a relationship;

- The place where the limitation is indicated (cardinality and optionality specification so that one can read from opposite ends of the relationship – Look Across, or towards the opposite end of the relationship – Look Here);
- There is a relationship attribute;
- There is a foreign key representation;
- How overlapping and disjoint entity subtypes are represented; and
- How complete or partial specialization is represented.

The authors in Song et al. (1995) showed a series of simple and complex data modelling methods. Based on that, the new KB system for data modelling that is proposed later in this chapter deals with entities, relationships, attributes and cardinality as basic constructs for data modelling.

Main Actors in Data Modelling

A planner, analyst, designer and developer are experts with different perspectives on information systems development. While a planner identifies major business organizations' sub-systems and their relationships, an analyst (in collaboration with the user) identifies and analyses in detail business processes that are performed in the organizations' sub-systems – which input/output data are used, which data must be stored and what the environment of the analysed system is. According to the input/output data used by business processes and data that must be stored, a designer determines the entities (objects), their attributes and relations (i.e. a data model) needed to describe the data that flow through the business system. Based on the data model, a developer (i.e. a database administrator) creates the database elements needed to store data (Panian & Ćurko, 2010).

In short – a planner and analyst identify business sub-systems, their business processes and data flows by which they are connected; a designer determines the data structure needed to store the data from data flows; the developer implements this data structure (by creating the database). This shows that the complex problem of the information system database creation breaks down into three sub-problems: required data identification, data structure determination, and data structure implementation (Panian & Ćurko, 2010).

In future work, the authors of this paper will analyse in detail the activity of the main actors in the data modelling process because it is expected that they will be the main users of the authors' new KB system for data modelling.

DATA MODELLING PROBLEMS AND CHALLENGES

Data modelling is a complex process and is prone to error. There are several generic reasons why problems may arise in the analysis and design phase and compromise the data model quality (consequently, the developed information system quality). Some of these reasons are:

- Complexity of the process model to data model translation,
- Lack of data modelling knowledge,
- Non-existent or insufficient data modelling knowledge formalisation required in computer-systems,
- Error occurrence in data modelling,

- Low efficiency of the process model to the data model translation (time, money, and other resources), and
- Possible low effectiveness of the data model in the case of business process changes.

These questions arise: What are the necessary data modelling cognitive, knowledge and experience requirements? and What solutions could the KB system for data modelling provide?

The information loss can occur in the very process of the data modelling because the data model is generated using the abstraction of the real world (Antony & Batra, 2002; Batini, Ceri & Navathe, 1992). Eid, (Eid,2012) describes five cognitive steps that are used during the process of data modelling using the ER method:

1. Description of the problem based on the business description.
2. Interpretation of the obtained business description to extract and define business rules.
3. For each business rule, the designer proceeds to identify entities and link them with relationships.
4. Identification of entity attributes, including keys.
5. Iteration of these steps leading to the gradual development of the data model, checking the accuracy and completeness of the model considering the business description.

These activities require a great cognitive effort and concentration, given the complexity and demanding intellectual processes such as abstraction, generalization, specialization, and it takes a lot of experience and knowledge to create a consistent ERD. And exactly the consistency is the core of the problem – it is necessary to represent user requirements from an informal description in natural language, in a formal description through ERD while preserving the consistency of user requirements. (Spanoudakis & Zisman, 2001) define consistency as: "A state in which two or more elements, which overlap in different models of the same system, have a satisfactory joint description". Consistency problem that arises in the analysis and design phases refers to the correct covering of all business specifications into a data model. According to (Lucas, Molina, &Toval, 2009) consistency problems in the development of the information system are there from the beginning and are usually associated with:

- The existence of multiple views of the business system – each of these views describes some area of interest whose parts may overlap, and this is a potential risk of preserving consistency,
- The existence of more developers to develop a single system, each with its own understanding of user requirements and different notations for developing process/data model, and
- Development of the system usually runs in several phases with iterations so it is possible that a problem occurs at some stage.

The same authors differentiate types of inconsistency: horizontal (intra model, at the same level of abstraction), vertical (inter model, at different levels of abstraction), syntactic (conforms to abstract syntax specified by metamodel) and semantic (semantically compatible behaviour of the model).

Another type of problem that occurs when modelling data refers to the designers who develop data model, to their knowledge, experience and representation ability and style. (Antony, Batra, & Santhanam, 2005) hold a claim that professional designers of databases are scarce and expensive, and therefore inexperienced designers sometimes take on the tasks of database development. Furthermore, a large number of end users, frustrated by delays and unresolved problems of development of the system, take up the development of a system by themselves using an easy-to-use software solution (Chidambaram, 1999; Brancheau & Brown, 1993). Such inexperienced designers or end users, under-educated in the process of developing a database are called novice designers (Rockart & Flannery, 1983; Storey & Goldstein, 1993) Research shows that systems developed by novice designers lead to unsatisfactory and inaccurate outputs (Turban, McClean, &Wetherbe, 1999;Edberg and Bowman, 1996). Therefore a KB systems can be used as a tool to help novice designers in developing better databases (Storey, 1988).

(Eid, 2012) lists the most common errors that students and novice designers make at data modelling: errors at identifying the relationships, semantics of optional, mandatory and maximum cardinality. The authors in (Kazi, Kazi, &Radulovic, 2012) suggest that students have the most difficulty with abstraction, generalization, specialization, analysis and synthesis activities. They describe the semantic and syntax errors of students. Semantic errors are: using derived attributes, incomplete set of attributes in an entity, no entity derived of a relationship that has important attributes, problems with composite and complex attributes, attribute attached to wrong entity, wrong and/or inadequate constructs nomination and others. Syntax types of student errors are manifested as various deficiencies (keys, data type for the constructs, relationship name ...) or redundancies.

(Batra & Antony, 1994) and (Antony, Batra, & Santhanam, 2005) also mention types of errors that novice designers do: slips, rule-based errors or knowledge based errors. Slips cannot be prevented by a KB system because they occur for lack of attention. Rule-based errors consist in applying a wrong set of rules or wrongly applying known rules for the task. Knowledge-based errors occur for lack of experience in situations that are new for the user. One third of committed errors are knowledge-based errors (Batra & Antony, 1994). In addition, inexperienced designers often translate sentences of business description in the ER model too literally, and tend to keep the original idea of the solution regardless of the facts (i.e. anchoring).

KB system, via smart navigation through the system (for example, a series of questions) could eliminate the rule-based and knowledge-based types of errors. Also, KB system with a knowledge base that stores a set of rules and the existence of a base of past cases could significantly reduce the incidence of rule-based and knowledge-based errors.

For the mentioned problems, current CASE tools that allow drawing and provide an attractive, but not necessarily correct look of the model, do little to help because they do not provide knowledge support or learning support for ER modelling.

KB system (in addition to reducing the inconsistencies, increasing the quality of the data model and reducing the cognitive effort of novice designers) can have an educational purpose; when users interact with the KB system and when they are concentrated on the execution of a task, they may implicitly learn about concepts, rules and principles in the problem domain (Antony &Santhanam, 2008).

After the review of various data modelling problems, the challenges and benefits of the use of KB system for data modelling could be synthesised as (Lo & Choobineh, 2002) suggest:

- Gathering rare and costly human expertise to perform and validate design activities.
- Creating an explanatory system which explains the rationale behind the actions and, therefore, educates a user.
- Constantly updating the knowledge base which improves performance of the KB system.

REVIEW OF KB SYSTEMS, METHODS AND TOOLS FOR DATA MODELLING

A fully automated system for generating data model using the ER method from the business description in natural language has not yet been developed. However, there are many approaches that have resulted in the development of systems for semi-automatic development of data models, which help students, novice designers or provide support to experienced designers. Most of these systems require interaction with the user of the system, and often manual maintenance and updating by the developers of the system. There are at least 5 approaches used in KB systems for conceptual data modelling: rule-based, reusable patterns-based, case-based, ontology-based, and multi-techniques-based. Generally, none of these techniques and/or approaches is the best solution. For the overall design of the KB system, it is recommended to combine and integrate more different techniques in different parts of the system (Thonggoom, Song, &An, 2011). In order to give an overview of different techniques, approaches and methods that are used by other authors in their research and development of KB systems to support the data modelling, a literature review follows. This review chronologically follows the comparison (Lo & Choobineh, 2002) of 23 systems for database design support in the period from 1982 to 1998. The authors in (Siau et al., 1996) suggest the need for the development of new knowledge representation schemes, inference, and learning techniques for intelligent database design tools as one of the guidelines for further research. It was also noted that such systems should have the ability of learning and upgrading the knowledge base and reasoning mechanism.

This review is based on papers that have been found in the databases EBSCO, ScienceDirect, IEEE, Google Scholar and on the scientific social network ResearchGate. The expressions "knowledge-based systems for data modelling", "formalisation of data modelling", and "entity- relationship method" were used as search strings. The search results were further filtered by relevance to the new KB system that the authors are developing. The relevance criteria included: user interaction methods, reasoning based on past cases, application of formal language theory (grammar, syntax analysis, parser), and rules for translation into entity-relationship model constructs. Finally, the search resulted in a total of 14 systems that support data modelling. Some of them have the characteristics of KB systems, while others are at the level of data modelling tools. The search also resulted in a number of methods that facilitate the creation of data models.

ER generator is a tool that semi-automatically creates data model based on the ER method (Gomez, Segami & Delaune, 1999). The first part of the system is the Natural Language Understander where (after parser output) a specific set of semantic rules are applied to construct semantically rich but enough formalized Knowledge Representation structures and Logical forms. Consequently specific rules are applied to identify verbal concepts that define relationships hierarchy, attributes and keys. Generic rules are applied in following steps that lead toward ER model construction. The system also systematically stores references among concepts in order to create a targeted question for a user if the system cannot draw a solution.

CODASYS was being developed from 1994 (Batra & Antony, 1994) and it gives maximum support for the area of relationships, because novice designers are successful in identifying the correct entities and modelling them, but have much more difficulty in modelling the relationships between them (Antony & Batra, 2002; Batra and Antony, 1994). In 2005, Antony, Batra, and Santhanam (Antony, Batra & Santhanam, 2005) evaluated it by applying restrictive and guidance user interface. Restrictive user interface provided the user with a limited number of paths in the process of data model development, while guidance user interface provided advice to the user without restricting the number of possible paths. Evaluation of the system showed that novice designers achieve better results when using guidance user interface. The authors (Antony, Batra & Santhanam, 2005) also emphasised the need to balance the application of guidance and restrictive user interface in KB systems. Authors also indicate that the more feedback the user provides in the KB system, it results in more understanding of the various design choices implications. These results indicate that the KB system for modelling data is useful and suggest that different user interfaces (restrictive and guidance) should be combined in different stages of supporting data modelling in KB system.

CABSYDD, (Choobineh & Lo, 2004) has 6 components: knowledge base, case base, inference engine, working memory, user interface, and help module. The system uses past cases because the authors believe that it is more efficient and productive than the system that only helps to construct the data model from the beginning. The authors of CABSYDD are driven by the idea that a tool for database design containing past models repository should be able to: store and retrieve previous cases of data models, guide the user to find the stored cases that are similar to the current problem and assist the user in adaptation of similar stored cases for successful creation of the new data model. CABSYDD consists of two subsystems where the first (SYDD) helps to form data model that is created for the first time, or when no similar cases exist in the past model repository. The second part of the system (CABSYDD) uses previous cases from the past model repository. This system activates SYDD for those parts when it cannot find the appropriate solution in the past model repository. So SYDD has the knowledge and ability to create a completely new data model, but has no ability of learning, while CABSYDD has the functionality of learning and reasoning from previous cases (Choobineh & Lo, 2004).

KERMIT, (Suraweera & Mitrovic, 2004), is an intelligent teaching system that represents a complement to classroom teaching, in which students practice database design using the ER data model. The system assists students during construction of ER schemas based on a given set of requirements. System provides tailored guidelines and feedback based on students' knowledge towards the correct solution. KERMIT has an interface, a pedagogical module and a constraint-based modeller. The interface contains the main working area where students draw the ER diagram and controls for next step or feedback. Pedagogical module determines the timing and content of pedagogical actions, and a constraint-based modeller analyses student answers and generates student models. KERMIT has no problem solver but contains a set of problems and their ideal solutions, which is the main method of checking correctness of the student's solution. Constraints cover syntactic and semantic knowledge (Mitrovic, Koedinger & Martin, 2003).

ER-Converter extracts relevant ER constructs from the business description based on the semantic relationships between words in business description sentences. Business description in natural language passes through the subsystems: parser, semantic analyser, heuristic rules application with user intervention for ER constructs identification (entities and attributes, relationships and cardinalities) (Omar, Hanna & Kevitt, 2006).

In (Kim, Lee & Moon, 2008) the process of ER constructs extraction from business description based on requirements-driven entity extraction methodology (REEM) is explained. REEM enables employees to autonomously perform conceptual data modelling without previous experience. The first phase is pre-processing to resolve possible semantic redundancy, performed by the tool SAM - Semantic Association Model. The expected result of the REEM methodology is an appropriate ERD. The authors also developed a tool called *BizData* based on REEM methodology which takes business description as an input and provides data needed for ER diagram as the output. The same authors in 2010 came up with the conclusion that SAM burdens the user with too many questions so he/she misses to capture the functionality and efficiency of the system. Therefore, the authors accentuate that a special attention should be paid to the format of input (Lee, Kim & Moon, 2010).

In (Al-Safadi, 2009) a tool called *DBDT* (Data Base Development Tool) which takes the business description in natural language as an input and produces an ER model is described. The main steps are: identification of the main objects from business description and their reduction to the singular, syntactic word categorization, mapping ER constructs with syntactic categories, search for non-identified constructs, redundancy elimination, synonyms and naming revision, preliminary model construction, human intervention.

In (Lee, Kim & Moon, 2010) the *ABCM* system is described. Main system parts are: ABCD generator (Association-Based Conceptual Diagram) and ERD generator. ABCD generator uses ABCD rules to extract objects and relationships from the business description while ERD generator (based on ERD rules) translates the ABCD generator's results into ER constructs. The main steps in ABCD system are:

1. Parser extracts an object from business descriptions (created by employee) and stores it in metadata vocabulary.
2. ABCD generator creates an ABC diagram.
3. Redundant relationships are identified and resolved.
4. ERD generator creates an ERD from the ABC diagram.

ERD generator is a KB system described in (Shahbaz, Ahsan, Shaheen & Nawab, 2011), which consists of three modules: reading and parsing the business description in natural language, heuristic classification of text and the module that generates textual form that contains everything needed for the creation of ERD.

The authors in (Kazi, Kazi & Radulovic, 2012) provide a comprehensive list of all possible students' errors in conceptual data modelling, which is the main motivator for creating the tool - *Data Model Validator*. The proposed tool assists a user in ER data model creation based on ontology. Ontology is used for describing semantic aspect of business domain and axioms are used for describing reasoning rules. System is an integration of ontology tool, CASE tool and transformation tool. They use the first order predicate logic calculus as a formal language in the process of data model formalization and then a set of axioms is applied for the process of transformation to ER constructs.

(Thonggoom, Song & An, 2011) present a method for automatic data model creation that uses artefacts which store knowledge of a certain domain: Entity Instance Repository (EIR) and the Relationship Instance Repository (RIR), which are the repositories of Entity Instance Patterns (EIPs) and Relationship Instance Patterns (RIPs). EIP is a pattern of one single entity and its properties, and RIP is a binary relationship with cardinality constraints between two entities. Both can be automatically extracted from the previous relational schemas. The authors developed two tools: *Heuristic-Based Technique (HBT) and Entity Instance Pattern WordNet (EIPW)*. HBT uses noun phrases, verb phrases, identification of hidden entities, and six independent domain modelling rules. EIPW works with noun phrases, an entity instance repository (EIR), entity categories, and WordNet. Relationship identification uses a relationship instance repository (RIR), and WordNet (Thonggoom, Song & An, 2011).

The main objective of developing a computer-based learning system proposed in (Eid, 2012) is to: provide a framework for more effective learning process of ER modelling and production of more accurate and complete ERD for users. Web based system named *A System for Teaching Entity Relationship Modelling* has 5 steps: Create Domain (Business description), Define Business Rules, Define Entities and Relationships, Resolve M-M relationships, and Define Entity Attributes (along with Keys). The system graphically supports every step and has appropriate assistance for the users.

Formalization of the semantics of natural language is mentioned in (Kleiner, Albert & Bézivin, 2009) as a special challenge in the field of natural language processing. In the past 10 years, SBVR (Semantics of Business Vocabulary and Business Rules) has been presented as a language for the semantic formalization of natural languages. So, one of the methods of transforming natural language description and capturing its semantics is based on the use of SBVR. The purpose of SBVR formalization is reducing the business description to a set of structured rules based on some SBVR method. Therefore, (Selway, Grossmann, Mayer & Stumptner, 2015) developed a tool that performs SBVR method formalization of the business description. The output of that process could be used for further transformation in ER constructs and ER model creation. In (Bajwa, Lee & Bordbar, 2011) a novel approach that automatically translates natural language specification of business rules to SBVR business rules is presented.

In order to formalise the business description, the concept of a controlled natural language (CNL) is described. CNL presents a subset of a natural language with restricted grammar and vocabulary with a purpose to reduce ambiguity and complexity of natural language (Hart, Johnson & Dolbear, 2008 ; Rolf, 2010). As a natural language that has a formal logical base (formal syntax and semantics), it serves as a good intermediary between natural and formal languages and could be suitable for knowledge representation and reasoning process (Njonko, Cardey, Greenfield, & Abed, 2014; Fuchs, Kaljurand & Kuhn, 2008).

In (Njonko et al. 2014) the *RuleCNL* – a system for formalised definition and representation of the business rules using special controlled natural language (CNL) is described. RuleCNL has its vocabulary and grammar with a parser that uses them. The business description is entered in CNL, syntactically validated and translated automatically in SBVR notation.

In (Btoush & Hammad, 2015) *ER generator* which extracts ER elements from natural language business descriptions is presented. The authors are motivated by the main problems of using NLP in the process of obtaining the data model from the business description in NL: ambiguity and incomplete information. The tool performs the process of obtaining ER model through 6 steps: sentence segmentation, tokenization, POS (Part-Of-Speech) tagging, chunking, parsing and ER generation. Chunking concatenates more POS tag symbols in order to provide more effective parsing. The authors emphasize that NLP technologies are not yet successful in processing and understanding information from the NL unrestricted text. They note that the NLP performed with a number of heuristics is more effective when used in a specific business domain.

The authors of this chapter are trying to reduce the problem of making the data model from user specifications to a problem of translating from one language (natural or CNL language of user specifications) into a second language (formal language of the data model). In their previous work, the authors described a new method of formalization of text-expressed knowledge (FMTEK) which translates textual knowledge in natural language into textual knowledge in formal language (Jakupović, Pavlić & Dovedan 2014). Its graphical version which uses textual knowledge to create conceptual schemes is also displayed, as well as its comparison to other graphical methods for knowledge representation (Jakupović, Pavlić, Meštrović & Jovanović, 2013; Pavlić, Jakupović & Meštrović, 2013; Pavlić, Meštrović & Jakupović, 2013).

The basic process of creating user questions and getting answers from the knowledge base in which knowledge is shown using FMTEK method is also shown (Pavlić, Dovedan & Jakupović, 2015). The results of such research will be the basis for further development of verbalisation based KB system for data modelling.

This overview of recent results in the field of computer system for data modelling indicates that it is possible to build a KB system to support the creation of ER model and, based on the conclusions of previous research, it is possible to identify shortcomings, advantages, and consider the guidelines and recommendations by various authors for further KB system development. It should be noted that only the systems and approaches that build the data model using the ER method were taken into account, and that only some systems used the theory of formal languages to help identify the ER constructs, which is exactly what the authors of this chapter intend for the construction of a new KB system.

NEW KNOWLEDGE BASED SYSTEM PROPOSAL

The initial result of the data modelling process is a conceptual data model (created through conceptual modelling). Conceptual modelling focuses on the conceptual aspects of a domain of interest and, unlike database modelling, excludes considerations relating to the database design and implementation. One of the main research topics in the domain of data modelling is related to the evaluation of conceptual modelling grammar, such as entity-relationship or business process modelling grammar (Burton-jones, Wand, & Weber, 2009; Siau & Rossi, 2011). It is considered that increased research focus on this type of grammar could result in improved conceptual modelling scripts. In this case, a script is a text-expressed conceptual model that is generated by the language grammar (e.g. text-expressed ER diagrams generated by ER grammar). The terms appearing in this research direction are "conceptual modelling grammar", "conceptual modelling script" and "conceptual modelling language" (Burton-Jones et al., 2009).

In accordance with this research direction, the translation process will be applied as a key mechanism of the new KB system for data modelling. Therefore, if data model development and construction are seen as a translation from one language to another, then business descriptions represent text-expressed knowledge in a natural language that should be translated into a data model formal language.

The translation process consists of two phases: a lexical and syntactic analysis of the input sentence (recognition) and generation of the output sentence (translation). The program for lexical and syntactic analysis is called the Recognizer, while the program for translation is called the Translator. The Translator that uses the Recognizer in the syntactic analysis phase is called the Transducer (Aho & Ullman, 1972; Dovedan, 2012; Dovedan, 2013; Jakupović et al., 2014;Pavlić et al., 2015). Figure 1. describes the Transducer model for the translation of business description to data model.

Based on lexicon and phrase structure grammar – PSG (implemented with the transition table), the Recognizer performs a lexical and syntactic analysis of the input business description. The result is a business description in sentential form. A morphosyntactic lexicon of a language contains word forms, lemmas and morphosyntactic descriptions, i.e. lexical items in the language and their linguistic properties. In their previous research, the authors used lexicon MULTEXT-East (Multilingual Text Tools and Corpora for Eastern and Central European Languages) – lexicon that is based on the results of the project MULTEXT and its spin-off name MULTEXT-East that was embraced by the European Commission and the U.S. National Science Foundation. Every lexical item in this lexicon has the following three attributes (Erjavec, 2010a)(Erjavec, 2010b):

- **Word-Form:** The inflected form of the word,
- **Lemma:** The base form of the word, and
- **MSD:** A morphosyntactic description of the lexical item.

Figure 1. Transducer model for business description to data model translation

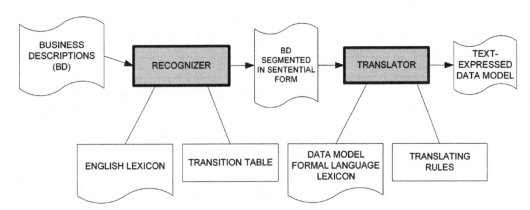

So far the authors have used PSG, which covers only some simple forms of declarative sentences. This PSG is synthesized from (Brinton & Brinton, 2010), (Celce-Murcia & Larsen-Freeman, 1999) and (Quirk, Greenbaum, Leech, & Svartvik, 1985) (see Table 1). Its rules are presented by the following symbols that are adapted to the format that is used in the MULTEXT-East morphosyntactic description (MSD) (Jakupović et al., 2014).

Certain word classes of the lexicon are represented with the following MULTEXT-East lexicon MSD category (see Table 2).

Table 1. PSG used by authors

S	→	*NP VP*
NP	→	*[D	NPs] N'	Np	Pro*
D	→	*Dd	Di	Dg	Ds*
NPs	→	*([Dd | Di | Dg | Ds | NPs] N' | Np |Pg) 's*
N'	→	*Nc*
N'	→	*AP Nc*
N'	→	*Nc PP*
N'	→	*AP Nc PP*
AP	→	*AP [Rs |AdvP]A| [Rs |AdvP]A*
AdvP	→	*[Rs]Rm*
PP	→	*PP [PSpec] Sp (NP	PP)	[PSpec]Sp (NP	PP)*
PSpec	→	*Rmp |Mc Nc*
Pro	→	*Pp |Pg*
VP	→	*Vm [NP' [NP'	PP	AP [PP]]	AP [PP]	PP [PP]]*
NP'	→	*[D	NPs] N'	Np	Pro'*
Pro'	→	*Pro	Px*
A	→	*Af*
V	→	*Vm*

Table 2. Word classes and corresponding MULTEXT-East lexicon MSD category

MSD Category	Word Class	MSD Category	Word Class
Dd	demonstrative determiner	Pg	general pronoun
Di	indefinite determiner	Rm	modifier adverb
Dg	general determiner	Rmp	positive modifier adverb
Ds	possessive determiner	Rs	specifier adverb
Nc	common noun	Mc	cardinal numeral
Np	proper noun	Sp	preposition
Pp	personal pronoun	Vm	main verb
Ps	possessive pronoun	Af	qualificative adjective
Px	reflexive pronoun		

For the sentence "The customer pays the invoice." the recognizer which uses the above lexicon and PSG would provide the next sentential form as the result: "Dd Nc Vm Dd Nc". For words that form the observed sentence, the MULTEXT-East lexicon contains the following lexical items (see Table 3).

By replacing the words in the sentence with the corresponding MSD, the following sentential forms are obtained:

- Dd Nc Vm Dd Nc,
- Dd Nc Vm Dd Vm,
- Dd Nc Nc Dd Nc, and
- Dd Nc Nc Dd Vm.

For the recognizer to discover which sentential form is valid, PSG is used. The validation process consists of finding the derivation sequence, starting with *S*, the result of which would be that sentential form. Only for sentential form "Dd Nc Vm Dd Nc", the derivation sequence can be found, so this sentential form is valid and this is the recognizer output.

Business description in sentential form is the input to translator. Translator (using translation rules) translates each sentential form into one or more sentential forms of the data model language.

Table 3. Word form, Lemma and MSD from MULTEXT-East lexicon for the sentence: "The customer pays the invoice"

Word-Form	Lemma	MSD
the	the	Dd
customer	customer	Nc
pays	pay	Nc
pays	pay	Vm
invoice	invoice	Nc
invoice	invoice	Vm

Then, by using its lexicon, it derives the final sentence into the data model language which eventually results in the data model. It is possible that the translation from sentential form of business description results in an incomplete sentential form in data model language. PSG for data model language will be used to find out which parts of the sentential form in data model language are missing. This will enable asking the user questions in order to complement the sentential forms.

The following potential users of the new KB system for data modelling have been identified: Business Domain Experts, IS Designers, IS Educators, IS Students and Researchers. Based on identified users, the basic KB system objectives were defined:

- Designer's knowledge and skills upgrade,
- Contribution to data modelling in business domain,
- Contribution to data modelling in education, and
- Contribution to conceptual modelling in scientific domain.

These objectives will be achieved through the following KB system functionalities:

- Translation of natural language business description into text-expressed data model
- Translation of text-expressed data model into natural language business description, and
- Explanation of both translation processes.

The KB system will have the ability to act in two ways: receive input in the form of a business description in natural language and translate it into a data model and vice versa, receive input in text-expressed data model and translate it into the corresponding business description. Having all requirements and functionalities in mind, a conceptual model of the new KB system composed of four major subsystems was developed:

1. Business description to data model translation:
   a. Business description update,
   b. Syntactic analysis and validation of business description, and
   c. ER constructs identification and model formation.
2. Data model to business description translation:
   a. Data model update,
   b. Syntactic analysis and validation of data model, and
   c. Word/phrase identification and business description formation.
3. Business description and/or data model view and explanation, and
4. Knowledge base updates.

All identified users of the new KB system are grouped into: Input provider user group, output consumer and KB system engineer.

In order to clearly describe the conceptual model of verbalisation based KB system for data modelling as well as its sub-systems and their information relationships, a variant of the basic Logic model that describes the system through the "if-then" (causal) relationships between the elements (subsystems) of the observed system are used (Figure 2.). Logic model consists of the following components: Purpose (What is the system/subsystem's purpose? What motivates the need for system/subsystem?), Context

Figure 2. Logical model of the new KB system for data modelling

<table>
<tr>
<td>

PURPOSE

To support the process of developing data models and conceptual models in general.
To support the process of education in data modelling domain.

</td>
<td>

MOTIVATION

Preserving consistency of user requirements.
Avoiding the problem of designers' lack of knowledge, experience and data model representation clarity.

</td>
</tr>
</table>

CONTEXT

Based on the KB system interaction type, three groups of users were identified: **Input providers**, **Output consumers** and **KBS engineer**.
Input providers: business domain experts, IS designers, IS educators, IS students and researchers.
Output consumers: business domain experts, IS designers, IS educators, IS students and researchers.
KBS engineer is the user with the ability to update the system knowledge base.

<table>
<tr>
<td>

INPUTS

Selection of operation: new, update or delete business description or data model.
Business description written in non formalised natural or controlled English Language.
Data model written in formalised language.
Users answers (when a system needs to interact to identify or to validate some constructs).
PSG and morpho-syntactic lexicon for declarative sentences in NL.
PSG and morpho-syntactic lexicon for Data model formalized sentences.
PSG and morpho-syntactic lexicon for interrogative sentences for the user in NL.
Translation rules from NL to data model language and vice versa.
Demand for specification view and/or data model view and/or explanation.

</td>
<td>

ACTIVITIES

KB system creates a new, deletes or updates existing business description and translates them to the data model.
KB system does syntactic analysis and validation of NL description (specification), provides feedback to users and stores each validation failed sentences in NL description.
KB system uses previous created data model for case based reasoning about new data model.
KB system stores each NL specification and corresponding data model.
KB system stores each step in process of translation from NL description to data model.
KB system stores translation rules and rules for QA system in corresponding data store.
KB system provides original NL specification, corresponding data model or explanation how it made translation from NL specification to corresponding data model.

</td>
</tr>
</table>

OUTPUTS

List of existing business descriptions and data models stored in KB system.
Information of business description or data model validation failed with explanation.
Polar questions for validation of proposed data model or NL sentences that represents business description.
NL specification view, corresponding data model view, translation steps explanation.

EFFECTS

Data model derived using KB system increases consistency of user requirements expressed in natural language during their translation into the formal language of the data model.
Possibility for business domain experts to create data model without IS design knowledge.
Support for IS designers in the development of data model.
Increased effectiveness and efficiency of IS education.
Other domain researchers are facilitated in the development of conceptual model applying the ER method for data modelling.

(What is the system/subsystem's environment? Who interacts with the system/subsystem?), Inputs (What are the system/subsystem's inputs?), Activities (What does system/subsystem do with inputs?), Outputs (What are the system/subsystem's outputs? What evidence is there that the activities were performed as planned?), Effects (What are the direct or indirect effects, results' consequences, outcomes, or impacts of the activities?) (McLaughlin & Jordan, 1999).

Outputs of the KB system for data modelling will be evaluated by a group of experts by comparing the business description and proposed data model, in order to verify the system (the extent to which the resulting data model represents the semantics of the business description) and validate it (whether the resulting data model includes all the essential semantics of a business description).

Identified effects of KB system for data modelling will be checked by specially developed questionnaires that will be filled in by different users of the system after its use in a given period of time.

CONCLUSION

The paper describes the process of data modelling and especially the entity-relationship method. The main actors involved in this process are also discussed. An overview of KB systems, methods, and tools for data modelling is shown.

The authors develop a new KB system for data modelling, which is based on verbalisation – the textual representation of knowledge. The main idea is to reduce the problem of data modelling based on the business description to the problem of translation from a controlled natural language in which the business description is verbalized into a specially defined formal language in which the data model is verbalized. The authors introduced the main sub-systems of the new KB system for data modelling and presented PSG and lexicon that will be used in the translation process.

The analysis of existing KB systems, methods and tools for data modelling, pointed out the elements of performance that are functional and effective and those that have proved to be ineffective and burdensome for the user. The elements of performance that various authors used in their systems are: restrictive and guidance user interface for data modelling, pre-processing (with a formalisation method) of business descriptions, elimination of semantic redundancy, syntactic and semantic analysis, special formal languages, CNL and/or SBVR languages, and existence of rules and reasoning based on the previous data model cases. The analysed systems are intended for employees of business domains that do not have experience in data modelling or designers, mostly beginners.

The new KB system for data modelling which the authors are developing will use a business description in the format of a subset of a natural language (CNL) as input. During the KB system development, special focus will be on the derivation of translation rules. The KB system should also have the ability to lead the user through the process of creating a completely new data model and also to consult past cases. The aim is to minimize the number of system questions for the user since a large number of questions have a negative impact on the user experience. Therefore, an extra sub-system for a question-answering dialogue will be developed. The output format of the data model produced by the system will be the formalised textual description, sufficient to create an ERD.

So far, a regular grammar for the system's input consisting in English language subset is completed. Subsequently, grammar is translated into finite deterministic automata, by which syntactic analysis of the input sentence is performed. Current research activities include derivation of the Entities-Attributes-Relations-Cardinalities (EARC) grammar and translation rules for translation of syntactically valid business description sentences (precisely their Multext-East categories) into EARC categories.

ACKNOWLEDGMENT

The research has been conducted under the project "Extending the information system development methodology with artificial intelligence methods" (reference number 13.13.1.2.01.) supported by the University of Rijeka (Croatia).

REFERENCES

Aho, A. V., & Ullman, J. D. (1972). The Theory of Parsing, Translation and compiling.: Vol. 1. *Parsing*. Prentice-Hall.

Al-Safadi, L. A. E. (2009). Natural Language Processing for Conceptual Modeling. *International Journal of Digital Content Technology and Its Applications*, *3*(3), 47–59.

Antony, S., Batra, D., & Santhanam, R. (2005). The use of a knowledge-based system in conceptual data modeling. *Decision Support Systems*, *41*(1), 176–188. doi:10.1016/j.dss.2004.05.011

Antony, S., & Santhanam, R. (2008). Could the Use of a Knowledge-Based System Lead to Implicit Learning? In International Handbook on Information Systems- Handbook on Decision Support Systems 1 Basic Themes (pp. 791–812). Springer. doi:10.1007/978-3-540-48713-5_35

Antony, S. R., & Batra, D. (2002). CODASYS: A consulting tool for novice database designers. *The Data Base for Advances in Information Systems*, *33*(3), 54–88. doi:10.1145/569905.569911

Bajwa, I. S., Lee, M. G., & Bordbar, B. (2011). SBVR business rules generation from natural language specification.*AAAI Spring Symposium - Technical Report, SS-11-03*, 2–8.

Batini, C., Ceri, S., & Navathe, S. B. (1992). *Conceptual Database Design An Entity-Relationship Approach*. Redwood City, CA: The Benjamin/Cummings Publishing Company.

Batra, D., & Antony, S. R. (1994). Novice errors in conceptual database design. *European Journal of Information Systems*, *3*(1), 57–69. doi:10.1057/ejis.1994.7

Brancheau, J. C., & Brown, C. V. (1993). The management of end-user computing: Status and directions. *ACM Computing Surveys*, *25*(4), 437–482. doi:10.1145/162124.162138

Brinton, L. J., & Brinton, D. M. (2010). *The Linguistic Structure of Modern English*. Philadelphia: John Benjamins Publishing Company. doi:10.1075/z.156

Btoush, E. S., & Hammad, M. M. (2015). *Generating ER Diagrams from Requirement Specifications Based On Natural Language Processing*. Academic Press.

Burton-jones, A., Wand, Y., & Weber, R. (2009). Guidelines for Empirical Evaluations of Conceptual Modeling Grammars * Guidelines for Empirical Evaluations of Conceptual Modeling Grammars. *Journal of the Association for Information Systems*, *10*(6), 495–532.

Celce-Murcia, M., & Larsen-Freeman, D. (1999). *The Grammar Book: An ESL/EFL Teacher's Course*. Boston: Heinle & Heinle.

Chen, P. P.-S. (1976). The Entity-Relationship Unified View of Data Model-Toward a. *ACM Transactions on Database Systems*, *1*(1), 9–36. doi:10.1145/320434.320440

Chidambaram, L. (1999). Knowledge transfer in conceptual modeling by end users. *Journal of End User Computing*, *11*(1), 40–51. doi:10.4018/joeuc.1999010105

Choobineh, J., & Lo, A. W. (2004). CABSYDD: Case-Based System for Database Design. *Journal of Management Information Systems*, *21*(3), 281–314. doi:10.1080/07421222.2004.11045813

Dovedan, H. Z. (2012). *Formalni jezici i prevodioci – sintaksna analiza i primjene*. Zagreb: Element.

Dovedan, H. Z. (2013). *Formalni jezici i prevodioci – prevođenje i primjene*. Zagreb: Element.

Edberg, D. T., & Bowman, B. J. (1996). User-developed applications: An empirical study of application quality and development productivity. *Journal of MIS, 13*(1), 167–186.

Eid, M. I. (2012). *A Learning System For Entity Relationship Modeling*. PACIS.

Elmasri, R., & Navathe, S. B. (2011). *Fundamentals of Database Systems* (6th ed.). Addison-Wesley.

Erjavec, T. (2010a). *MULTEXT-East - Morphosyntactic Specifications* (Version 4). Retrieved December 20, 2015, from http://nl.ijs.si/ME/V4/msd/html/index.html

Erjavec, T. (2010b). MULTEXT-East Version 4: Multilingual Morphosyntactic Specifications, Lexicons and Corpora. In *Proceedings of the LREC 2010*. Malta: European Language Resources Association.

Fuchs, N. E., Kaljurand, K., & Kuhn, T. (2008). Attempto controlled english for knowledge representation. Lecture Notes in Computer Science, 5224, 104–124.

Gomez, F., Segami, C., & Delaune, C. (1999). A system for the semiautomatic generation of E-R models from natural language specifications. *Data & Knowledge Engineering, 29*(1), 57–81. doi:10.1016/S0169-023X(98)00032-9

Hart, G., Johnson, M., & Dolbear, C. (2008). Rabbit: Developing a Control Natural Language for Authoring Ontologies. In *5th European Semantic Web Conference (ESWC'08)* (pp. 348–360). doi:10.1007/978-3-540-68234-9_27

Jakupović, A., Pavlić, M., & Dovedan, H. Z. (2014). Formalisation method for the text expressed knowledge. *Expert Systems with Applications, 41*(11), 5308–5322. doi:10.1016/j.eswa.2014.03.006

Jakupović, A., Pavlić, M., Meštrović, A., & Jovanović, V. (2013). Comparison of the Nodes of Knowledge method with other graphical methods for knowledge representation. In *Proceedings of the 36th international convention: Croatian Society for Information and Communication Technology, Electronics and Microelectronics MIPRO* (pp. 1276–1280).

Kazi, Z., Kazi, L., & Radulovic, B. (2012). Analysis of data model correctness by using automated reasoning system. *Technics Technologies Education Management, 7*(3), 1090–1100.

Kim, N., Lee, S., & Moon, S. (2008). Formalized Entity Extraction Methodology for Changeable Business Requirements. *Journal of Information Science and Engineering, 24*, 649–671.

Kleiner, M., Albert, P., & Bézivin, J. (2009). Parsing SBVR-Based Controlled Languages. In Lecture Notes in Computer Science: Vol. 5795. Model Driven Engineering Languages and Systems (pp. 122–136). Springer. doi:10.1007/978-3-642-04425-0_10

Lee, S., Kim, N., & Moon, S. (2010). Context-adaptive approach for automated entity relationship modeling. *Journal of Information Science and Engineering, 26*(6), 2229–2247.

Lo, A. W., & Choobineh, J. (2002). Knowledge-Based Systems as Database Design Tools: A Comparative Study. In V. Sugumaran (Ed.), *Intelligent Support Systems Technology: Knowledge Management*. IRM Press.

Lucas, F. J., Molina, F., & Toval, A. (2009). A systematic review of UML model consistency management. *Information and Software Technology, 51*(12), 1631–1645. doi:10.1016/j.infsof.2009.04.009

McLaughlin, J. A., & Jordan, G. B. (1999). Logic models: A tool for telling your programs performance story. *Evaluation and Program Planning, 22*(1), 65–72. doi:10.1016/S0149-7189(98)00042-1

Merson, P. (2009). Data Model as an Architectural View. *Solutions*, 1–10. Retrieved from http://www.sei.cmu.edu/reports/09tn024.pdf

Mitrovic, A., Koedinger, K., & Martin, B. (2003). A Comparative Analysis of Cognitive Tutoring and Constraint-Based Modeling. *Proceedings of Int. Conf. User Modeling, 2702*, 147.

Njonko, P. B. F., Cardey, S., Greenfield, P., & El Abed, W. (2014). RuleCNL: A controlled natural language for business rule specifications. Lecture Notes in Computer Science, 8625, 66–77. http://doi.org/doi:<ALIGNMENT.qj></ALIGNMENT>10.1007/978-3-319-10223-8_7

Omar, N., Hanna, P., & Kevitt, P. M. (2006). Semantic Analysis in the Automation of ER Modelling through Natural Language Processing. In *International Conference Computing & Informatics, ICOCI, Kuala Lumpur* (pp. 2–6). doi:10.1109/ICOCI.2006.5276559

Panian, Ž., & Ćurko, K. (2010). *Poslovni informacijski sustavi*. Zagreb: Sveučilište u Zagrebu.

Pavlić, M. (2009). *Informacijski sustavi*. Rijeka: Odjel za informatiku Sveučilišta u Rijeci.

Pavlić, M. (2011). *Oblikovanje baza podataka*. Rijeka: Odjel za informatiku Sveučilišta u Rijeci.

Pavlić, M., Dovedan, H. Z., & Jakupović, A. (2015). Question Answering with a Conceptual Framework for Knowledge-Based System Development Node of Knowledge.. *Expert Systems with Applications, 42*(12), 5264–5286. doi:10.1016/j.eswa.2015.02.024

Pavlić, M., Jakupović, A., & Meštrović, A. (2013). Nodes of knowledge method for knowledge representation. *Informatologia., 46*(3), 206–214.

Pavlić, M., Meštrović, A., & Jakupović, A. (2013). Graph-Based Formalisms for Knowledge Representation. In *Proceedings of the 17th World Multi-Conference on Systemics Cybernetics and Informatics (WMSCI 2013)* (pp. 200–204).

Quirk, R., Greenbaum, S., Leech, G., & Svartvik, J. (1985). *A comprehensive grammar of the English language*. New York: Longman Inc.

Rockart, J. F., & Flannery, L. S. (1983). The management of end-user computing. *Communications of the ACM, 26*(10), 776–784. doi:10.1145/358413.358429

Rolf, S. (2010). Controlled Natural Languages for Knowledge Representation. In *COLING '10,Proceedings of the 23rd International Conference on Computational Linguistics*, (pp. 1113–1121).

Sajja, P. S., & Akerkar, R. (2010). Knowledge-Based Systems for Development. In P. S. Sajja & R. Akerkar (Eds.), *Advanced Knowledge Based Systems: Model, Applications & Research* (Vol. 1, pp. 1–11). Sudbury, MA: Jones & Bartlett Publishers.

Selway, M., Grossmann, G., Mayer, W., & Stumptner, M. (2015). Formalising natural language specifications using a cognitive linguistic/configuration based approach. *Information Systems*, *54*, 191–208. doi:10.1016/j.is.2015.04.003

Shahbaz, M., Ahsan, S., Shaheen, M., & Nawab, R. M. A. (2011). Automatic Generation of Extended ER Diagram Using Natural Language Processing. *Journal of American Science*, *7*(8).

Shoval, P., & Shiran, S. (1997). Entity-relationship and object-oriented data modeling — An experimental comparison of design quality. *Data & Knowledge Engineering*, *21*(3), 297–315. doi:10.1016/S0169-023X(97)88935-5

Siau, K., & Rossi, M. (2011). Evaluation techniques for systems analysis and design modelling methods - a review and comparative analysis. *Information Systems Journal*, *21*(3), 249–268. doi:10.1111/j.1365-2575.2007.00255.x

Siau, K., Wand, Y., & Benbasat, I. (1996). When parents need not have children – cognitive biases in information modeling. In P. Constantopoulos, J. Mylopoulos, & Y. Vassiliou (Eds.), *Advanced Information Systems Engineering* (pp. 402–420). London: Springer-Verlag. doi:10.1007/3-540-61292-0_22

Spanoudakis, G., & Zisman, A. (2001). Inconsistency Management in Software Engineering: Survey and Open Research Issues. In S. K. Chang (Ed.), *Handbook of Software Engineering and Knowledge Engineering* (Vol. 1, pp. 329–380). World Scientific Publishing Co. doi:10.1142/9789812389718_0015

Storey, V. C. (1988). *View Creation: An Expert System for Database Design*. Washington, DC: ICIT Press.

Storey, V. C., & Goldstein, R. C. (1993). Knowledge-based approaches to database design. *Management Information Systems Quarterly*, *17*(1), 25–46. doi:10.2307/249508

Suraweera, P., & Mitrovic, A. (2004). An intelligent tutoring system for entity relationship modelling. *International Journal of Artificial Intelligence in Education*, *14*, 375–417.

Teorey, T. J. (1999). *Database Modeling and Design: The Fundamental Principle* (3rd ed.). St. Louis, MO: Morgan Kaufmann.

Thonggoom, O., Song, I., & An, Y. (2011). Semi-automatic Conceptual Data Modeling Using Entity and Relatinship Instance Repositories. *Conceptual Modeling – ER 2011*, *6998*, 219–232.

Turban, E., McClean, E., & Wetherbe, J. (1999). *Information Technology and Management*. New York: John Wiley.

KEY TERMS AND DEFINITIONS

Controlled Natural Language: A subset of a natural language with the restricted grammar and lexicon. Its purpose is to reduce ambiguity and complexity of the natural language.

Data Modelling: A process used to define and analyse the information needs of the information system users by applying some formal representation of a data and data relations (for example Bachman diagram, Barker's notation, Chen's notation, Martin's notation, IDEF1X, UML Class diagram etc.). The result of the data modelling is a data model. A Data model is an abstract model (usually graphically represented) that shows a data and data relations from some real world situation.

Entity-Relationship Method: A method for representing a data and data relations. The result is the Entity-Relationship (ER) model, graphically representation of a data and data relations from some real world situation. The ER model is composed of entity types (which classify the things of interest) and specifies relationships that can exist between instances of those entity types.

Knowledge-Based System: A computer system that uses the methods and techniques of artificial intelligence to solve problems. Such systems interact with the user in which they aid, train him/her and/or resolve problems. The general structure of the KB system includes: knowledge base inference engine, self-learning, explanation and reasoning and user interface.

Formal Language: A language designed for use in situations in which natural language is unsuitable (mathematics, logic, computer programming, process modelling, data modelling etc.). It can be symbolic or graphic. One of the methods for specification of the formal language uses formal grammar and lexicon. Type of the formal grammar is the phrase structure grammar (PSG). PSG consists of phrase-structure rules. Phrase-structure rules describe a language's syntax – syntactically correct sequence of words (sentence) from the lexicon (set of words and word characteristics in some language).

Parser: Software that provides syntactic analysis of a sentence using the rules of a formal grammar. A sentence is the sentence of the language if there is a set of grammar rules that generate analysed sentence.

Recognizer: A machine that takes a string (sentence) as input. The machine will accept string if the machine stops at an accepting state. Otherwise, a string is rejected. It is used for syntactic analysis of a sentence, i.e. to verify if a sentence is the sentence of the language.

Translator: Software that translates the input sentence in the source language into the output sentence in the targeted language. Translation process consists of a few phases: lexical and syntactic analysis of the input sentence (for example with the Recognizer) and output sentence generation. A Translator that uses Recognizer for the syntactic analysis is called Transducer.

Chapter 17
Six Sigma Project Teams and Rational Decision Making:
A Shared Leadership Perspective

Brian J. Galli
Long Island University, USA

Kathryn Szabat
La Salle University, USA

Mohamad Amin Kaviani
Islamic Azad University, Iran

ABSTRACT

An understanding of how teams make decisions in the team environment is of utmost importance to organizational leaders. This research aims to determine the relationship that a shared leadership environment has on a team's approach to decision-making. A systematic review of past research efforts has shown that a strong relationship exists between the internal and external conditions of shared leadership and that a strong relationship exists between shared leadership and six sigma team decision-making principles and approaches. Furthermore, a review of the relationship between shared leadership and team decision making techniques has shown that the consensual approach is the most effective method to achieve the functional conditions of shared leadership. Based on the presented research, a model of decision-making in shared leadership environments is proposed for use by teams to determine the type of decision-making method that should be employed as a team's level of shared leadership increases. This model has been shown to have many practical applications for business as well as for academic research.

DOI: 10.4018/978-1-5225-2382-6.ch017

INTRODUCTION

In the past two decades, organizations have increased their push for employees to work efficiently in completing projects in order to be competitive and to outperform competition. In order to meet the needs of the organization, more projects are being executed through the use of different team formats. These team formats enable the organization to quickly adjust to the various requirements and demands of its industry. The proper team format needs to be selected in order for a group of people to work effectively as a team, since it enables the group to make rational, timely, and effective decisions. Over the past twenty-five years, research into shared leadership models has significantly increased since this type of team format has proven to allow team members to complete projects on time and make decisions that were both logical and effective (Koschzeck, 2009).

In this study we examine two main hypotheses. First it is proposed that shared leadership environments have an effect on group/team decision making as well as the methods that are used to make group/team decisions (Hypothesis 1). Second, it is also proposed that the consensus decision-making method is the technique that is the most effective and closely related to the fundamental conditions and requirements of a shared leadership environment (Hypothesis 2). Furthermore, it is believed that a model of shared leadership decision-making can be developed from the results of these hypotheses. The purpose of this paper will be to answer the following questions: How does shared leadership in group/team environments affect the methods used in team decision-making? Based on the needs of shared leadership environments, what methods have proven to be the most effective in making group/team decisions in shared leadership environments?

In order to answer these questions, this paper aims to determine the relationship and effects (if any) that a shared leadership environment has on the team's approach to decision-making. Based on the internal and external environmental needs of a shared leadership, the final segment of the paper will investigate how decisions are made in shared leadership environments (i.e. the methods that have proven to be most effective in shared leadership environments) as well as outline a model for decision-making in shared leadership environments, which can be used by teams to determine the type of decision-making method that it should be employing as its level of shared leadership increases over time.

The remainder of this paper is organized as follows. Section 2 highlights recent research relevant to the topic of the paper. Section 3 outlines the methodology used in the research. Key findings are presented in Section 4. Section 5 discusses the implications of the research findings and proposes a model of shared leadership decision-making. Section 6 concludes the paper with final thoughts and suggested future steps for this area of research.

RESEARCH BACKGROUND

Shared Leadership

The concept of leadership is comprised of four main components: "leadership involves influence; leadership is a process; leadership involves goal attainment; and leadership occurs in a group context" (Northouse, 2007, p. 3). Based on the existed literature, shared leadership is a concept that is known by many names, including: team leadership, distributive leadership, co-leadership, collective leadership, shared governance, shared power, and blended leadership (Koschzeck, 2009). Shared leadership implies the idea that team members accept the responsibility and accountability of leadership in the team setting; team members actively share responsibility of the leadership role (Yukl, 2006). The team members work as one to accomplish a shared vision or set of objectives and act as both followers and leaders. Research into the different definitions of shared leadership has shown that shared responsibility, influence, accountability, and decision-making (shared power) were the most common factors associated with shared leadership (Northouse, 2007). The use of shared leadership enables individuals to increase their levels of empowerment, decision-making, team effectiveness, accountability, and responsibility. Past research efforts has shown that the use of shared leadership results in increased job satisfaction, shared sense of purpose and vision, improved communication, and reduced employee turnover (Koschzeck, 2009).

Pearce and Conger (2003) present the concern that there are many definitions or views of shared leadership and what it is; their paper goes into depth about the vast array of concepts and definitions of shared leadership, which in turn shows the lack of uniformity in the field of leadership. Their research also highlights the fact that currently there are very few empirical studies that investigate shared leadership; they point out that there are mostly theoretical studies, but they also concluded that there are many barriers that exist to performing empirical studies in this field. The researchers investigate the evidence around the idea that there is a temporal factor influencing shared leadership; the research concludes that there is evidence to support the idea that shared leadership is influenced by time.

Research shows that to have an effective shared leadership environment, a team must have two conditions satisfied: external coaching and internal team environment. External coaching (i.e. external leadership) is defined as "direct interaction with a team intended to help team members make coordinated and task-appropriate use of their collective resources in accomplishing the team's task" (Carson, Marrone and Tesluk, 2007, p. 1218). Supportive coaching from external leaders has shown to contribute to the development of shared leadership since it encourages the development of individual and team competence, as well as individual interdependence among team members. External coaching is critical since at the start of any project, members lack a sense of shared purpose, do not provide social support, nor do they encourage full engagement or participation. When a team has not developed a high level of voice, social support, and shared purpose, the supportive external coaching approach can aid in the emergence of shared leadership. This concept has been found to be directly linked to the second input condition since a strong external coaching condition can provide a team with the support it needs to develop its internal team environment (Carson et al., 2007).

The internal team environment is known to consist of three dimensions: shared purpose, social support, and voice. These three dimensions have been found to be "highly interrelated and mutually reinforcing, thereby representing a higher order construct" (Carson et al., 2007, p. 1219). Research shows that these three factors work as one unified concept in order to generate a team environment that encourages members to be willing to accept leadership responsibilities as well as be open to rely on other members to display leadership influence. These factors work in cooperation with each other in order to develop an atmosphere that consists of high levels of involvement, cooperation, shared understandings about team goals and purpose, and a sense of recognition. When shared purpose exists, the members have a mutual set of goals and tend to have higher levels of motivation, empowerment, and commitment to their team and their work. Social support is seen as the "interpersonal glue" that helps to build a team with strong internal relationships. Voice is related to the interactions that members have and behaviors that members display in the team setting. These interactions and behaviors result in members having higher levels of social influence, since they are involved more in the leadership responsibilities and team process.

Research by Carter and Justis (2010) sought to understand the development and impact of shared leadership in multi-generational family firms. The research identified that shared leadership is being used more in these settings due to the needs of the environments, and that in these settings, there were eight factors that impact shared leadership development and implementation, namely, close communication, shared understanding, long-term orientation, resistant to change, succession planning, failure to release control, reporting relationship confusion, increased decision time, and higher decision quality.

Ramthun and Matkin (2012) reviewed current literature in which they sought to develop a model of multi-cultural shared leadership. Their research found that previous conceptual models of shared leadership have argued that cultural diversity would be a challenge to shared leadership. But their research into multi-cultural shared leadership shows multi-cultural shared leadership does provide significant value and that previous models did not account for the potential impact that intercultural competence could have on enabling multi-cultural teams to form and sustain necessary relationships that would allow shared leadership to take place. Mendez and Busenbark (2015) examined the impact that shared leadership had on the gap between female and male leadership influence in groups. The study found that there are significant perceived differences in levels of influence when comparing the two genders. The study concluded that shared leadership had no significant impact on reducing the gender gap.

Research by Cawthorne (2010) studied how shared leadership is used in academic environments, such as libraries. The study examined how middle managers (from 22 academic libraries) take part in shared leadership and to what extent their environments used shared leadership principles. The results showed that shared leadership in this type of environment was not strongly present due to many organizational factors. The research concluded that as academic libraries change, they need to use more flexible and inclusive leadership approaches such as shared leadership in order to better position middle managers to influence change and the strategic direction of the organization.

According to Drescher and Garbers (2016), shared leadership, commonality (perceived similarities to others) and communication mode are related to each other. An experimental policy-capturing design study not only revealed that both shared leadership and high commonality had positive effects on team members' intended performance and predicted satisfaction but that commonality and communication modes had interactive effects. Moreover, the combined knowledge and competencies of individual team members lead to high performance for teams with shared leadership.

Nicolaides et al.'s (2014) study assesses factors (team confidence, task independence, and team tenure) that contribute to team effectiveness and performance as well as their contributions to the effects of shared leadership on team performance. Shared leadership, a new perspective in team leadership, is examined via meta-analysis methods by analyzing the relationship between shared leadership and team performance over and above vertical leadership. Big companies have implemented team-based structures in order to be successful, flexible, faster, and efficient. This study then concludes that there is a positive relationship between shared leadership and team performance.

Balkundi and Kilduff (2006) performed a study that examined how the synergy (combined effort) between leadership research and social network approaches (cognitive, 'ego' inter-organizational, and organizational networks) contribute to leadership effectiveness. Good leadership can create new perceptions of interactions between the minds of individuals and the networks through which actors exchange information. Moreover, perceptions of their daily interactions with organizational members of the different networks may or may not necessarily be connected with the leader but they can potentially influence the leader's cognition and inadvertently affect the leader's outcome by changing the way the leader operates throughout the whole organization, bypassing formal leaders and social clusters, and therefore fostering a more effective leadership. The study states that it is evident that the network perspective, emphasizing already known leadership researches, points to new directions.

Avolio et al. (2009) performed a study where a holistic view of leadership examined not only leadership models but the dynamic interactions of leader, followers, peers, supervisors, work setting context, culture, and their levels in private, public, and non-for-profit organizations. Leadership process was examined: how the leader and followers process information and how this interpretation affects their environment. Alternative approaches for examining leadership such as how integrating qualitative and quantitative methods, were highlighted. Because leadership is constantly evolving, the focus is on what is current in the field rather than on past research. However, this study states that over the next 10 years, there will be an increase demand for research and theory in leadership, especially in positive leadership and its impact in society, and technology.

Denis et al. (2010) performed a study that examined how practical knowledge developed within and around an organization can be a great asset for leaders to be able to move in different settings within an organization. The study states that effective leadership cannot be exercised in large, complex, and messy organizations without having numerous implications and that leadership in complex organizations cannot be viewed as an external authority that influences others from the outside. The inclusion of the dynamic, collective, situated, and dialectical nature of leadership practices is encouraged in research and training for awareness and effective leadership. However, more studies need to be performed to analyze practical activities of leaders in complex organizations (mostly large organizations) where multiple groups with different values, interests, and expertise compete for influence.

Detert and Burris's (2007) study focuses on leadership behavior (approachable and accessible) and their influence on employees to voluntarily voice their suggestions. Employees' suggestions and comments seem to be a good idea for organizations to improve their functioning and remain healthy in today's environment. However, employees provide insufficient feedback, possibly because employees might see it as a risky move that may outweigh its benefits. It was suggested that their behaviors should be measured to help companies differentiate between managers who welcome voice and those who do not. Cianci et al.'s (2014) study stated that authentic leaders not only promote positive psychological and ethical climate but they foster positive self-development in followers. Followers usually tend not to morally disengage from ethical decision-makings because of the guilt associated with such act. However, if temptation is not present, authentic leaders have no effect on ethical decision-making. Moreover, authentic leadership is low with followers with high morality.

Dane and Pratt's (2007) study stated that intuition can be used by management for critical or strategic decisions that must be made under time constraints as a way to make both fast and accurate decisions. These decisions usually arise through rapid, non-conscious, and holistic associations. However, Dane and Pratt (2007) indicated that the issue here is whether managers use their intuitions right and effectively. If not, it does create a problem. This study, suggests more research on intuition is important to build on the theory, and to increase attention on non-conscious processes. Spencer et al.'s (2011) study considered factors, such as ownership, leadership, leader's intuition, and preference, which influence small owner-managed travel firms' decisions in adopting new technologies. The article states that leadership of small firms, led by self-interest, not only affects firm strategy and resource used but also it seems to be the most significant driver in the decision-making process.

Six Sigma Team Decision-Making

One of the major requirements for any team to survive is the concept of decision-making (Northouse, 2007). A team decision "can be defined as a decision that would not have been thought of by an individual alone; is a sound solution to the problem; is a decision based upon input, as unbiased as possible, from each team member; and addresses the team's goal for the decision-making process" (Foundation Coalition, 2001). A team can reach a decision through a five-step procedure, including stating the problem, identifying any alternatives, evaluating the alternatives, making a decision, and finally, implementing it (Business Analysis Made Easy, 2006). Despite this commonly used procedure, often high-performing teams will modify it to meet their specific needs, especially since no one model can fit all situations.

In this section, we will discuss the seven methods for rational team decision-making that teams pursue for various reasons. They include decision made by authority without group discussion, also known as the single individual leader decision method, by expert, by averaging individual's opinions, by authority after group discussion, by minority, by majority vote, and by consensus (Resource International, 2009).

A situation in which a single leader makes all the decisions without consulting the team members is known as decision made by a single authority without group discussion. Research indicates the best time to use this method is when there is minimal time to make a decision, when there is a requirement for a routine decision to be made, and when the environment and team commitment are relatively low.

On the other hand, decision by expert is when the team selects an individual to take the role of expert. His/her task is to consider all the issues and make the final decisions. This method is most common when there is a clear choice in the selection of the expert. It also appears in situations in which results of the decision heavily rely on specific expertise or when the environment and six sigma team commitment is low.

Decision made by authority branches away from the two previously discussed methods in that the six sigma team develops and discusses different ideas, but the final decision is made by their designated leader. The leader will present an issue to the six sigma team, listen to their ideas, and then make the final decision while weighing the inputs of all the members. This method for decision-making is most common in environments where there is a clear consensus on who should have authority, there is just enough time for the members to interact and discuss but not reach a conclusion, and the environment and team commitment are only moderately low.

Decision by averaging individuals' opinions gives six sigma team members the chance to share their own inputs on a decision. The resulting decision is an average of all compiled inputs from six sigma team members. This is an appropriate method for teams in which active participation is necessary but lengthy interaction time is not feasible, time for reaching a decision is severely limited, and the environment and commitment is relatively low.

Decision by minority is another approach that capitalizes on the input of members that constitute less than 50% of the team to make the final decision. This method will be used most often when it is clear there is a minority group. It is also beneficial when time constraints prevent the entire team from meeting and when the environment and team commitment are moderately low.

Contrary to decision by minority and the other listed methods, decision by majority vote is more commonly implemented in the U.S. Typically, it includes a period of time for the team to discuss the issue at hand until 51% or more of the members agree on the final decision. This is popular in environments where group consensus supports a voting process, there is a time constraint on making decisions, and the environment and team commitment are moderately high.

Finally, decision by consensus is the method for decision-making most distant from decision by a single leader. This is a methodology that calls for a collective decision stemming from an effective communication process. This process ought to involve all members, giving them the chance to share and listen to all ideas. The participants are encouraged to agree to the option being discussed. Furthermore, should a member dissent to the alternative, they are encouraged to explain why. The key factors that comprise this method include listening and offering serious consideration for the minority's dissents and inputs (Resource International, 2009). The dissention educates and may have the power to change the final decision, therefore making this a successful process. It is most common in situations where the team has sufficient background and experience in achieving team consensus, time is ample for a consensus to be reached, and the environment and team commitment are high.

A Del Missier et al. (2012) study further expands the research in team decision-making. The study sheds light on components of team decision-making, especially focusing on executive functions (EF) and certain relationships between aspects of decision-making competence, specific cognitive control functions, and general cognitive abilities such as fluid intelligence and numeracy. They state a positive correlation between decision-making and EF components, in that different decision-making competence involves different EF components and that not all decision-making competence involves EF. Therefore, they conclude that decision-making competencies depend on different sets of abilities and skills, and involve a variety of decision-making aptitudes that are positively related to different fluid intelligence and numeracy abilities.

Finally, Snowden and Boone (2007) performed a study to evaluate the Cynefin framework, which was initially created to help executives view scenarios from new and differing perspectives. What qualifies a leader as a good one is if they can successfully deal with multiple demands at a time, be open to change, and make decisions that comply with the context, all while juggling uncertainty that exists in today's environment. Despite these demands, there is no formula for creating a good leader, and leadership is not quantified as an exact science. The Cynefin framework, therefore, is derived from five contexts defined by cause and effect. They include simple, complicated, complex, chaotic, and disorder. These contexts aid executives in the decision-making process: to make better decisions and to avoid mistakes. It is achievable by rapidly understanding the environment in which the executive is operating in.

Shared Decision-Making

Cervone (2005) found that in order for any team to make an effective decision, it must have a sound methodology that the team can use in order to achieve a decision. In order for a team to develop a sound decision-making methodology, the external leader must provide the guidance and experience that the team needs to help the members learn about decision-making and how effective decisions can be made in their team environment. Cervone's (2005) research also touched upon the fact that there is a delicate relationship between the external leader and the internal behaviors and actions of the team. The basic finding from this research study is that a team decision-making process must be supported by a sound methodology and by the external leader. If these elements are present, the team should have the necessary tools and support to handle any type of decision, regardless of the decision's complexity.

Bisol and Roy (2014) investigated how shared leadership could be used in a healthcare environment in order to improve the decision-making, competency, and regulatory performance of staff members. Their research showed that the introduction of a shared leadership model helped to create an environment that was interactive and employees felt more respect, collaboration, enthusiasm and progress in place of competition, frustration or burnout. Their research identified that shared leadership models are influence by three dimensions: social support, voice, and shared purpose; they found that all of these dimensions must be present in the environment in order to promote and sustain shared leadership.

Ledford et al. (2006) utilized a shared leadership approach in order to improve a hospital's performance in decision-making in relation to emergency room triage. The use of shared leadership decision-making models not only improve the decision-making while under the pressure of triage, but it also helped the organization to implement an improved documentation charting system as well as a streamline patient experience in the emergency department. Their research found that all of these outcomes occurred since the shared leadership model not only encouraged a voice from all of the staff, but it also empowered the staff to make the necessary changes to the work culture to successfully deploy and sustain this type of decision-making environment.

Hoegl and Muethel (2013) studied how shared leadership was utilized and what its impact was on independent (self-employed experts) teams. Using the concept of social exchange theory, they studied how decisions were made in these teams and the impact that shared leadership had on these decisions. They found that in order to make effective decisions in independent teams that deploy shared leadership, the teams need to display shared leadership from both the leader and follower perspectives. Their study identified that there are three stages of relationship development (calculus, knowledge, and identification based relationships) that impact the effectiveness of shared leadership in this type of team environment.

Caress and Scott (2005) found that shared decision-making empowers all staff members in the processes. Using this method not only provides members with a framework of how to work together in order to make effective decisions in a timely manner, but also with an environment where all aspects are changed from a single leadership perspective to a team-oriented perspective. This type of governance provides members with a sense of empowerment since they have a collective responsibility and accountability to complete the project at hand, with only support from an external leader. In order for a shared governance environment to exist, members need to rely on each other and share the responsibilities of leadership, especially the decision-making responsibility. Researchers were able to determine that some type of relationship should exist between the components of shared leadership and shared/team decision-making.

Shared decision-making, also known as worker involvement, results in "improved productivity, quality, job satisfaction, organizational commitment, and better acceptance of change among others" (Taveira, 2008, p. 509). Taveira (2008) found that participation was positively and statistically significant in relation to job performance satisfaction. The mentioned research also found that group efforts typically generate more effective solutions that would not be produced by the same individuals if they were working independently. A team's superior outcomes are due to a greater pool of knowledge, mutual influence on each member's thinking, and the interaction process among team members. One of the key elements in utilizing worker involvement is the support from external leaders and top management. This element was found to be essential for the team's functioning. Taveira's (2008) research concluded that management support (i.e. external coaching) is one of the fundamental conditions for implementation of any type of worker involvement initiative. His research also found that management support is critical during the internal team development portion of a project and concluded that the lack of external leadership/support is a critical impediment to team effectiveness and achievement.

Research by Jones and Roelofsma (2000) distinguished teams through the term differentiation, which involves the degree of task specialization, independence, and autonomy of the team members. Teams that have a high level of differentiation are most closely related to shared leadership since they have high levels independence, autonomy, and task specialization. Teams that have a high level of differentiation have a high level of shared decision-making since the members are willing to commit to the team and work as a team (i.e. high level of internal team environment). Jones and Roelofsma (2000) also found that a team's level of team effectiveness is dependent on "the degrees to which team members actively engage in decision-making relevant to the accomplishment of the task". In order to operate effectively, these types of teams need to be well coordinated, have the ability to adapt to change, manage their internal resources, have a strong base of outside support from a leader, and have a strong environment that is based on trust and commitment.

Kocher et al. (2006) found that teams existed in over 54.5% of U.S. firms and that decisions made by teams are expected to not only be better than ones made by individuals, but often be more easily accepted by the masses. The study performed by these researchers found that, when faced with the option to use single individual decision-making methods versus a shared decision-making method, over 60% of the subjects preferred the latter. In addition, the researchers found that decisions made in a team format were much more effective and successful when compared to the decisions made by single individuals. Overall, this research effort found that decisions made by teams outperform decisions made by individuals and members report much higher satisfaction and commitment to the decisions when they have an added input to the decision.

Kugler et al.'s (2012) study reviewed decision-makings by groups over the last 25 years and the results of differences between individual and group interactive decisions (the outcome of one might depend on the decision of another). It was noted that groups make more important decisions often based on collective knowledge, skills, and previous experience. Therefore, groups tend to be more rational and more competitive than individuals. Fath's (2008) study indicated that shared decision making concept is based on nursing practice and models that integrate professional values to achieve the best quality care. These professionals are all involved in decision making. However, this practice is attained by the creation of a collaborative infrastructure to facilitate shared governance, and to foster relationships and practice accountability at all levels. It was then stated that shared decision-making generates shared benefits.

In addition to the mentioned studies, Makoul and Clayman's (2006) study showed that there is no shared definition of a Shared Decision-Making (SDM) process for patients and providers due to the fact that it's been defined very loosely. In the provider-patient relationship model, SDM is positioned as a middle ground between physicians and patients. Part of the problem lies in the assigned roles and responsibilities of each party. More responsibility is usually placed on one party more than another. Therefore, the study concluded that the decision making process should be mutually shared. Zweifel and Haegeli (2014) investigated the aspects of group formation, leadership, and decision-making among winter recreationists when traveling in avalanche terrain. It is important to address weakness in group dynamics and in the group formation process because it not only leads to highly problematic leadership situations but also affects the safety (ability to make safe decisions) of individuals traveling in avalanche terrain. Therefore, the study concludes that forming groups with similar goals and skill levels dominated by favorable behaviors is best.

Patterns of leadership behavior were examined by Bergman et al. (2012) using cluster analysis; results indicate there is less conflict, higher intragroup trust, and cohesion, among team members who shared leadership. This study states that shared leadership can increase team effectiveness, performance, and success, leading to effective leadership. Elbana and Child (2007) performed a study that examined how a model is used to identify three perspectives (decision-specific, environmental, and firm characteristics) that influence the rationality of the decision process. Results of a study in Egypt indicated that the rationality of strategic decision-making process was shaped by variables identified by all three perspectives even though all three perspectives do not contribute equally in explaining the decision rationality. Moreover, while the national setting shapes the way decision makers take account of environmental characteristics, cognitive and political realities limit the decision making process.

Lovelace et al. (2007) performed a study that offers a proactive way for leaders to manage the stressful work environments, and create a positive and active work environment. High work demands, associated responsibilities and low job control hinders the leader's ability to successful manage today's organizations. While self-direction, self-motivation, physical fitness and greater job satisfaction are achieved through self-leadership; increased long-term job control and much of the burden that leads to stress can be eliminated through shared leadership. It was stated that the natural outcome of self and shared leadership practices (flow) creates active and positive work environments that support healthful regeneration and increased engagement as well as to better manage work stress.

Walter et al.'s (2012) research examines the interactive effect of strategic decision-making processes at both the firm and alliance levels. It also examines how both levels interact with each other, and jointly affect alliance performance. Research shows alliance performance depends on the quality decision processes that balance each partner's self-interest and collective actions with both within and between partners, both being dependent on each other's collaborations. The study shows that alliance performance is positively affected by procedural rationality on collective actions between alliance partners. However, it uncovers an unconditional reliance on procedural rationality at the firm level. Moreover, results show that politically charged decision processes compromise alliance performance because they impair alliance partners from making a consensual decision. Wallenius et al.'s (2008) study discussed multiple-criteria decision-making/multi-attribute utility theory (MCDM/MAUT) methods that help a decision maker think about the problem, maximize a utility or value on the basis of two or more criteria or attributes, as part of the decision-making process. This article is an update of a paper published five years ago and validates that conclusions remain valid. Much research has been performed in the MCDM/MAUT field in which it not only has matured but developments and methodologies are continuing to move into other fields, such as engineering, finance.

RESEARCH METHODOLOGY

Systematic review methodology was used to investigate the relationship between shared leadership and team decision-making. A systematic review is a review in which there is a comprehensive search for relevant studies on a specific topic, and those identified are then appraised and synthesized according to a pre-determined explicit method (Klassen et al., 1998). Systematic reviews start with a search of various electronic databases and hand-searches of journals. Because the returns from the first round of searches can be large in number, exclusion criteria are often established to reduce the studies down to a more manageable number; these are the relevant studies that then provide the basis for summary of results.

In order to identify all potential pieces of literature for this study, the following online databases were searched over a 20-year window: EBSCO Host, Elsevier's Scirus, Academy of Management, Google Scholar, Intute: Social Sciences, PROQUEST, Proquest Digital Thesis, Blackwell Publishing, Networked Digital Library of Theses & Dissertations, FirstSearch, Emerald Full Text Database, Academy of Management Perspectives, Executive Development, Journal of Management, and The Sociological Review. To run the queries within the online databases, the following keywords and phrases were explored (note: no filters were used and all combinations of these keywords and phrases were considered): Shared Leadership, Leadership, Decision-Making, Team Dynamics, Social Network Theory, Change Management, Organizational Development, and Shared Decision-Making.

Completing all of these searches returned a total of 600 pieces of literatures (N = 600). From these original pieces of literature and searches, database searches were performed again using the authors' names from the relevant studies identified in the initial searches. Using a search filter further refined this analysis; the main aim of a search filter is to unearth studies and articles of interest from a database. A simple filter for a query consists of single or combined words that are entered into search parameters of a database. Within many search parameters, Boolean algebra can be used to form relationships between words or phrases in order to further refine the output of query requests; the most commonly uses Boolean functions are "AND", "OR" and "NOT" functions.

For the search filter development, two aspects need to be considered and balanced; these are generally referred to as sensitivity and precision (Taylor et al. 2003, Popay et al. 2004, Vaughan, 2004). Sensitivity is the ability of the filter to find all relevant material in the database and precision is its ability to reject irrelevant material. A filter with a high emphasis on sensitivity will tend to include less and irrelevant material where a higher precision will tend to reject some potentially relevant information.

The study investigator's approach for this research was to initially develop a filter with a high level of sensitivity and then make further adjustments towards a desirable level of precision. More specifically, important material search listings obtained from early versions of the filter was closely examined. From there, common and key terms used within this material (and used in relevant cited literature) were incorporated to develop the filters sensitivity along with the wildcarding of some terms. From the precision perspective, examining common categories of irrelevant material returned by the now somewhat more developed filter made the precision adjustment. After some further experimentation, this adjustment was primarily made by changing the structure of the filter, in particular the usage and placement of the AND operators and bracketing of the OR functions. In practice the combination of the specific requirements linked by the AND operator largely excluded irrelevant material to a workable level.

For this study, the search filter included an "AND" relationship and "OR" (with brackets) that searched for keywords and phrases that included "shared leadership" and "decision-making." The filter developed for this study was then applied to the search parameters of each database utilized in the initial search.

From the literature found from the first set of queries, the reference sections of the identified studies were then examined as well as existing reviews of the literature. In addition, in some ways, the filter results had limited success in finding relevant studies and materials in the wider grey literature. Grey literature is typically considered to any material that is not commercially published and can include: working papers, business documents, government reports, educational reports, institutional reports, dissertations, technical reports, and conference proceedings. In addition, grey material could be found through manual searching, which involved examination of references lists from relevant studies obtained in: searches, qualitative studies, relevant journals or books, and articles. This involved the manual examination of relevant journal indexes. Manual searching also involved general and technically oriented Internet search engines and databases, which are maintained by government or commercial organizations. Some of the search engines included: Google, British Library, US Library of Congress, Yahoo, and National Technical Information Service. As a final measure of robustness, to add in the systematic review of the available and relevant material, based on critical literature obtained, the study also utilized direct correspondence with authors identified from the above processes in order to obtain additional information and studies that can be useful for this study.

This search process reduced the N of 600 pieces of literature to a more condensed and rich sample size of n=65 (10.8% of the total literature found). These 65 pieces of literature served as the basis for performing the subsequent analysis relevant to the research objectives and hypotheses.

FINDINGS ANALYSIS

Hypothesis 1

Research by Miskin and Gmelch (1985) has shown that team leadership requires team problem solving skills, since this type of structure provides a basis for productivity and achievement. Without this structure, the team may work well together but still not achieve the goals and objectives of the project. Their research also identified that when a team is supported by an external leader and given the ability to have a strong internal problem-solving structure, the members begin to act as one unit, which results in a strong sense of autonomy and internal team environment (Miskin and Gmelch, 1985). The researchers identified that the external support for the team is a critical component to its productivity and the development of its internal environment. The external leader must empower the team to make its own decisions but also provide the support the team needs. When the internal team environment is strong, the members will adopt more effective methods of communication and sharing with their team members. From these results, one can conclude that a relationship should exist between the components of shared leadership and shared decision-making.

Decisions are typically put into practice more effectively when they are made in a participative environment since they (who/what is they?) have a stronger sense of commitment and support towards the decision-making processes utilized by the teams (Meadows, 1990). In order for a team to have the ability to make an effective decision, the leader should distribute the decision-making power and influence among the team members and empower them to make decisions based on the whole team's input. In addition, Meadows points out that an external leader must provide a supportive environment for the team members since they need to aid the internal members in developing a strong sense of self. This signifies that the team needs to have a sense of self-management and self-identity in order to have the ability to make decisions without the influence of the external leader. Meadows points out that there appears to be some direct relationship with a team's level of self-management and the effectiveness of the decisions that are made by the team. In addition, there appears to be some type of relationship between a team's level of self-management and the level of support provided by an external figure. Based on this, one can again conclude that a relationship should exist between the components of shared leadership and shared decision-making.

According to the Guide to Collaborative Culture and Shared Leadership (Turning Points, n.d.), a relationship between shared leadership and decision-making does exist and this relationship is a primary component of a team's collaborative culture. In a shared leadership environment, decisions are made through participative methods (Ibid). A team that demonstrates shared leadership is one that has a strong collaborative (internal and external environmental conditions) culture as well as a strong ability to share in the decision-making responsibilities. In addition, the shared decision-making was made possible in shared leadership environments due to the level of support and interaction that the external leader provided to the team. In this sense, the external leader shared his/her decision-making power with the team in order to empower the members and provide them with a strong sense of autonomy. The research found that effective shared leadership teams demonstrated high levels of autonomy, empowerment, communication, member participation, and member commitment, especially in the realm of team decision-making. All of these benefits were shown to be the result of the strong levels of the internal and external team conditions.

Research by Gelzheiser et al. (2001) has found that shared leadership and shared decision-making are linked together and that both of these concepts have the potential to provide teams with more effective and efficient decisions. In shared decision-making strategies, there is a specific amount of power and influence that needs to be shared and distributed between the internal and external members. External leadership plays a significant role in the development and maintenance of shared leadership and shared decision-making. In addition, their research review found that an external leader's effectiveness in shared decision-making teams is maximized when he/she "(a) shared decision-making power with team members rather than exercising authoritative power and (b) helped to establish a vision that could guide and unify the team under a common purpose and understanding". Data from Gelzheiser et al. (2001) provides that the relationship between the internal and external environmental conditions for a team is critical towards a team's development of shared leadership and shared decision-making. The data proves that the team requires a high level of support and guidance from the external leader in order to develop shared decision-making among the team members. In environments where shared leadership showed positive signs, the external leader encouraged the members to adopt the distribution of power since the external leader understood that his encouragement would increase the members' willingness to utilize shared decision-making principles.

Gibson and Saxon (2005) found that there is a significant relationship between internal team environment conditions and external leadership in relation to decision-making. When external leadership (support and guidance) is present in a team environment, the internal team environmental conditions will be very strong and the decisions will be much more effective. The most significant finding from this research was that a strong relationship between internal team conditions and external leadership exists and is found to be directly related to the effectiveness of the team's decisions as well as the decision-making process.

Van Ginkel and Van Knippenerg's (2012) study suggested that team leaders may play an important role in shaping group member's mental representations and shared understanding of their teamwork. Groups may benefit from their information exchange and integration, which positively affect group members task representations, shared understanding, and decision quality. Leaders feel that they have to justify their decisions (reasons for and against the behavior) to others. Westaby et al. (2010) performed a study that examined the links between leadership decision-making, intentions, and behavior and how reasoning is related to leaders' attitudes, subjective norms and perceived control using the behavioral reasoning theory. Results indicated that the behavioral reasoning theory proposes that context-specific reasons are critical in decision-making, intension formation and behavior. Dane et al.'s (2012) study indicates that although empirical research on intuitive decision-making vs. analytical decision making is scarce, some researches indicate that domain expertise has a big impact on the effectiveness of intuitive decision-making. Traditionally, decisions based on intuition tended to be biased and risky. But in today's environment, some decisions must be made fast and must be effective. This study concluded that while decisions based on intuitions are thought to be at odds, extensive knowledge in the field in non-decomposable tasks demonstrated the effectiveness of intuition.

Hypothesis 2

With respect to Hypothesis 2, the authors originally intended to investigate the decision methods that have proven to be effective in making group/team decisions in a shared leadership environment. However, a paucity of substantial research exists relating the two topics to the core focus of which methods are proven to be most effective in this team setting. Due to an insufficient amount of research, a valid conclusion about the proven effectiveness of decision methods cannot be determined. Therefore, the scope has been modified to investigate the methods that should be the most effective in making decisions in this environment, based on the requirements of shared leadership.

Research from Turning Points found teams that demonstrated high levels of shared leadership usually relied on the consensus decision method in order to make team decisions, since it not only enabled all members to provide their input, but it enabled the team to communicate effectively. It also ensured that all members shared the same understanding and direction for the decision, all of which provided a strong sense of support and commitment from all members. Research detailed that when the teams relied on the consensus decision method, they were able to be much more autonomous, which enabled them to achieve a high level of self-management and self-identity (Turning Points, n.d.).

The research performed by Yang (2010) examined two dominant forms of decision-making in teams: consensus and single leader decision-making without team input. Both of these methods are quite different since one method accounts for the input from team members while the other does not. In addition, they are significantly different in the way that authority is applied to the final decision. Her research concluded that both of these methods are opposites of each other when considering the amount of group input and influence over the decision-making process as well as the quality of the decisions. Moreover, Yang's (2010) research found that the consensus decision method to be directly linked to "higher satisfaction within a group, higher interest in working with that group on future tasks, short decision making duration, and greater acceptance of decisions". The study results showed that single leader decision-making is faster than the consensus method, but the latter was found to lead to higher quality decisions since it typically results in buy in and support from all members. In addition, the results of her research point out that the consensus method was rated higher for quality of design choice, decision-making process, and in terms of efficiency. Overall, consensus was found to be the better decision-making method in teams since it was more effective in terms of decision quality, efficiency, and process, even though the decision-making time is slower

Meyer's (1997) longitudinal study of three teams points out that as teams develop in a shared leadership environment, they begin to adopt a more consensual form of decision-making and leadership. Meyers's research concluded that shared decision-making is a complex process and is not the same across teams. Her analysis indicates that there is a significant variation in the implementation of shared decision-making. Overall, it was identified that although shared decision-making is affected by a team's internal and external environmental conditions as well as several other variables, teams that made the most effective decisions were teams that utilized the consensus decision-making method.

Research from Gelzheiser et al. (2001) identified that there was variability in team leadership across the three teams studied. Two of the teams were found to have a high level of shared decision-making and positive group process procedures since all of the members were actively involved and contributed to the team in a positive manner. The third team was found to utilize a single individual decision model, which resulted in being much less productive when compared to the other two teams. In the first team observed, the researchers found that the external leader utilized a domineering form of leadership, which resulted in dissention in the team and ineffective results. The dissention from the team was obvious since the members expressed concern that the external leader was too involved and not providing the team with any autonomy; members stated that "he needs to step back so people realize he's a member, not the leader of the team" (Ibid, p. 282). Therefore, it was concluded that in this environment, a single individual decision method was the dominant strategy and it produced limited effective decisions. The team sought to have a shared leadership environment, but it was not possible due to the external leader.

Data from the second team indicates that the external leader and internal team members utilized shared leadership strategies and were moderately successful in having active participation from all members. All members had a high level of input and actively took part in making all decisions. The external leader was a significant driving force in pushing the members to take part in the shared decision-making process and actively pursued sharing his influence and power in order to have all members increase their levels of participation and involvement. But there was strain on the internal-external relationship, since some members were reluctant to actively take part in the shared leadership roles in fear of some conflict with the external leader. But with this environment, the team was effective in determining several significant decisions. The team's internal environment was very high and many members believed that there was a strong commitment by all members, as well as a strong relationship with their external leader (Ibid, p. 282).

Review of the data from the final team observed has shown that the team and external leader were functioning very well. Everyone participated in the shared decision-making process, which enabled the team to reach major decisions in a short time frame (Ibid, p. 283). The relationship between the internal and external factors was also very strong. The external leader was able to provide his support and input into the team decisions without deterring any of the members from expressing their opinions or participating in the decision-making process. The team appeared to move quickly through the development of the team-decision making method methodology and resulted in primarily utilizing the consensus decision method. Members found that the consensus method was most closely related to shared decision-making and the requirements of shared leadership. The external leader was a strong outlet for support and aided the team in developing its internal environment as well as motivating the members. As a result, members knew their opinions were valued and were more willing to share in the responsibilities of leadership and decision-making (Ibid, p. 283).

Dyer et al.'s (2009) study presented results of experiments taken of leadership and decision making in small and large human groups. Members of groups must make decisions (form of leadership) between two or more totally exclusive course of actions (with no known directional information) that suddenly emerge by making consensus decisions through collective behavior. The decision-makers or leaders can be elected or they just arise due to their personalities. Rowland and Parry's (2009) study examined the relationship between organizational design and leadership in decision-making teams and the effects in team member behavior. At the meso-level of leadership modeling, organizational design has a moderating impact between leadership and organizational outcomes for it influences both leadership style and decision-making by providing a level of assurance. At the micro-level (leadership), consensual commitment can be moderated by the impact of organizational design in generating the desirable outcomes. High levels of commitment influence organizational outcomes and vice versa. Organization design influences both leaders and team member's perceptions. This study suggests that leader behavior in relation to any given decision is situational specific.

McHugh et al.'s (2016) study examined collective decision-making as it relates to the performance metric of collective decision quality by incorporating leadership and collective intelligence using agent based simulations and content-coded field study data, for collective decision making. Collectives are united individuals with a common purpose, task, and expectations who are concerned with accomplishing its goals. Their individual intelligences and knowledge together becomes collective intelligence. Results of the study suggest that not only there is a positive relationship between individual and collective intelligence but also a positive relationship between collective intelligence and collective decision quality.

Relationship Between Shared Leadership and Decision-Making

The research outlined in the preceding sections lends support to the conclusion that there is a strong relationship between the major core conditions defined as internal team environment and external coaching and leadership within shared leadership. Both these conditions were proven to be mutually reinforcing. Furthermore, regardless of the type of shared leadership environment an organization is striving for, it is crucial to maintain high levels of external coaching and shared leadership. This factor is reflected in the team's level of internal team environment. For example, an external leader can demonstrate increased support and guiding influence on a team to ensure leadership and the team environment are not hindered by challenges and responsibilities presented towards them. As a result of this proactive influence, the team may very well exhibit a higher level of internal team environment, therefore reflecting the team's increased autonomy, self-confidence, -management, and -identity. Teams will reap benefits from an external coach that provides continuous support and guidance, especially in the form of increased self-awareness, greater commitment, shared understanding, and overall trust in the team. These are all values characteristic in a high level of internal team environment. Because of this delicate relationship, which was discussed in previous sections, if one condition does not exist or is not an equal to the other, then the resulting shared leadership will be inefficient when it comes to juggling the shared responsibilities of the leadership role.

The previous sections demonstrate that an external leader has the obligation to provide six sigma team members with opportunities to perform leadership responsibilities. This is one of the vital aspects of providing higher levels of external leadership. The most common form of leadership responsibilities to offer to six sigma team members is decision-making. This gives the external leader a two-fold role, in that he/she must willingly empower the team members to come to their own decisions, but also provide all the support the team needs to stay afloat. Let's take the scenario of project development. At first, the team lacks shared focus, purpose, and methodology to be able to achieve any level of team decision making. For the team to reach a level where they agree on a decision-making methodology, an external leader ought to provide guidance and expertise in how to make decisions that are effective in a team environment. Specifically, in a shared leadership environment, the external leader's task is even more important, as they must incorporate the core principles and ideas of shared leadership and shared decision-making into their lessons. This is primarily because the leadership role and decision-making responsibilities are foreign to all team members. Furthermore, the external leader's support and guidance creates another distinct relationship with the team's performance and internal team environment. It has been documented that the external leader's influence is an effective method to develop shared leadership and shared decision-making, but also to expand the acceptance of different aspects of the leadership role and responsibilities. If a strong internal team is evident, the members are more inclined to share a common purpose, to willingly participate in any leadership responsibilities, and to remain fully committed to the success of the team.

Due to the relationship between the two conditions of shared leadership and the impacts each yields on a team's concept and methodology in decision-making, it is concluded that there is a direct relationship between shared leadership and team decision-making. Previous research indicates this relationship, proving their linkage, and thus demonstrating the potential each condition has in providing a team with more effective and efficient decision-making. It is demonstrated that as a team gets more actively immersed in the shared leadership model and the six sigma team's shared leadership environment becomes stronger, over time, the decision-making approaches that a team utilizes will transform as a reflection of the distribution of decision-making responsibilities and roles each member plays on the final decision. Therefore, it becomes common for a team beginning to develop a shared leadership environment to pursue a decision-making model that parallels a "single leader individual decision method." This is because the ideas of sharing power, engaging as a leader, and inputting into the decision-making process are still foreign to the members. However, as the team's shared leadership environment matures, so do the levels of power, influence, and leadership that are increasingly distributed amongst the team members. As a direct result, the team will naturally shift from a decision-making approach that is more single leader/individual faceted to a shared decision-making method. This newly adopted method will enable members to have more input and influence in the decision-making process. In other words, decisions that were typically made by a single individual will be replaced by decisions made by an entire team that supports a shared leadership environment. Values such as influence, power, structure, decisions, and project processes will be diverted from a single leadership perspective to a team-oriented perspective.

As previously stated, research shows a direct relationship between shared leadership conditions and decision-making exists, in that as one concept evolves, so does the other. In this respect, as members in a six sigma team transfer from the individual leadership model to a shared leadership one, the six sigma team will also leave the individual decision-making methods for those based on each member's input, power, and influence over the entire process. This research already demonstrates the relationship's effectiveness, primarily through the natural ability of the six sigma team to be more effective in decision-making processes in which every member is engaged versus when an individual makes all the decisions. However, research indicates that this is effectiveness that is only apparent in a shared leadership environment in which the internal environment and external factor are both equally strong. With these high levels, the six sigma team has greater ability to pursue an effective decision-making methodology, and thus procure more effective decisions. As a direct result of this environment and its discussed conditions, the six sigma team will reap a stronger level of commitment and support for all decisions the team makes.

The direct relationship discussed throughout this research is further supported by Taveira's work as he identified just how shared leadership member participation in decision-making is positively and statistically relevant to the effectiveness of a team's decision-making and performance. This study's literature review further exemplifies this relationship, demonstrating the degree to which a team's level of effectiveness and success in decision-making is directly linked to the levels in which team members actively engage in the decision-making processes. Further proof of this relationship is found in the decisions made by the teams. Those that practice team decision-making methodology procure more effective decisions than those that pursue individual decision-making methodology. Primarily, this is the case because team members that are empowered to be actively involved in the team environment will harbor newfound beliefs that their input is valuable.

DISCUSSION

As the six sigma team more readily engages in a shared leadership model, it will also naturally pursue decision-making methods that show higher levels of distribution of power, influence, and responsibility. The six sigma team will also find it easier to leave behind single decision-making methods to pursue ones in which every member has input and six sigma team support and commitment are at their highest levels. The research demonstrates decision-making based on a consensual approach is the most effective method to achieve the functional conditions of shared leadership.

Many researchers lend support to the idea that consensus decision-making represents the relationship between shared leadership and decision-making, thereby being the optimal method to produce effective decisions. It most closely satisfies the needs and requirements of a shared leadership environment, including all internal and external conditions. A shared leadership environment is widely defined as an atmosphere that not only promotes but *requires* all participants to have the opportunity to provide individual input into the decision-making process, with increased accountability and responsibility on each participant. As a byproduct, members of this environment have a natural inclination to provide support for each other and enable everyone to have a voice in leadership. This constitutes a strong internal six sigma team environment.

The consensus decision-making method is one way in which a team can achieve the needs of shared leadership as it encourages members to express their opinions and decision inputs. In other words, every voice is heard and evaluated. In this method, the members are further provoked to actively listen and support all other members, so that this social support can make all members feel their opinions are valued and worthwhile being shared and developed. This method ensures a final decision is not made until all the members have the opportunity to share their ideas. This makes everyone responsible and accountable to reach a decision before the deadline. In general, this is a method that provides a shared leadership team with optimal benefits for the environment and project at hand. This is because the fundamental principles of the consensus method parallel those of a shared leadership environment, making them go hand-in-hand. As some research might dictate other decision-making methods as those effective enough to meet some needs of shared leadership teams, they do not provide the team with the ability to produce the *most* effective decisions and maintain the highest levels of shared leadership.

Recall that past research also demonstrates that as a team becomes more involved in shared leadership, the methods used to reach decisions change in such a way that the decision-making power becomes more evenly distributed amongst members. In other words, the team naturally moves away from single individual decision models towards a shared decision model. Based on the presented research and proven relationship between shared leadership conditions, including external coaching and internal team environment, and team decision-making, a continuum for decision-making in shared leadership environments is exemplified in Figure 1. This continuum dictates the recommended progression of decision-making methods that a team ought to use as it develops its degree of shared leadership.

Figure 1 demonstrates a trend in that as a team develops its sense of shared leadership, it also progresses through seven different methods of decision-making methods commonly adopted in teams. At first, in the shared leadership environment's infant stage, the most common and effective method is the single individual decision method. This "decision by single authority with no group input" does not rely on group decision-making practices or influence. As the shared leadership environment's internal and external conditions naturally develop, the team evolves to a consensus decision method. As previously mentioned, this is the optimal method to achieve the highest level of shared leadership in a team. The

Figure 1. Shared leadership decision-making continuum

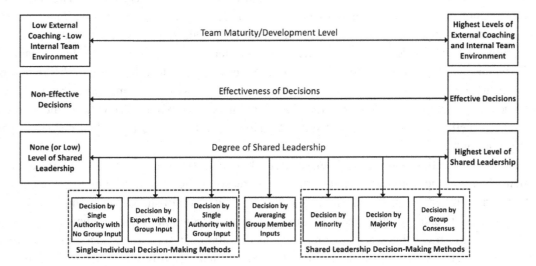

progression from a single decision method to a consensus one will also show the progression of the team through the different levels of distributed decision-making power and influence in the team.

The model demonstrates that in the case where shared leadership is nonexistent or very low, the six sigma team will progress with a single authority decision model lacking group input, but the next step in the six sigma team's progression is the "decision by expert with no group input." The six sigma team will naturally evolve from this method to the "decision by single authority with group input" method. This is the next point in the continuum because the leaders is just beginning to seek out the involvement of members in the decision-making process, even though the decision is still made by a single individual or authority. This is a sign that the six sigma team is heading towards a shared leadership model, because the single leading authority is still collecting input from all the six sigma team's members. These first three methods dictate the "single individual decision-making methods" in the entire model because the final decision is still made by a single individual or authority, regardless of how much input the team members have. Therefore, the relationship from left to right of these first three methods demonstrates that as a six sigma team gains more experience in the shared leadership model, the decision-making methods will change in order to reflect this increased power of member influence in the process. In the initial methods, member input is extremely low, however by the time the team progresses to the third method, they have been granted more input and influence over the decision-making process.

The midpoint of the model, and the fourth progression, is the "decision by averaging group member inputs." This is a method that demonstrates just how much the decision-making power and influence are moving towards a more distributed focus. It also demonstrates how the team is actively moving away from the idea that the members only provide input but have no actual authority over the final decision. It is the next three methods that represent the "shared leadership decision-making methods," because they are methods in which the power and influence of decision-making is entirely in the hands of the six sigma team members instead of a single authority. The six sigma team naturally evolves from the midpoint method into the decision by minority method and then the decision by majority method. As the team becomes more developed in shared leadership, influence is spread out to more members until the upper end of the spectrum is reached, which is the consensus method. In this final area of the model, more team members will gain the ability to yield decision-making power and influence. The continuum's endpoint is achieved only when all members yield influence, not only mere input. Once a team reaches this point, there is no need for a single individual authority to make decisions for the team anymore.

Something else to consider about this model is that as a team develops its level of shared leadership, the effectiveness of their decisions directly improves. Figure 1 is a perfect depiction of this relationship as it very clearly demonstrates the effectiveness of decisions made with single individual methods versus shared leadership methods. According to this figure, at an extreme point of view, it is safe to say that the consensus method produces more effective decisions than the single individual decision method without group input.

Finally, the last section of this model demonstrates how a six sigma team's level of maturity and development change as the degree of shared leadership increases in the six sigma team. Research indicates a positive correlation in that as the six sigma team increases its level of shared leadership, the team also increases in maturity and overall team development. This is reflected in Figure 1, where the top section of the figure demonstrates that when a team begins its development of shared leadership, it is expected that there are lower levels of external coaching and internal team environment. Because the members are "new" to this form of team environment, confusion and chaos is expected amongst the members and even the external leader. This is because they will not necessarily understand the roles and responsibilities accompanying the new environment. Thus, the six sigma team's levels of development and maturity are reflected in the naturally low levels of external coaching and internal six sigma team environment, which is therefore related to a team's low level of shared leadership. As a result, this section of the model also shows that as a team increases its degree of shared leadership, its levels of maturity and development also increase. In any shared leadership environment, the team will experience the highest levels of maturity and development if, and only if, they advanced to the highest degree of shared leadership--in other words, it implies the team exhibits the highest potential levels of external coaching and internal team environment conditions.

This developed model is applicable to numerous research fields and has its implications in the general business world. The model can be utilized by managers, leaders, and organizations to better enable them in gauging the proper levels of external coaching and support that will be needed in order to achieve progression to a shared leadership environment. To a leader, it would shed light on how to guide the team through the shared leadership development process. It may also have the additive benefit of aiding them to focus the team in the right direction and generate a shared sense of purpose and team support. A final application from the external leader point of view is that it can be used as a tracking tool, in which the external leader can gauge the development of shared leadership, how the team is making decisions, and how effective these decisions really are. From an organizational standpoint, the model will help with team development and training programs. The programs can be geared towards teaching teams about the value of shared leadership and decision-making in teams, as well as held the teaching managers guide the teams towards a shared leadership environment.

From the perspective of a team that is new to shared leadership, such a model can guide them to develop shared leadership. It can also act as a tracking tool for the reasons previously mentioned, especially since it has strength in ensuring that the team progresses in the right direction. A final, important note to make is that the academic world can also benefit from such a model, using it to test and compare the various theories of shared leadership and decision-making. Using this continuum will undoubtedly advance the fields of shared decision-making since this field currently lacks substantial enough research. This in turn prevents researchers from drawing accurate conclusions. And finally, the model depicted in Figure 1 can be used as a guide to design leadership and decision-making curriculums, in which students learn the proper methods in decision-making in a shared leadership environment, as well as how internal and external factors can contribute to the shared decision-making process.

CONCLUDING REMARKS

For any project, the proper six sigma team format needs to be determined since it enables the group to make rational, timely, and effective decisions. The concept of shared leadership means that multiple six sigma team members accept the responsibility of the leadership role, which is seen to result in the sharing of power, decision-making, and influence. In this sense, members work as one to accomplish a shared vision or set of objectives and members also act as both followers and leaders. In addition, it has been shown that in order to have an effective shared leadership environment, a six sigma team must have two conditions satisfied: external coaching and internal team environment. For the focus of this paper, it was proposed that shared leadership environments have an effect on team decision making as well as the methods that are used to make group/team decisions. It was also proposed that the consensus method is the technique that is the most effective and most closely related to the fundamental conditions and requirements of a shared leadership environment. In addition, it was also believed that a model of shared leadership decision-making could be developed from the results of this research.

A systematic review of past research efforts has shown that a strong relationship exists between the internal and external conditions of shared leadership. In addition, the research has also shown that a strong relationship exists between shared leadership and six sigma team decision-making principles and approaches. In this sense, as a six sigma team becomes more involved in the shared leadership model, the methods utilized to make decisions also change in such a way that the decision-making power is more distributed among members. As a six sigma team's degree of shared leadership increases, the six sigma team utilizes methods that are more in line with the ideals of shared leadership; the six sigma team moves away from single individual decision methods and it moves towards a shared decision method. Even though the author could not accurately identify the most effective decision method in a shared leadership environment (due to little research in the field), further review of research has shown that the consensus approach is the technique that is the most effective in satisfying the functional requirements of shared leadership. This is the method that should be used by six sigma teams in order to make decisions in a shared leadership environment.

From all of the past researches and conclusions, this paper developed a model for decision-making in shared leadership environments and this continuum represents the recommended progression of decision-making methods that a six sigma team should be using as it develops its degree of shared leadership. This model has been shown to have many practical applications for the real world as well as the academic/research world. Since this model has yet to be tested, future research should be performed to test the model in different six sigma team environments such as engineering six sigma teams. Another area of future research lies with using this model to test different theories of shared leadership, such as centralized and decentralized shared leadership. At the organizational level, future research could include the study of the relationship between this model and the organizational level.

REFERENCES

Avolio, B. J., Walumbwa, F. O., & Weber, T. J. (2009). Leadership: Current theories, research, and future directions. *Annual Review of Psychology*, *60*(1), 421–449. doi:10.1146/annurev.psych.60.110707.163621 PMID:18651820

Balkundi, P., & Kilduff, M. (2006). The ties that lead: A social network approach to leadership. *The Leadership Quarterly*, *17*(4), 419–439. doi:10.1016/j.leaqua.2006.01.001

Bergman, J. Z., Rentsch, J. R., Small, E. E., Davenport, S. W., & Bergman, S. M. (2012). The shared leadership process in decision-making teams. *The Journal of Social Psychology*, *152*(1), 17–42. doi:10.1080/00224545.2010.538763 PMID:22308759

Bisol, S., & Roy, A. (2014). Leveraging Shared Leadership in the Sterile Processing Department to Engage Staff in Process Improvement. *American Journal of Infection Control*, *42*(6), S29–S166. doi:10.1016/j.ajic.2014.03.167

Business Analysis Made Easy. (2006). *Decision Making Model in Five Steps*. Retrieved from http://www.business-analysis-made-easy.com/Decision-Making-Model-In-Five-Steps.html

Caress, A. L., & Scott, L. (2005). Shared governance and shared leadership: Meeting the challenges of implementation. *Journal of Nursing Management*, *13*(1), 4–12. doi:10.1111/j.1365-2834.2004.00455.x PMID:15613089

Carson, J. B., Marrone, J. A., & Tesluk, P. E. (2007). Shared Leadership in Teams: An Investigation of Antecedent Conditions and Performance. *Academy of Management Journal*, *50*(5), 1217–1234. doi:10.2307/20159921

Carter, J. J. III, & Justis, R. T. (2010). The Development and Implementation of Shared Leadership in Multi-Generational Family Firms. *Management Research Review*, *33*(6), 563–585. doi:10.1108/01409171011050190

Cawthorne, J. E. (2010). Leading from the middle of the organization: An examination of shared leadership in academic libraries. *Journal of Academic Librarianship*, *36*(2), 151–157. doi:10.1016/j.acalib.2010.01.006

Cervone, H. F. (2005). Making decisions: Methods for digital library project teams. *International Digital Library Perspectives*, *21*(1), 30–35.

Cianci, A. M., Hannah, S. T., Roberts, R. P., & Tsakumis, G. T. (2014). The effects of authentic leadership on followers ethical decision-making in the face of temptation: An experimental study. *The Leadership Quarterly*, *25*(3), 581–594. doi:10.1016/j.leaqua.2013.12.001

Dane, E., & Pratt, M. G. (2007). Exploring intuition and its role in managerial decision making. *Academy of Management Review*, *32*(1), 33–54. doi:10.5465/AMR.2007.23463682

Dane, E., Rockmann, K. W., & Pratt, M. G. (2012). When should I trust my gut? Linking domain expertise to intuitive decision-making effectiveness. *Organizational Behavior and Human Decision Processes*, *119*(2), 187–194. doi:10.1016/j.obhdp.2012.07.009

Del Missier, F., Mäntylä, T., & Bruin, W. B. (2012). Decision-making competence, executive functioning, and general cognitive abilities. *Journal of Behavioral Decision Making*, 25(4), 331–351. doi:10.1002/bdm.731

Denis, J. L., Langley, A., & Rouleau, L. (2010). The practice of leadership in the messy world of organizations. *Leadership*, 6(1), 67–88. doi:10.1177/1742715009354233

Detert, J. R., & Burris, E. R. (2007). Leadership behavior and employee voice: Is the door really open? *Academy of Management Journal*, 50(4), 869–884. doi:10.5465/AMJ.2007.26279183

Drescher, G., & Garbers, Y. (2016). Shared leadership and commonality: A policy-capturing study. *The Leadership Quarterly*, 27(2), 200–217. doi:10.1016/j.leaqua.2016.02.002

Dyer, J. R., Johansson, A., Helbing, D., Couzin, I. D., & Krause, J. (2009). Leadership, consensus decision making and collective behaviour in humans. *Philosophical Transactions of the Royal Society of London. Series B, Biological Sciences*, 364(1518), 781–789. doi:10.1098/rstb.2008.0233 PMID:19073481

Elbanna, S., & Child, J. (2007). The influence of decision, environmental and firm characteristics on the rationality of strategic decision-making. *Journal of Management Studies*, 44(4), 561–591. doi:10.1111/j.1467-6486.2006.00670.x

Fath, L. (2008). Shared decision making. *Paediatrics and Child Health (Oxford)*, 18, S90–S91. doi:10.1016/S1751-7222(08)70027-1

Foundation Coalition. (2001). *Effective Decision Making in Teams: Methods*. Retrieved from http://www.foundationcoalition.org/home/keycomponents/teams/decision2.html

Gelzheiser, L., Meyers, B., & Meyers, J. (2001). Observing leadership roles in shared decision making: A preliminary analysis of three teams. *Journal of Educational & Psychological Consultation*, 12(4), 277–312. doi:10.1207/S1532768XJEPC1204_01

Gibson, C. B., & Saxton, T. (2005). Thinking outside the black box: Outcomes of team decisions with third-party intervention. *Small Group Research*, 36(2), 208–236. doi:10.1177/1046496404270376

Hoegl, B., & Muethel, M. (2013). Shared Leadership Effectiveness in Independent Professional Teams. *European Management Journal*, 31(4), 423–432. doi:10.1016/j.emj.2012.11.008

Jones, P. E., & Roelofsma, P. H. M. P. (2000). The potential for social contextual and group biases in team decision-making: Biases, conditions, and psychological mechanisms. *Ergonomics*, 43(8), 1129–1152. doi:10.1080/00140130050084914 PMID:10975177

Klassen, T. P., Jahad, A. R., & Moher, D. (1998). Guides for reading and interpreting systematic reviews. *Archives of Pediatrics & Adolescent Medicine*, 152(7), 700–704. doi:10.1001/archpedi.152.7.700 PMID:9667544

Kocher, M., & Straub, S. (2006). Individual or team decision-making: Causes and consequences of self-selection. *Games and Economic Behavior*, 56(2), 259–270. doi:10.1016/j.geb.2005.08.009

Koschzeck, K. (2009). *You are the most important leader in your organization: Towards a shared leadership model*. Retrieved from Proquest Digital Dissertations. (MR52131).

Kugler, T., Kausel, E. E., & Kocher, M. G. (2012). Are groups more rational than individuals? A review of interactive decision making in groups. *Wiley Interdisciplinary Reviews: Cognitive Science*, *3*(4), 471–482. doi:10.1002/wcs.1184 PMID:26301530

Ledford, L., Lee, C., Bart, J., & Fuller, T. (2006). Shared Leadership Triage Process Redesign. Shared Leadership Triage Process Redesign. Journal of Emergency Nursing Conference. doi:10.1016/j.jen.2005.12.024

Lovelace, K. J., Manz, C. C., & Alves, J. C. (2007). Work stress and leadership development: The role of self-leadership, Shared leadership, physical fitness and flow in managing demands and increasing job control. *Human Resource Management Review*, *17*(4), 374–387. doi:10.1016/j.hrmr.2007.08.001

Makoul, G., & Clayman, M. L. (2006). An integrative model of shared decision making in medical encounters. *Patient Education and Counseling*, *60*(3), 301–312. doi:10.1016/j.pec.2005.06.010 PMID:16051459

McHugh, K. A., Yammarino, F. J., Dionne, S. D., Serban, A., Sayama, H., & Chatterjee, S. (2016). Collective decision making, leadership, and collective intelligence: Tests with agent-based simulations and a Field study. *The Leadership Quarterly*, *27*(2), 218–241. doi:10.1016/j.leaqua.2016.01.001

Mendez, M. J., & Busenbark, J. R. (2015). Shared leadership and gender: All members are equal… but some more than others. *Leadership and Organization Development Journal*, *36*(1), 17–34. doi:10.1108/LODJ-11-2012-0147

Meyers, B. (March1997). Getting better with practice? A longitudinal study of shared leadership. *Proceedings from the Annual Meeting of the American Educational Research Association*.

Miskin, V. D., & Gmelch, W. H. (1985, May). Quality leadership for quality teams. *Training and Development Journal*, 122–129.

Nicolaides, V. C., LaPort, K. A., Chen, T. R., Tomassetti, A. J., Weis, E. J., Zaccaro, S. J., & Cortina, J. M. (2014). The shared leadership of teams: A meta-analysis of proximal, distal, and moderating relationships. *The Leadership Quarterly*, *25*(5), 923–942. doi:10.1016/j.leaqua.2014.06.006

Northouse, P. G. (2007). *Leadership Theory and Practice* (4th ed.). Sage Publishing.

Popay, J., Roberts, H., Sowden, A., Petticrew, M., Arai, L., Roen, K., & Rodgers, M. (2004). *Guidance on the conduct of narrative synthesis in systematic reviews. Draft report from ESRC Methods Programme.* Lancaster, UK: Institute for Health Research, University of Lancaster.

Ramthun, A. J., & Matkin, G. S. (2012). Multicultural shared leadership a conceptual model of shared leadership in culturally diverse teams. *Journal of Leadership & Organizational Studies*, *19*(3), 303–314. doi:10.1177/1548051812444129

Resource International. (2009). *Decision Making and Resolving Conflicts in Teams*. Retrieved from http://www.resource-i.com

Rowland, P., & Parry, K. (2009). Consensual commitment: A grounded theory of the meso-level influence of organizational design on leadership and decision-making. *The Leadership Quarterly, 20*(4), 535–553. doi:10.1016/j.leaqua.2009.04.004

Snowden, D. J., & Boone, M. E. (2007). A leader's framework for decision making. *Harvard Business Review, 85*(11), 68.

Spencer, A. J., Buhalis, D., & Moital, M. (2012). A hierarchical model of technology adoption for small owner-managed travel firms: An organizational decision-making and leadership perspective. *Tourism Management, 33*(5), 1195–1208. doi:10.1016/j.tourman.2011.11.011

Taveira, A. D. (2008). Key elements on team achievement: A retrospective analysis. *Applied Ergonomics, 39*(4), 509–518. doi:10.1016/j.apergo.2008.02.007 PMID:18395695

Taylor, B. J., Dempster, M., & Donnelly, M. (2003). Hidden gems: Systematically searching electronic databases for publications for social work and social care. *British Journal of Social Work, 33*(4), 423–439. doi:10.1093/bjsw/33.4.423

Turning Points: Transforming Middle Schools. (n.d.). *Guide to Collaborative Culture and Shared Leadership.* Retrieved from http://www.turningpts.org

Van Ginkel, W. P., & Van Knippenberg, D. (2012). Group leadership and shared task representations in decision making groups. *The Leadership Quarterly, 23*(1), 94–106. doi:10.1016/j.leaqua.2011.11.008

Vaughan, L. (2004). New measurements for search engine evaluation proposed and tested. *Information Processing & Management, 40*(4), 677–691. doi:10.1016/S0306-4573(03)00043-8

Wallenius, J., Dyer, J. S., Fishburn, P. C., Steuer, R. E., Zionts, S., & Deb, K. (2008). Multiple criteria decision making, multiattribute utility theory: Recent accomplishments and what lies ahead. *Management Science, 54*(7), 1336–1349. doi:10.1287/mnsc.1070.0838

Walter, J., Kellermanns, F. W., & Lechner, C. (2012). Decision making within and between organizations rationality, politics, and alliance performance. *Journal of Management, 38*(5), 1582–1610. doi:10.1177/0149206310363308

Westaby, J. D., Probst, T. M., & Lee, B. C. (2010). Leadership decision-making: A behavioral reasoning theory analysis. *The Leadership Quarterly, 21*(3), 481–495. doi:10.1016/j.leaqua.2010.03.011

Yang, M. C. (2010). Consensus and single leader decision-making in teams using structured design methods. *Design Matters, 31*, 345–362.

Yukl, G. A. (2006). *Leadership in Organizations* (6th ed.). Upper Saddle River, NJ: Prentice Hall.

Zweifel, B., & Haegeli, P. (2014). A qualitative analysis of group formation, leadership and decision making in recreation groups traveling in avalanche terrain. *Journal of Outdoor Recreation and Tourism, 5*, 17–26. doi:10.1016/j.jort.2014.03.001

KEY TERMS AND DEFINITIONS

Continuous Improvement: Continuous Improvement comprises incremental and breakthrough improvements of processes in a persistent manner.

Decision-Making: The procedure of deciding about something significant, particularly in a group/organization.

Leadership: A process that occurs in a group context and involves influence and goal attainment.

Project Management: Organizing and planning the enterprises' resources to get the specific tasks or duties completed.

Shared Leadership: A leadership style in which team members accept the responsibility and accountability of leadership in the team setting; team members actively share responsibility of the leadership role.

Six Sigma: A data-driven and systematic methodology provides the enterprises tools for improving the capability of their business processes through eliminating the defects.

Team Cohesion: The degree to that all the team members have been tied to each other and to the team as a whole and would like to contribute to the group's capability to proceed as a functional work unit.

Team Performance: The effectiveness of the team/group which individual members should improve for achievement of team success.

Chapter 18

An Exploratory Study on the Influencers of the Perceived Relevance of CIO's Activities and Skills:
An Update

João Varajão
Centro ALGORITMI, University of Minho, Portugal

António Trigo
Polytechnic Institute of Coimbra- ISCAC, Portugal

Pedro Soto-Acosta
University of Murcia, Spain

ABSTRACT

This paper presents the results of an exploratory study developed to identify the current CIO's main activities, to verify whether CIO's demographics and CIO's business context influence the perception of the importance of CIO activities and to identify CIO's main skills. The results show that managing projects, interacting with top management teams, optimizing business processes and making strategic decisions are main CIO's activities; and that the importance recognized to these activities is influenced by characteristics such as the CIO's age or the hierarchical structure of the organization. Regarding CIO's skills, understanding business processes and operations, and strategic thinking and planning, are the ones CIOs identified as being the most important.

DOI: 10.4018/978-1-5225-2382-6.ch018

INTRODUCTION

Information Technology (IT) has come to assume many different roles in organizations since it began to be commercially available in the mid-twentieth century. Initially, its use was restricted practically to the operational level. But over time, with the development of new features and capabilities, companies found applications at various managerial levels and, currently, information technologies are embedded in Information Systems (IS) and in virtually all organizational activities (Varajão et al., 2009a; Varajão, 2005).

The Information Systems Function (ISF), as main responsible for IT/IS adoption and management, must ensure that organizations are adequately supported by IT. In this context, the Chief Information Officer (CIO) plays a central role as Head of the ISF, taking responsibility for the planning, organization, direction and control of the processes that are required to ensure the existence of an Information System (IS) that suits the organization's informational needs (Varajão et al., 2012b).

In fulfilling her/his role, the CIO needs to perform a rich and diversified set of activities. For several years, studies (Carvalho et al., 2009; Larson & Adams, 2010; Luftman & Ben-Zvi, 2010; Rusu et al., 2009; Trigo et al., 2009) have been developed aiming at identifying and ranking the activities performed by CIOs according to its relative importance. One of the aspects that stand out in these results is the fact that it is difficult to find two studies with similar rankings of activities, which is due, on one hand, to the evolving role of the CIO, and on the other hand to the characteristics of CIOs (Sobol & Klein, 2009) and of organizations.

The study presented in this paper is an extended version of the study previously published on International Journal of Enterprise Information Systems titled "An Exploratory Study on the Influencers of the Perceived Relevance of CIO's Activities" (Varajão et al., 2016), developed with two main objectives: 1) to identify the main activities currently carried out by CIOs in large enterprises; 2) identify whether certain variables related to the characteristics of the CIO and certain variables related to the business characteristics are influencers of the importance assigned to activities. This extended version presents also a list of the skills considered as the most important for a CIO good performance.

LITERATURE REVIEW

The literature review was conducted from two major sources of information: the community of practitioners, including the CIO Magazine in its yearly study "The state of the CIO" and Gartner in the yearly study "The CIO Agenda Report"; and the academic community, including Web of Science, Scopus and ScienceDirect. The main search expressions used were "CIO activities", "IS managers activities", "CIO skills", "IS managers roles", "CIO roles", "IS managers roles", "CIO characteristics", "IS manager characteristics", "CIO profile" and "IS manager profile".

Chief Information Officer

The CIO position emerged in the early 1980s as a result of increased importance placed on IS. Since its inception, the CIO position has gradually become more important as IT has been increasingly playing a more central role in the firm's daily operations, business processes, and overall business strategy. The most significant change in the role of the CIOs is their paradigm shift from technology to business. The

CIO's position in the corporate structure matured steadily and inexorably from the tactical/operational level to the strategic/management level (Polansky et al., 2004). The CIO can be characterized as someone who has a deep understanding of the organization's business as well as strong technical knowledge (Keen, 1991).

The importance of the CIO's roles depends on the context of the organization, namely the nature of the business, the dimension of the organization, the country, etc. (Grover et al., 1993; Stephens et al., 1992). In fulfilling its role, the CIO must plan its activities and those of ISF, establishing the interface between the ISF and other organizational areas, managing the overall conception of the IS, organizing resources and activities, directing and controlling operations, and evaluating performance. The analysis of the various activities that a CIO needs to develop gives a better perception of the CIO role in the organization (Varajão et al., 2012b).

CIO's Activities

Despite the wide variety of activities developed by the CIO, it is possible to find a limited set of activities that are most commonly part of his work (Carvalho et al., 2009). Based on the literature review carried out, various activities have been identified which together characterize the CIO's job duties. The identified activities are summarized in Table 1 and described next.

Table 1. CIO's activities

Code	Activity	Literature
A1	Interacting with top management team	(Broadbent & Kitzis, 2005; Ifinedo & Nahar, 2007; Preston, 2003; Varajão et al., 2009a)
A2	Making strategic decisions	(Bilhim, 1999; Ding et al., 2014; Lutchen, 2003; Muse, 2016; Preston, 2003; Sambamurthy & Zmud, 1992)
A3	Managing application development	(Muse, 2016; Varajão, 2002)
A4	Managing projects	(Bhatt et al., 2006; Gorgone et al., 2000; Heeks et al., 2001; Hirschheim et al., 2004; Iijima, 2007; Varajão et al., 2012a)
A5	Optimizing business processes	(Aron et al., 2015; Carvalho & Costa, 2007; Davenport & Short, 1990; Muse, 2016)
A6	Hiring, developing and managing the IT staff	(Chen et al., 2010; Hoving, 2007; Nelson, 1991; Polansky et al., 2004)
A7	Interacting with IT vendors and service providers	(Antero et al., 2014; Dibbern et al., 2004; Fraga et al., 2012; Leeney et al., 2011; Varajão, 2001; Varajão et al., 2009b).
A8	Managing crises	(Carvalho et al., 2009; CIOMAG, 2004; Varajão, 2002)
A9	Budgeting	(Marshall et al., 2005; Sutter, 2004)
A10	Interacting with customers	(Malladi & Krishnan, 2012; Muse, 2016).
A11	Seeking and evaluating IT/IS opportunities	(Aron et al., 2015; Benamati & Lederer, 2001; Johnson & Lederer, 2010; Karimi et al., 1996; Kearns & Lederer, 2003; Ross, 1996)
A12	Negotiating on behalf of the company	(Broadbent & Kitzis, 2005; Feeny & Willcocks, 1998; Rockart et al., 1996; Smaltz et al., 2006; Varajão, 2005)
A13	Representing the company in social events	(Varajão, 2002, 2005)

Interacting with the Top Management Team (TMT) is a crucial activity since both CIO and TMT have as one of the top concerns the IS strategic alignment. CIO and TMT need to have a common language and a common understanding regarding the role of IT/IS and ISF within an enterprise (Johnson & Lederer, 2007). The lack of a common language and understanding is one of the most cited reasons for the poor IS strategic alignment (Preston, 2003). The CIO must know what the TMT expects from his role and must be able to elucidate the TMT about the importance of certain initiatives, which may lead the business into new levels of competitiveness (Varajão, 2002; Vedder & Guynes, 2002). Mutual understanding between CIO and CEO on the IT role is a key factor to improve the IS contribution to the organization (Johnson & Lederer, 2010).

Making strategic decisions involves formulating IS objectives, defining strategies, policies and detailed plans to achieve them (Bilhim, 1999). The CIO must follow and understand changes, trends and innovations in the industry, in order to deliver new products and to discover new markets for the enterprise. Decision-making is one of the main roles which managers, such as the CIO, play in organizations. A CIO's strategic decision-making authority in the organization directly influences the contribution of IT to firm performance (Preston et al., 2008). Aligning IT/IS with business goals continues to be one of the CIOs main concerns (Muse, 2016). Therefore, organizations must cultivate the strategic roles of the CIO and treat them as strategic assets to derive value from IS (Ding et al., 2014).

Managing application development is an important area of ISF (Varajão, 2002), since software is a fundamental component of information systems. The CIO is commonly the main responsible for application development projects. Implementing new systems continues to be one of the majors CIOs concerns (Muse, 2016).

Managing projects consists of directing projects within an organization, including the processes related to the start, planning, implementation, monitoring and closure of a project, as well as controlling projects dimensions as time, cost, quality control and risk management (Bhatt et al., 2006; Gorgone et al., 2000). Currently project management faces new challenges since most of today's projects and applications are not built in-house. Inclusively, they tend to be partially or totally outsourced to countries with inferior costs like India (offshore outsourcing) (Heeks et al., 2001; Hirschheim et al., 2004; Iijima, 2007; Varajão et al., 2012a).

The IT activity of designing and optimizing business processes of the organization (Carvalho & Costa, 2007; Davenport & Short, 1990) is the activity where the CIO can prove the high value of IT, by applying and adjusting IT standards and technologies to business processes, enabling the digitalization of business functions. Digital has moved to a center stage of the CIO role (Aron et al., 2015).

Hiring, developing and managing the IT staff is also of the CIO's responsibility (Chen et al., 2010; Polansky et al., 2004). The CIO needs to avoid the shortage of qualified IS personnel that may threaten the IS department ability to deal with the information of the company's needs. The CIO needs to take into account which knowledge/skills are needed, determining areas of significant deficiencies and providing the appropriate education/training programs to its personnel, as well as the personnel personal career management and development (Hoving, 2007; Nelson, 1991).

IT outsourcing arrangements have been considered an undeniable trend (Antero et al., 2014). Outsourcing of IT started in the nineties and did not stop growing until today. Many enterprises even see it as the "holy grail" for all the problems within an organization and a way to achieve all the organizational goals (Dibbern et al., 2004). Therefore, the ability to interact with IT vendors, outsourcers and service providers is in growing demand. The CIO is in an Era where the IT function is shrinking rather than growing (Fraga et al., 2012; Leeney et al., 2011; Varajão, 2001; Varajão et al., 2009b) and where the outsourcing of IT activities have become a vital component of the IT plan (Varajão, 2001).

Managing crises is an activity that most CIO should not need to perform if everything went well and there were not any surprises along the way (Carvalho et al., 2009; Varajão, 2002). The truth is that a large number of CIOs, mainly in small medium enterprises (SME), end up performing this activity more than they would like (CIOMAG, 2004).

Budgeting is the process of predicting and controlling the spending of money. It consists of a periodic negotiation cycle to set budgets and a day-to-day monitoring of the current budgets (Sutter, 2004). The CIO must ensure that investment decisions are aligned with the strategic goals of the IS department, are well planned and justified, fit within the IS department's overall IT/IS strategy and enterprise architecture, and are managed effectively throughout the life cycle. The CIO must also assess the cost, risk, and return for all proposed expenditures on IT (Marshall et al., 2005).

Interacting effectively with clients and business partners is very important due to the fact that many of the IT projects are developed for external client use and not only for in-house use. One of the concerns of the CIO is to create value for the organization and to guarantee the IT alignment with the organization's goals (Muse, 2016). CIO responsibilities in interacting with customers, other executives of the firm and involving in product development processes are becoming an imperative to drive innovation (Malladi & Krishnan, 2012).

One of the most important activities is to constantly seek and evaluate IT/IS opportunities (Karimi et al., 1996; Ross, 1996), with the expectation of producing an IT-based competitive advantage (Kearns & Lederer, 2003) based on the innovation and capabilities provided by IT (Aron et al., 2015). The process of measuring the viability and hence, the adoption of new IT solutions to be employed in the organization, involve the evaluation of several factors, such as, assessing the severity of recent problems due to changes in IT; identifying mechanisms that could have prevented or reduced those problems; anticipating future problems due to changes in IT; and implementing such mechanisms to prevent or reducing these problems (Benamati & Lederer, 2001).

As organizations outsource more portions of their IT services, the oversight of the contractual arrangements has become important for CIOs. They are responsible for negotiating new IT contracts with external vendors, ensuring that contracts remain within scope and budget, and providing executive oversight for all external vendor IT contracts of the organization (Smaltz et al., 2006; Varajão, 2005). This activity encompasses managing supplier relationships, identifying potential of IT/IS service providers, recognizing the most profitable business relationships for the organization and ensuring that IT/IS service contracts are kept, protecting the position of the organization (Feeny & Willcocks, 1998; Rockart et al., 1996).

As maximum responsible for IT/IS and usually a member of the board, CIO's activities include the representation of the company in social events (Varajão, 2002, 2005).

This set of activities emphasizes the importance and complexity of the role that CIOs play in organizations (Varajão et al., 2012b): they are professionals who need to understand the IT together with business processes; respond and act strategically to the changes in the markets; possess the ability to interact and communicate effectively with senior management; and ensure that the organization is in a constant process of innovation and renewal, being the most recent challenge the digitalization of business functions (Aron et al., 2015; Muse, 2016).

CIO's Skills

The CIO, in order to execute the activities under its responsibility, needs to bring together a diverse set of skills. Some of the main required skills are summarized in Table 2 and described next.

The ability to communicate effectively is critical in working with business counterparts to learn and understand different business needs (Smaltz et al., 2006). If CIOs cannot communicate well, their projects will die either at the approval stage when the executive committee rejects them or at the implementation stage when users resist them. If CIOs do not get better at projecting themselves into the center of the corporate decision-making process (Ross & Feeny, 1999), their job will not steer the company toward its next competition-crushing opportunity, and will probably be taking orders and putting out fires.

Strategic thinking and planning skills are critical (Hawkins, 2004), because without them the CIO cannot help its company to respond to changes in the marketplace. In addition, good strategic planning and thinking skills can help the CIO to have influence beyond the IT department. As one of the few people who work with every business unit, the CIO is in a position to see more possibilities on how technology can help the enterprise to be more competitive.

Ability to lead and motivate staff is essential to get the job done (Lane & Koronios, 2007). If a CIO cannot lead and motivate its team to apply skills and techniques to solve dynamic problems and to get projects done in the approved deadlines, the CIO will be in serious problems.

Understanding of the business processes and operations is critical in order to prioritize projects so the TMT would not resent the CIO for wasting resources on the wrong projects (Yalin, 2007).

The global CIO should direct research and evaluation of emerging and advanced technologies of interest, examining the potential of these technologies to address a business requirement or to create a new business opportunity (Lee et al., 2002). Although the CIOs do not need to have in-depth knowledge of cutting-edge technology, they must be a "quick study" person, able to learn enough from the expert on staff who is watching the horizon to report intelligently on these technologies to the TMT, business-unit leaders, and other constituencies (Lutchen, 2003).

Table 2. CIO's skills

Code	Skill	Literature
S1	Ability to communicate effectively	(NASCIO, 2015; Prewitt & Ware, 2006; Ross & Feeny, 1999; Smaltz et al., 2006)
S2	Strategic thinking and planning	(Hawkins, 2004; NASCIO, 2015; Prewitt & Ware, 2006)
S3	Ability to lead and motivate staff	(Lane & Koronios, 2007; NASCIO, 2015; Prewitt & Ware, 2006)
S4	Understand business processes and operations	(Prewitt & Ware, 2006; Yalin, 2007)
S5	Ability to follow technological innovations	(Lee et al., 2002; Lutchen, 2003; Prewitt & Ware, 2006)
S6	Negotiation skills	(Ertel & Gordon, 2007; NASCIO, 2015; Prewitt & Ware, 2006; Reich & Nelson, 2003)
S7	Technical proficiency	(Polansky et al., 2004; Prewitt & Ware, 2006)
S8	Relationship skills	(Allison, 2010; NASCIO, 2015; Vreuls & Joia, 2011).

Negotiation skills are crucial for CIO (Ertel & Gordon, 2007), to be able to make trade-offs without compromising relationships. Sometimes TMT expectations are too high and the CIO, after carefully analyzing, must explain what is and what is not possible to do with IT/IS (Reich & Nelson, 2003).

Technical proficiency is often relegated to a second plan since the TMT already expects the CIO to possess this skill. Whilst CIOs are playing an increasingly business-focused role, the responsibility for running effective technology operations remains. The challenge is maintaining an appropriate level of technical competence without jeopardizing the focus on business (Polansky et al., 2004).

The multi-dimensional role of CIO with many, internal and external, touching points, such as, other executives within the organization, other areas of the organization, clients, suppliers, government, etc., require good relationship skills. These skills are important to build bridges between the IT and other departments (internal networking) and to build bridges with entities external to the organization (external networking) (Allison, 2010; NASCIO, 2015; Vreuls & Joia, 2011).

RESEARCH MODEL

In order to assess if the relative importance assigned to the CIO's activities is influenced by variables directly related to his personal characteristics (gender, age, education, years in the company, years as a CIO) and by variables related to the characteristics of the enterprise where s/he works (annual sales, number of employees, IT department budget, IT sourcing structure, IT hierarchical structure), was developed the illustrative theoretical model presented Figure 1.

METHODOLOGY

A survey was conducted to investigate several aspects of the IT/IS reality in large Iberian enterprises. Specifically, for this study, the survey aimed to identify the main CIO's activities and to test if the rela-

Figure 1. Illustrative theoretical model

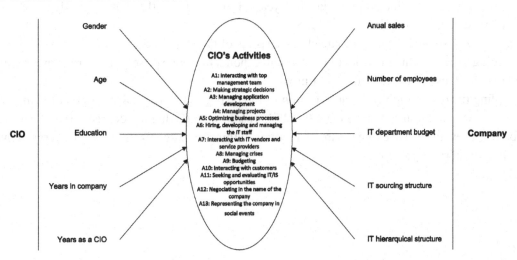

tive importance of those activities is influenced by variables regarding the CIO's characteristics and the characteristics of the enterprises where the CIO works.

Questionnaire

A structured questionnaire consisting of open and close-ended questions was developed from previous studies (Trigo et al., 2009; Varajão et al., 2009a). The questionnaire was divided into several sections (see Appendix 1).

The activities and skills considered in the study are the ones presented in Table 1 and Table 2 and were measured using a Likert scale from 1 to 5 (1 meaning "without importance" and 5 "very important").

The proposed questionnaire was pre-tested by four CIOs to validate its content and readability. The necessary changes were made to the final questionnaire, which was delivered to a sample of 1000 CIOs of Iberian large enterprises. With the questionnaire was sent a letter briefing the subjects about the scope and goals of the study, including a link to an Internet home page, which allowed filling the questionnaire online.

Data Collection

The survey was mailed to a sample group of 500 companies in Portugal and 500 companies in Spain. In order to obtain a representative sample, a casual stratified sample method was used, opting for a random sample of enterprises from the INE (Portuguese National Institute of Statistics) list of the 1000 largest national enterprises in Portugal (INE, 2007) and the SABI database list of the 1000 largest firms in Spain (Dijk, 2008).

In the first and second rounds of the data collection, the number of undelivered and returned questionnaires (by email) was 111 from Portuguese firms and 94 from Spanish enterprises, which reveals quite a significant number perhaps due to the email policies of the enterprises. In the third round, the invitation letter was sent by post and then the number of undelivered and returned questionnaires was 44 and 23 for Portuguese and Spanish firms, respectively. A total of 102 valid responses was obtained (59 responses from Portuguese enterprises and 43 from Spanish enterprises), yielding a final response rate of around 10%. This response rate did not come as a surprise as it is comparable with the response rates of others studies conducted in the last few years (Enns et al., 2001; Li et al., 2001; Lin & Pervan, 2003; Liu & Arnett, 2000; Sohal & Ng, 1998).

Table 3. and 4 show the demographic characteristics of the respondents.

According to Table 3 the majority of the sample respondents' enterprises had more than 500 employees and annual sales of up to 250 million Euros.

Regarding the demographic characterization of the respondents, Table 4 shows that the majority of CIOs that answered the survey were male (90.2%), possessed a Bachelor's degree (60.8%) and were in their forties. They have an average tenure of 10 years within their organization and an average tenure of 8 years in their current position.

Table 3. Demographic characteristics of respondents' enterprises

Characteristics	Number	%
Annual Sales (€)		
Up to 250 000 000	67	65.7
More than 250 000 000	28	27.5
Missing	7	6.9
Total	102	100
Number of Employees		
Up to 500	46	45.1
More than 500	56	54.9
Total	102	100
IT Budget		
Up to 1 000 000	49	48.0
More than 1 000 000	45	44.1
Missing	8	7.8
Total	102	100
IT Sourcing		
Up to 50% outsourcing	76	74.5
More than 50% outsourcing	26	25.5
Total	102	100
IT/CIO Reports		
CEO	61	59.8
Other (e.g. CFO)	41	40.2
Total	102	100

DATA ANALYSIS AND RESULTS

Figure 2 presents the ranking of CIO's activities, based on the score (importance) given by CIOs to each of the activities (see Table 1).

In the ranking obtained, three main groups of activities can be identified. The first group, includes the activities considered the most important, consisting of:

- **A4:** Managing projects;
- **A1:** Interacting with top management team;
- **A5:** Optimizing business processes; and
- **A2:** Making strategic decisions.

The second group contains seven activities of similar importance:

- **A3:** Managing application development;
- **A8:** Managing crises;

Table 4. Demographic characteristics of respondents

Characteristics	Number	%
Age		
Up to 40	41	40.2
More than 40	61	59.8
Total	102	100
Gender		
Male	92	90.2
Female	10	9.8
Total	102	100
Company Tenure		
Up to 10	57	55.9
More than 10	45	44.1
Total	102	100
CIO Tenure		
Up to 5	49	48.0
More than 5	53	52.0
Total	102	100
Education		
Graduated	71	69.6
Post-graduated	31	30.4
Total	102	100

Figure 2. Ranking of CIO's activities

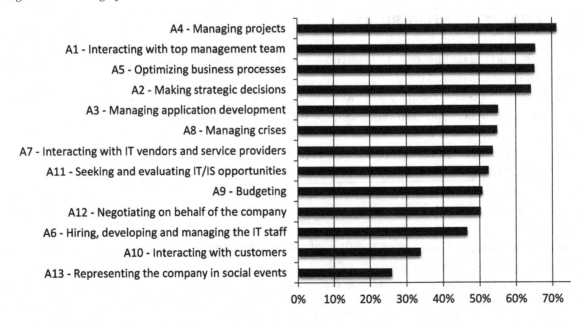

- **A7:** Interacting with IT vendors and service providers;
- **A11:** Seeking and evaluating IT/IS opportunities;
- **A9:** Budgeting;
- **A12:** Negotiating on behalf of the company; and
- **A6:** Hiring, developing and managing the IT staff.

Finally, the third group comprises of two activities which were regarded by CIOs as being less important:

- **A10:** Interacting with customers; and
- **A13:** Representing the company in social events.

The activities of the first group are consistent with some of today's CIOs top areas of focus, namely (Muse, 2016): improving IT operations/systems performance; security management; aligning IT initiatives with business goals; leading change efforts; implementing new systems and architecture.

Consistently with this view and the importance of the transformational CIO archetype, due to the emergence of digital business models (Muse, 2016), it is to mention the high importance attributed to the activity of "Managing projects", appearing in this study in the top of the CIO's activities ranking.

When comparing the activities in the first group with other study previous conducted by Trigo et al. (2009), it is interesting to notice that managing crises is not part of the first group of important activities, which is probably also related to the importance of transformational and business strategist CIO archetype.

Interacting with TMT is still the second most important activity for the CIO, probably due to the hierarchic position of the CIO in the organization structure. Today 46% of CIOs are part of the board, reporting directly to the Chief Executive Officer (CEO) (Muse, 2016).

In order to verify the influence of several variables on the perception of the importance of various activities, nonparametric tests were performed. More specifically, Mann-Whitney-Wilcoxon tests were performed. The detailed results of the tests can be found in Appendix 2. In Figure 4, a summary of the results obtained is presented and the significant results at $p < 0.05$ are identified.

Figure 3. Influence of the CIO's and organization's characteristics in the perception of the importance of the activities performed by the CIO

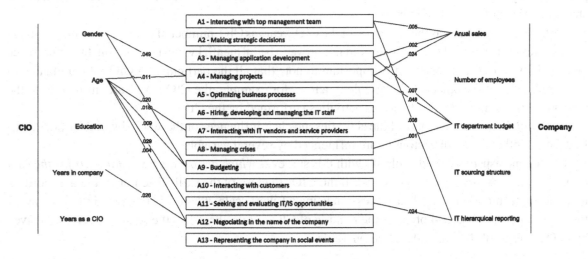

Figure 4. Ranking of CIO's skills

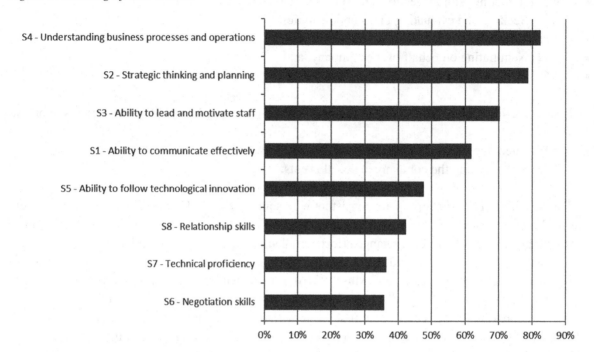

In the case of activities A2, A5, A6, A10 and A13, there is no a clear influence of the studied variables. Moreover, some activities, such as activities A7 and A8, appear to be influenced by only one variable. On its opposite is activity A4, whose importance is influenced by four variables: two concerning the CIO's characteristics; and two concerning the company's characteristics.

Interestingly, there are activities whose influences are easily understandable, as is the case, for example, of activity A1, whose perception of the importance is influenced by the position of the CIO in the hierarchical structure of the company. However, with respect to variables such as, for example, gender of the CIO, its influence is not so easy to explain in cases such as, for example, the A4 or A9 activities.

In summary, it is concluded that the perception of the relative importance of some of the activities performed by the CIO is influenced by several variables, including personal characteristics and the characteristics of the CIO's company.

Certain variables, such as the education of the CIO, years as CIO, number of employees of the company or IT sourcing structure of the company, did not prove to be influential when recognizing the importance of the CIO's activities. However it is important to note that all the participating CIOs are graduated or post-gradated. On the other hand, variables such as, for example, the CIO's age, are influential in the perception of the importance of various activities performed by the CIO.

In overall, in the case of some of the activities, no clear influences of the studied variables are identified. But in other cases, the activities are influenced by several variables.

The second aspect we tried to clarify with this survey is *which are the most pivotal skills for the CIO to perform its job successfully*. So we asked the CIOs to classify the skills listed on Table 2, according to the level of importance for their profession using a Likert scale, where 5 is the most important and 1 the least important. Figure 4 presents the ranking of CIO's skills, based on the score (importance) given by CIOs to each of the skills identified on Table 2.

In the ranking obtained, two main groups of skills can be found. The first group, includes the skills considered the most important, consisting of:

- **S4:** Understand business processes and operations;
- **S2:** Strategic thinking and planning;
- **S3:** Ability to lead and motivate staff; and
- **S1:** Ability to communicate effectively.

The second group comprises also four skills:

- **S5:** Ability to follow technological innovations;
- **S8:** Relationship skills;
- **S7:** Technical proficiency; and
- **S6:** Negotiation skills.

The two skills of the first group considered as most important by CIOs are aligned with the results from other studies (Magazine, 2009; Prewitt & Ware, 2006). Understanding business processes and operations was considered by the CIOs as the most important skill for their performance. Today, IT/IS importance and impact in the development of the organization business is well recognized and accepted, assuming the CIO a key role in today's process of business functions digitalization (Aron et al., 2015). These two skills are also aligned with the two of the activities (A5 - Optimizing business processes; A2 - Making strategic decisions) of the group of activities CIO considered as the most important and highlight once more the importance of the transformational and business strategist CIO's archetypes (Muse, 2016).

CONCLUSION

In recent years several studies have been conducted as well as papers published with the aim of presenting the CIO's activities. On the one hand, some studies have not organized the lists of activities, nor have weighed their importance (Chun & Mooney, 2009; Sellitto, 2012). On the other hand, some studies have shown rankings of activities regarding their relative importance to the performance of the CIO or regarding the time spent by CIO performing it (Chen & Wu, 2011; Luftman & Ben-Zvi, 2010; Trigo et al., 2009). These studies are extremely important because they enable a better understanding of the role played by the CIO as well as its evolution over time. However, there is quite often a change of position in the rankings of these activities, even when there is a similarity between the samples of the studies in which they are presented. This can be explained by the evolution of the CIO role or by some variables that can influence the recognized relative importance of the activities.

Research, based on a survey, was done with the aim of identifying whether or not some characteristics of the CIOs and of the enterprises they work for, influence the perceived importance of the CIOs' activities. Have participated in the study 102 CIOs from large enterprises and two main results stand out. First, a new ranking of the CIO activities was obtained, with the top four activities as follows: Managing projects; Interacting with top management team; Optimizing business processes; Making strategic decisions. Secondly, the study concluded that the relative importance recognized to some of the CIO activities is closely related to CIO characteristics as well as to the characteristics of the enterprise where the CIO works. Therefore, it can be concluded that the rankings of the CIO's activities should be seen as a whole, in groups of activities, and not only considering the individual position of each activity.

Concerning the skills that CIOs need to perform their job, the two most important were to understand business operations and strategic thinking and planning, which is in sync with today's emergence of new digital business models and the need of enterprises to digitalize business functions (Aron et al., 2015; Muse, 2016).

The findings of this research also suggest that it would be very interesting to carry out similar studies focusing other related aspects. Being this an explorative study, it would be also interesting to expand it with further studies considering other variables as, for instance, business sectors or business geographies.

REFERENCES

Allison, D. H. (2010). The future cio: Critical skills and competencies. *Research Bulletin (Sun Chiwawitthaya Thang Thale Phuket)*, 15.

Antero, M., Hedman, J., & Henningsson, S. (2014). Sourcing strategies to keep up with competition: The case of SAP. *International Journal of Information Systems and Project Management*, 2(4), 61–74.

Aron, D., Waller, G., & Weldon, L. (2015). *Flipping to Digital Leadership: The 2015 CIO Agenda (Executive Summary)*. Stanford, CA: Gartner.

Benamati, J., & Lederer, A. L. (2001). Coping with rapid changes in IT. *Communications of the ACM*, 44(8), 83–88. doi:10.1145/381641.381664

Bhatt, P., Shroff, G., Anantaram, C., & Misra, A. K. (2006). An influence model for factors in outsourced software maintenance. *Journal of Software Maintenance and Evolution: Research and Practice, 18*(6), 385-423. 10.1002/smr.339

Bilhim, J. (1999). *Metodologias e Técnicas de Avaliação, Avaliação na Administração Pública*. Lisboa, Portugal: INA.

Broadbent, M., & Kitzis, E. (2005). The New CIO Leader. *Harvard Business Review*.

Carvalho, R., Portela, L., Varajão, J., & Magalhães, L. (2009). *Actividades do Gestor de Sistemas de Informação*. Paper presented at the ADM 2009 - Congresso Internacional de Administração, Brasil.

Carvalho, R. A., & Costa, H. G. (2007). Application of an integrated decision support process for supplier selection. *Enterp. Inf. Syst.*, 1(2), 197–216. doi:10.1080/17517570701356208

Chen, D. Q., Preston, D. S., & Xia, W. (2010). Antecedents and effects of CIO supply-side and demand-side leadership: A staged maturity model. *Journal of Management Information Systems*, 27(1), 231–271. doi:10.2753/MIS0742-1222270110

Chen, Y.-C., & Wu, J.-H. (2011). IT management capability and its impact on the performance of a CIO. *Information & Management*, 48(4–5), 145–156. doi:10.1016/j.im.2011.04.001

Chun, M., & Mooney, J. (2009). CIO roles and responsibilities: Twenty-five years of evolution and change. *Information & Management*, 46(6), 323–334. doi:10.1016/j.im.2009.05.005

CIOMAG. (2004). *State of the CIO: Challenges Differ in SMBs, large Organizations*. CIO Magazine.

Davenport, T., & Short, J. (1990). The New Industrial Engineering: Information Technology and Business Process Redesign. *Sloan Management Review*, *31*(4), 11–27.

Dibbern, J., Goles, T., Hirschheim, R., & Jayatilaka, B. (2004). Information Systems Outsourcing: A Survey and Analysis of the Literature. *The Data Base for Advances in Information Systems*, *35*(4), 6–102. doi:10.1145/1035233.1035236

Dijk, B. v. (2008). *Sistema de Análisis de Balances Ibéricos*. Retrieved from http://www.bvdep.com

Ding, F., Li, D., & George, J. F. (2014). Investigating the effects of IS strategic leadership on organizational benefits from the perspective of CIO strategic roles. *Information & Management*, *51*(7), 865–879. doi:10.1016/j.im.2014.08.004

Enns, H. G., Huff, S. L., & Golden, B. R. (2001). How CIOs obtain peer commitment to strategic IS proposals: Barriers and facilitators. *The Journal of Strategic Information Systems*, *10*(1), 3–14. doi:10.1016/S0963-8687(01)00041-5

Ertel, D., & Gordon, M. (2007). *How to Negotiate When Yes Is Not Enough*. Harvard Business School Press.

Feeny, D. F., & Willcocks, L. P. (1998). Core IS capabilities for exploiting information technology. *MIT Sloan Management Review*, *39*(3), 9.

Fraga, M. G., Varajão, J., Amaral, L., & Bulas-Cruz, J. (2012). Information systems outsourcing in major Portuguese companies-contracting services. *Journal of Research and Practice in Information Technology*, *44*(1), 81.

Gorgone, J., Gray, P., Feinstein, D. L., Kasper, G. M., Luftman, J., Stohr, E. A., & Wigand, R. et al. (2000). MSIS 2000: Model Curriculum and Guidelines for Graduate Degree Programs in Information Systems. *Communications of the Association for Information Systems*, *3*(1). Retrieved from http://aisel.aisnet.org/cais/vol3/iss1/1

Grover, V., Seung-Ryul, J., William, J. K., & Lee, C. C. (1993). The Chief Information Officer: A study of managerial roles. *Journal of Management Information Systems*, *10*(2), 107–130. doi:10.1080/07421222.1993.11518002

Hawkins, B. L. (2004, November/December). A Framework for the CIO Position. *EDUCASE Review*, *39*, 94–102.

Heeks, R., Krishna, S., Nicholsen, B., & Sahay, S. (2001). Synching or sinking: Global software outsourcing relationships. *Software IEEE*, *18*(2), 54–60. doi:10.1109/52.914744

Hirschheim, R., George, B., & Wong, S. F. (2004). Information Technology Outsourcing: The Move Towards Offshoring. *Indian Journal of Economics & Businees*, *3*(Special Issue), 103–125.

Hoving, R. (2007). Information Technology Leadership Challenges - Past, Present, and Future. *Information Systems Management*, *24*(2), 147–153. Retrieved from http://www.informaworld.com/10.1080/10580530701221049 doi:10.1080/10580530701221049

Ifinedo, P., & Nahar, N. (2007). ERP systems success: an empirical analysis of how two organizational stakeholder groups prioritize and evaluate relevant measures. *Enterprise Information Systems, 1*(1), 25 - 48. Retrieved from http://www.informaworld.com/10.1080/17517570601088539

Iijima, T. (2007). Auditing your offshore outsource. *Journal of Corporate Accounting & Finance, 18*(4), 11-18. 10.1002/jcaf.20303

INE. (2007). *Lista das 1000 maiores empresas portuguesas. Ficheiro de Unidades Estatísticas - FUE - Base Belém*. Instituto Nacional de Estatística.

Johnson, A. M., & Lederer, A. L. (2007). The Impact of Communication between CEOs and CIOs on their Shared Views of the Current and Future Role of IT. *Information Systems Management, 24*(1), 85–90. doi:10.1080/10580530601038246

Johnson, A. M., & Lederer, A. L. (2010). CEO/CIO mutual understanding, strategic alignment, and the contribution of IS to the organization. *Information & Management, 47*(3), 138–149. doi:10.1016/j.im.2010.01.002

Karimi, J., Gupta, Y. P., & Somers, T. M. (1996). The congruence between a firms competitive strategy and information technology leaders rank and role. *Journal of Management Information Systems, 13*(1), 63–88. doi:10.1080/07421222.1996.11518112

Kearns, G. S., & Lederer, A. L. (2003). A Resource-Based View of Strategic IT Alignment: How Knowledge Sharing Creates Competitive Advantage. *Decision Sciences, 34*(1), 1–29. doi:10.1111/1540-5915.02289

Keen, P. G. W. (1991). *Shaping the future: business design through information technology*. Harvard Business School Press.

Lane, M. S., & Koronios, A. (2007). *Critical competencies required for the role of the modern CIO*. Paper presented at the ACIS 2007 - 18th Australasian Conference on Information Systems, Toowoomba, Australia.

Larson, E. C., & Adams, C. R. (2010). *Increasing Coordination Demands and the Impact on CIO Rank*. Paper presented at the System Sciences (HICSS), 2010 43rd Hawaii International Conference on.

Lee, S., Koh, S., Yen, D., & Tang, H.-L. (2002). Perception gaps between IS academics and IS practitioners: An exploratory study. *Information & Management, 40*(1), 51–61. doi:10.1016/S0378-7206(01)00132-X

Leeney, M., Varajão, J., Ribeiro, A. T., & Colomo-Palacios, R. (2011). Information Systems Outsourcing in Large Companies: Evidences from 20 Ireland Companies. *International Journal of Information Technology Project Management, 2*(4), 44–58. doi:10.4018/jitpm.2011100104

Li, E. Y., McLeod, R. Jr, & Rogers, J. C. (2001). Marketing information systems in Fortune 500 companies: A longitudinal analysis of 1980, 1990, and 2000. *Information & Management, 38*(5), 307–322. doi:10.1016/S0378-7206(00)00073-2

Lin, C., & Pervan, G. (2003). The practice of IS/IT benefits management in large Australian organizations. *Information & Management, 41*(1), 13–24. doi:10.1016/S0378-7206(03)00002-8

Liu, C., & Arnett, K. P. (2000). Exploring the factors associated with Web site success in the context of electronic commerce. *Information & Management, 38*(1), 23–33. doi:10.1016/S0378-7206(00)00049-5

Luftman, J., & Ben-Zvi, T. (2010). Key Issues for IT Executives 2009: Difficult Economy's Impact on IT. *MIS Quarterly Executive, 9*(1), 203–213.

Lutchen, M. D. (2003). *Managing IT as a Business: A Survival Guide for CEOs.* John Wiley & Sons, Ltd.

Magazine, C. (2009). *State of the CIO Survey '09.* CIO Magazine.

Malladi, S., & Krishnan, M. S. (2012). *Cloud computing adoption and its implications for CIO strategic focus–an empirical analysis.* Academic Press.

Marshall, P., McKay, J., & Prananto, A. (2005). Business Value Creation from IT Investments: Towards a process theory of IT governance. *Australasian Journal of Information Systems, 12*(2). doi:10.3127/ajis.v12i2.91

Muse, D. (2016). *State of the CIO.* Retrieved from United States: http://core0.staticworld.net/assets/2016/01/14/2016-state-of-the-cio-executive-summary.pdf

NASCIO. (2015). *The 2015 State of CIO Survey.* Retrieved from http://www.nascio.org/Portals/0/Publications/Documents/2015/NASCIO_2015_State_CIO_Survey.pdf

Nelson, R. R. (1991). Educational needs as perceived by IS and end-user personnel: A survey of knowledge and skill requirements. *Management Information Systems Quarterly, 15*(4), 503–525. doi:10.2307/249454

Polansky, M., Inuganti, T., & Wiggins, S. (2004). The 21st Century CIO. *Business Strategy Review, 15*(2), 29–33. doi:10.1111/j.0955-6419.2004.00310.x

Preston, D. (2003). Shared mental models between the CIO and CEO: Towards information systems strategic alignment. *AMCIS 2003 Proceedings*, 452.

Preston, D. S., Chen, D., & Leidner, D. E. (2008). Examining the Antecedents and Consequences of CIO Strategic Decision-Making Authority: An Empirical Study. *Decision Sciences, 39*(4), 605–642. doi:10.1111/j.1540-5915.2008.00206.x

Prewitt, E., & Ware, L. G. (2006). *The STATE of the CIO '06.* CIO Magazine.

Reich, B. H., & Nelson, K. (2003). In Their Own Words: CIO Visions About the Future of In-House IT Organizations. *The Data Base for Advances in Information Systems, 34*(4), 28–44. doi:10.1145/957758.957763

Rockart, J. F., Earl, M. J., & Ross, J. W. (1996). Eight imperatives for the new IT organization. *MIT Sloan Management Review, 38*(1), 43.

Romero, D., & Vernadat, F. (2016). Enterprise information systems state of the art: Past, present and future trends. *Computers in Industry, 79*, 3–13. doi:10.1016/j.compind.2016.03.001

Ross, J. W., Beath, C. M., & Goodhue, D. L. (1996). Develop Long-Term Competitiveness Through IT Assets. *Sloan Management Review, 38*(1), 31–65.

Ross, J. W., & Feeny, D. F. (1999). *The Evolving Role of the CIO. In Framing the Domain of IT Research: Glimpsing the Future Through the Past.* Cincinnati, OH: Pinnaflex Educational Resources Inc.

Rusu, L., Mekawy, M., & Hodosi, G. (2009). Information Technology Leadership in Swedish Leading Multinational Corporations. In M. Lytras, E. Damiani, J. Carroll, R. Tennyson, D. Avison, A. Naeve, & G. Vossen et al. (Eds.), *Visioning and Engineering the Knowledge Society. A Web Science Perspective* (Vol. 5736, pp. 511–522). Springer Berlin Heidelberg. doi:10.1007/978-3-642-04754-1_52

Sambamurthy, V., & Zmud, R. W. (1992). *Managing IT for success: The empowering business partnership*. Morristown, NJ: Financial Executives Research Foundation.

Sellitto, C. (2012). The Activities of the Chief Information Officer as Noted through Job Position Descriptions. *Communications of the IBIMA, 19*. doi:10.5171/2012.369727

Smaltz, D. H., Sambamurthy, V., & Agarwal, R. (2006). The antecedents of CIO role effectiveness in Organizations:An empirical study in the healthcare sector. *Engineering Management. IEEE Transactions on, 53*(2), 207–222. doi:10.1109/TEM.2006.872248

Sobol, M. G., & Klein, G. (2009). Relation of CIO background, IT infrastructure, and economic performance. *Information & Management, 46*(5), 271–278. doi:10.1016/j.im.2009.05.001

Sohal, A. S., & Ng, L. (1998). The role and impact of information technology in Australian business. *Journal of Information Technology, 13*(3), 201–217. doi:10.1080/026839698344846

Stephens, C., Ledbetter, W., Mitra, A., & Ford, F. (1992). Executive or functional? The nature of the CIOs job. *Management Information Systems Quarterly, 16*(4), 449–467. doi:10.2307/249731

Sutter, J. d. (2004). *The Power of IT: Survival Guide for the CIO*. North Charleston, SC: BookSurge, LLC.

Trigo, A., Varajão, J., Oliveira, I., & Barroso, J. (2009). Chief Information Officer's activities and skills in Portuguese large companies. *Communications of the IBIMA, 10*(9), 64–71.

Varajão, J. (2001). *Outsourcing de serviços de sistemas de informação*. Lisboa: FCA - Editora de Informática.

Varajão, J., Cruz-Cunha, M. M., da Glória Fraga, M., & Amaral, L. (2012a). Offshore outsourcing in large companies: Motivations and risks perceived. *African Journal of Business Management, 6*(36), 9936. doi:10.5897/AJBM11.669

Varajão, J., Pinto, J., Colomo-Palacios, R., & Amaral, L. (2012b). Modelo para a avaliação do desempenho potencial de gestores de sistemas de informação. *Interciencia, 37*(10), 724–728.

Varajão, J., Trigo, A., & Barroso, J. (2009a). Motivations and Trends for IT/IS Adoption: Insights from Portuguese Companies. *International Journal of Enterprise Information Systems, 5*(4), 34–52. doi:10.4018/jeis.2009090203

Varajão, J., Trigo, A., Figueiredo, N., Barroso, J., & Bulas-Cruz, J. (2009b). Information systems services outsourcing reality in large Portuguese organisations. *Int. J. Bus. Inf. Syst., 4*(1), 125–142. doi:10.1504/IJBIS.2009.021606

Varajão, J., Trigo, A., & Soto-Acosta, P. (2016). An Exploratory Study on the Influencers of the Perceived Relevance of CIOs Activities. *International Journal of Enterprise Information Systems, 12*(4), 1–15. doi:10.4018/IJEIS.2016100101

Varajão, J. E. Q. (2002). *Contributos para a melhoria do sucesso da adopção de tecnologias de informação e desenvolvimento de sistemas de informação nas organizações. (Tese de doutoramento PhD).* Guimarães: Universidade do Minho.

Varajão, J. E. Q. (2005). A Arquitectura da Gestão de Sistemas de Informação (3ª ed.). Lisboa: FCA - Editora de Informática.

Vedder, R. G., & Guynes, C. S. (2002). Cios Perspectives on Competitive Intelligence. *Information Systems Management, 19*(4), 49–55. doi:10.1201/1078/43202.19.4.20020901/38834.6

Vreuls, E. H., & Joia, L. A. (2011). An Exploratory Model for the Relevant Factors Related to the Professional Performance of the Brazilian CIO. *The Electronic Journal of Information Systems in Developing Countries, 47.*

Xu, L. D. (2011). Enterprise Systems: State-of-the-Art and Future Trends. *IEEE Transactions on Industrial Informatics, 7*(4), 630–640. doi:10.1109/TII.2011.2167156

Yalin, D. (2007). Business-savvy CIOs Step Up. *InformationWeek.* Retrieved from http://www.informationweek.com/shared/printableArticle.jhtml?articleID=199500669

KEY TERMS AND DEFINITIONS

Chief Information Officer (CIO): The person who determines the overall strategic direction and business contribution of the information systems function in a business.

CIO Activities: Set of doings developed by the CIO in the performance of its profession, usually grouped into the typical functions of management: planning, organizing, leading and controlling.

CIO Roles: Set of management roles performed by the CIO within the organization, categorized into three types: interpersonal, information and decisional. The CIO magazine defines three types of CIO archetypes: functional, transformational and business strategist. These last two roles are back in mode due to the new role played by the CIO, the role of the digital enabler of the organization within the scope of the digitalization of business functions.

CIO Skills: Set of abilities, coming from CIO's knowledge, practice, aptitude, etc., needed by the CIO to excel in its profession.

Information System (IS): Any organized system for the collection, organization, storage and communication of information.

Information System Function: Set of organizational activities aiming to optimize the organization's IS.

Information Technology (IT): A generic term that covers the collection, processing, storage and dissemination of information involving the use of computers and telecommunication technologies.

IT/IS Management: The discipline whereby all of the IT/IS resources of a company are managed in accordance with its needs and priorities. These resources may include hardware, software, data, networks and data center facilities, as well as the people hired to maintain them.

APPENDIX I: QUESTIONNAIRE

Figure 5.

1. Company characterization
   a. Number of employees (please choose only one of the following):
      - 1 to 200
      - 201 to 500
      - 501 to 2000
      - 2001 to 5000
      - More than 5000
      - Do not know/Do not answer
   b. Business volume (please choose only one of the following):
      - Less than 5 000 000 euros
      - 5 000 000 to 10 000 000 euros
      - 10 000 001 to 50 000 000 euros
      - 50 000 001 to 250 000 000 euros
      - 250 000 001 to 500 000 000 euros
      - More than 500 000 000 euros
      - Don't know / Don't answer
   c. International presence (number of countries excluding your own)? _____
   d. Sector of activity (please choose only one of the following):
      - Agriculture and agro-industry
      - Utilities
      - Cellulose and paper
      - Commerce
      - Car trade
      - Electric and electronic commerce
      - Building and construction
      - Food distribution
      - Fuel distribution
      - Artwork, DTP, publishing
      - Transportation equipment
      - Sanity and cleaning
      - Hotels and restaurants
      - Wood, cork and furniture
      - Electric and precision equipment
      - Metalworking and machinery
      - Metallic and non-metallic minerals
      - Medical and pharmaceutical products
      - Chemistry
      - Services
      - Telecommunications
      - Textiles
      - Transports and distribution
      - Footwear and leather
   e. IT/IS budget (please choose only one of the following):
      - Less than 1 000 000 euros
      - 1 000 000 to 5 000 000 euros
      - 5 000 001 to 10 000 000 euros
      - More than 10 000 000 euros
      - I do not know/ I do not answer
      - Other _____
2. IT/IS manager profile
   a. Sex (please choose only one of the following):
      - Female
      - Male
   b. Age (please choose only one of the following):
      - Less than 30
      - 31 to 35
      - 36 to 40
      - 41 to 45
      - More than 45
      - I do not know/ I do not answer
   c. Academic education and/or professional formation
      - Please choose "only one" of the following:
      - High school
      - Bachelor's
      - Post-Graduation
      - MBA
      - Master's
      - PhD
      - Other _____
   d. Original area of education/formation (please choose only one of the following):
      - IT/IS
      - Management
      - Sciences
      - Other engineering
      - Other _____
3. IT/IS manager position
   a. How long have you been in your current position (years)? _____
   b. How long have you worked in the company (years)? _____
   c. What was your previous function? _____
   d. To whom do you report (please choose only one of the following):
      - CEO, Administrator or Director of the company
      - CFO or Financial Director
      - Commercial Director
      - Commercial Director
      - Director of Production
      - Other _____
4. IT/IS manager activities
   a. Which are the most important activities in your job (where 1 is without importance and 5 the very important)?
      - Interacting with top management team (1-5) __
      - Making strategic decisions (1-5) __
      - Managing application development (1-5) __
      - Managing projects (1-5) __
      - Optimizing business processes (1-5) __
      - Hiring, developing and managing the IT staff (1-5) __
      - Interacting with IT vendors and service providers (1-5) __
      - Managing crises (1-5) __
      - Budgeting (1-5) __
      - Interacting with customers (1-5) __
      - Seeking and evaluating IT/IS opportunities (1-5) __
      - Negotiating in the name of the company (1-5) __
      - Representing the company in social events (1-5) __

APPENDIX 2: STATISTICS

Figure 6.

Test Statistics – Activities/Grouping variable GENDER

	A1	A2	A3	A4	A5	A6	A7	A8	A9	A10	A11	A12	A13
Mann-Whitney U	418.500	402.000	362.000	294.000	429.000	410.500	443.500	451.500	262.000	411.000	393.000	386.500	348.000
Wilcoxon W	4696.500	4680.000	4640.000	4572.000	4707.000	4688.500	4721.500	4729.500	4540.000	466.000	4671.000	4664.500	4626.000
Z	-.496	-.684	-1.145	-1.965	-.365	-.571	-.196	-.099	-2.318	-.571	-.783	-.858	-1.329
Asymp. Sig. (2-tailed)	.620	.494	.252	.049	.715	.568	.844	.921	.020	.568	.434	.391	.184

Test Statistics – Activities/Grouping variable EDUCATION

	A1	A2	A3	A4	A5	A6	A7	A8	A9	A10	A11	A12	A13
Mann-Whitney U	1029.000	1026.000	944.500	924.000	1086.500	920.000	994.500	1020.000	932.500	1096.500	983.500	1070.000	1072.500
Wilcoxon W	3585.000	1522.000	1440.500	1420.000	3642.500	3476.000	1490.500	1516.000	3488.500	3652.500	3539.500	3626.000	1568.500
Z	-.552	-.568	-1.178	-1.351	-.107	-1.347	-.815	-.608	-1.272	-.030	-.884	-.230	-.215
Asymp. Sig. (2-tailed)	.581	.570	.239	.177	.915	.178	.415	.543	.204	.976	.377	.818	.830

Test Statistics – Activities/Grouping variable AGE

	A1	A2	A3	A4	A5	A6	A7	A8	A9	A10	A11	A12	A13
Mann-Whitney U	1030.000	1217.500	1044.500	896.000	1031.000	1035.500	923.000	880.000	1117.500	1081.000	943.000	849.000	1150.500
Wilcoxon W	2921.000	3108.500	2935.500	2787.000	2922.000	2926.500	2814.000	2771.000	3008.500	2972.000	2834.000	2740.000	3041.500
Z	-1.598	-.236	-1.460	-2.545	-1.568	-1.505	-2.362	-2.623	-.944	-1.198	-2.180	-2.841	-.719
Asymp. Sig. (2-tailed)	.110	.813	.144	.011	.117	.132	.018	.009	.345	.231	.029	.004	.472

Test Statistics – Activities/Grouping variable YEARSCOMP

	A1	A2	A3	A4	A5	A6	A7	A8	A9	A10	A11	A12	A13
Mann-Whitney U	1071.000	1179.500	1191.500	1155.500	1218.500	1141.000	1178.500	1192.500	1221.000	1246.000	1043.000	963.500	1144.000
Wilcoxon W	2106.000	2214.500	2226.500	2190.500	2871.500	2176.000	2213.500	2227.500	2256.000	2899.000	2078.000	1998.500	2179.000
Z	-1.514	-.728	-.637	-.900	-.451	-.978	-.741	-.629	-.431	-.255	-1.676	-2.229	-.984
Asymp. Sig. (2-tailed)	.130	.467	.524	.368	.652	.328	.459	.529	.666	.799	.094	.026	.325

Test Statistics – Activities/Grouping variable YEARSCIO

	A1	A2	A3	A4	A5	A6	A7	A8	A9	A10	A11	A12	A13
Mann-Whitney U	1262.000	1271.000	1136.500	1264.000	1266.000	1291.000	1265.000	1207.000	1126.000	1250.500	1221.000	1245.000	1249.500
Wilcoxon W	2693.000	2496.000	2361.500	2489.000	2491.000	2722.000	2490.000	2432.000	2557.000	2681.500	2652.000	2676.000	2474.500
Z	-.260	-.193	-1.127	-.243	-.228	-.052	-.237	-.636	-1.202	-.333	-.539	-.372	-.346
Asymp. Sig. (2-tailed)	.795	.847	.260	.808	.820	.959	.813	.525	.229	.739	.590	.710	.729

Test Statistics – Activities/Grouping variable SALES

	A1	A2	A3	A4	A5	A6	A7	A8	A9	A10	A11	A12	A13
Mann-Whitney U	617.000	837.000	563.500	674.000	870.000	799.000	822.500	718.000	930.500	821.000	714.000	809.000	876.500
Wilcoxon W	1023.000	1243.000	969.500	1080.000	1276.000	1205.000	1228.500	1124.000	3208.500	3099.000	1120.000	1215.000	1282.500
Z	-2.786	-.863	-3.175	-2.261	-.581	-1.164	-.996	-1.862	-.064	-.989	-1.901	-1.092	-.530
Asymp. Sig. (2-tailed)	.005	.388	.002	.024	.561	.244	.319	.063	.949	.323	.057	.275	.596

Test Statistics – Activities/Grouping variable EMPLOYEES

	A1	A2	A3	A4	A5	A6	A7	A8	A9	A10	A11	A12	A13
Mann-Whitney U	1124.500	1208.000	1123.500	1279.000	1156.000	1257.500	1206.000	1105.500	1149.000	1182.000	1080.500	1191.000	1095.500
Wilcoxon W	2720.500	2289.000	2719.500	2875.000	2237.000	2338.500	2287.000	2701.500	2230.000	2263.000	2161.500	2272.000	2176.500
Z	1.168	.561	-1.149	-.064	-.929	-.210	-.583	-1.273	-.973	-.738	-1.449	-.676	-1.365
Asymp. Sig. (2-tailed)	.243	.573	.251	.949	.353	.833	.560	.203	.331	.460	.147	.499	.172

Test Statistics – Activities/Grouping variable ITBUDGET

	A1	A2	A3	A4	A5	A6	A7	A8	A9	A10	A11	A12	A13
Mann-Whitney U	1079.000	950.000	761.000	853.000	937.000	1058.000	872.000	661.000	1010.000	983.500	1075.000	1023.000	1082.000
Wilcoxon W	2304.000	2175.000	1796.000	1888.000	1972.000	2093.000	1907.000	1696.000	2045.000	2208.500	2110.000	2058.000	2307.000
Z	-.188	-1.208	-2.682	-1.976	-1.306	-.345	-1.852	-3.458	-.728	-.930	-.216	-.623	-.163
Asymp. Sig. (2-tailed)	.851	.227	.007	.048	.192	.730	.064	.001	.467	.352	.829	.533	.870

Test Statistics – Activities/Grouping variable ITSOURCING

	A1	A2	A3	A4	A5	A6	A7	A8	A9	A10	A11	A12	A13
Mann-Whitney U	910.000	858.000	915.000	814.500	894.000	853.500	907.000	789.000	974.000	780.500	964.500	912.000	933.500
Wilcoxon W	3836.000	1209.000	1266.000	3740.500	1245.000	1204.500	3833.000	1140.000	3900.000	3706.500	3890.500	3838.000	3859.500
Z	-.636	-1.046	-.582	-1.401	-.755	-1.059	-.657	-1.585	-.112	-1.650	-.187	-.605	-.441
Asymp. Sig. (2-tailed)	.525	.295	.561	.161	.450	.289	.511	.113	.911	.099	.851	.545	.659

Test Statistics – Activities/Grouping variable ITREPORT

	A1	A2	A3	A4	A5	A6	A7	A8	A9	A10	A11	A12	A13
Mann-Whitney U	882,5	1138	1079	1091,5	1177	1244,5	1186,5	1211,5	1155	1223,5	931,5	1140,5	1020,5
Wilcoxon W	1743,5	1999	1940	1952,5	2038	2105,5	2047,5	3102,5	3046	2084,5	1792,5	2001,5	1881,5
Z	-2,667	-0,805	-1,215	-1,142	-0,525	-0,042	-0,462	-0,276	-0,678	-0,191	-2,261	-0,778	-1,655
Asymp. Sig. (2-tailed)	0,008	0,421	0,224	0,254	0,6	0,966	0,644	0,782	0,498	0,849	0,024	0,436	0,098

Compilation of References

Abadi, D. J., Carney, D., Cetintemel, U., Cherniack, M., Convey, C., Lee, S., & Zdonik, S. et al. (2003). Aurora: A new model and architecture for data stream management. *The International Journal on Very Large Data Bases*, *12*(2), 120–139. doi:10.1007/s00778-003-0095-z

Abbott, M. (2006). The Productivity and Efficiency of the Australian Electricity Supply Industry. *Energy Economics*, *28*(4), 444–454. doi:10.1016/j.eneco.2005.10.007

Abdelghaffar, H. (2012). Success factors for ERP implementation in large organizations: The case of Egypt. *Electronic Journal of Information Systems in Developing Countries*, *52*(4), 1–13.

Abdel-Kader, M., & Nguyen, T. P. (2011). An investigation of enterprise resource planning implementation in a small firm: A study of problems encountered and successes achieved. *International Journal of Enterprise Information Systems*, *7*(1), 18–40. doi:10.4018/jeis.2011010102

Abid, A. A. (2010). *Perceived impacts and barriers to e-Business technology adoption: A preliminary study* (Unpublished Master's Dissertation). Caulfield School of IT, Monash University, Melbourne, Australia.

Ackoff, R. L. (1981). *Creating the Corporate Future*. New York: John Wiley & Sons.

Adam, F., & ODoherty, P. (2000). Lessons from enterprise resource planning implementations in Ireland - towards smaller and shorter ERP projects. *Journal of Information Technology*, *15*(4), 305–316. doi:10.1080/02683960010008953

Addy, R. (2007). *Effective IT Service Management*. Berlin: Springer.

Adele Berndt, F. H., & Roux. (2005). Implementing a customer relationship management programme in an emerging market. *Journal of Global Business and Technology*, *1*(2).

Adelman, S., & Moss, L. T. (2002). *Data Warehouse Project Management*. Boston: Addison Wesley.

Adrian Payne, P. F. (2004). The role of multichannel integration in customer relationship management. *Industrial Marketing Management*, *33*.

Agarwal, R., & Karahanna, E. (2000). Time flies when youre having fun: Cognitive absorption and beliefs about information technology usage. *Management Information Systems Quarterly*, *24*(4), 665–694. doi:10.2307/3250951

Agarwal, R., & Prasad, J. (1997). The role of innovation characteristics and perceived voluntaries in the acceptance of information technology. *Decision Sciences*, *28*(3), 557–582. doi:10.1111/j.1540-5915.1997.tb01322.x

Ahmad, M. M., & Cuenca, R. P. (2013). Critical success factors for ERP implementation in SMEs. *Robotics and Computer-integrated Manufacturing*, *29*(3), 104–111. doi:10.1016/j.rcim.2012.04.019

Aho, A. V., & Ullman, J. D. (1972). The Theory of Parsing, Translation and compiling.: Vol. 1. *Parsing*. Prentice-Hall.

Ahrari, M., & Amirusefi, R. (2012). Survey relationship between service quality and customer relationship management. *Journal of American Science, 8*(9).

Aier, S., & Schelp, J. (2009). A reassessment of enterprise architecture implementation. In *Proceedings of the 2009 International Conference on Service-Oriented Computing* (pp. 35-47). Berlin: Springer-Verlag.

Ajmal, M. M., & Kristianto, Y. (2010). Knowledge Sharing in Supply Chain. *International Journal of Strategic Decision Sciences, 1*(4), 44–55. doi:10.4018/jsds.2010100103

Akkermans, H. A., Bogerd, P., Yu, C. E. V., & Wassenhove, L. N. (2003). The impact of ERP on supply chain management: Exploratory findings from a European Delphi study. *European Journal of Operational Research, 146*(2), 284–301. doi:10.1016/S0377-2217(02)00550-7

Akkermans, H., & van Helden, K. (2002). Vicious and Virtuous Cycles in ERP Implementation: A Case Study of Interrelations between Critical Success Factors. *European Journal of Information Systems, 11*(1), 35–46. doi:10.1057/palgrave.ejis.3000418

Aladwani, A. M. (2001). Change management strategies for successful ERP implementation. *Business Process Management Journal, 7*(3), 266–275. doi:10.1108/14637150110392764

Alan, D. S., & Allen, R. L. (2005). Identity theft and e-fraud as critical crm concerns. *International Journal of Enterprise Information Systems, 1*(2), 17–36. doi:10.4018/jeis.2005040102

Albani, A., & Dietz, J. L. G. (2011). Enterprise ontology based development of information systems. *International Journal of Internet and Enterprise Management, 7*(1), 41–63. doi:10.1504/IJIEM.2011.038382

ALdayel, A. I., Aldayel, M. S., & Al-Mudimigh, A. S. (2011). The Critical Success Factors of ERP implementation in Higher Education in Saudi Arabia: A Case Study. *Journal of Information Technology & Economic Development, 2*(2).

Alekh, D., Maheshwari, N., & Kalicharan, S. (2013). A Business Intelligence Technique for Forecasting the Automobile Sales using Adaptive Intelligent Systems (ANFIS and ANN). *International Journal of Computers and Applications, 74*(1), 7–13.

Al-Hinai, H. S., Edwards, H. M., & Humphries, L. (2013). The Changing Importance of Critical Success Factors During ERP Implementation: An Empirical Study from Oman. *International Journal of Enterprise Information Systems, 9*(3), 1–21. doi:10.4018/jeis.2013070101

Alimazighi, Z., & Bouhmadi, A. (2011) Adapting goal oriented approaches in requirement engineering of Inter-Organizational Information System. *Proceedings of Fifth International Conference on Research Challenges in Information Science*, 1-7. doi:10.1109/RCIS.2011.6006847

Alison Cartlidge, e. a. (2007). *An introductory overview of ITIL v3*. UK Chapter of the itSMF.

Allan, G. (2003). A critique of using grounded theory as a research method. *Electronic Journal of Business Research Methods, 2*(1), 1–10.

Allison, D. H. (2010). The future cio: Critical skills and competencies. *Research Bulletin (Sun Chiwawitthaya Thang Thale Phuket)*, 15.

Al-Mashari, M., Al-Mudimigh, A., & Zairi, M. (2003). Enterprise resource planning: A taxonomy of critical factors. *European Journal of Operational Research, 146*(2), 352–364. doi:10.1016/S0377-2217(02)00554-4

Al-Mashari, M., & Zairi, M. (2000). Information and business process equality: The case of SAP R/3 implementation. *Electronic Journal of Information Systems in Developing Countries, 2*(4), 1–15.

Al-Mudimigh, A., Zairi, M., & Al-Mashari, M. (2001). ERP software implementation: An integrative framework. *European Journal of Information Systems*, *10*(4), 216–226. doi:10.1057/palgrave.ejis.3000406

Al-Safadi, L. A. E. (2009). Natural Language Processing for Conceptual Modeling. *International Journal of Digital Content Technology and Its Applications*, *3*(3), 47–59.

Alter, S. (2010). *Bridging the Chasm between Sociotechnical and Technical Views of Systems in Organizations.* Paper presented at the Thirty First International Conference on Information Systems, St. Louis, MO.

Alter, S. (2012). *The work system method: Systems thinking for business professionals.* Paper presented at the IIE Annual Conference.

Alter, S. (1999). A general, yet useful theory of information systems. *Communications of the Association for Information Systems*, *1*(13), 1–70.

Alter, S. (2003). 18 reasons why IT-reliant work systems should replace the IT artifact as the core subject matter of the IS field. *Communications of the Association for Information Systems*, *12*(23), 365–394.

Alter, S. (2006). Work systems and IT artifacts - does the definition matter? *Communications of the Association for Information Systems*, *17*(1), 14.

Alter, S. (2007). Could the work system method embrace systems concepts more fully? *Information Resources Management Journal*, *20*(2), 33–43. doi:10.4018/irmj.2007040103

Alter, S. (2008). Defining information systems as work systems: Implications for the IS field. *European Journal of Information Systems*, *17*(5), 448–469. doi:10.1057/ejis.2008.37

Alter, S. (2013). Work system theory: Overview of core concepts, extensions, and challenges for the future. *Journal of the Association for Information Systems*, *14*(2), 72–121.

Amid, A., & Kohansal, A. (2014). Organizational Levels Model for Measuring the Effectiveness of Enterprise Resource Planning System (Case Study TUGA Company, Iran). *Universal Journal of Industrial and Business Management*, *2*, 25–30.

Amid, A., Moalagh, M., & Ravasan, A. Z. (2012). Identification and classification of ERP critical failure factors in Iranian industries. *Information Systems*, *37*(3), 227–237. doi:10.1016/j.is.2011.10.010

Amoako-Gyampah, K. (2007). Perceived usefulness, user involvement and behavioral intention: An empirical study of ERP implementation. *Computers in Human Behavior*, *23*(3), 1232–1248. doi:10.1016/j.chb.2004.12.002

Anderson, J. C., & Gerbing, D. W. (1988). Structural equation modeling in practice: A review and recommended two-step approach. *Psychological Bulletin*, *103*(3), 411–423. doi:10.1037/0033-2909.103.3.411

Ang, J., & Pavri, F. (1994). A survey and critique of the impact of information technology. *International Journal of Information Management*, *17*(3), 122–130. doi:10.1016/0268-4012(94)90031-0

Antero, M., Hedman, J., & Henningsson, S. (2014). Sourcing strategies to keep up with competition: The case of SAP. *International Journal of Information Systems and Project Management*, *2*(4), 61–74.

Antony, S., & Santhanam, R. (2008). Could the Use of a Knowledge-Based System Lead to Implicit Learning? In International Handbook on Information Systems- Handbook on Decision Support Systems 1 Basic Themes (pp. 791–812). Springer. doi:10.1007/978-3-540-48713-5_35

Antony, S. R., & Batra, D. (2002). CODASYS: A consulting tool for novice database designers. *The Data Base for Advances in Information Systems*, *33*(3), 54–88. doi:10.1145/569905.569911

Antony, S., Batra, D., & Santhanam, R. (2005). The use of a knowledge-based system in conceptual data modeling. *Decision Support Systems*, *41*(1), 176–188. doi:10.1016/j.dss.2004.05.011

Anwar, A., Gulzar, A., & Anwar. (2011). Impact of Self-Designed Products on Customer Satisfaction. *Contemporary Research in Business*.

Appelbaum, S. H. (1997). Socio-Technical Systems Theory: An Intervention Strategy for Organizational Development. *Management Decision*, *35*(6), 452–463. doi:10.1108/00251749710173823

Apte, U., Sankar, C. S., Thakur, M., & Turner, J. E. (1990, December). Reusability-Based Strategy for Development of Information Systems: Implementation Experience of a Bank. *Management Information Systems Quarterly*, *14*(4), 421–433. doi:10.2307/249791

Arasu, A., Babcock, B., Babu, S., Cieslewicz, J., Datar, M., Ito, K., & Widom, J. et al. (2004). Stream: The stanford data stream management system. *A Quarterly Bulletin of the Computer Society of the IEEE Technical Committee on Data Engineering*, *26*(1), 19–26.

Armour, F. J., & Kaisler, S. H. (2001, November/ December). Enterprise architecture: Agile transition and implementation. *IT Pro*, 30-37.

Armour, F. J., Kaisler, S. H., & Liu, S. Y. (1999b, July/August). Building an enterprise architecture step by step. *IT Pro*, 31-39.

Armour, F. J., Kaisler, S. H., & Liu, S. Y. (1999a, January). A big-picture look at enterprise architectures. *IEEE IT Professional*, *1*(1), 35–42. doi:10.1109/6294.774792

Armstrong, A., & Hagel, J. III. (1996). The real value of online communities. *Harvard Business Review*, (May/June), 134–140.

Arnold, V. (2006). Behavioral research opportunities: Understanding the impact of enterprise systems. *International Journal of Accounting Information Systems*, *7*(1), 7–17. doi:10.1016/j.accinf.2006.02.001

Arnold, V., & Sutton, S. G. (2007). The impact of enterprise systems on business and audit practice and the implications for university accounting education. *International Journal of Enterprise Information Systems*, *3*(4), 1–21. doi:10.4018/jeis.2007100101

Aron, D., Waller, G., & Weldon, L. (2015). *Flipping to Digital Leadership: The 2015 CIO Agenda (Executive Summary)*. Stanford, CA: Gartner.

Askary, S., Goodwin, D., & Lanis, R. (2012). Improvements in audit risks related to information technology frauds. *International Journal of Enterprise Information Systems*, *8*(2), 52–63. doi:10.4018/jeis.2012040104

ASUG. (2007). *ASUG/SAP Benchmarking Initiative: Business Intelligence/Analytics*. Presentation at American SAP User Group Conference, Atlanta, GA.

Atre, S. (2003). *The Top 10 Critical Challenges For Business Intelligence Success*. C. C. Publishing. Retrieved from http://www.computerworld.com/computerworld/records/images/pdf/BusIntellWPonline.pdf

Auramo, J., Kauremaa, J., & Tanskanen, K. (2005). Benefits of IT in Supply Chain Management: An explorative study of progressive companies. *International Journal of Physical Distribution & Logistics Management*, *35*(2), 82–100. doi:10.1108/09600030510590282

Australian Institute of Health and Welfare (AIHW). (2012). *Residential aged care in Australia 2010-11: a statistical overview, Aged care statistics series no. 36, Cat. No. AGE 68*. Canberra: AIHW.

Avolio, B. J., Walumbwa, F. O., & Weber, T. J. (2009). Leadership: Current theories, research, and future directions. *Annual Review of Psychology*, *60*(1), 421–449. doi:10.1146/annurev.psych.60.110707.163621 PMID:18651820

Axelos. (2011). *ITIL Service Design.* TSO (The Stationery Office).

Aydin, A. O., & Tunali, S. (2007). Intelligent agent technologies promise in emerging arena: Mass customization. *Proceedings of the 6th WSEAS International Conference on Artificial Intelligent, Knowledge Engineering and Data Bases.*

Azad, B. & Faraz, S. (2011). Using signature matrix to analyze conflicting frames during the IS implementation process. *International Journal of Accounting Information Systems.*

Bacharach, S. B. (1989). Organizational Theories: Some Criteria for Evaluation. *Academy of Management Review*, *14*(4), 496–515.

Bailey, C., & Clarke, M. (2001). Managing knowledge for personal and organizational benefit. *Journal of Knowledge Management*, *5*(1), 58–68. doi:10.1108/13673270110384400

Bajwa, D. S., Garcia, J. E., & Mooney, T. (2004). An Integrative Framework for the Assimilation of Enterprise Resource Planning Systems: Phases, Antecedents, and Outcomes. *Journal of Computer Information Systems*, *44*(3), 81–90.

Bajwa, D., Rai, A., & Brennan, I. (1998). Key antecedents of executive information system success: A path analytic approach. *Decision Support Systems*, *22*(1), 31–43. doi:10.1016/S0167-9236(97)00032-8

Bajwa, I. S., Lee, M. G., & Bordbar, B. (2011). SBVR business rules generation from natural language specification. *AAAI Spring Symposium - Technical Report, SS-11-03*, 2–8.

Balazinska, M., Balakrishnan, H., Madden, S. R., & Stonebraker, M. (2008). Fault-tolerance in the borealis distributed stream processing system. *ACM Transactions on Database Systems*, *33*(1), 1–44. doi:10.1145/1331904.1331907

Balazinska, M., Balakrishnan, H., & Stonebraker, M. (2004). Load management and high availability in the medusa distributed stream processing system. In L. Liu (Ed.), *ACM SIGMOD International Conference on Management of Data*: (pp. 929-930). Paris, France: ACM. doi:10.1145/1007568.1007701

Balint, B. (2011). Difficulties in enterprise system implementation: The case of Millicent Homes. *Journal of Information Technology Case and Applications Research*, *13*(3), 72–84. doi:10.1080/15228053.2011.10856213

Balint, B. (2015). Obtaining Value from the Customization of Packaged Business Software: A Model and Simulation. *International Journal of Enterprise Information Systems*, *11*(1), 33–49. doi:10.4018/ijeis.2015010103

Balis, B., Kowalewski, B., & Bubak, M. (2011). Real-time grid monitoring based on complex event processing. *Future Generation Computer Systems*, *27*(8), 1103–1112. doi:10.1016/j.future.2011.04.005

Balkundi, P., & Kilduff, M. (2006). The ties that lead: A social network approach to leadership. *The Leadership Quarterly*, *17*(4), 419–439. doi:10.1016/j.leaqua.2006.01.001

Ball, D., Coelho, P. S., & Vilares, M. J. (2006). Service Personalization and Loyalty. *Services Marketing, 20*(6), 391-403.

Ballantyne, D. (2000). Internal relationship marketing: A strategy for knowledge renewal. *International Journal of Bank Marketing*, *18*(6), 274–286. doi:10.1108/02652320010358698

Ballou, D. P., & Tayi, G. K. (1999). Enhancing data quality in data warehouse environments. *Communications of the ACM*, *42*(1), 73–78. doi:10.1145/291469.291471

Banker, R., Charnes, A., & Cooper, W. (1984). Some Models for Estimating Technical and Scale Inefficiencies in Data Envelopment Analysis. *Management Science*, *30*(9), 1078–1092. doi:10.1287/mnsc.30.9.1078

Banker, R., & Morey, R. (1986). Efficiency analysis for exogenously fixed inputs and outputs. *Operations Research*, *34*(4), 513–521. doi:10.1287/opre.34.4.513

Barratt, M. (2004). Understanding the meaning of collaboration in the supply chain. *Supply Chain Management: An International Journal*, *9*(1), 30–42. doi:10.1108/13598540410517566

Barratt, M., & Oke, A. (2007). Antecedents of supply chain visibility in retail supply chains: A resource-based theory perspective. *Journal of Operations Management*, *25*(6), 1217–1233. doi:10.1016/j.jom.2007.01.003

Bartoli, A., & Phillipe, H. (2004). Managing change and innovation in IT implementation process. *Journal of Manufacturing Technology Management*, *15*(5), 5. doi:10.1108/17410380410540417

Barua, A., Konana, P., Whinston, A. B., & Yin, F. (2004). An empirical investigation of net-enabled business value: An exploratory investigation. *Management Information Systems Quarterly*, *28*(4), 585–620.

Baskerville, R., Pries-Heje, J., & Venable, J. (2009). Soft design science methodology. In *Proceedings of the 4th international conference on design science research in information systems and technology* (p. 9). ACM.

Basoglu, N., Daim, T., & Kerimoglu, O. (2007). Organizational adoption of enterprise resource planning systems: A conceptual framework. *The Journal of High Technology Management Research*, *18*(1), 73–97. doi:10.1016/j.hitech.2007.03.005

Bass, L., Clements, P., & Kazman, R. (2003). *Software Architecture in Practice* (2nd ed.). Boston: Addison-Wesley.

Batini, C., Ceri, S., & Navathe, S. B. (1992). *Conceptual Database Design An Entity-Relationship Approach*. Redwood City, CA: The Benjamin/Cummings Publishing Company.

Batra, D., & Antony, S. R. (1994). Novice errors in conceptual database design. *European Journal of Information Systems*, *3*(1), 57–69. doi:10.1057/ejis.1994.7

Beaumaster, S. (1999). *Information Technology Implementation Issues: An Analysis* (Thesis). Virginia Polytechnic Institute and State University.

Becerra-Fernandez, I., Gonzalez, A., & Sabherwal, R. (2004). *Knowledge management: Challenges, solutions, and technologies* (1st ed.). Upper Saddle River, NJ: Prentice Hall.

Beheshti, H. M., & Beheshti, C. M. (2010). Improving productivity and firm performance with enterprise resource planning. *Enterprise Information Systems*, *4*(4), 445–472. doi:10.1080/17517575.2010.511276

Belassi, W., & Tukel, O. I. (1996). A new framework for determining critical success/failure factors in projects. *International Journal of Project Management*, *14*(3), 141–151. doi:10.1016/0263-7863(95)00064-X

Benamati, J., & Lederer, A. L. (2001). Coping with rapid changes in IT. *Communications of the ACM*, *44*(8), 83–88. doi:10.1145/381641.381664

Benjamin, R. I., Rockart, J. F., Scott Morton, M. S., & Wyman, J. (1984). Information Technology: A Strategic Opportunity. *Sloan Management Review*, *25*(3), 3–10.

Bentler, P. M., & Chou, C.-P. (1987). Practical issues in structural modeling. *Sociological Methods & Research*, *16*(1), 78–117. doi:10.1177/0049124187016001004

Bergman, J. Z., Rentsch, J. R., Small, E. E., Davenport, S. W., & Bergman, S. M. (2012). The shared leadership process in decision-making teams. *The Journal of Social Psychology*, *152*(1), 17–42. doi:10.1080/00224545.2010.53876 3 PMID:22308759

Bergstrom, M., & Stehn, L. (2005). Matching industrialised timber frame housing needs and enterprise resource planning: A change process. *International Journal of Production Economics, 97*(2), 172–184. doi:10.1016/j.ijpe.2004.06.052

Bernard, S. A. (2005). *Introduction to Enterprise Architecture*. AuthorHouse.

Beynon-Davies, P., Owens, I., & Williams, M. D. (2004). Information systems evaluation and the information systems development. *The Journal of Enterprise Information Management, 17*(4), 276–282. doi:10.1108/17410390410548689

Bhatt, P., Shroff, G., Anantaram, C., & Misra, A. K. (2006). An influence model for factors in outsourced software maintenance. *Journal of Software Maintenance and Evolution: Research and Practice, 18*(6), 385-423. 10.1002/smr.339

Bhatt, G. D. (2001). Knowledge management in organizations: Examining the interaction between technologies, techniques, and people. *Journal of Knowledge Management, 5*(1), 68–75. doi:10.1108/13673270110384419

Bhatti, T. R. (2005). Critical success factors for the implementation of enterprise resource planning (ERP): empirical validation. *The Second International Conference on Innovation in Information Technology (IIT'05)*.

Bhatti, T. R. (2005, September). Critical success factors for the implementation of enterprise resource planning (ERP): empirical validation.*The Second International Conference on Innovation in Information Technology*, 110.

Biere, M. (2011). *The New Era of Enterprise Business Intelligence*. IBM Press.

Bilhim, J. (1999). *Metodologias e Técnicas de Avaliação, Avaliação na Administração Pública*. Lisboa, Portugal: INA.

Bingi, P., Sharma, M. K., & Godla, J. K. (1999). Critical Issues Affecting an ERP Implementation. *Information Systems Management, 16*(5), 7–15. doi:10.1201/1078/43197.16.3.19990601/31310.2

Bingi, P., Sharma, M. K., & Godla, J. K. (1999). Critical issues affecting an ERP implementation. *IS Management, 16*(3), 7–14.

Binney, D. (2000). The knowledge management spectrum-understanding the KM landscape. *Journal of Knowledge Management, 5*(1), 21–32.

Bisol, S., & Roy, A. (2014). Leveraging Shared Leadership in the Sterile Processing Department to Engage Staff in Process Improvement. *American Journal of Infection Control, 42*(6), S29–S166. doi:10.1016/j.ajic.2014.03.167

Blair, D. C. (2002). Knowledge Management: Hype, Hope or Help? *Journal of the American Society for Information Science and Technology, 53*(12), 1019–1028. doi:10.1002/asi.10113

Boahene, M. (1999). Information Systems Development Methodologies: Are you being served?. *Proceedings of the 10th Australasian Conference on Information Systems*, 88-99.

Boar, B. H. (1998). *Constructing Blueprints for Enterprise IT Architectures*. New York: John Wiley & Sons.

Bodoni, S. (2014). Kaupthing creditors, madoff, a-tec, lehman brothers: Bankruptcy. *Bloomberg News*. Retrieved January 12, 2014, from http://www.bloomberg.com/news/2010-11-25/kaupthing-creditors-madoff-a-tec-lehman-brothers-bankruptcy.html

Boh, W., & Yellin, D. (2006). Using enterprise architecture standards in managing information technology. *Journal of Management Information Systems, 23*(3), 163–207. doi:10.2753/MIS0742-1222230307

Bondarouk, T., & Rue, H. (2008). HRM systems for successful information technology implementation: Evidence from three case studies. *European Management Journal, 26*(3), 153–165. doi:10.1016/j.emj.2008.02.001

Boonstra, A. (2011). Aligning Systems, Structures and People: Managing Stakeholders. Managing Adaptability, Intervention, and People in Enterprise Information Systems, 157.

Borgonovi, F. (2008). Doing well by doing good. The relationship between formal volunteering and self-reported health and happiness. *Social Science & Medicine, 66*(11), 2321–2334. doi:10.1016/j.socscimed.2008.01.011 PMID:18321629

Borum, F., & Christiansen, J. (2006). Actors and structure in IS projects: What makes implementation happen? *Scandinavian Journal of Management, 22*(3), 213–237. doi:10.1016/j.scaman.2006.10.006

Bose, R. (2002). Customer relationship management, key component for IT success. *Industrial Management & Data Systems, 102*(2), 89–97. doi:10.1108/02635570210419636

Boster, M., Liu, S., & Thomas, R. (2000, July/August). Getting the most from your enterprise architecture. *IEEE - IT Pro*. Retrieved from http://app.search.lib.unimelb.edu.au/

Bostrom, R. P., & Heinen, J. S. (1977b). MIS Problems and failures: A socio-technical perspective. Part II: The application of socio-technical theory. *MIS Quarterly, 1*(4), 11-28.

Bostrom, R. P., & Heinen, J. S. (1977). MIS Problems and Failures: A Socio- Technical Perspective Part I: The Causes. *Management Information Systems Quarterly, 1*(3), 17–32. doi:10.2307/248710

Botta-Genoulaz, V., & Millet, P. A. (2005). A classification for better use of ERP systems. *Computers in Industry, 56*(6), 573–587. doi:10.1016/j.compind.2005.02.007

Boudreau, M. C., & Robey, D. (1999, January). Organizational transition to enterprise resource planning systems: theoretical choices for process research. In *Proceedings of the 20th international conference on Information Systems* (pp. 291-299). Association for Information Systems.

Boudreau, M.-C., & Robey, D. (2005). Enacting integrated information technology: A human agency perspective. *Organization Science, 16*(1), 3–18. doi:10.1287/orsc.1040.0103

Bouthillier, F., & Shearer, K. (2002). Understanding knowledge management and information management: the need for an empirical perspective. *Information Research, 8*(1), 8-1.

Bovet, D., & Martha, J. (2003). *Supply chain hidden profits*. Mercer Management Consulting.

Bowersox, D. J., & Daugherty, P. J. (1995). Logistics paradigms: The impact of information technology. *Journal of Business Logistics, 16*(1), 65–80.

Boyer, J., Frank, B., Green, B., Harris, T., & van De Vanter, K. (2010). *Business Intelligence Strategy: A Practical Guide for Achieving BI Excellence*. MC Press.

Boynton, A. C., Zmud, R. W., & Jacobs, G. C. (1994). The influence of IT management practice on IT use in large organizations. *Management Information Systems Quarterly, 18*(3), 299–318. doi:10.2307/249620

Bradley, J. (2008). Management based critical success factors in the implementation of enterprise resource planning systems. *International Journal of Accounting Information Systems, 9*(3), 175–200. doi:10.1016/j.accinf.2008.04.001

Bradley, R. V., Pratt, R. M. E., Byrd, T. A., Outlay, C. N., & Wynn, D. E. Jnr. (2012). Enterprise architecture, IT effectiveness and the mediating role of IT alignment in US hospitals. *Information Systems Journal, 22*(2), 97–127. doi:10.1111/j.1365-2575.2011.00379.x

Bramorski, T. (2003, August). A Case Study of ERP Implementation Issues. *ICEB Second International Conference on Electronic Business*.

Brancheau, J. C., & Brown, C. V. (1993). The management of end-user computing: Status and directions. *ACM Computing Surveys, 25*(4), 437–482. doi:10.1145/162124.162138

Brehm, L., Heinzl, A., & Markus, M. L. (2001). Tailoring ERP Systems: A Spectrum Of Choices And Their Implications. In *Proceedings of the 34th Annual Hawaii International Conference on System Sciences*. New York, NY: Institute of Electrical and Electronics Engineers. doi:10.1109/HICSS.2001.927130

Brinton, L. J., & Brinton, D. M. (2010). *The Linguistic Structure of Modern English*. Philadelphia: John Benjamins Publishing Company. doi:10.1075/z.156

Broadbent, M., & Kitzis, E. (2005). The New CIO Leader. *Harvard Business Review*.

Brookman, F., Smit, J., & Silvius, A. J. G. (2012). Perception of Information Technology Enablers for Supply Chain Management. *Communications of the IIMA*, *12*(2), 51–64.

Brown, C., & Vessey, I. (1999, January). ERP implementation approaches: toward a contingency framework. In *Proceedings of the 20th international conference on Information Systems* (pp. 411-416). Association for Information Systems.

Brown, D., & Wilson, S. (2005). *The Black Book of Outsourcing. How to manage the changes, challenges and opportunities*. John Wiley & Sons Inc.

Brown, S. A. (1997). *Revolution at the Checkout Counter: the explosion of the bar code*. London: Harvard University Press.

Bruce, M., Daly, L., & Towers, N. (2004). Lean or agile, a solution for supply chain management in the textiles and clothing industry? *International Journal of Operations & Production Management*, *24*(2), 151–170. doi:10.1108/01443570410514867

Bruls, W. A., van Steenbergen, M., Foothuis, R. M., Bos, B., & Brinkemper, S. (2010). Domain architectures as an instrument to refine architecture. *Communications of the Association for Information Systems*, *27*, 517–540.

Btoush, E. S., & Hammad, M. M. (2015). *Generating ER Diagrams from Requirement Specifications Based On Natural Language Processing*. Academic Press.

Buchanan, R. D., & Soley, R. M. (2002). *Aligning enterprise architecture and IT investments with corporate goals*. Object Management Group.

Bucher, D., & Meissner, J. (2010). *Automatic Parameter Configuration for Inventory Management in SAP ERP/APO* (Working Paper). The Department of Management Science.

Burdon, S. W., Al-Kilidar, H., & Mooney, G. R. (2013). Evaluating an Organizations Cultural Readiness for Innovation. *International Journal of Business Innovation and Research*, *7*(5), 572–589. doi:10.1504/IJBIR.2013.056179

Burton-jones, A., Wand, Y., & Weber, R. (2009). Guidelines for Empirical Evaluations of Conceptual Modeling Grammars * Guidelines for Empirical Evaluations of Conceptual Modeling Grammars. *Journal of the Association for Information Systems*, *10*(6), 495–532.

Business Analysis Made Easy. (2006). *Decision Making Model in Five Steps*. Retrieved from http://www.business-analysis-made-easy.com/Decision-Making-Model-In-Five-Steps.html

Buttle, F. (2004). *Customer relationship management: Concepts and tools*. Sydney: Elsevier.

Byrne, B. M. (1998). *Structural equation modeling with LISREL, PRELIS, and SIMPLIS: Basic concepts, applications, and programming*. Mahwah, NJ: Lawrence Erlbaum Associates, Inc.

Cameron, A. C., & Trivedi, P. K. (2010). *Microeconometrics using Stata*. College Station, TX: Stata Press.

Campos, R., Carvalho, R. A., & Rodrigues, J. S. (2007). Enterprise Modeling for Development Processes of Open-Source ERP. *18th Production and Operation Management Society Conference*.

Capaldo, G., Rippa, P., 2009. A planned-oriented approach for EPR implementation strategy selection. *Journal of Enterprise information Management, 22,* 642 – 659.

Caress, A. L., & Scott, L. (2005). Shared governance and shared leadership: Meeting the challenges of implementation. *Journal of Nursing Management, 13*(1), 4–12. doi:10.1111/j.1365-2834.2004.00455.x PMID:15613089

Carlock, P. G., & Fenton, R. E. (2001). System of systems (SoS) enterprise systems engineering for information-intensive organizations. *Systems Engineering, 4*(4), 242–261. doi:10.1002/sys.1021

Carlson, W. M. (1979). Business information analysis and integration technique (BIAIT) - The new horizon. *Database, 10*(4), 3–9.

Carolyn, C. Y., Melissa, D., & Chandana, U. (2003). *Organizational Transformation through CRM Implementation: a descriptive case study.* Working papers-series, School of Information Systems.

Carson, J. B., Marrone, J. A., & Tesluk, P. E. (2007). Shared Leadership in Teams: An Investigation of Antecedent Conditions and Performance. *Academy of Management Journal, 50*(5), 1217–1234. doi:10.2307/20159921

Carter, J. J. III, & Justis, R. T. (2010). The Development and Implementation of Shared Leadership in Multi-Generational Family Firms. *Management Research Review, 33*(6), 563–585. doi:10.1108/01409171011050190

Carter, S., & Yeo, A. C.-M. (2016). Students-as-customers satisfaction, predictive retention with marketing implications: The case of Malaysian higher education business students. *International Journal of Educational Management, 30*(5), 635–652. doi:10.1108/IJEM-09-2014-0129

Cartman, C., & Salazar, A. (2011). The influence of organizational size, internal IT capabilities and competitive and vendor pressure on ERP adoption in SMEs. *International Journal of Enterprise Information Systems, 7*(3), 68–92. doi:10.4018/jeis.2011070104

Carton, F., & Adam, F. (2003). Analysing the impact of ERP systems roll-outs in multi-national companies. *Electronic Journal of Information Systems Evaluation, 6*(2), 21–32.

Cartwright, C., Sankaran, S., & Kelly, J. (2008). *Developing a New Leadership Framework for Not-For-Profit Health and Community Care Organisations in Australia.* Lismore, Australia: Southern Cross University.

Carvalho, R., Portela, L., Varajão, J., & Magalhães, L. (2009). *Actividades do Gestor de Sistemas de Informação.* Paper presented at the ADM 2009 Congresso Internacional de Administração, Brasil.

Carvalho, R. A., & Costa, H. G. (2007). Application of an integrated decision support process for supplier selection. *Enterp. Inf. Syst., 1*(2), 197–216. doi:10.1080/17517570701356208

Cawthorne, J. E. (2010). Leading from the middle of the organization: An examination of shared leadership in academic libraries. *Journal of Academic Librarianship, 36*(2), 151–157. doi:10.1016/j.acalib.2010.01.006

Celce-Murcia, M., & Larsen-Freeman, D. (1999). *The Grammar Book: An ESL/EFL Teacher's Course.* Boston: Heinle & Heinle.

Cervone, H. F. (2005). Making decisions: Methods for digital library project teams. *International Digital Library Perspectives, 21*(1), 30–35.

Chandan, H. C., & Urhuogo, I. (2012). Organizational Challenges for Innovation in Information Systems. *SAIS 2012 Proceedings.*

Chand, D., Hachey, G., Hunton, J., Owhoso, V., & Vasudevan, S. (2005). A balanced scorecard based framework for assessing the strategic impacts of ERP systems. *Computers in Industry, 56*(6), 558–572. doi:10.1016/j.compind.2005.02.011

Chapman, R. L., Soosay, C., & Kandampully, J. (2003). Innovation in logistic services and the new business model: A conceptual framework. *International Journal of Physical Distribution & Logistics Management, 33*(7), 630–650. doi:10.1108/09600030310499295

Charnes, A. (1994). *Data Envelopment Analysis, theory, methodology and applications.* Kluwer Academic Publishers.

Charnes, A., Cooper, W., & Rhodes, E. (1978, November). Measuring the Efficiency of Decision Making Units. *European Journal of Operations Research,* 429-444.

Chase, R. B., & Aquilano, N. J. (1992). A Matrix for linking Marketing and Production Variables in Service System Design. In *Production and operations management* (6th ed.). Homewood, IL: Irwin.

Chatzoglou, P., & Diamantidis, A. (2009, April). IT/IS implementation risks and their impact on firm performance. *International Journal of Information Management, 29*(2), 119–128. doi:10.1016/j.ijinfomgt.2008.04.008

Chau, S. B., & Turner, P. (2002). A framework for analyzing factors influencing small to medium sized enterprises: Ability to derive benefits from the conduct of Web-based electronic commerce (EC).*Proceedings of Xth European Conference on Information Systems.*

Chauvel, D., & Despres, C. (2002). A review of survey research in knowledge management: 19972001. *Journal of Knowledge Management, 6*(3), 207–223. doi:10.1108/13673270210434322

Chen, D. Q., Preston, D. S., & Xia, W. (2010). Antecedents and effects of CIO supply-side and demand-side leadership: A staged maturity model. *Journal of Management Information Systems, 27*(1), 231–271. doi:10.2753/MIS0742-1222270110

Chen, I. J. (2001). Planning for ERP systems: Analysis and future trends. *Supply Chain Management Review, 7*(5), 374–386.

Chen, I. J., & Popovich, K. (2003). Understanding customer relationship management. *Business Process Management Journal, 9*(5), 672–688. doi:10.1108/14637150310496758

Chenoweth, T., Corral, K., & Demirkan, H. (2006). Seven key interventions for data warehouse success. *Communications of the ACM, 49*(1), 114–119. doi:10.1145/1107458.1107464

Chen, P. P.-S. (1976). The Entity-Relationship Unified View of Data Model-Toward a. *ACM Transactions on Database Systems, 1*(1), 9–36. doi:10.1145/320434.320440

Chen, Q., & Chen, H. (2004). Exploring the success factors of eCRM strategies in practice. *Database Marketing and Customer Strategy Management, 11*(4), 333–343. doi:10.1057/palgrave.dbm.3240232

Chen, T., & Wang, Y.-C. (2012). An integrated project management system for facilitating knowledge learning. *International Journal of Enterprise Information Systems, 8*(2), 30–51. doi:10.4018/jeis.2012040103

Chen, Y.-C., & Wu, J.-H. (2011). IT management capability and its impact on the performance of a CIO. *Information & Management, 48*(4–5), 145–156. doi:10.1016/j.im.2011.04.001

Chesbrough, H. (2010). *Business model Innovation: Opportunities and barriers.* Elsevier.

Chidambaram, L. (1999). Knowledge transfer in conceptual modeling by end users. *Journal of End User Computing, 11*(1), 40–51. doi:10.4018/joeuc.1999010105

Chin, W. W., Gopal, A., & Salisbury, W. D. (1997). Advancing the theory of adaptive structuration: The development of a scale to measure faithfulness of appropriation. *Information Systems Research, 8*(4), 342–367. doi:10.1287/isre.8.4.342

Chong, C. S. (2005). Critical factors in the successful implementation of Knowledge Management. *Journal of Knowledge Management,* (June): 21–42.

Choobineh, J., & Lo, A. W. (2004). CABSYDD: Case-Based System for Database Design. *Journal of Management Information Systems*, *21*(3), 281–314. doi:10.1080/07421222.2004.11045813

Chopra, S., & Meindl, P. (2001). *Supply Chain Management: Strategy, Planning, and Operation*. Upper Saddle River, NJ: Prentice Hall.

Chopra, S., & Meindl, P. (2007). *Supply chain management: Strategy planning, and operation* (3rd ed.). Upper Saddle River, NJ: Pearson Prentice Hall.

Chou, D. C., Tripuramallu, H. B., & Chou, A. Y. (2005). BI and ERP integration. *Information Management & Computer Security*, *13*(5), 340–349. doi:10.1108/09685220510627241

Chou, S. W., & Chang, Y. L. (2008). The Implementation Factors that Influence the ERP Benefits. *Decision Support Systems*, *46*(1), 149–157. doi:10.1016/j.dss.2008.06.003

Christensen, C., & Anthony, S. (2005). *Building Your Internal Growth Engine*. HBR, Strategy & Innovation, Jan/Feb.

Christensen, C., & Raynor, M. (2003). *The Innovator's Solution*. HBSP.

Christopher, M. (1998). *Logistics and Supply Chain Management Strategies for Reducing Cost and Improving service*. London, UK: Pittman Publishing.

Christopher, M., & Towill, D. (2000). Supply chain migration from lean and functional to agile and customized. *Supply Chain Management: An International Journal*, *5*(4), 206–213. doi:10.1108/13598540010347334

Chun, M., & Mooney, J. (2009). CIO roles and responsibilities: Twenty-five years of evolution and change. *Information & Management*, *46*(6), 323–334. doi:10.1016/j.im.2009.05.005

Churchill, G. A. J. (1979). A paradigm for developing better measures of marketing constructs. *JMR, Journal of Marketing Research*, *15*(1), 64–73. doi:10.2307/3150876

Chu, W. H. J., & Lee, C. C. (2006). Strategic information sharing in a supply chain. *European Journal of Operational Research*, *174*(3), 1567–1579. doi:10.1016/j.ejor.2005.02.053

Chwelos, P., Benbasat, I., & Dexter, A. S. (2001). Empirical test on EDI adoption model. *Information Systems Research*, *12*(1), 304–321. doi:10.1287/isre.12.3.304.9708

CIA World Fact Book. (2010). *Country Report*. Retrieved from www.cia.gov/cia/publications

Cianci, A. M., Hannah, S. T., Roberts, R. P., & Tsakumis, G. T. (2014). The effects of authentic leadership on followers ethical decision-making in the face of temptation: An experimental study. *The Leadership Quarterly*, *25*(3), 581–594. doi:10.1016/j.leaqua.2013.12.001

CIOMAG. (2004). *State of the CIO: Challenges Differ in SMBs, large Organizations*. CIO Magazine.

Cliffe, S. (1999). ERP Implementation. *Harvard Business Review*, 16–17.

Cohen, J. E., Lemley, M. A., & Lemleyt, M. A. (2012). Patent Scope and Innovation in the Software Industry. *California Law Review, 89*(1), 1-57.

Coiera, E. (2007). Putting the technical back into socio-technical systems research. *International Journal of Medical Informatics*, *76*, S98–S103. doi:10.1016/j.ijmedinf.2006.05.026 PMID:16807084

Commision, P. (2010). Contribution of the Not-for-Profit Sector. Research Report, Canberra.

Comondore, V. R., Devereaux, P. J., Zhou, Q., Stone, S. B., Busse, J. W., Ravindran, N. C., & Guyatt, G. H. et al. (2009). Quality of care in for-profit and not-for-profit nursing homes: Systematic review and meta-analysis. *BMJ (Clinical Research Ed.), 339*(aug04 2), b2732. doi:10.1136/bmj.b2732 PMID:19654184

Cooper, M. C., Lambert, D. M., & Pagh, J. D. (1997). Supply chain management: More than a new name for logistics. *The International Journal of Logistics Management, 8*(1), 1–14. doi:10.1108/09574099710805556

Cooper, R. B., & Zmud, R. W. (1990). Information Technology Implementation Research: A Technological Diffusion Approach. *Management Science, 36*(2), 123–139. doi:10.1287/mnsc.36.2.123

Coronado, A. E., Lyons, A. C., Michaelides, Z., & Kehoe, D. F. (2004). *Automotive supply chain models and technologies: A review of some latest developments.* Retrieved from, www.emeraldinsight.com/1741-0398.htm

Correia dos Santos, J., & Mira da Silva, M. (2015). Price management in IT outsourcing contracts. The path to flexibility. *Journal of Revenue and Pricing Management,* 1-23.

Correia dos Santos, J., & Mira da Silva, M. (2012). *Cost Management in IT Outsourcing contracts: The path to standardization. 19th International Business Information Management Association (IBIMA).* Barcelona: Ibima.

Correia dos Santos, J., & Mira da Silva, M. (2015). Mapping Critical Success Factors for IT Outsourcing: The Providers Perspective. *International Journal of Enterprise Information Systems, 11*(1), 62–84. doi:10.4018/ijeis.2015010105

Costa, P., Santos, J., & Mira da Silva, M. (2013). Evaluation Criteria for Cloud Services. *IEEE 6th International Conference on Cloud Computing.* Santa Clara, CA: IEEE.

Cotteleer, M. J., & Bendoly, E. (2006). Order Lead-Time Improvement Following Enterprise Information Technology Implementation: An Empirical Study. *Management Information Systems Quarterly, 30*(3), 643–660.

Cragg, P. B., and Mitchell, E. (2000). Benchmarking IT practices in small firms. *Proceedings of ACIS.*

Cragg, P. B., & King, M. (1993). Small-firm computing: Motivators and inhibitors. *Management Information Systems Quarterly, 17*(1), 47–60. doi:10.2307/249509

Crane, L. (2012). Trust me, Im an expert: Identity construction and knowledge sharing. *Journal of Knowledge Management, 16*(3), 448–460. doi:10.1108/13673271211238760

Cronbach, L. J. (1951). Coefficient alpha and the internal structure of test. *Psychometrika, 16*(3), 297–334. doi:10.1007/BF02310555

Cross, G. J. (2000). How e-business is transforming supply chain management. *The Journal of Business Strategy, 21*(2), 36–39. doi:10.1108/eb040073

Cullen, S., Seddon, P., & Willcocks, L. (2005, March). Managing Outsourcing: The Lifecycle Imperative. *MIS Quarterly Executive, 4*(1).

Cullen, S. (2009). *The Contract Scorecard: Successful Outsourcing by design.* England, UK: Gower Publishing Limited.

Cullen, S., Seddon, P., & Willcocks, L. (2005). IT Outsourcing configuration: Research into defining and designing outsourcing arrangements. *The Journal of Strategic Information Systems, 14*(4), 357–387. doi:10.1016/j.jsis.2005.07.001

D'Avanzo, R., Starr, E., & Von Lewinski, H. (2004). Supply chain and the bottom line: A critical link. *Outlook: Accenture, 1*, 39–45.

Dabic, M., Potocan, V., Nedelko, Z., & Morgan, T. R. (2013). Exploring the use of 25 leading business practices in transitioning market supply chains. *International Journal of Physical Distribution & Logistics Management, 43*(10), 833–851. doi:10.1108/IJPDLM-10-2012-0325

Dane, E., & Pratt, M. G. (2007). Exploring intuition and its role in managerial decision making. *Academy of Management Review, 32*(1), 33–54. doi:10.5465/AMR.2007.23463682

Dane, E., Rockmann, K. W., & Pratt, M. G. (2012). When should I trust my gut? Linking domain expertise to intuitive decision-making effectiveness. *Organizational Behavior and Human Decision Processes, 119*(2), 187–194. doi:10.1016/j.obhdp.2012.07.009

Daneva, M., & Wieringa, R. J. (2006). A requirements engineering framework for cross-organizational ERP systems. *Requirements Engineering, 11*(3), 194–204. doi:10.1007/s00766-006-0034-9

Das, K., & Dellana, S. A. (2013). A Quality and Partnering-Based Model for Improving Supply Chain Performance. *International Journal of Strategic Decision Sciences, 4*(3), 1–31. doi:10.4018/jsds.2013070101

Daugherty, P. J., Autry, C. W., & Ellinger, A. E. (2001). The impact of resource commitment on reverse logistics. *Journal of Business Logistics, 22*(1), 107–124. doi:10.1002/j.2158-1592.2001.tb00162.x

Davenport, T. H., & Brooks, J. D. (2004). Enterprise systems and the supply chain *Journal of Enterprise information Management, 17*(1), 8-19.

Davenport, T. H., & Prusak, L. (2000). Working Knowledge: How Organisations Manage What They Know. Harvard Business School Press.

Davenport, T. (1998). Putting Enterprise into the Enterprise system. *Harvard Business Review, 76*(4), 1–11. PMID:10181586

Davenport, T. (1998). Putting the enterprise into the enterprise system. *Harvard Business Review, 76*(4), 121–131. PMID:10181586

Davenport, T. (2000). *Mission Critical.* Boston, MA: Harvard Business School Press.

Davenport, T. H. (2000). *Mission critical: Realizing the promise of enterprise systems.* Harvard Business School Publishing.

Davenport, T. H., & Short, J. E. (1990). The New Industrial Engineering: Information Technology and Business Process Redesign. *Sloan Management Review, 31*(4), 11–27.

Davenport, T., Harris, J., & Cantrell, S. (2003). *The Return of Enterprise Solutions: The Director's Cut.* Accenture.

David, P. A. (1990). The Dynamo and the Computer: An historical Perspective on the Modern Productivity Paradox. *The American Economic Review, 80*(2), 355–361.

Davila, T., Estein, M., & Sheldon, R. (2005). Making Innovation work: How to make it, measure it and profit from it. Prentice Hall.

Davis, F. (1989). Perceived Usefulness, Perceived Ease of Use, and User Acceptance of Information Technology. *MIS Quarterly, 13*(3), 319-340.

Davis, G. B., & Olson, M. (1985). *Management information systems: Conceptual foundations, methods and development.* New York: McGraw Hill.

Dawson, J., & Owens, J. (2008). Critical success factors in the chartering phase: A case study of an ERP implementation. *International Journal of Enterprise Information Systems, 4*(3), 9–24. doi:10.4018/jeis.2008070102

Dawson, P. (2001). Organizational Change. In B. Millett & R. Wiesner (Eds.), *Management and Organizational Behavior* (pp. 211–223). Brisbane: John Wiley.

Dedrick, J., Gurbaxani, V., & Kraemer, K. (2003). Information Technology and Economic Performance: A Critical Review of the Empirical Evidence. *ACM Computing Surveys*, *35*(1), 1–28. doi:10.1145/641865.641866

Deep, A., Guttridge, P., Dani, S., & Burns, N. (2008). Investigating factors affecting ERP selection in made-to-order SME sector. *Journal of Manufacturing Technology Management*, *19*(4), 430–446. doi:10.1108/17410380810869905

Del Missier, F., Mäntylä, T., & Bruin, W. B. (2012). Decision-making competence, executive functioning, and general cognitive abilities. *Journal of Behavioral Decision Making*, *25*(4), 331–351. doi:10.1002/bdm.731

Deloitte-Consulting. (2000). *ERP's second wave: Maximizing the value of ERP-enabled processes*. Available at: www.dc.com/Insight/research

Delone, & McLean. (2003). The DeLone and McLean Model of Information Systems Success: A Ten-Year Update. *Journal of Management Information Systems, 19*(4).

DeLone, W. H., & McLean, E. R. (1992). Information systems success: The quest for the dependent variable. *Information Systems Research*, *3*(1), 60–69. doi:10.1287/isre.3.1.60

DeLone, W. H., & McLean, E. R. (2003). The DeLone and McLean model of information systems success: A ten-year update. *Journal of Management Information Systems*, *19*(4), 9–30.

Deng, Z., Lu, Y., Wei, K. K., & Zhang, J. (2009). Understanding customer satisfaction and loyalty: An empirical study of mobile instant messages in China. *International Journal of Information Management*, 30.

Denis, J. L., Langley, A., & Rouleau, L. (2010). The practice of leadership in the messy world of organizations. *Leadership*, *6*(1), 67–88. doi:10.1177/1742715009354233

Denolf, J. M., Trienekens, J. H., Wognuma, P. M., van der Vorst, J. G. A. J., & Omta, S. W. F. (2015). Towards a framework of critical success factors for implementing supply chain information systems. *Computers in Industry*, *68*, 16–26. doi:10.1016/j.compind.2014.12.012

Department of Health and Ageing (Australian Government) (DoHA). (2012). Living Longer. Living Better. Aged care reform package. DoHA.

Deshmukh, A. (2006). *Digital accounting: The effects of the internet and ERP on accounting*. IGI Global. doi:10.4018/978-1-59140-738-6

Desouza, K. C., & Awazu, Y. (2006). Knowledge management at SMEs: Five peculiarities. *Journal of Knowledge Management*, *10*(1), 32–43. doi:10.1108/13673270610650085

Detert, J. R., & Burris, E. R. (2007). Leadership behavior and employee voice: Is the door really open? *Academy of Management Journal*, *50*(4), 869–884. doi:10.5465/AMJ.2007.26279183

Devaraj, S., & Kohli, R. (2003). Performance Impacts of Information Technology: Is Actual Usage the Missing Link. *Management Science*, *49*(3), 273–289. doi:10.1287/mnsc.49.3.273.12736

Dezdar, S., & Sulaiman, A. (2009). Successful enterprise resource planning implementation: Taxonomy of critical factors. *Industrial Management + Data Systems, 109*(8), 1037-1052.

Dezdar, S., & Ainin, S. (2011). The influence of organizational factors on successful ERP implementation. *Management Decision*, *49*(6), 911–926. doi:10.1108/00251741111143603

Dezdar, S., & Sulaiman, A. (2009). Successful enterprise resource planning implementation: Taxonomy of critical factors. *Industrial Management & Data Systems*, *109*(8), 1037–1052. doi:10.1108/02635570910991283

Dhillon, G. (2004). Dimensions of power and IS implementation, Information & Management. *Information & Management*, *41*(5), 635–644. doi:10.1016/j.im.2003.02.001

Dhillon, G. (2005). Gaining benefits from IS/IT implementation: Interpretations from case studies. *International Journal of Information Management*, *25*(6), 502–515. doi:10.1016/j.ijinfomgt.2005.08.004

Dhillon, G., Caldeira, M., & Wenger, M. (2011). Intentionality and power interplay in IS implementation: The case of an asset management firm. *The Journal of Strategic Information Systems*, *20*(4), 438–448. doi:10.1016/j.jsis.2011.09.003

Di Maggio, P. (1995). What Theory is not. *Administrative Science Quarterly*, *40*(3), 391–397. doi:10.2307/2393790

Dibbern, J., Goles, T., Hirschheim, R., & Jayatilaka, B. (2004). Information Systems Outsourcing: A survey and analysis of the literature. *The Data Base for Advances in Information Systems*, *35*(4), 6–102. doi:10.1145/1035233.1035236

Dietz, J. L. G. (2006). *Enterprise ontology: Theory and methodology*. New York: Springer-Verlag Inc. doi:10.1007/3-540-33149-2

Dijk, B. v. (2008). *Sistema de Análisis de Balances Ibéricos*. Retrieved from http://www.bvdep.com

Dillman, D. (1978). *Mail and telephone surveys: The total design method*. New York: John Wiley & Sons, Inc.

Dillon, A. (2000). Group Dynamics Meet Cognition: applying socio-technical concepts in the design of information systems. In The New SocioTech: Graffiti on the Long Wall, (pp. 119-125). Springer Verlag.

Ding, F., Li, D., & George, J. F. (2014). Investigating the effects of IS strategic leadership on organizational benefits from the perspective of CIO strategic roles. *Information & Management*, *51*(7), 865–879. doi:10.1016/j.im.2014.08.004

Domberger, S., Fernandez, P., & Fiebig, D. (2000). Modelling the price, performance and contract characteristics of IT outsourcing. *Journal of Information Technology*, *15*(2), 107–118. doi:10.1080/026839600344302

Dong, L. (2008). Exploring the impact of top management support of enterprise systems implementations outcomes: Two cases. *Business Process Management Journal*, *14*(2), 204–218. doi:10.1108/14637150810864934

Doukidis, G. I., Smithson, S., & Lybereas, T. (1994). Trends in information technology in small business. *Journal of End User Computing*, *6*, 15–25.

Dovedan, H. Z. (2012). *Formalni jezici i prevodioci – sintaksna analiza i primjene*. Zagreb: Element.

Dovedan, H. Z. (2013). *Formalni jezici i prevodioci – prevođenje i primjene*. Zagreb: Element.

Dowlatshahi, S. (2005). Strategic Success Factors in Enterprise Resource Planning Design and Implementation: A Case-study Approach. *International Journal of Production Research*, *43*(18), 3745–3771. doi:10.1080/00207540500140864

Dreibelbis, A., Hechler, E., Milman, I., Oberhofer, M., van Run, P., & Wolfson, D. (2008). *Enterprise Master Data Management: An SOA Approach to Managing Core Information*. Pearson Education.

Drescher, G., & Garbers, Y. (2016). Shared leadership and commonality: A policy-capturing study. *The Leadership Quarterly*, *27*(2), 200–217. doi:10.1016/j.leaqua.2016.02.002

Dresner, H. J., Buytendijk, F., Linden, A., Friedman, T., Strange, K. H., Knox, M., & Camm, M. (2002), The Business Intelligence Competency Center: An Essential Business Strategy. Gartner Research, ID R-15-2248.

Drew, S. (2003). Strategic use of e-Commerce by SMEs in the east of England. *European Management Journal, 21*(1), 79–88. doi:10.1016/S0263-2373(02)00148-2

Drucker, P. (2000). *The Discipline of Innovation, HBR*. Financial Data.

Druker, P. F. (1956). *The Practice of Management*. Academic Press.

Duh, R., Chow, C. W., & Chen, H. (2006). Strategy, IT applications for planning and control, and firm performance: The impact of impediments to IT implementation. *Information & Management, 43*(8), 939–949. doi:10.1016/j.im.2006.08.007

Duncan, R. B. (1972). Characteristics of Organizational Environments and Perceived Environmental Uncertainty. *Administrative Science Quarterly, 17*(3), 313–327. doi:10.2307/2392145

Durst, S., & Runar Edvardsson, I. (2012). Knowledge management in SMEs: A literature review. *Journal of Knowledge Management, 16*(6), 879–903. doi:10.1108/13673271211276173

Dyché, J. (2002). *The CRM handbook: A business guide to customer relationship management*. Academic Press.

Dyer, J. R., Johansson, A., Helbing, D., Couzin, I. D., & Krause, J. (2009). Leadership, consensus decision making and collective behaviour in humans. *Philosophical Transactions of the Royal Society of London. Series B, Biological Sciences, 364*(1518), 781–789. doi:10.1098/rstb.2008.0233 PMID:19073481

Eckartz, S., Katsma, C., & Daneva, M. (2010). Inter-organizational Business Case in ES Implementations: Exploring the Impact of Coordination Structures and Their Properties. *ENTERprise Information Systems: Communications in Computer and Information Science Series, 10*, 188–197. doi:10.1007/978-3-642-16419-4_19

Eckerson, W. (2007). *Performance Dashboards: Measuring, Monitoring, and Managing Your Business*. Published by Wiley-Interscience.

Edberg, D. T., & Bowman, B. J. (1996). User-developed applications: An empirical study of application quality and development productivity. *Journal of MIS, 13*(1), 167–186.

Ehie, I., & Madsen, M. (2005). Identifying critical issues in enterprise resource planning (ERP) implementation. *Computers in Industry, 56*(6), 545–557. doi:10.1016/j.compind.2005.02.006

Eid, M. I. (2012). *A Learning System For Entity Relationship Modeling*. PACIS.

Ein-Dor, P., & Segev, E. (1978). Organizational context and the success of management information systems. *Management Science, 24*(10), 1064–1077. doi:10.1287/mnsc.24.10.1064

Eisenhardt, K. (1989). Building theories from case study research. *Academy of Management Review, 14*(4), 532-550.

Eisenhardt, K., & Graebner, M. E. (2007). Theory building from cases: Opportunities and Challenges. *Academy of Management Journal, 50*(1), 25–32. doi:10.5465/AMJ.2007.24160888

Elbanna, S., & Child, J. (2007). The influence of decision, environmental and firm characteristics on the rationality of strategic decision-making. *Journal of Management Studies, 44*(4), 561–591. doi:10.1111/j.1467-6486.2006.00670.x

Elmasri, R., & Navathe, S. B. (2011). *Fundamentals of Database Systems* (6th ed.). Addison-Wesley.

Enns, H. G., Huff, S. L., & Golden, B. R. (2001). How CIOs obtain peer commitment to strategic IS proposals: Barriers and facilitators. *The Journal of Strategic Information Systems, 10*(1), 3–14. doi:10.1016/S0963-8687(01)00041-5

Epetimehin, F. M. (2011). Market Segmentation: A Tool for Improving Customer Satisfaction and Retention in Insurance Service Delivery. *Journal of Emerging Trends in Economics and Management Sciences, 2*(1).

EPIC. (2016). *Radio Frequency Identification*. Retrieved 12 December, 2016, from http://www.epic.org/privacy/rfid/

Erikkson. (2008). *Ten Guidelines for the Implementation of Information Systems: Research in Progress*. IRIS31: The 31st Information Systems Research Seminar in Scandinavia, Are, Sweden.

Erjavec, T. (2010a). *MULTEXT-East - Morphosyntactic Specifications* (Version 4). Retrieved December 20, 2015, from http://nl.ijs.si/ME/V4/msd/html/index.html

Erjavec, T. (2010b). MULTEXT-East Version 4: Multilingual Morphosyntactic Specifications, Lexicons and Corpora. In *Proceedings of the LREC 2010*. Malta: European Language Resources Association.

Ertel, D., & Gordon, M. (2007). *How to Negotiate When Yes Is Not Enough*. Harvard Business School Press.

Espinoza, M. M. (1999). Assessing the cross-cultural applicability of a service quality measure: A comparative study between Quebec and Peru. *International Journal of Service Industry Management, 10*(5), 449–468. doi:10.1108/09564239910288987

Esteves, J., & Pastor, J. (1999). An ERP lifecycle-based research agenda. *International Workshop in Enterprise Management and Resource. Planning: Methods, Tools and Architectures–EMRPS*, 1-12.

Esteves, J., & Pastor, J. (2001). Enterprise Resource Planning: An Annotated Bibliography. *Communications of the AIS, 7*(8), 1–51.

Evans, P., & Wurster, T. (1997). Strategy and the new economics of information. *Harvard Business Review*, (September-October), 70–82. PMID:10170332

Faems, D., Looy, B. V., & Debackere, K. (2005). Interorganizational collaboration and innovation: Toward a portfolio approach. *Journal of Product Innovation Management, 22*(3), 238–250. doi:10.1111/j.0737-6782.2005.00120.x

Farzaneh, M., Vanani, I. R., & Sohrabi, B. (2013). A Survey Study of Influential Factors in the Implementation of Enterprise Resource Planning Systems. *International Journal of Enterprise Information Systems, 9*(1), 76–96. doi:10.4018/jeis.2013010105

Fasanghari, M., Roudsari, F. H., & Chaharsooghi, S. K. (2008). Assessing the Impact of Information Technology on Supply Chain Management. *World Applied Sciences Journal, 4*(1), 87–93.

Fath, L. (2008). Shared decision making. *Paediatrics and Child Health (Oxford), 18*, S90–S91. doi:10.1016/S1751-7222(08)70027-1

Feeny, D. F., & Willcocks, L. P. (1998). Core IS capabilities for exploiting information technology. *MIT Sloan Management Review, 39*(3), 9.

Ferreira, D., & Gillblad, D. (2009). Discovering process models from unlabelled event logs. In U. Dayal, J. Eder, J. Koehler, & H. Reijers (Eds.), *Business process management* (Vol. 5701, pp. 143–158). Heidelberg, Germany: Springer. doi:10.1007/978-3-642-03848-8_11

Filipowska, A., Hepp, M., Kaczmarek, M., & Markovic, I. (2009). Organisational ontology framework for semantic business process management. In W. Abramowicz (Ed.), *Business information systems* (Vol. 21, pp. 1–12). Heidelberg, Germany: Springer. doi:10.1007/978-3-642-01190-0_1

Finney, S., & Corbett, M. (2007). ERP implementation: A compilation and analysis of critical success factors. *Business Process Management Journal, 13*(3), 329–347. doi:10.1108/14637150710752272

Fitzsimmons, J., & Fitzsimmons, M. (2010). *Service Management: Operations, Strategy, and Information Technology* (7th ed.). Singapore: McGraw-Hill.

Flint, D. J., Larsson, E., Gammelgaard, B., & Mentzer, J. T. (2005). Logistics innovation: A customer value-oriented social process. *Journal of Business Logistics*, 26(1), 113–147. doi:10.1002/j.2158-1592.2005.tb00196.x

Folinas, D., & Daniel, E. (2012). Estimating the Impact of ERP Systems on Logistics System. *Enterprise Information Systems*, 8(3), 1–14. doi:10.4018/jeis.2012070101

Fornell, C., & Larcker, D. F. (1981). Evaluating structural equation models with unobservable variables and measurement error. *JMR, Journal of Marketing Research*, 18(10), 39–50. doi:10.2307/3151312

Foster, R., & Kaplan, S. (2001). *Creative Destruction*. New York: Doubleday Publishing.

Foundation Coalition. (2001). *Effective Decision Making in Teams: Methods*. Retrieved from http://www.foundationcoalition.org/home/keycomponents/teams/decision2.html

Fraga, M. G., Varajão, J., Amaral, L., & Bulas-Cruz, J. (2012). Information systems outsourcing in major Portuguese companies-contracting services. *Journal of Research and Practice in Information Technology*, 44(1), 81.

Francalanci, C. (2001). Predicting the implementation effort of ERP projects: Empirical evidence on SAP/R3. *Journal of Information Technology*, 16(1), 33–48. doi:10.1080/02683960010035943

Frei, F. X. (2006). Breaking the trade-Off Between Efficiency and Service. *Harvard Business Review*, (November), 1–12. PMID:17131566

Friedman, A. L., & Cornford, D. C. (1989). *Computer Systems Development: History, Organization and Implementation*. Chichester, UK: Wiley.

Fuchs, N. E., Kaljurand, K., & Kuhn, T. (2008). Attempto controlled english for knowledge representation. Lecture Notes in Computer Science, 5224, 104–124.

Gable, G. G., Chan, T., & Tan, W. (2001). Large packaged application software maintenance: A research framework. *Journal of Software Maintenance & Evolution: Research & Practice*, 13(6), 351–371. doi:10.1002/smr.237

Gable, G. G., Sedera, D., & Chan, T. (2003). Measuring Enterprise Systems Success: A preliminary model. *Proceedings of the 9th AMCIS Conference*, 576-591.

Gajic, G., Stankovski, S., Ostojic, G., Tesic, Z., & Miladinovic, L. (2014). Method of evaluating the impact of ERP implementation critical success factors–a case study in oil and gas industries. *Enterprise Information Systems*, 8(1), 84–106. doi:10.1080/17517575.2012.690105

Gal, U., & Berente, N. (2008). A social representations perspective on information systems implementation: Rethinking the concept of frames. *Information Technology & People*, 21(2), 133–154. doi:10.1108/09593840810881051

Garcia, D., Archer, T., Moradi, S., & Ghiabi, B. (2012). Waiting in Vain: Managing Time and Customer Satisfaction at Call Centers. *SciRes.*, 3(2).

Gargeya, V. B., & Brady, C. (2005). Success and failure factors of adopting SAP in ERP system implementation. *Business Process Management Journal*, 11(5), 501–516. doi:10.1108/14637150510619858

Garg, P., & Agarwal, D. (2014). Critical success factors for ERP implementation in a Fortis hospital: An empirical investigation. *Journal of Enterprise Information Management*, 27(4), 402–423. doi:10.1108/JEIM-06-2012-0027

Gartner. (2012). *Gartner Forecasts Global Business Intelligence Market to Grow*. Available at www.Gartner.com

Gartner. (2013). *Gartner Executive Program Survey of More Than 2,000 CIOs Shows Digital Technologies Are Top Priorities in 2013*. Available at http://www.gartner.com/newsroom/id/2304615

Gattiker, T. F., & Goodhue, D. L. (2004). Understanding the local-level costs and benefits of ERP through organizational information processing theory. *Information & Management, 41*(4), 431–443. doi:10.1016/S0378-7206(03)00082-X

Geels, F. W. (2004). From sectoral systems of innovation to socio-technical systems: Insights about dynamics and change from sociology and institutional theory. *Research Policy, 33*(6-7), 897–920. doi:10.1016/j.respol.2004.01.015

Gefen, D. (2004). What makes an ERP implementation relationship worthwhile: Linking trust, mechanism and ERP usefulness? *Journal of Management Information Systems, 21*(1), 263–288.

Gefen, D., & Ragowsky, A. (2005). A Multi-Level approach to Measuring the Benefits of an ERP system in Manufacturing Firms. *Information Systems Management, 22*(Winter), 18–25. doi:10.1201/1078/44912.22.1.20051201/85735.3

Gefen, D., & Straub, D. (2005). A Practical Guide to Factorial Validity Using PLS-Graph: Tutorial and Annotated Example. *Communications of the Association for Information Systems, 16*, 91–103.

Gelzheiser, L., Meyers, B., & Meyers, J. (2001). Observing leadership roles in shared decision making: A preliminary analysis of three teams. *Journal of Educational & Psychological Consultation, 12*(4), 277–312. doi:10.1207/S1532768XJEPC1204_01

Genete, L. D., & Tugui, A. (2008). From ERP Systems to Digital Accounting in Relations with Customers and Suppliers. *Selected Papers from the WSEAS Conferences in Spain September 2008,* 57-63.

Geremillo, M. (2000). *Information systems implementation: A social worker's perspective.* University of Sarasota.

Ghosh, S., & Skibniewski, M. J. (2010). Enterprise resource planning systems implementation as a complex project: a conceptual framework. *Journal of Business Economics and Management,* (4), 533-549.

Gibson, C. B., & Saxton, T. (2005). Thinking outside the black box: Outcomes of team decisions with third-party intervention. *Small Group Research, 36*(2), 208–236. doi:10.1177/1046496404270376

Gibson, N., Holland, C. P., & Light, B. (1999). Enterprise Resource Planning: A Business Approach to Systems Development. *Proceedings of the 32nd Hawaii International Conference on System Sciences.* doi:10.1109/HICSS.1999.772816

Glaser, B., & Strauss, A. (1967). *The Discovery of Grounded Theory: Strategies for Qualitative Research.* Chicago, IL: Aldine Publishing Company.

Glushko, R. J. (2010). Seven Contexts for Service System Design. In P. Maglio, C. Kieliszewski, & J. Spohrer (Eds.), *Handbook of service science* (pp. 219–249). New York: Springer. doi:10.1007/978-1-4419-1628-0_11

Goeke, R. J., & Faley, R. H. (2009). Do SAP Successes Outperform Themselves and Their Competitors? *Communications of the ACM, 52*(10), 113–117. doi:10.1145/1562764.1562793

Goguen, J. A. (1993). Social issues in requirements engineering. *Proceedings of IEEE International Symposium on Requirements Engineering.* Retrieved from http://ieeexplore.ieee.org/xpl/mostRecentIssue. jsp?punumber=896&filter %3DAND%28p_IS_Number%3A7734%29&pageNumber=2

Goguen, J. A. (1994). Requirements Engineering as the Reconciliation of Social and Technical Issues. In M. Jirotka & J. A. Goguen (Eds.), *Requirements Engineering* (pp. 165–199). Academic Press Professional, Inc.

Goh, H. P. (1995). The diffusion of Internet in Singapore: A Content analytic approach. Faculty of Business Administration, National University of Singapore.

Golany, B., & Storbeck, J. (1999). A Data Envelopment Analysis of the Operational Efficiency of Bank Branches. *Interfaces, 29*(3), 14–26. doi:10.1287/inte.29.3.14

Golden, W., & Powell, P. (1999). Exploring inter-organisational systems and flexibility in Ireland: A case of two value chains. *International Journal of Agile Management Systems, 1*(3), 169–184. doi:10.1108/14654659910296544

Golfarelli, M., Rizzi, S., & Cella, I. (2004), Beyond Data Warehousing: What's next in Business Intelligence?*Proceedings of the 7th ACM international workshop on Data warehousing and OLAP*, 1-6. doi:10.1145/1031763.1031765

Golicic, S. L., Davis, D. F., McCarthy, T. M., & Mentzer, J. T. (2002). The impact of e-commerce on supply chain relationships. *International Journal of Physical Distribution & Logistics Management, 32*(10), 851–871. doi:10.1108/09600030210455447

Gomez, F., Segami, C., & Delaune, C. (1999). A system for the semiautomatic generation of E-R models from natural language specifications. *Data & Knowledge Engineering, 29*(1), 57–81. doi:10.1016/S0169-023X(98)00032-9

Goodhue, D. L., Kirsch, L. J., Quillard, J. A., & Wybo, M. D. (1992). Strategic data planning: Lessons from the field. *Management Information Systems Quarterly, 16*(1), 11–34. doi:10.2307/249699

Goodhue, D. L., Wixom, B. H., & Watson, H. J. (2002). Realizing business benefits through CRM: Hitting the right target in the right way. *MIS Quarterly Executive, 1*(2), 79–94.

Goodpasture, V. (1995). Easton steps up to the plate. *Manufacturing Systems, 13*(9), 58–64.

Goomas, D. T., Smith, S. M., & Ludwig, T. D. (2011). Business activity monitoring: Real-time group goals and feedback using an overhead scoreboard in a distribution center. *Journal of Organizational Behavior Management, 31*(3), 196–209. doi:10.1080/01608061.2011.589715

Gorgone, J., Gray, P., Feinstein, D. L., Kasper, G. M., Luftman, J., Stohr, E. A., & Wigand, R. et al. (2000). MSIS 2000: Model Curriculum and Guidelines for Graduate Degree Programs in Information Systems. *Communications of the Association for Information Systems, 3*(1). Retrieved from http://aisel.aisnet.org/cais/vol3/iss1/1

GoToAssist. (2009). *Developing A True Multi-Channel Contact Center*. Author.

Gottlieb, J., & Willmott, P. (2014). *The digital tipping point*. McKinsey & Company.

Goulding, C. (1999). *Grounded Theory: some reflections on paradigm, procedures and misconceptions*. Working Paper Series, Number WP006/99, ISSN Number ISSN 1363-6839, pp.1-26.

Gourlay, S. (2006). Conceptualizing knowledge creation: A critique of nonakas theory*. *Journal of Management Studies, 43*(7), 1415–1436. doi:10.1111/j.1467-6486.2006.00637.x

Grabher, G., Ibert, O., & Flohr, S. (2008). The neglected king: The customer in the new knowledge ecology of innovation. *Economic Geography, 84*(3), 253–280. doi:10.1111/j.1944-8287.2008.tb00365.x

Grabski, S. V., Leech, S. A., & Schmidt, P. J. (2011). A Review of ERP Research: A Future Agenda for Accounting Information Systems. *Journal of Information Systems, 25*(1), 37–78. doi:10.2308/jis.2011.25.1.37

Graham, G., & Hardaker, G. (2000). Supply Chain management across the Internet. *International Journal of Physical Distribution & Logistics Management, 30*(3/4), 286–295. doi:10.1108/09600030010326055

Grant, K. A., & Qureshi, U. (2006, November). Knowledge Management Systems--Why So Many Failures? In Innovations in Information Technology, 2006 (pp. 1-5). IEEE.

Grant, D., & Mergen, E. (1996). Applying quality to Leavitts framework to solve information technology problems: A case study. *Information Technology & People, 9*(2), 43–60. doi:10.1108/09593849610121598

Grant, D., & Tu, Q. (2005). Levels of enterprise Integration: Study Using Case Analysis. *International Journal of Enterprise Information Systems, 1*(1), 1–22. doi:10.4018/jeis.2005010101

Grant, K. A. (2007). Tacit knowledge revisited–we can still learn from Polanyi. *Electronic Journal of Knowledge Management*, *5*(2), 173–180.

Grant, R. M. (1996). Toward a knowledge-based theory of the firm. *Strategic Management Journal*, *17*(S2), 109–122. doi:10.1002/smj.4250171110

Grawe, S. J. (2009). Logistics Innovation: A literature-based conceptual framework. *The International Journal of Logistics Management*, *20*(3), 360–377. doi:10.1108/09574090911002823

Gray, P., & Byun, J. (2001). *Customer Relationship Management. Center for Research on Information Technology and Organisations*. University of California.

Gregor, S., Hart, D., & Martin, N. (2007). Enterprise architectures: Enablers of business strategy and IS/IT alignment in government. *Information Technology & People*, *20*(2), 96–120. doi:10.1108/09593840710758031

Gregor, S., & Hevner, A. R. (2013). Positioning and Presenting Design Science Research for Maximum Impact. *Management Information Systems Quarterly*, *37*(2), 337–A6.

Greiner, T., Duster, W., Pouatcha, F., & Ammon, R. v. (2006). *Business activity monitoring of norisbank taking the example of the application easycredit and the future adoption of complex event processing*. Paper presented at the IEEE Services Computing Workshops, Chicago, IL.

Gronroos, C., & Ojasalo, K. (2004). Service productivity. Towards a conceptualization of the transformation of inputs into economic results in services. *Journal of Business Research*, 414–423.

Grossman, T., & Walsh, J. (2004). Avoiding the Pitfalls of ERP System Implementation. *Information Systems Management*, *21*(2), 38–42. doi:10.1201/1078/44118.21.2.20040301/80420.6

Groth, L. (1999). *Future Organizational Design: The Scope for the IT-based Enterprise*. Brisbane: John Wiley.

Group, G. (2008). Magic Quadrant for CRM Services Providers. G. R. C. Research.

Grover, V., Fiedler, K., & Teng, J. (1997). Evidence on Swansons Empirical Model of Information Systems Tri-Core Innovation. *Information Systems Research*, *8*(3), 273–287. doi:10.1287/isre.8.3.273

Grover, V., Seung-Ryul, J., William, J. K., & Lee, C. C. (1993). The Chief Information Officer: A study of managerial roles. *Journal of Management Information Systems*, *10*(2), 107–130. doi:10.1080/07421222.1993.11518002

Grover, V., & Teng, J. T. (1992). An examination of DBMS adoption and success in American organizations. *Information & Management*, *23*(5), 239–248. doi:10.1016/0378-7206(92)90055-K

Grublješič, T., & Jaklič, J. (2014). Three Dimensions of Business Intelligence Systems Use Behavior. *International Journal of Enterprise Information Systems*, *10*(3), 62–76. doi:10.4018/ijeis.2014070105

Guerreiro, S., Marques, R. P., & Gaaloul, K. (2016). *Optimizing business processes compliance using an evolvable risk-based approach*. Paper presented at the Hawaii International Conference on System Sciences (HICSS-49), Kauai, HI. doi:10.1109/HICSS.2016.699

Guimaraes, T., Cook, D., & Natarajan, N. (2002). Exploring the Importance of Business Clockspeed as a Moderator for Determinants of Supplier Network Performance. *Decision Sciences*, *33*(4), 629–644. doi:10.1111/j.1540-5915.2002.tb01659.x

Gumusluoglu, L., & Ilsev, A. (2009). Transformational leadership, creativity and organizational innovation. *Journal of Business Research*, *62*(4), 461–473. doi:10.1016/j.jbusres.2007.07.032

Gunasekaran, A. (2005). Enterprise Information Systems & Organizational Competitiveness. *International Journal of Enterprise Information Systems*, *1*(1), i–vi.

Gunasekaran, A., & Ngai, E. W. T. (2004). Information systems in supply chain integration and management. *European Journal of Operational Research*, *159*(2), 269–295. doi:10.1016/j.ejor.2003.08.016

Gunasekharan, A., & Ngai, E. W. T. (2004). Virtual Supply Chain Management. *Production Planning and Control*, *15*(6), 584–595. doi:10.1080/09537280412331283955

Gupta, A. (2000). Enterprise Resource Planning: The emerging organizational value systems. *Industrial Management & System*, *100*(3), 114–118. doi:10.1108/02635570010286131

Gupta, A. K., Raj, S. P., & Wilemon, D. (1986). A Model for Studying RID-Marketing Interface: The Product Innovation Process. *Journal of Marketing*, *50*(2), 7–17. doi:10.2307/1251596

Gu, V. C., Cao, Q., & Duan, W. (2012). Unified Modeling Language (UML) IT adoption — A holistic model of organizational capabilities perspective. *Decision Support Systems*, *54*(1), 257–269. doi:10.1016/j.dss.2012.05.034

Gyanendra, S., Rajeev, A., & Vivek, M. (2014). Emerging Trends in Supply Chain Management. *International Journal of Research in Engineering and Technology*, *3*(10), 100–103.

Haag, S., Cummings, M., & Philips, A. (2006). *Management Information Systems for the Information Age*. McGraw Hill College.

Hadzagas, C. (2011). Applying Customer Relationship Management Systems for Customer Satisfaction: An Empirical Approach for Small-and-Medium-Sized Companies. *European Journal of Economics, Finance and Administrative Sciences*, (40).

Hagan, P. J. (Ed.). (2004). *Guide to the (evolving) enterprise architecture body of knowledge* (Draft). Retrieved from http://www.mitre.org/work/tech_papers/tech_papers_04/04_0104/index.html

Haggie, K., and Kingston, J. (2003). Choosing your knowledge management strategy. *Journal of Knowledge Management Practice*, 1 – 20.

Haggie, J. K., & Kingston, J. (2003). Choosing a knowledge management strategy. *Journal of Knowledge Management*, (June): 33–56.

Haider, A. (2008). Information systems implementation in production environments. *Journal of Achievements in Materials and Manufacturing Engineering, 31*(2).

Hair, A., Tatham, & Black. (1998). Multivariate data analysis Englewood Cliffs, NJ: Printice-Hall Inc.

Hair, Black, Babin, Anderson, & Tatham. (2006). *Multivariate Data Analysis*. Upper Saddle River, NJ: Prentice-Hall.

Hair, J. F., Black, W. C., Babin, B. J., Anderson, R. E., & Tatham, R. L. (2006). *Multivariate Data Anaalysis*. Upper Saddle River, NJ: Prentice Hall.

Hair, J., Black, W., Babin, B., Anderson, R., & Tatham, R. (2006). *Multivariate Data Analysis* (6th ed.). Upper Saddle River, NJ: Pearson Prentice Hall.

Håkansson, H., & Persson, G. (2004). Supply chain management and the logic of supply chains and networks. *The International Journal of Logistics Managment*, *15*(1), 15–26.

Hall, R. (2003). *Knowledge Management in the New Business Environment*. A report prepared for the Australian Business Foundation, ACCIRT, University of Sydney.

Hall, R. (2003). *Knowledge Management in the New Business Environment (A report prepared for the Australian Business Foundation)*. Sydney: ACIRRT, University of Sydney.

Hamel, G. (2009). Moon Shots for Management. *Harvard Business Review, 87*(2), 91–98. PMID:19266704

Hammer, M., Champy, J., & Davenport, D. (1986, June). *Dispersion and Interconnection: Approaches to Distributed Systems Architecture*. Partnership for Research in Information Systems Management (PRISM). Retrieved from https://c.ymcdn.com/sites/www.globalaea.org/resource/collection/EAAC3D6C-D447-451C- AC5F-6E1DC7788D42/PRISM_Report.pdf

Hammer, M. (1990). Reengineering Work: Don't Automate, Obliterate. *Harvard Business Review, 68*(4), 104–112.

Hammer, M., & Champy, J. (1993). *Reengineering the corporation*. New York: Harper Business.

Hammer, M., & Santon, S. (1999). How process enterprises really work? *Harvard Business Review, 77*(6), 108–118. PMID:10662000

Hammer, M., & Stanton, S. (1999). How Process Enterprises Really Work. *Harvard Business Review*, 108–118. PMID:10662000

Han, J., Liu, R., Swanner, B., & Yang, S. (2010). *Enterprise resource planning*. Japansk produksjonsfilosofi, Toyota Production.

Hanafizadeh, P., Gholami, R., Dadbin, S., & Standage, N. (2010). The core critical success factors in implementation of enterprise resource planning systems. *International Journal of Enterprise Information Systems, 6*(2), 82–111. doi:10.4018/jeis.2010040105

Hanafizadeh, P., & Ravasan, A. Z. (2011). A McKinsey 7S model-based framework for ERP readiness assessment. *International Journal of Enterprise Information Systems, 7*(4), 23–63. doi:10.4018/jeis.2011100103

Hancox, M., & Hackney, R. (2000). IT Outsourcing: Frameworks for conceptualizing Practice and Perception. *Information Systems Journal, 10*(3), 217–237. doi:10.1046/j.1365-2575.2000.00082.x

Hansen, H. (1995). Conceptual framework and guidelines for the implementation of mass information systems. *Information & Management, 28*(2), 125–142. doi:10.1016/0378-7206(95)94021-4

Harison, E. (2012). Critical Success Factors of Business Intelligence System Implementations: Evidence from the Energy Sector. *International Journal of Enterprise Information Systems, 8*(2), 1–13. doi:10.4018/jeis.2012040101

Harland, C. M. (1996). Supply chain management: Relationships, chains, and networks. *British Journal of Management, 7*(s1), 63–80. doi:10.1111/j.1467-8551.1996.tb00148.x

Harrel, J. M. (2011). *Developing Enterprise Architectures to Address the Enterprise Dilemma Of Deciding What Should Be Sustained Versus What Should Be Changed* (PhD Thesis). George Mason University, Fairfax, VA.

Harris, J., & Davenport, T. (2006). *New Growth From Enterprise Systems*. Accenture.

Harter, D., Krishnan, M. S., & Slaughter, S. A. (2000). Effects of Process Maturity on Quality, Cycle Time, and Effort in Software Product Development. *Management Science, 46*(4), 451–466. doi:10.1287/mnsc.46.4.451.12056

Hart, G., Johnson, M., & Dolbear, C. (2008). Rabbit: Developing a Control Natural Language for Authoring Ontologies. In *5th European Semantic Web Conference (ESWC'08)* (pp. 348–360). doi:10.1007/978-3-540-68234-9_27

Hashemi, K. (2012). Customer Retention Strategies on Internet (e-CRM); Features and Principles. *Journal of American Science, 8*(2).

Hawking, P., & Sellitto, C. (2010). Business Intelligence (BI) Critical Success Factors *ACIS 2010 Proceedings*. Retrieved from http://aisel.aisnet.org/acis2010/4

Hawking, P., Stein, A., & Foster, S. (2004, January). Revisiting ERP systems: benefit realization. In *System Sciences, 2004.Proceedings of the 37th Annual Hawaii International Conference on* (pp. 1-8). IEEE.

Hawking, P., Stein, A., & Foster, S. (2004, January). Revisiting ERP systems: benefit realization. In *System Sciences, 2004.Proceedings of the 37th Annual Hawaii International Conference on* (pp. 8-pp). IEEE.

Hawking, P., & Rowley, C. (2012). *Tetra Pak's Journey to Business Intelligence Maturity. In Effective Strategy Execution: Improving Performance with Business Intelligence.* Springer.

Hawkins, B. L. (2004, November/December). A Framework for the CIO Position. *EDUCASE Review*, *39*, 94–102.

Heeks, R., Krishna, S., Nicholsen, B., & Sahay, S. (2001). Synching or sinking: Global software outsourcing relationships. *Software IEEE*, *18*(2), 54–60. doi:10.1109/52.914744

Henderson, R. (2006). The innovators dilemma as a problem of organizational competence. *Product Innovation Management*, *23*(1), 5–11. doi:10.1111/j.1540-5885.2005.00175.x

Henderson, R., & Mitchell, W. (1997). The interactions of organizational and competitive influences on strategy and performance. *Strategic Management Journal*, *18*(S1), 5–14. doi:10.1002/(SICI)1097-0266(199707)18:1+<5::AID-SMJ930>3.3.CO;2-9

Hendricks, K. B., Singhal, V. R., & Stratman, J. K. (2007). The impact of enterprise systems on corporate performance: A study of ERP, SCM, and CRM system implementations. *Journal of Operations Management*, *25*(1), 65–82. doi:10.1016/j.jom.2006.02.002

Henriques, A. (2009). *When radical innovation is not plausible*. Available at http://innovomics.wordpress.com/tag/innovation/page/4/

Hevner, A. R., March, S. T., Park, J., & Ram, S. (2004). Design science in information systems research. *MIS Quarterly*, *28*(1), 75–105.

Hevner, A., & Chatterjee, S. (2010). Design science research in information systems. In *Design research in information systems* (Vol. 22, pp. 9–22). New York: Springer. doi:10.1007/978-1-4419-5653-8_2

Hevner, A., March, S., Park, J., & Ram, S. (2004). Design Science in Information Systems Research. *Management Information Systems Quarterly*, *28*(1), 75–105.

Hewlett-Packard. (2007). *The HP Business Intelligence Maturity Model: describing the BI journey*. Hewlett-Packard.

Hillmer, M. P., Wodchis, W. P., Gill, S. S., Anderson, G. M., & Rochon, P. A. (2005). Nursing home profit status and quality of care: Is there any evidence of an association? *Medical Care Research and Review*, *62*(2), 139–166. doi:10.1177/1077558704273769 PMID:15750174

Hill, S. (1997). The wait is over. *Manufacturing Systems*, *15*(6), 11–X.

Himanshu, S. M., Murty, J. S., Senapati, S. K., & Khuntia, K. (2011). Importance of Information Technology for Effective Supply Chain Management. *International Journal of Modern Engineering Research*, *1*(2), 747–751.

Hindriks, C. (2007). Towards chain wide Business Intelligence. University of Twente.

Hirschheim, R., George, B., & Wong, S. (2004). Information Technology Outsourcing. The move towards offshoring. *Indian Journal of Economics and Business*.

Hirschheim, R. A. (1985). *Office Automation: A Social and Organizational Perspective.* Chichester, UK: Wiley.

Hirschheim, R., George, B., & Wong, S. F. (2004). Information Technology Outsourcing: The Move Towards Offshoring. *Indian Journal of Economics & Businees, 3*(Special Issue), 103–125.

Hitt, L. M., Wu, D. J., & Zhou, X. (2002). Investment in Enterprise Resource Planning: Business Impact and Productivity Measures. *Journal of Management Information Systems, 19*(1), 71–98.

Hjort-Madsen, K. (2006). Enterprise architecture implementation and management: A case study. *Proceedings of the 39th Hawaii International Conference on System Sciences*, 1-10. Retrieved from http://ieeexplore. ieee.org/xpl/login.jsp?tp= &arnumber=1579432&url=http%3A%2F%2Fieeexplore.ieee.org%2Fxpls%2Fabs_all. jsp%3Farnumber%3D1579432

Hoegl, B., & Muethel, M. (2013). Shared Leadership Effectiveness in Independent Professional Teams. *European Management Journal, 31*(4), 423–432. doi:10.1016/j.emj.2012.11.008

Hofmann, P. (2008). ERP is Dead, Long Live ERP. *IEEE Internet Computing, 12*(4), 84–88. doi:10.1109/MIC.2008.78

Holland, C. P., & Light, B. (1999). A critical success factors model for ERP implementation. *IEEE Software, 16*(3), 30–36. doi:10.1109/52.765784

Homburg, C. (2001). Using data envelopment analysis to benchmark activities. *International Journal of Production Economics, 73*(1), 51–58. doi:10.1016/S0925-5273(01)00194-3

Hong, K., & Kim, Y. (2002). The critical success factors for ERP implementation: An organizational fit perspective. *Information & Management, 40*(1), 25–40. doi:10.1016/S0378-7206(01)00134-3

Horngren, C., Foster, G., & Datar, S. (2000). Cost Accounting a managerial emphasis (6th ed.). Prentice-Hall International, Inc.

Hostmann, B., (2007, November). BI Competency Centres: Bringing Intelligence to the Business. *Business Performance Management.*

Hoving, R. (2007). Information Technology Leadership Challenges - Past, Present, and Future. *Information Systems Management, 24*(2), 147–153. Retrieved from http://www.informaworld.com/10.1080/10580530701221049 doi:10.1080/10580530701221049

Hoyer, W. D., & MacInnis, D. J. (2001). *Consumer Behavior.* Boston: Houghton Mifflin Company.

Hsu, L. L., & Chen, M. (2004). Impacts of ERP systems on the integrated-interaction performance of manufacturing and marketing. *Industrial Management & Data Systems, 104*(1/2), 42–55. doi:10.1108/02635570410514089

Huang, C. J., & Liu, C. J. (2005). Exploration for the relationship between innovation, IT and performance. *Journal of Intellectual Capital, 6*(2), 237–252. doi:10.1108/14691930510592825

Hufgard, A. (1994). *Betriebswirtschaftliche Softwarebibliotheken und Adaption: empirischer Befund, Produkte, Methoden, Werkzeuge, Dienstleistungen und ein Modell zur Planung und Realisierung im Unternehmen.* München: Vahlen.

Hughes, J., & Wood-Harper, T. (1999). Addressing organisational issues in requirements engineering practice: Lessons from action cases. *Australasian Journal of Information Systems, 6*(2), 64–74. doi:10.3127/ajis.v6i2.293

Hume, C., Clarke, P., & Hume, M. (2012). The role of knowledge management in the large non profit firm: Building a framework for KM success. *International Journal of Organisational Behaviour, 17*(3), 82–104.

Hume, C., & Hume, M. (2008). The strategic role of knowledge management in nonprofit organisations, International Journal of Nonprofit and Voluntary Sector Marketing. *Special Issue: Special Issue on Nonprofit Competitive Strategy*, *13*(2), 129–140.

Hume, C., Pope, N., & Hume, M. (2012). KM 100: Introductory knowledge management for not-for-profit organizations. *International Journal of Organisational Behaviour*, *17*(2), 56.

Hutchinson, V., & Quintas, P. (2008). Do SMEs do knowledge management? Or simply manage what they know? *International Small Business Journal*, *26*(2), 131–146. doi:10.1177/0266242607086571

Hwang, H.-G., Ku, C.-Y., Yen, D. C., & Cheng, C. C. (2004). Critical factors influencing the adoption of data warehouse technology: A study of the banking industry in Taiwan. *Decision Support Systems*, *37*(1), 1–21. doi:10.1016/S0167-9236(02)00191-4

Hwang, M., & Lin, J. (2012). Organizational factors for successful implementation of information systems: Disentangling the effect of top management support and training. *Proceedings of the Southern Association for Information Systems Conference*.

IBM. (2013). *The Case for Business Analytics in Midsize Firms*. Retrieved from http://www-03.ibm.com/innovation/us/engines/assets/ibm-business-analytics-case-study-1-22-13.pdf

IBM. (2014). *Better business outcomes with IBM Big Data & Analytics*. Retrieved from http://www-935.ibm.com/services/multimedia/59898_Better_Business_Outcomes_White_Paper_Final_NIW03048-USEN-00_Final_Jan21_14.pdf

IDC. (1996). *Financial Impact of Data Warehousing*. International Data Corporation.

Ifinedo, P. (2006). *Enterprise resource planning system success assessment: An integrative framework* (Unpublished doctoral dissertation). Department of Computer Science and Information Systems, University of Jyvaskyla, Jyvaskyla, Finland.

Ifinedo, P., & Nahar, N. (2007). ERP systems success: an empirical analysis of how two organizational stakeholder groups prioritize and evaluate relevant measures. *Enterprise Information Systems*, *1*(1), 25 - 48. Retrieved from http://www.informaworld.com/10.1080/17517570601088539

Ifinedo, P. (2008). Impact of business vision, top management support and external expertise on ERP success. *Business Process Management Journal*, *14*(4), 551–568. doi:10.1108/14637150810888073

Ifinedo, P., & Davidrajuh, R. (2005). Digital divide in Europe: Assessing and comparing the e-readiness of a developed and an emerging economy in the Nordic region. *Electronic Government: An International Journal*, *2*(2), 111–133. doi:10.1504/EG.2005.007090

Ifinedo, P., & Nahar, N. (2006). Quality, impact and success of ERP systems: A study involving some firms in the Nordic-Baltic region. *Journal of Information Technology Impact*, *6*(1), 19–46.

Iijima, T. (2007). Auditing your offshore outsource. *Journal of Corporate Accounting & Finance*, *18*(4), 11-18. 10.1002/jcaf.20303

Iivari, J. (2003). An empirical test of DeLone-McLean model of information systems success. *The Data Base for Advances in Information Systems*, *36*(2), 8–27. doi:10.1145/1066149.1066152

INE. (2007). *Lista das 1000 maiores empresas portuguesas. Ficheiro de Unidades Estatísticas - FUE - Base Belém*. Instituto Nacional de Estatística.

Information Technology Management Reform Act of. 1996, Sections 5001-5142. (1996). Retrieved from http:// govinfo. library.unt.edu/npr/library/misc/s1124.html

Injazz, J., & Chen, K. P. (2003). Understanding customer relationship management (CRM):People, process and technology. *Business Process Management Journal, 19*(5).

Institute of Electrical and Electronics Engineers. (2000). *1471-2000 - IEEE Recommended Practice for Architectural Description for Software-Intensive Systems.* IEEE Computer Society. Retrieved from http://www.enterprise-architecture. info/Images/Documents/IEEE%201471-2000.pdf

Ipeirotis, P. (2013, February 25). *WikiSynonyms: Find synonyms using Wikipedia redirects.* Retrieved from http://www. behind-the-enemy-lines.com/2013/02/ wikisynonyms- find- synonyms-using.html

Irani, Z., & Love, P. (2008). *Evaluating Information Systems in The Public and Private Sectors.* Oxford, UK: Elsevier.

Irefin, I. A., Abdul-Azeez, I. A., & Tijani, A. A. (2012). An investigative study of the factors affecting the adoption of ICT in SME in Nigeria. *Australian Journal of Business and Management Research, 2*(2), 1–9.

Isikdag, U., Underwood, J., Kuruoglu, M., & Acikalin, U. (2013). Data Integration Capability Evaluation of ERP Systems: A Construction Industry Perspective. *International Journal of Enterprise Information Systems, 9*(3), 113–129. doi:10.4018/jeis.2013070106

Isik, O., Jones, M., & Sidorova, A. (2013). Business intelligence success: The roles of BI capabilities and decision environments. *Information & Management, 50*(1), 13–23. doi:10.1016/j.im.2012.12.001

Iskandar, B. Y., Kurokawa, S., & LeBlanc, L. J. (2001). Business-to-business electronic commerce from first- and second-tier automotive suppliers perspectives: A preliminary analysis for hypotheses generation. *Technovation, 21*(11), 719–731. doi:10.1016/S0166-4972(01)00053-0

Ismail, Z., Doostdar, S., & Harun, Z. (2012). Factors influencing the implementation of a safety management system for construction sites. *Safety Science, 50*(3), 418–423. doi:10.1016/j.ssci.2011.10.001

Jacobs, F. R., & Whybark, D. C. (2000). *Why ERP a Premier on SAP Implementation?* New York: Irwin/McGraw-Hill.

Jacobs, R. F., & Weston, F. C. Jr. (2007). Enterprise resource planning (ERP)—A brief history. *Journal of Operations Management, 25*(2), 357–363. doi:10.1016/j.jom.2006.11.005

Jafari, S. M., Osman, R. M., Yusuff, & Tang, S. H. (2006). ERP implementation in Malaysia: The importance of critical success factor. *International Journal of Engineering & Technology, 3*(1), 125-131.

Jafarnejad, A., Ansari, M., Youshanlouei, H. R., & Mood, M. (2012). A Hybrid MCDM Approach for Solving the ERP System Selection Problem with Application to Steel Industry. *International Journal of Enterprise Information Systems, 8*(3), 54–73. doi:10.4018/jeis.2012070104

Jakupović, A., Pavlić, M., & Dovedan, H. Z. (2014). Formalisation method for the text expressed knowledge. *Expert Systems with Applications, 41*(11), 5308–5322. doi:10.1016/j.eswa.2014.03.006

Jakupović, A., Pavlić, M., Meštrović, A., & Jovanović, V. (2013). Comparison of the Nodes of Knowledge method with other graphical methods for knowledge representation. In *Proceedings of the 36th international convention: Croatian Society for Information and Communication Technology, Electronics and Microelectronics – MIPRO* (pp. 1276–1280).

James, M., Chui, M., Brown, B., Bughin, J., Dobbs, R., Roxburgh, C., & Byers, A. H. (2011, May). Big data: The next frontier for innovation, competition, and productivity. McKinsey Global Institute. October 2012. *Harvard Business Review,* 59–69.

Jamshidi, Rasli, & Yusof. (2012). Essential Competencies for the Supervisors of Oil and Gas Industrial Companies. *Procedia: Social and Behavioral Sciences*, 40.

Janssen, M., & Klievink, B. (2010). ICT-project failure in public administration: The need to include risk management in enterprise architectures.*Proceedings of the 11th Annual International Conference on Digital Government Research on Public Administration Online: Challenges and Opportunities*, 147-152.

Janssens, G., Kusters, R. J., & Heemstra, F. (2007). Clustering ERP Implementation Project Activities: A Foundation for Project Size Definition. In S. Sadiq, M. Reichert, K. Schulz, J. Trienekens, C. Moller, & R. J. Kusters (Eds.), *Proceedings of the 1st International Joint Workshop on Technologies for Collaborative Business Processes and Management of Enterprise Information Systems*, (pp. 23–32). Institute for Systems and Technologies of Information.

Janssens, G., Kusters, R., & Heemstra, F. (2008). Sizing ERP implementation projects: An activity-based approach. *International Journal of Enterprise Information Systems*, *4*(3), 25–47. doi:10.4018/jeis.2008070103

Jarrar, Y. F., Al-Mudimigh, & Zairi, M. (2000). ERP Implementation Critical Success Factors–The Role and Impact of Business Process Management. ICMIT (pp. 122–127). IEEE.

Jaruzelski, B., Loehr, J., & Holman, R. (2011). Global innovation 1000: why culture is key. *Strategy + Business, 65*. Available at http://www.strategybusiness.com/article/11404

Jayachandran, , & Hewett, , & Kaufman, P. (2004). Customer Response Capability in a Sense-and-Respond Era. The Role of Customer Knowledge Process. *Journal of the Academy of Marketing Science*, 32.

Jensen, M. C., & Meckling, W. H. (1976). Theory of the Firm: Managerial Behaviour, Agency Costs and Ownership Structure. *Journal of Financial Economics*, *3*(4), 305–360. doi:10.1016/0304-405X(76)90026-X

Jeong, S., & Keatinge, D. (2004). Innovative leadership and management in a nursing home. *Journal of Nursing Management*, *12*(6), 445–451. doi:10.1111/j.1365-2834.2004.00451.x PMID:15509274

Jeon, Y. H., Merlyn, T., & Chenoweth, L. (2010). Leadership and management in the aged care sector: A narrative synthesis. *Australasian Journal on Ageing*, *29*(2), 54–60. doi:10.1111/j.1741-6612.2010.00426.x PMID:20553534

Jeyaraj, A., Rottman, J. W., & Lacity, M. C. (2006). A review of the predictors, linkages, and biases in IT innovation adoption research. *Journal of Information Technology*, *21*(1), 1–23. doi:10.1057/palgrave.jit.2000056

Jharkharia, S., & Shankar, R. (2004). IT enablement of supply chains: Modeling the enablers. *International Journal of Productivity and Performance Management*, *53*(8), 700–712. doi:10.1108/17410400410569116

Jing, R., & Qiu, X. (2007). A Study on Critical Success Factors in ERP Systems Implementation.*International Conference on Service Systems and Service Management*, 1-6. doi:10.1109/ICSSSM.2007.4280192

Joha, A., & Janssen, M. (2014). Factors influencing the shaping of shared services business models: Balancing customization and standardization. *Strategic Outsourcing: An International Journal*, *7*(1), 47–65. doi:10.1108/SO-10-2013-0018

Johansson, W., Ba, S., & Chase, R. (2001). Virtual customer satisfaction: A service management perspective.*Proceedings of the Seventh Americas Conference on Information System*, 857-866.

Johnson, L.K. (2004). Strategies for Data Warehousing. *MIT Sloan Management Review*, *45*(3), 9.

Johnson, T., & Owens, L. (2003). *Survey response rate reporting in the professional literature*. Paper presented at the 58th Annual Meeting of the American Association for Public Opinion Research, Nashville, TN. Retrieved from www.sel.uic.edu/publist/Conference/rr_reporting.pdf

Johnson, A. M., & Lederer, A. L. (2007). The Impact of Communication between CEOs and CIOs on their Shared Views of the Current and Future Role of IT. *Information Systems Management, 24*(1), 85–90. doi:10.1080/10580530601038246

Johnson, A. M., & Lederer, A. L. (2010). CEO/CIO mutual understanding, strategic alignment, and the contribution of IS to the organization. *Information & Management, 47*(3), 138–149. doi:10.1016/j.im.2010.01.002

Johnson, G., & Scholes, K. (1999). *Exploring corporate strategy: text & cases*. London: Prentice-Hall.

Johnston, R., & Graham, C. (2008). *Service Operations Management, Improving Service Delivery* (3rd ed.). London, UK: Prentice Hall, Financial Times (UK).

Jones, N., Myers, M., & Jones, N. D. (2001). Assessing Three Theories of Information Systems Innovation: An Interpretive Case Study of a Funds Management Company. *PACIS 2001 Proceedings*.

Jones, N. B., Herschel, R. T., & Moesel, D. D. (2003). Using knowledge champions to facilitate knowledge management. *Journal of Knowledge Management, 7*(1), 49–63. doi:10.1108/13673270310463617

Jones, P. E., & Roelofsma, P. H. M. P. (2000). The potential for social contextual and group biases in team decision-making: Biases, conditions, and psychological mechanisms. *Ergonomics, 43*(8), 1129–1152. doi:10.1080/00140130050084914 PMID:10975177

Jonkers, H., Lankhorst, M., van Burren, R., Hoppenbrouwers, S., & Bonsangue, M. (2003). Concepts for modelling enterprise architecture. *Via Nova Architectura*. Retrieved from http://www.via-nova-architectura.org/ proceedings/lac-2003/concepts-for-modeling-enterprise-architectures-2.html

Jonsson, P., & Mattsson, S. (2013). The value of sharing planning information in supply chains. *International Journal of Physical Distribution & Logistics Management, 43*(4), 282–299. doi:10.1108/IJPDLM-07-2012-0204

Josey, A., Harrison, R., Homan, P., Rouse, M. F., van Sante, T., Turner, M., & van der Merwe, P. (2009). *TOGAF version 9 – A pocket guide*. Reading, UK: The Open Group.

Julien, P. and Raymond, L. (1994, Summer). Factors of new technology adoption in the retail sector. *Entrepreneurship Theory and Practice*, 79-90.

Kai, R. T., & Larsen. (2003). Development of the Information Systems Implementation Research Method. *Proceedings of the 36th Hawaii International Conference on System Sciences*.

Kamal, M.M. (2006). IT innovation adoption in the government sector : identifying the critical success factors. *Journal of Enterprise Information Management, 19*(1/2).

Kamariah, N. M., & Sentosa, I. (2008). *The Integration of Technology Acceptance Model and Technology of Puchasing Behavior (A Structural Equation Modeling Approach)*. Paper presented at the the Proceeding of Asia Pacific Conference on Management of Technology and Technology Entrepreneurship, Melaka, Malaysia.

Kamhawi, E. M. (2007). Critical Factors for Implementation Success of ERP Systems: An Empirical Investigation from Bahrain. *International Journal of Enterprise Information Systems, 3*(2), 34–49. doi:10.4018/jeis.2007040103

Kandall, J. D., Tung, L. L., Chua, K. H., Ng, C. H. D., & Tan, S. M. (2001). Receptivity of Singapore SMEs to e-commerce adoption. *The Journal of Strategic Information Systems, 10*(3), 223–242. doi:10.1016/S0963-8687(01)00048-8

Kane, R. (2003). Definition, Measurement, and Correlates of Quality of Life in Nursing Homes: Toward a Reasonable Practice, Research, and Policy Agenda. *The Gerontologist, 43*(Supplement 2), 28–36. doi:10.1093/geront/43.suppl_2.28 PMID:12711722

Kang, K. (2010). Considering Culture in Designing Web Based E-commerce. In E-Commerce. In-Tech.

Kaplan, R. S., & Cooper, R. (1998). *Cost & Effect, using integrated cost systems to drive profitability and performance.* Boston: Harvard Business School Press.

Karaarslan, N., & Gundogar, E. (2009). An application for modular capability-based ERP software selection using AHP method. *International Journal of Advanced Manufacturing Technology, 42*(10), 1025–1033. doi:10.1007/s00170-008-1522-5

Karimi, J., Gupta, Y. P., & Somers, T. M. (1996). The congruence between a firms competitive strategy and information technology leaders rank and role. *Journal of Management Information Systems, 13*(1), 63–88. doi:10.1080/07421222.1996.11518112

Karimi, J., Somers, T. M., & Gupta, Y. P. (2001). Impact of Information Technology Management Practices on Customer Service. *Journal of Management Information Systems, 17*, 125–158.

Karsh, B.-T. (2004). Beyond usability: Designing effective technology implementation systems to promote patient safety. *Quality & Safety in Health Care, 13*(5), 388–394. doi:10.1136/qshc.2004.010322 PMID:15465944

Katzenbach, J., von Post, R., & Thomas, J. (2014). The critical few: Components of a truly effective culture. *Strategy+Business, 74*, 1-9.

Kazi, Z., Kazi, L., & Radulovic, B. (2012). Analysis of data model correctness by using automated reasoning system. *Technics Technologies Education Management, 7*(3), 1090–1100.

Kearns, G. S., & Lederer, A. L. (2003). A Resource-Based View of Strategic IT Alignment: How Knowledge Sharing Creates Competitive Advantage. *Decision Sciences, 34*(1), 1–29. doi:10.1111/1540-5915.02289

Keen, P. G. (1981). Information systems and organizational change. *Communications of the ACM, 24*(1), 24–33. doi:10.1145/358527.358543

Keen, P. G. W. (1991). *Shaping the future: business design through information technology.* Harvard Business School Press.

Keen, P. G. W., & Scott-Morton, M. S. (1978). *Decision Support Systems: An Organizational Perspective.* Reading, MA: Addison-Wesley.

Kelle, P., & Akbulut, A. (2005). The role of ERP tools in supply chain information sharing, cooperation, and cost optimization. *International Journal of Production Economics, 93*, 41–52. doi:10.1016/j.ijpe.2004.06.004

Kemppainen, K., & Vepsäläinen, A. P. J. (2003). Trends in industrial supply chains and networks. *International Journal of Physical Distribution & Logistics Management, 33*(8), 701–719. doi:10.1108/09600030310502885

Kennedy, P. (2003). *A Guide to Econometrics* (5th ed.). Cambridge, MA: The MIT Press.

Kerlinger, F. N. (1986). *Foundations of Behavioral Research* (3rd ed.). New York: Holt, Rinehart, & Winston.

Kerner, D. (1979). Business information characterization study. *Database, 10*(4), 10–17.

Kettinger, J. (1994). National infrastructure diffusion and US information super highway. *Information & Management, 27*(6), 357–369. doi:10.1016/0378-7206(94)90016-7

Kettinger, W. J., Marchland, D. A., & Davis, J. M. (2010). Designing enterprise IT architectures to optimize flexibility and standardization in global business. *MIS Quarterly Executive, 9*(2), 95–113.

Keyes, J. (2005). *Implementing the IT blanced scorecard: aligning IT with corporate strategy.* Boca Raton, FL: Taylor & Francis Group. doi:10.1201/9781420031348

Khattak, M. A. O., She, Y., Memon, Z. A., Syed, N., Hussain, S., & Irfan, M. (2013). Investigating Critical Success Factors Affecting ERP Implementation in Chinese and Pakistani Enterprises. *International Journal of Enterprise Information Systems*, *9*(3), 39–76. doi:10.4018/jeis.2013070103

Kim, Suh, & Hwang. (2003). A model for evaluating the effectiveness of CRM using the balanced scorecard. *Interactive Marketing*, *17*(2).

Kim, H., & Pan, S. (2006). Towards a Process Model of Information Systems Implementation: The Case of Customer Relationship Management, Database for Advances in Information Systems; Winter 2006. *The Data Base for Advances in Information Systems*, (Winter), 2006.

Kim, N., Lee, S., & Moon, S. (2008). Formalized Entity Extraction Methodology for Changeable Business Requirements. *Journal of Information Science and Engineering*, *24*, 649–671.

Kim, Y., Lee, Z., & Gosain, S. (2005). Impediments to successful ERP implementation process. *Business Process Management Journal*, *11*(2), 158–170. doi:10.1108/14637150510591156

King, J. L., Gurbaxani, V., Kraemer, K. L., McFarlan, F. W., Raman, K. S., & Yap, C. S. (1994). Institutional factors in information technology innovation. *Information Systems Research*, *5*(2), 139–169. doi:10.1287/isre.5.2.139

King, J. L., & Kraemer, K. L. (1984). Evolution and Organizational Information Systems: An Assessment of Nolans Stage Model. *Communications of the ACM*, *27*(5), 466–475. doi:10.1145/358189.358074

Kini, R. B., & Basaviah, S. (2013). Critical Success Factors in the Implementation of Enterprise Resource Planning Systems in Small and Midsize Businesses: Microsoft Navision Implementation. *International Journal of Enterprise Information Systems*, *9*(1), 97–117. doi:10.4018/jeis.2013010106

Kinni, T. B. (1995). Process improvement, part 2. *Industry Week/IW*, *244*(4), 45.

Klassen, T. P., Jahad, A. R., & Moher, D. (1998). Guides for reading and interpreting systematic reviews. *Archives of Pediatrics & Adolescent Medicine*, *152*(7), 700–704. doi:10.1001/archpedi.152.7.700 PMID:9667544

Klaus, H., Rosemann, M., & Gable, G. (2000). What is ERP? *Information Systems Frontiers*, *2*(2), 141–162. doi:10.1023/A:1026543906354

Kleiner, M., Albert, P., & Bézivin, J. (2009). Parsing SBVR-Based Controlled Languages. In Lecture Notes in Computer Science: Vol. 5795. Model Driven Engineering Languages and Systems (pp. 122–136). Springer. doi:10.1007/978-3-642-04425-0_10

Kleis, L., Chwelos, P., Ramirez, R. V., & Cockburn, I. (2012). Information Technology and Intangible Output: The Impact of IT Investment on Innovation Productivity. *Information Systems Research*, *23*(1), 42–59. doi:10.1287/isre.1100.0338

Kline, R. B. (1998). *Principles and Practice of Structural Equation Modeling*. New York: The Guilford Press.

Koch, C. (2002, November 15). Hershey's Bittersweet Lesson. *CIO Magazine*.

Koch, C. (2004, July 15). Nike rebounds: How (and Why) Nike recovered from its supply chain disaster. *CIO Magazine*.

Koch, S., & Mitteregger, K. (2014). Linking customisation of ERP systems to support effort: an empirical study. *Enterprise Information Systems*, 1–27. http://doi.org/<ALIGNMENT.qj></ALIGNMENT>10.1080/17517575.2014.917705

Kocher, M., & Straub, S. (2006). Individual or team decision-making: Causes and consequences of self-selection. *Games and Economic Behavior*, *56*(2), 259–270. doi:10.1016/j.geb.2005.08.009

Ko, D., Kirsch, J. L., & King, W. R. (2005). Antecedents of knowledge transfer from consultants to clients in enterprise system implementations. *Management Information Systems Quarterly, 29*(1), 59–85.

Koen, A., Bertels, H. M., & Elsum, I. (2011). The three faces of business model innovation: Challenges for established firms. *Research-Technology Management, 54*(3), 52–59. doi:10.5437/08953608X5403009

Kohli, R., Devaraj, S., & Mahmood, A. M. (2004). Understanding Determinants of Online Customer Satisfaction:A Decision Process Perspective. *Journal of Management Information Systems, 21*(1).

Koh, S. C. L., & Simpson, M. (2007). Could enterprise resource planning create a competitive advantage for small businesses? *Benchmarking: An International Journal, 14*(1), 59–76. doi:10.1108/14635770710730937

Kontoghiorges, C. (2005). Key Organizational and HR Factors for Rapid Technology Assimilation. *Organization Development Journal, 23*(1), 26–39.

Kopczak, L. (1997). Logistics partnership and supply chain restructuration: Survey results from the U.S. computer industry. *Production and Operations Management, 6*(3), 226–247. doi:10.1111/j.1937-5956.1997.tb00428.x

Kornak, A., & Distefano, J. (2002). *Cap Gemini Ernst & Young Guide to Wireless Enterprise Application Architecture.* New York: John Wiley & Sons.

Koschzeck, K. (2009). *You are the most important leader in your organization: Towards a shared leadership model.* Retrieved from Proquest Digital Dissertations. (MR52131).

Kotler, P., & Armstrong, G. (2009). Principles of Marketing (13th ed.). Englewood Cliffs, NJ: Prentice-Hall Inc.

Kotler, P. (2000). *Marketing Management.* Upper Saddle River, NJ: Academic Press.

Krause, D. R., Pagell, M., & Curkovic, S. (2001). Toward a measure of competitive priorities for purchasing. *Journal of Operations Management, 19*(4), 497–512. doi:10.1016/S0272-6963(01)00047-X

Krippendorff, K. (2004). *Content Analysis: An Introduction to its Methodology.* Beverly Hills, CA: Sage Publications.

Kronbichler, S. A., Ostermann, H., & Staudinger, R. (2009). A Review of Critical Success Factors for ERP Projects. *The Open Information Systems Journal, 3*(1), 14–25. doi:10.2174/1874133900903010014

Krumbholz. M., and Maiden, N. (2001). The implementation of enterprise resource planning packages in different organizational and national cultures. *Information Systems, 26*(30), 185-204.

Kugler, T., Kausel, E. E., & Kocher, M. G. (2012). Are groups more rational than individuals? A review of interactive decision making in groups. *Wiley Interdisciplinary Reviews: Cognitive Science, 3*(4), 471–482. doi:10.1002/wcs.1184 PMID:26301530

Kukafka, R., Johnson, S., & Allegrantec, J. (2003). Grounding a new information technology implementation framework in behavioral science: A systematic analysis of the literature on IT use. *Journal of Biomedical Informatics, 36*(3), 218–227. doi:10.1016/j.jbi.2003.09.002 PMID:14615230

Kumar, V., Maheshwari, B., & Kumar, U. (2003). An investigation of critical management issues in ERP implementation: Empirical evidence from Canadian organizations. *Technovation, 23*(10), 793–807. doi:10.1016/S0166-4972(02)00015-9

Kwahk, K. (2006, January). ERP acceptance: organizational change perspective. In *System Sciences, 2006. HICSS'06. Proceedings of the 39th Annual Hawaii International Conference on System Sciences* (*Vol. 8*, pp. 172b-172b). IEEE. doi:10.1109/HICSS.2006.159

Kwak, Y. H., Park, J., Chung, B. Y., & Ghosh, S. (2012). Understanding end-users' acceptance of enterprise resource planning (ERP) system in project-based sectors. *Engineering Management. IEEE Transactions on*, *59*(2), 266–277.

Kwon, T. H., & Zmud, R. W. (1987). Unifying the Fragmented Models of Information Systems Implementation. In Critical Issues in Information Systems Research (pp. 227-51). John Wiley.

Lacity, M., & Fox, J. (2008). Creating global shared services: Lessons from Reuters. *MIS Quarterly Executive*, *7*, 17–32.

Lacity, M., & Hirschheim, R. (1993). *Information Systems Outsourcing: Myths, Methaphors and Realities*. Chichester, UK: Wiley.

Lahrmann, G., Marx, F., Winter, R., & Wortmann, F. (2011). Business Intelligence Maturity: Development and Evaluation of a Theoretical Model. Proceedings of HICSS.

Lai, I. K. (2006). The critical success factors across ERP implementation models: An empirical study in China. *International Journal of Enterprise Information Systems*, *2*(3), 24–42. doi:10.4018/jeis.2006070103

Lai, V., & Mahapatra, R. (1997). Exploring the research in information technology implementation. *Information & Management*, *32*(4), 187–201. doi:10.1016/S0378-7206(97)00022-0

Lam, C. F., & Brzenzinski. (2005). The Effects of Customization on Satisfaction with Mobile Systems. Idea Group Publishing.

Lambert, D. M., Cooper, M. C., & Pagh, J. D. (1998). Supply chain management: Implementation issues and research opportunities. *International Journal of Logistics Management*, *9*(2), 1–19. doi:10.1108/09574099810805807

Lambert, D. M., & Harrington, T. C. (1990). Measuring nonresponse bias in customer service mail surveys. *Journal of Business Logistics*, *11*(2), 5–25.

Lampel, J., & Mintzberg, H. (1996). Customizing Customization. *Sloan Management Review*, *38*(1), 21–30.

Lane, M. S., & Koronios, A. (2007). *Critical competencies required for the role of the modern CIO*. Paper presented at the ACIS 2007 - 18th Australasian Conference on Information Systems, Toowoomba, Australia.

Langer, N., Mani, D., & Srikanth, K. (2014). Client Satisfaction Versus Profitability: An Empirical Analysis of the Impact of Formal Controls in Strategic Outsourcing Contracts. In A. H. Rudy Hirschheim (Ed.), Information Systems Outsourcing (pp. 67-88). Springer Berlin Heidelberg.

Lankhorst, M. (2013). *Enterprise architecture at work: Modelling, communication and analysis*. Heidelberg, Germany: Springer. doi:10.1007/978-3-642-29651-2

Lankhorst, M. M., Iacob, M. E., & Jonkers, H. (2005). *Enterprise architecture at work: modelling, communication and analysis*. Berlin: Springer-Verlag.

Larsen, M. A., & Myers, M. D. (1997). BPR Success or Failure? A Business Process Reengineering Project in the Financial Services Industry. *Proceedings of the 18th International Conference on Information Systems*, 367-382.

Larson, E. C., & Adams, C. R. (2010). *Increasing Coordination Demands and the Impact on CIO Rank*. Paper presented at the System Sciences (HICSS), 2010 43rd Hawaii International Conference on.

Law, C. C. H., & Ngai, E. W. T. (2007). ERP systems adoption: An exploratory study of the organizational factors and impacts of ERP success. *Information & Management*, *44*(4), 418–432. doi:10.1016/j.im.2007.03.004

Le Duc, M. (2014). Critical success factors for implementing ERP in the curriculum of university business education: A case study.*Proceedings of the 8th European Conference on Information Management and Evaluation, ECIME 2014*, 128-135.

Leach, B. (2003). Success of CRM systems hinges on establishment of measureable benefits. *Pulp & Paper*, *77*(6), 48.

Leavitt, H. J. (1965). *Applying organizational change in industry: Structural, technological and humanistic approaches. In Handbook of Organizations.* Chicago: Academic Press.

Lech, P. (2011). Is it really so 'strategic'?: Motivational factors for investing in enterprise systems. *International Journal of Enterprise Information Systems*, *7*(4), 13–22.

Ledford, L., Lee, C., Bart, J., & Fuller, T. (2006). Shared Leadership Triage Process Redesign. Shared Leadership Triage Process Redesign. Journal of Emergency Nursing Conference. doi:10.1016/j.jen.2005.12.024

Lee, A. (2000). Researchable Directions for ERP and Other New Information Technologies, Editors Comments. MIS Quarterly, 24(1), iii-viii.

Lee, C., Lee, K. C., & Han, J. (1999). A Web-based Decision Support System for Logistics Decision-Making. *Proceedings of the Academy of Information and Management Sciences*, *3*(1).

Lee, J., Pi, S., Kwok, R. C., & Huynh, M. Q. (2003). The Contribution of Commitment Value in Internet Commerce: An Empirical Investigation. *Journal of the Association for Information Systems, 4*.

Lee, A. S. (2004). *Thinking about Social Theory and Philosophy for Information Systems*. In L. Willcocks & J. Mingers (Eds.), *Social Theory and Philosophy for Information Systems* (pp. 1–26). Chichester, UK: John Wiley & Sons.

Lee, H. L., & Whang, S. (1997). Bullwhip Effect in Supply Chains. *Sloan Management Review*, *38*(3), 93–102.

Lee, J. N., & Kim, Y. G. (1999). Effect of Partnership Quality on IS Outsourcing Sucess: Conceptual Framework and Empirical Validation. *Journal of Management Information Systems*, *15*(4), 29–61. doi:10.1080/07421222.1999.11518221

Leeney, M., Varajão, J., Ribeiro, A. T., & Colomo-Palacios, R. (2011). Information Systems Outsourcing in Large Companies: Evidences from 20 Ireland Companies. *International Journal of Information Technology Project Management*, *2*(4), 44–58. doi:10.4018/jitpm.2011100104

Lee, S. C., & Lee, H. G. (2004). The importance of change management after ERP implementation: An information capability perspective.*Proceedings of the 25th International Conference on Information Systems*.

Lee, S., Kim, N., & Moon, S. (2010). Context-adaptive approach for automated entity relationship modeling. *Journal of Information Science and Engineering*, *26*(6), 2229–2247.

Lee, S., Koh, S., Yen, D., & Tang, H.-L. (2002). Perception gaps between IS academics and IS practitioners: An exploratory study. *Information & Management*, *40*(1), 51–61. doi:10.1016/S0378-7206(01)00132-X

Lettieri, E., Borga, F., & Savoldelli, A. (2004). Knowledge Management in Nonprofit Organizations. *Journal of Knowledge Management*, *8*(6), 16–30. doi:10.1108/13673270410567602

Levary, R. R. (2000). Better Supply Chains through Information Technology. *Industrial Management (Des Plaines)*, *42*(3), 24–30.

Levasseur, R. E. (2001). People Skills: Change Management Tools - Lewin's Change Model. *Interfaces*, *31*(4), 71–73.

Lewin, K. (1952). *Field theory in social science: Selected theoretical papers* (D. Cartwright, Ed.). London: Tavistock.

Lewrick, M., & Raeside, R. (2010). Transformation and change process in innovation models: Start-up and mature companies. *International Journal of Business Innovation and Research, 4*(6), 515–534. doi:10.1504/IJBIR.2010.035711

Li, E. Y., McLeod, R. Jr, & Rogers, J. C. (2001). Marketing information systems in Fortune 500 companies: A longitudinal analysis of 1980, 1990, and 2000. *Information & Management, 38*(5), 307–322. doi:10.1016/S0378-7206(00)00073-2

Li, G., Field, J. M., Jiang, H., He, T., & Pang, Y. (2015). Decision Models for Workforce and Technology Planning in. *Service Science, 7*(1), 29–47. doi:10.1287/serv.2015.0094

Li, G., Yang, H., Sun, L., & Sohal, A. S. (2009). The impact of IT implementation on supply chain integration and performance. *International Journal of Production Economics, 120*(1), 125–138. doi:10.1016/j.ijpe.2008.07.017

Light, B. (2005). Going Beyond Misfit as a Reason for ERP Package Customization. *Computers in Industry, 56*(6), 606–619. doi:10.1016/j.compind.2005.02.008

Lin, C., Kuei, C., Madu, C. N., & Winch, J. (2010). Identifying Critical Success Factors for Supply Chain Excellence. *International Journal of Strategic Decision Sciences, 1*(3), 49–70. doi:10.4018/jsds.2010070104

Lin, C., & Pervan, G. (2003). The practice of IS/IT benefits management in large Australian organizations. *Information & Management, 41*(1), 13–24. doi:10.1016/S0378-7206(03)00002-8

Lindell, M. K., & Whitney, D. J. (2001). Accounting for common method variance in cross sectional research designs. *The Journal of Applied Psychology, 86*(1), 114–121. doi:10.1037/0021-9010.86.1.114 PMID:11302223

Liu, C., & Arnett, K. P. (2000). Exploring the factors associated with Web site success in the context of electronic commerce. *Information & Management, 38*(1), 23–33. doi:10.1016/S0378-7206(00)00049-5

Liu, P. L. (2011). Empirical study on influence of critical success factors on ERP knowledge management on management performance in high-tech industries in Taiwan. *Expert Systems with Applications, 38*(8), 10696–10704. doi:10.1016/j.eswa.2011.02.045

Lo, A. W., & Choobineh, J. (2002). Knowledge-Based Systems as Database Design Tools: A Comparative Study. In V. Sugumaran (Ed.), *Intelligent Support Systems Technology: Knowledge Management*. IRM Press.

Loh, L., & Venkatraman, N. (1992). Determinants of information technology outsourcing: A cross-sectional analysis. *Journal of Management Information Systems, 9*(1), 7–24. doi:10.1080/07421222.1992.11517945

Looi, H. C. (2005). E-commerce adoption in Brunei Darussalam: A quantitative analysis of factors influencing its adoption. *Communications of the AIS, 15*, 61–81.

Lovelace, K. J., Manz, C. C., & Alves, J. C. (2007). Work stress and leadership development: The role of self-leadership, Shared leadership, physical fitness and flow in managing demands and increasing job control. *Human Resource Management Review, 17*(4), 374–387. doi:10.1016/j.hrmr.2007.08.001

Loveman, G. (1991). Cash drain, no gain. *Computerworld, 25*(47), 69–70.

Lucas, H., et al. (1990). *Information Systems Implementation: Testing a Structural Model*. Alex Publishing Corporations.

Lucas, F. J., Molina, F., & Toval, A. (2009). A systematic review of UML model consistency management. *Information and Software Technology, 51*(12), 1631–1645. doi:10.1016/j.infsof.2009.04.009

Lucas, H. (1981). *Implementation: The Key to Successful Information Systems*. Columbia university press.

Lucas, H., Walton, E., & Ginzberg, M. (1988). Implementing packaged software. *Management Information Systems Quarterly, 12*(4), 537–549. doi:10.2307/249129

Luftman, J. N., Lewis, P. R., & Oldach, S. H. (1993). Transforming the enterprise: The alignment of business and information technology strategies. *IBM Systems Journal*, *32*(1), 198–221. doi:10.1147/sj.321.0198

Luftman, J., & Ben-Tvi, T. (2010). Key issues for IT executives 2010: Judicious IT investments continue post-recession. *MISQ Executive*, *9*(4), 263–273.

Luftman, J., & Ben-Zvi, T. (2010). Key Issues for IT Executives 2009: Difficult Economy's Impact on IT. *MIS Quarterly Executive*, *9*(1), 203–213.

Luo, W., & Strong, D. M. (2004). A Framework for Evaluating ERP Implementation Choices. *IEEE Transactions on Engineering Management*, *51*(3), 322–333. doi:10.1109/TEM.2004.830862

Lutchen, M. D. (2003). *Managing IT as a Business: A Survival Guide for CEOs*. John Wiley & Sons, Ltd.

Lyons, D. (2004). Too much information. *Forbes*, 110–115.

Lyytinen, K., Mathiassen, L., & Ropponen, J. (1996). A framework for software risk management. *Journal of Information Technology*, *11*(4), 275–285. doi:10.1057/jit.1996.2

Lyytinen, K., Mathiassen, L., & Ropponen, J. (1998). Attention Shaping and Software Risk – A Categorical analysis of Four Classical Risk Management Approaches. *Information Systems Research*, *9*(3), 233–255. doi:10.1287/isre.9.3.233

Lyytinen, K., & Newman, M. (2008). Explaining information systems change: A punctuated socio-technical change model. *European Journal of Information Systems*, *17*(6), 589–613. doi:10.1057/ejis.2008.50

Lyytinen, K., & Rose, G. M. (2003). Disruptive information system innovation: The case of internet computing. *Information Systems Journal*, *13*(4), 301–330. doi:10.1046/j.1365-2575.2003.00155.x

Mabert, V. M., Soni, A., & Venkataraman, M. A. (2000). Enterprise Resource Planning Survey of US Manufacturing Firms. *Production and Inventory Management Journal*, *41*(20), 52–58.

Mabert, V., Soni, A., & Venkataramanan, M. (2003). Enterprise resource planning: Managing the implication process. *European Journal of Operational Research*, *146*(2), 302–314. doi:10.1016/S0377-2217(02)00551-9

Macleod, M. (1994, July). What's new in supply chain software?. *Purchasing & Supply Management*, 22-25.

Magazine, C. (2009). *State of the CIO Survey '09*. CIO Magazine.

Maglio, P., Kieliszewski, C., & Spohrer, J. (2010). *Handook of Service Science*. New York: Springer Verlag. doi:10.1007/978-1-4419-1628-0

Maglio, P., & Spohrer, J. (2008). Fundamentals of service science. *Journal of the Academy of Marketing Science*, *36*(I), 18–20. doi:10.1007/s11747-007-0058-9

Mahgary, S., & Lahdelma, R. (1995). Data envelopment analysis: Visualising the results. *European Journal of Operational Research*, *85*(3), 700–710. doi:10.1016/0377-2217(94)00303-T

Makoul, G., & Clayman, M. L. (2006). An integrative model of shared decision making in medical encounters. *Patient Education and Counseling*, *60*(3), 301–312. doi:10.1016/j.pec.2005.06.010 PMID:16051459

Maldonado, M., & Sierra, V. (2013). User satisfaction as the foundation of the success following an ERP adoption: An empirical study from Latin America. *International Journal of Enterprise Information Systems*, *9*(3), 77–99. doi:10.4018/jeis.2013070104

Malhotra, N. K., Kim, S. S., & Patil, A. (2006). Common method variance in IS research: A comparison of alternative approaches and a reanalysis of past research. *Management Science*, *52*(12), 1865–1883. doi:10.1287/mnsc.1060.0597

Malladi, S., & Krishnan, M. S. (2012). *Cloud computing adoption and its implications for CIO strategic focus–an empirical analysis*. Academic Press.

Malone, T. W., Yates, J., & Benjamin, R. I. (1987). Electronic markets and electronic hierarchies. *Communications of the ACM, 30*(6), 484–497. doi:10.1145/214762.214766

Manes, A. T. (2003). *Web Services a managers guide*. Boston: Addison-Wesley.

Manz, C. C., Pearce, C. L., & Sims, H. P. Jr. (2009). The Ins and Outs of Leading Teams: An Overview. *Organizational Dynamics, 38*(3), 179–182. doi:10.1016/j.orgdyn.2009.04.005

Marble, R. (2003). A system implementation study: Management commitment to project management. *Information & Management, 41*(1), 111–123. doi:10.1016/S0378-7206(03)00031-4

March, S. T., & Storey, V. C. (2008). Design Science in the Information Systems Discipline: An Introduction to the Special Issue on Design Science Research. *Management Information Systems Quarterly, 32*(4), 725–730.

Mark Xu, J. W. (2005). Gaining customer knowledge through analytical CRM. *Industrial Management & Data Systems, 105*(7).

Markham, J. W. (2006). *Financial history of modern united states corporate scandals*. New York: M.E. Sharpe.

Markus, M. L., & Tanis, C. (2000). The Enterprise System Experience– from adoption to success. In Framing the Domains of IT Management: Projecting the Future through the Past (pp. 173-207). Pinnaflex Educational Resources, Inc.

Markus, M. L., & Tanis, C. (2000). The enterprise systems experience-from adoption to success. *Framing the domains of IT research: Glimpsing the future through the past, 173*, 207-173.

Markus, L., & Tanis, C. (2000). The enterprise systems experience from adoption to success. In R. W. Zmud (Ed.), *Framing the Domains of IT Research: Glimpsing the Future through the Past*. Cincinnati, OH: Pinnaflex Educational Resources, Inc.

Markus, L., Tanis, P. C., & Van, F. (2000). Multi-site ERP implementation. *Communications of the ACM, 43*(4), 42–46. doi:10.1145/332051.332068

Markus, M. L., Axline, S., Petrie, D., & Tanis, C. (2000). Learning from adopters experiences with ERP: Problems encountered and success achieved. *Journal of Information Technology, 15*(4), 245–265. doi:10.1080/02683960010008944

Marques, R. P., Santos, H., & Santos, C. (2013b). *An enterprise ontology-based database for continuous monitoring application*. Paper presented at the IEEE 15th Conference on Business Informatics, Vienna, Austria. doi:10.1109/CBI.2013.10

Marques, R. P. (2017). Continuous Assurance – The Use of Technology for Business Compliance. In M. Khosrow-Pour (Ed.), *Encyclopedia of Information Science and Technology* (4th ed.). Hershey, PA: IGI Global.

Marques, R. P., Santos, H. M. D., & Santos, C. (2013c). Organizational transactions with real time monitoring and auditing. *The Learning Organization, 20*(6), 390–405. doi:10.1108/TLO-09-2013-0048

Marques, R. P., Santos, H., & Santos, C. (2013a). A conceptual model for evaluating systems with continuous assurance services. *Procedia Technology, 9*, 304–309. doi:10.1016/j.protcy.2013.12.034

Marques, R. P., Santos, H., & Santos, C. (2015). Monitoring organizational transactions in enterprise information systems with continuous assurance requirements. *International Journal of Enterprise Information Systems, 11*(1), 13–32. doi:10.4018/ijeis.2015010102

Marques, R. P., Santos, H., & Santos, C. (2016). Evaluating information systems with continuous assurance services. *International Journal of Information Systems in the Service Sector*, *8*(3), 1–15. doi:10.4018/IJISSS.2016070101

Marshall, P., McKay, J., & Prananto, A. (2005). Business Value Creation from IT Investments: Towards a process theory of IT governance. *Australasian Journal of Information Systems*, *12*(2). doi:10.3127/ajis.v12i2.91

Martin, A. (2012). Enterprise IT architecture in large federated organizations: The art of the possible. *Information Systems Management*, *29*(2), 137–147. doi:10.1080/10580530.2012.662103

Martin, M. (1998). Enterprise Resource Planning. *Fortune*, *137*(2), 149–151.

Martinsons, M., & Hosley, S. (1993). Planning a strategic information system for a market-oriented non-profit organization. *Journal of Systems Management*, *44*(2), 14.

Matthew, L. (1996). IT outsourcing contracts: Practical issues for management. *Industrial Management & Data Systems*, *96*(1), 15–20. doi:10.1108/02635579610107684

McAdam, R., & Reid, R. (2001). SME and large organisation perceptions of knowledge management: Comparisons and contrasts. *Journal of Knowledge Management*, *5*(3), 231–241. doi:10.1108/13673270110400870

McAfee, A., & Brynjolfsson, E. (2008). Investing in the IT that makes a competitive difference. *Harvard Business Review*, *86*(7), 98–107. PMID:18271321

McBride, N. (2014, February). Business intelligence in magazine distribution. *International Journal of Information Management*, *34*(1), 58–62. doi:10.1016/j.ijinfomgt.2013.09.006

McCathie, L. (2004). *The advantages and disadvantages of barcodes and radio frequency identification in supply chain management*. School of Information Technology and Computer Science, Bachelor of Information and Communication Technology (Honours), University of Wollongong. Retrieved from http://www.ro.uow.edu.au/thesesinfo/9

McDonald, K. (2004). *Is SAP the Right Infrastructure for your Enterprise Analytics*. Presentation at American SAP User Group Conference, Atlanta, GA.

McFarlan, F. W. (1984). Information technology changes the way you compete. *Harvard Business Review*, *62*(3), 98–103.

McFarlan, F. W., & McKenney, J. L. (1983). The information archipelago - governing the new world. *Harvard Business Review*, *61*(4), 91–99.

McFarlan, F. W., McKenney, J., & Pyburn, P. (1983). The information archipelago - plotting a course. *Harvard Business Review*, *61*(1), 145–156. PMID:10299000

McHugh, K. A., Yammarino, F. J., Dionne, S. D., Serban, A., Sayama, H., & Chatterjee, S. (2016). Collective decision making, leadership, and collective intelligence: Tests with agent-based simulations and a Field study. *The Leadership Quarterly*, *27*(2), 218–241. doi:10.1016/j.leaqua.2016.01.001

McKenny, J. L., & McFarlan, F. W. (1979). The information archipelago - maps and bridges. *Harvard Business Review*, *60*(5), 109–114.

McKim, B. (2000). How to measure CRM success. *Target Marketing*, *23*(10), 138.

McKinsey. (2012). *Global Survey: Making Innovation Structures Work*. McKinsey & Company, McKinsey Insight. Available at: http://www.mckinsey.com/insights/organization

McKinsey. (2014). *McKinsey Global Survey results: The Digital Tipping Point*. McKinsey & Company.

McLaughlin, J. A., & Jordan, G. B. (1999). Logic models: A tool for telling your programs performance story. *Evaluation and Program Planning, 22*(1), 65–72. doi:10.1016/S0149-7189(98)00042-1

Melvin, F. (1975, October). Policy Making Under Discontinuous Change: The Situational Normativism Approach. *Management Science, 22*(2), 226–235. doi:10.1287/mnsc.22.2.226

Mendes, C., & Mira da Silva, M. (2012). DEMO-based Service Level Agreements. *3rd International Conference on Exploring Service Science.*

Mendez, M. J., & Busenbark, J. R. (2015). Shared leadership and gender: All members are equal… but some more than others. *Leadership and Organization Development Journal, 36*(1), 17–34. doi:10.1108/LODJ-11-2012-0147

Mengistie, A. A., Heaton, D. P., & Rainforth, M. (2013). Analysis of the critical success factors for ERP systems implementation in U.S. federal offices. *Lecture Notes in Information Systems and Organisation, 4*, 183–198. doi:10.1007/978-3-642-37021-2_15

Mentzer, J. T., Keebler, J. S., Min, S., Nix, N. W., Smith, C. D., & Zacharia, Z. G. (2001). Defining supply chain management. *Journal of Business Logistics, 22*(2), 1–25. doi:10.1002/j.2158-1592.2001.tb00001.x

Merson, P. (2009). Data Model as an Architectural View. *Solutions*, 1–10. Retrieved from http://www.sei.cmu.edu/reports/09tn024.pdf

META Group. (2004). *Market Research: The State of ERP Services.* Stamford, CT: META Group, Inc.

Mexas, M. P., Quelhas, G. O. L., Costa, H. G., & Lameira, V. (2013). A set of criteria for selection of enterprise resource planning (ERP). *International Journal of Enterprise Information Systems, 9*(2), 44–69. doi:10.4018/jeis.2013040103

Meyers, B. (March 1997). Getting better with practice? A longitudinal study of shared leadership.*Proceedings from the Annual Meeting of the American Educational Research Association.*

Mihelis, G., Grigoroudis, E., Siskos, Y., Politis, Y., & Malandrakis, Y. (2001). Customer Satisfaction Measurement in the Private Bank Sector. *European Journal of Operational Research, 130.*

Miles, M. B., & Huberman, A. M. (1994). *An Expanded Sourcebook:Qualitative Data Analysis* (2nd ed.). Sage Publications International.

Millman, G. J. (2004, May). What did you get from ERP and what can you get? *Financial Executive,* 38-42.

Mirani, R., & Lederer, A. L. (1998). An Instrument for assessing the organizational benefits of IS projects. *Decision Sciences, 29*(4), 803–838. doi:10.1111/j.1540-5915.1998.tb00878.x

Mirbagheri, F. A., & Marthandan, G. (2012). Success factors of ERP implementation in SMEs in Malaysia. *International Journal of Computing & Corporate Research, 2*(6). Retrieved from www.ijccr.com

Mishra, R. K. (2012). Measuring Supply Chain Efficiency: A Dea Approach. *Journal of Operations and Supply Chain Management, 5*(1), 45–68.

Miskin, V. D., & Gmelch, W. H. (1985, May). Quality leadership for quality teams. *Training and Development Journal*, 122–129.

Mithas, S., Krishnan, M. S., & Fornell, C. (2005). Why Do Customer Relationship Management Applications Affect Customer Satisfaction? *Journal of Marketing, 69*(4), 201–209. doi:10.1509/jmkg.2005.69.4.201

Mitrovic, A., Koedinger, K., & Martin, B. (2003). A Comparative Analysis of Cognitive Tutoring and Constraint-Based Modeling. *Proceedings of Int. Conf. User Modeling, 2702,* 147.

Monk, E. F., & Wagner, B. J. (2013). *Concepts in Enterprise Resource Planning*. Cengage Learning.

Mooney, G. R. (2009). *Enterprise Creativity and innovation, 1*. Berlin, Germany: Lambert Academic Publishing.

Moore, G. C., & Benbasat, I. (1991). Development of an instrument to measure the perceptions of adopting an information technology innovation. *Information Systems Research*, *2*(3), 192–222. doi:10.1287/isre.2.3.192

Morabito, V., Pace, S., & Previtali, P. (2005). ERP marketing and Italian SMEs. *European Management Journal*, *23*(5), 590–598. doi:10.1016/j.emj.2005.09.014

Morris, H. (2003). The Financial Impact of Business Analytics: Build vs. Buy. *DM Review*, *13*(1), 40-41.

Morris, M. G., & Venkatesh, V. (2010). Job Characteristics and Job Satisfaction: Understanding the Role of Enterprise Resource Planning System Implementation. *Management Information Systems Quarterly*, *34*(1), 143–161.

Mortara. L, Slacik. I, Napp. J. J, Minshall. T. (2010). Implementing open innovation: cultural issues. *Int. J. Entrepreneurship and Innovation Management, 11*(4).

Motwani, J., Madan, M., & Gunasekaran, A. (2000). Information technology in managing supply chains. *Logistics Information Management*, *13*(5), 320–327. doi:10.1108/09576050010378540

Motwani, J., Mirchandani, D., Madan, M., & Gunasekaran, A. (2002). Successful implementation of ERP projects: Evidence from two case studies. *International Journal of Production Economics*, *75*(1-2), 83–96. doi:10.1016/S0925-5273(01)00183-9

Motwani, J., Subramanian, R., & Gopalakrishna, P. (2005). Critical factors for successful ERP implementation: Exploratory findings from four case studies. *Computers in Industry*, *56*(6), 529–544. doi:10.1016/j.compind.2005.02.005

Mumford, E. (2006). The story of socio-technical design: Reflections on its successes, failures and potential. *Information Systems Journal*, *16*(4), 317–342. doi:10.1111/j.1365-2575.2006.00221.x

Murray, P., & Carter, L. (2005). Improving marketing intelligence through learning systems and knowledge communities in not-for-profit workplaces. *Journal of Workplace Learning*, *17*(7), 421–435. doi:10.1108/13665620510620016

Muscatello, J. R., & Chen, I. (2008). Enterprise resource planning (ERP) implementations: Theory and practice. *International Journal of Enterprise Information Systems*, *4*(1), 63–78. doi:10.4018/jeis.2008010105

Muscatello, J. R., Small, M. H., & Chen, I. J. (2003). Implementing enterprise resource planning (ERP) systems in small and midsize manufacturing firms. *International Journal of Operations & Production Management*, *23*(8), 850–871. doi:10.1108/01443570310486329

Muse, D. (2016). *State of the CIO*. Retrieved from United States: http://core0.staticworld.net/assets/2016/01/14/2016-state-of-the-cio-executive-summary.pdf

Mustonen-Ollila, E., & Lyytinen, K. (2003). Why organizations adopt information system process innovations: A longitudinal study using Diffusion of Innovation theory. *Information Systems Journal*, *13*(3), 275–297. doi:10.1046/j.1365-2575.2003.00141.x

Myers, M. D. (1997). Qualitative research in information systems. *Management Information Systems Quarterly*, *21*(2), 241–242. doi:10.2307/249422

Myers, M. D. (2013). *Qualitative Research in Business and Management* (2nd ed.). London: Sage.

Nagarjuna, B., & Siddaiah, T. (2012). Impact of information Technology – Paradigm shifts in SCM. *Journal of Exclusive Management Science*, *1*(3), 1–7.

Nah, F., Lau, J., & Kuang, J. (2001). Critical Factors for Successful Implementation of Enterprise Systems. *Business Process Management Journal*, *7*(3), 285–296. doi:10.1108/14637150110392782

Nair, J., Reddy, D. B., & Samuel, A. A. (2014). Conceptualizing Dimensions of Enterprise Resource Planning Systems Success: A SocioTechnical Perspective. *International Journal of Enterprise Information Systems*, *10*(1), 53–75. doi:10.4018/ijeis.2014010104

Nandhakumar, J., Rossi, M., & Talvinen, J. (2005). The dynamics of contextual forces of ERP implementation. *The Journal of Strategic Information Systems*, *14*(2), 221–242. doi:10.1016/j.jsis.2005.04.002

NASCIO. (2015). *The 2015 State of CIO Survey*. Retrieved from http://www.nascio.org/Portals/0/Publications/Documents/2015/NASCIO_2015_State_CIO_Survey.pdf

Nasershariati, F., & Khan, A. (2011). *CRM system benefits A case study of the banking sector*. Malardalen University.

Nasir, A., Ruiz, F., & Palacios, M. (2013). Organisational learning, strategic rigidity and technology adoption: Implications for electric utilities and renewable energy firms. *Renewable & Sustainable Energy Reviews*, *22*, 438–445. doi:10.1016/j.rser.2013.01.039

Neely, A., Gregory, M., & Platts, K. (2005). Performance measurement system design. *International Journal of Operations & Production Management*, *25*(12), 1228–1263.

Negi, T., & Bansal, V. (2013). A Methodology to Bridge Information Gap in ERP Implementation Life Cycle. *International Journal of Enterprise Information Systems*, *9*(2), 70–82. doi:10.4018/jeis.2013040104

Nelson, R. R. (1991). Educational needs as perceived by IS and end-user personnel: A survey of knowledge and skill requirements. *Management Information Systems Quarterly*, *15*(4), 503–525. doi:10.2307/249454

Newman, I., Ridenore, C. S., & Ridenore, C. (1998). *Qualitative-Quantitative Research Methodology: Exploring the Interactive Continuum* (1st ed.). Southern Illinois University Press.

Nexedi, S. A. (2014). *How to fill the Category Spreadsheet*. Retrieved January 28, 2014, from http://www.erp5.com/P-CLOUDIA-Category.Spreadsheet.HowTo

Nexedi, S. A. (2015). *The cloud-consulting git repository*. Retrieved February 19, 2015, from http://git.erp5.org/gitweb/cloud-consulting.git?js=1

Ngai, E. W. T., Law, C. C. H., & Wat, F. (2008). Examining the critical success factors in the adoption of enterprise resource planning. *Computers in Industry*, *59*(6), 548–564. doi:10.1016/j.compind.2007.12.001

Ngai, E. W., & Gunasekaran, A. (2004). Implementation of EDI in Hong Kong: An empirical analysis. *Industrial Management & Data Systems*, *104*(1), 88–100. doi:10.1108/02635570410514124

Ng, C. S. (2012). A Case on ERP Custom Add-On in Taiwan: Implications to System Fit, Acceptance and Maintenance Costs. *International Journal of Enterprise Information Systems*, *8*(4), 44–62. doi:10.4018/jeis.2012100102

Ng, C. S. (2013). Exploring Relationships in Tailoring Option, Task Category, and Effort in ERP Software Maintenance. *International Journal of Enterprise Information Systems*, *9*(2), 83–105. doi:10.4018/jeis.2013040105

Nicolaides, V. C., LaPort, K. A., Chen, T. R., Tomassetti, A. J., Weis, E. J., Zaccaro, S. J., & Cortina, J. M. (2014). The shared leadership of teams: A meta-analysis of proximal, distal, and moderating relationships. *The Leadership Quarterly*, *25*(5), 923–942. doi:10.1016/j.leaqua.2014.06.006

Nicolaou, A. I. (2004). Firms performance effects in relation to the implementation and use of ERP system. *Journal of Information Systems*, *18*(2), 79–105. doi:10.2308/jis.2004.18.2.79

Niederman, F. (2001). Global information systems and human resource management: A research agenda. *Global Perspective of Information Technology Management*, 30.

Nijaz, B. (2005). Continuous computing technologies for improving performances of enterprise information systems. *International Journal of Enterprise Information Systems*, *1*(4), 70–89. doi:10.4018/jeis.2005100105

Njonko, P. B. F., Cardey, S., Greenfield, P., & El Abed, W. (2014). RuleCNL: A controlled natural language for business rule specifications. Lecture Notes in Computer Science, 8625, 66–77. http://doi.org/ doi:<ALIGNMENT.qj></ALIGNMENT>10.1007/978-3-319-10223-8_7

Nonaka, I., & Takeuchi, H. (1995). The Knowledge Creating Company. Oxford University Press.

Northouse, P. G. (2007). *Leadership Theory and Practice* (4th ed.). Sage Publishing.

Nour, M. A., & Mouakket, S. (2011). A classification framework of critical success factors for erp systems implementation: A multi-stakeholder perspective. *International Journal of Enterprise Information Systems*, *7*(1), 56–71. doi:10.4018/jeis.2011010104

Nucleus Research. (2011). *IBM ROI Case Study: Becker Underwood*. Retrieved from http://www.nucleusresearch.com/research/roi-case-studies/ibm-roicase-study-becker-underwood/Becker%20Underwoo

Nunnally, J. C. (1970). *Introduction to Psychological Measurement*. New York: McGraw-Hill.

Nunnally, J. C. (1978). *Psychometric Theory*. McGraw-Hill.

Nwankpa, J. K. (2015). ERP system usage and benefit: A model of antecedents and outcomes. *Computers in Human Behavior*, *45*, 335–344. doi:10.1016/j.chb.2014.12.019

Offermann, P., Levina, O., Schönherr, M., & Bub, U. (2009). Outline of a design science research process. In *Proceedings of the 4th International Conference on Design Science Research in Information Systems and Technology* (Vol. 7, pp. 1–11). New York, NY: ACM. http://doi.org/ doi:10.1145/1555619.1555629

Office of Management and Budget. (1997). *Memorandum for the Heads of Executive Departments and Agencies, M-97-16, 18 June*. Retrieved from http://www.whitehouse.gov/omb/memoranda_m97-16/

Okrent, M. D., & Vokurka, R. J. (2004). Process mapping in successful ERP implementations. *Industrial Management & Data Systems*, *104*(8), 637–643. doi:10.1108/02635570410561618

Oldenborgh, M. V. (1994). Distribution superhighway. *International Business*, *7*(6), 80–84.

Oliva, R., & Kallenberg, R. (2003). Managing the transition from products to services. *International Journal of Service Industry Management*, *14*(2), 160–172. doi:10.1108/09564230310474138

Oliver, S., & Kandadi, K. R. (2006). How to develop knowledge culture in organizations? A multiple case study of large distributed organizations. *Journal of Knowledge Management*, *10*(4), 6–24. doi:10.1108/13673270610679336

Olson, D. L., Chae, B., & Sheu, C. (2005). Issues in multinational ERP Implementations. *International Journal of Services and Operations Management*, *1*(1), 7–21. doi:10.1504/IJSOM.2005.006314

Omar, N., Hanna, P., & Kevitt, P. M. (2006). Semantic Analysis in the Automation of ER Modelling through Natural Language Processing. In *International Conference Computing & Informatics, ICOCI, Kuala Lumpur* (pp. 2–6). doi:10.1109/ICOCI.2006.5276559

OpenERP SA. (2014). *Managing your Customers*. Retrieved January 27, 2014, from https://doc.openerp.com/book/2/3_CRM_Contacts/contacts/#categorizing-your-partners

OReilly, C. A., & Chatman, J. (1986). Organizational commitment and psychological attachment: The effects of compliance, identification, and internalization on prosocial behavior. *The Journal of Applied Psychology*, *71*(3), 492–499. doi:10.1037/0021-9010.71.3.492

Orlikowski, W., & Hoffman, D. (1997). *An Improvisational Model for Change Management: The Case of Groupware Technologies. In Inventing the Organizations of the 21st Century* (pp. 265–282). Boston, MA: MIT.

OSOE Project. (2014). *ERP: Theory, Practice and Configuration*. Retrieved February 22, 2014, from http://www.osoe-project.org/lesson/osoe-Lecture.ERP.Configuration. Introduction

OSOE Project. (2015). *OSOE Meetings*. Retrieved February 19, 2014, from http://www.osoe-project.org/meeting

Österle, H., Becker, J., Fank, U., Hess, T., Karagiannis, D., Krcmar, H., & Sinz, E. et al. (2010). Memorandum on design-oriented information systems research. *Journal of Information Systems*, *20*(1), 7–10. doi:10.1057/ejis.2010.55

OSullivan, H., & McKimm, J. (2011). Doctor as professional and doctor as leader: Same attributes, attitudes and values? *British Journal of Hospital Medicine*, *72*(8), 463–466. doi:10.12968/hmed.2011.72.8.463 PMID:21841592

Palmer, E., & Eveline, J. (2012).Sustaining low pay in aged care work. *Gender, Work and Organization*, *19*, 254–275.

Palmer, R. C. (1995). *The Bar Code Book: Reading, Printing and Specification of Bar Code Symbols* (3rd ed.). Helmers Publishing Inc.

Palvia, S. C., Sharma, R. S., & Conrath, D. W. (2001). A Socio-Technical Framework for Quality Assessment of Computer Information Systems. *Industrial Management & Data Systems*, *101*(5), 237–251. doi:10.1108/02635570110394635

Pandey, D. S. K., & Devasagayam, D. R. (2010). *Responsiveness as Antecedent of Satisfaction and Referrals in Financial Services Marketing*. Paper presented at the 10th Global Conference on Business & Economics.

Pan, G., Hackney, R., & Pan, S. (2008). Information Systems implementation failure: Insights from prism. *International Journal of Information Management*, *28*(4), 259–269. doi:10.1016/j.ijinfomgt.2007.07.001

Panian, Ž., & Ćurko, K. (2010). *Poslovni informacijski sustavi*. Zagreb: Sveučilište u Zagrebu.

Pan, S. L. (2005). Customer perspective of CRM Systems: A Focus Group Study. *International Journal of Enterprise Information Systems*, *1*(1), 65–68. doi:10.4018/jeis.2005010105

Pant, P. (2009). *Business Intelligence: How to build successful BI strategy*. Deloitte Consulting. Available at http://www.deloitte.com/assets/Dcom-SouthAfrica/Local%20Assets/Documents/Business%20intelligence%20that%20aligns%20with%20enterprise%20goals.pdf

Papazafeiropoulou, A., & Pouloudi. (2000). The government role in improving EC adoption. *Proceedings of European Conference on Information Systems*, 709-716.

Parasuraman, A., & Zeithaml, V. (2002). Measuring and Improving Service Quality:A Literature Reviewand Research Agenda. In B. Weitz (Ed.), *Handbook of Marketing*. Thousand Oaks, CA: Sage. doi:10.4135/9781848608283.n15

Parasuraman, A., Zeithaml, V., & Berry, L. (1988). SERVQUAL: A multiple-item scale for measuring consumer perceptions of service quality. *Journal of Retailing*, *64*(1), 12–40.

Parasuraman, A., Zeithaml, V., & Malhotra, A. (2005). E-S-Qual. A multiple-item Sclae for Assessing Electronic Service Quality. *Journal of Service Research*, 1–21.

Parr, A. N., & Shanks, G. (2000). A Taxonomy of ERP Implementation Approaches.*Proceedings of the 33rd Hawaii International Conference on System Sciences*, 1-10.

Parthasarathy, S., & Anbazhagan, N. (2007). Evaluating ERP implementation choices using AHP. *International Journal of Enterprise Information Systems, 3*(3), 52–65. doi:10.4018/jeis.2007070104

Parvatiyar, A., & Sheth, J. N. (2001). Conceptual framework of customer relationship management. In *Customer Relationship Management* (pp. 3–25). Emerging Concepts, Tools and Applications.

Pathak, J., & Vidyarthi, N. (2011). Cost Framework for Evaluation of Information Technology Alternatives in Supply Chain. *International Journal of Strategic Decision Sciences, 2*(1), 66–84. doi:10.4018/jsds.2011010104

Patro, C. S., & Raghunath, K. M. K. (2015). Impetus to Supply Chain Decisions with IT Tools: An Empirical Study. *International Journal of Enterprise Information Systems, 11*(3), 52–67. doi:10.4018/IJEIS.2015070104

Patterson, K. A., Grimm, C. M., & Corsi, T. M. (2003). Adopting new technologies for supply chain management. *Transportation Research Part E, Logistics and Transportation Review, 39*(2), 95–121. doi:10.1016/S1366-5545(02)00041-8

Patton, M. Q. (2002). *Qualitative evaluation and research methods* (3rd ed.). Thousand Oaks, CA: Sage Publications Inc.

Patton, Q. M. (1990). *Qualitative Evaluation and Research Methods* (2nd ed.). Sage Publications.

Paulraj, A., & Chen, I. J. (2005). Strategic supply management: Theory and practice. *International Journal of Integrated Supply Management, 1*(4), 457–477. doi:10.1504/IJISM.2005.006306

Pavlić, M. (2009). *Informacijski sustavi*. Rijeka: Odjel za informatiku Sveučilišta u Rijeci.

Pavlić, M. (2011). *Oblikovanje baza podataka*. Rijeka: Odjel za informatiku Sveučilišta u Rijeci.

Pavlić, M., Dovedan, H. Z., & Jakupović, A. (2015). Question Answering with a Conceptual Framework for Knowledge-Based System Development Node of Knowledge.. *Expert Systems with Applications, 42*(12), 5264–5286. doi:10.1016/j.eswa.2015.02.024

Pavlić, M., Jakupović, A., & Meštrović, A. (2013). Nodes of knowledge method for knowledge representation. *Informatologia., 46*(3), 206–214.

Pavlić, M., Meštrović, A., & Jakupović, A. (2013). Graph-Based Formalisms for Knowledge Representation. In *Proceedings of the 17th World Multi-Conference on Systemics Cybernetics and Informatics (WMSCI 2013)* (pp. 200–204).

Pawar, B. S. (2009). *Theory building for hypothesis specification in organizational studies*. Sage Publications.

Pearce, C. L., Manz, C. C., & Sims, H. P. Jr. (2009). Where Do We Go From Here?: Is Shared Leadership the Key to Team Success? *Organizational Dynamics, 38*(3), 234–238. doi:10.1016/j.orgdyn.2009.04.008

Peffers, K., Rothenberger, M., Tuunanen, T., & Vaezi, R. (2012). Design science research evaluation. In K. Peffers, M. Rothenberger, & B. Kuechler (Eds.), *Design science research in information systems. Advances in theory and practice* (Vol. 7286, pp. 398–410). Heidelberg, Germany: Springer. doi:10.1007/978-3-642-29863-9_29

Peffers, K., Tuunanen, T., Rothenberger, M., & Chatterjee, S. (2007). A Design Science Research Methodology for Information Systems Research. *Journal of Management Information Systems, 24*(3), 45–77. doi:10.2753/MIS0742-1222240302

Peppers, D., & Rogers, M. (1999). *The One to One Manager: Real-World Lessons in Customer Relationship Management*. Academic Press.

Pereira, J. V. (2009). The new supply chains frontier: Information management. *International Journal of Information Management, 29*(5), 372–379. doi:10.1016/j.ijinfomgt.2009.02.001

Pereira, R., & Mira da Silva, M. (2012). Designing a new integrated it governance and it management framework based on both scientific and practitioner viewpoint. *International Journal of Enterprise Information Systems, 8*(4), 1–43. doi:10.4018/jeis.2012100101

Peristeras, V., & Tarabanis, K. (2000). Towards an enterprise architecture for public administration using a top- down approach. *European Journal of Information Systems, 9*(4), 252–260. doi:10.1057/palgrave.ejis.3000378

Perks, C., & Beveridge, T. (2003). *A guide to enterprise architecture*. Berlin: Springer-Verlag.

Peslak, A. R. (2012). Industry variables affecting ERP success and Status. *International Journal of Enterprise Information Systems, 8*(3), 15–30. doi:10.4018/jeis.2012070102

Peterson, D. M., Gröne, D. F., Kammer, D. K., & Kirscheneder, J. (2009). *Multi-Channel Customer Management Delighting Consumers, Driving Efficiency*. Information Technology, Marketing & Sales.

Petter, S., DeLone, W., & McLean, E. (2008). Measuring information systems success: Model, dimensions, measures and interrelationship. *European Journal of Information Systems, 17*(3), 236–263. doi:10.1057/ejis.2008.15

Pheysey, D. C. (1993). *Organizational Cultures: Types and Transformation*. New York: Rutledge. doi:10.4324/9780203028568

Pigni, F., Ravarini, A., Sciuto, D., Zanaboni, C. A., & Burn, J. (2005). Business Associations as Hubs of Inter-Organizational Information Systems for SMEs – The 2Cities Portal. In S. B. Eom (Ed.), *Inter-organizational Information Systems in the Internet Age* (pp. 134–168). doi:10.4018/978-1-59140-318-0.ch006

Pinnington, A. (2011). Leadership Development: Applying the same leadership theories and development practices to different contexts? *Leadership, 7*(3), 335–365. doi:10.1177/1742715011407388

Pinto, J., & Millet, I. (1999). *Successful Information Systems Implementation*. Project Management Institute.

Plant, R., & Willcocks, L. (2007). Critical success factor in international ERP implementation: A case research approach. *Journal of Computer Information Systems, 47*(3), 60–70.

Plant, R., & Willcocks, L. (2007). Critical success factors in international ERP implementations: A case research approach. *Journal of Computer Information Systems, 47*, 60–71.

Podsakoff, P. M., & Organ, D. W. (1986). Self-reports in organizational research: Problems and prospects. *Journal of Management, 12*(4), 531–544. doi:10.1177/014920638601200408

Podsakoff, P., MacKenzie, S., Lee, J., & Podsakoff, N. (2003). Common method biases in behavioural research: A critical review of the literature and recommended remedies. *The Journal of Applied Psychology, 88*(5), 879–890. doi:10.1037/0021-9010.88.5.879 PMID:14516251

Polansky, M., Inuganti, T., & Wiggins, S. (2004). The 21st Century CIO. *Business Strategy Review, 15*(2), 29–33. doi:10.1111/j.0955-6419.2004.00310.x

Popay, J., Roberts, H., Sowden, A., Petticrew, M., Arai, L., Roen, K., & Rodgers, M. (2004). *Guidance on the conduct of narrative synthesis in systematic reviews. Draft report from ESRC Methods Programme*. Lancaster, UK: Institute for Health Research, University of Lancaster.

Porter, M. E., & Millar, V. E. (1985). *How information gives you competitive advantage*. Academic Press.

Porter, M. E., & Millar, V. E. (1985). How information gives you competitive advantage. *Harvard Business Review, 63*(4), 149–160.

Poston, R., & Grabski, S. (2001). Financial impacts of enterprise resource planning implementation. *International Journal of AIS*, *2*(4), 271–294.

Poutanen, J. (2012). The social dimension of enterprise architecture in government. *Journal of Enterprise Architecture*, *8*(2), 19–29.

Prabhaker, P. (2001). Integrating Marketing-manufacturing Strategies. *Journal of Business and Industrial Marketing*, *16*(2), 113–128. doi:10.1108/08858620110384141

Prahalad, C. K., & Ramaswamy, V. (2004b). Co-creation experiences: The next practice in value creation. *Journal of Interactive Marketing*, *18*(3), 5–14. doi:10.1002/dir.20015

Prasad, R. (2007). IT Enabled Supply Chain Management. *Serbian Journal of Management*, *2*(1), 47–56.

Prat, N., Comyn-Wattiau, I., & Akoka, J. (2014). Artifact Evaluation in Informtion Systems Design-Science Research–A Holistic View. *18th Pacific Asia Conference on Information Systems*.

Premkumar, G., & Ramamurthy, K. (1995). The role of inter-organizational and organizational factors on the decision mode for adoption of inter-organizational systems. *Decision Sciences*, *26*(3), 303–336. doi:10.1111/j.1540-5915.1995.tb01431.x

Preston, D. (2003). Shared mental models between the CIO and CEO: Towards information systems strategic alignment. *AMCIS 2003 Proceedings*, 452.

Preston, D. S., Chen, D., & Leidner, D. E. (2008). Examining the Antecedents and Consequences of CIO Strategic Decision-Making Authority: An Empirical Study. *Decision Sciences*, *39*(4), 605–642. doi:10.1111/j.1540-5915.2008.00206.x

Prewitt, E., & Ware, L. G. (2006). *The STATE of the CIO '06*. CIO Magazine.

Pries-Heje, J., Richard, B., & Venable, J. (2008). *Strategies for Design Science Research Evaluation*. ECIS.

Pries-Heje, L. (2008). Time, attitude, and user participation: How prior events determine user attitudes in ERP implementation. *International Journal of Enterprise Information Systems*, *4*(3), 48–65. doi:10.4018/jeis.2008070104

Princeton University. (2010). *About WordNet*. Retrieved February 13, 2014, from http://wordnet.princeton.edu

Productivity Commission. (2011). *Caring for Older Australians*. Report No. 53. Final Inquiry Report, Canberra.

Quinn, J., & Hilmer, F. (1994). Strategic Outsourcing. *Sloan Management Review*, 43–45.

Quintane, E., Casselman, R. M., Reiche, B. S., & Nylund, P. A. (2011). Innovation as a knowledge-based outcome. *Journal of Knowledge Management*, *15*(6), 928–947. doi:10.1108/13673271111179299

Quirk, R., Greenbaum, S., Leech, G., & Svartvik, J. (1985). *A comprehensive grammar of the English language*. New York: Longman Inc.

Raber, D., Wortmann, F., & Winter, R. (2013). Towards The Measurement Of Business Intelligence Maturity. *Proceedings of ECIS 2013*.

Radhakrishnan, A., David, D., Hales, D., & Sridharan, V. S. (2011). Mapping the Critical Links between Supply Chain Evaluation System and Supply Chain Integration Sustainability: An Empirical Study. *International Journal of Strategic Decision Sciences*, *2*(1), 44–65. doi:10.4018/jsds.2011010103

Rai, A., Patnayakuni, R., & Patnayakuni, N. (2006). Firm performance impacts of digitally enabled supply chain integration capabilities. *Management Information Systems Quarterly*, *30*(2), 225–246.

Rajapakse, J., & Seddon, P. (2005). Why ERP may not suitable for organizations in developing countries?*Proceedings of PACIS.*

Rajendran, R., & Elangovan, N. (2012). Response of small enterprise to the pressure of ERP adoption. *International Journal of Enterprise, 8*(1), 28–50. doi:10.4018/jeis.2012010103

Ramirez, P., & Garcia, R. (2005). Successful ERP in Chile: An empirical study. *Proceedings of European, Mediterranean and Middle Eastern Conference on Information System.*

Ram, J., & Corkindale, D. (2014). How critical are the critical success factors (CSFs)? *Business Process Management Journal, 20*(1), 151–174. doi:10.1108/BPMJ-11-2012-0127

Ram, J., Corkindale, D., & Wu, M.-L. (2013). Implementation critical success factors (CSFs) for ERP: Do they contribute to implementation success and post-implementation performance? *International Journal of Production Economics, 144*(1), 157–174. doi:10.1016/j.ijpe.2013.01.032

Ramthun, A. J., & Matkin, G. S. (2012). Multicultural shared leadership a conceptual model of shared leadership in culturally diverse teams. *Journal of Leadership & Organizational Studies, 19*(3), 303–314. doi:10.1177/1548051812444129

Randall, W. S., Wittmann, C. M., Nowicki, D. R., & Pohlen, T. L. (2014). Service-dominant logic and supply chain management: Are we there yet? *International Journal of Physical Distribution & Logistics Management, 44*(1/2), 113–131. doi:10.1108/IJPDLM-11-2012-0331

Rashid, M., Hossain, L., & Patrick, J. (2001). The Evolution of ERP Systems: A Historical Perspective. In L. Hossain, J. Patrick, & M. Rashid (Eds.), *Enterprise Resource Planning: Global Opportunities & Challenges* (pp. 1–16). Idea Group Publishing.

Ravasan, A. Z., & Mansouri, T. (2014). A FCM-Based Dynamic Modeling of ERP Implementation Critical Failure Factors. *International Journal of Enterprise Information Systems, 10*(1), 32–52. doi:10.4018/ijeis.2014010103

Ravasan, A. Z., & Rouhani, S. (2014). An Expert System for Predicting ERP Post-Implementation Benefits Using Artificial Neural Network. *International Journal of Enterprise Information Systems, 10*(3), 24–45. doi:10.4018/ijeis.2014070103

Raymond, L. (1985).Organizational characteristics and MIS success in the context of small business. *Management Information Systems Quarterly, 9*(1), 37–52.

Reich, B. H., & Nelson, K. (2003). In Their Own Words: CIO Visions About the Future of In House IT Organizations. *The Data Base for Advances in Information Systems, 34*(4), 28–44. doi:10.1145/957758.957763

Reinartz, W., Krafft, M., & Hoyer, W. D. (2004). The Customer Relationship Management Process: Its measurement and impact on performance. *JMR, Journal of Marketing Research, 41*(3), 293–305. doi:10.1509/jmkr.41.3.293.35991

Remneland-Wikhamn, B. (2011). Path dependence as a barrier for Soft and Open innovation. *International Journal of Business Innovation and Research, 5*(6), 714–730. doi:10.1504/IJBIR.2011.043207

Research, A. M. R. (2005). *The steady stream of ERP investment.* Retrieved from www.amrresearch.com

Resource International. (2009). *Decision Making and Resolving Conflicts in Teams.* Retrieved from http://www.resource-i.com

Reynolds, A. (2009). *The Myer Foundation 2020: A Vision for Aged Care in Australia.* Fitzroy, Victoria, Australia: Outcomes Review, Brotherhood of St Laurence.

Richardson, G., Jackson, B., & Dickson, G. (1990). A principles-based enterprise architecture: Lessons from Texaco and Star Enterprise. *Management Information Systems Quarterly, 14*(4), 385–403. doi:10.2307/249787

Richmond, B. (1993). Systems thinking: Critical thinking skills for the 1990s and beyond. *System Dynamics Review*, *9*(2), 113–133. doi:10.1002/sdr.4260090203

Riege, A. (2005). Three dozen knowledge sharing barriers managers must consider. *Journal of Knowledge Management*, *9*(3), 18–35. doi:10.1108/13673270510602746

Rivard, S. (Ed.). (2004). *Information Technology and Organizational Transformation: Solving the Management Puzzle*. Oxford, UK: Elsevier Butterworth-Heinemann.

Robbins-Gioia, L. L. C. (2006). *ERP survey result: Point to need for higher implementation success*. Retrieved from http://www.robbinsgioia.com/news_events/012802_esp.aspx.march

Robey, D., & Boudreau, M. C. (1999). Accounting for the Contradictory Organizational Consequences of Information Technology: Theoretical Directions and Methodological Implications. *Information Systems Research*, *10*(2), 167–185. doi:10.1287/isre.10.2.167

Rockart, F. (1979). Chief executives define their own data needs. *Harvard Business Review*, *57*, 81–93. PMID:10297607

Rockart, J. F., Earl, M. J., & Ross, J. W. (1996). Eight imperatives for the new IT organization. *MIT Sloan Management Review*, *38*(1), 43.

Rockart, J. F., & Flannery, L. S. (1983). The management of end-user computing. *Communications of the ACM*, *26*(10), 776–784. doi:10.1145/358413.358429

Roeleven, S. (2008). *Why two thirds of enterprise architecture projects fail* [Electronic version]. ARIS Expert Paper. Retrieved from http://www.softwareag.com

Rohm Andrew, J, S. V. (2004). A typology of online shoppers based on shopping motivations. *Journal of Business Research*, *57*(7).

Rolf, S. (2010). Controlled Natural Languages for Knowledge Representation. In *COLING '10, Proceedings of the 23rd International Conference on Computational Linguistics*, (pp. 1113–1121).

Romano, & Fjermestad. (2003). Electronic commerce customer relationship management. *Information Technology and Management, 4*(2-3), 233-258.

Romero, D., & Vernadat, F. (2016). Enterprise information systems state of the art: Past, present and future trends. *Computers in Industry*, *79*, 3–13. doi:10.1016/j.compind.2016.03.001

Rose, J., Jones, M., & Truex, D. (2005). Socio-Theoretic Accounts of IS: The Problem of Agency. *Scandinavian Journal of Information Systems*, *17*(1), 133–152.

Ross, J. W. (1998), *The ERP Revolution: Surviving Versus Thriving*. Centre for Information Systems Research, Research Report, CISR Working Paper No. 307, Sloan School of Management.

Ross, J. (2003). Creating a strategic IT architecture competency: Learning in stages. *MIS Quarterly Executive, 2*(1), 31–43.

Ross, J. W., & Beath, C. M. (2006). Sustainable IT outsourcing success: Let enterprise architecture be your guide. *MIS Quarterly Executive*, *5*(4), 181–192.

Ross, J. W., Beath, C. M., & Goodhue, D. L. (1996). Develop Long-Term Competitiveness Through IT Assets. *Sloan Management Review*, *38*(1), 31–65.

Ross, J. W., & Feeny, D. F. (1999). *The Evolving Role of the CIO. In Framing the Domain of IT Research: Glimpsing the Future Through the Past*. Cincinnati, OH: Pinnaflex Educational Resources Inc.

Ross, J., Weill, P., & Robertson, D. (2006). *Enterprise architecture as strategy: Creating a foundation for execution.* Boston: Harvard Business School Press.

Rowland, P., & Parry, K. (2009). Consensual commitment: A grounded theory of the meso-level influence of organizational design on leadership and decision-making. *The Leadership Quarterly, 20*(4), 535–553. doi:10.1016/j.leaqua.2009.04.004

Rozanski, N., & Woods, E. (2007). *Software systems architecture – Working with stakeholders using viewpoints and perspectives.* Upper Saddle River, NJ: Addison-Wesley.

Rubin, H. J., & Rubin, I. S. (2005). *Qualitative interviewing: The art of hearing data* (2nd ed.). Thousand Oaks, CA: Sage. doi:10.4135/9781452226651

Rushforth, J. A. (2007). *Maximizing relationship value with CRM systems: why commercial banks need to move beyond contact management to true customer relationship management.* Retrieved 10/30/2012, 2012, from http://www.access-mylibrary.com/article-1G1-158960824/maximizing-relationship-value-crm.html

Rushton, A., Oxley, J., & Croucher, P. (2000). *IT in the supply chain. The Handbook of Logistics and Distribution Management.* Bell & Bain Ltd., Glasgow.

Rusu, L., Mekawy, M., & Hodosi, G. (2009). Information Technology Leadership in Swedish Leading Multinational Corporations. In M. Lytras, E. Damiani, J. Carroll, R. Tennyson, D. Avison, A. Naeve, & G. Vossen et al. (Eds.), *Visioning and Engineering the Knowledge Society. A Web Science Perspective* (Vol. 5736, pp. 511–522). Springer Berlin Heidelberg. doi:10.1007/978-3-642-04754-1_52

Ryals, & Knox. (2001). Cross-Functional Issues in the Implementation of Relationship Marketing Through Customer Relationship Management. *European Management Journal, 19*, 534-542.

Sabherwal, R., & Robey, D. (1993). An Empirical Taxonomy of Implementation Processes Based on Sequences of Events in Information Systems Development. *Organization Science, 4*(4), 548–576. doi:10.1287/orsc.4.4.548

Sage, A. P., & Biemer, S. M. (2007, September). Processes for system family architecting, design, and integration. *IEEE Systems Journal, 1*(1).

Sahay, B. (2002). *Supply Chain Management in the Twenty First Century.* Macmillan Publishers.

Sajja, P. S., & Akerkar, R. (2010). Knowledge-Based Systems for Development. In P. S. Sajja & R. Akerkar (Eds.), *Advanced Knowledge Based Systems: Model, Applications & Research* (Vol. 1, pp. 1 11). Sudbury, MA: Jones & Bartlett Publishers.

Salipante, P., & Aram, J. D. (2003). Managers as knowledgeable generators: The nature of practitioner-scholar research in the non-profit sector. *Nonprofit Management & Leadership, 14*(2), 129–150. doi:10.1002/nml.26

Salo, J., & Karjaluoto, H. (2006). IT-Enabled Supply Chain Management. *Contemporary Management Research, 2*(1), 17–30. doi:10.7903/cmr.76

Sambamurthy, V., & Zmud, R. W. (1992). *Managing IT for success: The empowering business partnership.* Morristown, NJ: Financial Executives Research Foundation.

Sammon, D., & Finnegan, P. (2000). The ten commandments of data warehousing. *ACM SIGMIS Database, 31*(4), 82–91. doi:10.1145/506760.506767

Sammon, D., & Hanley, P. (2007). Case Study: Becoming a 100 per cent e-corporation: benefits of pursuing an e-supply chain strategy. *Supply Chain Management, 12*(4), 297–303. doi:10.1108/13598540710759817

Sanders, N. R., & Premus, R. (2002). IT applications in supply chain organizations: A link between competitive priorities and organizational benefits. *Journal of Business Logistics, 23*(1), 65–83. doi:10.1002/j.2158-1592.2002.tb00016.x

Sanin, C., & Szczerbicki, E. (2006). Using set of experience in the process of transforming information into knowledge. *International Journal of Enterprise Information Systems, 2*(2), 45–62. doi:10.4018/jeis.2006040104

Sankaran, S., Cartwright, C., Kelly, J., Shaw, K., & Soar, J. (2010). Leadership of non-profit organisations in the aged care sector in Australia. *Proceedings of the 54th meeting of the International Society for the Systems Sciences.*

Sankar, C. S. (2010). Factors that improve ERP implementation strategies in an organization. *International Journal of Enterprise Information Systems, 6*(2), 15–34. doi:10.4018/jeis.2010040102

Santos, C. (2009). *Modelo conceptual para auditoria organizacional contínua com análise em tempo real.* Penafiel: Editorial Novembro.

SAP AG. (2014). *Territory Hierarchy.* Retrieved January 28, 2014, from http://help.sap.com/saphelp_crm70/helpdata/en/de/d2fab855024f8d936fea84e9b9b551/content.htm

SAP. (2014). *Regional information and user groups.* Retrieved October 14, 2014 from https://websmp107.sap-ag.de/public/usergroups/list

Sarker, S. (2000). Toward a Methodology for Managing Information Systems Implementation: A Social Constructivist Perspective. *Informing Science, 3*(4), 195–205.

Sarkis, J., & Sundarraj, R. P. (2003). Managing largescale global enterprise resource planning systems: A case study at Texas Instruments. *International Journal of Information Management, 23*(6), 431–442. doi:10.1016/S0268-4012(03)00070-7

Sarmento, A. (Ed.). (2004). Preface. In Issues of human computer interaction. IGI Global.

Sarvari, P. A., Ustundag, A., & Takci, H. (2016). Performance evaluation of different customer segmentation approaches based on RFM and demographics analysi. *Kybernetes, 45*(7), 1129–1157. doi:10.1108/K-07-2015-0180

Sathish, S., Pan, S. L., & Raman, K. S. (2002). *Customer relationship management (CRM) network: A new approach to studying CRM.* Paper presented at the Eighth Americas Conference on Information Systems (AMCIS), Dallas, TX.

Saunders, C. S., & Clark, S. (1992). EDI adoption and implementation: A focus on inter-organizational linkages. *Information Resources Management Journal, 5*(1), 9–19. doi:10.4018/irmj.1992010102

Saunière, J.-C. (2013). Innovation that counts. PriceWaterhouseCoopers.

Sauter, V. L. (2005). Competitive intelligence systems: Qualitative DSS for strategic decision making. *ACM SIGMIS Database, 36*(2), 43–57. doi:10.1145/1066149.1066154

Schaffnit, C., Rosen, D., & Paradi, G. (1997). Best Practice Analysis of Bank Branches: An Application of DEA in a Large Canadian Bank. *European Journal of Operational Research, 98*(2), 269–289. doi:10.1016/S0377-2217(96)00347-5

Schein, E. H. (2010). Organizational culture and Leadership (4th ed.). John Wiley & Sons.

Schekkerman, J. (2004b). *Trends in enterprise architecture: How are organizations progressing?* Amersfoort, Netherlands: Institute for Enterprise Architecture Developments.

Schmenner, R. (1986). How can services businesses Survive and prosper? *Sloan Management Review, 27*(3), 21–32. PMID:10300742

Schmidt, C., & Buxman, P. (2011). Outcomes and success factors of enterprise IT architecture management: Empirical insight from the international financial services industry. *European Journal of Information Systems*, 20(2), 168–185. doi:10.1057/ejis.2010.68

Schneider, M. (2003). *Radio Frequency Identification (RFID) Technology and its Applications in the Commercial Construction Industry* (Thesis). University of Kentucky.

Schultz, R. L., Ginzberg, M. J., & Lucas, H. C. (1984). A structural model of implementation. In R. L. Schultz & M. J. Ginzberg (Eds.), *Management Science Implementation*. Greenwich, CT: JAI Press.

Scupola, A. (2003). Government intervention in SMEs e-Commerce adoption: An institutional approach. *Proceedings of 7th Pacific Asia Conference on Information Systems*, 184-195.

Seah, T. S., & Fjermestad, J. (1997). *Roles of government and the private sector: Electronic Commerce in Singapore*. Retrieved from http://www.hsb.baylor.edu/ramsower/ais.ac.97/papers/seah.htm

Sebastiani, F. (2002). Machine learning in automated text categorization. *ACM Computing Surveys*, 34(1), 1-47.

Seddon, P. B., Calvert, C., & Yong, S. (2010). A multi-project model of key factors affecting organizational benefits from enterprise systems. *Management Information Systems Quarterly*, 34(2), 305–328.

Sedra, D., & Tan, F. (2005). User Satisfaction: an overarching measure of enterprise systems success. Proceedings of the PACIS.

Seethmraju, R., & Seethmraju, J. (2008). Adoption of ERP in a middle-sized enterprise: A case Study. *Proceedings of 19th Australasian Conference on Information Systems*.

Segars, A. H. (1997). Assessing the unidimensionality of measurement: A paradigm and illustration within the context of information systems research. *Omega*, 25(1), 107–121. doi:10.1016/S0305-0483(96)00051-5

Sellitto, C. (2012). The Activities of the Chief Information Officer as Noted through Job Position Descriptions. *Communications of the IBIMA*, 19. doi:10.5171/2012.369727

Selway, M., Grossmann, G., Mayer, W., & Stumptner, M. (2015). Formalising natural language specifications using a cognitive linguistic/configuration based approach. *Information Systems*, 54, 191–208. doi:10.1016/j.is.2015.04.003

Senge, P. M. (1990). *The Fifth Dimension - The Art and Patience of The Learning Organisation*. New York: Doubleday.

Senge, P. M., Roberts, C., Ross, R. B., Smith, B. J., & Kleinter, A. (1994). *The Fifth Discipline Field Book: Strategies and Tools for Building a Learning Organisation*. New York: Doubleday.

Seppänen, V. (2009). *Experiences on enterprise architecture work in government administration*. Retrieved from www.vm.fi/vm/en/04_publications_and_documents/01_publications/04_public_management/20090121Experi/ name.jsp

Seyal, A. H., & Rahman, M. N. (2002). *Research report on Electronic Commerce adoption in small and medium enterprises in Brunei Darussalam*. Institut Teknologi Brunei.

Seyal, A. H., & Rahman, M. N. (2003). A preliminary investigation of E-Commerce adoption in small and medium enterprises in Brunei. *Journal of Global Information Technology Management*, 6(2), 6–26. doi:10.1080/1097198X.2003.10856347

Seyal, A. H., Rahman, M. N., & Mohamad, H. A. Y. (2007). A Quantitative analysis of factors contributing towards EDI adoption among Bruneian SMEs: A pilot study. *Business Process Management Journal*, 3(5), 728–746. doi:10.1108/14637150710823183

Shahbaz, M., Ahsan, S., Shaheen, M., & Nawab, R. M. A. (2011). Automatic Generation of Extended ER Diagram Using Natural Language Processing. *Journal of American Science, 7*(8).

Shaker, Xahar, & Hayton. (2004, Summer). Entrepreneurship in Family vs. Non-Family Companies. *Entrepreneurship Theory & Practice.*

Shank, G., Parr, A., Hu, B., Corbitt, B., Thanasankit, T., & Seddon, P. (2000). Difference in critical success factors in ERP systems implementation in Australia and China: A cultural analysis.*Proceedings of the 8th European Conference on Information Systems*, 537-549.

Sharma, R., & Yetton, P. (2003). The contingent effects of management support and task interdependence on successful information systems implementation. *MIS Quarterly, 27*(4), 533-555.

Shaul, L., & Tauber, D. (2013). Critical success factors in enterprise resource planning systems: Review of the last decade. *ACM Computing Surveys, 45*(4), 4. doi:10.1145/2501654.2501669

Shaw, B. (2010). *Enterprise architecture – Will yours fail?* Retrieved from http://www.itprojecttemplates.com/ WP_EA_Will_Yours_Fail.htm

Shehab, E. M., Sharp, M. W., Supramaniam, L., & Spedding, T. A. (2004). Enterprise resource planning: An integrative review. *Business Process Management Journal, 10*(4), 359–386. doi:10.1108/14637150410548056

Shen, Y., Chen, P., & Wang, P. (2015). A study of enterprise resource planning (ERP) system performance measurement using the quantitative balanced scorecard approach. *Computers in Industry, 75*, 127–139. doi:10.1016/j.compind.2015.05.006

Sherman, H., & Zhu, J. (2006). *Improving Service Performance using Data Envelopment Analysis (DEA).* Springer.

Sheu, C., Chae, C., & Yang, C. (2004). National differences in ERP implementations: Issues and challenges. *Omega, 32*(5), 61–371. doi:10.1016/j.omega.2004.02.001

Shieu, W. L., Hsu, P. Y., & Wang, J. Z. (2009). Development of measures to assess the ERP adoption of small and medium enterprises. *Journal of Enterprise Information Management, 22*(1/2), 99–118. doi:10.1108/17410390910922859

Shostack, L. (1987). Service Positioning through Structural Change. *Journal of Marketing, 51*(1), 34. doi:10.2307/1251142

Shoval, P., & Shiran, S. (1997). Entity-relationship and object-oriented data modeling — An experimental comparison of design quality. *Data & Knowledge Engineering, 21*(3), 297–315. doi:10.1016/S0169-023X(97)88935-5

Shuchih, E. C., & Boris, M. (2008). Monitoring enterprise applications and the future of self-healing applications. *International Journal of Enterprise Information Systems, 4*(2), 54–66. doi:10.4018/jeis.2008040104

Siau, K., & Rossi, M. (2011). Evaluation techniques for systems analysis and design modelling methods - a review and comparative analysis. *Information Systems Journal, 21*(3), 249–268. doi:10.1111/j.1365-2575.2007.00255.x

Siau, K., Wand, Y., & Benbasat, I. (1996). When parents need not have children – cognitive biases in information modeling. In P. Constantopoulos, J. Mylopoulos, & Y. Vassiliou (Eds.), *Advanced Information Systems Engineering* (pp. 402–420). London: Springer-Verlag. doi:10.1007/3-540-61292-0_22

Sidorova, A., & Kappelman, L. A. (2010). Enterprise architecture as politics: An actor-network theory perspective. In L. A. Kappelman (Ed.), *The SIM guide to enterprise architecture.* Boca Raton, FL: CRC Press.

Silva, F. (2009). *As tecnologias da informação e comunicação e o ensino da contabilidade* (Master's degree dissertation). University of Aveiro, Portugal.

Silvestro, R., Fitzgerald, L., Johnston, R., & Voss, C. (1992). Towards a Classification of Service Processes. *International Journal of Service Industry Management, 3*(3), 62–75. doi:10.1108/09564239210015175

Simchi-Levi, D., Kaminsky, P., & Simchi-Levi, E. (2000). *Designing and Managing the Supply Chain: Concepts, Strategies and Case Studies* (International Edition). Singapore: McGraw-Hill.

Simchi-Levi, D., Kaminsky, P., & Simchi-Levi, E. (2003). *Designing and Managing the Supply Chain: Concepts, Strategies, and Case Studies*. New York: McGraw-Hill.

Simon, D., Fischbach, K., & Schoder, D. (2013). An exploration of enterprise architecture research. *Communications of the Association for Information Systems, 32*, 1–72.

Simon, J. L., & Burstein, P. (1985). *Basic research methods in social science* (3rd ed.). New York: Random House.

Sims, R. R. (2002). Organizational Success through Effective HRM. Retrieved from www.books.goggle.com/books

Smaltz, D. H., Sambamurthy, V., & Agarwal, R. (2006). The antecedents of CIO role effectiveness in Organizations: An empirical study in the healthcare sector. *Engineering Management. IEEE Transactions on, 53*(2), 207–222. doi:10.1109/TEM.2006.872248

Smith, S., & Albaum, G. (2013). *Basic Marketing Research – Building Your Survey*. Qualtrics Labs, Inc.

Smolander, K., & Rossi, M. (2008). Conflicts, compromises, and political decisions: Methodological challenges of enterprise-wide e-business architecture creation. *Journal of Database Management, 19*(1), 19–40. doi:10.4018/jdm.2008010102

Snider, B., Da Silveira, G., & Balakrishnan, J. (2009). ERP implementation at SMEs: Analysis of five Canadian cases. *International Journal of Operations & Production Management, 29*(1), 4–29. doi:10.1108/01443570910925343

Snowden, D. J., & Boone, M. E. (2007). A leader's framework for decision making. *Harvard Business Review, 85*(11), 68.

Sobol, M. G., & Klein, G. (2009). Relation of CIO background, IT infrastructure, and economic performance. *Information & Management, 46*(5), 271–278. doi:10.1016/j.im.2009.05.001

Soffer, P., Boaz, G., & Dov, D. (2005). Aligning an ERP System with Enterprise Requirements: An Object-Process Based Approach. *Computers in Industry, 56*(6), 639–662. doi:10.1016/j.compind.2005.03.002

Sohal, A. S., & Ng, L. (1998). The role and impact of information technology in Australian business. *Journal of Information Technology, 13*(3), 201–217. doi:10.1080/026839698344846

Soh, C. K., & Tay-Yap, J. (2000). Cultural its and misfits: Is ERP a universal solution? *Communications of the ACM, 43*(4), 47–51. doi:10.1145/332051.332070

Soh, C., & Sia, S. K. (2005). The challenges of implementing "vanilla" versions of enterprise systems. *MIS Quarterly Executive, 4*(3), 373–384.

Soja, P. (2006). Success factors in ERP systems implementations Lessons from practice. *Journal of Enterprise Information Management, 19*(4), 418–433. doi:10.1108/17410390610678331

Somers, T. M., & Nelson, K. (2001, January). The impact of critical success factors across the stages of enterprise resource planning implementations. In *System Sciences, 2001. Proceeding of the 34th Hawaii International Conference on System Sciences*, 1-10. doi:10.1109/HICSS.2001.927129

Somers, T. M., & Nelson, K. G. (2004). A taxonomy of players and activities across the ERP project life cycle. *Information & Management, 41*(3), 57–78. doi:10.1016/S0378-7206(03)00023-5

Somers, T. M., Nelson, K., & Ragowsky, A. (2000). Enterprise Resource Planning (ERP) for the Next Millennium: Development of an Integrative Framework and Implications for Research. *AMCIS 2000Proceedings of the 2000 Americas Conference of Information Systems*, 998-1004.

Sowa, J. F., & Zachman, J. (1992). Extending and formalizing the framework for information systems architecture. *IBM Systems*, *31*(3), 590–616. doi:10.1147/sj.313.0590

Spanoudakis, G., & Zisman, A. (2001). Inconsistency Management in Software Engineering: Survey and Open Research Issues. In S. K. Chang (Ed.), *Handbook of Software Engineering and Knowledge Engineering* (Vol. 1, pp. 329–380). World Scientific Publishing Co. doi:10.1142/9789812389718_0015

Speed, R., & Smith, G. (1992). Retailing financial services segmentation. *The Service Industries, 12*.

Spencer, A. J., Buhalis, D., & Moital, M. (2012). A hierarchical model of technology adoption for small owner-managed travel firms: An organizational decision-making and leadership perspective. *Tourism Management*, *33*(5), 1195–1208. doi:10.1016/j.tourman.2011.11.011

Spender, J. C. (2002). Knowledge management, uncertainty, and an emergent theory of the firm. *The strategic management of intellectual capital and organizational knowledge*, 149-162.

Spewak, S. H. (1992). *Enterprise architecture planning: Developing a blueprint for data, applications and technology*. New York: John Wiley and Sons.

Spies, M., & Tabet, S. (2012). Emerging standards and protocols for governance, risk, and compliance management. In *Handbook of research on e-business standards and protocols: Documents, data and advanced web technologies* (pp. 768–790). Hershey, PA: IGI Global. doi:10.4018/978-1-4666-0146-8.ch035

Spohrer, J., Vargo, S., Caswell, N., & Maglio, P. (2008). The Service System Is the Basic Abstraction of Service Science.*41st Annual Hawaii International Conference on System Sciences (HICCS)*, 7(4), 104-116. doi:10.1109/HICSS.2008.451

Spruit, M., Vroon, R., & Batenburg, R. (2014). Towards healthcare business intelligence in long-term care: An explorative case study in the Netherlands. *Computers in Human Behavior*, *30*, 698–707. doi:10.1016/j.chb.2013.07.038

Sridharan, B., Deng, H., Kirk, J., & Corbitt, B. (2010). Structural equation modelling for evaluating the user perceptions of e-learning effectiveness in higher education.*18th European Conference on Information Systems*.

Srinivasan, M. (2010). E-Business and ERP: A Conceptual Framework toward the Business Transformation to an Integrated E-Supply Chain. *International Journal of Enterprise Information Systems*, *6*(4), 1–19. doi:10.4018/jeis.2010100101

Srinivasan, S. S., Anderson, R., & Ponnavolu, K. (2002). Customer loyalty in e-commerce: An exploration of its antecedents and consequences. *Journal of Retailing*, *78*(1), 41–50. doi:10.1016/S0022-4359(01)00065-3

Srite, M., Bennett, J., & Galy, E. (2008). Does within culture matter? An empirical study of computer usage. *Journal of Global Information Management*, *16*(1), 1–25. doi:10.4018/jgim.2008010101

Srivastava, M., & Gips, B. J. (2009). Chinese cultural implications for ERP implementation. *Journal of Technology Management & Innovation*, *4*(1), 105–113. doi:10.4067/S0718-27242009000100009

Stephens, C., Ledbetter, W., Mitra, A., & Ford, F. (1992). Executive or functional? The nature of the CIOs job. *Management Information Systems Quarterly*, *16*(4), 449–467. doi:10.2307/249731

Sternad, S., Bobek, S., Dezelak, Z., & Lampret, A. (2009). Critical success factors (CSFs) for enterprise resource planning (ERP) solution implementation in SMEs: What does matter for business integration. *International Journal of Enterprise Information Systems*, *5*(3), 27–46. doi:10.4018/jeis.2009070103

Stern, C., & Deimler, M. (2006). *The Boston Consulting Group on Strategy, classic concepts and new perspectives* (2nd ed.). John Wiley & Sons Inc.

Stewart, G., Milford, M., Jewels, T., Hunter, T., & Hunter, B. (2000). Organisational Readiness for ERP Implementation. *Americas Conference on Information Systems, AMCIS 2000 Proceedings*, 966 - 971. Retrieved from http://aisel. aisnet.org/amcis2000/291K

Storey, V. C. (1988). *View Creation: An Expert System for Database Design.* Washington, DC: ICIT Press.

Storey, V. C., & Goldstein, R. C. (1993). Knowledge-based approaches to database design. *Management Information Systems Quarterly, 17*(1), 25–46. doi:10.2307/249508

Subramani, M. (2004). How do suppliers benefit from information technology use in supply chain relationships? *Management Information Systems Quarterly, 28*(1), 45–73.

Sudevan, S., Bhasi, M., & Pramod, K. (2014). Distinct Stakeholder Roles Across the ERP Implementation Lifecycle: A Case Study. *International Journal of Enterprise Information Systems, 10*(4), 59–72. doi:10.4018/ijeis.2014100104

Sumner, M. (2000). Risk factors in enterprise-wide/ERP projects. *Journal of Information Technology, 15*(4), 317–327. doi:10.1080/02683960010009079

SunMicrosystems. (2004). *Web Services.* Retrieved 12 December, 2016, http://www.java.sun.com/webservices/docs/1.3/wsi-sampleapp/

Supply Chain Management, C. S. C. M. P. (2013). Retrieved Jan 10, 2013, from http://cscmp.org/about-us/supply-chain-management-definitions

Suraweera, P., & Mitrovic, A. (2004). An intelligent tutoring system for entity relationship modelling. *International Journal of Artificial Intelligence in Education, 14*, 375–417.

Sutter, J. d. (2004). *The Power of IT: Survival Guide for the CIO.* North Charleston, SC: BookSurge, LLC.

Swaminathan, J. (2001). Enabling Customization Using Standardized Operations. *California Management Review, 43*(3), 125–135. doi:10.2307/41166092

Swaminathan, J. M., & Tayur, S. R. (2003). Models for Supply Chains in E-Business. *Management Science, 49*(10), 1387–1406. doi:10.1287/mnsc.49.10.1387.17309

Swanson, E. B., & Ramiller, N. C. (1997). The Organizing Vision in Information Systems Innovation. *Organization Science, 8*(5), 458–474. doi:10.1287/orsc.8.5.458

Swift, R. (2001). *Accelerating Customer Relationship Management: Using CRM and Relationship Technologies.* Academic Press.

Symons, C. (2006). *Measuring the Business Value of IT, A Survey of IT Value Methodologies.* Forrester Research, Inc. Retrieved August 28, 2012, from http://www.cornerstone1.com/SAP/SAP_Forrester_Measuring_the_Business_Value_of_IT.pdf

Tan, C. W., & Pan, S. L. (2002). ERP success: The search for a comprehensive framework.*Proceedings of 8th Americas Conference on Information Systems.*

Tan, C., & Sia, S. (2006). Managing Flexibility in Outsourcing. *Journal of the Association for Information Systems, 7*(4), 179–206.

Tang, C. M., & Marthandan, G. (2011). An Analytical Model to Measure IS-Enabled Organizational Effectiveness. *International Journal of Enterprise Information Systems, 7*(2), 50–65. doi:10.4018/jeis.2011040104

Tan, N., & Teo, T. S. H. (1998). Factors influencing the adoption of the Internet. *International Journal of Electronic Commerce, 2*(3), 5–18. doi:10.1080/10864415.1998.11518312

Tavana, M. (2011). *Managing Adaptability*. Intervention, and People in Enterprise Information Systems; doi:10.4018/978-1-60960-529-2

Taveira, A. D. (2008). Key elements on team achievement: A retrospective analysis. *Applied Ergonomics, 39*(4), 509–518. doi:10.1016/j.apergo.2008.02.007 PMID:18395695

Taylor, S. (2007). *ITIL Service Design*. London: TSO, Office of Government Commerce.

Taylor, B. J., Dempster, M., & Donnelly, M. (2003). Hidden gems: Systematically searching electronic databases for publications for social work and social care. *British Journal of Social Work, 33*(4), 423–439. doi:10.1093/bjsw/33.4.423

Te'eni, D. (2005). In S. Nielsen & J. Beekhuyzen (Eds.), *Socio-technical aspects of ERP selection and implementation: The central role of communication. In Enterprise Systems in Academia* (pp. 1–21). Hershey, PA: IGP.

Teorey, T. J. (1999). *Database Modeling and Design: The Fundamental Principle* (3rd ed.). St. Louis, MO: Morgan Kaufmann.

Teo, T. S. H., & Tan, M. (2000). Factors influencing the adoption of Internet banking. *Journal of the Association for Information Systems, 1*(5), 36.

Thanassoulis, E., Boussofiane, A., & Dyson, R. (1996). A Comparison of Data Envelopment Analysis and Ratio Analysis as Tools for Performance Assessment. *Omega, 3*(3), 229–244. doi:10.1016/0305-0483(95)00060-7

The Open Group. (2003). *TOGAF (The open group architecture framework) version 8.1*. Retrieved from www. opengroup. org/architecture/togaf8/ downloads.htm

The Open Group. (2009). *TOGAF version 9 enterprise edition*. Zaltbommel, Netherlands: Van Haren Publishing.

Themistocleous, M., Zahir, I., & Love, P. (2004). Evaluating the integration of supply chain information systems: A case study. *European Journal of Operational Research, 159*(2), 393–405. doi:10.1016/j.ejor.2003.08.023

Thenent, N., Settanni, E., Parry, G., Goh, Y., & Newnes, L. (2014). Cutting Cost in Service Systems: Are You Running with Scissors? *Journal of Strategic Change: Briefings in Entrepreneurial Finance, 23*, 341–357.

Thomas, J. S., & Kumar, R. (2004). Getting the most out of all of your customers. *Harvard Business Review*, 116–123. PMID:15241958

Thome, R., & Hufgard, A. (2006). *Continuous system engineering: discovering the organizational potential of standard software*. Munich: OXYGON.

Thongchattu, C., & Buranajarukorn, P. (2007). The Utilisation of e-Tools of Information Technology towards Thorough Supply Chain Management.*Naresuan University Research Conference*.

Thonggoom, O., Song, I., & An, Y. (2011). Semi-automatic Conceptual Data Modeling Using Entity and Relatinship Instance Repositories. *Conceptual Modeling – ER 2011, 6998*, 219–232.

Thong, J. Y. L., & Yap, C. S. (1995). CEO characteristics, organizational characteristics and information technology adoption in small business. *Omega, 23*(4), 429–442. doi:10.1016/0305-0483(95)00017-I

Thong, J., Yap, C.-S., & Raman, K. S. (1994, Fall). Engagement of External Expertise in Information Systems Implementation. *Journal of Management Information Systems, 11*(2), 209–231. doi:10.1080/07421222.1994.11518046

Thong, J., Yap, C.-S., & Raman, K. S. (1996, June). Yap Chee-sing & Raman K.S (1996), Top Management Support, External Expertise and Information Systems Implementation in Small Businesses. *Information Systems Research, 7*(2), 248–267. doi:10.1287/isre.7.2.248

Timbrell, G., & Gable, G. (2002). The SAP ecosystem: a knowledge perspective. In *Proceedings of the Information Resources Management Association International Conference* (pp. 1115–1118). Hershey, PA: Information Resources Management Association.

Tiwana, A. (2001). The essential guide to knowledge management. *E-Business and CRM Applications.*

Toni, S. M., & Klara, N. (2001). The Impact of Critical Success Factors across the Stages of ERP Implementations. *Proceedings of the 34th Hawaii International Conference on Systems Science.*

Towill, D. (1997). The seamless supply chain - the predators strategic advantage. *International Journal of Technology Management, 13*(1), 37–56. doi:10.1504/IJTM.1997.001649

Transportation Statistics Annual Report. (2014). Bureau of Transportation Statistics.

Treleaven, L., & Sykes, C. (2005). Loss of organizational knowledge: From supporting clients to serving head office. *Journal of Organizational Change Management, 18*(4), 353–368. doi:10.1108/09534810510607056

Trigo, A., Varajão, J., Oliveira, I., & Barroso, J. (2009). Chief Information Officer's activities and skills in Portuguese large companies. *Communications of the IBIMA, 10*(9), 64–71.

Tsai, C-T., & Chang (2005). An integration framework of innovation assessment for the knowledge-intensive service industry. *International Journal of Technology Management, 30*(1-2), 85-104.

Tseng, S.-M. (2016). Knowledge management capability, customer relationship management, and service quality. *Journal of Enterprise Information Management, 29*(2), 202–221. doi:10.1108/JEIM-04-2014-0042

Tsoi, S. K., Cheung, C. F., & Lee, W. B. (2003). Knowledge-based customization of enterprise applications. *Expert Systems with Applications, 25*(1), 123–132. doi:10.1016/S0957-4174(03)00012-5

Tsoukas, H., & Vladimirou, E. (2001). What is organizational knowledge? *Journal of Management Studies, 38*(7), 973–993. doi:10.1111/1467-6486.00268

Turban, E., McClean, E., & Wetherbe, J. (1999). *Information Technology and Management.* New York: John Wiley.

Turning Points: Transforming Middle Schools. (n.d.). *Guide to Collaborative Culture and Shared Leadership.* Retrieved from http://www.turningpts.org

U.S. Department of Defense, Defense Science Board. (1994). *Report of the Defense Science Board Summer Study Task Force on Information Architecture for the Battlefield (October).* Retrieved from https://www.google. com.au/webhp?sourceid=chrome-instant&ion=1&espv=2&ie=UTF-8#q=report%20of%20the%20defense%20 science%20board%20summer%20study%20task%20force%20on%20information%20architecture%20for%20 the%20battlefield

Ullah, Z., Al-Mudimigh, A. S., Al-Ghamdi, A. A. M., & Saleem, F. (2013). Critical Success Factors of ERP Implementation at Higher Education Institutes: A Brief Case Study. International Information Institute Information, 16(10), 7369.

Umble, E. J., Haft, R. R., & Umble, M. M. (2003). Enterprise resource planning: Implementation procedures and critical success factors. *European Journal of Operational Research, 146*(2), 241–257. doi:10.1016/S0377-2217(02)00547-7

Umemoto, K. (2002). Managing existing knowledge is not enough. *The strategic management of intellectual capital and organizational knowledge*, 463-476.

Utomo, H., & Dodgson, M. (2001). Contributing factors to the diffusion of IT within small and medium sized firms in Indonesia. *Journal of Global Information Technology Management, 4*(2), 22–37. doi:10.1080/1097198X.2001.10856300

Uzoka, F. M. E., Abiola, R. O., & Nyangeresi, R. (2008). Influence of product and organizational constructs on ERP acquisition using an extended technology acceptance model. *International Journal of Enterprise Information Systems, 4*(2), 67–83. doi:10.4018/jeis.2008040105

Vaccaro, A., Parente, R., & Veloso, F. M. (2010). Knowledge management tools, inter organizational relationships, innovation and firm performance. *Technological Forecasting and Social Change, 77*(7), 1076–1089. doi:10.1016/j.techfore.2010.02.006

Van de Ven, A. H., & Poole, M. S. (2005). Alternative approaches for studying Organizational Change. *Organization Studies, 26*(9), 1377–1404. doi:10.1177/0170840605056907

Van der Raadt, B., Bonnet, M., Schouten, S., & van Vliet, H. (2010). The relation between EA effectiveness and stakeholder satisfaction. *Journal of Systems and Software, 83*(10), 1954–1969. doi:10.1016/j.jss.2010.05.076

Van der Raadt, B., Schouten, S., & van Vliet, H. (2008). Stakeholder perceptions of enterprise architecture, software architecture. In *Software Architecture, LNCS* (Vol. 5292, pp. 19–34). Berlin: Springer-Verlag. doi:10.1007/978-3-540-88030-1_4

van Gigch, J. P., & Moigne, J. L. L. (1990). The design of an organization information system: Intelligent artifacts for complex organizations. *Information & Management, 19*(5), 325–331. doi:10.1016/0378-7206(90)90046-K

Van Ginkel, W. P., & Van Knippenberg, D. (2012). Group leadership and shared task representations in decision making groups. *The Leadership Quarterly, 23*(1), 94–106. doi:10.1016/j.leaqua.2011.11.008

Van Velsen, L., Huijs, C., & Van der Geest, T. (2008). Eliciting User Input for Requirements on Personalization: The Case of a Dutch ERP System. *International Journal of Enterprise Information Systems, 4*(4), 34–46. doi:10.4018/jeis.2008100103

Varajão, J. E. Q. (2005). A Arquitectura da Gestão de Sistemas de Informação (3ª ed.). Lisboa: FCA - Editora de Informática.

Varajão, J. (2001). *Outsourcing de serviços de sistemas de informação*. Lisboa: FCA - Editora de Informática.

Varajão, J. E. Q. (2002). *Contributos para a melhoria do sucesso da adopção de tecnologias de informação e desenvolvimento de sistemas de informação nas organizações. (Tese de doutoramento PhD)*. Guimarães: Universidade do Minho.

Varajão, J., Cruz-Cunha, M. M., da Glória Fraga, M., & Amaral, L. (2012a). Offshore outsourcing in large companies: Motivations and risks perceived. *African Journal of Business Management, 6*(36), 9936. doi:10.5897/AJBM11.669

Varajão, J., Pinto, J., Colomo-Palacios, R., & Amaral, L. (2012b). Modelo para a avaliação do desempenho potencial de gestores de sistemas de informação. *Interciencia, 37*(10), 724–728.

Varajão, J., Trigo, A., & Barroso, J. (2009a). Motivations and Trends for IT/IS Adoption: Insights from Portuguese Companies. *International Journal of Enterprise Information Systems, 5*(4), 34–52. doi:10.4018/jeis.2009090203

Varajão, J., Trigo, A., Figueiredo, N., Barroso, J., & Bulas-Cruz, J. (2009b). Information systems services outsourcing reality in large Portuguese organisations. *Int. J. Bus. Inf. Syst., 4*(1), 125–142. doi:10.1504/IJBIS.2009.021606

Varajão, J., Trigo, A., & Soto-Acosta, P. (2016). An Exploratory Study on the Influencers of the Perceived Relevance of CIOs Activities. *International Journal of Enterprise Information Systems, 12*(4), 1–15. doi:10.4018/IJEIS.2016100101

Vasarhelyi, M., Alles, M., & Williams, K. T. (2010). *Continuous assurance for the now economy*. Sydney: Institute of Chartered Accountants in Australia.

Vasconcelos, J., Seixas, P., Kimble, C., & Lemos, P. (2005). Knowledge management in non-government organisations: A partnership for the future. *Proceedings of the 7th International Conference on Enterprise Information Systems*.

Vaughan, L. (2004). New measurements for search engine evaluation proposed and tested. *Information Processing & Management, 40*(4), 677–691. doi:10.1016/S0306-4573(03)00043-8

Vedder, R. G., & Guynes, C. S. (2002). Cios Perspectives on Competitive Intelligence. *Information Systems Management, 19*(4), 49–55. doi:10.1201/1078/43202.19.4.20020901/38834.6

Veloutsou, C., Gilbert, R.G., Moutinho, L.A. and Good, M. M. (2005). Measuring transactionspecific satisfaction in services. *European Journal of Marketing, 39*(5-6), 606-628.

Venkatesh, V. (2008). One-Size-Does-Not-Fit-All: Teaching MBA students different ERP implementation strategies. *Journal of Information Systems Education, 19*(2), 141–146.

Venkatraman, N. (1994). IT-Enabled Business Transformation: From Automation to Business Scope Redefinition. *Sloan Management Review, 35*(2), 73–87.

Venturato, L., & Drew, L. (2010). Beyonddoing: Supporting clinical leadership and nursing practice in aged care through innovative models of care. *Contemporary Nurse, 35*(2), 157–170. doi:10.5172/conu.2010.35.2.157 PMID:20950197

Verhoef, P. (2003). Understanding the effect of customer relationship management efforts on customer retention and customer share development. *Journal of Marketing, 67*(4), 30–45. doi:10.1509/jmkg.67.4.30.18685

Vermeulen, F., Puranam, P., & Gulati, R. (2010). Change for change's sake. *Harvard Business Review, 88*(6), 70–76.

Vestal, W. (2005). Making sense of KM costs. *KM World, 14*(7), 8–11.

Virtanen, I. (2011). Externalization of tacit knowledge implies a simplified theory of cognition. *Journal of Knowledge Management Practice, 12*(3).

Vreuls, E. H., & Joia, L. A. (2011). An Exploratory Model for the Relevant Factors Related to the Professional Performance of the Brazilian CIO. *The Electronic Journal of Information Systems in Developing Countries, 47*.

Vuksic, V., Bach, M., & Popovic, A. (2013). Supporting performance management with business process management and business intelligence: A case analysis of integration and orchestration. *International Journal of Information Management, 33*(4), 613–619. doi:10.1016/j.ijinfomgt.2013.03.008

Wagner, E. L., & Newell, S. (2004). Bestfor whom? The tension between best practiceERP packages and diverse epistemic cultures in a university context. *The Journal of Strategic Information Systems, 13*(4), 305–328. doi:10.1016/j.jsis.2004.11.002

Wagner, S. M., & Bode, C. (2008). An empirical examination of supply chain performance along several dimensions of risk. *Journal of Business Logistics, 29*(1), 307–325. doi:10.1002/j.2158-1592.2008.tb00081.x

Wallace, D. W., Giese, J. L., & Johnson, J. L. (2004). Customer retailer loyalty in the context of multiple channel strategies. *Journal of Retailing, 80*.

Wallenius, J., Dyer, J. S., Fishburn, P. C., Steuer, R. E., Zionts, S., & Deb, K. (2008). Multiple criteria decision making, multiattribute utility theory: Recent accomplishments and what lies ahead. *Management Science, 54*(7), 1336–1349. doi:10.1287/mnsc.1070.0838

Walter, J., Kellermanns, F. W., & Lechner, C. (2012). Decision making within and between organizations rationality, politics, and alliance performance. *Journal of Management, 38*(5), 1582–1610. doi:10.1177/0149206310363308

Wang, E. T. G., & Chen, J. H. F. (2006). Effect of internal support and consultant quality on the consulting process and ERP system quality. *Decision Support Systems, 42*(2), 1029–1041. doi:10.1016/j.dss.2005.08.005

Wang, E., Chou, H. W., & Jiang, J. (2005). The impacts of charismatic leadership style on team cohesiveness and overall performance during ERP implementation. *International Journal of Project Management, 23*(3), 173–180. doi:10.1016/j.ijproman.2004.09.003

Ward, J., & Griffits, P. (1996). *Strategic Planning for Information Systems* (2nd ed.). London: John Wiley & Sons Inc.

Ward, M. G., & Bawden, D. (1997). User-centered and User-sensitive Implementation of, and Training for, Information Systems: A Case Study. *International Journal of Information Management, 17*(I), 55–71. doi:10.1016/S0268-4012(96)00042-4

Watson, H. J., & Wixom, H. (2007). Enterprise agility and mature BI capabilities. *Business Intelligence Journal, 12*(3), 13–28.

Watson, H., Ariyachandra, T., & Matyska, J. Jr. (2001). Data Warehousing Stages Of Growth. *Information Systems Management, 18*(3), 41–50. doi:10.1201/1078/43196.18.3.20010601/31289.6

Watson, R. T., Akelsen, S., & Pitt, L. F. (1998). Building mountains in that flat landscape of the World Wide Web. *California Management Review, 40*(2), 36–56. doi:10.2307/41165932

Watts, S., & Henderson, J. C. (2006). Innovative IT climates: CIO perspectives. *The Journal of Strategic Information Systems, 15*(2), 125–151. doi:10.1016/j.jsis.2005.08.001

Wears, R. L., & Berg, M. (2005). Computer technology and clinical work. *Journal of the American Medical Association, 293*(10), 1261–1263. doi:10.1001/jama.293.10.1261 PMID:15755949

Wee, S. (2000). Juggling toward ERP success: Keep key success factors high. *ERP News*. Retrieved from http://www.erpnews.com/erpnews/erp904/02get.html

We, J., & Wang, S. (2005). What drives mobile commerce: An empirical evaluation of the revised technology acceptance model? *Information & Management, 42*, 719–729.

We, K. S., Loong, A. C. Y., Leong, Y. M., & Ooi, K. B. (2009). Measuring ERP systems success: A re-specification of the DeLone and McLean's IS success model.*Symposium on progress in Information and Communication Technologies.*

Wemmerlöv, U. (1990). A Taxonomy for Service Processes and its Implications for System Design. *International Journal of Service Industry Management, 1*(3), 20–40. doi:10.1108/09564239010002126

Wenger, E. C., & Snyder, W. M. (2000). Communities of practice: The organizational frontier. *Harvard Business Review, 78*(1), 139–145. PMID:11184968

Wen-Lung, S. (2014). Improving firm performance through a mobile auditing assistance system. *International Journal of Enterprise Information Systems, 10*(4), 22–35. doi:10.4018/ijeis.2014100102

Wenrich, K., & Ahmad, N. (2009). Lessons learned during a decade of ERP experience: A case study. *International Journal of Enterprise Information Systems, 5*(1), 55–73. doi:10.4018/jeis.2009010105

Westaby, J. D., Probst, T. M., & Lee, B. C. (2010). Leadership decision-making: A behavioral reasoning theory analysis. *The Leadership Quarterly, 21*(3), 481–495. doi:10.1016/j.leaqua.2010.03.011

Whetten, D. A. (1989). What Constitutes a Theoretical Contribution? *Academy of Management Review, 14*(4), 490–495. doi:10.2307/258554

Whitworth, B. (2009). *The Social Requirements of Technical Systems. In Handbook of Research on Socio-Technical Design and Social Networking Systems* (pp. 1–22). IGI Global; doi:10.4018/978-1-60566-264-0

Wiig, K. M. (1997). Integrating intellectual capital and knowledge management. *Long Range Planning, 30*(3), 399–405. doi:10.1016/S0024-6301(97)90256-9

Willcock, L. P., & Sykes, R. (2000). The role of the CIO and it functions in ERP. *Communications of the ACM, 43*(4), 32–38. doi:10.1145/332051.332065

Willcocks, L., Cullen, S., & Craig, A. (2010). *The Outsourcing Enterprise: From Cost Management to Collaborative Innovation (Technology, Work and Globalization)*. Palgrave.

Willcocks, L., & Lacity, M. (1998). The sourcing and outsourcing of IS: Shock of the new. In L. Willcocks & M. Lacity (Eds.), *Strategic Sourcing of Information Technology: Perspectives and Practices* (pp. 1–41). Chichester, UK: Wiley.

Willcocks, L., & Lacity, M. (2012). *The New IT Outsourcing Landscape: From Innovation to Cloud Services*. Palgrave Macmillan. doi:10.1057/9781137012296

Williams, J., Williams, M. D., & Morgan, A. (2013). A teleological process theory for managing ERP implementations. *Journal of Enterprise Information Management, 26*(3), 235–249. doi:10.1108/17410391311325216

Williams, L. R., Esper, T. L., & Ozment, J. (2002). The electronic supply chain. *International Journal of Physical Distribution & Logistics Management, 32*(8), 703–719. doi:10.1108/09600030210444935

Williamson, E. A., Harrison, D. K., & Jordan, M. (2004). Information systems development within supply chain management. *International Journal of Information Management, 24*(5), 375–385. doi:10.1016/j.ijinfomgt.2004.06.002

Williamson, O. E. (1985). *The Economic Institutions of Capitalism*. New York: Free Press.

Williams, S., & Williams, N. (2006). *The Profit Impact of Business Intelligence*. New York: Morgan Kaufmann.

Wixom, B. H., & Todd, P. A. (2005). A theorectical integration of user satisfaction and technology acceptance. *Information Systems Research, 16*(1), 85–102. doi:10.1287/isre.1050.0042

Wölfel, K. (2012). ERP5 Starter: Open-Source-ERP-Einführung durch standardisierte Beratung. *HMD - Praxis der Wirtschaftsinformatik, 283*, 58–67.

Wölfel, K. (2014). Suggestion-based Correction Support for MOOCs. In Tagungsband der Multikonferenz Wirtschaftsinformatik (MKWI), Paderborn, Deutschland.

Wölfel, K., & Smets, J.-P. (2012). Tailoring FOS-ERP Packages: Automation as an Opportunity for Small Businesses. In Free and Open Source Enterprise Resource Planning: Systems and Strategies (pp. 116–133). IGI Global.

Wolfswinkel, J. F., Furtmueller, E., & Wilderom, C. P. (2011). Using grounded theory as a method for rigorously reviewing literature. *European Journal of Information Systems, 22*(1), 45–55. doi:10.1057/ejis.2011.51

Worley, J. H., Chatha, K. A., Weston, R. H., Aguirre, O., & Grabot, B. (2005). Implementation and Optimization of ERP Systems: A Better Integration of Processes, Roles, Knowledge and User Competencies. *Computers in Industry, 56*(6), 620–638. doi:10.1016/j.compind.2005.03.006

Xu, L. D. (2011). Enterprise Systems: State-of-the-Art and Future Trends. *IEEE Transactions on Industrial Informatics, 7*(4), 630–640. doi:10.1109/TII.2011.2167156

Yalin, D. (2007). Business-savvy CIOs Step Up. *InformationWeek*. Retrieved from http://www.informationweek.com/shared/printableArticle.jhtml?articleID=199500669

Yang, M. C. (2010). Consensus and single leader decision-making in teams using structured design methods. *Design Matters*, *31*, 345–362.

Yap, C. S., Thong, J. Y. L., & Raman, K. S. (1994). Effect of government incentive in computerization in small business. *European Journal of Information Systems*, *3*(3), 191–200. doi:10.1057/ejis.1994.20

Yeoh, W., Koronios, A., & Gao, J. (2008). Managing the Implementation of Business Intelligence Systems: A Critical Success Factors Framework. *International Journal of Enterprise Information Systems*, *4*(3), 79–94. doi:10.4018/jeis.2008070106

Yi-fen, S., & Yang, C. (2010). Why are enterprise resources planning systems indispensable to supply chain management? *European Journal of Operational Research*, *203*(1), 81–94. doi:10.1016/j.ejor.2009.07.003

Yin, R. (1994). *Case Study Research, Design and Methods* (5th ed.). Newbury Park, CA: Sage Publications.

Yu, C. S. (2005). Causes influencing the effectiveness of the post-implementation ERP system. *Industrial Management & Data Systems*, *105*(1), 15–32. doi:10.1108/02635570510575225

Yukl, G. A. (2006). *Leadership in Organizations* (6th ed.). Upper Saddle River, NJ: Prentice Hall.

Yusuf, Y., Gunasekaran, A., & Abthorpe, M. S. (2004). Enterprise information systems project implementation: A case study of ERP in Rolls-Royce. *International Journal of Production Economics*, *87*(3), 251–266. doi:10.1016/j.ijpe.2003.10.004

Yu, Z., Yan, H., & Cheng, T. C. E. (2001). Benefits of information sharing with supply chain partnerships. *Industrial Management & Data Systems*, *101*(3), 114–119. doi:10.1108/02635570110386625

Zachman, J. (1987). A framework for information systems architecture. *IBM Systems Journal*, *26*(3), 276–292. doi:10.1147/sj.263.0276

Zachman, J. A. (1982). Business systems planning and business information control study: A comparison. *IBM Systems Journal*, *21*(1), 31–53. doi:10.1147/sj.211.0031

Zach, O., Munkvold, B. E., & Olsen, D. H. (2014). ERP system implementation in SMEs: Exploring the influences of the SME context. *Enterprise Information Systems*, *8*(2), 309–335. doi:10.1080/17517575.2012.702358

Zand, D. E., & Sorenson, R. E. (1975). Theory of change and the effective use of management science. *Administrative Science Quarterly*, *20*(4), 532–545. doi:10.2307/2392021

Zantow. (2009). *Understanding user attitudes in IS implementation through technological frames An interpretive, ethnographic case study* (Thesis). Department of Management Birkbeck, University of London.

Zarei, B., & Naeli, M. (2010). Critical Success Factors in Enterprise Resource Planning Implementation A Case-Study Approach. *International Journal of Enterprise Information Systems*, *6*(3), 48–58. doi:10.4018/jeis.2010070104

Zgener, S.-O., & I˙raz, R. (2006). Customer relationship management in small–medium enterprises: The case of Turkish tourism industry. *Tourism Management*, *27*.

Zhang, L., Lee, M. K., Zhang, Z., & Banerjee, P. (2003, January). Critical success factors of enterprise resource planning systems implementation success in China. In *System Sciences. Proceedings of the 36th Annual Hawaii International Conference on System Sciences* (pp. 1-10). IEEE. doi:10.1109/HICSS.2003.1174613

Zhang, Q., Vonderembse, M. A., & Lim, J. S. (2005). Logistics flexibility and its impact on customer satisfaction. *The International Journal of Logistics Management, 16*(1), 71–95. doi:10.1108/09574090510617367

Zhang, Z., Lee, M. K., Huang, P., Zhang, L., & Huang, X. (2005). A framework of ERP systems implementation success in China: An empirical study. *International Journal of Production Economics, 98*(1), 56–80. doi:10.1016/j.ijpe.2004.09.004

Zhu, J. (2000). Multi-factor performance measure model with an application to fortune 500 companies. *European Journal of Operational Research, 123*(1), 105–124. doi:10.1016/S0377-2217(99)00096-X

Zhu, Y., Li, Y., Wang, W., & Chen, J. (2010). What leads to post-implementation success of ERP? An empirical study of the Chinese retail industry. *International Journal of Information Management, 30*(3), 265–276. doi:10.1016/j.ijinfomgt.2009.09.007

Ziemba, E., & Oblak, I. (2013, July). Critical success factors for ERP systems implementation in public administration. *Proceedings of the Informing Science and Information Technology Education Conference*, 1-19.

Zikmund, McLeod, & Gilbert. (2003). *Customer Relationship Management, Integrating marketing strategy and information technology.* Academic Press.

Zmud, R. W. (2012). Diffusion of Modern Software Practices: Influence of Centralization and Formalization. *Management Science, 28*(12), 1421–1431.

Zuber-Skerritt, O. (2001). *Action Learning and action research: paradigm, praxis and programs. Effective change management using action research and action learning: Concepts, frameworks, process and applications.* Lismore, Australia: Southern Cross University Press.

Zweifel, B., & Haegeli, P. (2014). A qualitative analysis of group formation, leadership and decision making in recreation groups traveling in avalanche terrain. *Journal of Outdoor Recreation and Tourism, 5*, 17–26. doi:10.1016/j.jort.2014.03.001

About the Contributors

Madjid Tavana is Professor and Lindback Distinguished Chair of Business Analytics at La Salle University, where he serves as Chairman of the Business Systems and Analytics Department. He also holds an Honorary Professorship in Business Information Systems at the University of Paderborn in Germany. Dr. Tavana is Distinguished Research Fellow at the Kennedy Space Center, the Johnson Space Center, the Naval Research Laboratory at Stennis Space Center, and the Air Force Research Laboratory. He was recently honored with the prestigious Space Act Award by NASA. He holds an MBA, PMIS, and PhD in Management Information Systems and received his Post-Doctoral Diploma in Strategic Information Systems from the Wharton School at the University of Pennsylvania. He has published 11 books and over 200 research papers in international scholarly academic journals. He is the Editor-in-Chief of Decision Analytics, International Journal of Applied Decision Sciences, International Journal of Management and Decision Making, International Journal of Knowledge Engineering and Data Mining, International Journal of Strategic Decision Sciences, and International Journal of Enterprise Information Systems.

* * *

Mohammad Nazir Ahmad is a Senior Lecturer in the Information Systems Department, Faculty of Computing, Universiti Teknologi Malaysia (UTM). He received his Bachelor of Information Technology in Industrial Computing from Universiti Kebangsaan Malaysia (1998) and obtained an MSc in Information Systems from UTM (2002). In 2009, he was awarded a PhD in the field of Information Technology from The University of Queensland, Australia. Nazir has been a member of the academic staff in the Information Systems Department for more than fifteen years, and he is recently appointed as an academic fellow of Centre for Information and Communication Technology, UTM.

Bryon Balint is currently an Associate Professor of Management Information Systems in the Jack C. Massey College of Business at Belmont University. He earned his Ph.D. in Industrial Administration from Carnegie Mellon University in 2010, specializing in Information Systems. Dr. Balint's research focuses on using information technology for business process standardization and improvement, particularly in outsourcing and offshoring settings. His research interests also include electronic social networks and their implications for communications and privacy. His research has been published in several journals including *International Journal of Enterprise Information Systems and International Journal of Information Systems and Social Changes*.

Steve Burdon is Professor of Strategic Management & Technology at UTS, Sydney and Visiting Professor at Cass Business School, London. His research interests are Corporate Strategy, Disruptive Technology, Innovation and Government Digital Policy, with more than 50 published journal articles, conference papers and book chapters. Steve is currently working on research projects for the BBC (UK), and The CEO Circle, Australia. He has also been advisor to UK and Australian Government Ministers, and a number of leading Australian corporations including Telstra, Westpac and KPMG. He was previously Group Managing Director of Telstra and Managing Director of British Telecom, Asia Pacific.

João Correia dos Santos holds a MSc in E-Commerce. Currently he is doing a PhD in Management Science at the Technical University of Lisbon in Portugal. Additionally he develops a successfuly IT consultant career on one of the biggest IT providers in Portugal. João holds certifications on: Certified Information Systems Auditor by ISACA and ITIL Service Design by APMG International. His research work is focused on IT outsourcing, IT service design, IT service management and IT service pricing.

Mark Dale has over 25 years' experience in enterprise architecture, data, storage, and security architecture in the financial services, education and health services industries. He has worked as a senior consultant and manager for major Australian financial institutions and consultancies and holds a PhD in enterprise architecture (Swinburne University, 2015) and a PhD in music (Monash University, 2005). He teaches 1) enterprise architecture, strategy and governance, 2) system acquisition and implementation and 3) advanced business analysis at Swinburne University of Technology and 1) business process modelling and analysis at Melbourne University. His research interests are focused around enterprise architecture and the implementation of enterprise architecture.

Brian J. Galli holds a doctoral degree in Engineering Management from Old Dominion University, earned December 2013. He also holds a Bachelor's of Science in Industrial Engineering, earned May 2007, from Binghamton University (SUNY Binghamton), as well as Masters of Science in Engineering Management, earned July 2009, from Missouri University of Science & Technology. He is a licensed professional engineer in New York State and holds a certification as a Lean Six Sigma Blackbelt. The author's major field of study is continuous improvement in healthcare settings as well as deployment of continuous improvement and project management. He works as an Assistant Professor of Management Engineering at Long Island University – Post. He also owns Apex Strategies, Ltd, a company that that specializes in continuous improvement consulting and training initiatives. He has over 9 years of experience in applying industrial engineering and continuous improvement tools and concepts in a wide variety of arenas, including healthcare, manufacturing, transactional, and service environments. He has spent over 6 years working for Northwell Health (formerly known as North Shore LIJ Health System) in New York and 1 year in Health Plan in the EmblemHealth Service Company.

D. P. Goyal is Professor of Management Information Systems at Management Development Institute (MDI), Gurgaon. Earlier he has been Professor & Dean-Academics at Institute of Management Technology (IMT) Ghaziabad, Faculty at Punjabi University, Patiala and at Thapar Institute of Engineering & Technology, Patiala. He has held various administrative positions in the past including Chair of PGPM; Chair of Computer Centre and Computerisation initiatives at MDI. A Post-graduate in Business Management and Doctorate in Management Information Systems, Prof. Goyal has more than 27 years of corporate, teaching, and research experience to his credit. His teaching and research interest areas include Management Information Systems; IS Strategy; Knowledge Management; IS Value for Business; and Business Process Management.

Paul Hawking is an Associate Professor in the College of Business at Victoria University in Melbourne, Australia. Paul has published extensively on topics associated with enterprise resource planning systems, and business intelligence related to SAP solutions. His knowledge and experience in these areas is widely acknowledged by both academia and industry. Paul was the first academic to become a SAP Mentor. Further details about Paul can be found at http://www.business.vu.edu.au/staff/paulhawking/.

Margee Hume has 15 years' experience in the academe .Her teaching experience includes extensive postgraduate and MBA teaching in strategy and project subjects. She has held executive and management roles in both industry and in higher education administration. Her research specialises in service experience mapping and innovation and IT service management. Her focus is on sustainable business communities' and functional level strategy research. She has over 70 high quality publications.

Alen Jakupović is an assistant professor at the Business department, the Polytechnic of Rijeka. He is the author of 2 books and over 30 articles. His research interests are in Information Systems Design Methodology and Measurement, Knowledge Representation and KB System Development. Alen Jakupović has published in conference proceedings such as: International Conference on Information Systems Analysis and Synthesis (ISAS), International Conference on Enterprise Information Systems and Web Technologies (EISWT), International Conference on Software Engineering and Data Engineering (SEDE), and in Journal of Computing and Information Technology, International Journal of Enterprise Information Systems, Informatologia, Expert Systems With Applications.

Paul Johnston is an international business development executive, strategic planning specialist and research analyst with extensive internationalisation experience for emerging technology companies and projects targeting Asia (South East AND North) and The Americas. His industry expertise includes; Information and Communications Technology, Healthcare especially Aged Care. Paul has resided in Australia throughout his professional life, conducting research and industry sabbaticals to the United States of America, Brazil and The Philippines.

Kyeong Kang is an academic researcher and course coordinator for Bachelor of Science in IT (IS Management major)) at University of Technology Sydney. She is an expert in Innovative Digital Culture in E-service System Design particularly in E-commerce and E-government. Her research focuses on the system innovation towards positive impacts on people and society. She delivered excellent quality of industry and internationally collaborated research projects, and created industry projects with Australian governments and International organizations. Her research is widely published and cited. She is an executive member of the Korean Science and Engineering Association (Australia-New Zealand Chapter).

Mohamad Amin Kaviani is a PhD student of Industrial Engineering at Islamic Azad University (IAU), South Tehran branch, Tehran, Iran. He is also a researcher fellow at Young Researchers and Elite Club, IAU, Shiraz, Iran. He obtained his Bachelor degree in Industrial Engineering from IAU, Shiraz, Iran. After that he achieved his Master degree in Industrial Engineering from the same university as a top student. His main research interests include Decision sciences, Supply chain management, Operations management and Operations research. His publications have been appeared in prestigious journals such as *Applied Soft Computing, International Journal of Advanced Manufacturing Technology, Measurement, Management Decision, International Journal of Strategic Decision Sciences and Decision Science Letters.* He is a member of Decision Science Institute (DSI) and Production and Operations Management Society (POMS). He is also the editorial board member of *Management Decision, International Journal of Business Analytics, International Journal of Business and Systems Research, International Journal of Supply chain and Inventory Management.* In addition, he is the regular reviewer of some prestigious international scholarly journals.

Rui Pedro Figueiredo Marques received the PhD degree in Computer Science in 2014 from the universities of Minho, Aveiro and Porto, three of the top universities in the north of Portugal. In 2008 he concluded his Masters degree in Electronics and Telecommunications Engineering, at the University of Aveiro, and in 2005 he graduated in the same area, also from the University of Aveiro. He is a researcher at Centro Algoritmi, a research unit of University of Minho, and his main research interests are in Organizational Information Systems and Information Systems Auditing. He has been lecturing Information and Technology since 2007 at the Higher Institute for Accountancy and Administration, University of Aveiro.

Miguel Mira da Silva received a PhD in Computing Science from the University of Glasgow and more recently a "Sloan Fellowship" from the London Business School. Currently, he is a Professor of Information Systems at the Technical University of Lisbon and group leader at the INOV research institute.

Nastaran Mohammadhossein graduated from the University Technology Malaysia with a degree in Information Technology Management in the department of the Computing. She holds a B.Sc. in Information Technology Engineering from Parand Islamic Azad University in Iran. Her research interests are in Customer Relationship Management, E-commerce, Enterprise Systems and Cloud Computing. Nastaran Mohammadhossein has published in journals such as Journal of American Science, International Journal of Engineering Research and Application,, Journal of Basic and Applied Scientific Research, Applied, among others.

Grant Mooney is an Associate Industry Professor at the University of Technology Sydney (UTS). His research interests include Business Innovation, Organizational Leadership and Culture and Project Management, and has published two books plus a number of papers within these areas. Grant has nearly 30 years commercial, information systems and management experience in such firms as IBM, J.D. Edwards and Deloitte Consulting Group, engaging at senior levels in the finance, manufacturing, health and technology sectors. He has previously held positions as regional consulting manager, general manager and managing director in various multi-national information technology and services firms.

Joseph R. Muscatello, CFPIM, is an Associate Professor of Business Management and Technology at Kent State University- Geauga. He received his Doctorate from the Cleveland State University in 2002 and researches in the areas of enterprise systems, supply chain management, forecasting, project management and the impact of technology on organizations. He has extensive executive level industry experience in the Metals and Chemical industry and is the President of The Muscatello Group, a Supply Chain Consulting Company and has taught over 100 sessions of APICS certification classes. He has presented at academic and professional venues over 100 times and published over 50 articles in various journals including *IJES, Omega, IJOPM, BPMJ, IRMJ* among others.

Jessy Nair is an Associate Professor in Marketing, in Faculty of Management Studies at PES University, Bangalore, India. She received her PhD in Strategic Information Systems, from VIT University, Vellore, India. She has to her credit publications in many international and national journals. Her research interests include Consumer Behaviour, Digital Marketing, Strategic Information Systems and Technological Change.

Diane H. Parente is the Breene Professor of Management, Department Chair of Management, Program Chair for Interdisciplinary Programs in the Sam & Irene Black School of Business at Penn State Erie, The Behrend College. She received her PhD from the University at Buffalo. She has extensive industry experience including management positions in logistics, operations, sales management, management information systems, marketing, international business and strategic business unit management. She has been involved in numerous industry projects including systems implementation, manufacturing projects, new product introduction, and international manufacturing joint venturing. Her research interests revolve around the cross-functional aspects of business, especially the manufacturing – marketing interface, online procurement auctions, and supply chain management. She is the author of over 50 articles and conference proceedings in these areas and over 100 conference presentations.

Chandra Sekhar Patro is presently working as Assistant Professor in GVP College of Engineering (Autonomous), Visakhapatnam, India, and a doctoral student in Commerce and Management Studies of Andhra University of India. He has post-graduate degree in Master of Commerce (M.Com.) from Andhra University, Master in Financial Management (MFM) from Pondicherry University, and also MBA (HRM & Finance) from Jawaharlal Nehru Technological University. Mr. Patro has over 9 years of teaching experience in higher education. Mr. Patro has gained very good knowledge in Human Resource Management and Accountancy/Finance subjects. He has published number of research papers in reputed National and International Journals and also presented papers in National and International Conferences.

Mile Pavlić is a full professor at the Department of Informatics, the University of Rijeka. He is the author of 10 books and over 180 articles. His work focuses on the following methods: business system analysis, business process modeling, data modeling and software engineering. Mile Pavlić has published in conference proceedings such as: International Conference on Information Systems Analysis and Synthesis (ISAS), International Conference on Enterprise Information Systems and Web Technologies (EISWT), and in journals such as Journal of Computing and Information Technology, International Journal of Enterprise Information Systems, Journal of Information and Organizational Sciences, Informatologia, Expert Systems With Applications.

Kamakula Madhu Kishore Raghunath is a doctoral student in the School of Management Studies of National Institute of Technology-Warangal, India. He has Post-graduate degree in Management with Finance and Marketing specializations from Jawaharlal Nehru Technological University. He has over 3 years of teaching experience in higher education. Mr. Madhu has good knowledge in Finance and Marketing subjects. His research interests include Supply Chain Management, Marketing, and Finance topics.

Aparna Raman has pursued her doctorate from Management Development Institute, Gurgaon, India. She has published papers in international and national journals, and business cases in Harvard and Emerald Publishing. She has also attended and presented papers in many refereed national and international conferences. She has Bachelors of Engineering (Computer Science), MBA (IT and Systems), a postgraduate diploma in intellectual property rights, and MPhil (Management) degrees to her credit. She has twelve years' experience in the information technology industry and research.

Bhanu Sree Reddy is Professor at Business School, VIT University, Vellore, India. She holds a PhD from S V University, Tirupati and over 20 years of experience in teaching, consultancy and research. Dr Bhanu Sree has to her credit publications in many international and national journals and conducts executive development training programmes. Her broad areas of research interests include Organizational Change Management, Cross Cultural Management and International Business.

Arikan Tarik Saygili Associated Professor Arikan Tarik Saygili completed his BA and MBA degrees in University of South Dakota of USA and received his Phd in Bursa Uludag University in Turkey in 2002. He worked as a research assistant and assistant professor in Balikesir University between 1998 and 2007. Professor Saygili has been continuing his academic studies in Izmir University of Economics since 2007. His main fields of interest are managerial&cost accounting and financial audit with specific emphasis in Computer Aided Audit Tools and Techniques (CAATT's).

Ebru E. Saygili is an Assistant Professor at the Department of International Trade and Finance, Yasar University. She completed her BA and MBA degrees in Dokuz Eylul University and received her Phd in Celal Bayar University in 2011. She has eight years of working experience in banking sector and she is a CPA under Turkish laws. She has published papers in national and international journals and books about corporate governance, accounting information systems and enterprise resource planning (ERP).

Carmine Sellitto is a Senior Lecturer in the College of Business at Victoria University in Melbourne, Australia. Dr Sellitto also holds positions as a Research Associate with Victoria University's Centre for Applied Informatics and the Institute for Logistics & Supply Chain Management. Carmine has published widely with over 100 peer reviewed articles on topics associated with enterprise systems, information management and technology, tourism and IT, sport technology and small business technology adoption.

Pedro Soto-Acosta is a Professor of Management at the University of Murcia (Spain). He attended Postgraduate Courses in Management at Harvard University (USA) and received his PhD in Business Economics from Universidad de Murcia. He serves as Associate Editor and Senior Editor for several mainstream journals including *Decision Sciences*, *Electronic Commerce Research and Applications*, *Information Systems Management*, *Journal of Electronic Commerce Research*, and *Computational Economics*. His work has been published in journals such as *Computers in Human Behavior*, *Electronic Markets*, *Enterprise Information Systems*, *European Journal of Information Systems*, *European Management Journal*, *Journal of Business Research*, *Management Decision*, and *Technological and Economic Development of Economy*, among others. Further information is available at http://webs.um.es/psoto.

Sabrina Šuman, mag educ. math. et inf., is a doctoral student at the Department of Informatics (University of Rijeka) and a lecturer at the Business Department (Information science study) of the Polytechnic of Rijeka, Croatia. Her research interests are in Information systems development, Intelligent methods in data modelling, Knowledge discovery and representation methods, Data mining, Business Intelligence, Business process management tools and strategies and programming. Sabrina Šuman has presented at IN-TECH, DAAAM, MIPRO, DESIGN, WSEAS and other conferences, and published in journals such as the Journal of Polytechnic of Rijeka, Engineering Review and International Journal of Enterprise Information Systems.

Matthew Swinarski, is an associate professor in the Sam and Irene Black School of Business at Penn State University, The Behrend College. He received his Ph.D. from the State University of New York at Buffalo. His research interests include IS outsourcing, IS capabilities and IS education. Dr. Swinarski's papers have been published in the *European Journal of Information Systems, IEEE Transactions on Engineering Management, Communications of the ACM, Decision Support Systems,* and *Advances in Management Information Systems*, among others. His industry experience includes installation, configuration, and service contact management of enterprise systems for medium-size manufacturing companies.

Kathryn A. Szabat is Associate Professor in the Business Systems and Analytics Department at La Salle University. Her instructional responsibilities include teaching of business statistics and management science to undergraduate and MBA students. Her current interests include promoting the inclusion of business analytics in business school curriculums and the development of analytical capabilities of business students. She is actively involved in several academic and professional associations. She holds a BS in Mathematics from the State University of New York at Albany and a MS and PhD in Statistics, with cognate field in Operations Research, from the Wharton School of University of Pennsylvania.

António Trigo is an Assistant Professor of Management Information Systems at ISCAC – Coimbra Business School, which is part of the Polytechnic Institute of Coimbra, Portugal, where he teaches business intelligence, management information systems, software engineering and computer programming, supervising MSc students. He holds a Ph. D. in Information Systems and his research interests include Enterprise Information Systems and Project Management. He has publications in international journals, book chapters and international conferences. He serves as editorial board member for international journals and has served in the organization and scientific committees of international conferences.

João Varajão is currently professor of information systems and project management at the University of Minho. He is also a researcher of the Algoritmi research center. Born and raised in Portugal, he attended the University of Minho, earning his Graduate (1995), Masters (1997) and Doctorate (2003) degrees in Technologies and Information Systems. In 2012, he received his Habilitation degree from the University of Trás-os-Montes e Alto Douro. His current main research interests are in Information Systems Project Management (addressing, particularly, the success of project management). Before joining academia, he worked as an IT/IS consultant, project manager, information systems analyst and software developer, for private companies and public institutions. He has supervised more than 50 Masters and Doctoral dissertations in the Information Systems field. He has published over 250 works, including refereed publications, authored books, edited books, as well as book chapters and communications at international conferences. He serves as editor-in-chief, associate editor and member of the editorial board for international journals and has served in numerous committees of international conferences and workshops.

Klaus Wölfel implements ERP and Big Data projects for the open source publisher Nexedi, creator of the ERP package ERP5 and the data analysis framework Wendelin. He accomplished his doctorate on automation of ERP category configuration at the Chair of Information Systems, esp. in Manufacturing and Commerce in the Faculty of Economics of Technische Universität Dresden. His further research interests include data analysis, machine learning, business models for open source software, and Massive Open Online Courses (MOOCs). He presented his work at conferences such as the Fourth International Conference on Research and Practical Issues on Enterprise Information Systems (CONFENIS 2010), Natal and Multikonferenz Wirtschaftsinformatik (MKWI 2014), Paderborn. Klaus Wölfel published in HMD Praxis der Wirtschaftsinformatik and contributed a chapter to the book Free and Open Source Enterprise Resource Planning: Systems and Strategies, IGI Publishing.

Nor Hidayati Zakaria is a Senior Lecturer in the Information Systems Department, Faculty of Computing, Universiti Teknologi Malaysia (UTM). She received her Bachelor of Information Technology in Information Systems from Universiti Kebangsaan Malaysia (1999) and obtained a master degree in Computer Science from UTM (2002). In 2011, she was awarded a PhD from The Queensland University of Technology (QUT), Brisbane, Australia. Nor Hidayati has been a member of the Information Service Systems and Innovation (ISSI), a research group that focusing on both information and service systems type of innovation.

Index

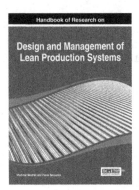
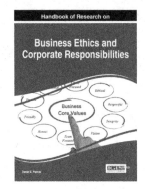

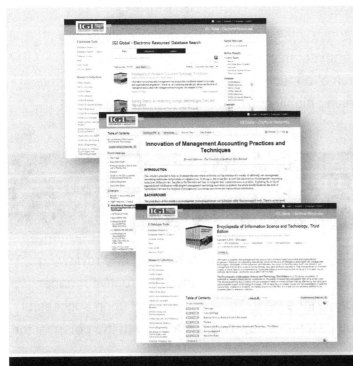

Printed in the United States
By Bookmasters